D1252490

THE OPEN BIBLE

BY

OLAF M. NORLIE

Ph. D., Pd. D., S. T. D., Litt. D.

ASSISTED BY

REV. JOHN N. ANDERSEN

1918
AUGSBURG PUBLISHING HOUSE
MINNEAPOLIS, MINN.

FOREWORD.

"Teaching them to observe all things whatsoever I have commanded you" (Matt. 28:20). This closing paragraph of Christ's Great Commission is one of the chief "martyrs of Christendom", sharing this sad distinction with the Lord's Prayer. Its terms are made to endure constant and glib quotation, while their import is often ignored, and their appeal too frequently goes unheeded.

It is, indeed, a great task which Christ here entrusts to His Church; even His most ardent followers would fear to undertake it, had He not promised to be "with them alway" in carrying it out. We are to teach those who have been baptized "all things whatsoever" He has commanded us—that is, the whole truth which Christ has revealed. And this teaching is to be done in such a manner that they may "observe" all these things. Those who through Baptism have been grafted into Christ—as branches into the Tree of Life—are to be trained to bear fruit of His whole truth; in brief, to *live* His truth in faith and love.

How has the Christian Church, at its best, endeavored to discharge its trust as Teacher of Christ's Truth? No doubt the Church has acted wisely in following the example of the apostles by way of presenting terse and simple summaries of Christ's truth for the benefit of the young and ignorant. These summaries have gradually crystallized into the Catechism, where the religion of Christ is viewed in Part I as a divine requirement, in Part II as an object of glad faith, in Part III as a treasure to be ever more our own by prayer, and in Parts IV and V as a salvation divinely assured and sealed unto us.

Under the head of the Catechism the various good Explanations of it deserve honorable mention, particularly those which confine themselves to a homely interpretation of its terms and to the citation of pertinent Bible passages in support of its teaching.

In the second place, sound sense, as well as the apostolic practice, justifies the Church in employing compends of Bible History as a means of teaching the truth of Christ. For the Christian religion rests upon facts of Sacred history and cannot be understood apart from them. Moreover, what Christ taught does not carry its full appeal to the heart unless it comes to us energized by His personality and life, and attested by its influence upon the nations and characters of the Bible era.

Still another primary means of instruction employed by the Church is, of course, the Common Service, with its collects and hymns, and above all its lessons from the Bible and their exposition in Christian preaching. And it would be unjust not to refer to the vast educational work accomplished by means of the Bible commentaries, by doctrinal and devotional treatises, by religious periodicals, and, last but not least, by the copious distributions of the Bible itself.

As we marshal these teaching forces before our mind the question presents itself, whether the Church, after all, has not lived up to the Great Commission.

If we test the educational work of the Church by the results, the answer is not very encouraging, as a rule. There is general complaint that a distressingly large percentage of those who have been baptized manifestly neglect to "observe" the "all things whatsoever" of Christ.

Space will not permit us to discuss the various reasons which may account, more or less clearly, for this partial failure of the teaching mission of the Church. In a general way it may be stated that the fault does not lie simply with the traditional systems, methods or agencies of instruction. They would prove efficient if the Church would make a more faithful use of them, and if the worldliness of so many Church members did not weaken their influence.

But in one respect, at least, there is constantly room for improvement in the teaching function of the Church. The point we would make is not a new one. It has been urged by the educational leaders of the Church in all ages, and may be put thus, *Train the young to study the Bible itself!* Whatever the form or method, let it be the constant aim of all Christian teaching to arouse interest in the Bible itself, to make men rest their faith on the Bible and draw from the Bible light and strength for their whole life.

It would appear superfluous to demonstrate to Christians the truth and value of this principle. But while all Christians hear or read a great deal about the Bible, and copies of the Bible are found in every home, it is only too evident that the great majority of church people do not read the Bible; still less do they study it prayerfully, diligently and systematically.

Yet it is the Bible which is the "all things whatsoever" Christ has commanded—directly, as it records His instructions to the disciples; indirectly, as His Spirit revealed to the Biblical writers the truth which they were to record and gave them the very words in which they were to record His truth. The Bible is Christ's own Word.

And concerning these words of His, Christ Himself declares that they are "spirit and life". In fact, Christ is the life of His Word;

the Scriptures "bear witness of Him"; He is the very sun whose rays are transmitted through all the parts of the Bible. How important to note this when we are to train men to "observe" His teachings! The Word of Truth itself is best fitted to influence men to live His truth. No one is content with water stored up in reservoirs when he may drink from the fresh flowing spring. For there is this difference between the Bible itself and the best systems incorporating its teaching, that the latter appeal more to the intellect, while the words of the Bible influence directly all the powers of the soul. Indeed "the Holy Scriptures are able to make thee wise unto salvation by faith which is in Christ Jesus".

For these reasons Christ and His apostles both by precept and example direct Christians to Scripture itself. And it is a well-known fact that the great characters of the Church have been great readers of the Bible.

The primary need of the Church in our day is men who, like Timothy, have been trained from youth to know the Holy Scriptures, so as to be at home in them, and reflect them in belief and conduct. It is for this reason chiefly that we bid this new book by Dr. Norlie a most hearty welcome.

As the title suggests, the purpose of the author is to open the Bible to our young people, to disclose to them its divine character, to give them a glimpse of the many wonders treasured up in it, and to attract and guide them to explore its sacred glories. The work is admirably adapted to serve this noble aim. Though arranged as a text-book, so that it may be used profitably by Bible Classes, Study Circles, and Christian high schools, no one will find it dry and uninteresting. Some of the readers may hesitate about endorsing every detail, but all will be impressed with the spirit of Christian sincerity and of genuine loyalty to the Bible which pervades the work. "The Open Bible" is in a class by itself as a brief, reliable, and comprehensive text-book of introduction to elementary Bible study. May it enjoy a wide use, and may an ever increasing circle of earnest Bible readers reward the author's labor of love.

O. E. BRANDT.

Luther Seminary, St. Paul,
MAY 20, 1918.

"Ye search the Scriptures, because ye think that in them ye have eternal life; and these are they which bear witness of Me" (John 5:39).

INTRODUCTION.

The object of this little handbook is to make young people interested in the Bible and to read it. The book is therefore divided into 52 lessons, one for each Sunday in the year. It can be used by Bible classes or young people's societies or even by religion classes at church schools. The lessons are not all of equal length. At the discretion of the teacher, additional assignments can be given when the lessons appear to be too short, and parts of the text can be omitted when the lessons are evidently too long.

It is called "The Open Bible", for two reasons: 1. The Bible is now an open book. It is like an open country to which immigrants from afar are heartily invited to come, in which they may freely and safely travel in every direction, enjoying the fat of the land and taking up their abode wherever they will. 2. The Bible has not always been an open book. For centuries it was to the average reader a sealed book, because it was to be had only in foreign and dead languages. It was, furthermore, bound with iron chains of Jewish or Roman tradition. Its reading was even by the Church made unlawful and subject to relentless persecution and awful punishments. But in 1517, four hundred years ago, Martin Luther began the Reformation, which again made the Bible an open book. It brushed away the laws regulating Bible reading. It broke away the chains of tradition. It translated the Bible into the languages of the people and laid it open before them, inviting them to come and read. Since then we have had an open Bible. But—sad to say—to many it is still a closed book. They know very little about it. They do not read it. They are not at all interested even when told that the Bible is the best book and God's Word. They are as indifferent as the scribes of Jerusalem, who told Herod that Christ, the expected King, was to be born at Bethlehem. The world had longed for His coming for 4000 years; now He was reported to have come. Bethlehem was only six miles distant, and yet not a scribe went down to find Him. Now, in writing this book the aim has been to glorify Christ and His Word, so that the reader may long to search the Scriptures to find Him.

The Bible may be likened to a foreign country. We may read about it, visit it and even make it our own native land. The more we know about it, the more we are apt to want to visit it, the more we shall see on our visit, and the more we shall want to occupy it and make it our home. It is devoutly to be hoped that those who read this little book will also want to read the Bible itself.

The author of the handbook takes great pleasure in acknowledging the assistance given him directly by Rev. J. N. Andersen and Prof. O. E. Brandt, D.D. Pastor Andersen suggested that this book be written, and assisted the author in planning it. To Pastor Andersen, too, is due, in large measure, many of the better features of the book, such as, orderliness and simplicity. Dr. Brandt has offered valuable suggestions besides adding a foreword. The mistakes and shortcomings of the book must not be charged up to either of these scholars.

The author wishes also to acknowledge the indirect help that he has had in preparing this book, from his former instructors in Biblical Introduction, namely, Profs. F. T. Kelly, Ph.D.; E. Kr. Johnsen, A.M.; M. O. Bøckman, D.D.; C. A. Blomgren, Ph.D.; and C. J. Södergren, D.D.

He is also under great obligation to other writers on the subject, Jewish, Catholic, Reformed and Lutheran, of negative as well as positive schools. Among those whose books have contributed in some measure to this handbook may be mentioned the following 100 authors:

J. Angus,	A. Edersheim,
A. Augustine,	F. W. Farrar,
K. Baedeker,	E. Friedberg,
F. C. Baur,	F. Godet,
W. J. Beecher,	A. L. Graebner,
J. Belsheim,	W. H. Green,
J. A. Bengel,	E. Greenwald,
N. Bentwich,	C. R. Gregory,
F. Bettex,	H. E. F. Guericke,
E. C. Bissell,	J. A. W. Haas,
C. A. Briggs,	A. Hahn,
F. W. Bugge,	A. Harnack,
J. Calvin,	H. L. Hastings,
C. P. Caspari,	E. W. Hengstenberg,
M. Chemnitz,	J. J. Herzog,
C. R. Conder,	H. V. Hilprecht,
J. E. Darras,	T. H. Horne,
J. D. Davis,	J. L. Hurlbut,
I. L. P. Dietrichson,	S. E. Jerome,
F. Delitzsch,	H. E. Jacobs,
S. R. Driver,	E. Kr. Johnsen,
A. Dächsel,	F. Josephus,

C. F. Keil,
L. S. Keyser,
J. N. Kildahl,
U. V. Koren,
A. Kuenen,
J. H. Kurtz,
E. König,
J. P. Lange,
F. Lenormant,
R. C. H. Lenski,
A. Levinson,
C. E. Lindberg,
C. E. Luthardt,
M. Luther,
T. MacCoun,
H. A. W. Meyer,
M. Mielziner,
G. C. Morgan,
R. G. Moulton,
M. Müller,
E. Nystrøm,
J. Orr,
F. N. Peloubet,
W. M. H. Petersen,
F. W. Putzger,
G. Rawlinson,
E. Renan,
A. H. Sayce,

P. Schaff,
J. Schaller,
T. E. Schmauk,
H. Schmid,
A. Schmidt,
G. H. Schodde,
E. Schrader,
E. Schurer,
J. Sether,
I. Singer,
Wm. Smith,
J. A. O. Stub,
G. Stöckhardt,
M. S. Terry,
C. Tischendorf,
H. B. Tristram,
J. Urquhart,
H. Ussing,
V. Vogt,
F. W. Weber,
R. F. Weidner,
J. Wellhausen,
G. B. Winer,
Joh. T. Ylvisaker,
R. Young,
T. Zahn,
A. C. Zenos,
O. Zoeckler,
and many others.

Finally, the author wishes to say that he is mostly indebted to his mother for his interest in and knowledge of the Bible. She herself was a constant and devout Bible reader and never tired of urging him to read it and obey its teachings. She departed from this life on the very day that he completed the proof reading of this book—May 27, 1918.

> Word of the ever-living God,
>   Will of His glorious Son;
> Without thee how could earth be trod,
>   Or Heaven itself be won?
> Lord, grant us all aright to learn
>   The wisdom it imparts;
> And to its heavenly teaching turn,
>   With simple, childlike hearts.
>
> O. M. NORLIE.

No. 1. Luther Discovers the Bible.

OUTLINE.

APPENDIX.

PART ONE.

CHARACTER OF THE BIBLE.

OUTLINE.

LESSON ONE. THE TITLES OF THE BIBLE.

Character (from the Greek word charassein—to make sharp, to cut into furrows, to engrave) is the distinctive mark, the peculiar quality, or the sum of qualities, by which a person or thing is distinguished from others. The Bible is in many respects very different from all other books; it is altogether more excellent and useful. It is therefore worth while for anyone to carefully consider some of the distinctive marks of this Book of Books.

It has many titles. The most familiar to us is perhaps that which we have already used, namely, the Bible. Some of the other names by which it is known are also very familiar, as, for example: The Scriptures, the Word, the Old and New Testaments, and the Canon. In addition to these, this good book has been known by many other terms, some of which are given below.

1. THE BIBLE.

The name Bible has come to us immediately from the French (bible). This, in turn, had received it from the Latin (biblia), and the Latin from the Greek. The word biblia in Greek is in the neuter plural and means the books, or a collection of books. The word biblia in Latin is a feminine singular and means the book. Now, by common consent we reverently apply the word only to one book, or, rather to one collection of books—our Bible, which is acknowledged to be the worthiest and best of all books, *the Book*. Originally, it might of course have applied to any collection of books, and even now the word, as already stated, means only the books, and nothing more. The term is absent from the pages of the Bible itself. Jesus and the apostles never called this book the Bible. It is a term that was invented by some churchman centuries after the apostolic age. It is believed that it was first applied to the

sacred books by John Chrysostom, patriarch at Constantinople from 398 to 404 A. D.

2. THE SCRIPTURE.

The word Scripture, from the Latin, meant at first simply
writing, no more, no less. Just as bible meant simply books,
so also scripture meant only anything written. But now
it is used, chiefly in the plural, by way of distinction to
apply only to the books of the Bible, the Sacred Writings
of the Christian Church. This term occurs frequently in
the New Testament, sometimes referring to all the Old Testament writings thought of as one book, at other times as
separate books, and then again as quotations from them.

Note the various uses in the following references:

(1) Search the Scriptures (John 5: 39).
(2) All Scripture is given by inspiration of God (2 Tim. 3: 16).
(3) Did ye never read in the Scriptures,
    "The Stone which the builders rejected,
    The Same was made the Head of the corner"?
                                        (Matt. 21:42).
(4) Have ye not read even this Scripture,
    "The Stone which the builders rejected,
    The Same was made the Head of the corner"?
                                        (Mark 12:10).

See also John 10:35; Luke 24:27; Mark 15:28; Gal.
3: 22; Rom. 1: 2; John 19: 37.

3. THE WORD.

The Bible is often called the Word of God, or simply,
the Word, because it is God's spoken and written message to humanity and is *the* Word above all other
words. As Peter says: "But the Word of the Lord endureth
forever. And this is the Word which by the Gospel is
preached unto you" (1 Pet. 1: 25). David, the sweet
psalmist of Israel, said: "The Spirit of the Lord was upon
me, and His Word was in my tongue" (2 Sam. 23: 1-2).
In Acts 11:1 we read that "The apostles and brethren that
were in Judea heard that the Gentiles had also received the

Word of God." People at that time were classified as Jews and Gentiles. The Jews had had the Word of God for centuries; now also the Gentiles were to have it. We—of Gentile race—have it to this day.

This title is very fitting also because its message can be summarized in the one word Jesus. He was called the Word before He came to this sinful earth in the form of a man. "In the beginning was the Word, and the Word was with God, and the Word was God . . . . . And the Word became flesh, and dwelt among us" (John 1: 1, 14).

4. THE OLD AND NEW TESTAMENTS.

The word for testament was berith in the Hebrew, diatheke in the Greek, and meant covenant. Covenant is derived from a Latin word which means to come together, to make an agreement or contract. God's dealings with Moses and the Israelites took the form of a covenant. He bound Himself forever to bestow upon them every temporal and spiritual blessing, provided they would obey and serve. There must be two parties to a covenant, but they need not be equals. Of course, in this Covenant the parties were not equals. God is faithful and has kept His Covenant, but Israel was not faithful. Therefore, a New Covenant was promised and entered into between God and the followers of His Son. The Old Covenant can be summarized in the one word the Law, the New Covenant in the one word the Gospel. Splendid comparisons of the two Covenants are made in the Epistles to the Galatians and to the Hebrews.

In the first translation of the Old Testament into Greek the word covenant was rendered both covenant and testament. Now testament does not mean exactly the same as covenant. It signifies making a last will, disposing of one's property for once and all. Later, the Old Latin version everywhere retained this new word—testament—instead of covenant. Other versions, upon the authority of the Greek and Latin versions, also kept it. And not only was it kept as a translation of the original words for covenant in the writings themselves, but in the course of time it was also applied to the writings which contained these Covenants. Thus, the books written before Christ, which particularly describe the Old Covenant, were consequently called Old Testament, and the books written after Christ, describing particularly the New Covenant, came to be called the New Testament. All of the modern versions have adopted these terms, though not all make the mistake of translating the Hebrew word berith—testament. Thus, we find that the Authorized Version of the English Bible renders the Hebrew word berith covenant 260 times, and not once does it render it testament. On the other hand, it translates the Greek word diatheke 20 times covenant and 13 times testament. The Revised Version never employs the word testament except as a title.

In a very real sense testament is, however, also a correct term for the New Covenant between God and man. This Covenant was sealed by the institution of the Lord's Supper, at which Jesus said: "This cup is the New Testament (Covenant) in My blood, which is shed for you" (Luke 22:20).

5. THE CANON.

The Bible has often been called the Canon, or the Sacred Canon. Canon is derived from the Latin word canon, which means a measuring line or rule. The Latin term, in turn, came from the Greek word kanon, which originally denoted any straight reed, hence a carpenter's rule. In a figurative sense it was applied to any rule whatsoever, as, the rules or canons of grammar. In Gal. 6:16 and 2 Cor. 10:13-16, it occurs in the original text and is translated rule in the Authorized Version and rule and province in the Revised. The early Christian writers began to speak of the sacred books of the Bible as the Canon, the Old Testament books as the Old Testament Canon and the New Testament books as the New Testament Canon. The word canon is used of the list of 66 books properly in the Bible, as distinguished from the apocryphal, or uninspired books. The Catholic and Lutheran editions of the Bible publish the following apocryphal Old Testament books, dealing with the later history of the Jews previous to the coming of Christ: 1 Esdras, 2 Esdras, Tobit, Judith, Additions to the Book of Esther, the Wisdom of Solomon, Ecclesiasticus (Sirach), Baruch, the Prayer of Manasseh, Additions to Daniel, 1 Maccabees, 2 Maccabees. The Catholic Church holds that these apocryphal books are sacred like the inspired books; the Lutheran Church holds that they contain many excellent maxims worth reading, but that they are in every way inferior to the canonical books; the Reformed Churches hold that since they abound in mistakes they ought not to be printed in the Bible at all. The New Testament apocryphal books are rejected by all the Denominations as spurious and unworthy of a place in the Bible. In the making of the Canon, all these apocryphal and other inferior books not mentioned here had to be excluded and all the inspired books had to be included. As to the Old Testament, this work was largely performed by Ezra and Nehemiah and a council of Jews, called the Great Synagogue, that met after the return from the captivity at Babylon. As to the New Testament, the Canon was gradually fixed by the agreement of the early Christians, and authoritatively settled by the Council of Carthage, 387 A. D.

6. OTHER TERMS.

The Old Testament writings have been called the Book of the Law (Josh. 1:8; 8:31; etc.). By the Law the Old Testament means the Word of God in general and the Moral Law in particular passages. Later, when other writings were added to the sacred collection the Book of the Law was held to designate only the five books of Moses, and the remainder of the Old Testament was known as the Prophets and the Sacred Writings, or merely the Prophets. Thus,

in the parable of Dives (Lazarus and the Rich Man, Luke
16: 19-31) Abraham answered the rich man who asked that
Lazarus might be sent to warn his father's house: "They
have Moses and the Prophets; let them hear them." In Ps.
119 the Word of God is called a "Lamp unto my feet
and a Light unto my path." In Rom. 3: 2 it is called
the "Oracles of God;" in Eph. 6: 17, "the Sword of the
Spirit." We often call the Bible Holy Writ, the Good Book,
the Book of Books.

———

What is meant by character? Why should a person carefully study
the character of the Bible? Mention some of the titles of the Bible?

What does the word Bible mean? Give its derivation. When
was the term first applied to the Sacred Books?

What did the word Scripture originally mean? How is it used
now? In what parts of the Bible does this term frequently occur?
Mention some of the passages in which the word Scripture or Scriptures is found.

Why is the Bible called the Word? Give examples where this
title is used. Why is this title very fitting?

What is the original word in the Bible for Testament? Give
derivation and meaning of the word Covenant? Why is God's dealings with the Israelites called a Covenant? What can you say of the
New Covenant? Where do you find splendid comparisons of the
two Covenants?

Give the meaning of the word Testament. How did it come to
be applied to the Scriptures? State how this term is used in some
of the versions of the Bible. Why is it a very fitting term, especially
for the New Covenant?

Why is the Bible called the Canon? Give the meaning of this
word. Of what books is the word Canon used now? What can
you say of the apocryphal books? Tell what you can about the
making of the Canon.

Mention some other terms applied to the Scriptures.

What does your Catechism say about the names of the Bible?
Your Bible history? Find appropriate hymns in your hymnal bear-
ing on this subject. Look up the Bible passages referred to in
your lesson, and find additional references to this subject in the
Bible. In what ways can the contents of this lesson help you in your
Bible study? In your faith and works?

LESSON TWO. THE ORIGIN OF THE BIBLE:
I. AUTHORSHIP.

By origin is meant the beginning of anything, the birth, foundation, source, cause, occasion. The study of origins is apt to be fascinating, at least instructive. In the case of the Bible one will find both pleasure and profit in pausing to meditate upon its origin. We shall look at this question from four points of view: authorship, revelation, inspiration, preservation.

1. DEFINITION.

Here we inquire as to who wrote the Bible. The answer is unmistakably that God Himself is the Author of the Bible. It is His Word. It was accepted as such by His people of old (the Israelites), and is verily believed to be nothing less than that by His people of today (the Christian Church). Jesus called it the Word of God (John 10:35; Mark 7:13). His witness is final. Now, strange to say, God employed men to do the writing, therefore it can also be said that the holy prophets, evangelists and apostles wrote the Bible.

2. NECESSITY.

Why was it necessary that the Lord should be the Author of the Bible? The answer is that, on the one hand, the human race had need of a Word of guidance from God, and, on the other hand, God was willing to speak this Word. Furthermore, it was not enough that this Word was merely spoken, for human memory is very treacherous, very apt to distort by additions and subtractions, and fully as liable to forget altogether. A written Record was necessary. In order that it might be thoroughly authoritative and inerrant God must needs be the Author. It was part of His wise plan to use men as His instruments, just as it is His plan even today to use us as His ambassadors in behalf of Christ, as though He were entreating by us (2 Cor. 5:20).

3. EXTENT.

To what extent is the Lord the Author of the Bible? In one sense He has not spoken everything which is recorded in the Bible. Satan spoke to our first parents; his words are not God's Words. In this sense also the words of Abraham, Isaac and Jacob and other characters are not God's Word. But in another sense they are, for God is telling in this book that Satan spoke such and such words, Abraham said this and that, etc. To what extent, then, did He use the sacred penmen as His scribes? In explaining this the dogmatician Hutter says that "He made use of their lips, their tongues, their hands, their pen" ("Loci Theologici," 30). The Spirit of God revealed to these men what they should write and moved them to record this revelation. The process may be likened to that of an employer dictating a letter to his stenographer. This explanation is often objected to as being too mechanical. It is argued that the work of the Biblical authors is not so machine-like as that of a-stenographer. This contention will readily be admitted. The Holy Spirit has seen fit to accommodate Himself to the individuality of the writer, making each person of himself speak divine words. Moses retains his personality in writing, as do also David, Solomon, Peter, Paul and the rest of the inspired writers. Moses has therefore a different style from that of David, and David is different from Solomon, just as they ordinarily were different in this earthly life and as they surely are different and speak differently in the life beyond.

4. PROOFS.

We assume at the start that there is a Triune God— Father, Son and Holy Spirit —Three in One. That there is a God is generally admitted by every people in all ages and places. Individuals and societies may, indeed, spring up to deny this common faith even as it is written:

> The fool saith in his heart,
> There is no God (Ps. 14: 1).

Robinson Crusoe lived alone on a deserted isle. One day, when out walking, he came across a foot-print different from his own. He concluded that some other human being had been there. In a similar way men have reasoned that there has been Some One like us, yet different, Who has created this universe, of which we are but a very, very tiny part, that He has planned it wisely and cares for it bountifully. Men have reasoned also that it is quite possible that this Being, Whom they call God, could communicate with His creatures. Furthermore, they have felt that it is quite probable that He would communicate His will to them so as to obtain the reverent obedience due Him. We have already stated the necessity of this. The facts are in full harmony with this course of reasoning. God has spoken to men. He has preserved His Word in a Written Book. This Word bears abundant witness to its being His Word and to His using men to record it. For example: He said to Moses: "Write this for a memorial in a book" (Ex. 17: 14), and "Moses wrote all the words of the Lord" (Ex. 24: 4) ; and in the same manner as He commanded Moses, the first of the writing prophets, to write did He also instruct John, the last of the writing apostles, to do likewise: "Write the things which thou hast seen, and the things which are, and the things which shall be hereafter" (Rev. 1: 19). Between Moses and John are about thirty other sacred writers, each one an instrument in the hand of God.   Thus David testifies concerning his own contribution in his last song:

> The Spirit of Jehovah spake by me;
> And His Word was upon my tongue (2 Sam. 23: 2).

Likewise, Peter, in a solemn warning concerning this matter, maintains that "the prophecy came not in old times by the will of man; but holy men of God spake as they were moved by the Holy Ghost" (2 Pet. 1: 21, A. V.).

What is meant by origin? What is the value of studying about origins? From what points of view is the origin of the Bible here studied?

Define authorship.   Who wrote the Bible?

Why was it necessary that God should be Author of the Bible? Why was it necessary to have the Word of God recorded in writing? Who was employed to write it?

To what extent is God the Author of the Bible?   To what extent did the sacred writers retain their personality?

Give proofs from reason and Scripture as to the authorship of the Bible.

What does your Catechism say about the authorship of the Bible? Your Bible history?   Find appropriate hymns in your hymnal bearing on this subject.   Look up the Bible passages referred to in the lesson, and find additional references to this subject in the Bible. In what ways can the contents of this lesson help you in your Bible study?   In your faith and works?

LESSON THREE. THE ORIGIN OF THE BIBLE:
II. REVELATION.

1. DEFINITION.

The word reveal means literally to unveil, or lift the veil, and thus make known what was previously concealed or unknown. Revelation is the act of disclosing to others what was before unknown to them. As used in connection with the Bible it is the act of God in making known His divine truth unto men.

2. NECESSITY.

A direct revelation from God was an absolute necessity, for sin had come into the world and the wages of sin is death. Everyone inherits the sinful nature; everyone struggles with it and suffers through it; everyone who is not saved by grace dies by sin and is damned on account of it. From this woeful state no creature can deliver mankind. But if there is a God, as men everywhere and at all times have assumed, and if this God is good and powerful, as has also been admitted, then everyone might expect of such a God that He would send a revelation that would warn of danger and guide into safe paths. We expect to see danger signs at every railway crossing and at each pitfall along the highway. The laws of the country demand that we have sign boards and red lights and whistles and horns and flags and watchmen to warn people of danger. Should not God cry out against sin and death, the Devil and hell-fire? He has done so. He has revealed Himself.

3. EXTENT.

God has revealed Himself to man in two ways: in a general and in a special way, or, in other words, in a natural and in a supernatural way. The creation, preserva-

tion and government of the world and the other heavenly
bodies occupying space tell us a good many things about
God, as, for example, His might and wisdom. As David,
Israel's psalmist-king, sings:

> The heavens declare the glory of God;
> And the firmament showeth His handiwork (Ps. 19: 1).

And, again, he says:

> O Jehovah, our Lord,
> How excellent is Thy name in all the earth!
> When I consider Thy heavens, the work of Thy fingers,
> The moon and the stars which Thou hast ordained;
> What is man, that Thou art mindful of him?
> And the son of man, that Thou visitest him?
> For Thou hast made him but little lower than God,
> And crownest him with glory and honor.
> Thou madest him to have dominion over the works of Thy hands;
> Thou hast put all things at his feet (Ps. 8).

This revelation of God through the world about us is
called a general or natural revelation. There is also another
source of natural revelation, namely, the world within us,
particularly our conscience, which fears when we do evil
and rejoices when we do good (Rom. 2: 14-15). God has
also revealed Himself to mankind in a special or supernatural way. He spoke in person and through angelic messengers, through visions and dreams, to Adam, Noah, Abraham, Jacob, Moses, Joshua, Isaiah, Jeremiah and the other
prophets. He told them His will unto their salvation. He
sent His Only-Begotten Son, Who revealed the Father's
goodness and mercy as well as His holiness and justice. He
sent the Holy Spirit, Who revealed to every prophet and
apostle what he should say and write. They wrote what had
been revealed to them. Hence, we call their writings the
Revealed Word. And because God does not now speak
directly to us as He did to Adam and Abraham and David
and Paul, but speaks to us through the Bible, we apply the
word Revelation not only to the act of disclosing divine
truth, but also to the truth which has been disclosed, namely,
the Bible.

4. PROOFS.

The Holy Scriptures witness repeatedly to the fact of revelation. God revealed Himself to the patriarchs and Moses and Joshua. He revealed Himself to the judges and kings and prophets. His Son revealed Himself to His disciples and the multitudes. After Christ's ascension the Holy Spirit revealed Himself to the disciples, as at Pentecost. Moses reminds his people of the fact "that the things that are revealed belong unto us and to our children forever, that we may do all the Words of this Law" (Deut. 29:29). It is said of the child Samuel, when the Lord was calling him by night, "that the Word of Jehovah was not yet revealed unto him" (1 Sam. 3:7). Isaiah prophesied of coming gloom and coming glory, specifying that "Jehovah revealed Himself in mine ears" (Isa. 22:14), and "the glory of Jehovah shall be revealed, and all flesh shall see it together, for the mouth of Jehovah hath spoken it" (Isa. 40:5). Both Joseph and Daniel were enabled to interpret dreams through consulting "Him That revealeth secrets" (Dan. 2:29). Jesus asked Peter, "But what say ye that I am?" Peter answered, "Thou art the Christ, the Son of the living God." Jesus said unto Him, "Blessed art thou, Simon Bar-Jonah; for flesh and blood hath not revealed it unto thee, but My Father Who is in Heaven" (Matt. 16:16-17). Just one more illustration from the Bible—the opening verses of the Epistle to the Hebrews: "God, having of old times spoken unto the fathers in the prophets by divers portions and in divers manners, hath at the end of these days spoken to us in His Son" (Heb.1:1-2). These and many other passages show conclusively that the Bible is given by revelation.

The Bible is itself a proof of revelation. Truly it contains things which the eye could not have seen, and the ear could not have heard, and which could not have entered into the heart of man, if God had not revealed it. "The Bible contains knowledge which no man could have discovered by his own power. It foretells events which no uninspired man could have foreseen. It contains teachings so exalted and holy that they could not have originated in the heart of man. It possesses a power such as no merely human book ever did or could possess. Its object is to make wise unto salvation. It is a lamp unto our feet and a light unto our path to guide us safely through this world to our Heavenly Home. It contains all that we need to know and all that we ever shall know in this world concerning God and His will. It is the final and absolute authority in all matters of religion" (Stump's "Explanation of Luther's Catechism").

———

Define revelation.

Why was a revelation from God an absolute necessity? Illustrate. To what extent has God revealed Himself? What is a natural revelation? A supernatural revelation? Give examples of each.

Give Bible passages testifying to special revelation. Give arguments from the contents and influence of the Bible in favor of revelation.

What does your Catechism say about revelation? Your Bible history? Find appropriate hymns in your hymnal bearing on this subject. Look up the Bible passages referred to in the lesson, and find additional references to this subject in the Bible. In what ways can the contents of this lesson help you in your Bible study? In your faith and works?

LESSON FOUR.   THE ORIGIN OF THE BIBLE:

III. INSPIRATION.

1. DEFINITION.

Inspiration (derived from the Latin inspirare, to breathe in) is, in general, the act of exercising a stimulating or elevating influence upon the intellect or the emotions. Here it has a more special meaning, namely, the influence of the Holy Spirit upon those who had received the revelation, whereby they were supernaturally guided so as to communicate this revelation without a mistake. They were told both the contents and the words which they were to write. "Men spake from God, being moved by the Holy Spirit" (2 Pet. 1: 21. R. V.).

Inspiration is not to be confused with revelation.   In revelation God has disclosed divine truth; in inspiration He has caused it to be recorded accurately and completely. He granted the prophet Elijah a revelation and an inspiration to speak, too, but not to write.   To the prophet Isaiah He granted both.   Here we want to limit ourselves only to the inspiration to write.   And here it should also be understood that our interest is not so much in the inspired men as in the inspired writings.   The men were inspired only so long as they had to write (or speak); when they had performed this task as the instruments of the Holy Spirit their inspiration ceased.   But the Scripture that they wrote is as inspired now as when it was first penned.   It may be urged that our present copies of the Bible are in every case only translations and reprints of the original text and that all the manuscripts from the original writers have been lost for centuries.   This must be admitted.   Now, it is not claimed for the men who have done the work of copying, translating and printing the Bible that they also are inspired, but, on the contrary, it is held that they were perfectly human and liable to make mistakes of many kinds, and on that account their translations or reprints may also have mistakes. It is only the original text as divinely preserved from the original records that is in every sense inspired and absolutely without error. It has always been the great passion of devout scholars, Jewish and Christian, to transmit the Holy Scriptures in copy or translation without error, and God has signally blessed their efforts. For all ordinary purposes the average Bible reader can take any standard, authorized translation of the Bible and look upon it as the Inspired Word.

2. NECESSITY.

Why was it necessary for the Lord to inspire the writers of the Bible? It was necessary that He inspire them so that their writings might be correct in substance and form. A revelation without inspiration would not have been sufficient to produce a perfect book that could command a believer's undivided trust. Human beings are very imperfect. They make mistakes of omission and commission. Memory plays them many a trick. Power to express themselves adequately, clearly, forcibly, elegantly, often lies slumbering.

3. EXTENT.

As to the extent of inspiration, it is maintained that the words as well as the contents of Holy Writ are inspired. God told the inspired writers not only what thoughts to express but also what words to convey them by. This is known as verbal or literal inspiration. Those who hold this theory argue that it is impossible to dissect inspiration into thoughts and words. Thoughts and words go together as tunes and notes, as sums and figures, as soul and body. When God gave the writers their thoughts He also added the words to convey them by. Men object to this explanation as too mechanical. They maintain that it would transform the sacred writers from living personalities into unconscious and inanimate tools of the Holy Spirit. Henry Ward Beecher, a great American divine, said: "I hold that the theory of the literal inspiration of Scripture is a theory of the Devil, and that it will lead a man who is logical and consistent as straight into infidelity as possible. The theory that every word and every letter of the Bible is inspired of God—in other words, that by an irresistible impulse God put certain thoughts in men's minds and hearts, without any volition on their part, so that they were impelled to say exactly what they did say—is the absolute destruction of any belief in inspiration" ("Bible Studies in the Old Testament," 34).

In answer to this statement by Beecher we shall cite the words of two other scholars, an Englishman and a German. Mr. Urquhart, the Englishman, in discussing the passage, "The Scripture cannot be broken" (Ps. 82: 6; John 10: 30-36), says:

"It is sometimes said that the doctrine of verbal inspiration recklessly imperils our faith. But does not our belief in the theory of gravitation do the same? You have only to show that one speck of dust, hovering in the air, does not obey the alleged 'law,' and you demolish the law utterly. If it fails to affect the dust, it cannot control the universe. Every principle carries its consequences, and if we believe that God gave the Scripture we dare not throw away our faith before the little things any more than we can throw it away before the great things. It is this position which is taken by our Lord. Show but one mistake in the Bible as originally given, and it is no longer true that all Scripture is eternally changeless. Prove that there is one exception to this law, and our Lord's argument falls to the ground. For it could then be no longer said that the Scripture could not be broken, and that therefore Psalm 82:6 and every other text in the Bible must be accepted as fully and everlastingly true" ("The Inspiration and Accuracy of the Holy Scriptures," 87).

F. Bettex, the German theologian, makes this positive
statement: "We care little for an inspiration that is not
verbal. We say, if the word wavers, the sense wavers. But
if we are to determine what parts of the Bible are inspired
or not, according as their content seems to us to be important
or unimportant, to pertain to the history of salvation or not,
we constitute ourselves masters of the Word, and are at
the mercy of our own caprice, and that of others. What
shall I do with this semi-faith in a semi-truth? Where and
how shall I distinguish? At every word of Scripture I
feel myself again benighted by doubts.

"Faith in verbal inspiration, many believing Christians
exclaim concernedly, is repulsive to people. Indeed, if
repulsion is to be avoided, many things must be changed,
and a wide field opened for inoffensive exposition. But we
do not see that Christ feared lest he might repel His listeners, or that He in any way took pains to make truth more
acceptable and credible to them. Even His disciples said,
'This is a hard saying'—and it was—'who can hear it?'
And, 'from that time many of His disciples went back, and
walked no more wih Him.' But Jesus did not take back a
single word, did not explain Himself, but asked, 'Will ye
also go away?' (John 6). He who fears lest he repel people
is on the way to seeking praise of people" ("The Bible,
the Word of God," 175-176).

4. PROOFS.

As to inspiration in general, it may briefly be stated that
the holy writers time and again affirm that their messages
came from God. The phrase, "The Lord spake unto Moses,
saying," recurs perpetually. The phrase, "Thus saith the
Lord," is said to occur 2,000 times. The New Testament
cites the Old Testament often and as though it were the Inspired Word. Not including duplicates it has 136 direct
quotations, including duplicates it has about 300 direct quotations, from the Old Testament. Genesis is quoted 19 times,

Exodus 24, Leviticus 5, the Psalms 59, Isaiah 50 times, etc.
These quotations cover so wide an area in both Testaments
and are so definite that we make no mistake as to the doctrine of inspiration in general being held by the New Testament writers. The attitude of Christ and the apostles, like
that of the prophets before them, was the same, "that no
prophecy ever came by the will of man, but men spake
from God, being moved by the Holy Spirit" (2 Pet. 1: 21.
R. V.).

As to verbal inspiration in particular, it can also be
clearly shown that not only the thought, but also the words
of the Bible, were inspired by God in their recording. It
is not here claimed that God has spoken everything that is
recorded in Scripture, for we know that also a host of other
characters come on the scene as speakers and actors. Thus,
even Satan appears in the Garden of Eden, speaking lies
to the first Adam, and in the desert, again speaking lies
to the Second Adam. Satan's words are Satan's words in
the sense that Satan uttered them, but they are God's Words
in the sense that God caused them to be recorded, and they
are inspired in the sense that they were caused to be recorded
accurately by the sacred writers. Both the Old and the New
Testament bear witness to verbal inspiration. In both the
witness is twofold—by example and precept.

Look at some of the examples where the words were
unmistakably given to the speakers. Read, for example, the
story of Balaam's curse frustrated in Num. 22:2—24:25.
It is said of Caiaphas, "who prophesied that Jesus should
die for the nation" (John 11: 51), that "he said not this
of himself." It is said of the disciples who were assembled
together on Pentecost morning that "they were filled with
the Holy Spirit, and began to speak with other tongues,
as the Spirit gave them utterance" (Acts 2:4). This is also
in harmony with the promise of Jesus: "When they deliver
you up, be not anxious how or what ye shall speak; for
it shall be given you in that hour what ye shall speak. For

it is not ye that speak, but the Spirit of your Father That speaketh in you" (Matt. 10: 19-20). This is also in harmony with the actions of the prophets, "who sought and searched diligently, who prophesied of the grace that should come unto you, searching what time the Spirit of Christ in them did point to" (1 Pet. 1:10-11). That is to say, these inspired prophets had to study the meaning of what they themselves had written.

Look now at some Bible passages which plainly teach that the words of the Bible are inspired. A few illustrations: When Moses was called upon to go to Egypt to lead his people out of bondage, he had many excuses for not accepting the call, one of which was, that he was slow of speech and slow of tongue. To this, Jehovah answered that He would be with his mouth and teach him what he should speak (Ex. 4: 10-12). This the Lord did. The psalmist speaks of the Law being perfect. This perfection is due to the fact that it was given verbatim by the Lord. Seven times does Moses tell the Chosen People that the Lord Himself had written the Law on the two tables of stone (See Ex. 31: 18; 32: 16; 34: 1, 28; Deut. 4: 13; 5: 22; 9: 10; 10: 2, 4). Jeremiah, like Moses, hesitated to be God's messenger to his people, pleading in excuse: "Ah, Lord, Jehovah! Behold, I know not how to speak, for I am a child" (Jer. 1: 6). The Lord answered him reassuringly: "Say not, 'I am a child'; for to whomsoever I shall send thee, thou shalt go, and whatsoever I shall command thee, thou shalt speak" (1: 7). "Then Jehovah put forth His hand, and touched my mouth; and Jehovah said unto me, 'Behold, I have put My Words into thy mouth'" (1: 9). As we read on in Jeremiah this phrase meets us time and again: "And the Word of Jehovah came unto me, saying." In Chapter 36 we are told that "Baruch wrote from the mouth of Jeremiah upon a roll of a book." Baruch was thereupon commanded to go and read this book before the people. This he did. The matter was reported to the king, who ordered the book

No. 2. Baruch and Jeremiah Writing. (G. Doré).

fetched and read. When he had heard three or four pages
the king took the book from the hands of the reader, cut
it in pieces with his knife and threw it into the fire. What
was now to be done, when the Word of God was burnt up?
This was done: "Then the Word of Jehovah came to Jeremiah, after that the king had burnt the roll, and the Words
which Baruch wrote at the mouth of Jeremiah, saying, 'Take
thee again another roll, and write in it all the former Words
that were in the first roll, which Jehoiakim the king of Judah
hath burnt'" (36: 27-28). In this way a new copy was
prepared which was word for word like the original.

In the New Testament the statement of Peter that "no
prophecy ever came by the will of man, for men spake from
God, being moved by the Holy Spirit" (2 Pet. 1: 21. R.
V.) is a proof of inspiration. The content of these prophecies never came by the will of man, and the words which
convey these prophecies never came by the will of man.
Men spake from God, being moved by the Holy Spirit.
Hence, we have, as Peter says, "the Word of prophecy made
more sure" (1: 19). The testimony of Paul is fully as assuring on this point as that of Peter. In Gal. 3: 16 he argues
concerning the spelling of a word in the Old Testament.
God had said to Abraham: "I will make thy seed as the
dust of the earth" (Gen. 13: 16). On the basis of this spelling Paul proceeds to argue in this fashion: "Now, to
Abraham were the promises spoken, and to his seed. He
saith not, 'And to seeds,' as of many; but as of one, 'and to
thy Seed,' Which is Christ" (Gal. 3:16). Concerning his
message Paul testifies on another occasion that he had
received "not the spirit of the world, but the Spirit That
is from God; that we might know the things that were freely
given to us of God. Which things also we speak, not in
words which man's wisdom teacheth, but which the Spirit
teacheth, combining spiritual things with spiritual words"
(1 Cor. 2:12-13). The Authorized Version renders 2 Tim.
3:16: "All Scripture is given by inspiration of God,

and is profitable," etc. The Revised Version is different only in diction: "All Scripture inspired of God is profitable," etc. Paul had been speaking of the Scriptures, which Timothy from his childhood had known. They are all inspired, all profitable, all on a par. If they were all inspired, then every single one is inspired, then every part is inspired, then every word is inspired. Christ teaches this even more directly. How often He appealed to the Written Word. He met the Tempter with this Word: "It is written." He met the Pharisees on this platform: "It is written." He warned His hearers: "Think not that I came to destroy the Law or the Prophets. I came not to destroy, but to fulfill. For verily I say unto you, Till heaven and earth shall pass away, one jot or one tittle shall in no wise pass away from the Law, till all things shall be accomplished" (Matt. 5: 17-18). The jot is the smallest Hebrew letter, called yod, and represented in the Hebrew character thus: (ׁ). The tittle is the horn, a short projection in certain Hebrew consonants extending the base line beyond the upright line which rests upon it, thus: (ב).

Give the literal meaning of inspiration. Its general meaning. Its special meaning. Give the distinction between revelation and inspiration.

Why was it necessary for God to inspire the holy prophets, evangelists and apostles who wrote the Bible?

To what extent was the Bible inspired? To what extent are our present printed Bibles inspired? Give the opinion of Beecher on verbal inspiration. Of Urquhart. Of Bettex. In cases of this kind, when great men disagree, who shall decide?

Give proofs from Scripture that the content of the Bible is inspired. That the words are inspired. Give examples from the Old Testament proving verbal inspiration. From the New Testament.

What does your Catechism say about inspiration? Your Bible history? Find appropriate hymns in your hymnal bearing on this subject. Look up the Bible passages referred to in the lesson, and find additional references to this subject in the Bible. In what ways can the contents of this lesson help you in your Bible study? In your faith and works?

LESSON FIVE.   THE ORIGIN OF THE BIBLE:
IV. PRESERVATION.

1. DEFINITION.

Preservation is the act or process of keeping safe from destruction or change. Every honest Christian wants his Bible to be just like the original, whose Author is God, whose message was revealed by Him, whose writers were inspired to write by Him. Everyone who has occasion to study the history of this Book can easily discover for himself that God has providentially, even miraculously, preserved His Book from being lost, mutilated or altered. Over a hundred years ago Voltaire, a noted skeptic, prophesied that within a century this Book would disappear from the earth. He stands before us as a false prophet. The Bible still lives, in over 500 more languages than in Voltaire's day, and in millions of new copies every year. It is reported that the very house of Voltaire is being used to store Bibles.

2. NECESSITY.

Why was it necessary for the Lord to preserve His Book? Because of its priceless value, the undying hatred of His enemies, the law of organic decay and the unwariness of man.

Its priceless value. When a person gets a large sum of money, he is careful not only to put it into his pocketbook, but also to have it securely locked up in a safe or vault. He does the same with valuable papers, such as deeds to land. The Bible is more precious than much fine gold. It is our deed to Heaven.

> The Word of God, our heritage,
> Our children shall inherit.

Because of its value God has guarded it from destruction.

The undying hatred of His enemies. Satan and the rest of the fallen angels are God's enemies as well as man's. The unconverted are also His enemies at heart, if not in conduct. "The mind of the flesh is enmity toward God" (Rom. 8: 7). Now, what does undying hatred prompt the Devil to do? It prompts him to rob mankind of this gracious gift, whereby salvation can be found. It prompts him to try to get it changed or corrupted, if he can not get it set aside. It prompts him to get men to disbelieve it or to misinterpret it, if he can not corrupt its text. So also have men hated this Good Book. King Jehoiakim took the roll that Baruch had written and threw it into the fire, which consumed it. But God was not going to see the book of Jeremiah thus lost to the world. Therefore He "dictated" another copy of it. When Luther began printing the Bible and spreading it out to the hungry multitudes throughout Europe, the Roman Church hastened to burn all the Bibles it could lay hands on as well as "heretics" who were bold enough to read it. God, however, saved His Book.

> Had God not come, may Israel say,
> Had God not come to aid us,
> Our enemies on that sad day
> Would surely have dismayed us   (Luther.)

The law of organic decay. Substances are either organic or inorganic. Inorganic are those of the mineral kingdom, organic are from the animal and vegetable kingdoms. Organic substances are specially liable to decay. Witness the stench from any dead animal, the rotting of any fallen tree. Now, the material from which books are generally made is organic. The Old Testament Scriptures were originally in the form of rolls, made of papyrus or parchment. Papyrus is from a plant, and parchment is from the skin of an animal. Both are subject to decay. Naturally, all of the original manuscripts of the Bible have, on account of this law, been lost. Therefore it was necessary that God kept watch over His Book.

The unwariness of man. Man is prone to be unwatchful

and to fall asleep even when on guard. He seems to understand the value of material things and takes great precau-
tions to guard his own. He uses locks and bolts and
alarms. He insures his life and property. He must have
a policeman on the street corner and an army and navy
on the border of his land or within ready call. In spiritual
matters he is not so wise or watchful. And even when his
heart is right with God and his intentions are of the best,
he is apt to blunder. Take, for example, in the matter of
copying the Bible or translating it. How easy it was to
make a blunder here—misspelling, omitting, interpolating,
faulty translations, etc. Some of the copies of the Bible
do have words misspelt; some, passages omitted; others,
passages added; and some versions do have some passages
incorrectly translated. Nevertheless, God has kept watch
over the copying and translating of the Bible, so that the
mistakes of omission and commission are speedily corrected by other zealous scholars whom He calls to the work.

3. EXTENT.

The original manuscripts as they came from the hands
of the holy prophets, evangelists and apostles have not
been preserved. They have all been lost. The manuscripts of the Old Testament now in the possession of
Christendom are but copies, according to Kennicott 630 in
number, according to De Rossi 751. Some of these are only
fragments. None of them is of great age. Kennicott
estimated the Reuchlin Ms. in the Imperial Library at
Vienna to be the oldest, being dated 1106 A. D. Pinner
describes in the Odessa collection three fragments, from
881, 843 and 580 A. D. Margoliouth reports having seen
in the possession of a Jewish family in Damascus a manuscript which according to a note upon its title page belonged
to the third century (Green). The original texts of the
New Testament are also lost. But the number of handwritten copies is quite numerous and constantly increasing
through the increasing interest in archaeological explora-

tions and search for ancient manuscripts. In 1884 there were 2,094 such manuscripts on hand (Belsheim's "Om Bibelen"). In 1903 the number had increased to 3,800 (Haas' "Biblical Criticism"). These are relatively older than the Old Testament copies, the oldest being now in the Imperial Library of Petrograd, dating from 330 A. D.

The manuscripts that we have—many of them fragmentary and of uncertain date—are the chief source of the original text of the Bible. Both Christians and Jews feel satisfied, however, that by means of these they have been able to get the Bible in its truth and purity as originally recorded by the servants of God. Scholars have examined every word and letter and compared all the manuscripts most minutely. They have marked and counted and discussed every variation. With comparatively few exceptions the manuscripts practically agree. The Old Testament copies have only 1,314 variant readings of value, of which only 147 affect the sense. The New Testament has indeed 200,000 variant readings (Haas), but only 400 influence the sense of a word, and only 50 are of any importance (H. G. Stub). Hort's final judgment is, that only one thousandth part of the whole text has any variation of importance (Westcott and Hort's "Greek Text"). Gregory finds that these substantial variations make one half page of fifteen lines ("Canon and Text of the New Testament", 528).

The method of comparison is about as follows: A standard is set up, say, from the most ancient and complete manuscript. Then each document is in turn compared with respect to that standard, word for word, letter by letter. Supposing we should compare the English versions in similar manner, would we be apt to get any variant readings? Let us take an example: Let us take from Heb. 1:1 ("God, having of old time spoken unto the fathers") the word time. Let us set up Tyndale's translation of 1525 as the standard. Tyndale renders it: "God

in tyme past." Tyme is, then, a variant reading, which
we shall call No. 1. Let us proceed to another version—
the Geneva Bible of 1560. This reads: "At sondrie times"
—variant reading No. 2. Next we go to the Rheims Version
of 1582, which has: "Diversely and many vvaies in times
past"—variation No. 3. We continue with the Authorized
Version of 1611 and find this reading: "God who at sundry
times"—variation No. 4. Here, then, out of five standard
English translations, no two have the same reading, and
yet the difference does not in this case at all affect the
sense. The Authorized Version of 1911 should be an exact
copy of that of 1611, yet we can find thousands of changes,
not unintentionally, but intentionally made. For example,
in the 1611 edition Heb. 1: 2 reads as follows: God "hath
in these last *dayes* spoken *vnto vs* by his *Sonne*." In the
1911 edition it reads: God "hath in these last *days* spoken
unto us by his *Son*."

God has guided the copying of the manuscripts and preserved them from extinction. He has used the consecrated
efforts of Biblical scholars at all times and places to try
to preserve the original text. The Old Testament was
originally written in Hebrew and the New Testament in
Greek. The Hebrew text of the Old Testament and the
Greek text of the New Testament as we now have them
represent the combined labors of all the scholars preceding,
and present a text which in all essential points surely agrees
with the apostolic original. It represents much more than
that—God's faithful preservation of His Word in its original
truth and purity.

4. PROOFS.

The Son of God has said: "Till heaven and earth pass
away, one jot or one tittle shall in no wise pass away from
the Law, till all things be accomplished" (Matt. 5: 18).
The Good Book shall stand. God wills it. He wants no one
to change it by adding to it or subtracting from it. He has
solemnly warned against such attempts: "I testify unto

every man that heareth the words of the prophecy of this book: <u>If any man shall add unto them, God shall add unto him the plagues which are written in this book; and if any man shall take away from the words of the book of this prophecy, God shall take away his part from the tree of life, and out of the Holy City, which are written in this book"</u> (Rev. 22: 18-19).

"The Old Testament was submitted to the calamities and miseries which befell the people of Israel. <u>The New Testament was persecuted by Jew and pagan alike.</u> Through seven (ten) pitiless persecutions, stretching through two and a half centuries, it shared the fate of the hunted and afflicted Christians. At times it seemed as though its holy light would be extinguished; but there was no one found who was able to quench its flame. Was there ever a book which has been subjected to such vindictive and persistent hate? Nevertheless, it still remains the One Great Book of the world. . . . We maintain: the preservation of this wonderful book is no less a miracle than its origin. That almighty God, Who was able to preserve His Word through the persecutions and vicissitudes of centuries, could, most assuredly, have preserved to us the original manuscripts, if He had found it expedient.

"It is more than passing strange that although no book so severely arraigns the Jews, nevertheless they have been largely instrumental in preserving its integrity. No book so utterly repudiates papacy; yet for centuries the Papal Church was its guardian. 'God moves in a mysterious way, His wonders to perform!' " (J. A. O. Stub's "Verbal Inspiration," 80-81).

As to the loss of the original manuscripts, even that may be regarded as a blessing. It is hard telling what extra benefits men would have derived from them or what extra hardships they would have had to endure. The history of sacred relics is not very uplifting, to say the least. It might, however, be worth while to hear a few lines on this subject from Walsh's "Curiosity of Popular Customs" (831-833): Europe was overflowed with relics. Whenever a town in the Holy Land was conquered, the Crusaders looked first for relics, as more precious than gold or gems. St. Louis made two unfortunate crusades, but he comforted himself with the relics he brought home. Chief among these was the holy crown of thorns. The court of France advanced as far as Troyes, in Champagne, to meet with devotion this inestimable relic. It was borne in triumph through Paris by the king himself, barefooted and clad only in his shirt. Among other treasures secured were a portion of the true cross, part of the baby linen of the infant Jesus, the bones of Moses, the sigh which St. Joseph heaved when he was splitting wood, feathers from the wings of Gabriel and Michael, the thorn in the flesh of Paul, the beam of the Bethlehem star, the perch whence the cock crew its reproach to Peter, the bones of the ass on which the royal entry was made, Moses' staff, manna from the desert, a piece of the rock from which he drew water, a portion of Pilate's staircase, the column where Jesus was scourged, drops of blood and hairs of Christ. Many of these relics are preserved to this day, as at Rome, Venice, Constance, Soissons, Paris, Corbie, Namur, St. Denis, Genoa and Aix-la-Chapelle.

"We also suggest that if we had owned one of the original manuscripts, this would have been misused. In His wise providence God has not permitted us to have any article which our Savior owned while He lived among men. It is common knowledge that considerable humbug—we came near saying idolatry—is permitted in connection with the fragments supposed to be from the original cross. We are to walk by faith, and not by sight. It is very likely that Protestantism would have received little benefit from the existence of such manuscript. It would in all probability have remained in the Vatican library. What an instrument with which to tyrannize Christendom!"

We have a sure, prophetic Word,
By inspiration of the Lord;
And though assailed on every hand,
Jehovah's Word shall ever stand.

By powers of empire banned and burned,
By pagan pride rejected, spurned,
The Word still stands the Christian's trust,
While haughty empires lie in dust.

(Stub's "Verbal Inspiration," 82-83.)

What is meant by preservation of the Bible? Show how Voltaire's prophecy came to naught.

Give four reasons why God should seek to preserve the Bible. Illustrate each.

To what extent has the original text been preserved? What is the present number of Old Testament manuscripts? Where are they kept? What is their age? Their value? How many New Testament manuscripts have been preserved? What became of the original text? Have we, then, no original text at present? Explain. What is the chief source of this text? How many variations have been found in the manuscripts? Do these variant readings essentially affect the sense of Scripture? Give an example of variations in modern versions. To what extent does a standard text now agree with the original text?

Give proofs that the original text has been preserved. In what way may the loss of the original text be regarded as a blessing?

What does your Catechism say about the preservation of the Bible? Your Bible history? Find appropriate hymns in your hymnal bearing on this subject. Look up references to this subject in the Bible. In what ways can the contents of this lesson help you in your Bible study? In your faith and works?

LESSON SIX. THE PROPERTIES OF THE BIBLE:
I. AUTHORITY.

1. DEFINITION.

Property means that which is proper to anything, its peculiar qualities or attributes, ownership. What peculiar qualities can we say is owned by the Bible, belongs essentially to this Book? We shall mention four such properties: Authority, perfection, clearness and efficacy.

By authority of the Bible is meant its right to claim "unrestricted acceptance of all its statements, full assent to all its teachings, unwavering confidence in all its promises, and willing observance of all its demands by those whom they concern" (Graebner's "Doctrinal Theology," 9). The Bible, like Jesus, when He was amongst men, calmly and majestically assumes this inherent right, "speaks as one with authority and not as the scribes."

2. NECESSITY.

The word authority is related to author, the beginner of a thing, the creator, the writer. It is but fair to suppose that He Who has created the world should have the right and the power to say something regarding its government; that He Who has written His Law in the human heart should have authority over it in life and in death. The need of authority is seen everywhere in society. The very smallest community must have its head, even as the home has it. The local authorities are subject to the state, and the state is subject to the nation. But all the powers that be are ordained of God and also subject to Him. The need of authority is preeminently apparent in the teaching of morals and religion. Supposing, for example, that the Moral Law be taught in the public schools of this country, in some community that does not permit any reference to God. How shall these Ten Commandments be taught which are at the basis of all good laws the world over? Take the First Commandment. That has to be omitted, because it mentions the name of God and even has Him to speak in the first person as a living God with absolute authority. The Second Commandment must be rejected on the same ground. The Third seems better, until we come to human legislation concerning the Sabbath. What a difference of opinion and of practice even in the same community. Who has the final word on the question? We can continue in this manner through all of the Ten Commandments, and shall get no satisfaction anywhere unless we accept God as the Authority. God must speak the authoritative Word. It is also necessary, as has been said before, that this Word be written.

3. EXTENT.

Now, to what extent shall we acknowledge the authority of the Bible? In the first place, we must without any restriction accept all of its statements, even though we can not understand them, and even though some of them may seem to conflict with other statements in the Bible. Shall we accept them if they, for example, conflict with the accepted teachings of modern scientists, moralists and historians? Yes, indeed. The Pharisees and Sadducees of Jesus' day were great scholars, and no doubt more learned in the Scripture than most scholars are today. They had worked out their theories and systems and were cock-sure that they were right. For example, with respect to Jesus, they were positive that He was not the One That they expected. But He showed them that they were wrong. Thus He spoke to them: "Ye search the Scriptures, because ye think that in them ye have eternal life; and these are they which bear witness of Me; and ye will not come to Me, that ye may have life" (John 5: 39-40). The trouble with these learned scribes was, that they really did not accept the Scripture as authority, hence they would not implicitly believe. This was also the trouble, at times even with the disciples, as it is shown in the story of the two who went to

Emmaus. You recall that Jesus drew near and went with them. He entered into conversation with them regarding the eventful last days. Finally He said to them: "O foolish men, and slow of heart to believe in all that the prophets have spoken!" (Luke 24: 25.)

In the second place, we must give full assent to all its teachings. The Samaritans, for example, accepted only a part of the Bible, the Pentateuch, or Five Books of Moses. Of this fraction of the Bible they accepted only such teachings as were agreeable to their politics or desires. The Jews accept the Old Testament as the Word of God, but not the New Testament. Of the Old Testament they follow only such teachings as suit their purposes. They reject the Savior, although, as Christ said, these Scriptures bear witness of Him. The Unitarians accept the whole Bible as the Word of God, but they accept only such teachings as conform to their views of sin and salvation. To them Christ was only a man, while the Bible teaches that He is a God-Man. They teach that we can save ourselves, but Scripture teaches that there is salvation only through Jesus, our crucified and risen Savior.

In the third place, we must believe all the promises given in the Bible. They are many, and precious, and pertain to all our wants and wishes, for body and soul, for time and eternity, and are all yea and amen in Jesus (2 Cor. 1: 20). In Samuel Clarke's little book entitled "Scripture Promises" there are listed about 2,000 Bible verses, each one containing one or more promises. These verses are grouped into 9 chapters and 107 topical sections. It is a handy little book and is very useful, for it presents in small space so many of the choicest promises of God. Not all of them, by any means, possibly not one-tenth of them, are in this list. Oh, if we only knew them every one and believed them! The trouble with the Children of Israel as they left Egypt was, that they did not believe in the promises of the Lord that He would give them the Promised Land.

Therefore they murmured on the way; therefore they rebelled and refused to enter the land; and therefore they had to lay their weary bones to rest in the wilderness. As we read about this Chosen People, how often we grow impatient with them and sigh: "If they had only believed." Take, for example, the case of King Ahaz (Isa. 7). He was threatened by an invasion, and sought an alliance with Assyria, promising to be an obedient servant and to pay tribute. Isaiah called upon the fearful king and promised him a better Ally, Jehovah, the Lord of hosts. Ahaz would not believe. Isaiah told the king he might demand any sign he pleased, in the depth below or in the height above, in testimony of the Lord's support. But Ahaz wanted no sign. Then the Lord Himself gave him a sign without his wish: "Behold, a virgin shall conceive, and bear a Son, and shall call His name Immanuel" (God-with-us). As we look back at Ahaz we think him worse than foolish, but, alas, we recognize in him our own weakness and the weakness of our fallen race. We find it so hard to believe. We begin to realize that we can not by our own reason or strength believe, but it is the work of the Holy Spirit, and we cry out: "Lord, I believe, help Thou my unbelief."

In the fourth place, we should willingly observe all of its demands and commands which apply to us. There are some demands in Scripture which do not now apply to us, as, for example, the ceremonial laws of the Old Covenant. The Jews of the Old Covenant had to offer the blood of goats and calves and sheep, but the children of the New Covenant escape this duty, since Christ once for all offered His body as a sacrifice for sins (Heb. 10). People are liable to make one or more of three serious mistakes with respect to the demands of the Bible. These are: Observing those demands which do not now apply to Christians, failing to observe those demands which do apply to Christians, and setting up new demands which are purely human, not divine. The Jews were forbidden to eat pork, for example.

This demand is clearly removed from the Christians. Yet there are members of the Christian Church who observe this Old Testament law as though it were still in force. There are others who go still further in this same connection and make a rule that no Christian shall eat any meat whatsoever. Like the Pharisees of old, they teach doctrines that are not the commands of God, but only of men (Mark 7: 6-8). The most common mistake of all is that of ignoring the commands which clearly apply to us, which include the Moral Law of the Old Covenant and the call of the Gospel of the New Covenant. We should willingly seek to obey His will in everything. We should have the same mind as was in Christ Jesus, Who said it was His meat to do His Father's will (John 4: 34). Even with this attitude we shall often be obliged to confess that we have done what we ought not to have done, and have left undone what we ought to have done.

In short, the Bible should be to us our only source and rule of faith, doctrine and works. We go to the Bible to find out what it has to say about every question of faith, doctrine and works. We use the Bible as a rule to measure up every belief, teaching and practice. Some deny the reality of sin. Why not believe that there is no sin, teach that there is no sin, and do exactly as we please according to the lust of the flesh, the lust of the eyes, and the vainglory of life? Look to the Bible as the source and rule. It teaches more forcibly than any other book, and more directly, the curse of sin, whose wages is death. Or, take another example. The world is full of religious and anti-religious sects and societies, with the most divergent creeds and practices. Some of these come to every man and woman, yes, to every boy and girl, saying: "Come and join us, for we have the truth." What shall one do who is beset by so tempting allurements from without and by doubts from within? Isaiah gives a good answer: "To the Law and to the Testimony" (Isa. 8: 20). That is, find out for cer-

tain what the Bible teaches, and say with Jesus, when
tempted: "It is written."

> God gave His Word by holy men,
> The words dictating to their pen;
> That Word shall shine with glorious ray
> When heaven and earth have passed away.
>
> It is not changeful human thought
> That here to darkened souls is brought,
> But everlasting truth and light,
> That shed on man their heavenly light.
>
> It makes the way of faith so plain
> That none in darkness need remain;
> Who meekly choose it as their guide
> Shall not in doubt and gloom abide.
>
> It makes the path of duty clear,
> That all may therein persevere;
> Who humbly heed its righteous way
> Shall not from right and virtue stray.
>
> For faith and life, for thought and deed,
> No other rule and guide we need:
> When God the King proclaims His will,
> 'Tis meet all others should be still.
>
> To this alone may we adhere,
> In faith and love and godly fear,
> And ever walking by His Word,
> Give glory to our sovereign Lord.   (M. Loy.)

4. PROOFS.

The proofs for the authority of the Sacred Scriptures
are practically the same as those for its authorship, revelation, inspiration and preservation. If it is God's Book,
revealed by Him, inspired by Him and preserved by Him, it
has the same authority as if He were present in person
speaking. Only this must be noted: That in case there is
any serious question as to the meaning of a passage, it is the
original text, and not the translations that must finally de-

cide. Any document is, before a court, authentic only in the language it was originally written in. The original text is genuine and authentic and authoritative beyond all versions. Still, under all ordinary circumstances, any standard translation is authoritative.

We speak of human books as being good and reliable authorities, if their authors were in a position to know whereof they wrote, and if they were honest, painstaking, and otherwise competent. It goes without saying that the Lord knew what He was going to say and how best to say it, when He made the Bible.

It is authoritative because it has no historical, moral or scientific blunders. God's Word is truth (John 17: 17). Infidels have stood up and boldly declared that the Bible is full of historical mistakes, but the inscriptions on the monuments silently bear witness to the truthfulness of the Biblical record. Philosophers have sneered at the value of the Moral Law, which the psalmist declared to be perfect (Ps. 19:7). And yet experience has proved that there is no better. The Moral Law is perfect and all inclusive, though containing scarcely over 100 words as given in the Ten Commandments. How imperfect are human laws, though numerous and long drawn out. Senator Smoot has called attention to the fact that 62,014 laws and 63,379 court decisions were made in the United States in the last five years. These filled over a million pages. God's Law is less than one page and written, in addition, on each human conscience. Besides, no human law is of any account or stability unless in its spirit it harmonizes with the Law of God. No wonder that Jesus said of it that He came to fulfill it, for He would certainly not have come down to earth just to fulfill the conflicting ordinances of men. No wonder that He said that "till heaven and earth pass away, one jot or one tittle shall in no wise pass away from the Law, till all things be accomplished" (Matt. 5: 18). Scientists have arrogantly proclaimed that the Biblical account of creation is incorrect, hence they can not accept it as an authority on this subject. Now, Scripture is not a book of science, but wherever it deals with scientific facts or principles it is inerrant and final authority. The men of science, no matter how learned they may be, at best understand only in part. Some day they will cast aside their present theory as to creation as they have cast aside many another interesting speculation. But the Word of God will remain unchanged till the end of time.

———

Define authority.

Why is it necessary that God should have absolute authority?

To what extent should we acknowledge the authority of the Bible? Illustrate.

Is there anything commanded in the Old Testament which has been revoked in the New Testament? Illustrate.

Prove that the Bible is authoritative.

What does your Catechism say about the authority of the Bible? Your Bible history? Find appropriate hymns in your hymnal bearing on this subject. Look up the Bible passages referred to in your lesson, and find additional references to this subject in the Bible. In what ways can the contents of this lesson help you in your Bible study? In your faith and works?

LESSON SEVEN. THE PROPERTIES OF THE BIBLE: II. PERFECTION.

1. DEFINITION.

By perfection of the Scriptures is meant that they do not contain any errors, that what they say is perfectly true, and that they "fully and perfectly instruct us concerning all the things necessary to salvation" (Gerhard's "Loci Theologici," II, 286).

2. NECESSITY.

"To err is human." Everything from the hand of man is more or less imperfect. In all the great issues of life, especially those relating to sin and salvation, nothing that man has thought of or attempted to do is of any avail. He stands helpless as at the Flood and the Confusion of Tongues at Babel. There is a need of a perfect Word, the Word of truth from the lips of God, Who is not a man that He should lie, and Who is the same today, yesterday and for ever.

3. EXTENT.

In the first place, the Word of God does not contain any mistake of any kind. A few years ago a certain lecturer went from town to town telling church people and others about the mistakes of Moses, charging his hearers a dollar for his oratory and robbing many of them of their childhood faith besides. All of his arguments have been disproved time and again. The only chance for errors to creep into the text of the Bible is through copying, translating or printing, but when these are detected they are at once rectified. No book in the world has been copied with such painstaking care, none translated with such careful preparation and arduous investigation, none printed and proof-read with such holy zeal and amazing diligence.

In the next place, the Bible contains everything needed by man in order to come to a knowledge of the truth and be saved. Some say that it must be supplemented by tradition. If that were so, it would not be perfect. Others say it must yield to reason. Reason would reject what it could not understand or what it did not wish to tolerate and would add an endless amount of new things, which would shift as often as the theories of scholars and the fashions of society.

4. PROOFS.

The very nature of the Book is proof of its perfection. It is God's Word, revealed, inspired, preserved by Him. It claims to be perfect, as David sings:

"The Law of Jehovah is perfect, restoring the soul;
The Testimony of Jehovah is sure, making wise the simple" (Ps. 19:7).

It claims to be sufficient, as Paul writes:

"In everything ye are enriched in Him (Christ), in all utterance and in all knowledge, even as the Testimony of Christ was confirmed in you, so that ye come behind in no gift" (1 Cor. 1:5-6). The main object of the Bible is to teach the great truth that Jesus is the Way of salvation to all believing souls, for, as John says: "These are written, that ye might believe that Jesus is the Christ, the Son of God; and that believing ye might have life through His name" (John 20:31). If any one will try to obey the Word and give it place in his heart, he will experience for himself that the Word is perfect. This was Christ's test before the unbelieving Pharisees: "If any man will do His will, he shall know of the doctrine, whether it be of God, or whether I speak of Myself" (John 7:17). This rule works as inevitably as testing the multiplication table to see if it is correct, or putting one's finger on the fire to see if it will burn.

Many comparisons of the relative perfection of the Bible and the products from uninspired writers might be made. The following is of interest:

"The Gospel narrative observes an almost unbroken silence as to the long abode of Jesus at Nazareth. Of the void thus left the Church became early impatient. During the first four centuries many attempts were made to fill it up. Some of these apocryphal gospels are still extant, notably that which deals with the infancy and youth of the Redeemer; and it is instructive to notice how those succeeded who tried to lift the veil which covers the earlier years of Christ. Let another state the contrast between the New Testament records and the spurious gospels: 'The case stands thus: our Gospels present us with a glorious picture of a mighty Savior, the mythic gospels with that of a contemptible one. In our Gospels He exhibits a superhuman wisdom; in the mythic ones this aspect of character is entirely wanting. In our Gospels not one stain of sinfulness defiles His character; in the mythic ones the Boy Jesus is both pettish and malicious. Our Gospels exhibit to us a sublime morality; not one ray of it shines in those of the mythologists. The miracles of the one and of the other stand contrasted on every point' (Row).

"These spurious gospels were written by men who lived not long after the apostolic age; by Christians who wished to honor the Savior in all they said about Him; by men who had the portraiture of Him before them which the Gospels supply. And yet these men, many of them better taught than the apostles, with the advantage of two or three centuries of Christian thought and study, could not produce a fancy sketch of the Child Jesus without violating our sense of propriety, and shocking our moral sense. The distance between the Gospels of the New Testament and the pseudo-gospels is measured by the distance between the product of the Spirit of God, and that of the fallen human mind.

"Let us take another illustration. The nineteenth century has been very fruitful in the production of what are commonly called 'Lives of Christ.' Contrast with the Gospels four such 'Lives,' perhaps the completest and the best, taken altogether, of those written by English-speaking people—Andrew's, Geikie's, Hanna's and Edersheim's. The authors of our Gospels had no models on which to frame their work. The path they trod had never before been pressed by human feet. The authors of the 'Lives' have not only these incomparable narratives as their pattern and the chief source of all their material, but numberless other such 'Lives' suggestive as to form and construction, and the culture and the research of eighteen centuries lying behind them. But would any one venture for a moment to set forth these 'Lives' as rivals of our Gospels? Much information and helpfulness are to be derived from the labors of these Christian scholars, and others who have toiled in the same field; but how far they all fall below the New Testament record it is needless to show. Indeed, all such writings are largely antiquated and scarcely read, though they are quite young in years, so soon does man's work decay and die.

"Let the contrast be noted as to size or bulk. Andrew's book contains 615 pages; Geikie's over 1,200; Hanna's over 2,100; Edersheim's, 1,500 pages. The four combined have no less than 5,490 pages, enough in these busy days to require months of reading to go but once through their contents. Bagster prints the Four Gospels in 82 pages; the Oxford, in 104; the Revised, 120. In the Bagster, Matthew has but 23; Mark, 13; Luke, 25; and John, 21. Less than one hundred pages of Four Gospels against more than five thousand four hundred of the four 'Lives.'

"Countless volumes, great and small, in the form of commentary, exposition, notes, harmony and history are written on these brief records. How happens it that such stores of wisdom and knowledge lie garnered in these short pieces? Who taught the evangelists this superhuman power of expansion and contraction, of combination and separation, of revelation in the words and more revelation below the words? Who taught them so to describe the person and work of the Lord Jesus that the description satisfies the most illiterate and the most learned, is adapted to minds of the most limited capacity, and to those of the widest grasp? Whence did they derive the infinite skill they display in grouping together events, discourses and actions in such fashion that vividly before us is the deathless beauty of a perfect Life? There is but one answer to these questions, there can be no other. The Spirit of the living God filled their minds with His unerring wisdom and controlled their human speech. To that creative Spirit Who has peopled the world with living organisms so minute that only the microscope can reveal their presence, it is not hard to give us in so brief a compass the sublime portrait of the Son of Man. To men it is impossible" (W. G. Moorhead's "Moral Glory of Jesus Christ a Proof of Inspiration," in "The Fundamentals," 56-58).

———

What is meant by the perfection of the Scriptures?
Why is it necessary that the Scriptures should be perfect?
To what extent are the Scriptures perfect?
Prove that the Scriptures are perfect.
What does your Catechism say about the perfection of the Scriptures? Your Bible history? Find appropriate hymns in your hymnal bearing on this subject. Look up the Bible passages referred to in your lesson, and find additional references to this subject in the Bible. In what ways can the contents of this lesson help you in your Bible study? In your faith and works?

LESSON EIGHT. THE PROPERTIES OF THE BIBLE: III. CLEARNESS.

1. DEFINITION.

Clearness is the quality or state of being clear, free from obscurity and ambiguity, unclouded. In all of the things the knowledge of which is necessary to salvation, the Bible is abundantly clear.

2. NECESSITY.

Since the message of the Holy Writ was intended by God for all mankind, it would have to be of such a nature that everybody with even less than average intelligence should be able to grasp it without difficulty, and should be stated in such language that both young and old, ignorant and educated might understand it. In preparing books for children, authors try to use language adapted to their ages and capacities. Necessity compels them to follow this rule in order that their books may be of use to the children. So necessity, humanly speaking, has kept the Bible message and language on a level with the masses of all times and places. "Why did not God, if He were a scientist," wrote one young man who was on the road to doubt and utter darkness, "why did He not tell Moses about electricity?" He knew everything about electricity, never fear, but the people of Moses' day did not, and would not then have understood the term. God revealed Himself progressively and adapted His revelation in deed and word according to the needs, conditions, environment, degree of culture and receptivity of men. (Cf. Heb. 1:1-2; Eph. 3:5; John 16:12.)

3. EXTENT.

In all matters, as stated above, the knowledge of which is necessary to salvation, the Bible is clear in all places, to all people and at all times. But it is not equally clear in all places, to all people and at all times.

It is not equally clear in all places. The story of Joseph being thrown into the pit and sold, is, for example, clear to young and old, but the vision of the Seventy Weeks is hard to see through. The account of the birth of Jesus gladdens every heart that listens to it, but the wonderful pictures in John's Revelation have puzzled the heads of the wisest of every generation. The Bible has been compared to the sea. On its shore the little child may frolic, but the tallest adult will soon, when wading, get beyond his depth. The oldest mariner has not visited every port, nor sounded every deep; the profoundest scientist does not know all of the secrets of the sea. So the Bible is clear to all, yet, in places, is too deep for all. Therefore Paul testifies that we know in part only, that we now see in a mirror, darkly, but beyond the grave we shall see more clearly, and know fully even as we are fully known by God (1 Cor. 13: 9-12; Cf. Rom. 11:33; 2 Pet. 3:15-16).

It is not equally clear to all people. This is also true of any other book. Arithmetic is not equally clear to everybody, nor is algebra, nor any other subject. A child does not, as a rule, understand as well as a grown-up. Hence we have graded courses at school and graded books for each course. Likewise graded lessons in Bible story and Bible doctrine. The Bible grows clearer as one progresses in knowledge and experience. Even the way of salvation becomes clearer—and dearer—with the growth in knowledge and the added light of years. It is clearest to those who have tried to live according to its precepts and who have permitted the Word to dwell in their hearts.

It is not equally clear at all times. In this respect, too, it is like other books. Today the pupil does not seem to understand his problem in fractions; yesterday it was clear to him; tomorrow, perhaps, the clouds will again pass away, and he will wonder why he did not understand the process or get the correct results.

When the Bible seems obscure to anyone, he should

remember two things: That he must study it as he studies any secular book, and that he must study it as God's Book ought to be studied. How should a secular book be studied? The meanings of the words as used in the text must, for example, be determined. Then the context, what goes before and what comes after, must be had in mind. Parallel passages must be examined, etc. How should God's Book be studied? Here we must bear in mind that sin has darkened the human understanding and that the Holy Spirit enlightens the understanding, brings to our hearts, if we ask Him, a living knowledge of the truth of the Bible. Therefore we should most earnestly pray for His enlightenment.

4. PROOFS.

How can we prove that the Lord chose to teach in His Book most clearly the elementary truths concerning the Law and the Gospel? We might ask: How can we prove that the sun shines or that we can see? For it is a fact that the Word of God is as the sun at high noon, while the absence of the Word leaves one in midnight darkness. And it is a fact that without the Word we walk about as children of darkness, blindly groping our way, while with the Word we see clearly and walk freely and work bravely as children of light. The Bible itself testifies to its clearness in many passages. Take, for example, a couple of chords from the ancient psalmist:

> Thy Word is a Lamp unto my feet,
> And a Light unto my path (Ps. 119: 105).

And again, in the same Psalm:

> The opening of Thy Words giveth light;
> It giveth understanding unto the simple (119: 130).

Paul writes to the Corinthians as follows:

> But if our Gospel be hid, it is hid to them that are lost; in whom the god of this world hath blinded the minds of them that believe not, lest the light of the glorious Gospel of Christ, Who is the image of God, should shine unto them (2 Cor. 4: 3-4).

Peter, also, likens the Word to a light:

We have also a more sure Word of prophecy; whereunto ye do
well that ye take heed, as unto a light that shineth in a dark place;
until the day dawn, and the day-star arise in your hearts (2 Pet.
1: 19).

In addition to these proof passages in the Bible as to
its perspicuity, the following will be representative of the
many warm and winged words which have been spoken on
this theme by thoughtful men.   The speaker is J. G. Fitch,
an English schoolmaster:

"Has it ever occurred to you to ask how it is that so many
of us have a much clearer knowledge of the history of the
Jews than of our own annals?   Is it not because the Bible is
in one respect the model of all history?   Look at it without
reference to its higher claims, simply as a piece of narrative.
Consider how it is that it conveys to its readers so full and
clear a knowledge of Jewish history during many centuries.

"There is, for example, a period of about one thousand
years from Abraham to Rehoboam, and how is the history
of the time told?   We have first the story of the patriarch's
personal career.   We are led to understand his character
and his motives; we see him as the center of a scene in which
pastoral life is attractively portrayed, and which affords us
glimpses of the patriarchal government, of life and manners, and of the social and domestic conditions of the
time.   In like manner we see Isaac and Jacob with their
families and their environments; and then the narrative,
disdaining to go into details about lesser matters, expands
into a copious biography of Joseph, whose personal history and fortunes make us incidentally acquainted with the
state of Egypt, its government, its political economy, and
many facts of great interest, which, had they been tabulated
in a book of outlines, we should not have cared to learn.

"The history then passes over four hundred years with
scarcely a sentence, and again becomes full and graphic
about the Exodus and the journey in the Wilderness, invest-
ing even the details of legislation with a special interest
by connecting them with the person, the character and the

private life of the lawgiver, Moses. And thus the story is continued, sometimes passing over a long interval of inaction or obscurity with a few words of general description, or a list of names; but, fastening here and there on the names of Joshua, of Gideon, of Samuel, of Saul, of David, and, narrating the history of the times with the circumstances of his life—.

"Who does not see that such a narrative precisely corresponds to the real picture of a nation's history? In the life of a people there are always great epochs of change and activity, occurring at irregular intervals and so marked and characteristic that if they be once understood, all the lesser details and intermediate become intelligible through their means.

"Moreover, the Scriptural story of the people of Israel curiously resembles the actual knowledge which even the most accomplished historical scholar possesses. That it is adapted to the needs and conditions of the human understanding will be evident to any one who will take trouble to recall his own experience, and will remember how he has secured one after another certain fixed points of interest, has grouped round them, little by little, the facts which he has subsequently acquired, filled up the intervals of time between them by slow degrees, but to the last has continued to retain his hold on these fixed points, and to refer every new acquisition to some one or other of them" (In N. C. Schaeffer's "Bible Readings for Schools," 11-12).

Finally, hear a strain or two from the songs of our modern psalmists:

> How shall the young secure their hearts,
>   And guard their lives from sin?
> The Word the choicest rules imparts
>   To keep the conscience clean.
>
> 'Tis like the sun, a heavenly Light,
>   That guides us all the day;
> And through the dangers of the night
>   A Lamp to lead our way   (I. Watts, 1719).

Thy Word, O God, the star resembles
    That led to Christ the Three Wise Men;
Its light with sweetest message trembles
    And fills the soul with joy again.
Lord, help each heart in every place
To find the Bethlehem of Grace (K. B. Garve, 1825).

———

Define clearness.

Why is it necessary that the Bible should be clear? Illustrate.

Is the Bible equally clear in all places, to all people, and at all times? Illustrate each point.

Prove that the Bible is clear.

What does your Catechism say about clearness of the Bible? Your Bible history? Find appropriate hymns in your hymnal bearing on this subject. Look up the Bible passages referred to in your lesson, and find additional references to this subject in the Bible. In what way can the contents of this lesson help you in your Bible study? In your faith and works?

LESSON NINE. THE PROPERTIES OF THE BIBLE:
IV. EFFICACY.

1. DEFINITION.

Efficacy is the power to produce effects, or results; as, the efficacy of medicine in counteracting disease, or the efficacy of prayer in securing help from God. The efficacy of the Bible is that property by which it produces in the hearts and minds of those who properly hear and read it the blessed effects God desires: Living knowledge, true faith, regeneration, conversion, sanctification, preservation. It is the Holy Spirit Who operates through the Word, when taught in its truth and purity. Hence the Word has "an active, supernatural and truly divine power of producing supernatural effects; in other words, of converting, regenerating and renewing the minds of men" (H. Schmid's "Doctrinal Theology," 505).

2. NECESSITY.

Again we face the terrible fact of sin. There are many other awful things in this world, that strike terror into the bravest hearts. Take, for instance, some dread disease, such as, leprosy, yellow fever, smallpox, consumption, bubonic plague and the like. For a person to be told that he has contracted any one of these sicknesses has been almost equivalent to a death doom. Yet sickness is not so fearful as sin. Sickness is a result of sin, one of a host of results. Disease may be inherited; sin always is. There is near Trondhjem, Norway, a hospital for lepers. A certain pastor visited this hospital, and on the way back began a conversation with his coachman, who seemed to have an unusual sympathy with the unfortunates in the hospital. "Perhaps you have some relative at the hospital who is a leper," the pastor ventured to ask. "Worse than that, sir," answered the coachman, with tears in his eyes, "I myself am a leper." He had inherited or gotten the disease, and realized that his turn would come to be interned in the hospital and to die in agony. Now, we all have inherited sin, and as sinners we are lost and condemned creatures. There is no help from any human source. Humanity needs a Savior. God has furnished one in Jesus, Who came to save from sin, and death, and the power of the Devil. Men need to be told about their lost condition and the way of salvation. God has furnished such a Word, most appropriately called a Means of Grace, for it is a means, and the chief means, by which the Lord rescues the perishing. Speaking again of disease, we might say that it makes the various organs and members of the body helpless and useless, and finally causes death and corruption. This also, in a spiritual sense, is the case with sin. Sin has darkened the understanding. It has made the will powerless for what is good, and inclined to all that is evil. It has disturbed the joy and peace of conscience. The human soul in this condition must have help. Such help the Word of God alone can give, having the power to regenerate. The Word, then, would enlighten the understanding. It would create in the will a holy desire, power and longing. It would give the conscience true peace and joy.

3. EXTENT.

To what extent is the Word of God efficacious? It meets every want of the human soul completely. It has the power to produce for every human being every blessed effect desired by man or God. By it the Holy Spirit awakens in our hearts a knowledge of sin, and invites us to accept God's grace in Christ. The reason why so many are not blessed through the Word is, that they resist the Holy Spirit, and will not repent and believe. If they would accept the Word as the only source and rule of their faith, teachings and life, they would experience, in great measure, the blessings which it can bring.

4. PROOFS.

The Bible has hundreds of passages regarding the efficacy of the Word. Meditate upon the following:

"For as the rain cometh down and the snow from heaven, and returneth not thither, but watereth the earth, and maketh it bring forth and bud, and giveth seed to the sower and bread to the eater; so shall My Word be that goeth forth out of My mouth; it shall accomplish that which I please, and it shall prosper in the thing whereto I sent it" (Isa. 55: 10-11).

"The Law was our schoolmaster to bring us to Christ" (Gal. 3: 24).

"For I am not ashamed of the Gospel; for it is the power of God unto salvation to every one that believeth; to the Jew first, and also to the Greek" (Rom. 1:16).

"Every Scripture inspired of God is also profitable for teaching, for reproof, for correction, for instruction which is in righteousness: that the man of God may be complete, furnished completely unto every good work" (2 Tim. 3:16-17).

"If any man willeth to do His will, he shall know of the teaching, whether it be of God, or whether I speak of Myself " (John 7: 17).

The Bible has thousands of living witnesses to its efficacy, of male and female, old and young, rich and poor, high and low, slave and free, who have been called, enlightened, regenerated, converted, sanctified and preserved by its divine message. Think of the Bible characters who obeyed its counsel—from Creation down to Revelation—and compare them with those unfortunates who chose to resist or disobey the Word! Take any known person you please, and you will find that the Word was efficacious in his case. In the case of Adam it warned him of danger and death. We know how truthfully and effectively:

In Adam's fall
We sinnéd all.

In the case of Noah it promised rescue and life. We

know again that it produced results: Those who heeded it
were saved.

Concerning the efficacy of this Book of books Philip Schaff
says in his Preface to Lange's "Commentary on Matthew:"

"Viewed merely as a literary production, the Bible is a
marvelous book, and without a rival. All the libraries of
the world could not furnish material enough for so rich
a treasure of the choicest gems of genius, wisdom and
experience. It embraces works of about forty authors,
representing the extremes of society, from the throne of the
king to the boat of the fisherman; it was written during a
period of sixteen centuries, on the banks of the Nile, in the
desert of Arabia, in the Land of Promise, in Asia Minor, in
classical Greece and in Imperial Rome; it begins with the
creation, it ends with the new heavens and the new earth,
and describes all the intervening stages in the revelation
of God and in the spiritual development of man. It uses
all forms of literary composition; it rises to the highest
heights and descends to the lowest depths of humanity; it
is acquainted with every joy and every woe; it contains
the spiritual biography of every human heart; it is suited
to every class of society; it is as universal as the race, and
as boundless as eternity. This matchless combination of
human excellencies points to its divine character and origin;
as the absolute perfection of Christ's humanity is an evidence of His divinity. But the Bible is first and last a
book of religion. It is a book of life for all ages and
nations. It presents the religion of God, both in its pre-
paratory growth under the Law and promise, and in its
completion under the Gospel. It speaks to us as immortal
beings on the highest themes, and with irresistible authority. It can instruct, edify, warn, terrify, appease, cheer
and encourage, as no other book. It seizes man in the hidden depths of his intellectual and moral constitution, and
goes to the quick of the soul, to that mysterious point where
it is connected with the unseen world and with the great

Father of spirits. It purifies, ennobles, sanctifies man, and brings him into living union with God. It has light for the blind, strength for the weak, food for the hungry, drink for the thirsty; it has, in precept or example, a counsel for every relation in life, a comfort for every sorrow, a balm for every wound. Like the diamond, it casts its luster in every direction; like a torch, the more it is shaken, the more it shines; like a healing herb, the harder it is pressed, the sweeter is its fragrance. Of all the books in the world, the Bible is the only one of which we never tire, but which we admire and love more and more in proportion as we use it. What an unspeakable blessing, that this inexhaustible treasure of divine truth and comfort is now accessible, without material alteration, to almost every nation on earth in its own tongue, and, in Protestant countries at least, even to the humblest man and woman that can read or hear!"

In the same strain is the following beautiful tribute by F. Bettex in his "The Bible the Word of God " (52) :

"The Bible! Indeed, not an ordinary Book! Hated and hounded as no other book has ever been, and yet indestructible; despised, and yet honored; derided, and yet highly esteemed; declared dead, and yet alive. Mighty emperors and kings and priests have shunned no toil and no guilt in order to exterminate it; wise and scholarly men have, in the sweat of their brow, thoroughly refuted it; and now, that higher criticism lords over it and science has done away with it, it is spreading over the whole earth with astonishing rapidity in millions of copies and hundreds of languages, and is being read and preached from pole to pole; and, in the faith and power of the Word, Negroes submit to being burned alive, and Armenians and Chinese to being tortured to death. Ho, all ye scholars and critics! do but write such a book, and we will believe you! Complete in itself—'accursed any man that shall add unto or take away'—unchanged and unchangeable, this Bible stands for centuries, unconcerned about the praise and the reproach of men; it does not accommodate itself to progress, does not recant a single word, remains grandly simple and divinely overpowering, and in its sight all men are equal and feel their impotency." "The grass withereth, and the flower thereof falleth away; but the Word of the Lord endureth forever" (1 Pet. 1:24-25).

———

Define efficacy.

Why is it necessary that the Word of God should be efficacious?

To what extent is the Word of God efficacious?

Give five Bible passages proving the efficacy of the Word.

Give the testimony of two scholars on this point.

What does your Catechism say about the powerful effects of the Word? Your Bible history? Find appropriate hymns in your hymnal bearing on this subject. Look up the Bible passages referred to in your lesson, and find additional references to this subject in the Bible. In what ways can the contents of this lesson help you in your Bible study? In your faith and works?

LESSON TEN. THE STRUCTURE OF THE BIBLE.

When a small boy gets a toy he soon takes it to pieces to find out how it is put together—he is studying its structure. By structure is meant the arrangement of parts, the manner of building or organization. At school the pupil is set to study the structure of the human body or of animals, with head, trunk, limbs and various other organs. He is required to analyze sentences into subject, predicate and modifiers, and the parts of speech. He must study the different forms of literature and analyze the different parts of a book. This is all very interesting and useful study. Why not subject the Bible to this same analysis? Let us see what structural facts we can find.

1. TWO-FOLD.

Our first and most important discovery as to the structure of the Bible is, that it has two main divisions—it has a two-fold, or dual structure. These divisions are the Old Testament and the New Testament, already somewhat described in a previous section (under Titles). In point of size the Old Testament occupies fully 75 per cent of the whole volume; the New Testament, hardly 25 per cent. One edition of the American Revised has 893 pages for the Old Testament and 276 for the New. Find the ratio in your Bible.

2. THREE-FOLD.

As we begin to examine the content and form of the compositions which fill the pages of the Bible, we soon discover that there is a three-fold division in each of the two main divisions—the Old Testament has a triple structure, and the New Testament has a triple structure. The Old Testament begins with a historical section, continues with a poetical section and ends with a prophetical section. The New Testament begins with a historical sec-

Old Testament Books

(1) Law	1	Genesis	
	2	Exodus	
	3	Leviticus	
	4	Numbers	
	5	Deuteronomy	
2) History	6	Joshua	Historical (1)
	7	Judges	
	8	Ruth	
	9	1 Samuel	
	10	2 Samuel	
	11	1 Kings	
	12	2 Kings	
	13	1 Chronicles	
	14	2 Chronicles	
	15	Ezra	
	16	Nehemiah	
	17	Esther	
3) Poetry	1	Job	Didactic (2)
	2	Psalms	
	3	Proverbs	
	4	Ecclesiastes	
	5	Song of Solomon	
4) Major Prophets	1	Isaiah	Prophetical (3)
	2	Jeremiah	
	3	Lamentations	
	4	Ezekiel	
	5	Daniel	
5) Minor Prophets	6	Hosea	
	7	Joel	
	8	Amos	
	9	Obadiah	
	10	Jonah	
	11	Micah	
	12	Nahum	
	13	Habakkuk	
	14	Zephaniah	
	15	Haggai	
	16	Zechariah	
	17	Malachi	

No. 3. The Old Testament Books.

New Testament Books

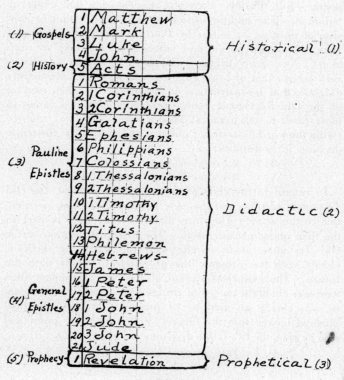

No. 4. The New Testament Books.

tion, continues with an epistolary (letter) section and ends with a prophetical section. Arranged side by side the divisions are:

O. T.: Historical—poetical—prophetical.
N. T.: Historical—epistolary—prophetical.

The first and last sections of the two divisions are identical. The middle section of the Old Testament consists of poems—Job, Psalms, Proverbs, Ecclesiastes and Song of Solomon. The middle section of the New Testament consists of epistles, or letters by Paul, James, Peter, Jude and John. Do these poems and letters have anything in common? Yes, many things. The purpose of the epistles is very largely that of conveying instruction. They are mainly didactic, that is, instructive, in tendency. A hasty reading of the Old Testament poetry reveals that it, too, aims in most cases to teach moral lessons—it is didactic. Substituting the word didactic for poetical and epistolary, the triple division is as follows:

O. T.: Historical—didactic—prophetical.
N. T.: Historical—didactic—prophetical.

In regard to the class of the composition, then, the Old Testament sections and the New Testament sections are identically the same. They are identical also with respect to the time under consideration. The historical section of the Old Testament dealt chiefly with the past; the didactic, chiefly with the present; the prophetical, chiefly with the future. The historical section of the New Testament likewise was chiefly a record of things accomplished; the didactic was chiefly an analysis of present problems; the prophetical looked into the future. Stated point by point and side by side, the two triple divisions are identical, as follows:

O. T.: Past—present—future.
N. T.: Past—present—future.

3. MANI-FOLD.

Let us now examine the structure of the Bible a little more closely. A feature that is at once noticeable is, that it is made up of a number of individual books. There are 66 of these books, 39 in the Old Testament and 27 in the New Testament, and they were written at God's command by the holy prophets, evangelists and apostles at various times and places. There are at least 30 men, probably more, who have acted as God's penmen. Between Moses and John, the first and the last of them, is a span of sixteen centuries. Moses wrote in the Sinaitic Peninsula, Daniel wrote in Babylon, Paul wrote in Rome, Greece and Asia Minor, most of the writers wrote in Palestine. Their writings contain all of the many types of prose and poetical composition: history, biography, oration, essay, letter, drama, lyric, epic, didactic, etc. Therefore the Bible has been called a library, a national library, a divine library. The 66 books are listed and grouped in the following diagrams. It will be noted that in addition to the three-fold division of the Old and New Testaments, a five-fold division is also possible.

THE SIXTY-SIX BOOKS.

Sixty-six *singers*, singing sweet and true,
And setting all the world to singing, too.

Sixty-six *soldiers*, vigorous and strong,
Valiantly attacking cruelty and wrong.

Sixty-six *judges*, learned in the law,
Uttering decisions free from fear and flaw.

Sixty-six *artists*—wondrously they paint
Kings and sages, common folk, angel, Devil, saint.

Sixty-six *explorers*, keen to search and find
All the hidden secrets of life and death and mind.

Sixty-six *masons*, marvelously skilled,
One majestic temple they unite to build.

Sixty-six *farmers*, planting holy seed,
Happily upspringing in thought and word and deed.

Sixty-six *teachers*, keeping perfect school,
Where faith the law, and charity the rule.

Sixty-six *doctors*, knowing well to cure,
Masters of a medicine healing swift and sure.

Sixty-six *sailors*, bearing us away
To a better country, to a brighter day   (A. Wells).

4.   ONE-FOLD.

.   We have just noted that the Bible is, as Jerome called
it, a whole library, and that it presents a most dazzling
variety of subjects, written by thirty or more different
men, in different walks of life, three different languages, in
different periods of time, in lands far apart, among hostile
peoples, in all of the types of composition and literary
style. Can there be any unity in this bewildering variety?
Yes. The "sixty-six" sweet singers are singing in sweet harmony. The sixty-six books are unified. There is unity.
It is a unity on a vast scale, such as that of the planet we
live on. It is a unity impossible in any other national
library, but essential to God's library. It is a real and
positive unity, admitted by the most careful and judicial
minds in the world, and recognized even by the simple and
the young.

Examine it. It begins with a declaration of God and
ends with a declaration of God. Beginning and end seem
to have been written by the same hand and at the same time.
Yet a span of some 1,600 years marks the time from Moses
writing in the Wilderness of Midian to John writing on the
Island of Patmos. The first chapter begins with the creation of our heaven and earth; the last chapter ends with the
creation of a new heaven and earth. It begins with the first
Adam in Paradise; it ends with the Second Adam in Paradise. It begins with a tree of knowledge and streams of
life; it ends with a tree of knowledge and streams of life.
It begins with Satan coming to destroy; it ends with Satan
having got his reward. It begins with sin and sorrow and

death entering the world; it ends with sin and sorrow and death put aside forever. In fact, the whole Book is one united and connected whole. The sixty-six books are one Book. There is a red thread from the first to the last word. The English navy is said to have a red thread in all of its ropes, as much present in short as in long pieces. The Bible has likewise one message running through its whole length and all its parts—that "we should believe that Jesus is the Christ, the Son of God, and that believing we might have life through His name" (John 20:31). Everywhere we can read that God wants us to win back the Paradise we have lost, and to accept the Helper and Savior He has provided in Jesus. The Old Testament looked forward to that glad day when Jesus should come; the New Testament celebrates it and looks back to it. The whole book is unified in Jesus and could be summed up in That Word.

What is meant by structure of the Bible? Discuss the two-fold division. The three-fold division. Can you think of a four-fold division? The five-fold division? Discuss the manifold division. The one-fold division.

Study the poem entitled "The Sixty-Six Books."

What does your Catechism say about the structure of the Bible? Your Bible history? Find appropriate hymns in your hymnal bearing on this subject. Look up the Bible passages referred to in your lesson, and find additional references to this subject in the Bible. In what ways can the contents of this lesson help you in your Bible study? In your faith and works?

The First Pentecost.

PART TWO.

TEXT OF THE BIBLE.

OUTLINE.

LESSON ELEVEN.   THE ORIGINAL TEXT:
I. THE LANGUAGES OF THE BIBLE.

It is the original text of the Bible that is of most value
and interest to the Church, for that is the only text that is
inspired and inerrant.   Now, it is everywhere admitted that
the first manuscripts have been lost.   How can we then
know whether we now have the original text?   A brief
answer to this question is given in the following lessons
under the headings: Languages of the Original Text, Sources
of the Original Text, and History of the Original Text.

1. THEIR NUMBER.

The sacred penmen were all descendants of Abraham,
Isaac and Jacob.   Abraham, being a descendant of Heber,
(Gen. 14: 13), and these holy writers being Abraham's descendants, were therefore Hebrews by race and language.
The Old Testament was written entirely in the Hebrew, with
the exception of one verse in Jeremiah (10:1), 67 verses in
Ezra (4: 8—6: 18; 7: 12-26), and 200 verses in Daniel (2:
4—7: 28), which were written in Aramaic, the language of
Aram and Mesopotamia, the country between the Tigris
and the Euphrates.   The Aramaic was closely related to
the Hebrew and was destined to supersede it even as the
language of the descendants of Abraham.   In 722 B. C.
the Ten Tribes were taken captive into the Mesopotamian
country and beyond.   In 586 the Two Tribes were led captive into Babylonia, where also Aramaic was spoken.   After
the 70 years of capitivity the Jews returned to Jerusalem,
but they had neglected Hebrew so long that they hardly
understood it (Neh. 8: 8, 13: 24).   From this time on
Hebrew gradually disappeared as the spoken language.
Aramaic took its place and, in the time of Christ, was the
popular language of Palestine.   The Aramaic of Palestine,
having been spoken in Babylonia or Chaldea, is often called

Chaldee, while the Aramaic of Mesopotamia, being later spoken in Syria, is often called Syriac. About 300 years before the birth of Christ all of Western Asia, including Palestine, had been conquered by Greece. Through this conquest the Greek language became the language of general communication between all parts of Western Asia and the rest of the civilized world. Christ and His disciples spoke Greek as well as Aramaic. The New Testament was written in Greek. The original text of the Old Testament is, then, Hebrew; that of the New Testament is Greek.

2. THEIR ORIGIN.

It is of value to know what relationship one language has to another, even as it is of value to know how one people is related to another, or to trace one's own lineage. But it is no easy task to trace one's lineage—very few can get much further back than to their grandparents. And it is no easy task to classify the races and the languages of the world from the beginning of time up to the present day. So much has happened that has not been recorded; so many things even of that which has been recorded cannot be explained. Truly we know, as Paul says, only in part.

The Bible states that there was originally one race and one language. "The whole earth was of one language and of one speech" (Gen. 11:1). What this language was, is not stated. Formerly, the general opinion among Christian scholars was, that this language was the Hebrew. The Pali grammarian Katyayana thought "that there is a language that is the root of all language. It is the Magadhi" (or Pali, a dead language of the island of Ceylon, the language of the Buddhist sacred books). (Spence Hardy's Legends of the Buddhists, 23). As a curiosity from the realm of speculation in this field Max Müller relates that Andre Kempe, in his work on Paradise, maintains that God spoke to Adam in Swedish, Adam answered in Danish, and the serpent spoke to Eve in French. Goropius, a Dutchman, published a book in Antwerp, in 1580, to prove that Dutch was the language of Paradise. Others may have tried to prove that some other language was the original one. Still, amongst Christian scholars, as already stated, the idea was current and established that Hebrew was the original language.

When the first attempts at classifying the languages were made, the scholars (Guichard, Thomassin, etc.) started out with the assumption that there had been one original language for all mankind, and that this original language was undoubtedly the Hebrew. The problem then was: "How can we explain the process by which Hebrew became split up into so many languages; and how can these numerous languages, such as Greek and Latin, Coptic, Persian, Turkish, be traced back to their common source, the Hebrew?" Leibniz was the first to conquer the prejudice that Hebrew was the language of Adam and Noah. For a time many philologists did not believe that there had been any one original language at all. Then they began to believe that the language known as Indo-European (from the two geographical extremes where they are spoken) must have had an original parent, which they have tried to reconstruct and have called the Aryan. The Aryans, they suposed, were a primitive people who lived in prehistoric times in Central Asia, east of the Caspian Sea, and north of the Hindu Kush Mountains. They are supposed to have been the parent stock from which have sprung Hindu, Persian, Greek, Latin, Celtic, Teutonic and Slavic. Now they are pretty well agreed that not only have the Indo-European, or Japhetic, languages a common ancestor, but the Semitic languages also have a common ancestor and other languages likewise, and finally that all languages go back to an original language. What this language is, no one knows. The Bible does not say. Nobody else so far can say.

Thus Bunsen speaks in his "Philosophy of Universal History" (I, 474-476), where he is tracing language and religion as two primitive and universal manifestations of the human mind: "But over the languages of the primitive Asiatic continent of Asia and Europe a new light begins to dawn, which in spite of perplexing appearances reveals more and more clearly the possibility of their common origin". Just so we might continue to cite the testimony of other students of philology, as Max Müller, J. Grimm, W. Steinthal, A. P. E. Lefevre, E. Renan, A. J. Johnes, John Peile, Henry Sweet, etc., the believers in evolution as well as the believers in special creation, to show that there is quite a consensus of opinion on this point that there was a parent language, now lost.

The Biblical account is no doubt the only solution. To our mind the case is forever settled, because the Sacred Scriptures have said that "the whole earth was of one language and of one speech" (Gen. 11:1). But as to what the original language was, no one knows. It will always remain a matter of interesting, if not profitable, speculation.

As to the time and manner of the breaking up of the original language into many languages, scholars differ greatly. Formerly, they quietly accepted without questioning the simple account of Scriptures on this point, where we read that God in His righteous judgment came down to the builders of the Tower of Babel and confounded their language, so they might not understand one another, and scattered them abroad from thence upon the face of the earth (Gen. 11:5-9). Therefore is the name of it called Babel (confusion); therefore and from that time we have had a confusion of tongues. This happened, according to Ussher, in 2247 B. C.

Now we can not say for sure that Ussher has determined the dates exactly in every instance. But we see no reason why the Biblical account of the Confusion of Tongues as well as the account of the Flood and the Creation can not stand as thoroughly reliable. It is stated clearly that there was no long development, but a sudden confusion of languages (Gen. 11:7-8). Not all of the changes in the earth's surface are caused by slow weathering. Terrific storms, floods, earthquakes and volcanoes are also historical realities. The Biblical stories of Creation and of the Flood are the most reasonable accounts that have yet been set forth. That of the rise of many languages is the only one that can at all satisfy the intellect.

3. THEIR CLASSIFICATION.

There are now about 50 nations in the world, speaking about 500 distinct languages, and probably 5,000 dialects. Some of the distinct languages we know to be quite closely related, as Icelandic, Norwegian, Danish, Swedish; or Italian, Portuguese, Spanish, French. All of the languages, in fact, are related, and go back to the Confusion of Tongues at Babel, just as all of the races of men—white, yellow, red, brown, black—trace their origin to Shem, Japheth and Ham, the sons of Noah. The position of Hebrew and Greek among the languages may be shown in several ways, as by classifying them according to use, structure or source (genealogy). The last method is followed in the following table:

(1) SEMITIC.

(I) East—Babylonian, Assyrian, etc.
(II) South—Arabic, Abyssinian, etc.
(III) West—Hebrew, Phoenician, etc.
(IV) North—Aramaic (Syriac, Chaldee, etc.).

(2) JAPHETIC.

(I) East—Indian (Sanskrit, Pali, Hindustani, etc.).
       Iranian (Zend, Persian, Armenian, etc.).
(II) South—Greek (Classical Greek, New Testament, or Hellenistic Greek, Modern Greek, etc.).
       Latin (Classical Latin, Italian, French, Spanish, Portuguese, Rumanian, etc.).
(III) West—Celtic (Irish, Scotch, Welsh, etc.).
(IV) North—Teutonic (Gothic, German, Dutch, English, Scandinavian, etc.).
       Slavic (Russian, Polish, Serb, Bulgar, Bohemian, etc.).

As the English belongs to the Teutonic group, it may be worth while to classify the members of this group a little more closely.

Teutonic languages:

East—Gothic.

South—German, etc.

West—English (Anglo-Saxon, Old English, Middle English, Modern English, etc.).

North—Scandinavian (Swedish, Danish, Norwegian, Icelandic, etc.).

(3) HAMITIC.

(I) White—Ancients (Egyptian, etc.).
    Moderns (Turkish, etc.).

(II) Yellow—Mongolians, Finns, Esquimaux, etc.

(III) Brown—Tamil, Polynesian, Malagassi, etc.

(IV) Black—Hottentot, Kaffir, etc.

(V) Red—Sioux, Chocktaw, etc.

———

What is meant by the original text of the Bible?

To what race did the sacred penmen belong? What languages did they speak? What languages did they write? What parts of the Bible are written in Hebrew? What parts are written in Aramaic? What parts are in Greek?

What was the original language? What were some former opinions on this subject? Modern opinions? What does the Bible say? How did it come about that we got so many languages?

How many nations are there in the world? How many languages?

What are the three chief divisions and races of the languages of the world? Subdivide the Semitic languages. The Japhetic. The Hamitic. To which of these groups does the English language belong? How is the English related to the French? To the German? To the Greek? To the Scandinavian? To the Hebrew?

Look up the Bible passages referred to in your lesson, and find additional references to this subject in the Bible. In what ways can the contents of this lesson help you in your Bible study? In your faith and works?

LESSON TWELVE. THE ORIGINAL TEXT:
II. THE FITNESS OF THE BIBLICAL LANGUAGES.

There can be very little dispute about the historical position of the Semitic and Japhetic races of mankind. Historians agree that the curse and prophecy of Noah (Gen. 9: 25-27) have so far been the course of history. Shem gave to the world the worship of Jehovah—Judaism and Christianity; Japheth "has become enlarged," controlling now about 90 per cent of the land area of the earth; he has "dwelt in the tents of Shem," having since the time of Christ occupied the Christian Church. There can be very little disagreement as to the position of the Hebrews among the Semitic peoples and the Greeks among the Japhetic peoples. The Hebrews were the most typical and the most highly developed Semitic people, and the Greeks were the most typical and the most highly developed Japhetic people of the ancient world. As to language, the consensus of opinion is, that Hebrew is the most representative and most perfect Semitic language, while Greek is the most representative and highly developed Japhetic language. "Both, having accomplished their highest purpose, soon afterward became stereotyped in form, or, as they are commonly called, dead languages; so that henceforth all successive generations, and indeed all the families of the earth, might resort to them and find the common, divine revelation in the same fixed and unalterable forms" (Briggs' "Languages of the Bible").

1. HEBREW.

"As long as the heir is a child," says the apostle Paul, "he differeth nothing from a bond servant, though he is lord of all; but is under guardians and stewards until the term appointed of the father." Paul goes on to apply this to the time when "we were children" before "the fulness of time." This applies certainly to the time of the Old Testament. The Hebrews were under the Law, guarded and kept as children. The Word of God to them was essentially the Law, but also the Gospel promise of heirship through faith, as, for example, to Abraham. The language to children must be simple in its words and construction. It must be homely and natural, concrete and realistic, picturesque and majestic. The language of Law should be clear and stable. The Hebrew language possessed all of these characteristics in

בְּרֵאשִׁית בָּרָא אֱלֹהִים אֵת הַשָּׁמַיִם וְאֵת הָאָרֶץ: וְהָאָרֶץ א 2
הָיְתָה תֹהוּ וָבֹהוּ וְחֹשֶׁךְ עַל־פְּנֵי תְהוֹם וְרוּחַ אֱלֹהִים
מְרַחֶפֶת עַל־פְּנֵי הַמָּיִם: וַיֹּאמֶר אֱלֹהִים יְהִי אוֹר וַיְהִי־ 3
אוֹר: וַיַּרְא אֱלֹהִים אֶת־הָאוֹר כִּי־טוֹב וַיַּבְדֵּל אֱלֹהִים בֵּין 4
הָאוֹר וּבֵין הַחֹשֶׁךְ: וַיִּקְרָא אֱלֹהִים לָאוֹר יוֹם וְלַחֹשֶׁךְ ה
קָרָא לָיְלָה וַיְהִי־עֶרֶב וַיְהִי־בֹקֶר יוֹם אֶחָד: פ

No. 5.   Gen. 1:1-5 in Hebrew with Massoretic Points (Hahn Edition).

the highest degree. Three fourths of the Bible is in the Hebrew. The record—from Moses to Malachi—covers over 1,000 years, yet the language had scarcely changed during all these centuries. The nature of the language, and of the people, and of their isolation on the hills of Judea, all favored stability of language. As soon as the Old Testament Canon was established, the Hebrew language as a living language had served its purpose, and the language was dropped, giving way to the Aramaic (called also Chaldee) as the spoken language.

2. GREEK.

The Greek language represented a people in their maturity. They had toiled upwards toward the light and had reached the highest pinnacles of fame in literature and art, in philosophy and statecraft, apart from the influence of Holy Writ. Their achievements are to this day amazing.

The language was, like the people, fullgrown. The Hebrew mind was strong on perceiving; the Greek, on conceiving. The Hebrew contemplated; the Greek reflected. The Hebrew must see with his eyes; the Greek must know the reason why. How many the roots and few the forms in the Hebrew tongue; how few the roots and many the forms in the Greek. The Greek was a world conqueror politi-

¹Ἐγένετο δὲ ἐν ταῖς ἡμέραις ἐκείναις ἐξῆλθεν δόγμα παρὰ Καίσαρος Αὐγούστου ἀπογράφεσθαι πᾶσαν τὴν οἰκουμένην. ²αὕτη ἀπογραφὴ ἐγένετο πρώτη ἡγεμονεύοντος τῆς Συρίας Κυρηνίου. ³καὶ ἐπορεύοντο πάντες ἀπογράφεσθαι, ἕκαστος εἰς τὴν ἑαυτοῦ πόλιν. ⁴ἀνέβη δὲ καὶ Ἰωσὴφ ἀπὸ τῆς Γαλιλαίας ἐκ πόλεως Ναζαρὲθ εἰς τὴν Ἰουδαίαν εἰς πόλιν Δαυεὶδ ἥτις καλεῖται Βηθλεέμ, διὰ τὸ εἶναι αὐτὸν ἐξ οἴκου καὶ πατριᾶς Δαυείδ, ⁵ἀπογράψασθαι σὺν Μαριὰμ τῇ ἐμνηστευμένῃ αὐτῷ, οὔσῃ ἐγκύῳ. ⁶Ἐγένετο δὲ ἐν τῷ εἶναι αὐτοὺς ἐκεῖ ἐπλήσθησαν αἱ ἡμέραι τοῦ τεκεῖν αὐτήν, ⁷καὶ ἔτεκεν τὸν υἱὸν αὐτῆς τὸν πρωτότοκον, καὶ ἐσπαργάνωσεν αὐτὸν καὶ ἀνέκλινεν αὐτὸν ἐν φάτνῃ, διότι οὐκ ἦν αὐτοῖς τόπος ἐν τῷ καταλύματι.

No. 6. Luke 2:1-7 in Greek (Tischendorf-Gebhardt edition).

cally and intellectually. His mind and his hands were into everything. His language, like his acts, is complex and finished. How complex and minute are the rules of syntax and prosody in Greek, how beautiful the style, how convincing the argumentation, how persuasive the oratory. It was the language of Homer, the greatest of epic poets; of Demosthenes, the greatest of orators; of Plato, the most idealistic, and of Aristotle, the most scientific, of philosophers. It was a language fit to proclaim the Day of the Lord and His Gospel of freedom, a message far surpassing the heroic action of Homer, the fervent appeal of Demosthenes, the great flights of imagination of Plato, or the practical systems of Aristotle.

In the passage just cited from Paul we learn that "when the fulness of time came, God sent forth His Son, born of a woman, born under the Law that He might redeem

them that were under the Law, that we might receive the
adoption of sons" (Gal. 4:-4-5). The Son of God did come
to earth in human flesh in the fulness of time. We can think
of no time in the world's history so opportune for His coming. No period before His coming was in point of religious
need, of political, social, educational, commercial, philosophical and linguistic standing, so opportune, and none since. As
to language, Greek was then the universal language, the common speech of the nations in intercourse with one another.
The Jews were dispersed throughout all the world, and having
quit using the Hebrew as a living language, spoke the languages of the countries in which they lived. Behold the Jews
at the first Pentecost hearing the Gospel from the lips of the
disciples in the various tongues: "And how hear we, every
man in our own language, wherein we were born? Parthians
and Medes and Elamites, and the dwellers in Mesopotamia,
in Judea and Cappadocia, in Pontus and Asia, in Phrygia
and Pamphylia, in Egypt and the parts of Libya about
Cyrene, and sojourners from Rome, both Jews and proselytes, Cretans and Arabians, we do hear them speaking in
our tongues the mighty works of God" (Acts 2:8-11).

It is quite apparent that the Jews of that day, as also
of our own times, knew the language of the country in
which they were born. It is also reasonable to suppose that
they were familiar with the Greek, the language of culture and of commerce. Already 250 years or more B. C. the
Jews in Alexandria, Egypt, had found it necessary to have
the Old Testament translated into Greek, and their translation, the Septuagint, became the accepted Scriptures of the
Jews of the Dispersion and even of Judea. It was used by the
Jews for spreading the Hebrew faith among the heathen
and for making proselytes; it was used by Christ in His
conflicts with the scribes, and by the apostles in spreading
the teachings of Christianity. Although the Jews of Palestine spoke Aramaic amongst themselves, they were also
familiar with the Greek. The New Testament Scriptures,

as stated, are all written in Greek, both because it was a familiar language and because it was the universal language, the only language that could be used as a medium of communication even among the soldiers of many nationalities that maintained the Roman authority in Palestine (Zahn's "Introduction to the New Testament," 1, 38). It is claimed that Matthew wrote his Gospel also in Hebrew, because he wrote particularly for the Jews. Yet it is a significant fact that none of the New Testament writings was originally written in Aramaic. Paul was indeed a "Hebrew of the Hebrews" in more ways than one (Phil. 3: 5). In point of language he was familiar with the Hebrew and the Aramaic and no doubt held both dear (Acts 21:37—22:2). Yet for the sake of Christ he used the Greek, counting "all things loss for the excellency of the knowledge of Jesus Christ." Greek was therefore Paul's language, at least when recording the Word of God in writing.

It was the language "predestined," as P. Schaff says in his "History of the Apostolic Church," to "form the pictures of silver in which the golden apple of the Gospel should be preserved for all generations." For ten centuries and more the Greek had been in preparation as a literary language, and has freely been pronounced the most beautiful, rich, harmonious and perfect language ever spoken or written. For three centuries it had been the universal language, and by the Jews modified to express the Jewish Scriptures and spirit. The Hellenistic Greek of the Jews and the early Christians is therefore strongly Hebraistic. Hebrew thought and idiom take on a Greek dress. It is a sort of compromise language—largely Hebrew in sentence structure, mainly Greek in diction. "The language of the New Testament has a Greek body, a Hebrew soul, and a Christian spirit. It is the noble language of classical civilization and the venerable language of revealed religion. It combines the best elements of the ancient world, regenerated and controlled by the spirit of a new religion, and made subservient to the

highest ends. It is, moreover, so plain and simple in its
diction that, both in the original and in translations, it
comes home to the capacity of the common people. The New
Testament is not a book for scholars only or chiefly, but
for all classes and conditions of men" (Schaff's "Propaedeutics," 128). "The inscription on the cross was threefold
(John 19: 20), in Hebrew—the language of religion, in
Greek—the language of civilization, and in Latin—the language of the law and power. This foretokens the universal-
ity of Christianity."

W. H. Green characterizes the respective fitness of these
two languages thus: "The Semite abides substantially unal-
tered from age to age. Travellers find the same dress, the
same manners, habits and modes of life in Palestine at
the present day that existed in the days of Abraham. With
the Europeans there is constant change; fashions in dress
vary from season to season, the conveniences and comforts
of life, customs and laws undergo perpetual alteration.
The Semite abides on the same spot on which he was born.
With the exception of the trading colonies of the Phoenicians (Hamites by race, Semites by language) and the fana-
tical conquests of the Saracens, the Semite populations have
remained fixed in the same territory from the dawn of history, and that one of very limited extent (except dispersion
through persecution). The restless, moving Indo-European
population has spread itself across both the continents of
Europe and Asia, occupying a broad belt from Great Britain
to the peninsula of Hindoostan, and is now filling the new
continent of America and settling on the islands of the
ocean, ever the same energetic, progressive race. May not
this suggest a reason why the Old Testament was given to a
Semitic people, a steadfast adherence to what was delivered
being the chief quality demanded in that traditionary dis-
pensation? But when the period was come for aggression,
for breaking over the old boundaries, giving up ancient

usages, and carrying the Gospel to the ends of the earth, the work was given in charge to Europeans" ("Text," 9-10).

What is the historical position of the Semitic race? Of the Japhetic? Of the Hamitic? How is this position connected with the prophecy of Noah?

In what respect were the Chosen People under the Old Covenant like children? In what respect must language be adapted to children? In what respect can it be said that the Hebrew language is the language of childhood?

In what respect are the people of the New Covenant mature? In what respect was the Greek language full grown? What is meant by the fullness of time? How is the Greek language particularly fitted to present the Gospel to the world? What did the inscription on the cross foretoken? Characterize the respective fitness of Hebrew and Greek as Bible languages.

Look up in the Bible the passages referred to in your lesson, and find additional references to this subject in the Bible. In what ways can the contents of this lesson help you in your Bible study? In your faith and works?

LESSON THIRTEEN. THE ORIGINAL TEXT:
III. THE SOURCES.

1. ANCIENT MANUSCRIPTS.

Printed books date back only to 1456, the year in which
Johann Gutenberg of Mentz published a Latin version of
the Bible, known as the Mazarin Bible.

The books of the Middle Ages were not printed, but
handwritten, copied by the monks, clerks and students of the
monasteries and schools. Naturally, the books produced by
this laborious method were very bulky, costly and rare.
The custom of chaining the books in libraries and churches
arose as a matter of course on account of their great expense and rarity. As comparatively few could read in
those days those in authority regarded the Evil One as more
likely to steal or destroy the sacred books than the people.
The tale is told that the Devil once came to the church
of St. Wallberg at Zupphen, in Holland, which had a
number of books, but none chained. The Devil thereupon
despoiled this church of some of its best volumes, but left
the mark of his cloven hoof upon the flagged floor, which
gave a clue to the identity of the thief. The custodian had
the remaining books "secured by chains sprinkled with holy
water, by which the malice of the Evil One was made of
none effect" (G. S. Rawling's "Story of Books," 66).

The books of ancient times were also handwritten, the
work of copyists, both slave and free. Without the patient
and efficient labor of their hands we should never have had
the Bible or any other book of classic age and worth. The
history of the printed book is less than 500 years long,
beginning practically 1,500 years after Christ; that of the
manuscript books is at least 3,000 years long, going back
to the time of Moses, 1,500 years before Christ.

The actual beginning of writing no one knows with certainty. But we all feel certain with Thomas Carlyle that "the art of writing is one of the most miraculous of all things man has devised." There is also much truth in Carlyle's further remark that "with the art of writing, of which printing is a simple, an inevitable and comparatively insignificant corollary, the true reign of miracles for mankind commenced." No wonder then that the ancients attributed its origin to the gods. Thus, the Scandinavians honor Odin as the first cutter of the mysterious runes, the Greeks give Hermes credit for the invention of the Greek script, the Assyrians Nebo, the Hindus Buddha. No wonder either that the art of writing has, from time immemorial, been considered a high and honorable accomplishment, and closely connected with the holy functions of priesthood. The scribes of the Gospel story, the Talmud scholars of the Dispersion, the monks of the mediaeval monasteries, were men of high and acknowledged standing among their fellows. The words clerk and clergy have the same source and retain to some extent the former Low Latin meaning of scholar and copyist.

The writing materials of the ancients were of many kinds, such as stone, metal, clay bricks, wood, the papyrus plant, the skins of animals. Clay tablets of various sizes were used by the peoples inhabiting the Tigris-Euphrates valleys; papyrus (cf. paper) was the choice writing material of Egypt and no doubt also of Greece and Rome. The Old Testament Scriptures were in the form of rolls, made of papyrus or parchment.

The original New Testament writings were also of parchment, but not in rolls. Copies were of paper made of rags or linen. The manuscripts now extant are written on vellum (calf-skin) or parchment (sheep-skin). The number of Old Testament copies now extant is about 750, of which none is much over nine centuries old. The number of New Testament manuscripts in 1903 was 3,800, of which none is quite sixteen centuries old. About 120 of these are called uncials, from the Latin uncia, meaning an inch, because the letters in these copies are printed by hand an inch high. They are all Greek capitals with no break between the words or sentences. For examples of ancient manuscripts see diagram 7.

The remainder of the manuscripts are called cursives, from the Latin curro, meaning run, because they were written in a running hand. The manuscripts are the chief source of the original text.

2. ANCIENT VERSIONS.

The Old Testament, in whole or in part, was translated into Greek, Samaritan, Syriac, Latin, Aramaic, Gothic and other languages. These ancient versions do not hold rank with the Hebrew manuscripts as sources of the original text, except in cases of omissions or interpolations. The first Greek translation was the Septuagint (from the Latin septuaginta—seventy), for tradition says it was the work of seventy (or rather 72) translators, who completed the task in 70 (72) days, to the great delight of King Ptolemy Philadelphus of Egypt, who had ordered the work to be done. The Septuagint seems to have been begun somewhere in the third century and completed somewhere in the second century B. C. At the time of Christ, Hebrew was already a dead language, although it was used in the synagogue. Greek was the language of culture, and the Septuagint was the only Greek translation. Horne finds that the Gospels quote the Septuagint verbatim 88 times, with variation in the translation 64 times, and giving the sense, but not the words, 37 times. When the Christians began to use the Septuagint the Jews began to look upon it with suspicion. In about 130 A. D. Aquila, a Jewish proselyte of Pontus, made a new Greek translation. In 180 A. D. Theodotion made a revision of the Septuagint. In 201 A. D. Symmachus made a freer translation that expressed the sense rather than the words of the original. Besides these Greek versions may be mentioned the following:

(1)

ΧΕΤΕΔΕΑΠΟΤΩΝ
ΑΝΩΝΠΑΡΑΔΩ
ϹΟΥϹΙΝΓΑΡΥΜΑ
ΕΙϹϹΥΝΕΔΡΙΑΚΑΙ
ΕΝΤΑΙϹϹΥΝΑΓΩ
ΓΑΙϹΑΥΤΩΝΜΑϹΤΙ
ΓΩϹΟΥϹΙΝΥΜΑ
ΚΑΙΕΠΙΗΓΕΜΟΝΑ
ΔΕΚΑΙΒΑϹΙΛΙϹΑ
ΧΘΗϹΕϹΘΑΙΕΝΕ
ΚΕΝΕΜΟΥΕΙϹΜΑΡ

(2)

ΚΑΛΥΜΜΑΕΠΙΤΗΝΚΑΡ
ΔΙΑΝΑΥΤΩΝΚΕΙΤΑΙΗΝΙ
ΚΑΔΑΝΕΠΙϹΤΡΕΨΗΠΡΟϹ
ΚΝΠΕΡΙΕΡΕΙΤΑΙΤΟΚΑ

(3)

(4)

ΕΤΟΙΧΙΙ
ΤLUSTHSAMEN
AMENDICOUO

(5)

ITE ETINTERROGA
TEDILIGENTERDE

(6)

ΔΙϹΥΝΕΛΕΖΑΝΛΥΤΟΡΩΙΠ̅Ρ̅Ω̅Ι
ΕΚΑϹΤΟϹΤΟΚΛΘΗΚΟΝΛΥΤΩΙΗΝΙ
ΚΛΕΔΙΕΘΕΡΜΕΝΕΝΟΗΛΙΟϹΕΤΗ

(7)

ΥΕΙΗΝΛΙΝΛΜΛΘΕΙΝ· ϹΙΜΛΙΦΙΝΗ
ΝΛϹϹΝϹϹΘΕΙΝ·S· ΥΛΙΚΦΛΙΥΙΛϹΛ

No. 7.   Specimens from the Manuscripts (see p. 98 for key).

A translation of the Pentateuch, or Five Books of Moses, into Samaritan, for the people of Samaria. Author unknown.

A translation, or paraphrase, of the Old Testament into Aramaic (Chaldee), for the Jews of Palestine. The author of this was Jonathan, an older contemporary of Christ.

A translation of the Old Testament into Aramaic (Syriac), for the use of Jewish Christians. It was made from the Hebrew original and is called Peschito, or Peshito (Simple), to this day.

A translation of the Old Testament into Latin from the Septuagint. This was called Itala. The great scholar Jerome revised this in 382. While he was at work on the revision of the Itala he was persuaded by some of his friends to undertake making a new translation directly from the Hebrew. He was a good Hebrew scholar and a man of vast learning and patience. He had access to many Hebrew manuscripts of ancient date, long since lost, and was acquainted with many translations. He had spent three years in the work of revision. With this equipment he set to work in 385 and continued with great zeal until its completion in 405. This became later known as the Vulgate (from vulgus—people), meaning common. It was violently attacked at the time of its first publication and has frequently been revised. Nevertheless, the Catholic Church in 1546, at the Council of Trent, exalted his translation above

---

1. Matt. 10: 17, from the Greek Sinaitic Ms. (Codex Sinaiticus— Aleph), at Petrograd.
2. 2 Cor. 3: 15, from the Greek Vatican Ms. (Codex Vaticanus—B), at Rome.
3. Title of John's Gospel, from a Syriac Ms., at Rome.
4. John 1: 51, from the Latin Palatinate Ms., at Vienna.
5. Matt. 2: 8, from the Latin Golden Ms., at Stockholm.
6. Ex. 16: 21, from the Alexandrian Ms. (Codex Alexandrinus—A), at London.
7. Matt. 6: 9, from the Gothic Silver Ms., at Upsala.

(J. Belsheim's "Om Bibelen".)

every other version, and above the texts in the original languages (Session 4, Decretal 2). In 1907 Pius X made preparations to have it revised again (Herbermann's "Catholic Encyclopaedia," XV, 515).

With the spread of Christianity among the nations of the earth and the decay of the Greek language as the common language of commerce and culture, the demand for translations of the Bible into other languages than those already mentioned soon arose. In the latter part of the third century the Septuagint was translated into the Coptic, the dialect of Lower Egypt, and into the Sahidic, the dialect of Upper Egypt; in the fourth century it was translated into the Ethiopic; and (together with the New Testament) into the Gothic (by Ulfilas); in the fifth century the Armenians obtained a translation of the Bible, based, in the Old Testament, on the Septuagint; also one in the sixth century, and in the tenth century the Book was rendered into Arabic. Bede's translation of the Bible in the eighth century and Aelfric's translation of the Pentateuch and Joshua into Anglo-Saxon in the tenth century were based on the Vulgate. All of these versions, Samaritan, Greek, Chaldee, Syriac, Latin, Coptic, etc., are of value in ascertaining the original text. Modern versions are in several hundred languages, but are of course of no account in determining the original.

In the above sketch of Old Testament versions the chief ancient New Testament versions were also included: Syriac, Latin, Gothic and Armenian.

3. EARLY CHRISTIAN WRITINGS.

The successors of the apostles, the Christian writers in the early centuries of the Church, in their attempts to explain and defend the Scriptures quote often from both of the Testaments and thus afford another source for determining the original text. Those writers who were the immediate successors of the apostles are called Apostolic Fathers. Those who wrote between 150 and 325, mainly in defense of Christianity, are called Ante-Nicene Fathers. The greatest of all the battles for the Christian faith in the early Church was fought ou. at Nice, a town in Asia Minor, in 325, between the followers of Arius, who denied that Christ was God, and the followers of Athanasius, who maintained that He was true God and true Man. Those who took part in this struggle between 325 and 381 are called Nicene Fathers. Those who wrote between 381 and 750 are called Post-Nicene Fathers. The amount that these "fathers" have written is not inconsiderable. The Ante-Nicene Fathers, for example, in the Roberts and Donaldson edition, fill 5400 large quarto pages. The Nicene and Post-Nicene authors occupy about 15,600 pages of the Schaff edition. All of these ancient Christian writers quote the Bible, now literally, and then again freely, just as Christians do to this very day. To give a few specific illustrations, Burgon discovered 387 quotations from the New Testament in Justin Martyr's writings, 1819 in Irenaeus', 2406 in Clement's of Alexandria, and 17,922 in Origen's works (Angus-Green's "Cyclopedic Handbook of the Bible", 57).

The original texts have been lost. And yet God has not taken His Word of truth from us; He has not left us in darkness. By means of the source material at hand, and still accumulating with every new archaeological exploration, the true text can be approximately restored. In fact, we can feel perfectly sure that the text of the modern standard Hebrew Old Testament (called Massoretic) and the Tischendorf, Gebhardt, Nestle, or Westcott and Hort Greek recensions are in every essential the same as that from the hands of the inspired prophets, evangelists and apostles. God has most wonderfully preserved His Word. He has employed the scribes and Pharisees, who crucified His Beloved Son, as the custodians of the Old Testament manuscripts, and their tribe as the faithful copyists of the same. He has used the Roman Church, which has burnt multitudes for reading the Bible and whose chief doctrines and practices

4-2393

are condemned by the Bible, in copying the Bible and preserving it. The reading of the patristic authors of the first
centuries of the Christian era is rather difficult, even in
translation. These writers were vastly inferior to the New
Testament writers in kind as well as in degree. They were
not inspired. Their language was not classical. And yet
their writings like their lives are fascinating and a powerful witness to the power of the Gospel and the truth of the
saying of Paul that "God chose the foolish things of the
world, that He might put to shame them that are wise; and
God chose the weak things of the world, that He might put to
shame the things that are strong"; and of the other saying:
"The foolishness of God is wiser than men; and the weakness of God is stronger than men" (1 Cor. 1: 27, 25).
These early Christians, most of them from the humbler
walks of life, learnt Scripture and in speech and writing,
in season and out of season, proclaimed the Gospel. The
Ante-Nicene Fathers in A. Roberts and J. Donaldson's English edition contain about 20,000 quotations from the Bible,
about 12,000 from the Old Testament and 8,000 from the
New, an average of about four to the page. We are impressed
with the familiar ring of these quotations. Their Bible was
the same as our Bible. More remarkable still are these
quotations when we consider that during the Ante-Nicene
period the New Testament Canon had not yet been established, and very few people had all of the Biblical books,
and most of them had never seen even a single one of them,
but had committed to memory passages they had heard.
Equally remarkable is the life of these first witnesses (many
of them martyrs). They reared the Christian home in a
world that knew no such sacred ties. To the terms wife,
mother, brotherhood, patience, charity, mercy, law, grace and
Christian—they gave content in a world that had no conception of Christianity. The study of the sources is, thus, in
many and striking ways of great importance. It is a scientific and satisfactory enterprise.

ASSYRIAN ACCOUNT OF THE CREATION.

A clay tablet from the library of Assurbanipal, king of Assyria, 668-626 B. C., at Nineveh.

(From the "Oxford Helps to the Study of the Bible.")

A LETTER FROM THE GOVERNOR OF TYRE TO THE KING OF EGYPT.

One of the Tel el Amarna Letters written on clay bricks in cuneiform characters during the Period of Bondage.

(From the "Oxford Helps to the Study of the Bible.")

When was the first book printed? What is the name of the first book printed? Before the invention of printing, how were books made? Why was the Bible chained in the churches during the Middle Ages?

How far back does the art of writing go? What can you say about the importance of this invention? To whom do the ancients attribute its origin? What is the meaning of clerk? Of clergy? What were used as writing materials in Biblical times by the Christian copyists? How many manuscripts do we have of the Old Testament? What is the most ancient of these? How many manuscripts do we have of the New Testament? How far do they go back in time? What is the difference between an uncial and a cursive copy?

What is a version? Into how many ancient languages do we find the Old Testament translated? What is the Septuagint? The Samaritan Pentateuch? The Peschito? The Itala? The Vulgate? What other ancient versions of the Old Testament can you name?

What event took place at Nice in 325? Who were the Ante-Nicene fathers? Who were the Nicene fathers? When did they live? Who were the Post-Nicene fathers? When did they live? What can you say about the number and character of their quotations from the Bible?

Look up in the Bible passages referred to in your lesson, and find additional references to this subject in the Bible. In what ways can the contents of this lesson help you in your Bible study? In your faith and works?

LESSON FOURTEEN.   THE ORIGINAL TEXT:
IV. THE HISTORY OF THE OLD TESTAMENT TEXT.

By text is meant the original words of the inspired writers. But the original text has been lost. Can we then be sure that the precise words of the original have been faithfully handed down to us? The determination of this is a matter of the greatest moment. We have noted the position of the Hebrew and Greek languages amongst their sisters, also their character. We have considered the sources from which the original text has to be determined—the ancient manuscripts primarily, but also the ancient versions and patristic quotations. What has been done to arrive at the true text? In other words, what is the history of the text?

The history of the Old Testament text may be considered divided into four periods: Moses-Ezra, 1500-400 B. C.; Scribes, 400 B. C.-600 A. D.; Massorites, 600-1477 A. D.; and Printed Text, 1477—.

1. PERIOD FROM MOSES TO EZRA, 1500-400 B. C.

All the texts from this period are lost. The Old Testament itself has few notices about the recording and preservation of the text. The materials used were stone, lead, papyrus and parchment. The Ten Commandments were written on stone; Joshua set up at Ebal stones with the Law inscribed on them (Josh. 8: 32; cf. Deut. 27: 2-4). Job and Jeremiah make mention of writing with an iron pen and the point of a diamond (Job 19: 24; Jer. 17: 1).

The books came in the form of a roll (Ps. 40: 7; Jer. 36: 2, 23; Ezek. 2: 9; Zech. 5: 2). It was written with ink (Jer. 36: 18; Ezek. 9: 2), and a pen (Ps. 45: 1; Isa. 8: 1). The Tables of the Law were preserved in the Ark (Ex. 25: 16; 1 Kings 8: 9; Heb. 9: 4). A standard copy of the Pentateuch was kept in the Temple. There it was found by

Josiah's high priest (2 Kings 22:8). Copies of it had been made, for after the destruction of the Temple and the return from the Captivity it is related that Ezra the scribe brought the book of the Law and read it before the Congregation from early morning until midday (Neh. 8:3). It was Ezra also who completed the making of the Old Testament Canon.

2. PERIOD OF THE SCRIBES, 400 B. C.—600 A. D.

Every text from this period also is lost. For 1,000 years after the work of Ezra was completed the sacred text was in the custody of the scribes. It was their holy purpose to protect it from corruption in copying and interpretation. Their banner was the letter of the Law. They adopted the square character of the Hebrew script in copying the Scriptures, while retaining the running script for more hurried writing. They fixed rules for writing the sacred text, numbered the words and letters of each book, determined the spaces between the words and sections, and established a tradition as to the correct reading. The Targums of Jonathan and Onkelos, contemporaries of Christ, and the Greek versions by Aquila and Theodotion in the following century, all indicate that there was already then an established form of the text. And the Talmudic writings refer to the rules in use as ancient and as the work of the early scribes. One of the greatest scholars of the period, Origen (186-253), tried to correct the Septuagint by comparing it with the Hebrew original and four Greek translations. He placed the six side by side on a page and hence called it "Hexapla" (Six-fold). In his writings there is not a hint that there was any controversy about the Hebrew text and the reading of it.

3. PERIOD OF THE MASSORITES, 600-1477.

The Massorites were learned Jewish scholars continuing the work of the scribes, enlarging upon their rules for copying the Old Testament, reading and classifying the great mass of traditional matter handed down by the scribes. Their object was to preserve the text accurately. Their special contribution to the sum of knowledge was their invention of the points which represent the Hebrew vowels and accents. Their critical notes on the correct reading are called Massora, that is, tradition, the traditional reading.

4. PERIOD OF THE PRINTED TEXT, 1477—.

The first book to be printed was the Latin Vulgate, in 1456. The first book to be printed in Hebrew was the book of Psalms, in 1477. The whole Hebrew Old Testament appeared from the press in 1488. Since then many others have followed, accurately revised after the manuscripts and critical notes of the Massorites.

What is meant by the original text? What has become of the original text? How can you be sure that the precise words of the original text have been faithfully handed down to us? Into how many periods may the history of the text be divided? Name these periods, together with the years that they cover.

Describe the periods from Moses to Ezra. What Old Testament books were written during this period? Describe the writing materials. Where were standard copies of the Law and Pentateuch kept?

Describe the period of the scribes. What was the motto of the scribes? What was their chief work? What was their contribution to the text?

Who were the Massorites? What are we indebted to them for? When was the first Bible printed in Latin? In Hebrew?

Look up the Bible passages referred to in your lesson, and find additional references to this subject in the Bible. In what ways can the contents of this lesson help you in your Bible study? In your faith and works?

LESSON FIFTEEN.   THE ORIGINAL TEXT:

V. THE HISTORY OF THE NEW TESTAMENT TEXT.

The history of the New Testament Text may also be divided into four periods: From the Apostles to the Canon, 50-397; the Copyists, 397-1516; the Received Text, 1516-1770; the Restored Text, 1770—.

1. PERIOD FROM THE APOSTLES TO THE CANON, 50-397.

This period begins with the writing of the New Testament books by the evangelists and apostles and ends with the closing of the Canon at the council of Carthage, in 397, under the influence of Augustine.   Our two best manuscripts belong to this period, the Aleph, from 330, and the B, from about the same time.   But the original manuscripts of the sacred writers are all lost, and were no doubt already lost in the second century.

2. PERIOD OF THE COPYISTS, 397-1516.

According to the custom of that day the text was not divided into chapters, paragraphs, sentences and words, with notation, spacing, punctuation, accents and capitalization. Everything was one continuous writing, with nothing to distinguish one word from another, or one sentence from another.   In the Old Testament the words had been separated by spaces and the verses by colons (:).   The verses were not numbered one by one, but the sum total of verses was placed at the end of each book.   Thus, after Isaiah was placed the figure 1,295 to indicate the number of verses in that book.   The present chapter division was not known in the Old Testament, therefore Christ, in referring, for example, to Ex. 3:6, did not say "Ex. 3:6," but "in the place concerning the bush" (Luke 20: 37). Since the Old Testament was regularly used in the synagogues, the Jews divided it up into sections for use at these services (Parshioth). The Pentateuch had 54 such divisions, subdivided into 669 smaller sections. The remainder of the Old Testament had 85 larger sections (Haftaroth). (Cf. as to the reading of Moses and the prophets: Acts 13: 15; 15: 21; Luke 4: 17; 2 Cor. 3: 14). The present chapter division was made by the Spanish Cardinal Hugo of St. Caro (1262). As to the New Testament also the necessities of worship required some kind of chapter division. Ammonius of Alexandria in 220 made a division of the Gospel into sections all numbered according to the sense. This method was followed by Eusebius of Calsona (before 340), who grouped the sections into 10 classes, or "canons," and introduced in the margin the parallel passages. He divided Matt. into 355 sections, Mark into 233, Luke into 342, and John into 232, total 1162. The present number of chapter divisions for the Gospels is 89. We owe the present divisions of the New Testament into chapters also to Hugo of St. Caro.

In the earliest writings there was nothing to distinguish one sentence from another, nor even one word from another. The first two sentences in the Bible, according to this method of writing, would then appear as one solid mass, as follows: inthebeginninggodcreatedtheheavenandtheearthand theearthwaswithoutformandvoidanddarknesswasupontheface ofthedeep. . . . As this method of writing made rather difficult reading the mediaeval copyists experimented with dividing the lines into stichs, or sense verses. But as this took more space, and according to reckoning, wasted much valuable parchment, they went back to the continual writing, setting off each stich by a period. This act is said to have been the beginning of the present system of interpunctuation (Weber's "Indledning"). The necessities of study called for a better system, but no satisfactory answer was given until the mediaeval period was over. Then Henry Stephens, the printer, divided the New Testament into verses and numbered them, the whole work being done on horse back on his journey from Paris to Lyons (Stephens' "Concordance," preface). In 1551 he printed an edition of the Bible with this method of division, and it met at once with universal approval, and has since been used in nearly all editions. Considering that the work was done on horseback, and rather mechanically, a division for each step of the horse, it is a wonder that the verses are so well divided as they are. They ought, in the poetical parts, to be identical with the sentence; but they are not, of course. The Authorized Version of the English Bible, for example, does not have logical divisions into chapters and verses, and has no paragraphing at all. Therefore, the reader is in danger of beginning or leaving off in the middle of his topic, and if he reads a stated number of verses at a time he may begin in the middle of one sentence and end in the middle of another. The Revised Version has grouped the sentences into paragraphs, but has retained the numbering of the "verses." The poetical verses have been printed as poetry.

3. PERIOD OF THE RECEIVED TEXT, 1516-1770.

During this period of two and a half centuries the "Received Text" reigned. By "Received Text" may be meant any text accepted by translators as the basis of their version. But specifically it is applied to either of two editions of the New Testament in Greek—that of Stephens, in 1550, used, for example, by the King James' translators, or that of the Elzivir Brothers, in 1633, which contained in its preface the words: "You have therefore the *Text*, now received by everybody." The first New Testament in Greek appeared in 1516, and was edited by the great scholar Erasmus. But it was hurriedly gotten up by an enterprising Dutch publisher. Erasmus worked only six months at preparing the copy for the printer and used only eight manuscripts, none of which was older than the eleventh century. It was a good edition, though not perfect, having been, to use Erasmus' own words, "precipitated instead of edited."

4. PERIOD OF THE RESTORED TEXT, 1770—.

During the last 150 years the many manuscripts of the New Testament have been most carefully studied and compared, and the minor inaccuracies of the "Received Text" have been removed, through the consecrated labors of a host of brilliant scholars like Griesbach, Lachmann, Tischendorf, Tregelles, Nestle, Winer, Alford, Westcott and Hort. The corrected text is the Restored Text, probably as close to the original as we can ever come.

Into what periods may the history of the New Testament text be divided? Describe the period from the apostles to the closing of the Canon. What has become of their original manuscripts? How old are the oldest New Testament manuscripts?

Describe the period of the copyists. What is meant by continuous writing? Illustrate. What efforts were made to divide the text into words, sentences, paragraphs and chapters? Tell how the Bible came to be divided into "verses". What are the advantages of this method of division? Name some of the disadvantages.

What is meant by Received Text? Describe the period of the Received Text.

What is meant by Restored Text? Describe the period of the Restored Text.

Look up the Bible passages referred to in your lesson, and find additional references to this subject in the Bible. In what ways can the contents of this lesson help you in your Bible study? In your faith and works.

LESSON SIXTEEN. VERSIONS:
I. THE NEED OF TRANSLATIONS.

1. THE COMMAND TO MAKE DISCIPLES OF ALL THE NATIONS.

The Lord has given His disciples the great commission to "make disciples of all the nations, baptizing them into the name of the Father and of the Son and of the Holy Spirit, teaching them to observe all things whatsoever He has commanded them" (Matt. 28:19-20). It is His gracious will that everyone shall own and read His Word. It shall be an Open Book. He wants the people to have it in a language that they understand. But now the nations of the world speak many languages. F. N. Finck has described 2,176 languages and dialects in his book "Die Sprachstamme des Erdkreises." The Bible has been translated into only 653 of these. It is clear to anyone who loves the cause of foreign missions that the work of Bible translation is very imperative, even when it is recognized that the languages that do not have the Bible are minor languages, none of them spoken by a large population. In every new missionary field some one is assigned to this task as soon as he can acquire the languages of the country. It goes without saying that every translation should be made from a standard text of the Hebrew and Greek originals, with reference to the best modern versions.

2. THE WORK OF THE CHURCHES AND BIBLE SOCIETIES.

The chief modern agencies for translating and distributing the Bible are the Bible societies and mission societies. In addition to the independent societies each Denomination has usually a literature department (board), with publishing plant, and a foreign mission department (board), with organized work in heathen (and even Christian) foreign lands. The earliest Bible society was the one in Halle,

Germany, founded in 1712. The largest of the Bible societies is the British and Foreign Bible Society, founded in 1804. Its work has been increased from an annual output of 20,000 to over 10,000,000 copies yearly. The following list from H. O. Dwight's "Story of the American Bible Society for 1915" includes the names of the Bible societies which publish the whole Bible or parts of it. An idea is thereby gained of the number of volumes of Scripture annually published by the Bible Societies throughout the world (statistics of 1913). The statistics of denominational publishers are not included in this list.

UNITED STATES

American Bible Society (1816) 6,406,323

GREAT BRITAIN

British and Foreign Bible Society (1804) 10,162,413
National Bible Society of Scotland (1861) 2,762,616
Trinitarian Bible Society (1831) 344,165
Scripture Gift Mission 5,748,293

FRANCE

Bible Society of France (1864) 60,908
Protestant Bible Society of Paris (1818) 6,879

GERMANY

Bavarian (or Central) Bible Society of Nuremberg (1823) 11,123
Bergische Bible Society, Elberfeld (1814) 117,437
Canstein Bible Institution of Halle (1712) 33,208
Prussian Bible Society (1814), as Berlin Bible Society (1806) 207,746
Saxony Bible Society (1814) 61,478
Wurtemberg Bible Institution (1812) 621,775

HOLLAND

Netherlands Bible Society (1815) 85,757

RUSSIA

Russian Bible Society, by Imperial Sanction (1869) ....No statistics
Russian Evangelical Bible Society (1835) 22,219
Finnish Bible Society (1812) 2,422

SCANDINAVIA

Danish Bible Society (1814)............................   57,000
Norwegian Bible Society (1815).......................   83,643
Swedish Bible Society (1809)..........................   12,255

SWITZERLAND

Basel Bible Society (1804)............................   28,344

BELGIUM

Bible Society of Belgium (1909).....................   126,402

Total 26,963,408

Statistics are not at hand showing the number of Bibles issued by the denominational publishing houses.

The history of each individual denominational publishing house as well as each Bible society is worthy of study. In May, 1916, for example, the American Bible Society celebrated its first centennial, and May 7th of that year was generally observed as Bible Sunday by the Reformed Churches and some others. Some of the results of the work of this one society during its first 100 years of labor was made known to the public. It had distributed in the United States during the century 68,828,334 Scriptures; in foreign lands, 41,097,880, a total of 109,926,214 volumes. It had circulated the Bible in 150 languages and types, 90 of the languages being spoken in the United States. With the help of the European Bible societies and the other publishing houses it had made the Bible the cheapest book, and the best seller in the world. It had received as a free will gift over $38,000,000.00, by means of which it could give the Bible away through many agencies and sell it at a small price through others. The chief agencies supporting their output are branch societies, Bible colporteurs or book agents, evangelists and teachers, pastors and missionaries, the denominational publishing houses and book stores.

Of the issues from the Bible House in New York during the twelve months ending March 31, 1915, 1,852,754 volumes were in the English language. This total is made up of 237,057 Bibles, 360,876 New Testaments and New Testaments and Psalms, 1,263,080 portions, and 1,741 volumes in the various raised characters for the blind. Of the Bibles and Testaments, 20,193 were the American Revised Edition.

Scriptures were issued in the same twelve months from the American Bible House in ninety-one languages and dialects other than English. The following table classifies these issues according to language:

LANGUAGE.	VOLUMES.	LANGUAGE.	VOLUMES.
Albanian	31	Latin	355
Arabic	3,023	Lettish	265
Arapahoe	11	Lithuanian	4,139
Armenian	3,281	Luragoli	1,940
Armeno-Turkish	459	Malay	39
Benga	2	Marshall Islands	3,001
Bengali	16	Mortlock	1,001
Bicol	4	Mpongwe	2
Bohemian	9,302	Muskokee	6
Bohemian-Slovak	2	Navaho	521
Bulgarian	1,383	Norwegian	4,502
Bulu	2	Ojibwa	32
Chamorro	1	Pampanga	4
Cherokee	60	Panjabi	106
Chinese, Easy Wenli	45	Panayan	3
Chinese, Mandarin	737	Pangasinan	2
Chinese, Canton Colloquial	1,360	Persian	4
Chinese, Classical	722	Polish	31,610
Choctaw	201	Ponape	2
Croatian	3,273	Portuguese	23,130
Dakota	96	Rumanian	7,337
Danish	5,924	Ruk	1
Dikele	1	Russian	14,132
Dutch	4,678	Ruthenian	1,155
Esperanto	271	Sanskrit	6
Esthonian	18	Scotch "Broad"	3
Finnish	2,718	Seneca	5
Flemish	391	Serb	1,714
French	21,377	Sheetswa	209
Gaelic	4	Slavic	294
German	32,971	Slovak	3,117
Gilbert Islands	4	Slovenian	2,408
Grebo	5	Spanish	214,189
Greek	13,517	Swedish	13,082
Hawaiian	673	Syriac (Ancient)	215
Hebrew	915	Syriac (Modern)	658
Hindi	3	Tagalog	27
Hungarian	10,945	Tonga	51
Ibanag	3	Urdu	62
Icelandic	3	Visayan	40
Ilcano	10	Welsh	825
Irish	13	Winnebago	6
Italian	97,138	Yiddish	4,427
Japanese	2,064	Zapotec	8
Korea n.	12	Zulu	10 025
Kuesien	351	Total	560,043

Why do we need translations of the Bible? Into how many languages has the Bible already been translated? Into how many languages and dialects has it not yet been translated? From what text should every translation be made?

What are the chief modern agencies for translating and distributing the Bible? What other agencies are there? What is the name of your own church publishing house? Name some of the great Bible houses of the world.

Look up the Bible passages referred to in your lesson, and find additional references to this subject in the Bible. Show that it is the will of God that the Word shall be available in every language. In what way can the contents of this lesson help you in your Bible study? In your faith and works?

LESSON SEVENTEEN. VERSIONS:
II. THE NEED OF REVISIONS.

Every language that has a translation, no matter how good and popular, is sure sometime to get a revision, if not an entirely new translation. There are at least four reasons for this: 1. Corrections in the Standard Text; 2. Mistakes in the Standard Translations; 3. Changes in the Spoken Language; 4. Unpopularity of Existing Translations.

1. DUE TO CORRECTIONS IN THE STANDARD TEXT.

A standard text is the original text as we have it. The original text as it was prepared by the inspired writers is lost. The first copies made from these texts have also been lost. The oldest manuscripts now in existence are copies of copies, and probably copies of copies of copies. Very few of the manuscripts are complete. In the work of copying, mistakes may have been made, rather trifling in character, it is true, and yet mistakes withal. The first printed texts in the original were hurriedly prepared, without access to the earliest and most correct manuscripts, and without a critical comparison of all of the sources. These first editions of the original text were at once accepted by the translators as the standard. More recent scholars have carefully corrected this early standard text. The corrected text should therefore be translated, or the old translation should be revised and brought up to the latest standard of consecrated construction of textual scholarship. For this reason revisions have been in progress of making in every land of Christendom. Even the "infallible" Latin translation, called Vulgate, has been revised time and again on this very score. The Revised Version in English is an answer to this demand, brought on by the great accumulation of ancient texts and various readings and by the greater perfection of the science of textual criticism.

2. DUE TO MISTAKES IN THE STANDARD TRANSLATIONS.

A standard translation is one that has been accepted by Church, State or popular opinion. Such a translation may have occasional mistakes or unhappy renderings. This was held to be the case of the Authorized Version, and a strong reason for the preparation of the Revised. The 47 translators who had done the work of translation for King James, it was held, had, in a great many instances, misunderstood the sense (Schaff's "Bible Revision," 47). "To make this as evident as it may be made we should need to write a volume. Such volumes have been written: among which Dr. Lightfoot's work on 'A Fresh Revision of the English New Testament' may be commended as the best. In this brief paper we can only say that the main deficiency in our translation proceeds from want of exact knowledge of the Hebrew and Greek languages" (T. D. Woolsey's "Reasons for a New Revision of the Scripture in English"). As an example of a faulty translation, that of Matt. 28: 19-20 will perhaps suffice. This is translated as follows in the Revised Version: "Go ye therefore, and make disciples of all the nations, baptizing them into the name of the Father and of the Son and of the Holy Spirit; teaching them to observe all things whatsoever I commanded you." The verse in the original reads as in the Revised Version: "Make disciples—baptizing—teaching." Formerly, this was translated "Make disciples—and baptize—teaching—." This occurred first in the Itala, the first Latin version, then in the Vulgate, the standard Latin version. It passed on to Italian, Spanish, French, Portuguese and Rumanian translations. Luther retained this defective translation in his version and passed it on to Dutch, Danish, Norwegian, Swedish, Icelandic and English versions. The Russian, Polish and

Bohemian versions have it; also the oldest New Testament translation, the Syriac Peschito. The King James,' or Authorized, had it, but has changed it to conform to the original. Nevertheless, the faulty English translation has had a mighty influence on the many versions of the Bible societies, and thus this incorrect translation has been passed on to all parts of the earth. Still every competent text critic and commentator of modern times is of the opinion that the words baptizing and teaching should be translated as coordinates. The first to render it correctly was Theodor Beza, in his Latin Bible of 1565.

3. DUE TO CHANGES IN THE SPOKEN LANGUAGE.

Every living tongue that has translations of the Bible is apt to need new translations, too, from time to time, for the reason that a language that is spoken is constantly undergoing change, notwithstanding the retarding influence of Bible translations, standard literature, grammar, government, travel, commerce, etc. Every translation will have to be revised to catch up with the spoken language.

If we take, for example, the very popular and excellent translation of 1611, called King James,' or the Authorized, we note that it has lately been put through a very thorough revision. A group of 52 English and 34 American scholars began working together at this revision in 1870 and continued zealously at it for 10 years. Most of these were professors of Hebrew and Greek at theological seminaries or writers of commentaries. The English committee lost by death 15 and the American 7, but this number was supplied by the appointment of other eminent scholars, making the total number that worked at this revision 101. Both committees were virtually one organization, with the same principles and objects, and in constant correspondence with each other. They did not intend to issue two separate and distinct revisions, but one and the same revision for both nations. Their object was to adapt Kings James' Version

to the present state of the English language, without changing the idiom and vocabulary, and to the present state of
Biblical knowledge, which has since 1611 made much progress in geography, archaeology, philology, textual criticism
and literary criticism. It was not the intention to furnish
a new version, but a revision.

Attention was called to the gradual change to which standard English—like all other living languages—has been
subject. "Old words drop out of use, or lose certain meanings, so as to puzzle many readers; or, by being used in
a new sense, they acquire a certain ambiguity, which needs
to be removed, for the sake of the common reader. It is
true that a well executed version, like our English one (the
King James'), tends to preserve a language from a number of changes which would otherwise be inevitable; but it
is true, also, that an ancient translation, preserved on
account of the veneration which is felt towards it, may
even do harm to religion by obscuring thoughts which would
otherwise be clear."

A few examples of obsolete words in the King James,'
or Authorized Version, which have been given a more modern rendering in the Revised:

	AUTHORIZED	REVISED
Ex. 9: 16	shew	show
Ex. 36: 38	chapiters	capitals
2 Chron. 9: 14	chapmen	merchants
Isa. 16: 3	bewray	betray
Joel 2: 24	fats	vats
Luke 17: 7	by and by	straightway
Acts 28: 13	fetched a compass	made a circuit
1 Pet. 3: 11	eschew	turn away from

The work of the Anglo-American committee on the New
Testament was completed in 1881, and on the Old Testament
in 1885, and the world has as a result a new version to adopt
or reject. The committee expected that their work should
pass through a severe ordeal of criticism, as everything else
that is new and pretentious must do.

The following examples from English translations of the Lord's Prayer illustrates that a living language is constantly undergoing change (G. F. Bergholtz' "The Lord's Prayer in the Principal Languages of the World"):

OLD ENGLISH (ANGLO-SAXON), 700.

Uren Fader thic arth in heofnas, sic gehalgad thin noma. To cymeth thin ric. Sic thin willa sue is in heofnas und in eortho.

OLD ENGLISH (DANISH-SAXON), 875.

Fader ure, thu the earth on heofunum, si thin nama gehalgad. To becume thin rice. Gewurthe thin wille on eorthan swa swa on heofunum.

MIDDLE ENGLISH, 1200.

Ure Fadir that hart in hevene, halged be thi name with giftes sevene. Samen cume thi kingdom. Thi wille in herthe als in heven be don.

MIDDLE ENGLISH (WYCLIF), 1380.

Oure fadir that art in heuenes halovid be thi name. Thi kyngdom come to—Be thi wille don in erthe as in heuene.

MODERN ENGLISH (AUTHORIZED), 1611.

Our father which art in heauen, hallowed be thy Name. Thy kingdome come. Thy will be done, in earth as it is in heauen.

MODERN ENGLISH (REVISED), 1881.

Our father, who art in Heaven, hallowed be Thy name. Thy
. Thy will be done, as in Heaven, so on earth.

---

4. DUE TO UNPOPULARITY OF EXISTING TRANSLATIONS.

If a new translation or revision does not in time win popular approval, no matter how good it is otherwise, it will have to be set aside and a new attempt will have to be made. It took the Vulgate 200 years to win out over the old Itala. Translations of the Bible into the vernaculars of Europe had been circulated long before Luther's day. During the 61 years from the invention of the printing press (in 1456) to the advent of Luther as reformer (in 1517), in Germany alone 14 editions of the Bible appeared in High German, besides a few in Low German. These were based on the German Bible of the so-called Codex Eplensis, translated by some unknown Waldensian. Each edition was a sort of revision, an attempt to make the translation popular (Mueller's "History of the Christian Church," II, 543). These translators lacked Luther's tremendous knowledge of Greek and Hebrew and his fine and almost unerring linguistic feeling, hence their versions never became popular. (Cf. P. Pietsch's "Luther und die hochdeutsche Schriftsprache," 1883).

The popularity of King James' Version like Luther's can not be questioned. It has received tributes of most excellent praise from high and low. Thus, from a longer eulogy by Dr. F. W. Faber, a Catholic: "Who will say that the uncommon beauty and marvellous English of the Protestant Bible is not one of the great strongholds of heresy in this country? It lives on the ear, like music that can never be forgotten, like the sound of church bells, which the convert hardly knows how he can forego. Its felicities often seem to be almost things rather than words. It is part of the national mind, and the anchor of national seriousness." Yet it was not popular at first. Thomas Ward, for example, accused King James' translators of "blasphemy, most damnable corruptions, intolerable deceit, and vile imposture" (Schaff's "Companion to the Greek Testament," 327). Moulton's "Literary Study of the Bible" (91) gives this account of its first reception: "The Authorized Version had itself to encounter the same opposition. It is said to have been a full half century before the work of King James' translators came into general use; and in the interval we have on record the opinion of a scholar and divine, who, asked by the king, declared he would be torn by wild horses rather than urge so badly executed a version upon the Churches."

As to the Revised Version, the Anglo-American committee naturally urged the adoption of their work. Thus they reasoned: If the Churches adopted it they would have "a bond of interdenominational and international union in a common Bible;" if they did not adopt it, "the irrepres-

sible task of correcting King James' Version will be carried
on more zealously than ever by unauthorized individuals, and
by sectarian enterprise, which will increase the difficulty by
multiplying confusion and division." "But," they add,
"we never had the least fear of the final result. There never
has been such a truly providential combination of favorable
circumstances, and of able and sound Biblical scholars from
all the evangelical Churches of the two great nations speaking the English language, for such a holy work of common
Christianity, as is presented in the Anglo-American Bible
revision committees. This providential juncture, the remarkable harmony of the revisers in the prosecution of
their work, and the growing desire of the Churches for a
timely improvement and rejuvenation of our venerable English version, justify the expectation of a speedy and general
adoption of the new Revision in Great Britain and America "
(Schaff's "Bible Revision," 21).

It might be added here that Dr. Schaff's fears have been
fully realized—the Revised Version has been attacked, and
several new individual and sectarian translations have appeared. His hopes have been blasted—the Revised Version
has not become popular, is not being bought by the public, does not seem to meet the demand, in spite of its
great merits and the "truly providential combination of
favorable circumstances" which brought it forth. It has
been found necessary not only to publish an English Revised
Version (1881, 1885), but also an American Revised
(1901), containing the preferences of the American committee. Even this has not made this excellent revision
popular.

Not every version true to the original is popular. The
Revised Version is not popular, at least not yet, even after
35 years of trial. Yet it is much more than a mere external,
grammatical and lexicographical translation. The spirit
of the original has also been apprehended and conveyed in
more modern phraseology. The content has been grouped

into paragraphs, so that the reader may get not only texts, but also context. Still, it is not popular. Some day another translation will therefore be forthcoming.

———

State four reasons why there is need of Bible revision?

Explain why it is necessary to make corrections in the standard text.

Explain how it happens that there are mistakes in the standard translations. Illustrate.

Explain how the changes in the spoken language affect the Bible versions. Tell in brief the composition of the Anglo-American committee to revise the King James' Version. Give examples of the changes in the language called attention to by this committee. Illustrate from the Lord's Prayer how the English language has changed in the course of the centuries.

If a translation or revision does not become popular, what must be done with it? Why will it be necessary to make a new attempt at translation or revision? How many attempts were made in Germany before Luther's became popular? What was the opposition in England to King James' Version before it became popular? Why should the Revised Version become popular? Why is it not popular?

Look up in the Bible passages referred to in your lesson, and find additional references to this subject in the Bible. In what ways can the contents of this lesson help you in your Bible study? In your faith and works?

LESSON EIGHTEEN. THE ENGLISH BIBLE:
I. EARLY VERSIONS, 680-1611.

In the United States English is spoken, not American. English is the chief language of England and all her colonies, past and present. In order to understand the story of the Bible in English we are obliged to enter upon English soil and into English history. At the dawn of history the British Isles were occupied by the Celts. Just before the birth of Christ they were conquered by the Romans under Caesar. In 550 A. D. they were overrun by the Germanic tribes (from Denmark, Sweden and Germany) called Jutes, Angles and Saxons. They spoke many dialects, which are often grouped under one hyphenated term: Anglo-Saxon. The term English is derived from the name Angles. The Celts had been Christianized during the Roman occupation, but neither Irish, Welsh nor Scotch "felt any inclination to help these barbarians who had robbed them of their lands, to secure a title to the heavenly inheritance" (Myers' "Mediaeval and Modern History," 31). Pope Gregory the Great was the first one to take any interest in their conversion. As he was walking through the slave market at Rome one day, he chanced to see some English captives, and was struck by their fine form and fair features. He made inquiry as to what people they were and was told that they were called Angles. "Right," said he, "for they have an angelic face, and it becomes such to become coheirs with the angels in Heaven." Gregory shortly afterwards dispatched Augustine to Britain to do mission work amongst the invaders from the Baltic coasts. This was in 597. It took a long time for this sturdy people to forget the worship of Thor (Cf. Thursday) and Odin, or Woden (Cf. Wednesday), and the rest of the Northern gods and to accept in their place the Prince of Peace. It took a still longer time for them to secure the Bible in their own language. They have, however, the honor of being amongst the first of the modern nations to secure the Bible in their own language, and they rank first in their zeal to have it translated into the other languages of the earth. The story of the English Bible versions falls naturally into three groups: The Early Versions, the Authorized Version and the Revised Version.

The first attempt to translate the Bible into Anglo-Saxon was rather a poetical paraphrase, made in 680 by Caedmon, a Saxon cowherd. His poem is composed of four parts: Genesis, Exodus, Daniel, and Christ and Satan. The historian Bede, born 673, has this to say in his "Ecclesiastical History" about Caedmon and his "Paraphrase:"

"Caedmon, having lived in a secular habit until he was well advanced in years, had never learned anything of versifying; for which reason, being sometimes at entertainments, where it was agreed for the sake of mirth that all present should sing in their turns, when he saw the instrument come toward him, he rose up from the table and returned home.

"Having done so at a certain time, and gone out of the house where the entertainment was, to the stable, where he had to take care of the horses that night, he there composed himself to rest at the proper time; a person appeared to him in his sleep, and, saluting him by his name, said, 'Caedmon, sing some song to me.' He answered, 'I cannot sing; for that was the reason why I left the entertainment and retired to this place, because I could not sing.' The other who talked to him replied, 'However, you shall sing.' 'What shall I sing?' rejoined he. 'Sing the beginning of created beings,' said the other. Hereupon he presently began to sing verses to the praise of God.

"He sang the creation of the world, the origin of man, and all the history of Genesis: and made many verses on the departure of the children of Israel out of Egypt, and their entering into the Land of Promise, with many other histories from Holy Writ; the incarnation, passion, resurrection of our Lord and His ascension into Heaven; the coming of the Holy Ghost and the preaching of the apostles; also the terror of future judgment, the horror of the pains of Hell and the delights of Heaven."

After Caedmon other poets, such as Cynewulf, also attempted to write on Biblical themes after the manner of Caedmon. Others attempted prose translations of Scripture, among whom may be mentioned Bede and King Alfred the Great and Aelfric. Bede translated the Gospel, Alfred the Psalms, and Aelfric the Pentateuch and Joshua. Although Alfred's translations of Scriptures are now lost, his work is nevertheless still bearing fruit; for he founded schools, among which may be numbered the famous university at Oxford, established libraries and sought to translate the best books into the Anglo-Saxon, the language of his people.

Alfred died in 901. He had spent much of his time in defending his country against the attacks of the Danish barbarians from the Baltic. The Anglo-Saxons were substantially of the same blood as the Danes, and had the same institutions and customs. Their languages, too, were so nearly alike that they could readily converse together without an interpreter, in the same manner as Norwegians, Danes and Swedes of today can readily understand one another. The Danes, through the activity of St. Ansgar (826), had recently accepted Christianity, but had not yet as a people submitted to its message of peace. Hence they continued their raids on England and eventually made that country a province of Denmark (1013-1042). The crown came back to the Saxon line in 1042, only to remain there a brief space of 24 years. Meanwhile the Northmen (Norwegians) were also making viking raids on the countries of the South, often settling in the conquered territory and mingling with the native population. From the eighth to the twelfth century they made invasions and settlements in various countries, as: England (Northumberland), Ireland,

Scotland, the Faroe Islands, Iceland, Greenland, Vinland, France, etc. The occupation of France by Ganger Rolf in 912 has a direct bearing on the present topic. The Northmen who settled in Normandy adopted the French language and customs. In 1066 William, Duke of Normandy, claiming that Harold, the English prince, had promised him the English crown, since he had once been a shipwrecked captive in Normandy, invaded England and made himself its king. One of the effects of this conquest was, that out of the struggle between the Anglo-Saxon, spoken by the conquered, and the French, spoken by the conquerors, a new, composite tongue arose, namely, the English, which is about equally Anglo-Saxon and French-Latin in its makeup. During these 300 years and more of struggle there was little attempt made to translate the Bible. The Latin was sufficient for the use of the Catholic clergy. The first English translation was made in 1382 by John Wiclif, the "Morning Star of the Reformation," whose fight against the abuses in the Catholic Church had led him to see the need of the Bible in the language of the people. The Church did not look with favor upon Wiclif's work. Soon he was forced to retire from his position as teacher and preacher at Oxford, and his followers, who were nicknamed Lollards, were persecuted. In 1401, only 19 years after the publication of this translation, the burning at the stake of the Bible readers, or "heretics," was begun, a practice which had the sanction of Church and State in England for nearly two centuries.

In spite of the persecutions and the severity of the laws against Bible reading and "heresy," the English people continued to read the Bible and English scholars continued to study it and translate it. Many epoch-making events combined to promote the desire for the Scriptures in the language of the common people. There were discoveries and inventions, revivals, revolts and reformations. In 1492 Columbus discovered San Salvador. In 1497 Vasco de

Gama sailed around Africa. A host of other discoverers and explorers followed in their wake. Gunpowder and cannon were used as early as 1346, at the battle of Crecy. The printing press was invented in 1456, and the first book published was the Bible, in Latin. In 1488 the first Hebrew edition of the Old Testament was printed, and in 1516 the first Greek edition in western Europe after the fall of Constantinople, in 1453, caused a profound interest in Greek language and literature, giving learning a new impetus and range. The excessive tyranny of the nobility and the worldliness of the clergy caused deep mutterings and open revolts, which were cruelly suppressed. Wiclif's followers in England and Holland were hunted down and burnt. The Bohemian reformers, Huss and Jerome, were likewise condemned and sentenced to the flames (1415), and their adherents were almost totally exterminated in a desolating war of fifteen years. In 1498 the Florentine Reformer Savonarola was burnt at the stake for having denounced the corruptions of the Church. Ferdinand and Isabella of Spain established the Inquisition for the detection and punishment of heresy, creating a reign of terror in which thousands were consigned to the flames and tens of thousands were condemned to endure penalties scarcely less terrible (Cf. Prescott's "Ferdinand and Isabella"). In 1517 Luther nailed his Ninety-five Theses to the Church at Wittenberg, protesting against the many abuses of the Church, particularly that of indulgences, or the buying of the forgiveness of sins. In 1523 he published the New Testament in German, and in 1534 the whole Bible in German. Schools were founded in which the Word of God was taught in its truth and purity. Catechisms were written in which the essential doctrines of the Bible were made plain to young and old. The Gospel was again preached with power from the pulpit. The Protestant Churches came into being. Unfortunately, they divided into many factions with varying teachings. In order to decide which party or teaching was in the right, one would have to search the Scriptures. The Order of Jesuits was founded to counteract the zeal and energy of the reformers and by means of the terrible machinery of the Inquisition to uproot all heresy. Yet, notwithstanding the ban and the curse of the Pope, the rack and the fires of the Jesuits, the edicts and armies of kings, the reformers continued to translate the Bible and the people to read it. Here is an old woman, for example, who has secured a New Testament that she can read. She nails it to the bottom of an old armchair, where no one can see it. She turns the chair upside down and reads it when all alone and unseen by human eye. But, ah, she cannot hide the light of the Gospel which has lightened up her own soul. Men begin to suspect that she, too, is a Bible reader. They search her apartments and find her Book. For this great transgression of the law of the land and of the Church she is bundled off to the flames.

In such times it was that William Tyndale set about to translate the Bible into more modern English on the basis of more correct manuscripts. He printed at Worms his New Testament Version in 1525, and thereupon set to work to render the Old Testament into English. But he found this work of translating a very dangerous occupation, therefore he had to flee from country to country and from place to place and remain in hiding. Finally he was betrayed at Brussels, kept by Henry VIII of England for 18 months in a dungeon, then strangled and burned (1536). Shortly afterwards, when this same arbitrary monarch discovered that the Bible could be used as an effective instrument against the Pope, with whom he was at outs, he ordered a number of successive revisions of the Bible to be printed and sold. Nearly all of these versions are merely revisions of Tyndale's translation. Even the famous Authorized Version and the modern Revised Version are to a large extent revisions of Tyndale's. Tyndale's translation, in turn, both in form and substance generally follows Luther's translation and in places minutely copies Luther—(L. F. Gruber's "The Truth about Tyndale's New Testament").

Among the successors to Tyndale's are the following:

The Miles Coverdale Version, 1535, translated principally from Luther's Bible and the Vulgate. It was the first version printed on English soil.

The Matthew's Bible, 1537. This was 60 per cent Tyndale and 40 per cent Coverdale, that is, Gen.—2 Chron. and the New Testament were a reprint of Tyndale's, and Esra—Malachi was a reprint of Coverdale's translation. The editor was John Rogers (alias Matthew), the martyr. It was published with the King's license and was the first "authorized" Bible in English.

The Taverner's Version, 1539, which is partly a revision of the Matthew's Bible and partly an original rendering by Taverner.

The Cranmer's Bible, also called on account of its size the Great Bible, 1539. This was a revision of Coverdale's Bible. Its melodious rendering of the Psalms is still used in the English "Prayer Book."

The Whittingham Version, 1557. This was published at Geneva during the bloody reign of Queen Mary, and is therefore known also as the Geneva Bible. It was the first English Bible printed in verses and Roman letter. It used a different type to denote the words in the translation not found in the original, but inserted to make the meaning plain, like the italics of our Bibles. Thus, in the following sentence the word "him" is not found in the original Greek text:

And King Herod heard of *him* (Mark 6:14).

This version, on account of its marginal notes, was very popular with the masses, but distasteful to those in authority. It is related that King James, too, found that it taught sedition and treason. As, for example, in Ex. 1:19, disobedience to kings was allowed in a marginal note. This passage tells of the disobedience of the midwives in order to save the male children of the Israelites from being killed at birth.

The Bishops' Bible, 1568, being a revision of the Great Bible, made by nine bishops and other theologians. This version was popular with the High Church party.

The Thomson New Testament, 1576. Very popular.

The Rheims New Testament, 1582. Made from the Latin Vulgate by Catholic refugees in the reign of Queen Elizabeth.

The Douai Old Testament, 1609. Made from the Latin by the aforesaid Catholic refugees, who had moved from Rheims to Douai, France. It has been subject to several revisions and is the standard English Catholic Version to this day.

———

Where did the English people originally come from? From what is the name derived? When did this people become Christian? What was their original religion? What was their original language? When was the first attempt made to translate the Bible into this language? Name some other early attempts. Show that English now is a composite tongue. What were the first attempts made to translate the Bible into modern English? Who was Wiclif? Who were the Lollards? What opposition did Wiclif and the Lollards have? Give some of the epoch-making events just preceding the Reformation. Why was there such opposition to the Bible and to those who translated, published, distributed and read it? Give examples of some who braved the wrath of the Church in order to read the Good Book. What was the work of Tyndale? On whose work is his translation largely based? What succeeding translations follow Tyndale to a considerable extent? Name nine other English translations of the Bible preceding the King James' Version. Give the date and chief characteristics of each.

Look up the Bible passages referred to in your lesson, and find additional references to this subject in the Bible. In what ways can the contents of this lesson help you in your Bible study? In your faith and works?

LESSON NINETEEN. THE ENGLISH BIBLE: II. THE AUTHORIZED, OR KING JAMES' VERSION, 1611—.

Due to the fact that there were getting to be so many different versions of the Bible, and all of them were coming into use, much confusion arose, and disputes as to which translation was correct. At the Hampton Court Conference, in 1604, King James was petitioned by the Puritans to grant, among other reforms, a new and standard translation of the Bible to be authorized for use in all the Churches. The petition was granted, a commission of 54 eminent scholars was appointed to make the revision, rules to govern the translators were prepared, and the work was begun by 47 of the appointed men. The Bishops' Bible was taken as the basis for revision. It was to be altered as little as the truth of the original would permit. All of the other English translations were to be consulted, besides the standard translations in German, French, Spanish, Italian and Dutch. In 1611 the revision was ready from the press, but met with violent opposition or cold contempt. The first edition was disfigured by several misprints, such as in Matt. 26:36, where the name of Judas was substituted for that of Jesus. It had no marginal notes such as made the Geneva Version so popular. The king's own printer continued therefore to print the Geneva Bible and to place it on the market side by side of the King James.' Not until 1649, after it had passed 160 editions and its marginal notes had been transferred to the King James' Version, was the Geneva Bible finally taken from the market. People were as yet, however, not satisfied. In 1653, the Rump Parliament debated a bill to revise the King James,' a project which failed purely on account of the sudden dissolution of the Parliament by Oliver Cromwell. Those were tempestuous days for England, for she was engaged in bitter domestic and foreign wars. It is no wonder, then, that the faults and shortcomings of the King James' translation was for the moment lost sight of. In 1660, the Commonwealth, or Republic, established by Cromwell in 1649, came to an end. Monarchy was again restored. Puritans and dissenters of every class were crushed and persecuted. High Church men and royalists were in seats of power and authority. Naturally they would favor the use of King James' Version. Opposition to this version began to wane. It became the standard version and found its way into the hands of the common people as well as of the royalists. It began to win favor and to call forth the most lavish praise ever bestowed on any English book. And, indeed, this version is truly the chief classic in the English language, having been for nearly 300 years the fountain head of English language and literature, the inspiration of English Christianity. It owes very much to Tyndale's Version, from which it had gotten its general phraseology and style. It owes also much to the Geneva Version, from which it had borrowed the versification and marginal notes. It has been printed in thousands of editions, of which no two are alike except those that are printed from the same stereotyped plates. Thus, a committee of the American Bible Society, in 1851, upon examining six editions of this version, discovered nearly 24,000 variations in the text and the punctuation. In the 1611 edition, for example, this spelling occurs: "heauen;" now the public wants the word spelt thus: "heaven." The changes made are but trifling in character, although appalling in number. It is very necessary, too, that some of these changes shall be made, for it will be remembered that this version dates from 1611, over 300 years ago, and uses the English of 300 years ago, with words often different in spelling and meaning. Forty English dictionaries have been issued to keep pace with the changes in the language. On account of the changes already made in the different editions of this version, and on account of the changes that ought yet to be made in order to make it correspond to the standard original text and the present usage of English, Bible scholars began about 60 years ago earnestly to advocate the making of a new revision.

EXAMPLES OF ENGLISH IN THE AUTHORIZED AND AMERICAN REVISED VERSIONS.

(N. B. The spelling in the Authorized is from the 1748 edition. Note that it has two variants—judgement, instead of judgment, and Mars, instead of Mars').

AUTHORIZED.	REVISED.

Ex. 3:22.

22. But every woman shall borrow of her neighbour,	22. But every woman shall ask of her neighbor,

Ps. 19:3.

3. *There is* no speech nor language, *where* their voice is not heard.	3. There is no speech nor language; Their voice is not heard.

Isa. 10:2.

2. To turn aside the needy from judgement, and to take away the right from the poor of my people, that the widows may be their prey, and *that* they may rob the fatherless!	2. To turn aside the needy from justice, and to rob the poor of my people of their right, that widows may be their spoil, and that they may make the fatherless their prey!

Acts 2:47.

47. Praising God, and having favour with all the people. And the Lord added to the church daily such as should be saved.	47. Praising God, and having favor with all the people. And the Lord added to them day by day those that were saved.

1 Cor. 13:1.

1. Though I speak with the tongues of men and of angels, and have not charity,	1. If I speak with the tongues of men and angels, but have not love,

Acts 17:22-23.

22. Then Paul stood in the midst of Mars hill and said, Ye men of Athens, I perceive that in all things ye are too superstitious.

23. For as I passed by, and beheld your devotions,

22. And Paul stood in the midst of the Areopagus, and said,

Ye men of Athens, in all things I perceive that ye are very religious. 23. For as I passed along, and observed the objects of your worship,

Jas. 5:16.

The effectual fervent prayer of a righteous man availeth much.

The supplication of a righteous man availeth much in its working,

---

Why do we call our Standard Version the King James'? Why do we call it the Authorized? Give the history of its origin. Tell briefly the first opposition to it. Its succeeding popularity. What does it owe to preceding versions? What can you say about variations found in later editions? Why are such variations necessary and inevitable? Why was the Revised Version planned and undertaken? Give examples of the English in both Versions.

Look up the Bible passages referred to in your lesson, and find additional references to this subject in the Bible. In what ways can the contents of this lesson help you in your Bible study? In your faith and works?

LESSON TWENTY. THE ENGLISH BIBLE:
III. THE REVISED VERSION, 1881—.

In 1870 a commission of noted British scholars was appointed to undertake the revision of the King James,' or Authorized Version. The leading Protestant Bible scholars of the United States were also asked to co-operate with the British Commission and to constitute the American Revision Committee. It was hoped that by this co-operation the whole English-speaking world could get one uniform, standard, authorized version of the Bible, instead of the hundred and one varying editions of the Authorized then (and now) in use. The British Committee devoted 10 years to the task; the American Committee, not being satisfied, continued 20 years longer at the work. Every member of both committees worked without pay. In 1881 the Joint Committee issued the Revised New Testament; in 1885, the Revised Bible. In 1901 the American Committee issued the American Standard Revised Version, containing a few variations from the British Standard Revised Version of 1885.

The American Revised Version ought to be the best version in English, for several reasons: A hundred of the best Biblical scholars in the English world labored at the revision from 10 to 30 years. They had at their command everything that former translators had had, and very much more.

They had the most important and authentic manuscripts, most of which have been discovered since 1611. They had the great storehouse of knowledge of ancient lands, peoples and languages, acquired through a century of unexampled zeal and fruitfulness in exploration, excavation and study. They had for references the recent scholarly revisions made in Germany, Holland, Sweden, Norway, Denmark and France.

The American Revised Version is no doubt the best English Version on the market, for several reasons: It is based on the oldest and most authentic manuscripts. It has sought to correct every mistranslation in the Authorized. It has tried to give the exact meaning of the original in the language of today instead of the language used 300 years ago. It has printed prose as prose and poetry as poetry and has grouped the prose selections into paragraphs. It has in the margin a much more accurate and systematic set of helps than the Authorized. Its marginal translations are of two forms: literal translations of the Hebrew and Greek, where the English idiom requires a different turn of expression, and second choice translations in doubtful cases. Its marginal references have been carefully corrected and classified. Some editions of the Bible have no marginal references; others have a greater or less abundance of this kind of help, ranging from a few hundred to 63,000 references. The earlier English editions had, in addition to parallel passages, a number of expository notes dealing with the grammar, doctrine or application of the verse. Later versions left out these explanations, but encumbered the margin with an ever-increasing number of references to parallel passages. The revisers have struck out a large number of these references that are erroneous, farfetched or non-applicable, and have inserted others that are more to the point. The summaries of the chapters in the Authorized Version are omitted in the Revised, because they do not belong to Scripture and do not add anything to its clearness.

The most striking alterations in the text are: In 1 John 5: 7 the words "and these Three are one" are omitted; in Mark 16:9-20, Luke 22:43-44, John 7:53—8:11 and a few other passages footnotes are given, stating that these passages are omitted in some ancient manuscripts.

Examples of changes in translation are: In Gen. 12: 6 the Authorized reads that Abram went to the plain of

Moreh; the American Revised reads the oak of Moreh.   In
1 Kings 10: 28 the Authorized Version reads: "And Solomon had horses brought out of Egypt, and linen yarn; the
king's merchants received the linen yarn at a price."   The
American Standard reads: "And the horses which Solomon
had were brought out of Egypt; and the king's merchants
received them in droves, each drove at a price."   In 1 Tim.
6: 10 the A. V. reads: "For the love of money is the root
of all evil;" the R. V. reads: "For the love of money is
a root of all kinds of evil."

Examples of current words in place of older and obsolete
words are quite numerous.   The following are illustrative:

Astonied (Job 17: 8) in A. V. is changed to astonished in R. V.
Charity (1 Cor. 13) in A. V. is changed to love in R. V.
Eschew (1 Pet. 3: 11) in A. V. is changed to turn away from in R. V.
Minish (Ex. 5: 19) in A. V. is changed to diminish in R. V.
Wot (Gen. 21: 26) in A. V. is changed to know in R. V.

For illustrations of the advantage of the prose selections
being grouped in paragraph units compare 2 Kings 6:24—
7: 2 in both versions.   Compare in the same manner Isa.
52:13—53:12; 1 Cor. 10:14—11:1.   See also Moulton's
"Modern Readers' Bible."

For examples of the poetical sections printed as poetry
see Ex. 15; parts of Num. 21—24; Deut. 32:1-43; Job;
Psalms, etc.   Compare the two versions with each other and
with the more elaborate versification in Moulton's "Modern Readers' Bible."

Here is an illustration of a Biblical lyric as printed in
the Authorized Version, the Revised Version and Moulton
(2 Sam. 1:19-27).   Compare it with the prose printing in
the older versions.

DAVID'S LAMENT (2 SAM. 1:24-27).

24. Ye daughters of Israel, weep over Saul, who clothed you in
scarlet, with other delights, who put on ornaments of gold upon
your apparel.
25. How are the mighty fallen in the midst of the battle! O
Jonathan, thou wast slain in thine high places.

26. I am distressed for thee, my brother Jonathan: very pleasant hast thou been unto me: thy love to me was wonderful, passing the love of women.

27. How are the mighty fallen, and the weapons of war perished!

_____ (Authorized Version).

24. Ye daughters of Israel, weep over Saul,
   Who clothed you in scarlet delicately,
   Who put ornaments of gold upon your apparel.
25. How are the mighty fallen in the midst of the battle!
   Jonathan is slain upon thy high places.
26. I am distressed for thee, my brother Jonathan:
   Very pleasant hast thou been unto me:
   Thy love to me was wonderful, ·
   Passing the love of women.
27. How are the mighty fallen,
   And the weapons of war perished!

_____ (Revised Version).

Thy glory, O Israel,
Is slain upon thy high places!
   How are the mighty—
   Fallen!
Tell it not in Gath,
Publish it not in the streets of Ashkelon;
   Lest the daughters of the Philistines rejoice,
   Lest the daughters of the uncircumcised triumph.
Neither fields of offerings:
Ye mountains of Gilboa, let there be no dew nor rain upon you,
   For there the shield of the mighty was vilely cast away,
   The shield of Saul, as of one not anointed with oil.
From the blood of the slain,
From the fat of the mighty,
   The bow of Jonathan turned not back,
   And the sword of Saul returned not empty.
Saul and Jonathan were lovely and pleasant in their lives,
And in their death they were not divided!
   They were swifter than eagles,
   They were stronger than lions.
Ye daughters of Israel,
Weep over Saul,
   Who clothed you in scarlet delicately,
   Who put ornaments of gold upon your apparel.
      How are the mighty—
      Fallen in the midst of the battle!
         O Jonathan,
         Slain upon the high places.

I am distressed for thee, my brother Jonathan:
Very pleasant hast thou been unto me:
    Thy love to me was wonderful,
    Passing the love of woman.
        How are the mighty—
           Fallen!
        And the weapons of war—
           Perished!
(R. G. Moulton's "Masterpieces of Biblical Literature," 158-159).

Nearly every Protestant Denomination has recognized the merits of the American Standard Version by making it the basis of all their explanatory notes in their school texts. Besides this, The American Bible Society, which since 1816 has published only the King James' Version, has recently amended its constitution to enable it to publish the American Standard Version to meet the demands of Churches and Sunday schools for this Version. There is scarcely a prominent college, theological seminary or leading Christian scholar who does not recognize and use this latest version of the Scriptures, because it brings the plain reader into closer contact with the thought of the original writers than any other English version.

State again the composition of the committee that undertook to revise the King James' Bible. How long did this committee work at it? When did they get through? What is the difference between the American Revised Version and the British Revised Version? Name some of the qualifications of this committee. Name some of the advantages they had over the earlier translators and revisors.

Give five or more reasons why the American revision is the best English version on the market. Give examples of alterations in the text. Of changes in translation. Of current words instead of older and obsolete ones. Of the advantage of paragraph divisions over the so-called "verses". Of the advantage of printing poetry as poetry and not as prose. If nearly everybody admits that the American Revised Version is better than the Authorized, why does it not become popular?

Look up the Bible passages referred to in your lesson, and find additional references to this subject in the Bible. In what way can the contents of this lesson help you in your Bible study? In your faith and works?

PART THREE.

GEOGRAPHY OF THE BIBLE.

OUTLINE.

LESSON TWENTY-ONE. PLACE OF GEOGRAPHY.

Geography (from the Greek ge—earth, and graphein—to describe) is a description of the earth or a portion of the earth, including its structure, features, products, political divisions and the people by whom it is inhabited. Biblical geography is such a description of the lands mentioned in the Bible in connection with the history of the Chosen People, particularly the land of Canaan.

1. LOCAL SETTING.

The study of Biblical geography makes the story of the Chosen People more real and vivid. Like chronology, it has been called one of the eyes of the Bible student. The history of every country has a definite local setting. We can not, for example, understand our own country's history unless we know something about its location and boundaries, its divisions and neighbors, its resources and towns, etc. We cannot appreciate the merits of the contending forces in the present world war without a clear view of the geographical questions involved. We must approach the study of the Chosen People also through their country—Canaan. For they were to live in the world, even though they were to be not of the world. Their story, too, has a definite local setting. Geographical landmarks are even more necessary than chronological.

2. RELIGION.

If we look deeper we shall find that the geography of Palestine had a definite influence upon the inhabitants thereof. For example, in matters of religion. Every people, savage as well as civilized, is religious. Traces of the Common Story of the Fall and the Flood are to be found in the myths and folk lore of every tribe and nation.

The true account of these great events was in the course of
time forgotten, due to the fact that memory is notably un-
reliable at best.   In place of the historical truth we therefore meet a host of legends, the product of the imagination
and superstition.   For the early races, being in their childhood, were imaginative, and being religious, were superstitious.   They did not worship the One True God, but the
many gods of their own fancies.   The heathen attributed
his own nature to natural phenomena, thought nature was
alive with supernatural beings in disposition much like himself, only on a greater scale, whose wrath and enmity he must
seek to ward off by offerings and sacrifice.   He saw no beauty
in mountains, seas, clouds, storms and winter snows, for he
had to fight to overcome these forces that he might live.   But
when nature was lavish in her gifts, he attributed his good
fortune to the kindness of some benevolent deity, or to the
value placed by the hostile deities upon his offerings.   In
Canaan and its near neighbors, Syria and Phoenicia, too,
the natural tendency was toward polytheism, the worship
of many gods, but, strange to say, this section has given
to the whole world its only monotheistic religions—Judaism,
Christianity and Mohammedanism.   The presence of Mohammedanism can be accounted for by the Jewish and Christian
religions as prototypes and the near-by desert with its
silence, monotony and illiberality, where Mohammed spent
much of his time.   But Judaism and Christianity can not
be accounted for in this way, for these had their rise, not
in Arabia, the monotonous desert, but in Palestine, the
"land flowing with milk and honey."   Here we might expect
not the worship of One God, but the worship of many gods.
Here we find exactly what we expect.   The original occupants of Palestine and the contemporaries of the Twelve
Tribes, Philistines, Amorites, Amalekites, Canaanites, and
all other heathen tribes that secured a foothold in Palestine,
were polytheistic.   The strong bent towards nature-worship
can have no better illustration than in the history of the

Twelve Tribes, for no sooner had these forsaken the Wilderness of Sinai and the plateaus of Moab than they "also built them high places, and images and groves on every high hill and under every green tree, and there were also Sodomites in the land; and they did according to all the abominations of the nations which the Lord cast out before the children of Israel" (1 Kings 14: 23-24). The fact is, that the physical geography of Canaan was, like the presence of the idolatrous neighbors, an obstruction to the religion of the Jews. Therefore, the character and spirit of Judaism and Christianity are the more conspicuous. Everything points to the presence and power of a Higher Spiritual Force shaping the destiny of the People of God.

3. WORLD HISTORY.

The position of the Jews in relation to other peoples in the world is also brought out by a study of the geography of Biblical lands. Palestine lay in the center of the ancient civilized world, not in some far-away, hidden nook. Jerusalem was a city set on a hill, and could not be hid (Matt. 5:14). Although Jerusalem, on account of her distance away from water and her position on top of an inland mountain, did not like other world cities have any natural conditions of a great city, yet it "was here that she arose who, more than Athens and more than Rome, taught the nations justice and gave her name to the Ideal City men are ever striving to build on earth, to the city of God that shall one day descend from Heaven—the new Jerusalem" (G. A. Smith). Because to the east lay the Great Arabian Desert and to the west the Great Mediterranean Sea, Palestine became the highway of the nations in commerce and in war, and the Chosen People came into touch with the nations of the earth. Fitting also this position among the nations, for Israel was chosen not only to receive a great blessing, but to be a great blessing. To Abraham God had said: "I will make of thee a great nation, and I will bless thee, and make thy name great; and thou shalt be a blessing. . . . . and in thee shall all the families of the earth be blessed" (Gen. 12: 2-3). We can safely conclude that Israel's geographical position was like her position as the Chosen Servant of God, not one of pure chance, but of divine appointment.

4. ARCHAEOLOGY.

A good knowledge of Biblical geography is indeed valuable and indispensable to the excavators and explorers and students of archaeology. The findings of these excavators and explorers and scholars when thoroughly sifted are invariably the same, namely: that the Bible has stated facts of geography and history correctly. It never makes a mistake.

5. INTERPRETATION.

"The Bible lands are the best commentary on the Bible, as the Bible is the best guide-book in the Bible lands. The Land and the Book mutually illustrate and confirm each other. Palestine has been called (by Renan) 'the fifth Gospel,' lacerated and torn, but still legible. It furnishes the illustrations to the other four Gospels. It is nature's framework to the life of Christ. . . . . . . Every student should visit Bible lands, if he can, and finish his theological education there. They will make a deeper impression and be of more practical use to him for sermonizing and for the religious instruction of youth than many commentaries. Palestine is a ruin, but an eloquent ruin, surrounded by sacred memories. Travel in the East takes away much of the poetry, but deepens and enlivens the sense of the reality" (Schaff). To this splendid advice to students of theology might be added the following to daily Bible readers: If you can not visit Palestine, you can at least study its geography.

Define geography. Biblical geography.

In what sense can the study of geography be called one of the eyes of the Bible student? What is the relation of the study of geography to the local setting?

How does geography influence religion? Illustrate. Has it influenced the religion of the Jews and of the Christians? Give examples. What is meant by mythology? How has geography influenced mythology?

In what way is the knowledge of Biblical geography valuable to students of archaeology? Does the Bible ever make a mistake in stating facts of geography?

In what sense are the Bible lands the best commentary on the Bible? What is the "Fifth Gospel"? What does your Bible history say about Bible geography?

Look up the Bible passages referred to in your lesson, and find additional references to this subject in the Bible. In what ways can the contents of this lesson help you in your Bible study? In your faith and works?

LESSON TWENTY-TWO. LANDS OF THE BIBLE.

1. TWELVE CANAANITE TRIBES.

The Canaanites were descendants of Canaan, the son of Ham (Gen. 9: 25). They occupied the land of Canaan between Jordan and the Mediterranean, and at times parts of the adjoining territories to the east. The southwestern part of their land was taken from them by the Philistines before 1921 B. C., and the central part was conquered by Joshua during 1451-1443 B. C. They were in the land when Abraham became a "sojourner in the Land of Promise, as in a land not his own, dwelling in tents" (Heb. 11: 9). Their wickedness at Sodom and Gomorrah was punished by the destruction of those cities (Gen. 19: 13), and the Dead Sea now occupies the fair plain where once these cities flourished. Their land was promised to Abraham, Isaac, Jacob and the Chosen People (Gen. 12: 7; 13: 14; 17: 8; etc.).

The Canaanites were a mighty people, therefore 10 of the 12 spies that Moses had sent into Canaan reported that it would be impossible to drive them out of the land (Num. 13: 28-29). At this gloomy prospect the Israelites rebelled and were sentenced to wander in the Wilderness 40 years (Num. 13:30—14:45). In his farewell addresses Moses charged Israel to cast out the people though mightier than Israel (Deut. 7:1-5), "for Jehovah. shall deliver them up before thee, and thou shalt smite them."

Joshua set out to drive them out of the land, and was very successful. In 7 years he defeated 31 kings of cities. As Joshua was then getting old, he was commanded to divide the land amongst the Israelites by lot. The work of expelling the Canaanites should continue, each tribe being responsible for its territory (Josh. 12:1—13:7).

After the death of Joshua, Judah and Simeon and Ephraim did subdue a few Canaanite cities, but did not utterly drive them out. The other tribes let them dwell in comparative peace (Judges 1). Therefore the angel of the Lord prophesied that the Canaanites should be as thorns in the sides of the Israelites, and their gods should be a snare unto them (Judges 2: 1-3). And truly was this judgment and prophecy fulfilled. The Canaanites tempted the Israelites to worship their idols. The Israelites forsook the Lord and served the Baalim and provoked the Lord to punish them. He delivered them into the hands of spoilers until they in their sore distress repented and called upon His name again. Then He raised them up judges, and He was with the judge, and saved them from their enemies. The Israelites were always warned not to walk in the ungodly ways of the Canaanites (Lev. 18:3, 24, 30; 20:23; etc.)

a. CANAANITES (?—1551-1351 B. C.).

The Canaanite tribe, in the narrower sense, dwelt along the coast between Philistia and Phoenicia. They fought under Jabin against Joshua (Josh. 11: 1-9), and 200 years later under another Jabin they fought against Deborah and Barak (Judges 4-5).

b. ANAKIM (?—1492-1063 B. C.).

The Anakim were a people "great and tall" (Num. 13:33), a race of giants, occupying several cities in southern Canaan at the time of the Conquest. Their reported size discouraged the faint-hearted pilgrims so that they refused to enter the Promised Land. Joshua destroyed them (Josh. 11:21) as a tribe. Some descendants, however, came to notice in later history, as, for example, Goliath, who was killed by the lad David (1 Sam. 17:4, 10).

c. AMORITES (?—1921-400 B. C.).

The Amorites (Mountaineers) at the time of Abraham were his neighbors on the east. At the Conquest they had moved across the Jordan and their lands became the possession of Reuben.

d. GIRGASHITES (?—1921-1451 B. C.).

This tribe is thought by Origen and Jerome to have lived to the east of the Sea of Galilee, near Gergesa.

e. HITTITES (?—1921-1000 B. C.).

The Hittites were descendants of Heth, the son of Canaan. They lived in southern Canaan and were on friendly terms with Abraham. From the children of Heth he bought a burying place for his beloved Sarah (Gen. 23), guarded by the Mohammedans to this day. Esau married two Hittite wives. Uriah, the husband of Bathsheba, was a Hittite. That they were a powerful people during the Bondage of Israel is seen from the brick tablets known as Tel el Amarna letters.

f. HIVITES (?—1921-400 B. C.).

The Hivites occupied the central part of Canaan, with Gibeon and Shechem as principal cities. The city of Shechem plays an important role in the story of Jacob (Gen. 34) and Abimelech, 500 years later (Judges 8).

g. JEBUSITES (?—1492-1000 B. C.).

The Jebusites held the city of Jebus (Jerusalem) at the time of Joshua and until its capture by David, 400 years later.

h. KENITES (?—1921-1000 B. C.).

The Kenites dwelt in Canaan when Abraham migrated there. Moses' father-in-law was a half Kenite. His family cast their lot with the tribe of Judah and settled in southern Judah, their old camping ground.

i. KENIZZITES (?—1921-1397 B. C.).

The Kenizzites occupied some portion of south-eastern Canaan. Caleb, the spy, was a half Kenizzite. Othniel, his brother, was the first judge after the Conquest.

j. PERIZZITES (?—1921-1000 B. C.).

The Perizzites lived in central Canaan west of Shechem. The tribes of Judah and Simeon slew 10,000 of them after

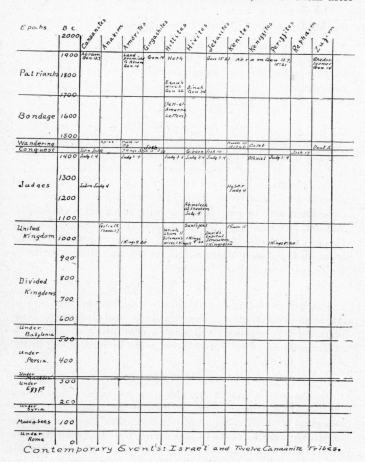

No. 8. Contemporary Events: Israel and Twelve Canaanite Tribes.

the death of Joshua (Judges 1:4-5). Solomon made them bond servants (1 Kings 9:20-21).

k. REPHAIM (?—1921-1451 B. C.).

The Rephaim were a race of giants, joint occupants of the land promised Abraham and conquered by Joshua.

l. ZUZIM (?—1921-1451 B. C.).

The Zuzim, living to the east of the Jordan, were conquered by Chedorlaomer and exterminated 400 years later by the Ammonites.

2. TWELVE SMALLER NATIONS.

a. MESOPOTAMIA (?—1926-1000 B. C.).

Mesopotamia was a country lying between the Euphrates and the Upper Tigris, hence the name, meaning "Between the Rivers." It was the adopted home of Terah, Abraham's father. Abraham had lived at Haran for a time. Isaac had procured his wife from there. Thither Jacob had fled to escape Esau and to get himself a wife from his own people. Balaam, the hireling prophet, hailed from there. The first of the oppressors of Israel was a Mesopotamian. Visitors from Mesopotamia at Jerusalem on the first Pentecost heard the Good News in their tongue.

b. ARABIA (1910 B. C.—).

The progenitor of the Arabians was Ishmael, the son of Abraham and Hagar. The Arabians sold Joseph to Potiphar. They opposed Nehemiah's rebuilding of the walls of Jerusalem. Paul spent three years in meditation in the Arabian solitudes.

c. MIDIAN (1850-1322 B. C.).

Midian was a son of Abraham by Keturah. He became the father of a large tribe, occupying the land between the two arms of the Red Sea. Moses had spent 40 years of exile in Midian and 40 years of wandering together with his people. The Midianites opposed Joshua in 1452 and were defeated by Gideon in 1322 B. C.

d. MOAB (1896-400 B. C.).

The Moabites were descendants of Moab, Lot's eldest son, and lived east of the Dead Sea. In 1452 they hired Balaam to curse Israel. At Shittim they tempted Israel to idolatry. They invaded Canaan until Ehud expelled them. Ruth was a Moabite who settled in Bethlehem, and became the great-grandmother of David. The Moabites paid tribute to Omri and Ahab (894 B. C.). Jehoshaphat won a victory over them without a blow. They were conquered by Nebuchadnezzar and thenceforth disappear as a nation, but not as a race.

e. AMMON (1896-163 B. C.).

The Ammonites were descendants of Lot's youngest son, Ben-ammi, and lived to the north of their cousins, the Moabites. They fought with Joshua (1452), Ehud (1369), Jephthah (1130), Saul (1095), David (1038), Jehoshaphat (900), Jehoiakim (606), Gedaliah (586), Nehemiah (444), and Judas Maccabeus (163) B. C.

f. EDOM (1837 B. C.—70 A. D.).

The Edomites were descendants of Isaac's first born son, Esau (meaning Hairy), or Edom (meaning Red). Red was the color of the pottage Esau bought (Gen. 25:27-34; Heb. 12:16-17). Esau lost his right to the land of Canaan and settled in the hilly country to the south of the Dead Sea. The history of the cousin tribes, Edom and Israel, touches at many points in the Bible. Edom opposed Moses (Num. 20:18-21), Saul (1 Sam. 14:47), David (1 Chron. 18:13), Solomon (1 Kings 11: 14-22), Jehoshaphat (2 Chron. 20: 22-30) Joram (2 Kings 8:20-22), Amaziah (2 Kings 14:7), Ahaz (2 Chron. 28: 17). Herod was an Edomite, or Idumean. The country was also known as Idumea or Mt. Seir.

g. AMALEK (1680-1056 B. C.).

The Amalekites were descendants of Amalek, the grandson of Esau (Gen. 36: 12). At the time of the Exodus they inhabited the Wilderness to the southwest of Canaan. On account of their open enmity to Moses their utter destruction was commanded (Deut. 25:17-19; Ex. 17:8-16). In 1397 they aided Eglon the Moabite in wresting Jericho from Israel. In 1329 they opposed Gideon. Saul was rejected partly because he refused to "smite Amalek and destroy all that they had." David destroyed them at Ziklag (1 Sam. 30:11-31). Balaam's prophecy came true (Num. 24:20).

h. PHILISTIA (?—1921-64 B. C.).

The Philistines (meaning Immigrants) were Hamites by race, descendants of Misraim, the founder of the Egyptians (Gen. 10:14), but they spoke a Semitic language. They possessed the maritime plains and foothills of southwestern Canaan already when Abraham arrived there. Gasa, Askalon, Ashdod, Gath and Ekron were their chief cities. Moses at God's command avoided them (Ex. 13:17). Joshua did not expel them (Josh. 13:1-3). Shamgar fought with them (Judges 3:31), as did also Samson, Samuel, Saul, David, Nadab, Jehoram, Ahaz, Uzziah and Hezekiah in turn.

i. SYRIA (?—1055-732 B. C.).

The Syrians were descendants of Amram, the fifth son of Shem. Their country lay on the plateau bounded on the north by Asia Minor, on the east by the Euphrates, on the south by the Arabian Desert and Bashan, on the west by the Lebanon Mountains. The language of the country was Aramaic, the language of commerce from 800 to 300 B. C. At times Syria consisted of a number of small kingdoms, such as, Damascus, Zobah and Hamath; at other times it included these and parts of adjoining countries, even Palestine. Syria and Israel often met each other on the battle field. The stories of Benhadad I of Syria and Ahab of Israel (1 Kings 22) and of Naaman and Elisha (2 Kings 5: 1-27) are two of the most dramatic in the Bible.

j. ETHIOPIA (?—957 B. C.—37 A. D.).

Ethiopia lay to the south of Egypt. The country and its people are mentioned 40 times in Scripture. The Ethiopians invaded Judah in the days of Asa (2 Chron. 14:9-15). The psalmist foretold that this people should stretch out their hands to God, a prophecy that began to be fulfilled in the conversion of the Eunuch (Acts 8:27-39). The people were black, hence the saying (Jer. 13:23) : "Can the Ethiopian change his skin, or the leopard his spots? Then may ye also do good that are accustomed to do evil."

k. SHEBA (?—990—?).

Sheba was a country probably in southwestern Arabia. Its people, called Sabeans, were, through intermarriage, both Hamitic and Semitic (Gen. 10:7, 28; 25:3). One of the queens, having heard of the fame of Solomon, came to Jerusalem to see him. The Sabeans are mentioned in the story of Job. The Abyssinians claim descent from the Queen of Sheba and Solomon.

l. SAMARIA (722 B. C.—37 A. D.).

The Samaritans were the people who occupied Samaria, the central part of Canaan, after the captivity of the Ten Tribes in 722 B. C. It was the policy of the Assyrian conquerors to plant the subdued nations in colonies far away from their native lands. The Ten Tribes were carried to Hamath, Media, etc. Other peoples, from Elam, Babylon, Arabia, Hamath, etc., were transported to Samaria (2 Kings 17:24; Ezra 4:9). In this melting pot a new race was created, a people that adopted the language of Israel, which in time became known as the Samaritan, and also the five books of Moses with some modifications to suit their political interests (Samaritan Pentateuch). They were a mixed people with a mixed language and a mixed religion. The Samaritans had lived in Samaria nearly 200 years when the Jews returned from Babylon, in 536. They wished to take part in the building of the Jewish Temple, but were flatly refused. From that time a mutual hatred arose. They built a rival temple on Gerizim in 400 B. C., which the Maccabees destroyed in 129 B. C. It was not customary for a Jew to trespass on Samaritan ground. But with Christ a new order was to prevail.

Epochs	B.C 2000	Mesopotamia	Arabia	Midian	Moab	Ammon	Edom	Amalek	Philistia	Syria Aram	Hamath	Zobah	Samaria
Patriarchs	1900	Abram's call	Ishmael Abram's Son		Moab Son of Lot	Ammon S - of Lot	Esau son of Isaac		Abimelech				
	1800			Midian Abrams Son			Vs Jacob						
	1700	Jacob's ? Laban	Buying Joseph										
Bondage	1600							Amalek grandson of Esau					
	1500			Moses									
Wandering Conquest		Balaam		Vs Joshua Balaam	Hired Balaam Baalam		Vs Israel		Rephidim				
Judges	1400	1st op-pression Othniel			2nd op-pression Ehud		2nd op-pression Ehud	2nd op-pression	2nd op-pression Shamgar				
	1300												
	1200			4th op-pression Gideon			4th op-pression Gideon						
	1100				Ruth		6th op-pression Jephthah	Agag	7th op-pression Samson				
United Kingdom	1000	Vs David				Vs Saul / Vs Dan & Solomons wives	Vs Saul / Vs David	Vs Saul / Vs David Ziklag	Vs Saul Gilboa	David Solomon		David David Solomon Solomon	Vs Saul
Divided Kingdoms	900	Vs Jehoram Uzziah			Vs Omri Vs Joash	Vs Jehosh-aphat Vs Joash	Vs Jehosh-aphat	Vs Nadab	Vs Ahab Ramoth Naaman Vs Samaria			Vassal of Syria	
	800				Vs Uzziah		Vs Jehoram	Vs Jehoram	Vs Samaria	Resin ally of Syria	Vassal of Assyria		Colonization of Elamites, etc.
	700			Isa 60	Vs Jotham	Vs Ahaz	Vs Hezekiah	Vs Ahaz Ashdod	Ten tribes Vassal of Assyria				
	600				Vs Jehoiachin								
Under Babylonia	500		Jer 49			Vs Gedaliah	Vs Gedaliah						Vs Zerubbabel Vs Ezra Vs Nehemiah
Under Persia	400		Vs Nehemiah			Vs Nehemiah	Vs Nehemiah	Haman the Agagite					
Under Macedonia	300												
Under Macedonian Egypt	200												
Under Mac. Syria													
Maccabees	100					Vs Maccabees	Vs Maccabees Herod	Vs Maccabees					Destruction of Temple at Gerizim
Under Rome	0	1st Pentecost 1st Pentecost											Christ at Sychar

Contemporary Events Israel and Twelve Smaller Nations

No. 9. Contemporary Events: Israel and Twelve Smaller Nations.

3. TWELVE LARGE EMPIRES.

a. EGYPT (?—1921-345 B. C.).

The Egyptians were Hamitics, and spoke a Hamitic language. When the sons of Jacob went to Egypt to buy corn they had to employ an interpreter, an act which would hardly have been necessary amongst the Semitics. There is no country in the Bible, with the exception of Canaan, mentioned so often as Egypt. Israel spent 430 years in bondage there, counting from the time that Abraham sojourned there. Even Christ spent some time of His life there, "that it might be fulfilled which was spoken of the Lord by the prophet. 'Out of Egypt have I called My Son.'"

b. ELAM (?—1911-645 B. C.).

The country of Elam got its name from Elam, a son of Shem. It lay beyond the Tigris, east of Babylonia. Its capital was Shushan (Susa). In 1913 B. C., its king, Chedorlaomer, the first empire builder, conquered Babylonia and even the territory along the Jordan, including Sodom and Gomorrah. Abraham defeated this powerful monarch and his allies and rescued Lot. About 1200 years later Isaiah prophesied that Elam and Media should capture Babylon (Isa. 21:2-9). Later it became a province of Persia, with Susa as capital of the empire. Here Daniel had his vision of the he-goat. Here Darius issued his decree to rebuild the Temple. Here Esther reigned as queen. At the first Pentecost Elam was represented (Acts 2:9).

c. CHALDEA, OR EARLY BABYLONIA (?—1996-1250 B. C.).

Chaldea, in a narrower sense, was the southern province of Babylonia, at the head of the Persian Gulf. In a wider sense, it was all of Babylonia, with varying boundaries. The names Chaldea and Babylonia are used interchangeably in secular books and the Bible itself (2 Kings 25: 1, 4; 2 Chron. 36:7, 17; Isa. 13:19; etc.). The people traced their origins from Nimrod, the Hamite, and Arphaxad, the Semite, but spoke a Semitic language. Like the Hebrews they wrote from right to left. Their writing was wedge-shaped, due to the soft clay tablets which they used for books. This country is mentioned 2C0 times in the Bible. The Confusion of Tongues took place here. Abraham came from Ur of the Chaldees. In 1250 the nation became a province of Assyria.

d. ASSYRIA (?—854-625 B. C.).

Assyria got its name from Asshur, one of the sons of Shem. The Assyrians in the course of time raised Asshur to the position of their national god. The country in its narrowest extent lay to the north of Elam and Babylonia and to the east of Mesopotamia. In its widest extent it held dominion over all the lands from the Caspian to the Mediterranean, and from the Black Sea to the Persian Gulf. The Assyrians came down like a wolf on the fold and carried away the Ten Tribes in 722 B. C. The Assyrian king Sennacherib shut up Hezekiah of Judah in Jerusalem, but the angel of the Lord came to the defence of the beleaguered city, slaying 185,000 of the Assyrians. After this the power of Assyria waned and her light was snuffed out as a candle by the wind. Nineveh was the capital of Assyria, the object of the prophecies of Jonah and Nahum. It was taken by the Babylonians in 606 B. C.

e. CHALDEA, OR LATER BABYLONIA (625-538 B. C.).

This Babylonia is a continuation of the former empire by this name, which had been forced to remain an Assyrian province for 600 years. When Sennacherib fled in dismay from Jerusalem the king of Babylon, Merodach-Baladan, sent messengers to Hezekiah to congratulate him on his recovery and probably to seek an alliance with such a brave little nation against a common foe. In 606 Nebuchadnezzar pounded at the gates of Jerusalem. In 586 he destroyed the city and put an end to the Theocratic Nation. In 555 Nabonadius usurped the throne. He appointed his son Belshazzar his associate, and Belshazzar in turn appointed Daniel the third in authority. On the night the city was taken by the Medes the strange handwriting on the wall foretold the fall of the city. The famous city is now according to prophecy a barren heap, a dwelling place for jackals, an astonishment and a hissing.

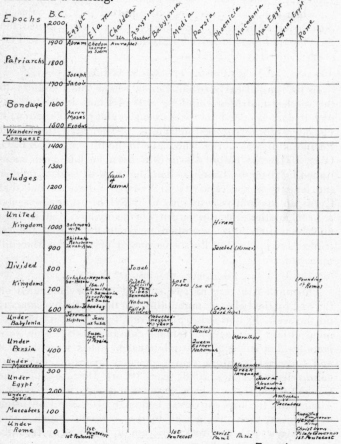

Contemporary Events: Israel and Twelve Large Empires

No. 10. Contemporary Events: Israel and Twelve Large Empires.

f. MEDIA (?—625-536 B. C.).

This country lay to the east of Asia Minor and Assyria and to the north of Babylonia and Elam. The people were Japhetics. They were probably subject to Assyria in 722 B. C., when the Ten Tribes were transported into the cities of the Medes (2 Kings 17:6; 18:11). The Medes joined the Babylonians and destroyed Assyria. They joined the Persians in destroying Babylonia.

g. PERSIA (?—558-330 B. C.).

In its limited early extent Persia was a small country to the southeast of Media and the east of Elam, in its full extent it corresponded to the present country of Persia with considerable territories additional. The first prominent Persian king was Cyrus, who came to the throne in 558 B. C. Over 150 years before Cyrus was born he had been mentioned by name by Isaiah as the appointed of God to deliver the Jews from the captivity in Babylon. Ezra relates that Cyrus, in his first year as king of Babylon, promptly issued a proclamation for the return of the exiles. Later, Ezra and Nehemiah were permitted to go to the aid of the returned Jews. In 330 Persia became a part of the Macedonian Empire.

h. PHOENICIA (?—1050-332 B. C.).

Phoenicia is a very narrow strip of territory bounded on the east by the Lebanon mountains; on the south, by Canaan; on the west, by the sea. Sidon and Tyre were its two famous cities; Carthage, its famous colony. The people were Hamites, but spoke a Semitic language. They were the first and foremost maritime power in early history. They circumnavigated Africa 2088 years before Diaz rounded the Cape of Good Hope. They were the missionaries of culture. Theirs was the first universal language after the Confusion of Tongues, then giving way to the Aramaic, which again later gave way to the Greek. Hiram of Tyre was on friendly terms with David and Solomon and furnished workmen and material for the Temple. A century later (918 B. C.) Ahab married a princess of Sidon, the wicked Jezebel. Our Lord visited the coasts of Tyre and Sidon (Matt. 15: 21), as did also Paul and Barnabas (Acts 15: 3; 21: 2-3).

i. MACEDONIA (?—776-146 B. C.).

Macedonia, or Greece, became a world empire in 330 through Alexander the Great. The Greeks were Japhetics, descendants of Javan, inhabiting at first the isles of the Sea, later Greece proper, and finally conquering nearly the whole civilized ancient world. The country is ancient, for the great poet Homer sang his "Iliad" about the time of Solomon. Its actual points of contact with the Hebrews are not many. Its influence is immeasurable. For 300 years before the birth of Christ the Greek language was preparing the way for the Gospel, which was "the power of God unto salvation to everyone that believeth, to the Jew first, and also to the Greek" (Rom. 1: 16). The New Testament is written in Greek. Paul, the chief apostle, took up his labors also in Macedonia proper and Greece proper, establishing Congregations at Philippi and Thessalonica (in Macedonia) and in Corinth (in Greece).

j. MACEDONIAN EGYPT (321-198 B. C.).

At the death of Alexander the Great, his empire was divided up amongst his generals. Egypt fell to the lot of Ptolemy. The boundaries of Egypt during the reign of the Ptolemies included at times also Palestine.

k. MACEDONIAN SYRIA (321-166 B. C.).

The largest section of Alexander's empire became known as Syria and included nearly everything in Asia Minor and modern Persia. The Syrian kings laid claim to Palestine and struggled with Egypt for its possession. From 198 to 166 Palestine was a province of Syria.

l. ROME (754 B. C.—476 A. D.).

Rome was the last and mightiest of the world empires of antiquity, and with Israel and Greece one of the elect nations of the world. The inscription on the cross was in three languages: Hebrew, because Christ was a Hebrew; Greek, because that was the universal language; and Latin, because the Romans ruled the world. Roman history began with the reputed founding of the city 754 B. C. and extended 1200 years—to the downfall of the city in 476 A. D. For 250 years it comprised a small district—Latium (hence Latin), and was ruled by kings. After this it was a republic for 450 years. After the death of Julius Caesar it became an empire, with Augustus Caesar as the first emperor. "And it came to pass in those days, there went out a decree from Caesar Augustus, that all the world should be enrolled" (Luke 2:1)—the fullness of time had come, the world was ready for the coming of Christ. Rome governed Palestine at first through King Herod. After his death his kingdom was parcelled out to four rulers called tetrarchs. Archelaus, the tetrarch of Judea, was deposed in 6 A. D., and Judea became a province under Roman governors. One of these was Pilate, who crucified Christ. In 70 A. D. the Jews revolted from the hated Roman tyranny and were besieged in their capital city. After 5 months of desperate defence and untold starvation the city was taken. Over a million Jews perished; 30,000 were crucified by the victorious Romans in a single day (Josephus "Jewish War").

Who were the Canaanites? Where did they live? Name twelve of their tribes. Why were these tribes dispossessed of their land? What right did Abraham and his descendants have to the land? When the Israelites did not utterly drive them out of the land, what prophecy did the angel of the Lord make concerning the relationship of the Canaanites to the Israelites?

Describe the Canaanite tribes in the narrower sense. Tell where they lived, and name two Biblical events connected with them.

Who were the Anakim? Mention two events in which they figure.

Who were the Amorites?

Who were the Girgashites?

Who were the Hittites? Mention three events in connection with them.

Who were the Hivites? Mention two events of their history.

Who were the Jebusites? What was their chief city?

Who were the Kenites? Mention two events in their history.

Who were the Kenizzites? Mention two men in Israel who were half Kenizzites.

Who were the Perizzites? Rephaim? Zuzim?

Locate Mesopotamia. Mention five events in its history.

Locate Arabia. Mention four events in its history.

Locate Midian. Mention three events in its history.

Locate Moab. Mention seven events in its history.

Locate Ammon. Mention some of the wars of the Ammonites against the Chosen People.

Locate Edom. Mention some of the wars of the Edomites against the Chosen People.

Locate Amalek. Why did the Lord command the Amalekites to be utterly destroyed?

Locate Philistia. Mention some of the wars between Israel and Philistia.

Locate Syria. For what is it noted in Biblical history?

Locate Ethiopia. Quote two Bible passages referring to the Ethiopians.

Locate Sheba. For what is the Queen of Sheba noted? The Sabeans?

Locate Samaria. When was Samaria founded? By whom? Why was there enmity between the Samaritans and the Jews?

Locate Egypt. For what is it noted in Biblical history?

Locate Elam. For what is it noted?

Locate Chaldea. For what is it noted?

Locate Assyria. For what is it noted?

Locate Babylonia. For what is it noted?

Locate Media. For what is it noted?

Locate Persia. For what is it noted?

Locate Phoenicia. For what is it noted?

Locate Macedonia. For what is it noted?

Locate Macedonian Egypt. For what is it noted?

Locate Macedonian Syria. For what is it noted?

Locate Rome. Bound the Roman Empire at the time of Christ. Who was the emperor at the birth of Christ? Who was king of Judea? Why was there no king at the time of Christ's crucifixion? When did Rome destroy Jerusalem? And why?

What is said in your Bible history about the twelve Canaanite tribes? The twelve smaller nations, and the twelve large empires mentioned in this lesson? Look up the Bible passage referred to in your lesson, and find additional references to this subject in the Bible. In what ways can the contents of this lesson help you in your Bible study? In your faith and works?

LESSON TWENTY-THREE. PHYSICAL GEOGRA-PHY OF CANAAN.

The chief land of the Bible is Canaan, called also the Promised Land, the Holy Land, Jehovah's Land, Immanuel's Land, Palestine, Syria, etc.

1. ITS LOCATION AND SIZE.

a. ITS LOCATION.

Canaan was situated in the center of the ancient world, half way between Egypt and the Tigris-Euphrates nations, equally distant from the heart of Asia, Africa and Europe. It was bounded on the north by Phoenicia, the Lebanon Mountains and Syria, on the east by the Arabian Desert, on the south by deserts, and on the west by the Great Sea. On account of its position, it was the connecting link between the East and the West; it was the door to Egypt from the east and to the Eastern nations from the west, it was a "highway of the nations." It was a big oasis between the deserts and the sea, a land flowing with milk and honey, the center of travel and traffic, of culture and conquest. Yet, Israel was in large measure secluded— not only by the Lord's commands, by training and inclination, but also by the peculiar structure of the country. The highways of nations proper crossed the lowlands and followed the maritime plain, while the Jews occupied the highlands chiefly, thus, to a large extent, escaping contact with the wayfaring merchants and armies.

b. ITS SIZE.

The importance of Canaan does not lie in its size. Canaan proper consists of the land lying between the Jordan River and the Mediterranean Sea, a narrow strip about 120 miles long and an average of 50 miles in width, 6,600 sq. miles in area. The part of West Canaan actually occupied by the Israelites, or by the Kingdom of Judah after the time of the downfall of the Ten Tribes, could not at times have exceeded 1,000 sq. miles. The area of the country under David and Solomon never exceeded 60,000 sq. miles. These figures should not be forgotten when the importance of the country is under consideration. They often throw light also on other matters. For example, Isaiah warned against foreign alliances. He urged Hezekiah to trust only in God. The area of Judah was in his day reduced to probably less than 1,000 sq. miles. If we take 1,000 sq. miles as the size of this country, then it will be seen that West Canaan was 6 times as large, that David's kingdom was 60 times as large, that Assyria was about 600 times as large, that Minnesota is 80 times as large, that the United States

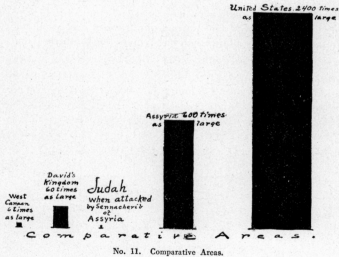

No. 11. Comparative Areas.

is 2,400 times as large, and that the British Empire is 12,000 times as large. "Fear not, O little flock, the foe."

2. ITS STRUCTURE.

a. CROSSWISE.

(1) *Through Galilee.*—Proceeding from west to east in Galilee, a traveler will first have to cross a sandy sea-coast plain for a few miles, then he will have to cross a hilly country, with the low plains of Esdraelon and back of it Mount Carmel, 1,400 ft. high, to the south and the high mountains of Lebanon to the left. Here and there are hills of considerable height, such as the Nazareth hills and Mount Tabor, 1,800 ft. high. To the north-east rises Mount Hermon, 8,300 ft. high. Descending from Nazareth, the traveler goes eastward through a rough country towards the Sea of Galilee. This Sea is 14 miles long and 9 wide, lies 682 ft. below sea level, and is surrounded by high hills.

(2) *Through Samaria.*—A trip through Samaria is somewhat similar, although over more rugged country. Beginning to the south of Mount Carmel, the traveler crosses about two miles of sandy plain, then he ascends the foothills from

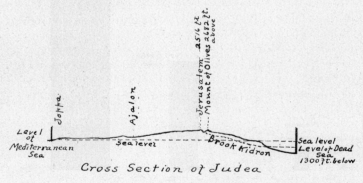

No. 12.   Cross Section of Judea.

300 to 500 feet high. The Samaritan plateau lies before him, considerably higher than the highlands of Galilee, but lower than those of Judea. Several mountain peaks appear

to the right, such as Mount Gerizim and Mount Ebal, 3,000 feet high. The approach to the Jordan is steep and rugged.

(3) *Through Judea.*—This trip is the most rugged of all. Starting from Joppa, the traveler crosses a maritime plain for about 15 miles, then ascends the foothills (shephelah) also for about 15 miles. Before him now rises the mountain country of Judea, varying from 2,000 to 4,000 feet in height. From Olivet, 2,682 feet above sea level, there is a rapid descent to the Dead Sea, 1,300 feet below sea level, a 3,982 foot drop in 12 miles. The eastern slope of the Judean Mountains is very steep, rocky, wild and desolate.

b. LENGTHWISE.

(1) *Along the Coast.*—A trip along the coast from the south to the north of Canaan would take one through the level maritime plain, 20 miles wide at the south and two at Carmel. The plain is cut off at Carmel, but opens up wide in the Plains of Esdraelon on the north. These plains were once very fruitful, being occupied by the Philistines (to the west of Judea), the Canaanites (Sharon, to the west of Samaria), and the Phoenicians (to the west of Galilee). The foot-hills to the east of them were also rich and populous at one time.

(2) *Along the Central Range.*—Beginning in the Negeb or South Country of the desert, the traveler ascends a gradual slope until he reaches Hebron, 3,546 feet above him. Fifteen miles to the left are the fruitful foothills a half mile below; fifteen miles to the right is the Dead Sea nearly a mile below. From Hebron to Bethlehem and Jerusalem is a descent of nearly 1,000 feet in 20 miles. The country north of Jerusalem has a general downward slope all the way to Galilee, with the exception of Shechem and Samaria. Galilee in the southern portion is the Kishon Valley and the Plains of Esdraelon, in the northern portion it is the foothills of the Lebanon Mountains.

(3) *Along the Jordan Valley.*—Beginning at the southern

end of the Dead Sea, the saltest and lowest sea in the world, with the rising hills and mountains of Edom behind, the mountains of Judea nearly a mile above to the left, the table land of Moab about as high to the right, the traveler crosses a body of water 46 miles long and from 20 to 1,300

No. 13.   On the Road from Jericho to Jerusalem.

feet deep. At the north end of the sea the Plains of Jericho
stretch out about 14 miles wide, but the Jordan Valley is
seldom as wide as this anywhere else. The name Jordan
means Descender. It gets its name from its rapid descent
from the mountains of Syria to Lake Merom, and then on
to the Sea of Galilee and the Dead Sea, a drop of a mile
in a distance of 200 miles. It is the natural boundary between Canaan proper and East Palestine. Going up along
the east bank of the Jordan was the road from Judea to Galilee, taken by Jews who did not like to trespass on Samaritan
soil. The sea of Galilee, 682 feet below sea level, is surrounded by lofty country, with mountains rising 1,000
feet from the water on the east, and slightly set back on
the west. The water is fresh and full of fish, on account
of which at the time of Christ the lake was covered with
fishing boats, and its shores were lined with villages and
houses. Gusts from the mountains nearby meeting strong
hot winds from the desert cause sudden, terrific and dangerous squalls on this little lake, such as when the Lord lay
asleep in the boat (Mark 4: 35-41), and, being awakened by
His fearful disciples, He rebuked the wind and said unto
the sea: "Peace, be still." And the wind ceased, and there
was a great calm. The source of the Jordan is only 26
miles above this lake, but in that distance there is a fall of
1,682 feet, or 85 feet to the mile.

3. ITS LAND AND WATER.

a. LAND.

Nearly all of Canaan is land area, only 7 per cent being
water. At present nearly all of the land is desert or arid;
formerly nearly all of it was fruitful. What was not fruitful was at least excellent for grazing in the days of Abraham, David and Jeremiah. The Jordan Valley, which in the
flourishing days of Canaan cultivated the palm and other
tropical vegetation, was sometimes termed the desert in the
prophetical books, on account of its excessive heat and

parched condition and the encroaching of the real desert during times of apostasy. John the Baptist lived in this desert a part of his stay here below. Christ was tempted in the Wilderness, another term for desert. The particular Wilderness in which Christ was tempted is doubtless the wild tract of land to the east and southeast of Jerusalem. Here also John the Baptist no doubt preached (Matt. 3:1). Here amongst the rocks and the caverns, as at Engedi, David sought refuge from Saul (1 Sam. 23—24).

b. WATER.

The water surface consists of three lakes—the Waters of Merom, the Sea of Galilee and the Dead Sea. The Waters of Merom is a little triangular lake, three miles across, far to the north, the scene of Joshua's last battle with the Canaanites (Josh. 11:5-7). The Sea of Galilee (Luke 5:1) was the scene of many of the events in the life of our Lord and His disciples. The Dead Sea receives the waters of the Jordan, but has no outlet, therefore its waters are very salt and bitter, containing four or five times as great a percentage of salt as the ocean. On this account animal life can not exist in its waters, and vegetable organisms thrive only near the inlets. This was once a fair plain, chosen by Lot for pasturage. But God destroyed Sodom and Gomorrah and three other cities of this plain on account of their shameful iniquities (Gen. 19) and converted the plain into a lake of salt. The coast line of Canaan has no harbors, therefore the sea did not invite the Hebrews as it did their neighbors, the Phoenicians. The Great Sea became in this way a solid wall of protection and seclusion from the west, more impregnable than the Arabian desert on the east.

Jordan was the chief river, but little utilized. Its descent is steep; it is full of rapids, meandering and deep. The valley is excessively hot, with approach to the desert, so that villages and habitations were scarce. Near the mouth of the Jordan was the scene of the miraculous crossing by Joshua (Josh. 3—4). Above its eastern tributary, the Jabbok, are many fords, over one of which Jacob crossed (Gen. 32: 10, 22). At this place the fleeing Midianites, pursued by Gideon, crossed (Judges 7: 24; 8: 4-5). At these fords the Gileadites killed the Ephraimites who could not give the password (Judges 12: 5-6). When pursued by Absalom, David twice crossed lower down, between Jericho

No. 14. The Sea of Galilee.

and Jabbok (2 Sam. 17: 22-24; 19: 15-18). Elijah and Elisha crossed at Jericho (2 Kings 2: 5-15). Naaman the Syrian dipped seven times in the Jordan, in obedience to the Lord's command, and was cured of his leprosy (2 Kings 5: 14). Christ was baptized in the Jordan (Matt. 3: 6-17).

The most famous smaller streams are the Jabbok, the Arnon, the brook Kidron and Kishon. The Jabbok empties into the Jordan from the east, and was the scene of Jacob's struggle with the angel of the Lord (Gen. 32: 24-28). The Arnon was a rivulet emptying into the Dead Sea from the east. The brook Kidron has its rise near Jerusalem, passes between the Mount of Olives and the city and flows in a south-

No. 15. The Dead Sea.

(From Wm. Smith's "Old Testament History", by permission of Harper and Bros.).

easterly direction into the Dead Sea. It is the scene of many Biblical events. The Kishon is the largest stream of Galilee. It flows through the Plain of Esdraelon in a northwesterly direction to the Great Sea. It is named in connection with the rout of the Canaanites by Deborah and

Barak (Judges 4—5), and with the slaughter of the prophets
of Baal by Elijah (1 Kings 18:40).

In addition to the seas, lakes, rivers and brooks, there
is frequent mention made of springs, wells, cisterns and
dams. In the geography of Canaan, with the desert and the
desert winds on nearly all sides, with only two rainy seasons and almost no snow, with only one fresh-water lake
and only a few running brooks, it goes without saying that
the question of getting water from springs and wells, cisterns
and dams, was highly important at all times.

4. ITS MOUNTAINS AND VALLEYS.

a. Its Mountains.

Hebrew history is peculiarly connected with the names
of mountains. There is Ararat, on which Noah's Ark settled after the Flood; there is Sinai, from which Jehovah gave

No. 16. Mount Sinai.

the Law; there is Hor, where Aaron died and was buried; there is Nebo, on top of which Moses could take a view of the Promised Land, but could not enter; there is Lebanon, from which material was furnished for the Temple of Solomon; and Hermon, yielding its waters to the supply of the Jordan. But all of these mountains are outside of Canaan. In Canaan are also a number of famous mountains, in fact the chief part of Canaan is one vast mountain ridge. The most famous of the Judean mountains are Mount Zion, the seat of the Temple; the Mount of Olives, the seat of Gethsemane; and Mount Moriah, the place where Isaac was to be offered up and where the Temple was located. In Samaria are Mount Gerizim and Mount Ebal, seats of rival altars, and Carmel, where Elijah met the prophets of Baal. In Galilee is Mount Tabor and Mount Gilboa and the mounts on which the Lord spoke His "Sermon on the Mount" and was transfigured.

b. Its Valleys.

There are five words in Scripture which denote valley and seven which denote plain. The most prominent valleys in Canaan are the Jordan, Hinnom, Jehoshaphat, Jezreel, Megiddo and Tyropaeon. The most prominent plains are the maritime plains of Philistia, Sharon, Akka and Esdraelon (also central), the central plains of Aijalon, Moreh and Mamre, and the eastern plains of Baashan, Jericho and Sodom. In addition to these, the Shephelah, or foothills, were gently sloping plains to the west of the central range. The Valley of the Jordan is a great fault or crack in the earth's surface extending from Antioch to the eastern arm of the Red Sea, but by far the deepest part is from Galilee to the Dead Sea. In fact, this is the lowest place on the earth's surface. The maritime plains were once the most fruitful parts of Canaan, blossoming as the rose, dotted with thriving cities. The Plain of Esdraelon, called also the Valley of Megiddo, about 250 feet above sea level, was

No. 17. The Plain of Sharon.

the great battle field of Canaan. A part of this plain, the middle arm, is the famous Valley or Plain of Jezreel, where stood the palace of Ahab and the vineyard of Naboth. Hinnom was a deep and narrow gorge west and south of Jerusalem, the site of many heathen idols and temples. On the southern brow, overlooking the valley, stood the idol of Molech, erected by Solomon (1 Kings 11:7). Ahaz and Manasseh made their children pass through the fire in this valley (2 Kings 16: 3; 2 Chron. 28: 3; 33: 6). The southeastern extremity was termed Tophet, the scene of many infant sacrifices to the fire gods of Ammon and Moab (2 Kings 23: 13; Jer. 7: 31). Josiah made a wholesale cleaning out of these heathen altars and turned the valley into a dumping ground and cesspool (2 Chron. 34: 4-5; 2 Kings 23: 10-14). From the fact that it was the scene of unclean worship and the sewer and burning ground of the city, the place where dead animals and executed criminals were cast away, the place began to be called Ge Hinnom, or Gehenna (Matt. 5: 22), and became the symbol and type of the place of eternal torment. Mamre was the name of an Amorite chieftain, a friend of Abraham's, under the shade of whose oak tree the patriarch dwelt for a while. The name was also applied to the place, which was level as a plain (Gen. 23: 17, 19; 25: 9; 35: 27).

What is the chief land of the Bible? Give seven or more names by which it is known.

Locate the land of Canaan with respect to Asia, Africa and Europe. Bound it.

Compare its size with that of other countries.

Make a journey through Galilee from the west to the east, stating what you see. Make a similar journey through Samaria, likewise, describing the surrounding country. Make a third journey through Judea, again describing the landscape.

Now, make a journey along the coast from the south of Canaan to the north, describing the country and places. Make another journey along the central range, beginning in the south and proceeding as far as the Lebanon Mountains. Mention objects of interest.

Make a third journey along the Jordan Valley from the southern end of the Dead Sea to the source of the Jordan. Describe interesting sights.

How much of Canaan is land? How much water? Describe the land area and the water surface. Name some of the lakes. Some of the rivers. Some of the smaller streams. What can you say of the importance of the springs, wells, streams and dams in this country?

Name some of the principal mountains, outside of Canaan, mentioned in the Bible. Name the most famous of the mountains in Canaan. What are some of the prominent plains and valleys of Palestine?

What is said in your Bible history about the location of Canaan? Its size? Its structure? Its land and water? Its mountains and valleys? Look up the Bible passages referred to in your lesson, and find additional references to this subject in the Bible. In what ways can the contents of this lesson help you in your Bible study? In your faith and works?

LESSON TWENTY-FOUR. THE WORLD IN THE EARLY AGES.

1. THE ANTEDILUVIAN AGE.

a. THE CREATION.

The first verse of the first chapter of the first book of the Bible states the fact that in the beginning God created heaven and earth. This chapter goes on to say that He created this heaven and earth in six days, according to the following orderly plan:

1st day: Light.   4th day: Sun, moon, stars.
2nd day: Firmament.   5th day: Fish and fowl.
3rd day: Land and sea, vegetation. 6th day: Animals and man.
7th day: Rest.

It is generally maintained by scientists that the process of creation has covered an inconceivably long stretch of time. In order to reconcile the Mosaic account of the Creation with the discoveries of geology and astronomy, scholars have generally concluded that the six days of creation need not mean days of 24 hours each, but periods of unknown length during which the earth has been slowly and gradually taking form.

There are, however, those who still believe that God could have created the earth in six days and that He did do so because He has said so. It would certainly not detract anything from His wisdom and power if it had taken Him billions of years to do this vast work, but it is not necessary to extend the time in that way to the Almighty.

It is admitted even by such geologists who require up to billions of years to explain the story of the earth, that the course of nature is not always slow and orderly, but, on the contrary, rapid and freakish. Thus N. S. Shaler, in his

"Interpretations of Nature," says that "the world is a place
of surprises which take place under natural law, but are
quite as revolutionary as if they were the products of chance,
or a result arising from the immediate intervention of the
Supreme Power." Now, we do not believe in chance, but we
do believe in a Supreme Being, Who does not permit a
sparrow to fall without His consent (Matt. 10: 29). If we
knew more about the circumstances attending the sudden

No. 18. The Creation.

changes in nature, we should also see the hand of God
directing those changes. Thus, in 1908, when Sicily was
visited by a terrible earthquake, it was stated in the current papers that an infidel editor had published an editorial
on Christmas day asking the Lord to send an earthquake
to show that He was still alive. The earthquake began
promptly that day and destroyed 200,000 souls.

Again, the students of ethnology find it difficult to harmonize the story in Genesis and the classification of the

human race except by the interposition of God in a miraculous manner such as is related in Gen. 11. It still holds true, as in the time of Jeremiah, that "the Ethiopian can not change his skin, nor the leopard his spots" (Jer. 13: 23), just as it has ever been true that a monkey or an ape-man has never developed into a man. It must then have taken a fearfully long time to produce the white, and yellow, and brown, and black, and red races of the earth, if God had not seen fit to do it more rapidly than the laws of evolution permit Him to work.

b. THE GARDEN OF EDEN.

"And the Lord God planted a garden eastward in Eden; and there He put the man He had formed" (Gen. 2:8). "And a river went out of Eden to water the garden; and from thence it was parted, and became into four heads" —Pison, compassing the land of Havilah; Gihon, compassing the land of Ethiopia; Hiddikel, going toward the east of Assyria; and the river Euphrates. This description of Eden includes three names familiar in later history and geography, and four names entirely unknown to us. There is absolutely no agreement as to the location of the Garden of Eden. Josephus believed that it extended from India to Egypt; Hartmann, that it was in Thibet; Weidner, that it was in India; Sayce, that it was near the Persian Gulf; Le Clerc, that it was at Damascus; Delitzsch, that it was in Babylonia; Warren, that it was at the North Pole; Jerome, that it was beyond the limits of the world; Luther, that the Flood had wiped out all traces of it. Rashi maintained that the Pison was the Nile; Ewald, that it was the Indus. Calvin conjectured that the Pison was the most easterly of the four rivers; Huet, that it was the most westerly. The data are insufficient and speculations are futile.

We have definite data, however, about our first parents living in bliss in the Garden, about their temptation and fall, about God's righteous wrath and gracious promise of a Redeemer in the Seed of the woman. On account of their sin Adam and Eve were expelled from the Garden and the earth was accursed.

c. THE DESCENDANTS OF ADAM.

Only three of the children of Adam and Eve are mentioned by name in the Bible—Cain, Abel and Seth. Cain and Seth represent types of two classes of character—the children of the Devil and the children of God (1 John 3: 10). Cain's race seemed to excel in worldly accomplishments; Seth's line became the bearer of the promise of salvation to mankind. Cain lived in the land of Nod, to the east of the Garden of Eden, and there built the city of Enoch. Crime became more and more prevalent. Wickedness increased, the two lines intermingled, causing the "sons of God"—the descendants of Seth—also to become ungodly (Gen. 6). Then came the Deluge, sweeping away the whole race with the exception of one faithful family—that of Noah. The lineage of the two families of Cain and Seth, placed side by side, is as follows:

(Gen. 4: 1-23) (Gen. 4: 25—5: 32; 1 Chron. 1: 1-4; Luke. 3: 36-38).

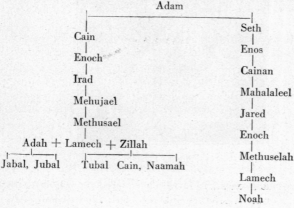

```
                        Adam
         |---------------------------------|
         Cain                              Seth
          |                                 |
         Enoch                             Enos
          |                                 |
         Irad                             Cainan
          |                                 |
        Mehujael                        Mahalaleel
          |                                 |
        Methusael                        Jared
          |                                 |
 Adah + Lamech + Zillah                   Enoch
 |----|----|    |------|------|            |
Jabal, Jubal   Tubal  Cain, Naamah     Methuselah
                                          |
                                        Lamech
                                          |
                                         Noah
```

2. THE POSTDILUVIAN AGES.

a. THE FLOOD.

Modern evolutionists reject in one breath the Biblical account of the Creation, the Deluge and the Confusion of Languages. We have now briefly shown that the account of the Creation is very reasonable to anyone who believes that Almighty God can create the world in six days, if He wants to, and has done so, since He has said so. Now we shall briefly show that He also has sent the Flood to destroy the sinful creatures upon this earth, even as it is recorded in Holy Scriptures. This should in turn help to make it easier to believe the account of the Judgment at Babel.

No. 19.   The Flood.

If there has been a Flood which covered the whole earth, even the mountain tops, so that all flesh died (Gen. 7: 20-22), with the exception of the people and beasts within the Ark, then there must still remain some evidences thereof on and in the earth itself. Geologists are unanimous in declaring that in almost every part of the earth may be seen piles of stone, gravel and sediment which water alone could have deposited. Older geologists called these evidences Diluvium (Latin, flood). But modern geologists have seemed to avoid the story of the Biblical Deluge altogether unless they have felt called upon to sneer at it. But they admit that the deposits have been made by water, and set out to account for the presence of this water. Fifty different theories have been propounded, of which the following three have been most widely defended: the sinking and rising of continents, the presence of overflowing streams and the glacial epochs.

Now, as to the sinking and rising of continents, it seems rather strange that every continent shall have sunk deep below the sea and then have risen again. If a continent had been under the sea it would have innumerable traces of sea organisms, nevertheless geologists maintain that every foot of European and American soil has been coast line and sea bottom and has no evidences of sea life left. But there are evidences in great plenty of prehistoric animals and men huddled together, especially along the mountain slopes, and there are evidences of debris and drift being piled up over the tops of the highest mountains, of a flood having covered the whole earth, and remaining but for a short while.

And as to the presence of mighty rivers overflowing and destroying everything in their courses, it is a great puzzle to know where these rivers got their supply of water from. In Patagonia Darwin discovered a ridge of stones 700 miles long, and, in places, 200 feet deep. Well can J. Urquhart ("Jordlagenes Vidnesbyrd om Syndfloden," 12) ask what stream that might have been that carried these flint blocks down the mountains, washed them clean, and left them free from sediment. J. Le Conte ("Compend of Geology," 54), says that blocks of stone of many hundreds of tons weight, such as are often found in the path of glaciers, would require, if carried by water, an almost incredible velocity. But glaciers carry materials resting on their surfaces, and therefore of all sizes, with equal ease. Rock fragments of thousands of tons weight are carried by them and left in their path by retreat. Fragments carried by water, are, moreover, more or less bruised, worn and rounded, while fragments carried on the surface of glaciers are angular. Again, water currents set down blocks of stone in secure positions; while glaciers, in their slow melting, often leave them perched in insecure positions, and even sometimes as rocking-stones. Now, Le Conte is by no means trying to defend the Scriptural Deluge. In his "Compend" he never even hints that there ever was such an account. In his larger work, "Elements of Geology," he is equally silent on this question. He simply does not believe very much in the theory that the boulders and drifts have been transported by monster streams. His pet theory is that of the glacial epochs.

The glacial epoch theory presumes that there was an upward movement of the crust in high latitude regions, and the continents stood 2,000 ft. above their present height. An arctic rigor of climate prevailed and vast portions were covered with glacial sheets of ice. Thus, these ice barriers lay over all the northern part of North America where now is found almost everywhere heaps of unsorted, unstratified and unfossiliferous rocks, pebbles and clay. Through sudden change of climate these ice sheets melted and broke off, carrying debris along with them and producing violent mountain torrents.

But this theory does not account for the presence of such debris in British Guiana (Urquhart), nor the presence of massive blocks of Norwegian rock in Germany. Glaciers and streams do not cross oceans and move up hill (Th. Kjerulf's "Istiden"). Nor does this theory account for the fact that the civilized ancients and the savage heathens of to-day all have some version of the Flood story, even as they have stories about their descent from God and the fall into sin and degradation. Very striking is the title of Sir Henry Howorth's book, written not to defend the Biblical account —far from it —but to puncture this theory. He calls his book "The Glacial Nightmare and the Flood."

While everybody knows that glaciers can carry debris and that rivers can overflow their beds and that islands can disappear and reappear, no one yet can satisfactorily account for the geological phenomena of the boulders and debris piles free from seafossils, but full of land fossils, of prehistoric animals, men and tools, except by means of the Biblical Flood. Sir William Dawson is an illustration of a great modern geologist who does not care for the sneers of Voltaire, but actually states his belief in the scientific truth of the Bible story.

b. Descendants of Noah.

Noah's Ark settled down on Mount Ararat in Armenia. Then Noah and his family went forth, built an altar and offered a thank offering. God made a covenant with Noah —the Covenant of the Rainbow—and signally blessed him and his house. From his three sons have descended all of the races of the world.

c. The Dispersion of the Race.

Noah and his family made their way down from Mount Ararat. One of the far-reaching events in their history is the blessing which he pronounced upon Japheth and Shem and the curse upon Ham, a prophecy which has been in fulfillment until this day (Gen. 9: 21-27). Another event, later on, was the movement of the descendants of Noah to the Plain of Shinar, where they in their unbelief and pride began building the Tower of Babel. God saw the danger of their scheme to them, and confounded their language and scattered them abroad upon the face of the earth (Gen. 11). Before that time there was only one language, after that

No. 20.   The Confusion of Tongues (J. Schnorr).

event there has been an evergrowing babel of tongues.
The Japhetic peoples drifted toward the east and northwest,
the Semitic remained in southwestern Asia, the Hamitics
settled in Africa, Canaan, Phoenicia, Asia and farther east.
For the lands which each race occupied see map.

What does Gen. 1 state as to Who created heaven and earth?
As to how long it took Him? What is the opinion of scientists as
to the length of time taken for the work of creation? Why is it
not necessary to agree with the modern scholars in their many conflicting opinions?

What was the Garden of Eden? Where was it located? Who
lived there in the beginning? Why were they expelled?

How many children did Adam and Eve have? How many of these
are mentioned by name? What can you say about the lineage of
the Cainites? Sethites?

What was the Flood? Why did it come? What did it accomplish?
Mention three theories suggested by geologists to account for the
deposits made by water ever present all over the earth. Show that
none of these theories can be defended.

Where did the descendants of Noah settle? Give the names of his sons from whom all of the races of the world have descended. From which of these sons have you descended?

Describe Noah's prophecy and curse. Account for the building of the Tower of Babel. What was the result of this building?

What does your Catechism say about Creation and the Flood? Your Bible history? Find appropriate hymns in your hymnal bearing on the subject. Look up the Bible references referred to in your lesson, and find additional references to this subject in the Bible. In what ways can the contents of this lesson help you in your Bible study? In your faith and works?

LESSON TWENTY-FIVE. PALESTINE DURING THE THEOCRACY (1921-1095 B. C.).

1. PERIOD OF PATRIARCHS (1921-1706 B. C.).

This is the period of Abraham, Isaac and Jacob. Up to the beginning of the sojourn in Egypt, Abraham had lived in Ur of Chaldea. At the command of the Lord he had migrated northward to Haran of Mesopotamia. While there the Lord had appeared again unto him and commanded him to leave the house of his father Terah, and to go into the land that the Lord would show him, where he would become the father of a great nation. Abraham had made the journey to Canaan and had settled first in the Valley of Shechem. He had not been long in Canaan when the famine compelled him to go to Egypt. As he was exposed to some danger there, he soon returned and settled in Judea. After his separation from his nephew Lot, he made his abode on the

No. 21. So Shall Thy Seed Be (J. Schnorr).

Plains of Mamre. It was while he dwelt there that Chedorlaomer, King of Elam, conquered Sodom and in turn was

No. 22. The Journeys of Abraham.

conquered by Abraham. It was also while he lived at
Mamre that Sodom was destroyed. After the destruction of
Sodom, Abraham moved southward to Gerar, where he had

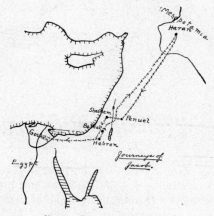

No. 23. The Journeys of Jacob.

trouble with King Abimelech, with whom he later concluded a treaty of peace at Beersheba, which signifies "The

Well of the Oath." During the period of the patriarchs
other events were: Abraham's journey to Mt. Moriah for
the purpose of offering up his son Isaac; Eliezer's journey
to Nahor for the purpose of finding a wife for Isaac; and
Jacob's flight to Mesopotamia and return, as well as his
journey to Egypt.

2. PERIOD OF BONDAGE (1706-1491 B. C.).

Although Canaan had been promised and given to Abra-
·ham for his posterity, it was during his life and throughout
the patriarchal period really in the possession of the Canaanite tribes.   The patriarchs themselves dwelt in the land as
strangers.   Abraham even bought a part of his own land

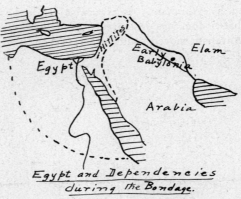

No. 24.   Egypt during the Period of Bondage.

for a burying place.   There was no central government in
Canaan, and each tribe was independent and often at war
with its neighbors.   During the period of bondage these
Canaanite tribes were more or less subject to Egypt, and
the descendants of Jacob all dwelt in Egypt, where they had
been reduced to the lowest depths of slavery.   There is
very little in the Biblical record concerning this long period

No. 25. Making Bricks without Straw—Ex. 5:9 (G. Hoet).

of 215 years which has anything to do with geography. The "Tel el Amarna Letters," 330 letters written from the Canaanite tribes to King Amenophis IV of Egypt during the period of bondage, add many interesting touches to the vivid descriptions of Ex. 1, and indicate that the Canaanite tribes, though nominally independent, were in fact under the rule of Egypt and at times under Chaldea.

3. PERIOD OF WANDERING (1491-1451 B. C.).

During the period of wandering, the Israelites, under the command of Moses, escaped from the bondage in Egypt, re-

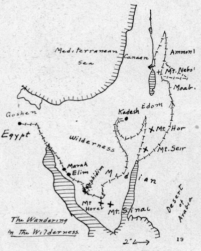

No. 26. The Wanderings in the Wilderness.

ceived the Law at Sinai and were compelled to wander about in the Wilderness of Midian for forty years. Canaan was in the hands of the Canaanites as in the preceding ages. All of the five books of Moses, excepting the first, are devoted to this period. The first book of Moses, Genesis, enables us to describe the journey into Egypt. The second book of Moses,

No. 27. The Water from the Rock—Ex. 17:6 (E. J. Poynter).

Exodus, describes the going out of Egypt. The third book, Leviticus, describes the stay at Mt. Sinai. The fourth book, Numbers, describes the wandering from Sinai to Canaan; and the fifth book, Deuteronomy, describes the review before entering the land.

4. PERIOD OF CONQUEST (1451-1435 B. C.).

Before the death of Moses East Canaan had been conquered by Israel. After his death, under Joshua, the central range of West Canaan was conquered. Thirty-one Canaanite cities

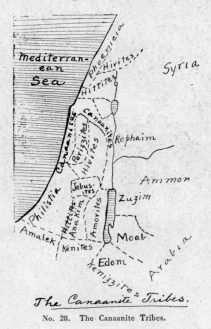

No. 28. The Canaanite Tribes.

were taken by the invaders, and the whole land both east and west of the Jordan was partitioned among them. When Joshua rested from his labors, his intention was, that the work of

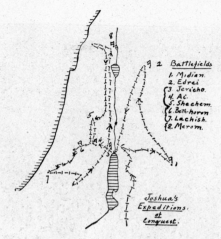

No. 29. The Conquest of Canaan.

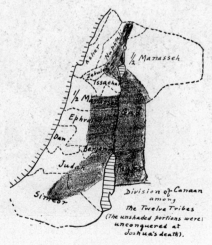

No. 30. The Division of Canaan.

No. 31. The Five Kings in the Cave —Josh. 10:17 (E. G. Dalziel).

conquest should continue until each tribe had expelled or exterminated the Canaanites in its territory. But this was not done. Only three tribes tried to continue the good work so auspiciously begun. These Canaanites were a mighty people, or rather mighty peoples, for they were divided into twelve or more smaller factions. On this account ten of the twelve spies that Moses had sent into Canaan reported that it would be impossible to drive them out of the land (Num. 13: 28-29). The accompanying maps show where they lived, what military expeditions were undertaken against them, and what portions of the land were wrested from them and how the land was apportioned.

5. PERIOD OF THE JUDGES (1435-1095 B. C.).

During the later years of Joshua Israel lived in peace, notwithstanding that the work of conquest had not been completed. Joshua, realizing that his days were numbered, assembled all the tribes at Shechem and made them renew their Covenant with the Lord. During Joshua's days and all the days of the elders that outlived him Israel did serve the Lord. Three of the Israelite tribes made rather half-hearted, yet successful, attempts to expel the heathen tribes, but the remaining tribes preferred to rest on their laurels. Little by little the people began to adjust themselves to the ways of the natives and heathenism began to corrupt the Israelites, as a rotten apple contaminates its neighbors in the barrel. Thus Scripture puts the state of affairs: "And there arose another generation after them, which knew not the Lord, nor yet the works He had done for Israel...... And they forsook the Lord, and served Baal and Ashtaroth. And the anger of the Lord was hot against Israel, and He delivered them into the hands of spoilers that spoiled them .... and they were greatly distressed. Nevertheless the Lord raised up judges, which delivered them " (Judges 2: 10-16). This describes the political situation during the four centuries of this period. The people forgot the benefits of the Lord,

and disobeyed His express commands; He allowed them
as a punishment to be oppressed by their heathen neighbors;
they called upon Him in their great need; He sent them
judges to rescue them. This happened again and again, for

No. 32.   The First Oppression.

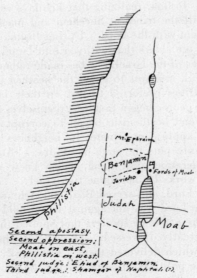

No. 33.   The Second Oppression.

their sorrow was only momentary and their repentance was not lasting. The book of Judges records seven apostasies, with accompanying servitudes and rescues. During this time there was no central government in Canaan. The Canaanites had no central government for all of their tribes, and the Israelites were hardly united as one nation even when they had a judge to rule them. Theoretically, the form of government of the Israelites was a theocracy: God should be their King, and His Word should be their Law. But practically they rejected Him. Therefore, near the close of Samuel's judgeship, the people demanded a king like their neighbors. Samuel protested, but yielded to their

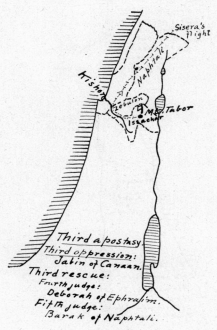

No. 34. The Third Oppression.

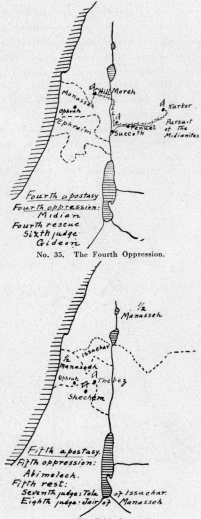

Fourth apostasy
Fourth oppression:
   Midian
Fourth rescue
Sixth judge:
   Gideon

No. 35. The Fourth Oppression.

Fifth apostasy.
Fifth oppression:
   Abimelech.
Fifth rest:
   Seventh judge:Tola of Issachar.
   Eighth judge:Jair of Manasseh.

No. 36. The Fifth Oppression.

No. 37. The Sixth Oppression.

No. 38. The Seventh Oppression.

No. 39. Samuel Given to God—1 Sam. 1:24-28 (W. W. Topham).

No. 40. The Anointing of Saul—1 Sam. 10:1 (J. S. Davis).

urgency, at God's order: "Hearken unto the voice of the people in all that they say unto thee: for they have not rejected thee, but they have rejected Me, that I should not be King over them" (1 Sam. 8:7). Samuel was instructed to show them what manner of rule a monarchy would be, and to go and anoint Saul as king.

The accompanying outline maps locate the oppressors, battle-fields, expeditions and journeys of this period.

———

Where did Abraham live before being called to Canaan? Describe his journeying from Ur to Egypt. Describe Eliezer's journey to Nahor. Describe Jacob's flight to Laban. Describe the journey back to Canaan and on to Egypt.

From where were the Tel el Amarna letters written?

Make a journey together with the Israelites from Egypt through the Wilderness and into the Promised Land.

Follow Joshua and the conquering army to Jericho, Ai, against the five kings, to the north and to the south. State what part of Canaan fell to the lot of each of the twelve tribes of Israel.

Why were there oppressions during the time of the judges? Why were judges appointed? Locate on the map each of the seven oppressions and campaigns against the oppressors. Why did the people demand a king?

What does your Catechism say about Israel during the theocracy? Your Bible history? Find appropriate hymns in your hymnal bearing on this subject. Look up the Bible passages referred to in your lesson, and find additional references on the subject in the Bible. In what ways can the contents of this lesson help you in your Bible study? In your faith and works?

LESSON TWENTY-SIX. PALESTINE DURING THE MONARCHY (1095-586 B. C.).

1. PERIOD OF UNION (1095-975 B. C.).

This was the golden age of the Hebrew political history. It was the age of Saul, David and Solomon, during which the Canaanite tribes were conquered one by one, and most of them forever subdued, and the neighboring nations were made subject and their lands from Egypt to Euphrates made

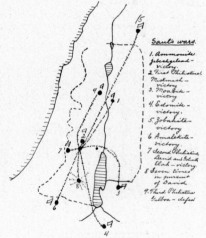

Saul's wars.

1. Ammonite
Jabeshgilead —
victory
2. First Philistine
Michmash —
victory
3. Moabite —
victory.
4. Edomite —
victory.
5. Zobahite —
victory
6. Amalekite —
victory.
7. Second Philistine
Beand and Elah
Elah — victory.
8. Seven times
in pursuit
of David
9. Third Philistine
Gilboa — defeat

No. 41. The Wars of Saul.

a part of the Israelite realm. Never before or since has the geography of the Hebrew people included so much territory. The accompanying outline maps illustrate the wars of Saul and David and the boundaries during the reigns of the three kings.

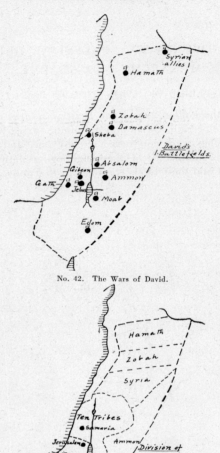

No. 42. The Wars of David.

No. 43. The Division of Solomon's Kingdom.

2. PERIOD OF DIVISION (975-586 B. C.).

At the death of Solomon the Kingdom of the Twelve Tribes divided into two kingdoms: That of the Ten Tribes, known as the Kingdom of Israel, and that of the Two Tribes, known as the Kingdom of Judah.

a. KINGDOM OF THE TEN TRIBES, OR ISRAEL (975-722 B. C.).

The causes of the division of the Kingdom of the Twelve Tribes were both remote and immediate. Remote causes were such as: Ancient jealousy between the tribe of Ephraim and the tribe of Judah (Cf. 2 Sam. 19:15, 40-43); the breaking of national and religious ties due to foreign alliances, heathen marriages and the encouragement given to heathen religions; discontent due to heavy taxes and forced labor to support Solomon's enormous household (1 Kings 4: 22-26; 5: 13-16; etc.). The immediate cause was the insolent refusal of Solomon's son, Rehoboam, to grant the people's request for relief (1 Kings 12: 3-16).

Ten of the tribes revolted: Ephraim, Manasseh, Gad, Simeon, Naphtali, Reuben, Dan, Issachar, Zebulon and Asher. Their allotted territory at the Conquest was over 10,000 sq. miles, against 1,700 for the two remaining tribes. Through the conquests of David their territorial possessions were nominally over four times as extensive as the first allotment. But they soon lost all of their lands to the north and northeast, and even that east of the Jordan. At times the Kingdom of the Ten Tribes was hardly larger than that of the Two Tribes.

The Kingdom of the Ten Tribes lasted 254 years. It falls into four periods: First, Judah and Israel at war; second, Judah and Israel as allies; third, Judah and Israel at war again, not alone, but in alliance with foreigners; fourth, Israel as vassal and captive. Nineteen kings, belonging to nine houses, reigned in turn, as follows:

First Period: Judah and Israel at War, Chiefly Alone.

House of Jeroboam I *(Ephraim)*, 975-953, 24 years.
       Jeroboam I, 22 years, 975—954 (1 Kings 12:25—14:20).
       Nadab, 2 years, 954-953 (1 Kings 15:25-32).

House of Baasha *(Issachar)*, 953-929, 24 years.
       Baasha, 24 years, 953-930 (1 Kings 15: 33—16: 6).
       Elah, 2 years, 930-929 (1 Kings 16: 7-10).

House of Zimri *(Simeon)*, 929, 7 days.

House of Omri *(Ephraim)*, 929-884, 45 years.
       Omri, 12 years, 929-918 (1 Kings 16: 21-28).

       Second Period: Judah and Israel as Allies.

       Ahab, 22 years, 918-898 (1 Kings 16: 29—22: 40).
       Ahaziah, 2 years, 898-896 (1 Kings 22:51-53; 2 Kings 1:1-18).
       Jehoram, 12 years, 896-884 (2 Kings 2: 1—8: 15).

House of Jehu *(Ephraim)*, 884-762, 124 years.
       Jehu, 28 years, 884-856 (2 Kings 9: 1—10: 36).
       Jehoahaz, 17 years, 856-840 (2 Kings 13: 1-9).

  Third Period: Judah and Israel at War Again, with Allies.

       Jehoash, 16 years, 840-825 (2 Kings 13:10-25).
       Jeroboam II, 41 years, 825-784 (2 Kings 14: 23-29).

    Fourth Period: Submission to Foreign Nations.

       Interregnum.
       Zachariah, 6 months, 762 (2 Kings 15: 10-12).

House of Shallum, 762, 1 month (2 Kings 15: 13-15).

House of Menahem, 761-750, 13 years.
       Menahem, 12 years, 761-752 (2 Kings 15: 16-22).
       Pekahiah, 2 years, 752-750 (2 Kings 15: 23-26).

House of Pekah, 750-730, 20 years (2 Kings 15: 27-31).

House of Hoshea, 730-722, 9 years (2 Kings 17: 1-41).

The capital of the Northern Kingdom was at first Shechem, in the land of Ephraim; later it was moved to Tirzah,
in Issachar; but with the return of Ephraim to power the
capital was removed to the territory of Ephraim. King
Omri founded Samaria and made it his capital city. The
name means the Place of Watch (1 Kings 16: 24) and,
indeed, was very appropriate, for it was situated on a hill
with fertile valleys surrounding it. Scarcely had it been

No. 44. The Prophecy to Jeroboam.—1 Kings 11:31 (B. Picart).

established when it was attacked by Benhadad I of Syria
and forced to allow the Syrians to open up a market there
(1 Kings 20: 34). It was twice besieged by Benhadad II
while Ahab and Jehoram reigned (1 King 20:1-21; 2 Kings
6: 8—7: 20). At the order of Jehu the 70 sons of Ahab were
slaughtered in this city (2 Kings 10: 1-10). The city was
well provided with altars to Baal and Astarte, against which
Hosea (7: 1-8: 13: 6), Amos (4: 1; 8: 14), Elijah (1 Kings
18), Isaiah (7: 9; 8: 4), Jeremiah (31: 5), Ezekiel (16:
46-55) and Micah (1: 5-9) wrote and spoke. It was taken
after a three years' siege begun by the Assyrians under Shal-
maneser and concluded by Sargon. The Israelites were
transported to Media and the East, and the city was re-peo-
pled by unruly peoples from other lands subject to Assyria.
The Ten Tribes have been called the "Lost Tribes," because
they never returned. Some have conjectured that the Jap-
anese are the lineal descendants of these lost tribes. Others

No. 45.   First Period of the Divided Kingdoms.

No. 46. Second Period of the Divided Kingdoms.

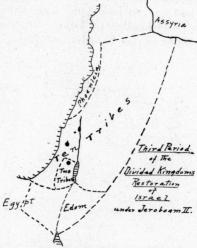

No. 47. Third Period of the Divided Kingdoms.

hold that the Mound Builders of the United States have that distinction. Yet others believe the Indians are their descendants. The Mormons believe that when Christ said: "And other sheep I have, which are not of this fold" (John 10:16), He then meant the Lost Tribes who had wandered to the American continent and had received the Mormon religion from God. E. J. Banks says in his book, "The Bible and the Spade" (171): "The 'Lost Tribes' are not lost; one needs only to go to Babylonia to find them." Their descendants live there now, intermixed with other peoples.

The captivity of the Ten Tribes was a punishment upon them for choosing to follow in the ways of the heathen neighbors rather than according to God's revealed Word. They worshipped the heathen idols, practised the licentiousness of the idolators, warred against Judah, persecuted the prophets of Jehovah, utterly rejecting the Statutes of the Lord. Their ways were all wicked. The people as a nation was thoroughly apostate, in spite of the fact that at the time of Elijah 7,000 had not yet bowed the knee unto Baal (1 Kings 19:18). The Kingdom of Israel had many times the extent of territory of the Kingdom of Judah, twice as

No. 48. Fourth Period of the Divided Kingdoms: the Ten Tribes in Captivity.

many people, and the best of promises from the Lord if Jeroboam had chosen to serve the Lord; but Israel's king and people chose to reject Him and to be rejected by Him in turn.

b. KINGDOM OF THE TWO TRIBES, OR JUDAH (975-586 B. B.).

The Two Tribes were Judah and Benjamin. The priests and Levites also, that is, the tribe of Levi, chose to cast their lot with Judah and Jerusalem (2 Chron. 11:13-14). The Kingdom received its name from the tribe of Judah, because it was by far the largest tribe in Israel (Num. 1: 26; 2 Sam. 24: 9). From Judah is derived the name Jew.

The Kingdom of Judah lasted 389 years. Like its neighbor on the north it had four periods: First, Judah and Israel at war; second, Judah and Israel as allies; third, Judah and Israel at war again, not alone, but in alliance with foreign nations; and fourth, Judah as vassal and cap-

No. 49. Josiah's Lamentations—2 Chron. 34:19 (J. Schnorr).

tive. Nineteen kings and one queen, all of the house of
David, reigned in turn, as follows:

First Period: Judah and Israel at War, Chiefly Alone.

Rehoboam, 975-959, 17 years (1 Kings 14: 21-31).
Abijah (Abijam), 959-957, 3 years (1 Kings 15: 1-8).
Asa, 957-917, 41 years (1 Kings 15: 9-24).

Second Period: Judah and Israel as Allies.

Jehoshaphat, 917-893, 25 years (1 Kings 22: 41-50).
Jehoram, 893-885, 8 years (2 Kings 8: 16-24).
Ahaziah, 885, 1 year (2 Kings 8: 25-29).
Athaliah, 885-879, 6 years (2 Kings 11: 1-21).
Joash, 879-840, 40 years (2 Kings 12: 1-21).

Third Period: Judah and Israel at War Again, with Allies.

Amaziah, 840-811, 29 years (2 Kings 14: 1-20).
Uzziah, 811-759, 52 years (2 Kings 15: 1-7).
Jotham, 781-742, sole ruler only 16 years (2 Kings 15: 32-38).
Ahaz, 742-726, 16 years (2 Kings 16: 1-20).
Hezekiah, 726-697, 29 years (2 Kings 18: 1-20: 21).

Fourth Period: Submission to Foreign Nations.

Manasseh, 697-642, 55 years (2 Kings 21: 1-18).
Amon, 642-640, 2 years (2 Kings 21: 19-26).
Josiah, 640-609, 31 years (2 Kings 22: 1—23: 30).
Jehoahaz, 609, 3 months (2 Kings 23: 31-34).
Jehoiakim, 609-598, 11 years (2 Kings 23: 35—24: 7).
Jehoiakin, 598, 3 months (2 Kings 24: 8-17).
Zedekiah, 597-586, 11 years (2 Kings 24: 18—25: 30).

The capital of the Southern Kingdom remained at Jerusalem, one of the best built and strongest cities in history,
the most famous city in the world. The greatest attraction
of the city was the Temple of Solomon, erected at great
expense and labor. No less than 180,000 men had worked
on the construction of this marvelous work of art for the
space of seven years. (See under Sacred Places). During the reign of Rehoboam, Shishak, king of Egypt, forced
his way into the city and robbed the temple and the king's

palace of all of their treasures (1 Kings 14:25-28). The king had to be satisfied with brass shields as a substitute for the golden ones taken by Shishak. About the year 890, during Jehoram's reign, the Arabians and Philistines raided the city and carried away the treasures that had been accumulated during the century (2 Chron. 21: 16-17). About the year 840 the Israelites broke down a portion of the city wall and despoiled the Temple again (2 Kings 14: 13-14). Uzziah and Jotham repaired the ruins caused by this attack and by a severe earthquake (Amos 1: 1; Zech. 14: 5; 2 Chron. 26: 9; 27: 3; Josephus' "Antiquities," 9: 10). A century later, under Ahaz, the city was besieged by the allied forces of Israel and Syria (2 Kings 16: 5), but it was not taken. Ahaz was inclined to heathenism and foreign alliance with Assyria, therefore he closed the Temple (2 Kings 16: 14; 2 Chron. 28: 24; 29: 7), which was not opened again for service until Hezekiah ascended the throne. Hezekiah was forced to strip the Temple again of its vessels and ornaments to pay the Assyrian for the support he gave to Ahaz. Even by so doing he was not able to ward off the Assyrians permanently. The Assyrian troops were soon afterward at the city walls calling aloud to surrender. But through the statesmanship of Isaiah and the providential help of the angel of the Lord the city held out and the remnant of the slaughtered Assyrian army fled homeward (2 Chron. 32: 21; 2 Kings 19: 36; Isa. 36-38). When Manasseh came to the throne he began to undo the good work of his illustrious father Hezekiah by building altars to Baal and Astarte and the hosts of heaven, even within the courts of the Temple, causing his own son to pass through the fire, and spilling the innocent blood of the prophets who warned him. Esarhaddon and Ashurbanipal made him pay tribute to Assyria, and Ashurbanipal placed him in captivity at Babylon for a period of years. There he repented of his sins, and the Lord brought about his reinstatement as king of the Jews (2 Chron. 33: 11-19; "Prayer of Manasseh"). Upon

No. 50. The Burning of Jerusalem—2 Chron. 36:19 (J. Goeree).

his return he reinstated the worship of Jehovah and repaired the city walls and fortifications. Nebuchadnezzar captured the city three times, the last time razing it to the ground.

The reason for the fall of Jerusalem, and with it, of Judah, was the apostasy of the kings, priests and people of Judah. A few of the kings had served the Lord—rather half-heartedly, it must be admitted. Most illustrious of these were Jehoshaphat, Hezekiah and Josiah. The rest of the kings were more or less like the kings of Israel and the heathen

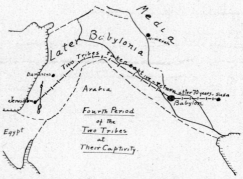

No. 51. Fourth Period of the Divided Kingdom: the Two Tribes in Captivity.

nations round about, spokesmen of the naturalistic heathen religions with their idolatrous practices and low morality. Prophet after prophet was sent to awaken and warn against apostasy and accompanying disaster. Judah would not listen.

Why was the age of Saul, David and Solomon the Golden Age of Hebrew political history? Study the maps showing the wars of Saul. Of David. Of the boundaries of the Kingdom of Solomon.

Describe the division of the Kingdom at the death of Solomon.

How long did the Kingdom of the Ten Tribes last? How many kings reigned? How many houses? Describe the four periods. Why were the Ten Tribes taken captive? Why were they not allowed to return?

How long did the Kingdom of the Two Tribes last? How many kings reigned? How many houses? Describe the four periods. Why were the Two Tribes taken captive? Why were they allowed to return?

What does your Bible history say about the period of monarchy? Find appropriate hymns in your hymnal bearing on this subject. Look up the Bible passages referred to in your lesson, and find additional references to this subject in the Bible. In what ways can the contents of this lesson help you in your Bible study? In your faith and works?

LESSON TWENTY-SEVEN. PALESTINE AS A DEPENDENCY (586 B. C.—4. B. C.—).

1. UNDER BABYLONIA (606-536, or 586-516 B. C.).

The prophets had foretold that the Jews should be led captive to Babylon and that they should return after 70 years (Isa. 46:11; Micah 4:10; Jer. 25:1-12). The beginning of the Captivity may be reckoned from the first captivity by Nebuchadnezzar, in 606, or from the third and final captivity by him, in 586. The beginning of the Return can be reckoned either from the decree of Cyrus, in 536, when 42,360 of them embraced the opportunity to go back (Ezra 2: 64), or from the completion of the restored Temple, in 516.

The Jews in exile enjoyed many privileges. They were allowed to have their own homes and engage in business (Jer. 29: 5-7; Ezra 2: 65). They were allowed to have priests and prophets with them to instruct them and comfort them (Jer. 29:1; Ezra 2:65). Their bright young men, such as Daniel and the three friends and Nehemiah, had a chance to rise to positions of highest trust in the State (Dan. 2:48; Neh. 1:11). A Jewish girl later became the queen of Persia (Esther). The majority of the people enjoyed life so much in the exile, in spite of the disadvantage of not having a country or a temple, that they were loath to go back. They therefore remained by the rivers of Babylon, voluntarily joining that great multitude of Israelites that had been taken into captivity never to return. Unlike the Ten Tribes the Jews of the Diaspora (Dispersion) retained their faith and made pilgrimages to the Temple on the great festive occasions (Zech. 6: 10; Acts. 2: 9).

The handful of Jews left behind under Nebuchadnezzar's appointive Gedaliah soon had troubles enough and to spare. The governor was killed by the assassin Ishmael (2 Kings

No. 52. The Building of the Temple of Zerubbabel—Ezra 3:10-13 (E. van Dargent).

No. 53. The Renewal of the Covenant—Ezra 10:10-14 (A. Sacchi).

25:22-26; Jer. 39:14; 40:5—41:18). The remnant picked up their belongings and fled to Egypt, taking with them the prophet Jeremiah much against his will. Arabian and Samaritan bands took possession of the land at their departure.

2. UNDER PERSIA (516-330 B. C.).

Jerusalem lay waste 50 years. In 536 B. C., 42,360 of the exiles returned under Zerubbabel and began rebuilding the city, with its walls and Temple (Ezra 2:64-65; 3-8). On account of the opposition of the Samaritans the Temple was not completed before the sixth year of the reign of Darius the Great, or 516 B. C., 20 years after its foundations had been

No. 54. The Hanging of Haman—Esther 7:10 (L. de Later).

laid (Ezra 3:8; 6:15). The dedication in 516 marks the end of the 70 years. To bring about the completion of the Temple diplomatic correspondence had to be carried on between Jerusalem and Darius, and the prophets Haggai and Zechariah had to appear on the scene to urge the people to build the Temple. The successor of Darius was Xerxes I (486—465), the Ahasuerus of the book of Esther. Artaxerxes succeeded Xerxes to the throne of Persia. He permitted Ezra in 456 B. C. to go to Jerusalem to establish law and order (Ezra 7). Thirteen years later, in 444, he permitted his cupbearer, Nehemiah, to go to Jerusalem with

No. 55. Judah a Persian Province.

workmen and supplies to superintend the rebuilding of the walls of the city. In 432 he allowed him to go a second time, this time to bring about needed reforms. About the same time (400) the Samaritans built a rival temple on Mount Gerizim, intensifying the mutual dislike of these neighbors for each other. Very little is known about the state of the restored Judah from 400 to 330, except that it was a weak province of a weakening world empire.

3. UNDER MACEDONIA (330-321 B. C.).

Greece (Macedonia) subjugated Persia in 330 and became master of the Persian provinces, also Judah. Alexander granted the Jews many special privileges, allowing them to retain their worship. He made Palestine a part of Syria, on account of which it became a bone of contention among Alexander's generals at his death. The most important effect of the Macedonian conquest of Asia was the spread of Greek culture and language in Western Asia.

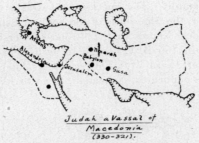

No. 56.   Judah a Macedonian Province.

4. UNDER MACEDONIAN EGYPT   (321-198 B. C.).

In the year 321 B. C. Palestine was partitioned to Egypt, and the Greek rulers of Egypt, the Ptolemies, ruled Canaan for 123 years. The high priests were the virtual rulers during this period. The most important event

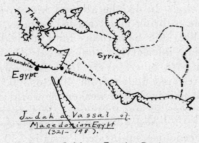

No. 57.   Judah an Egyptian Province.

of the epoch was the translation of the Old Testament into Greek. This translation is the famous Septuagint, perhaps the first translation of any book in the world. During this epoch, too, the Greek language and culture became the common heritage of all the nations.

5. UNDER MACEDONIAN SYRIA (198-166 B. C.).

In 198 occurred the battle of Mount Panium, by which the kings of Syria wrested from the Ptolemies the land of Canaan. Antiochus Epiphanes, the Syrian king, took the city of Jerusalem in 203 and lost it to the Egyptians in 199; he again captured it in 170, desecrating the Temple

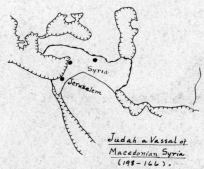

Judah a Vassal of
Macedonian Syria
(198-166).

No. 58. Judah a Syrian Province.

and setting up a statue of Jupiter in the Holy of Holies. He broke down the walls of Jerusalem, commanded the people to eat swine, forbade circumcision, destroyed copies of Scripture that he could find, and tortured those who protested or disobeyed (1 Macc. 1; 2 Macc. 5—7; Heb. 11:35-37). The violence of his intolerance and tyranny led to a determined revolt and eventual independence.

6. UNDER THE MACCABEES—INDEPENDENT (166-63 B. C.).

The family that secured Jewish independence was called Maccabean or Asmonaean. The name Asmonaean refers back to Eashman, an ancestor of the Maccabees (1 Chron. 24:7; 1 Macc. 2:1; Josephus' "Antiquities," 12:6). The name Maccabean was first applied to Judas, the first general against the Syrians (1 Macc. 2: 40), but later was trans-

No. 59. The Revolt of Mattathias Maccabaeus—1 Macc. 2:24 (G. Doré).

ferred to the whole family. It is said to mean hammer, in allusion to the crushing blows Judas dealt his enemies. The first to raise the flag of revolt was Mattathias, an aged Jewish priest. He fled to the mountains of Judea, followed by his sons and others, a growing band. Judas, his third son, became the first general, and won out in every conflict with the invading armies. He took Jerusalem, purified the Temple and restored the Jewish worship. When Judas fell in battle, in 160, his brother Jonathan assumed leadership for 17 years. When Jonathan was treacherously slain, in 143, the leadership fell to his brother Simon, the last of the six brothers alive. John and Eleazar, the first and the fourth

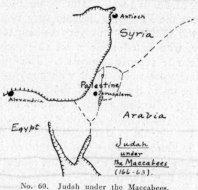

No. 60. Judah under the Maccabees.

of the brothers, had already met death. Under Simon Syria acknowledged the independence of Judah.

So far the Maccabean rule had been a theocracy. With the accession of John Hyrcanus as king it became a monarchy. Not only did the form of government change, but also the spirit. There was a rapid decline in politics and morals. The history of the Maccabees from 135 to 37 B. C. is far from heroic. It is a record of awful domestic crimes, civil wars and defeats by outside enemies. Brother fought brother for leadership, sect fought sect. During the Macedonian, Egyptian and Syrian periods the Greek language and culture were taking a hold of the Jews and threatening the extinction of the Jewish religion. The Syrian king Antiochus Epiphanes had tried by means of the utmost cruelty to force the Jews to live as heathen. His tyranny had brought about the political revolt of the Maccabees and the organization of the religious sect later known as Pharisees (1 Macc. 2: 42; Josephus' "Antiquities"). They took a determined stand under the Maccabees for the purity of the old religion of Israel, as opposed to the high priestly house, later known as Sadducees, which was worldly and inclined to accept the Greek and Syrian demands as inevitable (2 Macc. 4: 14-16). During the theocratic rule of the Maccabees the Pharisees became very popular with the rulers and the multitude, but very odious to the cultured and wealthy, who hated their strict rules and their growing pretensions to superior morality. The Pharisees in the course of time were not content with copying and explaining and living up to the letter of the Law of God, but were also very busy collecting many traditions and making new ordinances, besides meddling with everybody's affairs. In their attempt to dictate to Hyrcanus he broke with them and joined the Sadducees. This stand resulted in civil wars, which were fought periodically with the utmost violence even until the day that Jerusalem was destroyed. From 135 to 78 the kings favored the Sadducees, from 78 to the time of Christ they favored the Pharisees. The result of the dissensions was, that the Romans interfered to arbitrate the quarrel. The result of the whole arbitration was, that the Maccabees were deposed and Herod, an Edomite (Idumean), was appointed king, with the understanding that Palestine should become a Roman province.

7. UNDER ROME (63-4 B. C.).

In 37 Herod became king, at the appointment of Rome. It was during his reign that Christ was born in Bethlehem.

Herod was very cunning and cruel. On account of these traits he had endeavored to strengthen his position by the removal of possible rivals. Among those he murdered to secure his throne may be mentioned his father-in-law, brother-in-law, one of his ten wives and three of his fifteen sons.

No. 61.   Birth of Christ.

No wonder then that he was not a little troubled at the news that a king was born in Bethlehem. No wonder, either, that he ordered the slaughter of the infants. Soon afterwards, when he was on his death-bed, one of his last commands was to put to death the most prominent Jews of the nearest town, Jericho, that there might be mourning at his death. His kingdom at his death was divided into four parts, each called a tetrarchy. His son Archelaus became his successor in Judea and Samaria; another son, Herod Antipas, became tetrarch of Galilee and Perea; a third son, Philip, became tetrarch of Iturea, the country east of the Sea of Galilee; and Lysanias became tetrarch of Abilene, to the north of the Sea of Galilee. Palestine continued a vassal of

Rome after the birth of Christ until the fall of Jerusalem in 70 A. D., and beyond.

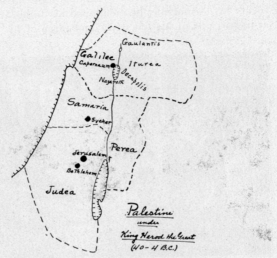

No. 62. Judah a Roman Province: under King Herod.

How did the Jews fare in the Exile? How did the Jews fare who were left behind in Canaan?

How long did Jerusalem lay waste? How long were the Jews kept in Exile? Why were they permitted to return? How many did return? Who were the leaders from the time that they returned until Jerusalem and the Temple were restored? Show on the map the contemporary countries at the time of the return.

When did Macedonia conquer Persia and her provinces? Show on the map the extent of the Macedonian territory before and after the Conquest.

Show on the map the relation of Canaan to Macedonian Egypt. Name one event of importance happening while the Jews were under Macedonian Egypt.

Who was Antiochus Epiphanes? Describe his tyranny.

Who were the Maccabees? Why did they revolt against Syria?

Describe the state of the Maccabean kingdom from the time of Mattathias down to Herod the Great.

Describe the boundaries of Judea under Herod. Why was Herod
afraid of the new born King? How was his kingdom divided up at
his death?

What does your Bible history say about Canaan as a province
of Babylonia? Of Persia? Of Greece? Of Egypt? Of Syria?
Independent under the Maccabees? Subject to Rome? Find appropriate hymns in your hymnal bearing on this subject. Look up
the Bible passages referred to in your lesson, and find additional
references to this subject in the Bible. In what ways can the contents
of this lesson help you in your Bible study? In your faith and works?

LESSON TWENTY-EIGHT. PALESTINE AT THE TIME OF CHRIST: I. HIS FIRST YEARS

(4 B. C.—29 A. D.).

1. THE POLITICAL DIVISIONS.

The Roman Empire included all of the lands of Southern Europe from Great Britain to the Black Sea, all of the lands of Northern Africa and all of the lands of Western Asia. Palestine at the birth of Christ was a small kingdom at the beckoning of Rome. At the death of Herod, in 4 B. C., it was divided into four provinces governed by tetrarchs.

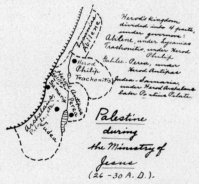

No. 63. Judah a Roman Province: under Governors.

The first tetrarchy consisted of Judea and Samaria. In 6 A. D., Archelaus, the son of Herod, was deposed, and his tetrarchy was annexed directly to Rome and ruled by appointed governors, of whom Pontius Pilate was the sixth.

The second tetrarchy consisted of Galilee and Perea. It was governed by Herod Antipas, a brother of Herod Archelaus. This Herod divorced his wife and married

Herodias, the wife of his half-brother Philip (not the tetrarch), on account of which he was reprimanded by John the Baptist. Herodias demanded of Herod the head of John. Most of Christ's ministry was performed in Herod's domain, particularly in Galilee. When Christ's fame began to spread, Herod's guilty conscience imagined that John the Baptist had risen from the dead (Matt. 14: 1-2). He was present at the Passover during which Jesus was tried and crucified, and was pleased to think that he would have a chance to see Jesus perform a miracle. When Pilate learnt that Jesus was a Galilean, he sent Him to Herod to be tried. "And Herod and Pilate became friends with each other that very day; for before they were at enmity between themselves" (Luke 23: 12).

The third tetrarchy was that east of the Sea of Galilee, ruled by Philip, not the husband of Herodias, but a half-brother of his, son of Herod the Great and Queen Cleopatra of Egypt. This Philip built the city of Caesarea Philippi and rebuilt Bethsaida, to which he gave the name Julias in honor of Julia, the daughter of Emperor Augustus. His tetrarchy came to an end in 33.

The fourth tetrarchy—of Abilene—plays no part in the life of Christ.

2. THE JOURNEYS OF CHRIST.

a. HIS PRIVATE LIFE.

About 30 years of the earthly life of our Lord was lived in comparative obscurity. In this period of obscurity the sacred records tell only of four journeys which He made. The first of these was from Bethlehem, when He was born, to Jerusalem, where He was to be presented unto the Lord at the Temple on the fortieth day. The second was from Bethlehem to Egypt, where Joseph and Mary had to flee with the Child, in order to escape the suspicious Herod. The third was from Egypt to Nazareth, where Joseph and Mary took Him, for they feared Herod Archelaus. The fourth was when as a child of 12 He visited the Temple and questioned the doctors.

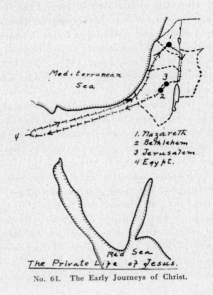

Med.terranean
Sea

1. Nazareth
2 Bethlehem
3 Jerusalem.
4 Egypt.

Red Sea

The Private Life of Jesus.

No. 61.   The Early Journeys of Christ.

b.   HIS FIRST YEAR OF MINISTRY.

The prelude to the ministry of Jesus is the ministry of His forerunner, John the Baptist.   John preached in the Wilderness of Judea and near the Jordan.   John's father, Zacharias, was a priest.   He himself was no doubt trained for the priesthood.   All that we know of his early life is, that "he grew and waxed strong in spirit, and was in the deserts till the day of his showing unto Israel" (Luke 1: 80).   He had been consecrated to his office before his birth (Luke 1: 13-15), but did not enter upon it until ripe manhood, his whole life having been spent in self-denial and solitude. With scant clothing of camel's hair, and locusts and honey for food, his very appearance and manner were a contrast

to the luxury of his day and excited attention. His heart
was profoundly stirred by the prevailing sins of his day
and by the conviction that a new day was at hand. His
words of denunciation were bold and sweeping, demanding
repentance of high and low, for the Kingdom of Heaven
was at hand. He was the last and greatest of the Old
Testament prophets. From the very first he declared that
he was not the Christ, the Messianic King, that had been

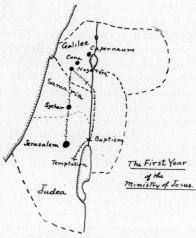

No. 65. The First Year of Christ's Ministry.

promised to David and Moses and Jacob and Abraham and
Adam, but that he was only His voice crying in the wilderness. John declared also that the King had come, and that
He was the "Lamb of God, That taketh away the sin of the
world" (John 1: 29). Immense crowds went to hear him,
many of them swept away by the religious revival. Jesus
Himself came down from Nazareth and presented Himself
for Baptism. John hesitated at first, under a sense of
unworthiness, but at the command of Jesus baptized Him.

Then the Holy Spirit descended like a dove, and a voice from Heaven proclaimed: "This is my beloved Son, in Whom I am well pleased" (Matt. 3: 17). After His Baptism Jesus was driven by the Spirit into the Wilderness to be tempted by the Devil (Matt. 4: 1-11). This ended the preparation for the public ministry of our Lord.

Together with six disciples: Andrew and Peter, two brothers; John and James, also two brothers; and Philip and Nathanael (Bartholomew)—Jesus began His ministry at the marriage feast at Cana (John 2: 1-12). Shortly afterwards He visited Jerusalem during the Passover season, cleansed the Temple and discoursed with Nicodemus (John 3). Eight months later, contrary to the Jewish custom, He went directly through Samaria to reach Galilee. At Sychar He converted the Samaritan woman (John 4). At Capernaum His first miracle of healing was performed—the nobleman's son was saved by faith (John 4:43-54). Again, after a few weeks spent in retirement, He went to Jerusalem for the celebration of the second Passover, and there healed an impotent man at the Pool of Bethesda on a Sabbath, whereupon arose His first conflict with the Pharisees.

c. His Second Year of Ministry.

He returned to Galilee, took up His abode at Capernaum, called His disciples to become "fishers of men" (Luke 5:1-11), taught in the synagogues and healed the sick and possessed. He made His first preaching circuit of Galilee, took His disciples into the desert to pray and taught them the cost of following Him. In crossing the Sea of Galilee He stilled the storm. At Gergesa He restored the demoniacs (Mark 5: 1-20). He returned to Capernaum and healed a paralytic (Matt. 9: 1-8).

At this point He called a seventh disciple, Matthew the publican. He raised the daughter of Jairus to life, effected other cures and preached to vast multitudes, especially in parables (Matt. 13). He made a visit to His home town Nazareth, but was rejected (Mark 6: 1-6).

Now He chose the Twelve, preached on a mount the famous "Sermon on the Mount" (Matt. 5—7), performed many
miracles of healing, raised the widow's son of Nain, made
a second preaching circuit of Galilee and sent forth the
Twelve. He crossed over to Bethsaida to get rest for His
wearied body, but was followed by the curious multitude.
He fed 5,000 in the Wilderness. He walked on the sea.

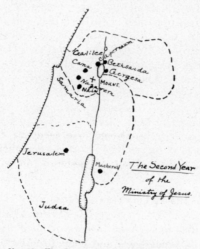

No. 66.   The Second Year of Christ's Ministry.

Arriving at Capernaum, He was forced into an argument
regarding the Bread of Life (John 6) and also an argument
regarding the Sabbath (Matt. 12). Thereupon He healed
on the Sabbath a man with a withered hand (Mark 3:1-6)
and laid bare the hypocrisy of the Pharisees (Matt. 15).

Bound the Roman Empire at the time of Christ. What political
changes were made in Palestine after the death of Herod? Describe
the territory of each of the four tetrarchies. Name the ruler of
each of these provinces at the time of Christ's ministry.

Describe the journeys of Christ during His private life. During
His first year of ministry. During His second year of ministry.

What does your Bible history say concerning Palestine at the
time of Christ, and His journeys in the first and second years of
His ministry? Find appropriate hymns in your hymnal bearing
on this subject. Look up the Bible passages referred to in your
lesson, and find additional references to this subject in the Bible.
In what ways can the contents of this lesson help you in your Bible
study? In your faith and works?

LESSON TWENTY-NINE. PALESTINE AT THE TIME OF CHRIST: II. HIS LAST YEAR (30 A. D.).

1. THE CITIES VISITED BY CHRIST.

There is no period in the world's history so crowded with strange and important events as the short three years of Christ's ministry. Our Savior moved about from place to

No. 67. Cities Visited by Christ.

place, His time from early morning to late at night fully taken up with giving sight to the blind, making the lame walk, cleansing the lepers, giving hearing to the deaf, raising

up the dead and preaching the Good Tidings to the poor
(Matt. 11:5). Even when He retired into the desert for rest
and prayer the multitudes followed Him, sometimes in such
haste that they forgot to take bread along. Yet it is more
than passing strange that there are really very few places
mentioned by name as having been visited by Jesus. In the
following brief notice are mentioned the cities visited by
Him during His earlier years and during His last year, particular attention being paid to Jerusalem. They are grouped
by provinces:

a. Judea.	b. Samaria.	c. Galilee.	d. Perea.	e. Iturea
(1) Bethlehem	(1) Sychar	(1) Nazareth	(1) Bethabara	(1) Gergesa
(2) Jerusalem		(2) Cana		(2) Bethsaida
(3) Bethany		(3) Capernaum		(3) Caesarea
(4) Jericho		(4) Nain		. Philippi
(5) Ephraim		(5) Dalmanutha		
(6) Emmaus				

a. THE CITIES OF JUDEA.

(1) *Bethlehem.*—Bethlehem means House of Bread. It
was originally called Ephrah and was also known as Bethlehem Judah to distinguish it from Bethlehem Zebulun. It
was a city on a hill 6 miles south of Jerusalem. Here
Benjamin was born, and Jacob's beloved wife, Rachel, died
(1729 B. C). Here Boaz and Ruth were married. Here
David was born (1085 B. C.), hence it was called the city
of David. To this city Joseph and Mary came at the order
of Augustus Caesar, to enroll. And it came to pass while
they were there and shepherds watched their flocks by night
that Jesus was born to them, and He was laid in a manger,
for there was no room for them in the inn (Luke 2). Then
it was that the angels sang:

> Glory to God in the highest, and on earth peace among men in
> whom He is well pleased.

No. 68. Bethlehem.

O little town of Bethlehem,
　　How still we see thee lie;
Above thy deep and dreamless sleep
　　The silent stars go by;
Yet in the dark streets shineth
　　The everlasting Light;
The hopes and fears of all the years
　　Are met in thee tonight.

(2) *Jerusalem.*—Jerusalem means Foundation of Peace, Secure Habitation. It is known in the Old Testament as Salem, Jebus and Jerusalem. The name Salem occurs in Gen. 14: 18, when Melchizedek went out to meet Abraham. The name Jebus was applied to it until David made it his capital and called it Jerusalem. It is 18 miles west from the meeting point of the Jordan and the Dead Sea and 31 miles east of the Mediterranean. It has a horse-shoe shape and is built on four hills: Mount Moriah, in the eastern part, reaching up to an elevation of 2,432 feet; Mount Zion, in the southern part, 2,516 feet above sea level; Acra, just north of Mount Zion, 2,482 feet high; and Bezetha, north of Acra, 2,520 feet high. Between Mount Moriah and Mount Zion lay the Tyropaean Valley. East of Mount Moriah was a gorge from 200 to 400 feet deep, through which the Brook Kidron flowed. South of Mount Zion was another deep valley called Hinnom or Gehenna. In this valley Solomon in his old age erected an altar to the idol Moloch, being led to do so by his Ammonite wives, and in the following centuries children were burnt there to Moloch (2 Chron. 28: 3; 2 Kings 21: 6). From the horrible sins practised there and from the fact that offal was burnt in it, the Valley of Gehenna became a type of the place of eternal punishment— Hell. The three valleys meet at the southeastern point of the city. Opposite Mount Moriah to the east is the Mount of Olives, 2,682 feet above the Mediterranean to the west and 3,982 feet above the Dead Sea to the east. The city

No. 69. A Tower on the Walls of Jerusalem.

with these tremendous natural defences of deep ravines and surrounding mountains made a very strong fastness.

Zion stands with hills surrounded.

In addition to the national defence it was surrounded by walls with towers, and was about 4½ miles in circumference.

No. 70. The Kidron Valley.

(From J. D. Davis' "Dictionary of the Bible", by permission of the Westminster Press.)

The city has had a very chequered career. Some of its varying fortunes are seen in the following events:

1913 (?) B. C. Melchizedek meets Abraham.
1442 (?) B. C. Judah sets the city on fire.
1049 B. C. David captures it.

1011-04	Solomon builds the Temple.
970 B. C.	Shishak of Egypt plunders it.
884 B. C.	Philistines and Arabians plunder it.
808 B. C.	The Ten Tribes plunder it.
710 B. C.	Sennacherib of Assyria besieges it.
610 B. C.	Pharaoh-Necho of Egypt besieges it.
586 B. C.	Nebuchadnezzar destroys it.
536 B. C.	The Exiles begin to rebuild it.
536-16	Zerubbabel rebuilds the Temple.
444 B. C.	Nehemiah rebuilds the city walls.
332 B. C.	Alexander the Great of Macedonia captures it.
320 B. C.	Ptolemy Soter of Egypt captures it.
170 B. C.	Antiochus Epiphanes of Syria destroys it.
63 B. C.	Pompey of Rome captures the restored city.
44 B. C.	Antipater, the Edomite, rebuilds its walls.
19 B. C.	Herod the Great begins restoring the Temple.
30 A. D.	Christ, the King of the Jews, is crucified.
70 A. D.	Tatian of Rome destroys the city.
130 A. D.	Hadrian rebuilds it.
614 A. D.	The Persians capture it.
637 A. D.	The Saracens capture it.
1076 A. D.	The Seljukan Turks capture it.
1099 A. D.	The Crusaders capture it.
1187 A. D.	Saladin of Egypt captures it.
1517 A. D.	The Ottoman Turks capture it.
1917 A. D.	The English capture it.

In the New Testament period the city was divided into three main sections: The upper city on Mount Zion, the lower city on Acra and Bezetha, and Mount Moriah. The Temple stood on Mount Moriah, and Herod's palace on Mount Zion. The room where Jesus instituted the Lord's Supper was on Mount Zion, as was also the house of Caiaphas, where He was tried by the Jews. Otherwise Herod's headquarters were at Caesarea. Gethsemane was on the west slope of the Mount of Olives. Golgotha was outside of the lower city, north or west. The Pool of Siloam was at the south end of the Tyropaean Valley. The Pool of Bethesda was north of the Temple, near the sheep market. Six main roads led up to the city—one from the Shittim on the north, a second from Jericho on the east, a third from Bethlehem on the south, a fourth from Gaza on the southwest, a fifth from Emmaus on the west, and a sixth from Joppa on the northwest.

Jerusalem was the capital of the Theocratic Nation and is today the symbol of the city of God, both in the humble likeness of the Church here below and the glorious likeness of Heaven above.

> Jerusalem, thou city fair and high,
>   Would God I were in thee!
> My longing heart fain, fain to thee would fly,
>   It will not stay with me.
>   (J. M. Meyfarth.)

No. 71. Bethany and the Dead Sea.

(3) *Bethany.*—This little village lay on the east slope of the Mount of Olives, two miles from Jerusalem. It was the home of Martha and Mary and Lazarus and the scene of their hospitality to our Lord and His restoring Lazarus to life. It was the starting place of the royal entry on Palm Sunday and the nightly resting place of Jesus during the Passion Week prior to His arrest.

(4) *Jericho.*—Jericho was situated near the site of the Jericho destroyed by Joshua and rebuilt by Hiel 600 years later. In connection with the rebuilding by Hiel it is important to note that the curse upon the man who should rebuild it (Josh. 6: 26) was literally fulfilled (Kings 16: 34). Jericho was the scene of the cure of the blind Bartimaeus and Christ's visit to Zaccheus.

(5) *Ephraim.*—Ephraim was a city in the Wilderness, to which Christ retired with His disciples after having raised Lazarus from the dead. It lay five miles east of Bethel and 16 northeast of Jerusalem.

(6) *Emmaus.*—Emmaus was a village probably 8 miles west of Jerusalem, the scene of our Lord's conversation with the two disciples on Easter day (Luke 24).

b. A CITY OF SAMARIA.

(1) *Sychar.*—Sychar was a village of Samaria, about two miles east of Shechem. About ½ mile southwest of the village of Sychar was a well dug by Jacob nearly 1,800 years before. This was the place where Jesus, weary with his hot and dusty journey, had the memorable interview with the prodigal woman of Samaria. In this city He staid two days teaching.

c. THE CITIES OF GALILEE.

(1) *Nazareth.*—Nazareth was a little retired village in southern Galilee, the home of Joseph and Mary, the scene of the annunciation, the home of Jesus after the return from Egypt until His Baptism and the scene of His preaching to His neighbors and subsequent rejection by them. The city is set on a hill and has an almost perpendicular precipice, about 50 feet high, over which the infuriated townsmen were going to hurl Jesus (Luke 4: 29). The people of Galilee were regarded in contempt by the people of Judea because of their alleged lack of culture. The people of Nazareth were a special object of contempt even by the Galileans themselves, as can be inferred from the ques-

tion of Nathanael, himself a Galilean: "Can any good come out of Nazareth?" Philip, to whom the question was put, answered: "Come and see" (John 1:46).

(2) *Cana.*—Cana lay about nine miles to the northeast of Nazareth. It was the home town of the disciple Nathanael (John 21:2), the scene of Christ's first miracle (turning water into wine), and the healing of the nobleman's son who lay sick at Capernaum, 20 miles distant (John 4:46-54).

(3) *Capernaum.*—Capernaum was a city on the northwest shore of the sea of Galilee and the residence of Jesus during His two years of ministry in Galilee. This was the home also of Simon Peter and Andrew and Matthew the publican. Here Jesus had performed several of His miracles: restoring a demoniac (Mark 1: 21-28), curing Peter's wife's mother (Matt. 8: 14-17), healing a paralytic (Matt. 9: 1-8), raising Jairus' daughter to life (Matt. 9: 18:26) and healing the centurion's servant. Here Jesus taught in the synagogues, explained fasting, blasphemy and kinship. Here He argued with the Pharisees about the Bread of Life and the Sabbath and exposed their hypocrisy. This city, exalted unto Heaven by the fact that Jesus made His home there, is now no more. Its very site is uncertain. The doom which He announced upon it has been amply fulfilled (Luke 10: 15).

(4) *Nain.*—Nain was a city of Galilee, two miles south of Mount Tabor, where Jesus restored a widow's son to life (Luke 7: 11-17).

(5) *Dalmanutha.*—This is a village on the west shore of the Sea of Galilee, straight across the lake from Gergesa. The Lord came into the parts of Dalmanutha after having fed the 4,000 (Mark 8: 10).

d. A City of Perea.

(1) *Bethabara.*—Bethabara means House of the Ford. It was one of the principal fords of the Jordan. Its traditional site is east of Jericho. At this place Jesus was baptized by John the Baptist.

e. THE CITIES OF ITUREA-GAULANITIS.

(1) *Gergesa, Gadara, or Gerasa.*—This was one of the cities of Decapolis, a district lying east and southeast of the Sea of Galilee. Jesus had crossed over from Galilee into the country of the Gadarenes, and there He met a man who had a legion of demons. After Jesus had driven these out and permitted them to enter a herd of swine, the people of the neighborhood asked Him to depart from them (Luke 8: 26-39). Jesus did not really enter their city, nor did He ever come back to visit them.

(2) *Bethsaida.*—There was a Bethsaida in Galilee, the native city of Peter, Andrew and Philip, and also a Bethsaida in Gaulanitis, to the northeast of the Sea of Galilee. In His second year of ministry Jesus had withdrawn to a desert place belonging to Bethsaida (Luke 9: 10), and there He fed 5,000 who had followed Him. In His last year of ministry He healed a blind man near Bethsaida (Mark 8: 22-26).

(3) *Caesarea Philippi.*—This was a town near the source of the Jordan, the most northerly point of Christ's journeys. It was called Caesarea Philippi to distinguish it from the Caesarea in Samaria on the coast. The city on the coast had been built by Herod the Great in honor of the emperor. The city inland was built by Herod Philip the tetrarch, also in honor of the emperor and himself. At this place Peter acknowledged that Christ was the Son of God (Matt. 16: 13-16), and on one of the neighboring peaks of Hermon Christ was transfigured (Matt. 17: 1).

2. THE JOURNEYS OF CHRIST.

The opposition of the leaders against Him intensified from year to year. At the end of the first year Jesus had healed at Bethsaida a helpless man who had been sick for 38 years. Because He had performed this deed of mercy on the Sabbath the Pharisees, who had been watching Him with growing fear and hatred, used this as a pretext to accuse Him.

Jesus defended Himself with power (John 5:1-47). At the end of the second year the opposition was still bolder. His enemies brought a man with a withered hand into the synagogue on the Sabbath, that they might tempt Him to cure the man and thus bring Him to trial for Sabbath-breaking. He did cure the man, and the Pharisees did go out to counsel how they might destroy Him (Matt. 12:1-14). Jesus laid bare their hypocrisy in the plainest of terms (Matt. 15:1-20). At the end of the third year His enemies had organized their forces and succeeded in bringing Him to trial and execution. The last year of the earthly life of our Lord is the saddest, yet sweetest, story ever told. In this year Christ went up to Jerusalem to suffer and die for our sins. "He humbled Himself and became obedient unto death, even the death of the cross" (Phil. 2:8). "He was wounded for our transgressions, He was bruised for our iniquities" (Isa. 53:5).

About 60 per cent of the Gospel narrative is devoted to telling the events of His last year of ministry. This is about equally divided between the last year up to the time of His passion and the Passion Week. The story of the Passion Week occupies 25 of the 89 chapters of the Gospels, or 1,149 of the 3,679 verses (Peloubet's "Matthew," 244). A few pages are also devoted to the events of His Forty Days from resurrection to ascension.

a. THE LAST YEAR.

The events up to the Passion Week may be divided into two parts—the Galilean journeys and the Perean journeys.

(1). *The Galilean Journeys.*—The Galilean journeys did not confine themselves to Galilee, but radiated from Galilee. They were six in number:

The first journey, in June, 29, was toward Sidon, where Christ healed the Syro-Phoenician woman (Matt. 15:21-28).

The second journey, in July, was into Decapolis, where He

cured a deaf-mute, fed the 4,000 in the desert, and was asked by the Pharisees for a sign (Matt. 15:30—16:4).

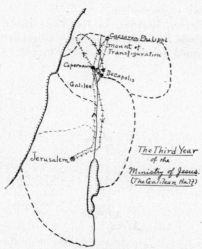

No. 72. The Third Year of Christ's Ministry: the Galilean Half.

The third Journey, in July, was across the Sea of Galilee by boat to the north shore. Landing there He walked up to Bethsaida and healed a blind man (Mark 8: 13-26).

The fourth journey, in Oct., was to celebrate the Feast of Tabernacles at Jerusalem (John 7: 1—10: 21) and to visit Martha and Mary at Bethany (Luke 10: 38-42).

The fifth journey, in Nov., was to Caesarea Philippi, where He foretold His death for the first time, was transfigured, and cured a demoniac boy (Luke 9: 18-43).

The sixth journey, in Nov., was in Galilee. Here He foretold His approaching death a second time (Matt. 17: 22-23), paid tribute money (Matt. 17: 24-27) and discoursed concerning Christian duties (Matt. 18).

(2) *The Perean Journeys.*—The Perean journeys were

three in number—the first from Galilee past Samaria into
Perea to Jerusalem, the second from Jerusalem into Perea to
Bethany, and the third from Bethany past Ephraim into
Perea and back to Jerusalem.

The first Perean journey, in Nov. and Dec., 29, was intended to include Samaria. But being rejected by the Samaritans, He turned into Perea (Luke 17:11-19). On His way

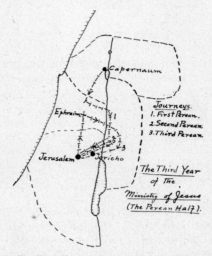

No. 73. The Third Year of Christ's Ministry: the Perean Half.

He healed the 10 lepers, sent forth the Seventy, rejoiced with
them at their success, gave the parable of the Good Samaritan, answered questions concerning divorce, blessed little
children, directed a young ruler to eternal life, gave the parable of the Laborers in the Vineyard. He arrived at Jerusalem in time to celebrate the Feast of Dedication (at the time
of our Christmas).

The second Perean journey, in Jan. and Feb., 30, is
crowded with warnings (vs. the Pharisees, hypocrisy, the

unforgivable sin and Herod), teachings (concerning divisions, salvation, the lost, forgiveness, faith, the nature and coming of His Kingdom) and parables (the Fruitless Fig Tree, the Great Supper, the Lost Sheep, the Lost Penny, the Prodigal Son, the Unfaithful Steward, Dives, the Unrighteous Judge and the Pharisee and the Publican). This routine of warning, teaching and speaking in parables was broken by only a few incidents. He refused to act as judge in a civil dispute (Luke 12: 13-21). He healed a woman on the Sabbath (Luke 13: 10-21). He healed a man with dropsy (Luke 14). He was called to Bethany to raise His friend Lazarus to life (John 11).

The third Perean journey, in March, 30, was marked by the following incidents: Withdrawing into Ephraim, foretelling for the third time His passion, healing two blind men at Jericho, visiting Zaccheus and being anointed by Mary at Bethany. The story of the healing of the two blind men at Jericho is interesting also because it contains two apparent discrepancies: Matthew (20:29-34) records that there were two blind men; Mark (10: 46-52), that there was one, whose name was Bartimæus; Luke (18: 35-43), that there was one. The larger number may include the smaller, hence this disagreement has been easy to reconcile. Matthew relates that the miracle occurred as they went out from Jericho; Luke, that it happened as He drew nigh unto Jericho. This has been explained this way, that there were two Jerichos, the old city destroyed by Joshua and the new city of Christ's day, that the miracle was performed between the two cities, and that Matthew mentions the old city while Luke the new city (Ylvisaker's "De Fire Evangelier," II, 128).

b.   THE LAST WEEK.

(1) *The Journey on Sunday.*—Christ came up from Jericho to Bethany on Saturday. At the home of Simon the Leper a supper was given in His honor. During the feast Mary,

the sister of Lazarus, came and anointed His head with
precious ointment (Matt. 26: 6-13). The disciples, especially Judas, were indignant at this waste. Jesus understood that the principle of her act was good and rebuked
the disciples. Judas Iscariot, angry at the reproof, left the
house, going to the chief priests to betray His Master. The
priests hated Jesus because He explained the Scriptures with
more truth and power than they could; He exposed their
false teachings and hypocritical lives; He claimed to be
the promised Messiah, but was so different from what they

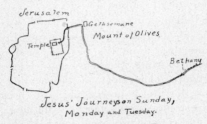

No. 74. Christ's Journeys on Sunday, Monday and Tuesday of the Passion Week.

expected the Messiah to be; and, finally, He claimed to be
the Son of God. They had for a long time been conspiring
to get Him to transgress some of their laws. His wonderful words of life, His miracles, His hold on the people,
His power to silence them in debate, awakened the most
intense jealousy and hatred in their hearts. The chief priest
advised His death. The priests, therefore, soon came to
terms with Judas, the price for the betrayal being 30 pieces
of silver, about $15.30 in our money, the usual price of a
slave.

On Palm Sunday morning Jesus sent His disciples to
fetch the ass on which He was to ride. Riding on this
humble beast, the Son of David, the King of Zion, proceeded
across the top of the Mount of Olives. This was during
the Passover season, the very day the paschal lamb was

to be selected. A census at the time of Nero showed that there were 2,700,000 Jews present at the Passover. Jerusalem was then filled with a multitude, which suddenly began to sing "Hosanna to the Son of David" and spread their garments and branches in His way. Going down Mount Olivet, Jesus passed Gethsemane and entered the Temple Gate. This was a day of triumph.

(2) *The Journey on Monday.*—Jesus retired to Bethany over night. On His way to Jerusalem on Monday morning He pronounced a curse on a barren fig tree (Matt. 21: 18-19). He proceeded to the Temple and cleansed it a second time, casting out those who bought and sold there. This was a day of authority.

(3) *The Journey on Tuesday.*—He spent the night again at Bethany and the day in the Temple. On His way to Jerusalem His disciples marvelled because the fig tree had withered at His curse (Mark 11: 20-26). In the Temple He was soon approached by a question as to His authority (Matt. 21:23-27). He answered by a counter question. He taught in parables—the Two Sons, the Wicked Husbandmen and the Marriage of the King's Son— but His enemies hardened their hearts. He replied to the questions of the Herodians as to tribute, the Sadducees as to resurrection, the Pharisees as to the Great Commandment, and put another counter question to the Pharisees. He invoked woe on the leaders, praised the widow's mite, was sought by the Gentiles, rejected by His own, prophesied the destruction of Jerusalem and foretold, for the fourth time, His own death. The chief priests and Judas met again in conspiracy. It was a day of conflict.

(4) *The Journey on Thursday.*—Wednesday was a day of retirement. On Thursday He was again in Jerusalem preparing for the Last Supper. The room where it was held was in a house on Mount Zion. With the Twelve about Him He instituted the Sacrament of the Lord's Supper, after which Judas went out to betray Him. The Eleven remained

with Jesus to hear His farewell discourses and His high priestly prayer before breaking up from the feast. It was a day of farewells.

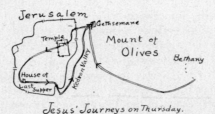

Jesus' Journeys on Thursday.

No. 75. Christ's Journeys on Thursday of the Passion Week.

(5) *The Journey on Friday.*—Having sung a hymn, Jesus and His disciples left the upper room and went in the darkness of night down the Kidron Valley to Gethsemane.

> Over Kidron Jesus treadeth
> To His passion for us all.

On the way He foretold His capture that night and Peter's denial. Around midnight He entered Gethsemane to pray, taking Peter, John and James with Him. For an hour He struggled in prayer and deepest agony of soul, even sweating blood, while His tired disciples slept.

> Go to dark Gethsemane,
>   Ye that feel the Tempter's power;
> Your Redeemer's conflict see,
>   Watch with Him one bitter hour;
> Turn not from His griefs away,
>   Learn of Jesus how to pray.

Judas, having meanwhile gone to the high priest, suddenly appeared with a company of Roman soldiers, armed and carrying torches. Judas betrayed Jesus with a kiss. They took Jesus to the palace of Annas and then to the house of Caiaphas to be tried by the Jewish Sanhedrin at daybreak. During the trial by the Jewish authorities He was denied thrice by Peter. Having been condemned by

No. 76. The Nailing to the Cross—Mark 15:24 (J. Fuhrich).

the Sanhedrin and spit upon and mocked by the Jews, He
was surrendered to the Roman governor, who had come up
from Caesarea during the Passover and was at his palace.
The charges before the Jews were, that He had said that He
would destroy the Temple and rebuild it in three days and
that He had spoken blasphemy. The charges before the
governor were, of course, quite different. They were three-
fold: That He had perverted the nation, refused to give
tribute to Caesar, and said that He Himself was Christ, a
king (Luke 23:2). Meanwhile Judas came with his blood
money and pronounced Jesus innocent. Pilate examined
Him and also pronounced Him innocent. As Herod was
in town and Christ was from Galilee, Pilate then turned Him
over to Herod, who questioned and mocked Him. When

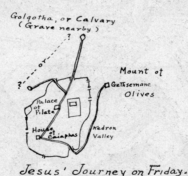

No. 77.   Christ's Journeys on Friday of the Passion Week.

Herod did not do anything more with Him Pilate thought
that he would excite the pity of the Jews by chastising Him.
He therefore placed Him with bleeding back before the
mob, saying "Behold the Man!" But they shouted "Crucify!"
Seeing they wanted blood, and that some prisoner might
be freed on the Passover, Pilate offered them the choice
between Jesus and Barabbas, an infamous murderer. They

No. 78. The Crucifixion—Mark 15:33 (G. Doré).
(Nos. 79 and 80 on page 102.)

cried: "Release Barabbas, crucify Christ!" Pilate washed his hands of the guilt and surrendered Jesus to be crucified. The trial over, they stripped Him, crowned Him with thorns, spit on Him, struck Him, mocked Him, forced Him to carry His cross, and crucified Him at Golgotha between two thieves. This was at 9 o'clock. At noon a darkness came over all the land. At 3 in the afternoon He died. Meanwhile He had spoken Seven Words. On the cross Pilate had written in Hebrew, Greek and Latin the accusation: Jesus of Nazareth the King of the Jews (I. N. R. I.). On account of the next day being the Passover Sabbath it was necessary to bury Him before night. The soldiers found that He was dead, but to make sure they ran a spear into His side. His disciples had fled. His nearest friends were not there to bury Him. Then Joseph of Arimathea and Nicodemus, secret disciples, begged that they might do so. There was no time for embalming. His body was placed in the tomb. A stone was rolled across the entrance. A heavy guard was set to watch that His disciples should not steal the body and then say that He had arisen. It was a day of suffering.

c. THE FORTY DAYS.

(1) *The Journeys on Resurrection Day.*—At Easter dawn Mary Magdalene and Mary the mother of James and Salome went to anoint His body. But He had arisen. An angel had rolled the stone away. The soldiers had fled. Jesus appeared at this time to Mary Magdalene in the garden (Mark 16: 9), a little later to the women returning from the sepulchre (Matt. 28: 9-10), still later, to Peter alone (Luke 24: 24), in the late afternoon to two disciples going to Emmaus (Luke 24: 13-31), and in the evening to the disciples, excepting Thomas, holding secret conference in Jerusalem (John 20: 19-25).

(2) *The Later Journeys.*—Jesus appeared on six other occasions after His resurrection. On Sunday evening, one week after Easter, He again met the disciples within closed doors,

Thomas also being present (John 20: 26-29). About two weeks later He appeared before seven disciples fishing on the Sea of Galilee (John 21). Soon afterwards He appeared unto the Eleven on a mountain in Galilee (Matt. 28: 16-20); to about 500 brethren at once (1 Cor. 15: 6); and to James alone, probably in Jerusalem (1 Cor. 15: 7); and, finally, 40 days after Resurrection Day, on Ascension Day, to all the disciples on the Mount of Olives (Luke 24: 50-51; Acts 1: 6-12).

———

Mention all of the cities visited by Christ. Locate them on the map. State some important incident in connection with each of the cities: Bethlehem, Jerusalem, Bethany, Jericho, Ephraim, Emmaus, Sychar, Nazareth, Cana, Capernaum, Nain, Dalmanutha, Bethabara, Gergesa, Bethsaida, Caesarea Philippi.

Describe the journeys of Christ during His last year. The six Galilean journeys. The three Perean journeys. The journey on Sunday of Passion Week. On Monday. On Tuesday. On Thursday. On Friday of Passion Week. Locate: Bethany, Mount of Olives, Gethsemane, Kidron Valley, the House of Caiaphas, the House of the Last Supper, the Palace of Pilate, the Temple of Golgotha and the grave where Christ was buried.

Describe the journeys on Resurrection Day. The six later journeys. What does your Catechism say about the ministry of Christ and the places visited by Him? Your Bible history? Find appropriate hymns in your hymnal bearing on this subject. Look up the Bible passages referred to in your lesson, and find additional references to this subject in the Bible. In what ways can the contents of this lesson help you in your Bible study? In your faith and works?

LESSON THIRTY. THE ROMAN WORLD IN THE TIMES OF THE APOSTLES.

1. THE POLITICAL DIVISIONS.

The Roman armies had conquered all the countries bordering on the Mediterranean Sea. The fate of these countries was to become subject kingdoms or provinces, paying

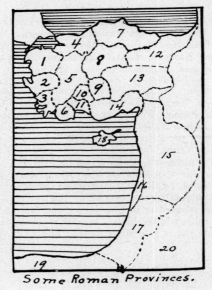

Some Roman Provinces.

No. 81. Some Roman Provinces.

1. Mysia.	8. Galatia.	15. Syria.
2. Lydia.	9. Lycaonia.	16. Phoenicia.
3. Caria.	10. Pisidia.	17. Palestine.
4. Bithynia.	11. Pamphylia.	18. Cyprus.
5. Phrygia.	12. Pontus.	19. Egypt.
6. Lycia.	13. Cappadocia.	20. Arabia.
7. Paphlagonia.	14. Cilicia.	

heavy tribute to Roman tax collectors. At the time of the apostles there was a general peace within the empire with considerable intercourse and commerce between various parts of the empire. We shall notice twelve of the provinces in which the apostles labored.

a. ACHAIA.

The name Achaia signifies in the New Testament a Roman province which included nearly the whole of modern Greece. Paul had worked in two of its famous cities —Athens and Corinth. He had visited Athens on his first journey from Macedonia (Acts 17), and there he delivered his famous oration on the Unknown God to the scholars of Greece. He also disputed with the Jews in the synagogue and the market place. After his stay at Athens he proceeded to Corinth. Corinth was then the commercial metropolis of the Mediterranean, due to the fact that nearly all the trade from the East to the West must pass through it. It was a wealthy and wicked city. Paul staid there 18 months, working as a tentmaker during the working days and preaching on the Sabbaths and Sundays. As was his custom he began preaching amongst the Jews, but being persecuted he wo 'ked more with the Gentiles (Acts 18: 1-16). He organized a Congregation there in 52. Soon afterward he is supposed to have dispatched a letter to the Galatians (Epistle). About May, 53, he wrote his First Epistle to the Thessalonians, and about August of the same year his Second Epistle to the Thessalonians. The Jews who opposed Paul had him arrested, but Gallio, the deputy of Achaia, dismissed the case (Acts 18: 12-23). When Paul left Corinth Apollos served for a while. By his eloquence Apollos attracted much attention, and some members of the Congregation began to create factions on account of these pastors, some professing loyalty to Paul, others to Apollos, still others to Peter and, finally, some to Christ. When Paul came to Ephesus on his third missionary journey the news of these strifes and other disorders in the Congregation

reached him at Ephesus, and he wrote, therefore, in 57, his
First Epistle to the Corinthians, promising also to come in
person.   Anxious to find out the effect of his letter, Paul
sent Titus ahead.   Meanwhile occurred the riot at Ephesus,
by which Paul was obliged to leave that city.   In Macedonia
he met Titus returning.   He learnt that there were people in
the Congregation who would not submit and denied his apostolic authority.   He answered these critics in his Second
Epistle to the Corinthians, defending his right to enforce
church discipline.   At New Year's, 58, he came again to
Corinth and remained three months, during which he wrote
his Epistle to the Romans (Acts 20: 3; Rom. 15: 25; 16: 1).

b. MACEDONIA.

The Macedonia of the New Testament lay to the north
of Achaia and was a Roman province including Thessaly
and Illyria.   It was the first part of Europe that had received the Gospel directly from Paul.   On his second journey he had visited five of its cities—Philippi (Acts 16:
12-40), Amphipolis (Acts 17:1), Apollonia (Acts 17:1),
Thessalonica (Acts 17:1-9) and Berea (Acts 17:10-13).
On his third journey also he visited this province.   The
Macedonians receive much praise for their Christian virtues.   The openmindedness of the Bereans and the liber-
ality of the Philippians are commended.   Paul's affection
for the Thessalonians is stated most positively (1 Thess.
2: 8, 17-20; 3: 10).

c. CAPPADOCIA.

This highland province of Asia Minor is interesting
to Bible readers chiefly for two reasons: Some of its Jewish residents were present in Jerusalem at Peter's first Pentecost sermon (Acts 2:9), and some of its Christian residents were readers of his First Epistle (1 Pet. 1:1).

d. CILICIA.

This province of Asia Minor, bordering on the Mediterranean Sea, is mentioned several times in connection with Paul. Its capital, Tarsus, was his native town (Acts 9:11, 30; 21:39; 22:3). He visited the province soon after his conversion (Acts 9:30; Gal. 1:21) and on his second missionary journey (Acts 15:41).

e. GALATIA.

Galatia was a province occupying the north central part of Asia Minor. Its people were Gauls, who had emigrated from France and occupied the country by force in 280 B. C. In 189 B. C. they had been defeated by the Romans and made subject to Rome. Paul visited Galatia on his second missionary journey (Acts 16: 6). On account of sickness he was obliged to remain there for some time, during which he organized Congregations (Acts 16:6; Gal. 4:13-16). He visited his Churches again on his third journey to strengthen them (Acts 18: 23; Gal. 1: 9; 4: 16; 5: 3). There were many Jews in the province. Most of these remained Jews in faith; others became Christians; and some, who were called Judaizers, combined the two religions, laying special stress on the Law. These Judaizers worked very hard to undo Paul's work in Galatia. When the news of the falling away of the Galatian Christians reached Paul at Corinth he wrote them his Epistle to the Galatians, proving that they could not be justified if they went back to the Law. Justification is by faith. Peter's First Epistle is also addressed to Christian pilgrims in Galatia (1 Pet. 1: 1).

f. LYCAONIA.

Lycaonia was a very small inland province of Asia Minor south of Galatia and north of Cilicia. Paul preached in three of its cities—Iconium, Derbe and Lystra—on his first missionary journey. At Iconium he was assaulted by Jews and Gentiles (Acts 14:1-5), and at Lystra he was stoned and thrown out of the city as dead (Acts 14:8-19).

g. LYDIA.

Lydia was a small province in Southwestern Asia Minor. Its inhabitants were originally Semitics (Gen. 10: 22), descendants of Lud, the son of Shem. Their most famous king was Croesus, who is proverbial for his wealth. In 546 B. C. the land was subdued by Cyrus the Great of Persia. The burning of the capital, Sardis, in 499 B. C., by the Greeks, was the immediate cause of the war against Greece by Persia. In 334 it became a province of Greece and in 190 a province of Rome. Five of its cities were noted in New Testament history. Thyatira, Sardis and Philadelphia were seats of three of the seven Churches of Asia addressed in the book of Revelation (Rev. 2: 8—3: 13). Ephesus was one of the largest cities of the Roman world, a political, commercial and religious center. This city had a theater that could seat 50,000, and a temple of the Greek goddess Diana which was reckoned as one of the seven wonders of the world. Paul visited Ephesus in 53 on his homeward voyage to Jerusalem (Acts 18:19-21). He left behind him two Corinthian Christians, Aquila and Priscilla, man and wife. Soon afterwards, Apollos, an Alexandrian Christian, also arrived there to preach the Gospel. Paul returned in 54 and remained three years (Acts 19: 1-20). From there he wrote, in 57, his First Epistle to the Corinthians. In this letter he mentions that he had fought with beasts on the city race course (1 Cor. 15: 32). Owing to a riot led by Demetrius, a silversmith, who made silver shrines for Diana, and whose trade was suffering by Paul's preaching, he had to depart in haste from Ephesus. When he returned from his visit to Greece, he hastened past Ephesus, but stopped at Miletus and sent for the elders of the Ephesian Church, warning them against false teachers (Acts 20: 1-12.). At a later period Timothy served as pastor there (1 Tim. 1: 3). Still later, the apostle John became bishop there, exerting a wide influence, which included the leveling of the temple of Diana to the ground. Ephesus is one of the seven Churches mentioned in Revelation (2:1-7). The island Patmos lies off the coast of

Lydia about 40 miles. To this island the apostle John had been banished in 95, an exile for the Word of God (Rev. 1:9). Later he was allowed to return to Ephesus. At Patmos he penned his book called Revelation. At Ephesus he wrote his three Epistles and his Gospel.

h. MYSIA.

Mysia was a small province in the extreme northwest of Asia Minor, separated from Europe by the Hellespont and the Propontis (now the Sea of Marmora). Three of its cities are connected with New Testament history— Troas, Assos and Pergamos. Troas was the ancient Troy, made famous by Homer's "Iliad." On his second missionary journey Paul was moved by the Holy Spirit to come down to Troas. From there he could dimly see the coasts of Europe on the west. There a vision appeared unto him of a man of Macedonia calling to him: "Come over and help us" (Acts 16: 6-11). On his third return journey Paul sailed from Philippi in Macedonia back to Troas, remaining there a week with the Church. One night while Paul was preaching a young man named Eutychus, sunk down in sleep, fell out of a window and was taken up dead. He was restored to life again by the apostle (Acts 20: 6-12). Paul continued on foot to the city of Assos, 19 miles from Troas. At Assos he was taken on board his ship, bound for Palestine (Acts 20: 13-16). Pergamos was the most important city of Mysia, famous for its temples and libraries. Parchment, called in Greek pergamene, gets its name from Pergamos, because it was first obtained there. The third of the seven epistles of John in the book of Revelation was addressed to the Church of Pergamos (Rev. 2: 12-17). This letter states that Satan's seat was located there, meaning, no doubt, that it was a stronghold of idolatry and wickedness.

i. PHRYGIA.

Phrygia was a narrow, high inland province of Asia Minor to the east of Lydia and Mysia and to the west of

Galatia. Three of its towns are named in the New Testament—Colosse, Laodicea and Hierapolis. Antiochus the Great had settled 2000 Jewish families in this province from Babylonia and Mesopotamia (Josephus' "Antiquities," 12: 3-4). At the first Pentecost Jews from Phrygia heard the Gospel in their Phrygian tongue (Acts 2: 8-10). Paul passed through Phrygia on his second and third missionary journeys (Acts 16: 6; 18: 23). There was a Church at Colosse, which may have been formed by Paul. At any rate, while he was a prisoner at Rome in 62, he was visited by two Colossians—Epaphras, a preacher at Colosse, and Onesimus, a runaway slave (Col. 1: 7; 4: 9, 12; Philemon 9). From Epaphras he had learned that the Congregation was threatened by a dangerous teaching, partly heathen, partly Christian (Col. 2: 8, 16, 20). Christian freedom was set aside for asceticism. Christ was set aside for angels. Paul therefore wrote his Epistle to the Colossians, which he sent by Tychicus, who was about to return to Ephesus together with Onesimus. In this letter he states that he is also zealous for the Christians in Hierapolis and Laodicea (Col. 4: 13). Laodicea was one of the seven Churches addressed in the book of Revelation (Rev. 3: 14-22).

j. PONTUS.

Pontus, located in Northwestern Asia Minor, had been an independent kingdom from about 400 to 63 B. C. Rome had reduced it to a province with limited boundaries and powers. Jews from Pontus were at Jerusalem at the first Pentecost (Acts 2: 9). Aquila, Paul's fellow tentmaker and preacher at Corinth, Ephesus and Rome, was born in Pontus (Acts 18: 2). Peter addressed the Christians of Pontus in his First Epistle (1 Pet. 1: 1).

k. CYPRUS.

Cyprus is an island in the Northeast Mediterranean, considerably larger than the state of Delaware or Long Island, New York. It is first mentioned in Gen. 10: 4 as Chittim, from the name of one of the descendants of Japheth. It was colonized in early times by Greeks (Japhetics) and Phoenicians (Hamitics) and later by Jews (Semitics). The ships of Chittim are mentioned in the prophecies of Balaam (Num. 24:24), Isaiah (Isa. 23:1, 12), Ezekiel (Ezek. 27: 6) and Daniel (Dan. 11:30). It was the birthplace of Barnabas, the assistant of Paul (Acts 4:36). It early received the Gospel and passed it on to others (Acts 11: 19-20; 21:16). It was visited by Paul on his first missionary journey (Acts 13:4-13).

1. SPAIN.

This is the present country of that name, but at the time of Christ only a Roman province. In the Old Testament it was known as Tarshish and was noted for its silver, iron, tin and lead (1 Kings 10:22; 2 Chron. 9:21; Isa. 2:16; Jer. 10:9; Ezek. 27:12). Jonah had tried to flee to Tarshish in order to escape delivering the Lord's doom upon Nineveh (Jonah 1:3). Paul desired to visit Spain in order to preach the Glad Tidings there at the uttermost western end of the ancient world (Rom. 15:24, 28).

2. THE JOURNEYS OF PAUL.

The Gospels tell about the work of Christ in His humiliation; the Acts of the Apostles tells about His work after His exaltation. Christ promised to send His Holy Spirit. Acts shows how the Holy Spirit works—calling, gathering, enlightening, sanctifying the whole Christian Church on earth and preserving it in union with Jesus Christ in the one true faith. All of the work of salvation may be said to be performed by the Holy Spirit. The Holy Spirit works ordinarily through the Means of Grace (the Word of God and the Sacraments). The Means of Grace are administered by the Church through men. Therefore, it may also be said that the work of salvation is performed by the Holy Spirit through men, "ambassadors in Christ's stead". Acts of the Apostles is a continuation of the Gospel story. It shows

how Christ still is at work, sending His Spirit, Who estab-
lishes the Church and sends out men with the Means of
Grace.

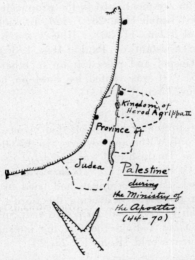

No. 82.   Palestine in the Times of the Apostles.

Acts 1: 4-26 records that there were 120 disciples at
prayer awaiting the outpouring of the Holy Ghost. The
Holy Ghost descended on them on Pentecost morning. What
a change came over the unbelieving, helpless, hopeless, fear-
ing disciples. Peter, who had denied Christ, stood up and
boldly preached Him (Acts 3). All of the disciples seem
to have gone out in Jesus' name preaching with spirit and
power. Not all are mentioned. Not a word, for example,
is recorded in Acts about Matthew except his being listed
as one of the Twelve. And yet we know that Matthew must
have been at work just as well as Peter and John, for
he was the instrument in recording the first Gospel. Most
of the missionary activity recorded in Acts and the Epistles

is attributed to Paul. The work of the others, with the exception of a few notices, is unrecorded. All, with the exception of John, are said to have died as martyrs. Not even tradition is agreed in the field of activity of each of the Twelve. The list of the Twelve Apostles with their probable fields is as follows:

Apostles	Fields
(1) Simon Peter	Judea, Asia Minor, Babylon, Rome
(2) Andrew, his brother	Asia Minor, Greece, etc.
(3) James the Great, son of Zebedee	Jerusalem
(4) John, his brother	Ephesus
(5) James the Less	Jerusalem
(6) Jude, or Lebbeus Thaddeus, his brother	Libya, Arabia, etc.
(7) Philip	Phrygia, etc.
(8) Nathanael Bartholomew	India, Phrygia, Armenia, etc.
(9) Thomas	Persia, India, Ethiopia
(10) Matthew	Judea, Ethiopia, Persia, etc.
(11) Simon Zelotes	Africa, Britain, etc.
(12) Matthias	Judea, Russia

The work of the apostles was at first limited to Jerusalem. For seven years they did not seem to realize that the Gospel was intended for Gentiles as well as for Jews, and for all the world as well as for Jerusalem. During these seven years the Congregation at Jerusalem increased in numbers to such an extent that the Twelve could not take charge of all of the work. An organization for charity work was effected in the election of deacons (Acts 6: 1-7). The Jews continued their hostility. Peter and John were imprisoned and forbidden to preach in Jesus' name (Acts 4). Stephen the deacon was stoned (Acts 6—7). The whole Congregation was scattered by the persecutors. One of these, Saul, better known as Paul, carried the persecution even beyond the confines of Jerusalem and Palestine. But on his way to persecute the Christians of Damascus he was converted and became the chief apostle (Acts 9), the "Apostle to the Gentiles." The scattering of the Congregation in Jerusalem

turned out to be a blessing, for it brought the Gospel to
Judea and Samaria and all other parts where the fleeing
Christians went (Acts 8). Philip the deacon baptized an
Ethiopian eunuch (Acts 8:26). Peter baptized the Roman
Cornelius (Acts 9—11). The Gospel spread to Antioch,
where the disciples first (in 42) became known as Christians, and even to Rome. Agrippa killed James the Great
by the sword and imprisoned Peter in 44 (Acts 12). In
63 the Jews conspired against James the Less and threw
him down from the pinnacle of the Temple. John was
*in his old age exiled to the Island of Patmos. Emperor
Nerva gave him his freedom, and he went back to Ephesus,
where he served as bishop until 100.

The work of Paul is tremendous in its scope, influence
and interest. It may be grouped under five headings:
Early Journeys, First Missionary Journey, Second Missionary Journey, Third Missionary Journey, and Last Journeys.

a. PAUL'S EARLY JOURNEYS (37-45).

The early journeys of Paul were 6 in number and cover 8
years of time:

(1) *From Jerusalem to Damascus.*—On this trip Paul
was converted (Acts 9).

(2) *From Damascus to Arabia.*—Paul spent three years
in retirement and meditation (Gal. 1:17-18).

(3) *From Arabia to Jerusalem.*—Some of the Jews at
Damascus laid a plot to kill Paul, but he escaped by being
lowered down from the walls in a basket and then hastened
on to Jerusalem to meet Peter. He staid with Peter two
weeks (Acts 9:27; 22:17-21; Gal. 1:18-19).

(4) *From Jerusalem to Tarsus.*—Tarsus was Paul's home
town, to which he retired (Acts 11:24).

(5) *From Tarsus to Antioch.*—Through Barnabas he received a call to Antioch, where he began his wonderful career
(Acts 11:19-30).

(6) *From Antioch to Jerusalem.*—After a year of preach-

ing at Antioch Paul and Barnabas went to Jerusalem over-
land, bringing with them a contribution for the poor.

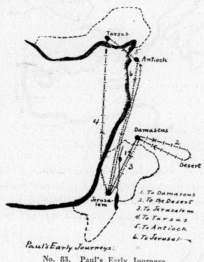

No. 83.   Paul's Early Journeys.

b. Paul's First Missionary Journey (45-46).

Barnabas and Paul, with Mark as an assistant, were called
to preach to the heathen. They embarked at Seleucia and set
sail for Cyprus, the early home of Barnabas (Acts 4: 36).
From Salamis to Paphos, about 100 miles, they walked,
preaching in the synagogues. At Paphos Paul rebuked a fortune teller and smote him with blindness (Acts 13: 6-13).
They embarked again for the mainland, visiting Antioch in
Pisidia, Iconium, Lystra and Derbe. Paul was believed by
the Gentiles at Antioch, driven out by the Jews at Iconium
and stoned at Lystra. On his homeward trip he confirmed the
believers (Acts 14: 25-28). This ended, not the first missionary journey of Paul, but his first missionary journey
after his official call as an apostle.

No. 84. Paul's First Missionary Journey.

c. PAUL'S SECOND MISSIONARY JOURNEY (51-53).

The report of the first missionary journey made it plain to many that God had opened the door of faith unto the Gentiles. Yet certain Jews insisted that circumcision and observance of

No. 85. Paul's Second Missionary Journey.

the Jewish ceremonial law were essential to salvation. Paul and Barnabas resisted this claim most emphatically. A committee consisting of these two and others were sent to Jeru-

salem to confer with the apostles there. The Council of
Jerusalem, after a memorable debate, decided for the Christian liberty championed by Paul (Acts 15). Titus returned
with Paul.

Paul proposed to Barnabas that they revisit the places
from the first tour. Barnabas wanted to take Mark along.
Paul refused. Barnabas and Mark thereupon set out together for Cyprus (Acts 15: 37-39). Paul, taking Silas as
his companion, set out by land through Cilicia until he
reached Derbe, Lystra and Iconium. At Derbe he added
Timothy to his company. At Antioch he started on a new
track, which led him into Galatia and even to Troas, on
the coast. At Troas he met Luke the physician, who joined
his Gospel band. There he had a vision of the man calling
him to Macedonia. He went to Macedonia, brought the
Gospel work into Europe, won Lydia, a woman, as his first
convert, established thriving Congregations at Philippi,
Thessalonica, Berea, all in Macedonia, and proceeded on
to Athens and Corinth in Achaia. In Corinth he staid 18
months. There he wrote three of his Epistles—to the Galatians and the Thessalonians. On his homeward journey
Paul stopped at Ephesus, Rhodes and Jerusalem. At Ephesus he was urged to remain, but would not consent to do
so, although he promised to return if the Lord was willing
(Acts 18: 21). At Jerusalem he had a chance to meet at
the feast a great body of Jewish Christians and tell them
of his success in foreign missions, besides presenting the
poor in Jerusalem with the contributions from Europe that
he had collected.

d. Paul's Third Missionary Journey (54-58).

Paul soon set out a third time upon his old track in Asia
Minor. His heart was set on Ephesus this time. But first of
all he turned aside to visit his Churches in Galatia, sorely
troubled by Judaizers. At Ephesus he worked with great
power for three years. Near the close of his stay there, he

learnt about the disorders at Corinth and wrote his First Epistle to the Corinthians. Due to the influence of his preaching,
a great tumult was aroused in the name of the goddess Diana
by Demetrius the silversmith, whose trade was suffering on
account of the Gospel preaching.   Paul left Ephesus in order

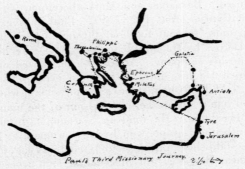

No. 86. Paul's Third Missionary Journey.

to visit Corinth. On his way he dispatched his Second
Epistle to the Corinthians. At Corinth he wrote to the
Romans. Having taken up contributions in the Churches for
the poor at Jerusalem he again, together with deputies, set
sail for Jerusalem, stopping at Philippi, Troas, Miletus and
Tyre.

e. PAUL'S LAST JOURNEYS.

The last journeys of Paul are less known than the great
missionary journeys, but full of interest and instruction.
There may have been seven such journeys.

(1) *As a Prisoner to Rome.*—Acts 21: 17 reports that
Paul and his companions were gladly received by the
brethren in Jerusalem. The day after his arrival he re-
hearsed before James and the elders the progress of the
missions. The elders had heard bad rumors about Paul's
rejection of Moses and proposed that Paul should set

himself right by the public performance of a Levitical
ceremony (Acts 21: 18-25). Paul consented to do so
on the principle of being careful not to cause a weaker
brother to stumble (Rom. 14: 21). Being recognized, he
was seized by a Jewish mob, who would have killed him

Paul's Last Journeys.

No. 87. Paul's Last Journey.

in the Court of the Gentiles had not the Roman temple guard
rescued him. The captain of the guard, pleased at hearing
Paul speak good Greek, granted his request to address the
people. Paul delivered an oration in Hebrew (Chaldee)
from the stairs at the fort. As he proceeded in describing
his mission to the Gentiles the fury of the mob knew no
bounds (Acts 21—22). He was scourged, tried before the
Sanhedrin, escorted under a strong guard to Caesarea, kept
prisoner there two years, defended his case before Herod
Agrippa II and appealed to Caesar. Since he had made this
appeal he was sent to Rome in bonds to be tried. He set
sail in 60 for Italy. This proved to be a most remarkable
voyage. The first part of the voyage was from Caesarea
to Myra in Lycia, via Sidon. Here he embarked upon another ship. This ship had to put in at Crete on account of

No. 88. Paul Writes from His Prison (R. van Ryn).

strong winds and suffered shipwreck at Malta. This is most vividly described by Luke, who was on board (Acts 27). They had to remain on Malta for 3 months until navigation opened in the spring. At Rome Paul was allowed considerable freedom. He wrote four Epistles from his prison, to the Ephesians, Colossians, Philemon and Philippians.

(2) *To Ephesus.*—Very little is known concerning Paul's trial. We do not even know whether he was tried before Nero or one of his representatives. In 63 he was released. Acts closes with Paul's first imprisonment at Rome. The Epistles have only an occasional allusion as to his later work. The order in which these visits were made can not be decided. From 1 Tim. 1: 3 it can be inferred that he had made a tour to his beloved Ephesus again.

(3) *To Macedonia.*—From 1 Tim. 1: 3 it can also be inferred that he had visited Macedonia again.

(4) *To Crete.*—He had touched at Crete on his voyage to Rome. Now he went there to organize a Church, leaving it in charge of Titus (Titus 1: 5).

(5) *To Nicopolis.*—He had determined to winter at Nicopolis (Titus 3:12).

(6) *To Troas.*—Paul had evidently passed through this place, for he wrote to Timothy asking him to bring the cloak he had left behind with Carpus, and to bring his books and especially his parchments (2 Tim. 4: 13).

(7) *A Prisoner to Rome.*—Paul was arrested again, some think at Ephesus, and brought to Rome accompanied by Titus, Tychicus and Luke. From Rome he wrote earnestly to Timothy to come bringing Mark with him. It is pleasant to note that Mark had at last found favor in his eyes (2 Tim. 4:9, 11). Paul was executed in 67.

———

What countries were subject to Rome at the time of Christ? What is meant by Roman province? Bound each of the following

provinces and tell some interesting facts about each: Achaia,
Macedonia, Cappadocia, Cilicia, Galatia, Lycaonia, Lydia, Mysia,
Phrygia, Pontus, Cyprus, Spain.

What book in the Bible especially tells about the work of the
apostles? Name the twelve apostles, and their respective fields of
labor. Follow in particular Peter from the first day of Pentecost
until his death, stating where he worked. Likewise the work of
John. Who was the chief of the apostles? Who was the thirteenth
apostle.

Describe in brief Paul's early journeys. Picture his conversion.
Describe his first missionary journey.
Picture the events at Lystra.

Describe his second missionary journey. Make believe you attended the council at Jerusalem, and give a report of the journey
that you took and the proceedings of the convention. Where was
Paul when he was asked to come over to Macedonia to give his help?

Describe Paul's third missionary journey. Imagining that you
were present at the tumult at Ephesus, describe the events that took
place.

Accompany Paul on his first journey as a prisoner to Rome. Mention his last journeys. How did he meet his death?

What does your Bible history say about the acts of the apostles,
and the countries visited by Peter, John, Paul and other apostles?
Find appropriate hymns in your hymnal bearing on this subject.
Look at the Bible passages referred to in your lesson, and find
additional references to this subject in the Bible. In what ways can
the contents of this lesson help you in your Bible study? In your
faith and works?

PART FOUR.

CHRONOLOGY OF THE BIBLE.

OUTLINE.

LESSON THIRTY-ONE. PLACE OF CHRONOLOGY.

Chronology is derived from the Greek words chronos—time, and logos—discourse. It is the science of the computation of time, here the investigation or arrangement of events in the order of time. It is impossible to get a historical perspective without chronology. Like geography, chronology has been called one of the eyes of historical study.

1. RELATION TO HISTORY.

History is derived from the Greek word historein—to examine into, to know by inquiry, to narrate. It is a systematic record of past events, especially the record of events in which man has taken part. It treats of the rise, growth and decay of the nations, the deeds of their men and women in peace and in war, in the home and in society, in industry and commerce, in religion and education, in intellectual and mechanical achievements, and everything else pertaining to man's life here on earth. It may be in the form of a story, in which particular attention is given to the narration of the events. It may also be in the form of a chronicle, in which particular attention is paid to the dates on which events took place. Or, it may be a philosophical study, in which particular attention is paid to cause and effects. If it deals only with the Bible record it is commonly called sacred history; if it deals with events outside of the Bible record, it is often called profane, or secular, history. Biblical history is here taken to include sacred history and as much of secular history as will throw light on the secular nations and events mentioned in the Bible.

Sacred history runs parallel with secular history from

Adam to John. After that the history of God's Old Covenant People (Jews) is known as the history of the Jews, and the history of His New Covenant People (Christians) is known as church history. The sons of God here on earth have always lived amongst the sons of men. They have been in the world, though in many respects not of the world.

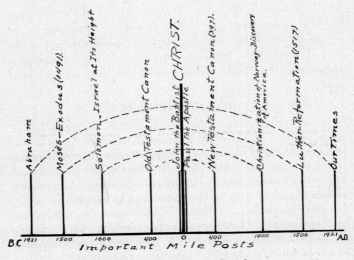

No. 89. The Center Point in Chronology.

Their history therefore runs parallel with that of secular history. It has matched secular history in friendly or hostile contact at a thousand places, and has influenced secular history and in turn been subject to influence.

Thus, dates are reckoned from the birth of Christ, the central point in history. Just as in creation "all things were made through Him" (John 1: 3), and in salvation "neither is there any other name under Heaven, that is given among men, wherein we must be saved" (Acts 4: 12), so also in the long stretch of time between creation and final judgment, the multitudinous events of history and the countless problems in the story of mankind, Christ looms up as the central figure. "All history before Him was a preparation for His coming, all history after Him is the execution of His work. He appeared in the fulness of time (Mark 1: 15; Gal. 4: 4), when everything was ripe for Him, and from His birth we justly date our chronology. He is the Desire of all nations. He came to 'fulfill the Law and the Prophets', and all the nobler aspirations and unconscious prophecies of the ancient world. He is the Prophet, Priest and King of redeemed humanity. All events must directly or indirectly, positively or negatively, nearly or remotely, advance His Kingdom, until He shall reign King of nations as He now rules King of saints in His Church. The great empires of the world are rising and passing away one by one, but His Kingdom is constantly advancing and will last forever" (Schaff's "Propaedeutics," 241).

2. RELATION TO BIOGRAPHY.

Biography is derived from the Greek words bios—life, and graphein—to write. It is the life account of a person. The lives of persons are also touched upon in history, in fact, all historical events center around persons, and persons are the most interesting facts of history. But history deals with persons more in mass; biography, more individually. In a history, one hardly gets so close to his heroes as he gets to his acquaintances on the street; in a biography, one is invited to go along into every nook and crook of life, at home and abroad, and is told even the innermost thoughts of his friend. Biography appeals to old and young. From the first dawn of intelligence to the last, biography never loses its magic interest. Nothing comes sooner home to the child than biographies of good men and great. Anything concerning the life of a person has an appeal: work, play, virtues, vices, friends, enemies, successes, disasters, rewards, punishments. Most fascinating of all lives, more fascinating

by far than Plutarch's famous "Lives," is that of the Bible
characters, particularly that of our Lord and Savior, Jesus
Christ, "the chiefest among 10,000," and "altogether lovely"
(Cant. 5: 10,16).

The life of Christ is the great and abidingly interesting
and profitable biography. He is the perfect Man, having
the image of God, unblemished by sin. He is true man, like
unto us, "born of a woman, born under the Law," yet without sin. He is also true God, begotten of the Father in
eternity, "for God so loved the world that He gave His
only begotten Son." He is our Savior and our Example.
He was God from all eternity, yet He became flesh and
dwelt amongst us. He was rich, yet for our sakes He became poor, that we through His poverty might become rich.
All we like sheep went astray; He came to seek and to save
that which was lost. He is the Good Shepherd Who gave
His life for His sheep. He had time for every individual.
He promised in no wise to cast out anyone who would come
to Him. He promised rest. He promised forgiveness of
sins, righteousness, peace, joy and salvation full and free.
His promises are all yea and amen. He has all power in
Heaven and on earth. He is with His disciples always.
No wonder the people of God never grow tired of hearing
in Scripture and sermon about the God-Man, their King
and Prophet and High Priest, their Master and Friend and
Brother; no wonder they ever honor Him in song and
praise, in prayer and thanksgiving:

> Praise to Thee, and adoration,
> Blessed Jesus, Son of God,
> Who, to serve Thine own creation,
> Didst partake of flesh and blood;
> Teach me that I never may
> From Thy fold or pastures stray,
> But with zeal and joy exceeding
> Follow where Thy steps are leading.

Let me never, Lord, forsake Thee,
E'en though bitter pain and strife
On my way shall overtake me;
But may I through all my life
Walk in fervent love to Thee,
In all woes for comfort flee
To Thy birth, Thy death and passion;
Till I see Thy full salvation (T. Kingo, 1689).

———

What is meant by chronology? In what sense can it be called one of the eyes of historical study?

What is meant by history? What is meant by story? By chronicle? What is the philosophical study of history? What is sacred history? Profane history? To what extent have sacred and profane history run parallel? To what extent have they influenced each other? What is the central date in history? Why?

What is meant by biography? Compare biography and history. What is the most fascinating of all lives? What is the most profitable biography? Why?

What does your Catechism say about the relation of chronology to history and biography? Your Bible history? Find appropriate hymns in your hymnal bearing on this subject. Look up the Bible passages referred to in your lesson, and find additional references to this subject in the Bible. In what ways can the contents of this lesson help you in your Bible study? In your faith and works?

LESSON THIRTY-TWO. DIFFICULTIES IN COMPUTING CHRONOLOGY.

In spite of the seemingly abundant material in the Bible and other ancient books, on monuments, coins, etc., relating to chronology, there are many and grave difficulties connected with computing and arranging a safe chronology. Some of the difficulties are: Lack of Complete Records, Lack of Fixed Time to Count from, Lack of Fixed Unit of Time, Overlappings and Discrepancies.

1. LACK OF COMPLETE RECORDS.

Very little of historical facts has been recorded. The ancient monuments have only a few inscriptions. The Bible only briefly mentions that Adam begat, in addition to Cain, Abel and Seth, other sons and daughters (Gen. 5: 4), but it is silent as to how many, what they were called, and other facts of vital interest. Genesis covers a period of over 2,000 years of history, but it spends 50 times as much space on Abraham as on the degenerate nations that were destroyed by the Flood. In the genealogy of Christ in Matt. I there is an omission of three names of Christ's royal ancestors, namely: Ahaziah, Joash and Amaziah. A whole century is here skipped in the royal lineage. Joram was really the great-great-grandfather of Uzziah, in spite of the fact that in Matt. 1: 8 it is said that "Joram begat Uzziah." This statement is not a mistake, but in accordance with a Hebrew use of the word beget. It might have reference to child, or to grandchild (Gen. 46: 12, 15, 18), or to great-grandchild (Gen. 46: 12, 21, 22), or to a still more remote offspring. Similarly, the word father might mean grandfather or forefather, as: Father Abraham; and the word son might mean grandson or other descendant, as: Jesus, the son of David.

No people of antiquity has such a complete written

record as have the Hebrews.   What other nations may have
had no one can tell.   The uncovered ancient cities reveal
many libraries, many books and inscriptions, but not one
has yet been able to make out from the recovered material
a record so chronologically complete as that of the Bible.
Besides, much of that which is written can not be relied
on, as many of the ancients were "some tall liars."   For
example, after Sennacherib's defeat at Jerusalem, he had a
monument put up saying that he had made Hezekiah a captive at Jerusalem, but not a word did he say about his own
disaster.   Berosus tells of ten primeval kings that ruled in
Babylonia for 432,000 years.

2. LACK OF FIXED TIME TO COUNT FROM.

We have a fixed time to count from—the birth of Christ.
We say 1 year after Christ (A. D.—Anno Domini, or, in
the year of our Lord), 2 years after Christ, 100 years A. D.,
1000 years A. D., 1918 A. D.   Similarly we reckon the time
before Christ as 1 year before Christ (B. C.), 2 years B.
C., 100 B. C., 1000 B. C., 1918 B. C., etc.   The birth of
Christ is our fixed point in history.

It was not so with the ancients.   The Greeks sometimes
reckoned from the first Olympic Games; at other times, in
the archonship of So and So, that is, during the reign of So
and So.   The Romans sometimes reckoned from the year of
the building of the city of Rome (A. U. C.—Annus Urbis
Conditae, the year of the building of the city) ; at other
times they reckoned an event as having happened in the con-
sulate of a certain person.   Every nation had its own way
of reckoning dates, but there was no point to count from.
No ancient nation, not even the Israelites, began with the
act of creation, calling that year 1, and continuing with the
next as 2, the one thereafter as 3, and so on in unbroken
line up to the coming of Christ.   The Jews, like other
nations, had various modes of dating, such as an important past event and in the reign of So and So.   For example,

in 1 Kings 6: "And it came to pass in the 480th year after
the children of Israel were come out of the land of Egypt,
in the fourth year of Solomon's reign over Israel, in the
month Ziv, which is the second month, that he began to build
the house of Jehovah."

3. LACK OF FIXED UNIT OF TIME.

The exact length of the solar year was variously determined by the ancients. The Hebrews observed the lunar
month of 29.5 days, sometimes 12 and at other times 13
months making one year. The Romans observed a year of
365 days, whereas the year is actually 365 days, 5 hours, 48
minutes and 45.5 seconds, a trifle less than 365¼ days, in
length. In 45 B. C. Julius Caesar found that the Roman
calendar had run behind three months, thus making spring
occur in summer. He therefore reformed the calendar by
making the year have 445 days, the three succeeding years
365 days each, followed by one of 366 days. His year
was a little over 11 minutes too long, or about ¾ of a
day for each century. This made a loss of three days
for each 400 years, and each succeeding century started
farther and farther behind time. In 1582, by order of Pope
Gregory XIII the Julian Calendar was reformed, so that
Oct. 4th of that year became Oct. 15th, and to avoid future
difficulty the last year of each century three times out of
four should not be a leap year. Only such century years
as are divisible by 400 should be reckoned as leap years.
Thus, 1900 was not a leap year, but 2,000 will be. At the
present time Russia and Greece still follow the old style of
Julian reckoning and are about two weeks behind the rest
of Christendom in their datings.

In addition to not having an exact and fixed measure-
ment for the solar year, the ancients did not agree on the
beginning of the year and the length of the months. The
Hebrew sacred year began with the Passover, around the
first of April; the civil year began with the Feast of Trum-

pets, six months later (Ex. 12: 1-51; Lev. 23: 24; Num. 29: 1). The Roman year began April 21st. The Babylonian year began Feb. 26th; the Assyrian, in March; the Syrian, Sept. 1st; the Mohammedan, July 16th. (Cf. the present Chinese New Year.)

4. OVERLAPPINGS.

Cases of overlappings are found in the Bible as well as in secular books. In the genealogy of Christ already referred to we note not only omissions, but also overlappings. Matt. 1: 17 reads: "So all of the generations from Abraham unto David are 14 generations; and from David unto the carrying away to Babylon are 14 generations; and from the carrying away to Babylon unto Christ are 14 generations." Here are then 42 generations assumed. Yet the list of generations enumerated in Matt. 1:1-16 does not give 42 generations, but only 40. The list is as follows:

1. Isaac	1. Solomon	1. Jechoniah
2. Jacob	2. Rehoboam	2. Shealtiel
3. Judah	3. Abijah	3. Zerubbabel
4. Perez	4. Asa	4. Abiud
5. Hezron	5. Jehoshaphat	5. Eliakim
6. Ram	6. Joram	6. Azor
7. Amminadab	7. Uzziah	7. Sadoc
8. Nahshon	8. Jotham	8. Achim
9. Salmon	9. Ahaz	9. Eliud
10. Boaz	10. Hezekiah	10. Eleazar
11. Obed	11. Manasseh	11. Matthan
12. Jesse	12. Amon	12. Jacob
13. David	13. Josiah	13. Joseph
14. Solomon	14. Jechoniah	14. Christ.

From Abraham to Isaac is one generation, and from Abraham to David are only 13 generations, not 14 generations, unless either Abraham is taken along as one generation or Solomon's name is repeated. There are but 13 generations mentioned from the Babylonian Capitivity to Christ, unless Jechoniah's name be repeated. In that case there is an overlapping—the last generation of one list overlaps the first of the following list (See the names underlined in the table). In the same manner parts of a day were often by the Hebrews reckoned whole days, or parts of a year reckoned whole years. For example: Christ was three days in the grave—Friday evening, all of Saturday and Sunday morning.

An interesting example of overlapping in secular history is that of ancient Egypt. It is customary to divide the history of Egypt into three periods—the Old Empire, the Middle Empire and the New Empire. In the Old Empire the pyramids were built, in the Middle Empire Jacob moved to Egypt, and in the New Empire the Israelites were oppressed and escaped. Manetho reckons 30 dynasties from the accession of the first king to the fall of the New Empire, in 345 B. C. Rawlinson has shown in his "Ancient History" (78) that in the Old Empire there existed up to six kingdoms at the same time, just as there exists today in the Austrian Empire two kingdoms side by side, and in the German Empire four kingdoms and other political divisions, and in the United States 48 states, besides colonies. If Egypt had six kingdoms existing side by side, then Manetho's dynasties are not in every case successive, but parallel. The dynasties overlapped. Historians who accept this overlapping as a fact shorten the history of Egypt; those who do not accept this explanation, lengthen it.

5. APPARENT DISCREPANCIES.

Discrepancies are disagreements as to facts. Such disagreements are not only quite possible, but highly probable. When two persons set out to write about a certain thing, they are almost sure to disagree on certain details. Take the case of the great newspapers with their immense facilities for getting at the facts. How often do they not differ from one another in presenting the news and even contradict themselves in the same number. During the recent attempt of the United States to capture the Mexican bandit Villa, for example, he was reported killed, buried, exhumed, captured, allowed to escape, seen in various parts of this country, etc. Not all of these reports could be true. Yet disagreements need not be contradictions or mistakes. There are apparent discrepancies in the Bible, but no errors in the original text. Some of these discrepancies are indeed very puzzling and hard to explain, but we are not ready to conclude that there are any mistakes in the original text. Our understanding is only relative at best, and even the most learned understand only in part. Furthermore, our understanding is progressive. We understand better at maturity than at childhood. Some day we hope to know as we are known. However, in all things the knowledge of which is necessary to salvation, the Bible is amply and perfectly clear, and there is no contradiction or variation of sense.

The chief discrepancies are found in parallel passages. For example, one of the most difficult of these disagreements is the statement in 1 Kings 6: 1 that the Temple was begun 480 years after the Exodus and Acts 13: 20, where Paul assigns to the Judges "about the space of 450 years." This apparent contradiction has caused much dismay and speculation. Some of the attempts at a solution will be stated in Lesson Thirty-Five.

In addition to the chronological disagreements just noted, there is another class of disagreements which have made it hard for historians to make a safe chronology. The Septuagint has already been mentioned as the oldest Greek translation of the Old Testament. Another old translation —of the five books of Moses only—is the Samaritan Pentateuch. These two translations ought to agree with the original Hebrew text in chronology, but in some places they do not. Nobody knows why this is so. This difference between the original text and the translations has led to much discussion and vain speculation. Some historians follow the Hebrew text, others the Septuagint or the Samaritan, still others combine the three sources or disregard all of them. On this account there is a most unpleasant variety of estimates on all dates preceding the foundation of the Temple. Estimates and guesses become more varied and bewildering the further back the chronologist is working. Thus, with respect to the age of creation, the dates vary from less than 4000 B. C. to more than 6,000,000,000 B. C. Des Vignoles has collected over 200 estimates on the date of creation ("L'art de verifier les dates," I, 27-36, Herzog's "Real-Encyklopädie," XVIII, 421, "The New International Cyclopaedia," V, 300).

What materials outside of the Bible relating to chronology do we have? Name some of the principal difficulties connected with computing a safe chronology.

What ancient people has the most complete written records? Did they have complete records? Explain and illustrate. What is the fixed time that we count from? Did the ancients count from the same point in history? Give examples.

Discuss the lack of fixed unit of time. How long is our solar year? What was the Julian Calendar? The Georgian Calendar? Why are Russia and Greece about two weeks behind us in date? On what day did the ancient Hebrews begin their year? The Greeks? The Romans? The Egyptians?

What is meant by overlappings? Give an example of overlapping from Matt. 1:1-17. Explain how the forty generations enumerated can be forty-two. Give an example of overlapping from secular history.

What is a discrepancy? Are there any real discrepancies in the Bible? Give an example of an apparent discrepancy. What is the date for the creation of the world agreed (?) upon by the scientists?

What does your Bible history say about the difficulties of computing chronology? Look up the Bible passages referred to in your lesson, and find additional references to this subject in the Bible. In what ways can the contents of this lesson help you in your Bible study? In your faith and works?

LESSON THIRTY-THREE.   SYSTEMS OF CHRO-
NOLOGY.

The present method of dating everything B. C. or A. D. began with the Roman Abbot Dionysius (556 A. D.), who in his Easter tables counted from the birth of our Lord. He reckoned that Christ was born 750 years after the founding of the City of Rome and called the year of His birth 0. It has now become established that Rome was founded 754 years before the Christian era and that Christ also was born four years earlier than the date ascribed to Him by Dionysius. He was born 4 B. C., instead of 0. Instead of making the corrections necessary due to this error, chronologists found it convenient to date His birth back four years to 4 B. C., or rather, Dec., 5 B. C., instead of letting it occur at 0. He appears thus to have been born about four years before His own era.

1. IN GENERAL.

Considering the many and serious difficulties connected with chronology, it is quite remarkable that the Bible chronology is so well established as it is. The reader should bear in mind that no system of chronology is absolutely authoritative in all its parts. The question of date in some parts of the Bible can perhaps never be solved to the satisfaction of everybody. No system of chronology is in any sense a part of the Bible, although any good system is of untold value in furnishing a skeleton outline of history.

2. USSHER'S.

The Received Chronology of the Bible is that prepared by Archbishop Ussher in 1650 and since then accepted by most English Bible readers as correct or nearly so. It is found in the margins of many of the Authorized Bibles, but was rejected by the revisers as being inaccurate in many particulars. Ussher followed the Hebrew and Greek texts and is considered even by recent chronologists, such as W. J. Beecher, as being in most points admirably correct. Other chronologists may perhaps have prepared better tables than Archbishop Ussher, but this remains yet to be proved and

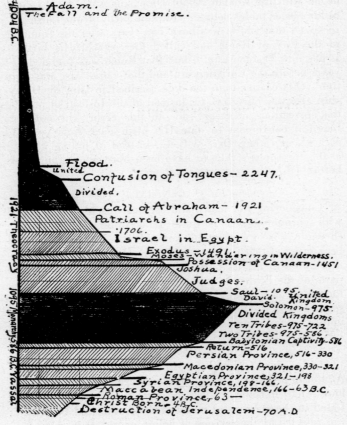

No. 90. 4000 Years of Bible Chronology.

accepted by the English reading public. Since the Usserian (Ussher's) tables are still acknowledged as being in the main correct and trustworthy and no other system is at all likely soon to challenge it in general trustworthiness and popularity, it is profitable for the Bible student to acquaint himself with its principal divisions and dates. These will be mainly followed in the following tables. (For greater detail see Appendix).

NO. OF YEARS	DATES	PERIODS
2083	1. BEFORE THE FOUNDING OF ISRAEL.	4004 B. C.-1921 B. C.
1656	a. ANTEDILUVIAN AGE.	4004 B. C.-2348 B. C.
427	b. POSTDILUVIAN AGE.	2348 B. C.-1921 B. C.
101	(1) *Period of Union.*	2348 B. C.-2247 B. C.
326	(2) *Period of Dispersion.*	2247 B. C.-1921 B. C.
1917	2. DURING THE OLD COVENANT.	1921 B. C.- 4 B. C.
826	a. THEOCRACY.	1921 B. C.-1095 B. C.
215	(1) *Period of Patriarchs.*	1921 B. C.-1706 B. C.
215	(2) *Period of Bondage.*	1706 B. C.-1491 B. C.
40	(3) *Period of Wandering.*	1491 B. C.-1451 B. C.
16	(4) *Period of Conquest.*	1451 B. C.-1435 B. C.
340	(5) *Period of Judges.*	1435 B. C.-1095 B. C.
509	b. MONARCHY.	1095 B. C.- 586 B. C.
120	(1) *Period of Union.*	1095 B. C.- 975 B. C.
389	(2) *Period of Division.*	975 B. C.- 586 B. C.
582	c. DEPENDENCY.	586 B. C.- 4 B. C.
70	(1) *Period under Babylonia.*	586 B. C.- 516 B. C.
186	(2) *Period under Persia.*	516 B. C.- 330 B. C.
9	(3) *Period under Macedonia.*	330 B. C.- 321 B. C.
123	(4) *Period under Egypt.*	321 B. C.- 198 B. C.
32	(5) *Period under Syria.*	198 B. C.- 166 B. C.
103	(6) *Period under Maccabees.*	166 B. C.- 63 B. C.
59	(7) *Period under Rome.*	63 B. C.- 4 B. C.
?	3. DURING THE NEW COVENANT.	4 B. C.- ? A. D.
104	a. NEW TESTAMENT TIMES.	4 B. C.- 100 A. D.
34	(1) *Times of Christ.*	4 B. C.- 30 A. D.
70	(2) *Times of Apostles.*	30 A. D.- 100 A. D.
?	b. DISPERSION.	70 A. D.- ? A. D.

When was the system of dating B. C. or A. D. begun? When was Christ really born?

Is there any system of chronology that is absolutely authoritative in all its parts? Can all the events of the Bible be accurately dated? Is there any system of chronology that is in any sense a part of the Bible? If not, what is the value of any good system of chronology?

Who is the author of the Received Chronology? How long has this system been followed by the English speaking people? Study the table in the lesson, and be able to give all the periods together with the years marked with letter notation. Likewise all the subdivisions of each period with the respective years of each. Study the chart and be able to make a chart showing the relative length of the different periods of Biblical history.

What does your Bible history say about chronology? Find references to this subject in the Bible. In what ways can the contents of this lesson help you in your Bible study? In your faith and works?

LESSON THIRTY - FOUR. THE EARLY AGES
(2083 YEARS).

1. AN ADDED DIFFICULTY IN COMPUTING DATES.

The early ages of the world's history are the most difficult to arrange in chronological tables. Yet the chief difficulty is not so much in the subject itself as in the attitude and theory of the chronologist.

Stated briefly, the attitude of the average chronologist is this: He shakes his head at the abundant material relating to chronology in the Bible and expresses doubt and dismay at every point; but his face brightens when excavators in Biblical lands find any inscription upon monument or brick, however fragmentary, and he accepts with most sanguine assurance almost any theory propounded by modern "scientists." And yet he knows that there are no records of ancient chronology so complete and exact as those of the Bible and none so incomplete and inexact as the records of the ancient countries of the East. A large part of the work in fixing the dates of ancient history is downright guess work at best. Yet, no matter how few the records or how difficult to translate the fragments, or how desperately impossible the contents and their interpretations, modern historians as a rule laugh at the difficulties and accept almost any solution but the right one. They are about like the San Francisco audience listening to a man imitating the squeal of a pig and shouting themselves hoarse in approval. One of the actors thought he would give them the real article and placed a young porker in his bosom. Every time he wanted a squeal he twitched the porker's tail and the squeal was forthcoming. "Ah, wot are you giving us," roared a disgusted critic; "get off the stage, you cheap imitator."

As to the theory of the chronologist, it is sufficient to

say that most modern scholars are followers of the theory of evolution. Briefly stated, the word evolution is used by most writers in a very loose sense. It is derived from the Latin evolvere, meaning to unroll, unfold, develop, and is the act or process of growing or developing. We behold growth and development and progress on every hand, therefore in a popular sense this word is used to mean simply any growth or progress. In a scientific sense it means something entirely different. It refers to the explanation by modern scholars that the various types of animals and plants have developed by descent with modifications from pre-existing types, as opposed to the old theory of the separate creation of each species. It involves, therefore, the descent of man from the lower animals, the lower animals from plants, the living beings from non-living substances, and everything from an original atom.

The particular point to be considered in this connection is, that this theory can not tolerate the Bible chronology. For example: The Bible says that Creation was the work of 6 days; evolution requires that many periods of untold duration each, thousands or millions or even billions of years. The Bible says that the Confusion of Tongues was instantaneous; evolution knows nothing about the Judgment at Babel, but finds that the development of the original language into the present confusion has been the slow process of untold ages. The Bible makes the antediluvian men from Adam to Noah attain high ages, even up to 969 years; evolution says that here the reader ought to substitute some other measure instead of years. We recall reading once in some Chicago daily an incident from a university class room. The professor was insisting that it was impossible that Abraham was 100 years old and Sarah 90 years old when they became parents of Isaac. He insisted on that the correct word was months, not years. "Are you sure?" asked a student. "Of course, I am," answered the learned evolutionist. "You see it is unreasonable that a woman of 90 should bear a son: It must mean months. That is the only reasonable thing. Next." "But," persisted the dull student, "I have been figuring at this new version of yours, and I cannot make out that it is more reasonable. If Abraham were 100 months old at Isaac's birth, he would have been only 8 years and 4 months old; and if Sarah were 90 months old at that time, she would have been only 7 years and 6 months old. Is that more reasonable?"

We often find strange inconsistencies in the figures of the evolutionists. In Haydn's "Dictionary of Dates" it is stated that Menes came to the throne of Egypt in 5004 B C., and that previous to his ascension to the throne the country had been ruled by fabulous god-kings for 13,900 years and demi-gods 4000 years, making the beginning of Egypt go back to 22,904 B. C. Now, the nations of the Tigris-Euphrates Valley are usually conceded to have history even more ancient than that of Egypt. Yet this same book by Haydn tells us that the Tower of Babel was built in 2247 B. C., that the earliest astronomical observations at Babylon were made in 2234 B. C., and that Asshur built Nineveh in 2218 B. C. These first events in the Tigris-Euphrates Valley are thus seen to have taken place 20,000 years after the first events in Egypt, although these were contemporary events.

The assurance of the chronologists is, as a rule, perfectly astounding, yet hardly more amazing than their disagreements. For instance, Haydn's date for the beginning of Menes' reign in Egypt is 5004 B. C. Barnes places him at 2700 B. C.; Lepsius, at 3542; Breasted, at 4251; Brugsch, at 4455; Petrie, at 4777; Bøckh, at 5702. That is, in the case of these seven authorities no two agree, and the amount of disagreement varies from 9 to 3011 years. As to the length of prehistoric time most of the historians do not commit themselves. Thus, West says in his "Ancient History:" "Through thousands and thousands of years, man has been lifting himself from this earliest savagery to our many sided civilization."

2. ANALYSIS OF THE TABLES.

The Usserian system is constructed on the theory that the beginning of the earth occurred exactly 4000 years before Christ. The Bible does not say so, even as it does not give the date of Christ's coming to the world. This date, computed by Ussher, may not be absolutely exact, but should be remembered because it is the one in general use. The Early Ages cover a stretch of 2083 years, considerably more than the whole length of the history of Israel from the Call of Abraham to the Fall of Jerusalem, in 70 A. D.

It is divided into two very unequal periods of 10 generations each, as follows:

Antediluvian Age (1656 years).
Postdiluvian Age (427 years).

The first age extended from Creation to the Flood; the second, from the Flood to the Call of Abraham.

The Postdiluvian Age is naturally divided into two periods by the Confusion of Tongues at Babel. These periods are as follows:

Union, 101 years.
Dispersion, 326 years.

Of the 20 patriarchs whose names are given in the table seven attained an age of over 800 years. Adam was 930 at his death, and Seth was 912. Methuselah, the oldest of all men, reached the age of 969, and passed away the year of the Deluge. Noah was born in 2948 B. C., and died at the good old age of 950, in 1998 B. C., two years before the birth of Abraham. The span from Adam to Abraham was almost covered by the lives of two men—Adam and Noah, and fully covered by one additional before the Flood and one additional after the Flood. The leading chronological feature of these ages is the length of life just noted. We believe the statements of the Bible on this point, because the Word of God is truth. It is also in accordance with the traditions of ancient nations, such as the Egyptians, Chaldeans, Greeks, Romans, Hindus and Chinese. The only dif-

No. 91.   The Distribution of the Human Race (Gen. 10).
(From Wm. Smith's "Old Testament History," by permission of Harper and Brothers.)

ference seems to be, that the Bible limits the age of the antediluvian patriarchs to a few hundred years, while many of the
other nations used much less moderation. It has already
been mentioned that Berosus, for example, assigns to 10 Chaldean kings a period of 432,000 years.   The ancient Jewish
historian, Josephus, states in his "Antiquities of the Jews"
(I, 3:9) that Manetho, Berosus, Mochus, Hestiaeus, Hier-
onymus, Hesiod, Hecataeus, Hellanicus, Acusilaus, Ephorus

and Nicolaus bear witness to the extraordinary long lives
of the early patriarchs. This divine arrangement tended
to promote the increase of the race and the preservation of
the primitive revelation concerning God and His work,
concerning creation and redemption.

What period of the world's history is the most difficult to arrange
chronologically? Why? What is the chief difficulty in connection
with this subject?

What is generally the attitude of the average modern chronologist? Illustrate. What theory does he usually hold? What is
meant by evolution in a scientific sense? Illustrate. What does
Haydn state as to the age of Egypt? Of Babylon? Of Assyria?
What strange inconsistency do you find in his figures? Show how the
scholars disagree as to the beginning of Menes' reign in Egypt.

What is the Usserian system of chronology? According to Ussher,
how many years are included by the so-called Early Ages? Into
what two periods are the Early Ages divided? What is the Antediluvian Age noted for? How many generations lived during this
period? What was the Postdiluvian Age noted for? How many
generations did it include? Give one reason for the extraordinary
long lives of the early patriarchs.

What does your Catechism say of the Early Ages? Find appropriate hymns in your hymnal bearing on this subject. Look up the
Bible passages referred to in your lesson, and find additional references to this subject in the Bible. In what ways can the contents
of this lesson help you in your Bible study? In your faith and
works?

LESSON THIRTY-FIVE. THEOCRACY
(826 YEARS).

1. AN ILLUSTRATION OF DISAGREEMENT AMONG THE CHRONOLOGISTS.

By theocracy is meant the government of a state under the immediate direction of God. The Chosen People were a theocratic nation from the Call of Abraham until the establishment of the monarchy, a period of over 800 years. We have no certain chronological data for this period, on account of which there is no end to the disagreements among chronologists regarding the dates of this period. The two chief points of dispute are the length of the sojourn in Egypt and the length of the rule of the judges.

Let us take the case of the judges as an illustration. In 1 Kings 6:1 it is said that the Temple was begun 480 years after the Exodus. In Acts 13:20 it is said that the judges before Samuel reigned about 450 years. Here is a discrepancy that has baffled many of the bravest students of history. Note some of the attempts to unravel the mystery.

W. Smith, in his "Old Testament History" (336-341), believes that 1 Kings 6:1 is without error. His table is as follows:

		YEARS	B.C.
(1)	In the Wilderness	40	1491-1451
(2)	Joshua	40	1451-1411
(3)	Othniel	40	1411-1371
(4-5)	Ehud and Shamgar	80	1371-1291
(6)	Deborah and Barak	40	1291-1251
(7)	Gideon	40	1251-1211
(8-9)	Abimelech to Abdon	80	1211-1131
(10)	Eli, Samson, Samuel	40	1131-1091
(11)	Saul	40	1091-1051
(12)	David	40	1051-1011

480

(3-10) Properly belonging to judges, 320 years.

No allowance is made for the years of servitude as they are supposed to have been included in the years of the judges. Smith finds that the number 450 stated in Acts 13:20 is the exact total of the numbers given in the Book of Judges arranged consecutively.

Thus:

First servitude: Mesopotamia............................	8	years
First judge: Othniel...................................	40	”
Second servitude: Moab................................	18	”
Second and third judges: Ehud and Shamgar............	80	”
Third servitude: Jabin................................	20	”
Fourth and fifth judges: Deborah and Barak............	40	”
Fourth servitude: Midian..............................	7	”
Fifth judge: Gideon...................................	40	”
Sixth judge: Abimelech................................	3	”.
Seventh judge: Tola...................................	23	”
Eighth judge: Jair.....................................	22	”
Fifth servitude: Ammon................................	18	”
Ninth judge: Jephthah.................................	6	”
Tenth judge: Ibzan....................................	7	”
Eleventh judge: Elon..................................	10	”
Twelfth judge: Abdon..................................	8	”
Sixth servitude: Philistia..............................	40	”
Thirteenth judge: Samson..............................	20	”
Fourteenth and fifteenth judges: Eli, Samuel............	40	”
	450	”

T. E. Schmauk, in his "Bible Geography" (152), and W. J. Beecher, in his "Dated Events of the Old Testament" (79-119), proceed on the theory that the time from the Exodus to the foundation of the Temple was exactly 480 years. But, since the sum of the numbers assigned to Moses, Joshua, the servitudes, judges, Saul, David and Solomon is 589 years instead of 480, they assume that there is an overlapping somewhere. They both present the judges as ruling consecutively, but allow the periods of oppression and peace to overlap in sufficient instances so as to make the total number of years amount to 480. They do not agree on details. Keil rejects both 1 Kings 6:1 and Acts 13:20 as incorrect. His table for the judges covers a period of 390 years ("Introduction to the Old Testament" I, 225). Hales extends the period from the Exodus to the Temple to 612 years. Clement of Alexandria estimates 566 years; Julius Africanus, 744 years; Bede, 490 years; Seyfarth, 880 years; Jatho, 605 years; etc. (Herzog's "Real Encyklopädie," XVIII, 454).

R. Anderson, in his "Daniel in the Critics' Den" (90), gives the following solution:

1 KINGS 6: 1	YEARS	ACTS 13: 17-21		YEARS
(1) Wilderness	70	(1) Wilderness		40
(2) Joshua	40	(2) Joshua	40	
Judges (not including		Judges	317	450
years of servitude)	317	Servitude	93	
(3) Saul	40	(3) Saul		40
(4) David	40	(4) David		40
(5) Solomon	3	(5) Solomon		3
	480	From Exodus to Temple		573
Servitude	93			
From Exodus to Temple	573			

Anderson observes that the period of servitude was 93 years, the exact number of years that Israel had not kept the Sabbatical years (Cf. Lev. 25: 1-7, the command to allow the land to rest every seventh year). He insists that the 93 years of bondage were not counted in 1 Kings 6: 1. If he is right we shall have to move the date of Exodus back 93 years.

The Usserian chronology for this period is made on the theory that it is entirely probable that the oppressions and deliverances were not always successive, but at times contemporary, since they were in every case local struggles. It is both possible and probable that while one part of the land was enjoying peace and prosperity under a judge, another part of the land was troubled by the oppressor.

2. ANALYSIS OF THE TABLES.

The theocracy covers a stretch of 826 years, according
to the Usserian reckoning. This is subdivided as follows:

a. Period of Patriarchs.....................	215	years
b. Period of Bondage......................	215	"
c. Period of Wanderings...................	40	"
d. Period of Conquest.....................	16	"
e. Period of Judges........................	340	"
Total.................................	826	"

In the table on the Patriarchs it will be interesting to
note that the parallel columns give the ages of the chief
patriarchs Abraham, Isaac, Jacob and Joseph at certain
events. Thus, at the birth of Jacob Abraham was 160 and
Isaac 60. For the source of the information see Gen. 25:
26. Or, when Joseph was sold, he was 17 years old, Jacob
was 108, Isaac was 168, and Abraham had been dead 93
years (See Gen. 37: 2).

In the table on the Bondage there are not many events
recorded. This period is held by Ussher to be 215 years.
Some chronologists, like Rawlinson, interpret Ex. 12: 40;
Gen. 15: 30 and Acts 7: 6 to mean that the Israelites were
to be in bondage in Egypt for 430 years. Ussher, together
with Petavius, Clinton, Hales, Jackson, Beecher, etc., inter-
prets the 430 years of Ex. 12:40 to mean the period beginning with Abraham's visit to Egypt almost immediately after
arriving in Canaan, and ending with the Exodus. This
agrees with Paul's statement in Gal. 3: 17. During the
whole period of the Patriarchs the Chosen Family were
strangers in their own land, hence it may be taken as a
part of the bondage. It may be objected that the 215 years
of the period of the Patriarchs were not years of real bondage. In like manner it may be said that the 215 years from
the departure of Jacob to Egypt to the Exodus were not all
years of real bondage. Joseph lived on into this period for
about 70 years. Sometime after this—exactly how long we

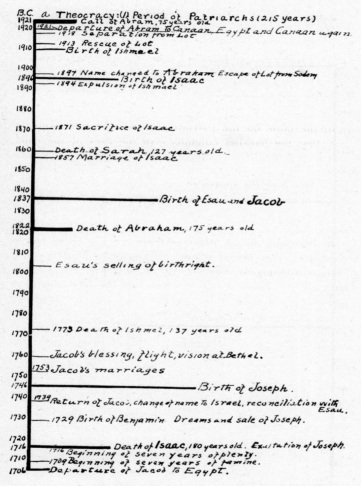

B.C.
1921 — a Theocracy:(1) Period of Patriarchs (215 years)
1921 — Call of Abram, 75 years old
1920 — 1921 Departure of Abram to Canaan, Egypt and Canaan again.
— 1918 Separation from Lot
1910 — 1913 Rescue of Lot
— Birth of Ishmael

1900
1896 — 1897 Name changed to Abraham, Escape of Lot from Sodom
— Birth of Isaac
1890 — 1894 Expulsion of Ishmael

1880

1870 — 1871 Sacrifice of Isaac

1860 — Death of Sarah, 127 years old
— 1857 Marriage of Isaac
1850

1840
1837 — Birth of Esau and Jacob
1830

1822
1820 — Death of Abraham, 175 years old

1810

1800 — Esau's selling of birthright.

1790

1780

1770 — 1773 Death of Ishmael, 137 years old

1760 — Jacob's blessing, flight, vision at Bethel.

1750 — 1753 Jacob's marriages
1746 — Birth of Joseph.

1740 — 1739 Return of Jacob, change of name to Israel, reconciliation with Esau.
1730 — 1729 Birth of Benjamin. Dreams and sale of Joseph.

1720
1716 — Death of Isaac, 180 years old. Exaltation of Joseph.
— 1716 Beginning of seven years of plenty.
1710 — 1709 Beginning of seven years of famine.
1706 — Departure of Jacob to Egypt.

No. 92. Period of the Patriarchs, 1921-1706 B. C.

cannot say—"there arose a king over Egypt that knew not
Joseph" (Ex. 1:8). Note that the order to kill male in-
fants must have been given shortly before the birth of
Moses.

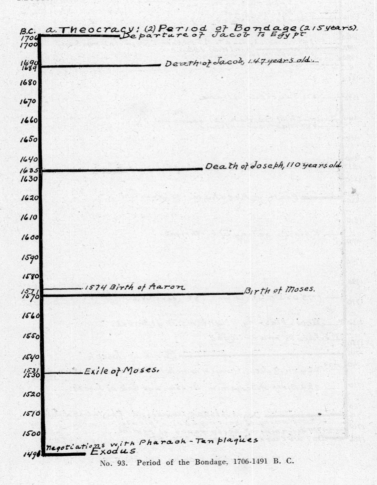

B.C.   *a. Theocracy: (2) Period of Bondage (215 years).*
1706   *Departure of Jacob To Egypt*
1700

1690   *Death of Jacob, 147 years old.*
1689

1680

1670

1660

1650

1640   *Death of Joseph, 110 years old.*
1635
1630

1620

1610

1600

1590

1580

1576   *.1574 Birth of Aaron*   *Birth of Moses.*
1576

1560

1550

1540

1531   *Exile of Moses.*
1536

1520

1510

1500

1491   *negotiations with Pharaoh - Ten plagues*
             Exodus

No. 93.   Period of the Bondage, 1706-1491 B. C.

In the table on the Wandering the first two and the last two years of the 40 are crowded with events, which occupy fully one-eighth of the whole Bible, or one-sixth of the Old Testament. The other 38 years—the years of actual wandering—are passed over hurriedly in a single verse—Deut.

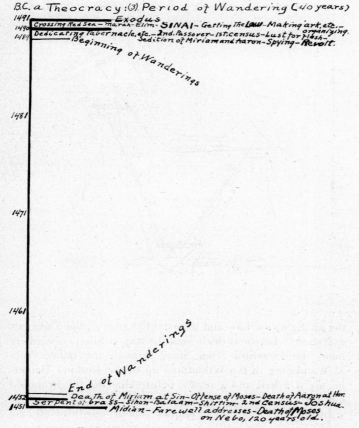

B.C. a Theocracy: (3) Period of Wandering (40 years)

1491

1490 Crossing Red Sea — Marah - Elim - SINAI - Getting The Law - Making ark, etc. —

1489 Dedicating Tabernacle, etc. — 2nd. Passover - 1st. census - Lust for flesh — organizing. Sedition of Miriam and Aaron - Spying - Revolt.

Beginning of Wanderings

1481

1471

1461

End of Wanderings

1452 Death of Miriam at Sin - Offense of Moses - Death of Aaron at Hor.

1451 Serpent of brass - Sihon - Balaam - Shittim - 2nd Census - Joshua - Midian - Farewell addresses - Death of Moses on Nebo, 120 years old.

No. 94. Period of the Wandering, 1491-1451 B. C.

2: 14. The student should with the aid of the map take the
trip with Moses from Egypt to Nebo and mark the events
which happened each year, as noted in the table.—It might
be remarked that the Book of Genesis is largely occupied
with the geography from Mesopotamia along a bee line to
Egypt. The Book of Exodus covers the geography and
period of time from Egypt with its bondage to Sinai with

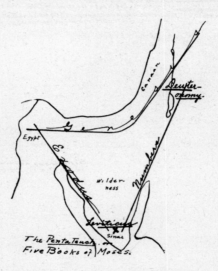

No. 95. The Geography of the Pentateuch.

the giving of the Law and the establishment of the Theocratic Nation. Leviticus deals with the stay at Sinai. Numbers
takes the Israelites from Sinai through the many years
of Wandering in the Wilderness up to the Jordan. Deuteronomy is a halt and a review before entering the Promised
Land.

In the table on the Conquest about one-third of the
events bear on the brilliant conquests of the first seven years,

another third is devoted to the division of the land, and a
final third is devoted to convocations and supplementary
conquests. Each of these groups should receive careful

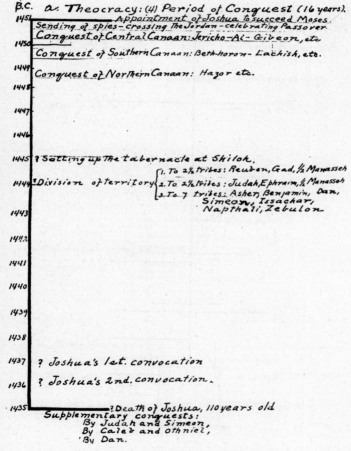

B.C. *a. Theocracy: (4) Period of Conquest (16 years).*
1451 ──────── *Appointment of Joshua to succeed Moses.*
Sending of spies — crossing the Jordan — celebrating Passover.
Conquest of Central Canaan: Jericho-Ai-Gibeon, etc.
1450
Conquest of Southern Canaan: Beth-horon-Lachish, etc.

1449 *Conquest of Northern Canaan: Hazor etc.*

1448

1447

1446

1445 ? *Setting up the tabernacle at Shiloh.*
                                    1. To 2½ tribes: Reuben, Gad, ½ Manasseh
1444 *Division of territory* 2. To 2½ tribes: Judah, Ephraim, ½ Manasseh
                                    3. To 7 tribes: Asher, Benjamin, Dan,
1443   Simeon, Issachar,
                                                Napthali, Zebulon

1442

1441

1440

1439

1438

1437 ? *Joshua's 1st. convocation*

1436 ? *Joshua's 2nd. convocation.*

1435 ?*Death of Joshua, 110 years old*
Supplementary conquests:
     By Judah and Simeon,
     By Caleb and Othniel,
     By Dan.

No. 96. Period of the Conquest, 1451-1435 B. C.

study. The dates in the third group are all a matter of conjecture.

In the table on the Judges this formula repeated seven times should be noted: apostasy—servitude—rescue.

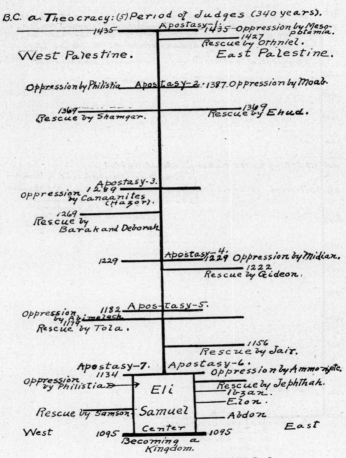

B.C. *a. Theocracy: (5) Period of Judges (340 years).*

1435 — Apostasy-1435-Oppression by Mesopotamia.
1427
Rescue by Othniel.

West Palestine. East Palestine.

Oppression by Philistia Apostasy-2 · 1387 Oppression by Moab.

1369 1369
Rescue by Shamgar. Rescue by Ehud.

Apostasy-3.
Oppression 1289
by Canaanites (Hazor).

1269
Rescue by Barak and Deborah.

1229 Apostasy-4. 1229 Oppression by Midian.
1222
Rescue by Gideon.

Oppression 1182 Apostasy-5.
by Abimelech.
Rescue by Tola.

1156
Rescue by Jair.

Apostasy-7. Apostasy-6.
1134 Oppression by Ammon, etc.
Oppression
by Philistia Rescue by Jephthah.
Eli Ibzan.
Elon.
Rescue by Samson Samuel Abdon.

West 1095 Center 1095 East
Becoming a Kingdom.

No. 97. Period of the Judges, 1435-1095 B. C.

What is meant by theocracy? How long were the Chosen People a theocratic nation? Why do the chronologists disagree concerning certain dates in the period? Give two important points in dispute. How does W. Smith manage to harmonize the apparent disagreement between 1 Kings 6:1 and Acts 13:20? T. E. Schmauk? C. F. Keil? R. Anderson?

What years and how many does the theocracy cover? What are its five main divisions? Give the chief events together with dates in the table on the Patriarchs. In the table on the Bondage. In the table on the Wandering. In the table on the Conquest. In the table on the Judges.

What does your Bible history say about the theocracy? Find appropriate hymns in your hymnal bearing on this subject. Look up the Bible passages referred to in your lesson, and find additional references to this subject in the Bible. In what ways can the contents of this lesson help you in your Bible study? In your faith and works?

LESSON THIRTY - SIX. MONARCHY
(509 YEARS).

1. AN ILLUSTRATION OF AGREEMENT AMONG THE CHRONOLOGISTS.

In the chronology of the earlier ages there were the wildest kinds of disagreements among the chronologists. In the period of theocracy there was also very much difference of opinion as to dates for the sojourn in Egypt and the rule of the judges. In the periods of the monarchy the differences as to dates are small and trifling. In addition to the Biblical data archaeological explorers have discovered many records of temples, laws, business transactions, including dated events, an immense body of facts which have been classified and which are found to agree in all essentials with the chronological references of the Bible. Thus, the date of the fall of Samaria at 722 B. C. and the date of the fall of Jerusalem at 586 B. C., seem to be recognized as reasonably authentic by leading scholars everywhere.

2. ANALYSIS OF TABLES.

The period of monarchy is divided into two unequal parts:

The United Kingdom..........120 years,
The Divided Kingdoms........389 years.

a. THE UNITED KINGDOM.

Three kings reigned 40 years each during the period of union—Saul, David and Solomon.

Saul's reign falls into three periods, as follows:

(1) From anointing of Saul to birth of David—10 years.

(2) From birth of David to his anointing—20 years.

(3) From anointing of David to death of Saul—10 years.

The chief events in the first period of Saul's reign were

the wars with Ammon and Philistia, Saul's disobedience in sacrificing at Gilgal and first rejection. The chief events of the second period were the war against Amalek, Saul's disobedience in sparing King Agag and second rejection. The chief events of the third period were David's victory over Goliath, Saul's consequent jealousy and relentless persecution of David and death in battle against the Philistines.

David's reign also falls into three periods:
(1) His rise—20 years.
(2) His fall—10 years.
(3) His restoration—10 years.

During his first period he reigned for 8 years over Judah alone and 12 years over all of Israel. He defeated all opposition from within the Twelve Tribes and without and extended the boundaries of Israel so that it included all the Promised Land from Egypt to the Euphrates. Jerusalem became his capital. The Ark was moved to Mount Zion. During his second period he committed adultery with Bathsheba and was humbled unto repentance. Domestic and political troubles broke out through the wicked acts of his sons Ammon and Absalom. During his third period, due to his repentance he was granted victory over Absalom and Sheba. For his sinful census a plague visited his people. In his last year he crowned Solomon, his son by Bathsheba, instead of Adonijah, the heir.

Solomon's reign falls into only two periods:
(1) One of firmness—25 years.
(2) One of weakness—15 years.

The first year of Solomon's reign was marked by the execution of his brother and other political enemies, his fateful marriage to an Egyptian princess, his prayer for wisdom and first wise judicial decision. The third year marked the foundation of the Temple; the eleventh, its dedication. The period of weakness witnessed Solomon's growing polygamy, idolatry and luxury and the insurrections of Hadad, Rezon and Jeroboam.

b. THE DIVIDED KINGDOMS.

At his death the house of Solomon became divided against itself. Two kingdoms were formed—Judah, or the Two Tribes, with capital at Jerusalem, and Israel, or the Ten Tribes, with capital at Samaria. The Kingdom of Israel

B.C. **b. Monarchy: (I) Period of Union (120 years).**

King Saul.

- 1095 — Anointing, election by lot, inauguration of Saul.
- 1096 — Defeat of Ammon, second inauguration. War with Philistia, Saul's disobedience in sacrificing at Gilgal.
- 1093 — Defeat of Philistines by Jonathan, Saul's vow. and doom.
- 1090 — Victories over Moab, Ammon, Edom, Philistia, etc.

- 1084 — Birth of David.
- 1079 — War on Amalek. Saul's disobedience in sparing king and cattle. His rejection.

- 1065 — Anointing of David.
- 1063 — David and Goliath.
- 1062 — David in exile, Saul in pursuit.
- 1060
- 1057 — David in Philistia.
- 1055 — Death of Saul.

King David.

David King of Judah, Ishbosheth king of Israel—civil war.

- 1048 — David sole King, with capital at Jerusalem. Defeat of Philistia.
- 1042 — Bringing of ark to Zion. Extension of boundaries.
- 1035 — Various victories over heathen neighbors. David's fall. Nathan. Birth of Solomon.

- 1027 — Domestic troubles.
- 1023 — Absalom's rebellion.

Census and pestilence.
- 1015 — Death of David.

King Solomon.

- 1012 — Beginning of building of Temple, 480 years after Exodus.

- 1004 — Dedication of Temple.

- 992 — Completion of palace. Visit of Queen of Sheba.

Solomon's idolatry and taxation.
Enmity of Hadad of Edom, Rezon of Syria.
Revolt of Jereboam.
- 975 — Death of Solomon. Division of kingdom.

No. 98. Period of the United Monarchy, 1095-975 B. C.

lasted 253 years, until 722 B. C., and the Kingdom of
Judah lasted 389 years, 136 years longer than Israel, until
586 B. C.

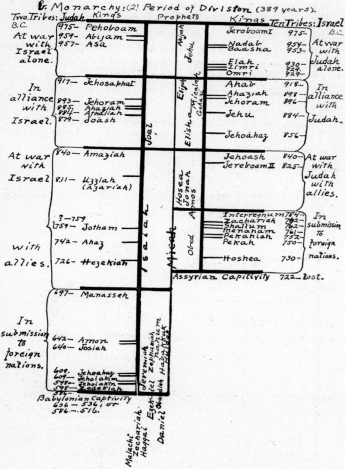

No. 99.   Period of the Divided Monarchies, 975-586 B. C.

The story of the Ten Tribes has four distinct epochs:

(1) At war with the Two Tribes, mainly alone—58 years.

(2) In alliance with the Two Tribes—77 years.

(3) At war again with the Two Tribes, with allies—56 years.

(4) In submission to foreign nations—62 years.

The story of the Two Tribes has similar epochs:

(1) At war with the Ten Tribes, mainly alone—58 years.

(2) In alliance with the Ten Tribes—77 years.

(3) At war again with the Ten Tribes, with allies—143 years.

(4) In submission to foreign nations—111 years.

The following table gives the number of kings in each kingdom:

Two Tribes—19 kings and 1 queen.

Ten Tribes—19 kings and 1 interregnum.

975-586 B. C. Two Tribes.		Ten Tribes.	975-722 B. C.
975-959	(1) Rehoboam	(1) Jeroboam 1.	975-954
959-957	(2) Abijam		
957-917	(3) Asa	(2) Nadab	954-953
		(3) Baasha	953-930
		(4) Elah	930-929
		(5) Zimri	929-929
		(6) Omri	929-917
917-893	(4) *Jehoshaphat	(7) Ahab	917-898
		(8) Ahaziah	898-896
893-885	(5) Jehoram	(9) Jehoram	896-884
885-884	(6) Ahaziah		
884-879	Athaliah (Queen)	(10) Jehu	884-856
879-840	(7) *Joash		
		(11) Jehoahaz	856-840
		(12) Jehoash (Joash)	840-825
840-811	(8) Amaziah	(13) Jeroboam II.	825-784
811-759	(9) *Uzziah (Azaria)		
		(Interregnum)	784-762
		(14) Zachariah	762-762
		(15) Shallum	762-762
759-742	(10) Jotham	(16) Menahem	761-752
		(17) Pekahiah	752-750

| 742-726 | (11) Ahaz | (18) Pekah | 750-730 |
| 726-697 | (12) *Hezekiah | (19) Hoshea | 730-722 |

697-642	(13) Manasseh
642-640	(14) Amon
640-609	(15) *Josiah
609-609	(16) Jehoahaz (Shal- lum)
609-598	(17) Jehoiakim (Eli- akim)
597-597	(18) Jehoiakin
597-586	(19) Zedekiah

All of the kings of the Ten Tribes and nearly all of the kings of the Two Tribes were wicked. The most godly of the kings were Jehoshaphat, Joash, Uzziah, Hezekiah and Josiah, all of Judah, and the most wicked of all was no doubt Ahab of Israel. These 389 years were crowded with events of more than passing interest. The student should refer to the chronological table in the Appendix for a catalog of the most important events.

Give examples of dated events concerning which Bible chronologists generally agree.

What is the meaning of monarchy? Divide the Hebrew monarchy into two periods, and give the length of each.

Give the subdivisions of Saul's reign together with the chief events in each. Of David's reign. Of Solomon's reign.

Why was the kingdom divided? What kingdoms were formed at the division? Give the constituent tribes and the territorial boundaries of each kingdom. How long did the Kingdom of Israel last? Give the dates. How long did the Kingdom of Judah last? Give the dates.

Give the four distinct epochs of the Northern Kingdom with the years for each. Give a list of the kings, and the chief events in the Northern Kingdom.

What were the four distinct epochs of the Southern Kingdom, with the years for each? Give a list of the kings, and the chief events in the Southern Kingdom.

What does your Bible history say about the monarchy? Find appropriate hymns in your hymnal bearing on this subject. Find references to this subject in the Bible. In what ways can the contents of this lesson help you in your Bible study? In your faith and works?

LESSON THIRTY - SEVEN.   DEPENDENCY
(582 + YEARS).

1. THE ORDER OF THE OLD TESTAMENT WRITINGS.

The Theocratic Nation disappeared as such with the fall of Jerusalem in 586 B. C.   From then on until the fall of Jerusalem in 70 A. D., was a long stretch of 656 years, during which the Chosen People were more or less subject to foreign powers.   From the fall of Jerusalem to the birth of Christ was 582 years.

One of the most important and far-reaching events during the centuries of dependency was the completion of the Old Testament Canon.   The books in the Canon are by no means all of the Hebrew writings that had been produced, for mention is made in the Bible itself of such works as "The Books of the Wars of the Lord" (Num. 21:14), "The Book of Jasher" (Josh. 10: 13; 2 Sam. 1: 18), "The History of Samuel the Seer and the History of Nathan the Prophet and the History of Gad the Seer" (1 Chron. 29: 29. R. V.), "The Book of the Acts of Solomon" (1 Kings 11: 41), "The Histories of Shemaiah the Prophet and of Iddo the Seer" (2 Chron. 12: 15), "The Book of the Chronicles of the Kings of Judah" (1 Kings 14: 29), "The Book of the Chronicles of the Kings of Israel" (1 Kings 14: 19), etc.   These books are not now in existence, and we do not know how much we have lost thereby.   We are convinced, however, that the books that were canonized or accepted as God's Word, that is, the present Old Testament, were chosen because men perceived from the character of these books that they were the Word of God. It is from these books that most of the chronological data relating to the history of mankind before Christ are taken. The student has now followed the Chosen People from the early ages to their disappearance as a nation.   It might be profitable, therefore, to take a glance at the books which tell this story and the approximate dates at which they were written.

NAME OF BOOK	THEME	AUTHOR	YEAR B. C.
(1) Genesis	The Beginnings..........	Moses	
(2) Exodus	The Establishment of the Theocratic Nation......	Moses	
(3) Leviticus	The Laws of the Theocratic Nation	Moses	1491-1451
(4) Numbers	The Discipline of the Theocratic Nation..........	Moses	
(5) Deut.	The Review before Possession	Moses	
(6) Joshua	The Possession of the Promised Land........	Joshua	1451-35
(7) Judges	Dark Pictures of Unfaithfulness and Punishment	Samuel(?)	1100(?)
(8) Ruth	Bright Pictures of Faithfulness and Reward....	Samuel(?)	1100(?)
(9) 1 Samuel	The Beginning of the Theocratic Monarchy.......	(?)	1115(?)-1015(?)
(10) 2 Samuel	The Height of the Theocratic Monarchy	(?)	
(11) 1 Kings	The Disruption of the Theocratic Monarchy...	(?)	
(12) 2 Kings	The Passing of the Divided Monarchies	Jeremiah(?)	586(?)
(13) 1 Chron.	The Necessity and Conception of the Temple.....	Ezra(?)	450(?)
(14) 2 Chron.	The Construction and Destruction of the Temple	Ezra(?)	450(?)
(15) Ezra	The Restoration and Reformation under Zerubbabel and Ezra........	Ezra(?)	450(?)
(16) Nehemiah	The Restoration and Reformation under Nehemiah	Ezra	450(?)

NAME OF BOOK	THEME	AUTHOR	YEAR B. C.
(17) Esther	God's Protection of His People in Dispersion...	Ezra (?)	450(?)
(18) Job	The Testing Value of Pain	(?)	(?)
(19) Psalms	Songs of Worship........	David, etc.	1060, etc.
(20) Proverbs	Practical Wisdom—Applied Religion.........	Solomon	1000(?)
(21) Eccl.	The Despair of the Materialist Dispersed.......	Solomon	977(?)
(22) Song of Songs	Bridegroom and Bride....	Solomon	1010(?)
(23) Isaiah	Redemption from the World	Isaiah	800(?)-700(?)
(24) Jeremiah	The Fall of Jerusalem....	Jeremiah	626-586
(25) Lament.	The Fall of Jerusalem....	Jeremiah	586
(26) Ezekiel	The Fall and Restoration of Jerusalem...........	Ezekiel	592-570
(27) Daniel	God the Ruler of State and Church	Daniel	534-464
(28) Hosea	The Restoration of an Adulterous Wife (Israel)	Hosea	792-727
(29) Joel	The Day of the Lord......	Joel	874-836 (?)
(30) Amos	The Fall of Israel........	Amos	807-756
(31) Obadiah	The Fall of Edom and the Restoration of Judah...	Obadiah	586-583
(32) Jonah	God's Mercy unto Repentant Nineveh...........	Jonah	825-784
(33) Micah	The Trial of God's Chosen	Micah	722(?)
(34) Nahum	God's Vengeance upon Unrepentant Nineveh.....	Nahum	661(?)-606(?)
(35) Habakkuk	Judgment, the Result of Sin	Habakkuk	610(?)
(36) Zephaniah	Sin, the Cause of Judgment	Zephaniah	629-623
(37) Haggai	The Blessings in Building the House of God......	Haggai	520
(38) Zechariah	Judah Militant and Triumphant	Zechariah	520
(39) Malachi	God, Loving, Holy, Righteous	Malachi	436(?)

2. ANALYSIS OF THE TABLES.

The 582 years of dependency, from the capture of Jerusalem by Nebuchadnezzar to the birth of Christ, are divided into the following seven epochs:

a. 70 years under Babylonia (586-516 B. C.).
b. 186 years under Persia (516-330).
c. 9 years under Macedonia (330-321).
d. 123 years under Macedonian Egypt (321-198).
e. 32 years under Macedonian Syria (198-166).
f. 103 years under the Maccabees (166-63).
g. 59 years under Rome (63-4 B. C.).

a. 70 YEARS UNDER BABYLONIA (586-516).

The first epoch is the 70 years under Babylon. In 606 B. C., the first deportation of Jews to Babylon took place; in 586 B. C., the third and last. The end of the first reckoning of 70 years was 536, when 42,360 exiles were permitted by Cyrus, the Persian conquerer of Babylon, to return. The end of the second reckoning of 70 years was 516, when the Temple was completed and dedicated. Daniel found favor with the kings of Babylonia and Persia in turn, though one king (Darius the Mede) was persuaded to have him thrown into a den of lions. These kings were as follows:

OF BABYLONIA.

Nebuchadnezzar (Dan. 1-4)	604-561 B. C.
Evil—Merodach (2 Kings 25: 27)	561-559
Neriglissar	559-556
Labossoracus	556-555
Nabonadius	555-538
Belshazzar co-regent (Dan. 5)	(?)-538
Darius the Mede (Dan. 6)	537-536

OF PERSIA.

Cyrus (Dan. 10)	536(558)-529 B. C.
Cambyses	529-522
Pseudo-Smerdis	522-521
Darius I (Ezra 6)	521-486

Others, too, of the Jews, being treated as colonists rather than slaves, got along fairly well by the rivers of Babylon and at the court of Susa and preferred not to return in 536 to rebuild the city of Jerusalem. They kept up their national distinctions, became known as the Jews of the Dispersion (John 7: 35; 1 Pet. 1: 1) and played an important role in the early history of the Christian Church. A remnant of the Jews had been left to hover around the ruins of Jerusalem. Most of these, at the murder of the governor, in fear fled to Egypt, taking the prophet Jeremiah with them. Judah was then overrun by the desert tribes until the exiles returned. These tribes, particularly the Samaritans, interrupted the restoration of the Temple by Joshua and Zerubbabel in 536. In 520, 16 years later, a second attempt to rebuild the Temple was promoted by the prophets Haggai and Zechariah and brought to a successful conclusion. The epoch ends with the dedication of the Temple in spite of enemies on every hand. The Lord had kept His promise to restore Judah.

b. 186 Years under Persia (516-330).

The second epoch is the 186 years under Persia. This period is in reality 20 years longer, dating from 536, when Cyrus assumed control at Babylon, but we prefer to date it from 516, when the Babylonian Captivity came to an end. The kings of Persia were as follows:

Cyrus	558-529 B. C.
Cambyses	529-522
Pseudo-Smerdis	522-521
Darius I.	521-486
Xerxes I (Ahasuerus)	486-465
Artaxerxes I.	465-425
Xerxes II.	425-425
Sogdianus	425-424
Darius II.	424-405
Artaxerxes II (Mnemon)	405-359
Artaxerxes III.	359-338
Arses	338-336
Darius III.	336-330

C. Period of Dependency (656 years).

B.C. 586		
	Under Babylonia	—536 Daniel First return Temple begun. —516 End of captivity Haggai and Zechariah Temple dedicated
516		
	Under Persia	Esther queen. —456 Ezra and second return. —444 Restoration of wall under Malachi. Nehemiah Reforms Making of Old Testament Canon
330 321	Under Macedonia	Introduction of Greek.
	Under Egypt	Septuagint
198 166	Under Syria	Tyranny of Antiochus
	Theocracy	Revolt of The Maccabees Re-dedication of Temple.
	Independent under Maccabees	Rise of Pharisees and Sadducees
63	Monarchy	Pompey's capture of Jerusalem.
	Under — Kingdom	40 Herod King of Judea. —19 Rebuilding The Temple ★ Birth of Christ.
0		
	Rome — Province	His life. ✝ Death of Christ. Pentecost
	Kingdom	
	Province	Missionary labors of The Twelve and Paul.
A.D. 70	70	Destruction of Jerusalem.
	Dispersion	Dispersion of Jews. Persecution of Christians

No. 100. Period of Dependency, 586-4 B. C.—

There are five outstanding events in this epoch which have Biblical as well as secular interest, namely:

(1) 479 B. C. The elevation of Esther as queen of Persia.

(2) 456 B. C. The return of Ezra to Jerusalem to direct its restoration.

(3) 444 B. C. The return of Nehemiah to Jerusalem to rebuild its walls.

(4) 430 (?) B. C. The prophecies of Malachi.

(5) 400 (?) B. C. The completion of the Old Testament Canon.

c. 9 YEARS UNDER MACEDONIA (330-321).

The third epoch is the 9 years under Greece. These were eventful years—Alexander the Great established a world empire, whose boundaries were more extensive, whose influence was more intensive, than that of any of the great empires that had flourished before. The most important contributions of Macedonia to the conquered countries were the Greek language and culture. These became also the possession of the Jews .

d. 123 YEARS UNDER MACEDONIAN EGYPT (321-198).

The fourth epoch is the 123 years under Macedonian Egypt. At the death of Alexander no one was found strong enough to wield his sword and none wise enough to govern his state. The empire broke up into four larger and several smaller states. One of the larger states was Egypt. For two and a half centuries Egypt had been a dependency of other empires—of Babylonia, Persia and Greece in turn. Now, under the Macedonian rulers, called Ptolemies, not Pharaohs, Egypt was again to raise her head proudly amongst the nations of the world. The first Ptolemy, surnamed Soter, wrested from Seleucus, king of Syria, Palestine and transported 100,000 Jews to Alexandria. This city became one of the metropolises of the world and a center of Greek culture, with schools, libraries, museums and the like. The three events of most interest to Bible students are:

(1) 320 B. C. The establishment of Jewish colonies in Egypt.

(2) 284 (?) B. C. The Septuagint translation of the Old Testament.

(3) 321-198 B. C. The wars between Syria and Egypt for the possession of Palestine.

e. 32 YEARS UNDER MACEDONIAN SYRIA (198-166).

The fifth epoch is the 32 years under Macedonian Syria. Upon the death of Alexander Syria fell to the lot of Seleucus Nicator. Syria then included nearly all of Western Asia, also Palestine. Seleucus was a man of might and a patron of Greek learning and art. He built Seleucia, a city of 600,000, as his capital. He built 6 other cities named Seleucia, after himself; 16 cities named Antioch, after his father; 5 cities called Laodicea, in honor of his mother; and still others which bore the names of his wives. These were schools of Greek culture. The three events of most interest to Bible students are:

(1) 321-198 B. C. The wars between Egypt and Syria for the possession of Palestine.

(2) 198-168 B. C. The excessive tyranny of the Syrian king, Antiochus Epiphanes, which resulted in the revolt of the Maccabees.

(3) 321-168 B. C. The rise of the Sadducees, who favored Greek culture, and of the opposing sect, the Pharisees, who emphasized the traditions of the Jews.

f. 103 YEARS UNDER THE MACCABEES (166-63).

The sixth epoch is the 103 years of independence under the Maccabees. This falls into two parts:

(1) 168-135 B. C. The theocracy under Judas, Jonathan and Simon. During these 33 years Syria was defeated time

and again and the freedom of Palestine was recognized even by Rome.

(2) 135-63 B. C. The monarchy under Hyrcanus I and his successors. These 70 years are marked by persistent civil feuds between rival claimants to the throne and between the rival sects. At the end of the period two brothers, Aristobulus II and Hyrcanus II, brought their dispute before the Roman general Pompey for settlement. Pompey hesitated in answering, but hastened to capture Jerusalem, profaned the Temple, carried Aristobulus a prisoner to Rome, and forbade Hyrcanus to assume the crown, but allowed Antipater, an Edomite, the father of Herod, to govern under Hyrcanus as nominal king.

g. 59 YEARS UNDER ROME (63-4).

The seventh epoch is the 59 years under Rome up to the time of Christ (63-4 B. C.). During the first 26 years of this period the Maccabeans were nominally rulers. During the weak rule of Hyrcanus II the Temple was plundered in 55 by the Roman general Crassus, and the Pharisees revolted and put Antipater to death in 44. The son of Antipater, Herod, governor of Galilee, espoused the cause of his father and Rome against the Pharisees and their leader Antigonus, son of Aristobulus II. By marrying the daughter of Hyrcanus II Herod won also the favor of a large portion of the Jews, who became known as Herodians. For three short and troubled years (40-37), Antigonus was able to rule in Jerusalem, at the end of which he was put to death by Mark Anthony, and Herod was declared king in his stead. Herod, miscalled the Great, was king 34 years—years crowded with murders, massacres, infidelity and intrigue. The Roman Empire was established in 27 B. C. In order to win favor with the young emperor, Augustus Caesar, Herod built Caesarea, which became the official capital of Judea-Samaria henceforth. In order to win favor with the Jews he began, in 19 B. C., to restore the Temple that had been dedicated 500 years before. During his reign occurred the event which is the center, the turning point in history— Christ, the Son of God, was born in Bethlehem of Judea.

When did the Theocratic Nation disappear as such? How long were the Chosen People more or less subject to foreign powers? Mention one of the most important events between the fall of Jerusalem and the birth of Christ. What is meant by Canon? Does the Old Testament Canon include all of the books written by the Jews before Christ? If not, mention some Hebrew books that are not in this Canon. What is the character of each book that has found a place in the Old Testament?

Be able to name in their consecutive order all of the books of the Old Testament, and to give the approximate date of their writing.

What were the seven epochs stretching from the capture of Jerusalem in 586 to the birth of Christ?

How many years were the Jews under Babylonia? What are some of the outstanding events during those years?

How many years were the Jews under Persia? Mention five outstanding events.

How many years were the Jews under Greece? What was the chief contribution of the Greeks to the Jews?

How many years were the Jews under Macedonian Egypt? Mention three events of interest.

How many years were the Jews under Macedonian Syria? Mention three important events.

How many years were the Jews independent under the Maccabees? Describe this period.

How many years were the Jews under Rome up to the time of Christ? Mention some of the events.

What does your Catechism say about the period of dependency? Your Bible history? Find appropriate hymns in your hymnal bearing on this subject. Look up the Bible passages referred to in your lesson, and find additional references to this subject in the Bible and the Old Testament Apocrypha. In what ways can the contents of this lesson help you in your Bible study? In your faith and works?

LESSON THIRTY - EIGHT. TIMES OF CHRIST:
I. HIS FIRST YEARS.

1. HARMONIES OF THE GOSPELS.

A harmony (from the Greek harmonia—music, concord) is a work displaying the agreement of different books of history. Thus there are four Gospels, each giving the words and works of Christ. The four different authors are writing to four different classes of people with four different objects in view. Some of the events in the life of Christ are told by all four, some by three, some by two, and some by only one of the Gospel writers. The chronological order is not observed with equal strictness by all; the manner of grouping varies with each writer. The first three (Matthew, Mark and Luke) have most in common and are called "Synoptic Gospels" (from the Greek synopsis—a seeing together). These relate particularly the life of the Lord in Galilee, while John relates particularly His life in Judea. All are authentic and truthful to the smallest detail. Displaying the agreement of the four is called a harmony—"Harmony of the Gospels."

Tatian (150) was perhaps the first to prepare a harmony of the Gospels, called "Diatessaron." Since then many devout and painstaking Bible students have tried their hand at it. J. A. Broadus, who himself spent 30 years at this task, mentions in his "Harmony" 82 other important works of the same nature by such scholars as Eusebius (315), Augustine (400), Gerson (1420), Osiander (1537), Calvin (1553), Chemnitz (1593), Gerhard (1608), Lightfoot (1654), Le Clerc (1699), Griesbach (1776), De Wette (1818), Clausen (1829), Robinson (1845), Tischendorf (1851), Caspari (1876), Stevens and Burton (1894), etc. In addition to these may be mentioned J. Th. Ylvisaker's, which is followed in this book.

By means of the "Harmony of the Gospels" the life of Christ becomes more of a unit, and the Gospels become not so much the "Four Gospels" as "The Gospel." But it is not only, though principally, this part of the Bible that needs to be viewed in this fashion. The story in Acts and in the Epistles needs also the same treatment. Likewise the accounts in Kings and in Chronicles must be harmonized, and this result again must tally with the books of the 16 Prophets.

The Gospel according to Matthew was designed especially for Jewish readers, and seeks to prove that Jesus is the promised King. It contains many (41) allusions to the Old Testament prophecies as fulfilled. Thus, in Matt. 1:22: "Now all of this is come to pass, that it might be fulfilled which was spoken by the Lord through the prophet, saying——." The genealogy of Christ shows that He was the son of Abraham and of David, the legal heir to the throne.

The Gospel according to Mark was designed especially for Roman Gentiles, and seeks to show that Jesus is a mighty King and a servant King (a King Who Serves). The book is short, full of action and vivid details. Its favorite expression is "straightway."

The Gospel according to Luke was designed especially for the Greeks. They were an educated and philosophical people, and in their speculations had conceived of man approaching God Himself in perfection. Luke presents Christ as the Son of Man, the perfect Man, in Whom are found all of the virtues of man and woman. Furthermore, this Man is very God and the Savior of all men.

The Gospel according to John was designed especially for Christians, and seeks to correct errors about Christ's true nature and teachings. It presents Christ as the Son of God, revealed as such first to the Jews, and then to the Christians. The favorite expression seems to be "verily, verily."

It might be well at this point to take a look at the outlines of the four Gospels. The themes and main divisions placed side by side are as follows:

MATTHEW	MARK	LUKE	JOHN
Christ the Prophesied King.	Christ the Servant King.	Christ the Son of Man.	Christ the Son of God.
A. His Person.	A. His Person.	A. His Person.	A. His Person.
B. The Nature of His Kingdom.	B. His Service.	B. His Perfection.	B. His Revelation to the Jews.
C. The Foundation of His Kingdom.	C. His Sacrifice.	C. His Sacrifice.	C. His Revelation to His Disciples.

We are fortunate in having four Gospels (cf. Gregory's "Why Four Gospels?"). Here we get a four-sided view of Christ; we hear the precious truth from four inspired witnesses. And yet the picture of Christ which one of the evangelists paints does not conflict with that of the other three. The experience of every careful student of the Gospel is similar to that which A. Anderson relates in his "Life of Christ" ("Menneskets Søn"). He had set to work to read each Gospel separately, trying not to think of any other representation of Christ than that which he had in that particular book. He found that after he had made four separate pictures of Christ, one for each Gospel, they were remarkably alike—it was the same Christ portrayed in each of the books, only seen from a different angle. Likewise, Paul's representation of Him as the crucified and risen Lord is in perfect harmony with the Gospel portraits. So also that in Hebrews, and in the rest of the New Testament, and in the Old Testament, in fact, in all of the Bible. Jesus Christ is everywhere and always consistently portrayed as "true God, begotten of the Father from eternity, and also true man, born of Virgin Mary, my Lord Who has redeemed me, a lost and condemned creature, purchased

and won me from all sins, from death and from the power
of the Devil, not with gold or silver, but with His holy,
precious blood, and with His innocent sufferings and death,
in order that I might be His own, and serve Him in everlasting righteousness, innocence and blessedness, even as
He is risen from the dead, lives and reigns to all eternity.
This is most certainly true" (Luther's "Smaller Catechism").

2. ANALYSIS OF TABLES.

The Gospel story of the life of Christ is grouped by
Ylvisaker in his "De fire evangelier" into 160 sections.
63 of these tell the story from His birth up to His last
year of ministry, 87 record the events of the last year, and
10 the events of the 40 days beginning with His resurrection. The life of John the Baptist was closely associated
with that of Jesus and runs parallel to it. In this lesson
we shall study the chronology of the first 63 events of
Ylvisaker's classification.

JOHN.			JESUS.		
YEAR	NO.	EVENT	YEAR	NO.	EVENT
6 B. C.	(4)	Annunciation to Zacharias.	5. B. C.	(5)	Annunciation to Mary.
5 B. C.	(8)	Birth of John the Baptist.	Dec. 5. B. C. 4 B. C.	(9)	Birth of Jesus.
			4 B. C.	(12)	Flight into Egypt.
			2 B. C.	(13)	Return to Naza-reth.
			8 A. D.	(14)	Jesus in the Tem-ple.
26	(15)	Beginning of min-istry.			
Jan., 27	(16)	Baptism of Jesus.	Jan., 27	(16)	Baptism of Jesus.
			Jan.-Feb., 27	(17)	Temptation of Je-sus.
27	(18)	First testimony concerning Jesus.			

a. *With Six Disciples.*

JOHN			JESUS		
YEAR	NO.	EVENT	YEAR	NO.	EVENT
			Feb., 27	(19)	First disciples.
			Feb., 27	(20)	First miracles.
			Apr., 27	(21)	First cleansing of Temple.
			Apr., 27	(22)	First recorded discourse—with Nicodemus.
Fall, 27	(23)	Last testimony concerning Jesus.			
			Dec., 27	(24)	First convert in Samaria.
Dec., 27	(26)	Imprisonment.	Dec., 27	(25)	First healing—nobleman's son.
			Mch., 28	(27)	First conflict with Pharisees, following healing at Bethesda.
			Apr., 28	(28)	Taking up abode at Capernaum.
			Apr., 28	(29)	Calling four fishermen.
			May, 28	(32)	Making first preaching circuit of Galilee.
			May, 28	(33)	Teaching the disciples to pray.
			May, 28	(34)	Teaching concerning the cost of discipleship.
			May, 28	(35)	Stilling the storm.
			May, 28	(36)	Restoring the demoniacs.

b. *With Seven Disciples.*

JOHN			JESUS		
YEAR	NO.	EVENT	YEAR	NO.	EVENT
			June, 28	(38)	Calling Matthew.
			June, 28	(40)	Raising Jairus' daughter.
			June, 28	(42)	Warning against blasphemy.
			June, 28	(43)	Being asked for a sign.
			June, 28	(44)	Defining kingship.
			June, 28	(45)	Preaching in parables.
			June, 28	(46)	Rejected at Nazareth.

c. *With Twelve Disciples.*

JOHN			JESUS		
			July, 28	(47)	Choosing the Twelve.
			July, 28	(48)	Preaching on the Mount.
Fall, 28 (52)		Sending messengers to Jesus.	Fall, 28	(52)	Witnessing concerning John.
			Fall, 28	(54)	Making a second preaching circuit of Galilee.
			Winter 28,	(55)	Sending forth the Twelve.
Mch., 29 (56)		Death of John.			
			Apr., 29	(58)	Feeding 5000.
			Apr., 29	(60)	Laying bare the hypocrisy of the Pharisees.

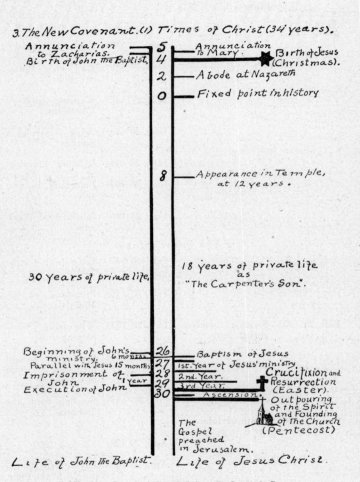

3. *The New Covenant.* (1) *Times of Christ* (34 *years*).

No. 101. Period of Christ's Life, 4 B. C.—30 A. D.

What is meant by harmony? By harmony of the Gospels? Mention some who have prepared Gospel harmonies. What is the value of a harmony? What other parts of the Bible besides the Gospel can be harmonized?

What is the general design of the Gospel of Matthew? Of the Gospel of Mark? Of the Gospel of Luke? Of the Gospel of John? Give these themes and main divisions of each of the four Gospels. What is the value of having four Gospels? In what sense are they only one Gospel?

Study the tables and the diagrams of the first years of the life of Christ. Be able to mention somewhat fully the events in their chronological order.

What does your Catechism say about the first years of Christ's life on earth? Your Bible history? Find appropriate hymns in your hymnal bearing on this subject. Look up the Bible passages referred to in your lesson, and find additional references to this subject in the Bible. In what ways can the contents of this lesson help you in your Bible study? In your faith and works?

LESSON THIRTY-NINE. TIMES OF CHRIST:
II. HIS LAST YEAR.

1. SYNOPSIS OF THE GOSPELS.

The word Gospel is a modern spelling of the old English God-spell, meaning God-story, or a story about God. It was early confused with good-spell, which meant a good story, glad tidings, and was used in this sense by Wiclif in translating the Greek word Evangelium, meaning Good News. Each of the four Gospels tells the Good News about the life of our Savior. The four Gospels are, however, really only one Gospel, under four aspects. The work of displaying the agreement of the four different books is called a Harmony of the Gospels. The arrangement of the Gospels is not in strict chronological order or according to the same plan. The work, then, of displaying every event in its proper chronological place can be called a Synopsis of the Gospels.

2. ANALYSIS OF THE TABLES.

The closing year of Christ's stay on earth may be divided into three periods:

a. The Last Year of Ministry.
b. The Last Week.
c. The 40 Days.

a. THIRD AND LAST YEAR OF MINISTRY (29-30 A. D.).

PLACE	TIME	NO.	EVENT
In Phoenicia	June	(64)	Healing Syro-Phoenician woman.
In Decapolis	July	(66)	Feeding 4000.
In Galilee	July	(69)	Healing blind man near Bethsaida.
In Judea	Oct.	(70)	Celebrating Feast of Tabernacles.
In Caesarea Philippi	Nov.	(72)	Foretelling His death.
	Nov.	(73)	Transfigured.
In Galilee	Nov.	(75)	Foretelling again His death.

PLACE	TIME	NO.	EVENT
In Perea—			
1st journey	Nov.	(78)	Rejected by the Samaritans.
	Nov.	(79)	Healing the lepers.
	Dec.	(80)	Sending forth the Seventy.
	Dec.	(82)	Giving parable of the Good Samaritan.
	Dec.	(84)	Blessing little children.
	Dec.	(87)	Celebrating the Feast of Dedication.
In Perea—			
2nd journey	Jan.	(88)	Uttering woes vs. the Pharisees.
	Jan.	(89)	Warning vs. hypocrisy and blasphemy.
	Jan.	(98)	Discoursing on counting the cost.
	Jan.	(99)	Giving the parables of the Lost Sheep, Lost Penny, Lost Son.
	Jan.	(103)	Teaching concerning faith.
	Jan.	(104)	Teaching concerning the nature of His Kingdom.
	Jan.	(105)	Teaching concerning the coming of His Kingdom.
	Feb.	(108)	Raising Lazarus to life.
In Perea—			
3rd journey	Mch.	(110)	Foretelling for the third time His passion.
	Mch.	(112)	Visiting Zaccheus.
	Mch.	(113)	Anointing by Mary.

b. THE PASSION WEEK.

PLACE	TIME	NO.	EVENT
Jerusalem	Sunday	(114)	Entering as King.
Temple	Monday	(116)	Second cleansing of the Temple.
Temple	Tuesday	(118)	Questioned as to His authority.
		(120)	Giving parable of the Wicked Husbandmen.
		(121)	Giving parable of the Marriage of the King's Son.
		(122)	Replying to the Herodians as to tribute.
		(123)	Replying to the Sadducees as to resurrection.
		(124)	Replying to the Pharisees as to the Great Commandment.
		(130)	Prophesying the destruction of Jerusalem and the world.
		(131)	Foretelling for the fourth time His passion.
		(132)	Conspired against by the priests and Judas.
Jerusalem	Thursday	(134)	Instituting the Lord's Supper.
		(135)	Delivering His farewell discourse.
		(136)	Offering His intercessory prayer.

PLACE	TIME	NO.	EVENT
Gethsemane	Friday	(138)	In agony and prayer.
		(139)	Betrayed by Judas.
Jerusalem		(140)	Condemned by the Jewish Sanhedrin.
		(143)	Pronounced innocent by Judas.
		(144)	Pronounced innocent by Pilate.
		(146)	Condemned by Pilate.
		(147)	Crucified between two thieves.
		(149)	Dead.
		(150)	Buried.

c. THE FORTY DAYS.

PLACE	TIME	NO.	EVENT
Jerusalem			
	Sunday, April 9	(151)	Appearing, risen, to the women at the tomb.
		(152)	Appearing unto Peter.
Emmaus		(153)	Appearing to Two Disciples.
Jerusalem		(154)	Appearing to Ten Disciples.
Jerusalem			
	Sunday, Apr. 16	(155)	Appearing to the Eleven.
Sea of Galilee	Apr.	(156)	Appearing to Seven Disciples.
Galilee	May	(157)	Appearing to 500 Disciples.
Bethany	May, 18	(159)	Ascending to Heaven.

———

What is meant by a synopsis? What is meant by Gospel? How does a synopsis of the Gospels differ from a harmony?

Study the tables and the diagrams of Christ's last year of ministry. Give the events during the Galilean journeys. During the Perean journeys. During the Passion Week. During the Forty Days.

What does your Catechism say about the last year of Christ on earth? Your Bible history? Find appropriate hymns in your hymnal bearing on this subject. Look up the Bible passages referred to in this lesson, and find additional references to this subject in the Bible. In what ways can the contents of this lesson help you in your Bible study? In your faith and works?

LESSON FORTY. TIMES OF THE APOSTLES.

1. THE ORDER OF THE NEW TESTAMENT WRITINGS.

In the following table the dates are on the authority of T. Zahn's "Introduction to the New Testament" (III, 481-485).

NO. NAME OF BOOK	THEME	AUTHOR	YEAR
(1) Matthew	Christ, the Prophesied King........	Matt.	62
(2) Mark	Christ, the Servant King...........	Mark	67
(3) Luke	Christ, the Son of Man...........	Luke	75
(4) John	Christ, the Son of God............	John	80-90
(5) Acts	The Holy Spirit at Work..........	Luke	75
(6) Romans	Justification by Faith a Universal Law..	Paul	58
(7) 1 Cor.	A Case of Church Discipline.......	Paul	57
(8) 2 Cor.	A Defense of Church Discipline.....	Paul	57
(9) Gal.	Justification is by Faith, not by Law	Paul	53
(10) Eph.	The Church: Its Nature and Appearance......................	Paul	62
(11) Phil.	Christian Joy	Paul	63
(12) Col.	The Church: Its Sufficiency in Christ..	Paul	62
(13) 1 Thess.	The Manner of Advent............	Paul	53
(14) 2 Thess.	The Time of Advent.............	Paul	53
(15) 1 Tim.	The Church and the Ministry......	Paul	65
(16) 2 Tim.	Zeal in the Ministry..............	Paul	66
(17) Titus	A Bishop's Duties.................	Paul	66
(18) Philemon	Christianity and Slavery...........	Paul	62
(19) Heb.	The Superiority of Christianity to Judaism......................	(?)	80(?)
(20) James	The Demonstration of Faith........	James	50
(21) 1 Peter	The Pilgrim's Conduct under Trials from Without (Persecutions).......	Peter	64
(22) 2 Peter	The Pilgrim's Conduct under Trials from Within (Heresies)...........	Peter	62
(23) 1 John	Christians, the Children of God.....	John	80-90
(24) 2 John	The Right Attitude towards False Teachers	John	80-90
(25) 3 John	A False Attitude towards Right Teachers	John	80-90
(26) Jude	Apostasy	Jude	75
(27) Rev.	The Church Militant and Triumphant	John	95

The date of the authorship of some of the New Testament writings is often a matter of conjecture, therefore the student must expect that scholars will not always agree on every detail. In the following table Zahn's dates are given in chronological order:

NO.	BOOK	YEAR	NO.	BOOK	YEAR
(1)	James	50	(15)	1 Timothy	65
(2)	Galatians	53	(16)	Titus	65
(3)	1 Thessalonians	53	(17)	2 Timothy	66
(4)	2 Thessalonians	53	(18)	Mark	67
(5)	1 Corinthians	57	(19)	Jude	75
(6)	2 Corinthians	57	(20)	Luke	75
(7)	Romans	58	(21)	Acts	75
(8)	Ephesians	62	(22)	Hebrews	80
(9)	Colossians	62	(23)	John	80-90
(10)	Philemon	62	(24)	1 John	80-90
(11)	2 Peter	62	(25)	2 John	80-90
(12)	Matthew	62	(26)	3 John	80-90
(13)	Philippians	63	(27)	Revelation	95
(14)	1 Peter	64			

2. ANALYSIS OF TABLES.

The times of the Apostles may be marked off into three parts:

a. The Church in Jerusalem.

b. The Extension of the Church to Judea and Samaria.

c. The Extension to the Uttermost Parts of the Earth.

a. THE CHURCH IN JERUSALEM.

This period covers seven years and includes the following momentous happenings:

In the year 30, the election of Matthias to succeed Judas Iscariot; the descent of the Holy Spirit at Pentecost, and the establishment of the Christian Church; the activity of the apostles and the hostility of the Jews; Peter and John in prison.

In the year 31, the growth of the Congregation and of the hostility.

In the year 34, the organization for charity work.

In the year 37, the martyrdom of Stephen.

b. THE EXTENSION TO JUDEA AND SAMARIA.

This happened in 37, when the Congregation at Jerusalem was scattered by the persecution of the Jews.

c. THE EXTENSION TO THE UTTERMOST PARTS OF THE EARTH.

There were thirteen apostles to bring the Gospel to the ends of the earth—the Eleven, Matthias and Paul. Tradition tells us that all of these were efficient ambassadors in Christ's stead and faithful until the end. The New Testament is silent on the work of nearly all of them. It has most to say about Paul, although it certainly omits to record much of his work also, some of which is briefly hinted at in his own writings and some is supplied by tradition. As to the work of the other apostles, little or nothing is said about most of them. The only exceptions are Peter and John, whose early work in Jerusalem is described in the opening chapters of Acts (1—12), and whose later work can be partly surmised from the Epistles that they wrote.

THE TWELVE.		PAUL.	
37	Conversion of the Ethiopian eunuch.	37	Conversion of Paul.
37	Peter's call to baptize Cornelius and defense of foreign missions.	38	Retirement into Arabia.
		41	Retirement to Tarsus.
41	Spread of the Gospel to Antioch.	42	Call to Antioch.
		44	Visit to Jerusalem with gifts to famine sufferers.
42	Calling the disciples Christians.	45-46	First missionary journey into Asia Minor.
44	Martyrdom of James.	51	Council of Jerusalem, determining circumcision.
		51-53	Second missionary journey into Asia Minor and Greece.
		54-58	Third missionary journey, Ephesus and Greece.
		58	Arrest at Jerusalem.
		58-60	Imprisonment at Caesarea.
		61	Voyage to Rome.
		62	First imprisonment at Rome.
		64	Journeys to Crete, Ephesus, etc.
		65	Second imprisonment at Rome.
		67	Martyrdom.

Name the books of the New Testament in the order in which they appear in the Bible. In the order in which they were written, together with the date for each.

Into how many parts may the times of the apostles be marked off?

Describe the period when the apostles were at Jerusalem only. Mention the chief events.

Describe the period of extension to Judea and Samaria.

Describe the period of extension to the uttermost parts of the earth.

What does your Catechism say about the times of the apostles? Your Bible history? Find appropriate hymns in your hymnal bearing on this subject. Look up the Bible passages referred to in your lesson, and find additional references to this subject in the Bible. In what ways can the contents of this lesson help you in your Bible study? In your faith and works?

PART FIVE.

ANTIQUITIES OF THE BIBLE.

OUTLINE.

LESSON FORTY-ONE. PHYSICAL ANTIQUITIES.

Biblical natural history is limited in this book to the study of the minerals, plants, animals and races of mankind of the Bible.   The division of natural objects into three primary classes, or kingdoms, as they are called, dates from time immemorial.   Thus: mineral kingdom, vegetable kingdom and animal kingdom.   Linnaeus (1707-1778) , the Swedish botanist, in his "Systema Naturae" follows this classification and distinguishes thus: "Minerals are concrete bodies, possessing neither life nor sensibility; vegetables are organized bodies possessed of life, but without sensibility; animals are organized bodies possessing life and sensibility, together with voluntary motion" ("Standard Dictionary").   According to this three-fold classification man would also be classed among the animals.   But he is also higher than a mere animal, therefore we must have a fourth kingdom in which to place him for the purpose of study.   A certain king is said once to have visited an elementary school and to have listened to a recitation on the three kingdoms.   He thought he himself would test the class and asked them to determine the kingdom of various objects he mentioned.   Finally, he asked: "And to what kingdom do I belong?"   They did not like to say the animal kingdom, and hesitated to reply.   At last a child volunteered: "Please, sire, you belong to the Kingdom of Heaven".   The reply was entirely correct, but in the present discussion the spiritual and heavenly side of man's nature is not under consideration.   Here we limit ourselves to a small portion of the natural history of man, namely, his position in the human kingdom, the natural division of mankind into races and families.   In the following enumeration the four kingdoms are had in mind, and a very few references to them in the Bible are cited.

1. MINERALS.

The references to the mineral kingdom can be grouped under three heads: a. Mineral Substances; b. Metals; c. Precious Stones.

a. MINERAL SUBSTANCES.

Of mineral substances may be enumerated earth, clay, dust, sand, stone, slime and mire, besides salt and sulphur. In their substantive forms these words occur in the Bible the following number of times:

(1)	Earth..	953	(6)	Slime.	3
(2)	Clay	31	(7)	Mire	14
(3)	Dust.	102	(8)	Salt..	41
(4)	Sand	28	(9)	Sulphur	15
(5)	Stone.	419	(10)	Others (Adamant, etc.)	41

Total   1,647

The word earth occurs even in the first verse of the first chapter in the first book: "In the beginning God created heaven and earth" (Gen. 1:1). Clay is used to mean earth in general and to mean the soft, plastic earth used by us, as by the people of Bible lands, for making bricks and pottery and even houses. Dust is mentioned about a hundred times. Thus: "The Lord God formed man out of the dust" (Gen. 2:7). The Holy Land was surrounded by sandy wastes, hence the term sand was very impressive. Jehovah promised Abraham: "I will multiply thy seed as the sand which is upon the sea shore" (Gen. 22:17). Stones are mentioned hundreds of times in Scripture. The patriarchs made altars of stones, and pillars, mills, houses, and walls for defense. The Law was given on two tables of stone. Jesus was the Chief Corner Stone laid in Zion. Slime is mentioned in connection with the building of the tower of Babel (Gen. 11:3), etc. Mire occurs oftener, as: "Deliver me out of the mire, and let me not sink" (Ps. 69: 14). Salt is often mentioned in the Bible. There is the

Salt Sea, the Valley of Salt, the salt pits, Lot's wife, who became a pillar of salt. Jesus said: "Ye are the salt of the earth" (Matt. 5:13). Sulphur, or brimstone, was used by the Lord in the destruction of Sodom and Gomorrah, and will be used by Him in the destruction of the world.

b. METALS.

Metal (from the Greek metallon—a mine; from metallan —to search after. Cf. medal, mettle) is a term applied to elements such as gold, silver, copper, tin, lead and zinc, which fuse readily, and also to mixed metals, such as brass, bronze, steel, etc., which are already combinations of two or more pure metals. Six of the metals—gold, silver, iron, copper, lead and tin—were well known to the ancients and are mentioned repeatedly in the Bible. The Bible also mentions two alloys—brass (a mixture of copper and zinc) and steel (a mixture of iron and carbon). These words used as nouns occur in the Bible the following number of times:

(1)	Gold	397	(5)	Tin		5
(2)	Silver	317	(6)	Lead		9
(3)	Iron	97	(7)	Copper		2
(4)	Steel	4	(8)	Brass		123

Total 954

Gold is the first metal mentioned in Scripture. In Gen. 2:11-12 it is stated that there was gold in the land of Havilah, "and the gold of that land is good". Abraham was rich in cattle, in silver and in gold (Gen. 13:2). Gold was used by him as money, but was weighed, not counted (Gen. 23:16; 24:22). Pharaoh put a gold chain about Joseph's neck (Gen. 41:42). The Israelites made a golden calf at Sinai. The street of the New Jerusalem was pure gold, as if it were transparent glass (Rev. 21:21). Silver was used as money, jewels, utensils and images. "The silver is Mine, and the gold is Mine, saith the Lord of hosts" (Hag. 2:8).

Iron is undoubtedly the most important metal. Unlike gold
and copper and tin it does not occur in nature in a pure state.
Iron ores, therefore, do not readily attract attention. Besides, their reduction is no easy process. Nevertheless, iron
is mentioned early in Scripture—the first time in Gen. 4:22,
where Tubal-cain is said to be "instructor of every artificer
in brass and iron". Canaan was said to be a land "whose
stones were iron, and out of whose hills they might dig
brass" (Deut. 8: 9). Steel is mentioned four times (2 Sam.
22:35; etc.); tin, five times (Isa. 1:25; etc.); lead, nine
times (Num. 31: 22; etc.); and copper, twice (Ezra 8: 27).
Brass is a compound of about one part of zinc to two parts
of copper. Brass is mentioned as early as Gen. 4: 22,
therefore it is reasonable to suppose that the two elements
from which brass is made—zinc and copper—were also
known at that time. Copper, as just stated, is mentioned
only twice in the Bible, and zinc is not mentioned at all.
It is well to bear in mind that the Bible does not give an
exposition, not even a catalog, of everything which existed
in the time that it was written. As to brass, it should be
noted that it is mentioned 80 times and brazen about 30
times. It was used in the manufacture and embellishment
of the vessels and furniture of the Tabernacle and the Temple. It was also used for money and helmets and gates.
Moses made a serpent of brass and lifted it up in the Wilderness for the salvation of the snakebitten Israelites, and
as an emblem of the crucified Savior (Num. 21: 9; John
3:14).

c. PRECIOUS STONES.

Precious stones, or gems, are stones of great rarity and
beauty, usually cut and polished for ornamental purposes.
The list of gems is a long one, over 100 being named
in the "Standard Dictionary" of 1916. The art of polish-
ing and engraving precious stones is as old as civilization
itself. Gen. 2: 12 mentions the bdellium and the onyx stone.
Nearly all of the principal gems are recorded in the

Bible. Some of these are mentioned only once; some, up to a dozen times; all together they are mentioned about 100 times. From earliest times gems have been associated with symbolic meanings, and it is quite possible that in many Scripture passages mentioning them, symbolism was intended. The symbolic association will occasionally be given in connection with the stones listed below. In the Bible there are three almost identical lists of precious stones: The description of the high priest's breastplate, in Ex. 28:17-20; the visionary ornaments of the king of Tyre, in Ezek. 28:13; and the foundations of the New Jerusalem, in Rev. 21:19-20. The three lists are as follows, the numbers referring to the consecutive order in each:

BREASTPLATE	ORNAMENTS	FOUNDATIONS	SYMBOLICAL MEANING
(1) Sardius	(1) Sardius	(6) Sardius	
(2) Topaz	(2) Topaz	(9) Topaz	Fellowship
(3) Carbuncle	(9) Carbuncle		
(4) Emerald	(8) Emerald	(4) Emerald	Immortality
(5) Sapphire	(7) Sapphire	(2) Sapphire	Truth
(6) Diamond	(3) Diamond		Innocence
(7) Jacinth		(11) Jacinth	Modesty
(8) Agate			Health
(9) Amethyst		(12) Amethyst	Sincerity
(10) Beryl	(4) Beryl	(8) Beryl	Youth
(11) Onyr	(5) Onyx	(5) Sardonyx	Married happiness
(12) Jasper	(6) Jasper	(1) Jasper	Wisdom
		(3) Chalcedony	Joy
		(7) Chrysolite	Gladness
		(10) Chrysoprase	

The term precious stones occurs thirteen times in the Bible. David prepared all manner of precious stones for the Temple (1 Chron. 29:2). "And they with whom precious stones were found gave them to the treasurer of the house of Jehovah" (1 Chron. 29:8). Daniel beholds a strange god honored with precious stones (Dan. 11:27). The foundations of the wall of the City of God were adorned

with all manner of precious stones (Rev. 21:19). A list
of precious stones is herewith submitted:

NAME	TIMES MENTIONED	ILLUSTRATIONS
(1) Adamant	2	Zech. 7:12
(2) Agate	4	Ex. 28:19
(3) Amber	3	Ezek. 1:4
(4) Amethyst	2	Ex. 28:19
(5) Bdellium	2	Gen. 2:2
(6) Beryl	8	Ezek. 28:19
(7) Carbuncle	3	Isa. 54:12
(8) Chalcedony	1	Rev. 21:19
(9) Chrysolite	1	Rev. 21:20
(10) Chrysoprase	1	Rev. 21:20
(11) Diamond	4	Jer. 17:1
(12) Emerald	6	Rev. 4:3
(13) Jacinth (Hyacinth)	2	Rev. 9:17
(14) Jasper	7	Rev. 4:3
(15) Ligure	2	Ex. 28:19
(16) Onyx	11	Ex. 28:9
(17) Ruby	6	Prov. 3:15
(18) Sapphire	12	Ezek. 1:26
(19) Sardius (Sard)	5	Ex. 28:17
(20) Sardonyx	1	Rev. 21:20
(21) Topaz	5	Ex. 28:17
(22) Precious Stones	13	1 Kings 10:2
Total	101	

CLASS	TIMES MENTIONED IN THE BIBLE
a. Mineral Substances	1647
b. Metals	954
c. Precious Stones	101
Total	2702

2. PLANTS.

The references to the vegetable kingdom will be treated
under seven heads: a. Timber Trees; b. Fruit Trees;
c. Grains and Grasses; d. Vegetables; e. Herbs; f. Flowers; g. Perfumes and Medicines. The following table
groups the individual species under these seven heads and
gives the number of times the name of each occurs in the
Bible.

a. TIMBER TREES.

(1) Algum (Almug) 6
(2) Ash (Fir) 1
(3) Bay 1
(4) Box 2
(5) Cedar 72
(6) Chestnut (Plane) 2
(7) Cypress 1
(8) Ebony 1
(9) Elm (Terebinth) 1
(10) Fir 21
(11) Gopher 1
(12) Juniper 4
(13) Mulberry (Sycamine) . . . 5
(14) Myrtle 6

(15) Oak 21
(16) Oil 3
(17) Pine 3
(18) Poplar 2
(19) Shittim 27
(20) Teil (Oak) 1
(21) Terebinth (Oak) 11
(22) Thyine 1
(23) Willow 6
(24) Withe 1

Specific 200
General 220

Total 440

b. FRUIT TREES.

(1) Almond 2
(2) Apple 3
(3) Fig 16
(4) Husk 3
(5) Olive 41
(6) Nut 2

(7) Pomegranate 30
(8) Sycamore 8

Specific 105
General 170

Total 275

c. GRAINS AND GRASSES.

(1) Barley 36
(2) Bulrush 3
(3) Corn (Grain) 63
(4) Fitch 4
(5) Flag (Bulrush) 4
(6) Flax 11
(7) Grass 58
(8) Reed (Bulrush) 31

(9) Rush (Bulrush) 4
(10) Tares 8
(11) Wheat 52

Specific 274
General 62

Total 338

d. VEGETABLES.

(1) Bean 2
(2) Cucumber 2
(3) Garlic 1
(4) Gourd 6
(5) Leek 1
(6) Lentil 4

(7) Mandrake 6
(8) Melon 1
(9) Onion 1
(10) Pulse 2
(11) Vine (Grapes) 110

Total 136

e. HERBS.

(1) Anise 1		(11) Mallow 1
(2) Bramble 5		(12) Mint 2
(3) Brier 14		(13) Mustard 5
(4) Cockle 1		(14) Nettles 5
(5) Coriander 2		(15) Rue 1
(6) Desire 1		(16) Thistle (Bramble) 8
(7) Gall 8		(17) Thorn (Bramble) 52
(8) Hemlock 2		(18) Wormwood 9
(9) Herb 35		
(10) Hyssop 11		Total 163

f. FLOWERS.

(1) Lily 15   (2) Rose 2

Total 17

g. PERFUMES AND MEDICINES.

(1) Aloes 5		(10) Galbanum 1
(2) Balm (Balsom) 6		(11) Myrrh 16
(3) Calamus 3		(12) Onycha 1
(4) Camphire 2		(13) Saffron 1
(5) Cane, Sweet 2		(14) Spice 34
(6) Cassia 3		(15) Spikenard 5
(7) Cinnamon 4		(16) Stacte 1
(8) Cummin 4		
(9) Frankincense 16		Total 104

SUMMARY OF PLANTS MENTIONED IN THE BIBLE.

a. Timber Trees . . . . : 440
b. Fruit Trees 275
c. Grains and Grasses 338
d. Vegetables 136
e. Herbs 163
f. Flowers 17
g. Perfumes and Medicines 104

Total 1473

a. TIMBER TREES.

Palestine was at one time one of the most fertile countries in the world, with great diversities of climate, elevation, soil, and rain in season. Its vegetation, on the whole, was as rich and diversified as its elevations and climatic changes. Recent explorers have catalogued over 1000 species of plants now found in the country, and the whole number of native species is held to be at least 2000. A very small portion of these—barely 100—are referred to in the Bible. But these are illustrative of the great diversity of vegetation and climate producing them. In the Lebanon regions the climate approaches Arctic severity, and the vegetation is that of Northern Europe. On the central highlands the climate is temperate, with a vegetation somewhat like that of Central Europe. Along the coast and the southern foothills the climate and vegetation are like those of Southern Europe. In the Jordan Valley tropical heat and plants are in evidence. At one time the country may have been well wooded, but the forests fell beneath the axe of the Israelite farmers and the many ruthless conquerors that from time to time swept down upon this fair land (Isa. 37:24; Jer. 22:7).

There are six principal terms in the Hebrew original, four in the English Authorized Version, to denote trees collectively, namely: Forest (46 times), wood (122 times), grove (40 times) and thicket (6 times). The first of these is generally applied to the larger groups of trees, the second to groups of smaller dimensions, the third to places of idolatrous worship, and the fourth to the thicker portions of vegetation, especially the shrubbery of which the country is so full. The great forests of Palestine were those of Lebanon, Carmel, Judah and Mahanaim. From the cedars of Lebanon it was that Solomon built the famous "House of the Forest of Lebanon", an armory in Jerusalem, fitted up with cedar and with forest-like rows of cedars (1 Kings 7:2; 10:17, 21; 2 Chron. 9:16, 20). The account by Josephus of the destruction of Jerusalem by the Romans is sad in more than one respect. As to the trees, they were cut down to supply the engines of the besiegers. When the city was taken, wood failed to supply crosses in sufficient abundance on which the wretched survivors of the siege might be nailed ("Wars", V. 3:2; 1; VI. 1:1).

The following list mentions the trees of the Bible in

alphabetical order, but any student who has studied botany
will find it interesting to group them into scientific classes.
Algum (almug) was a very hard and fine grained wood,
of a beautiful red color inside, with a black exterior.   It
was used by Solomon in the construction of musical instruments as well as his Temple and palace.   The Hebrew
"oren" in Isa. 44:14 is translated by the Authorized Version ash, by the Revised Version fir tree.   It was used in the
making of idols.   The word bay occurs only once in the Scripture: "I have seen the wicked . . . . . spreading himself like a

No. 102.   Cedars of Lebanon.

green bay tree" (Ps. 37:35).   The box is a small tree, or
shrub, widely distributed.   In Isa. 60:13 it is, together with
the fir tree and the pine tree, spoken of as the glory of Lebanon.   The cone-bearing trees are perhaps the most important of the monarchs of the forest, and the cedars of Lebanon
are, at least in historical interest, the most important of the

numerous tribe which includes amongst its members the pines, spruce trees, fir trees, larches, arbor vitae, cypresses, junipers, yews, besides the loftiest, thickest and oldest trees in existence in the world—the sequoias of California. The cedar is mentioned 74 times in the Old Testament. It is a large tree reaching up to 100 feet in height and 50 in circumference. It supplied the timber for the Temples of Solomon, Zerubbabel and Herod. It was used for building ships as well as palaces (Ezek. 27:5), for making idols (Isa. 44:14) as well as temples. It was used in ceremonial purifications (Lev. 19:4; Num. 19:6), and often was employed to express symbolic truth. It symbolized stateliness, solemn grandeur, great strength. The chestnut was used by Jacob in his stratagem to get rich (Gen. 30:37). There is some doubt as to the translation of the word tirzah, which occurs only in one passage: "He heweth him down cedars, and taketh the cypress and the oak" (Isa. 44:14). In the above rendering, from the Authorized Version, tirzah is translated cypress. In the Revised Version it is rendered holm tree. Others have proposed beech, oak, fir or ilex, all of which denote wood with a fairly hard grain, from which idols could be made. This also is an illustration of the difficulty, at times, of translation, and the limitation of scholarship. In Ezek. 27:15 the prophet is speaking of the commerce of the famous commercial center of his day (Tyre) and the costly ebony wood as one of the commodities. The word elm occurs only once in the Authorized Version: "They burn incense upon the hills, under oaks and poplars and elms". The Revised Version, the Norwegian and other versions render it terebinth. The fir was used in the manufacture of musical instruments (2 Sam. 6:5) and spears (Nah. 2:3 R. V.), and in the building of temples and ships (Ezek. 27:5). It is promised as one of the signs of the coming of the glory of the Lord: "Instead of the thorn shall come up the fir tree" (Isa. 55:13). God commanded Noah to make him an ark of gopher wood (Gen. 6:14).

Gesenius has suggested that gopher was another form of kopher, meaning pitch, and argued that cypress was most likely the tree intended. Elijah lay and slept in the desert under a juniper tree (1 Kings 19:4-5). The mulberry is a native of Palestine, and its leaves can rustle in the wind as well as those of the aspen or poplar (2 Sam. 5:23-24). Isaiah prophesied of a better day, when the Lord would plant the myrtle in the wilderness (Isa. 41:19), of a time when "instead of the brier shall come up the myrtle" (Isa. 55:13). The oak was a familiar tree in Palestine. Among the incidents of Scripture in connection with oaks may be mentioned that Abraham dwelt by the oaks of Mamre (Gen. 14: 13). Absalom lost his life by being entangled in an oak (2 Sam. 18). It symbolized strength. The oil tree is a small tree, or shrub, with silvery leaves and small flowers. It bears a green berry of a bitter taste, and yields an oil inferior to olive, used for medicine, but not for food (Isa. 41:19). Of the pine tree the prophet said: "The glory of Lebanon shall come unto thee, the fir tree, the pine tree, and the box together" (Isa. 60:13). The poplar is familiar to all parts of Palestine (Hos. 4:13). The shittah was the tree that furnished the wood of which the ark, tables, altars, bars and pillars of the Tabernacle were made, now believed to have been the wood of the acacia, which is very hard, close grained, orange brown in color, very durable and adapted for cabinet work. The teil and the terebinth were varieties of oak. Thyine wood was an article on the markets of mystic Babylon(Rev. 18:12). By the rivers of Babylon repentant exiles sat down, when they remembered Zion, and hung their harps upon the willows in their midst (Ps. 137:2). Samson was bound by rope made of withes (Judg. 16:7-9).

b. FRUIT TREES.

Palestine is more noted for its fruit trees than for its standing timber, and more famous for its gardens, orchards and vineyards than for its great forests. With its rich soil, abundant and seasonable rain and varied climate, the country was well adapted to fruit raising and farming. It seems that everybody, high and low, took a hand in the cultivation of the fruit trees in those "good old days". Solomon relates about himself that he made himself gardens and orchards, and planted trees in them of all kinds of fruit (Eccl. 2:5). Micah prophesies of the time coming when every man shall sit under his vine and fig tree (Micah 4:4). It seems that the country was dotted with gardens and vineyards. The word garden occurs over 60 times and the word vineyard over 100 times. Palestine was called not only a "land of milk and honey" (Ex. 13:5), but also a "land of bread and vineyards" (2 Kings 18:32). It is possible that the vineyard was regarded by the Israelites as their most precious possession, and on that account the Lord, in seeking to gain their attention and obedience, threatens time and again to destroy their vineyards. The Lord likened the Chosen People to a vineyard, carefully planted, cultivated and watched over by Himself, the Good Husbandman (Isa. 5).

The following is a reference to each of the fruit trees mentioned in the Bible: In the test as to who had the right of the office of high priest, it was found that Aaron's rod had "brought forth buds and bloomed blossoms and bare ripe almonds" (Num. 17:8). In Prov. 25:11 we are told that "a word fitly spoken is like apples of gold in a network of silver". In Mark 11:13-14 is related the incident of the cursing of the fruit tree. In Luke 15:16 the Prodigal Son is said to have fain satisfied his hunger with the husks that the swine ate. In Gen. 43:11 the sons of Jacob are instructed to take, amongst other things, nuts as a present to the ruler of Egypt. In Rom. 11:24 the Gentiles are spoken of as a wild olive tree. In Luke 19:4 it is recorded that Zaccheus climbed up into a sycamore tree. In John 15:5 Jesus says: "I am the Vine, ye are the branches: He that abideth in Me, and I in him, the same bringeth forth much fruit; for without Me ye can do nothing". In Ps. 92:12 we are told that the "righteous shall flourish like the palm tree".

c. GRAINS AND GRASSES.

The chief industry of Canaan was farming. Raising of herds and flocks was also at all times a popular occupation. Abraham and Lot had vast herds. Saul and David were shepherds. On Christmas Eve there were shepherds keeping watch over their flocks by night. Canaan was well adapted for grazing and agriculture. The Lord promised, too, that he would bring His Chosen People "into a good land, a land of brooks, of water, of fountains and depths that spring out of valleys and hills; a land of wheat and barley; and vines, and fig trees and pomegranates; a land of oil olive and honey; a land wherein thou shalt eat bread without scarceness, and not lack anything in it" (Deut. 8:7-9).

Herewith is given one reference to each of the grains and grasses mentioned in the Bible. In Ruth 1:22 Ruth came to Bethlehem in the beginning of the barley harvest. In Ex. 2:3 Moses' mother made for him an ark of bulrushes. In Gen. 41:49 Joseph laid up corn, grain, as the sand of the sea, very much. In Isa. 28:27 the fitches are beaten out with a staff. In Ex. 9:31 the plague of hail smote the flax and the barley in Egypt. In Job 8:11 Bildad asked: "Can the flax grow without water?" In Ps. 90:5 Moses likens the life of man to the grass, which in the morning flourisheth, and in the evening is cut down. In Matt. 11:7 Jesus asks whether John the Baptist was a reed shaken by the wind. In Isa. 9:14 it was prophesied that the Lord will cut off from Israel head and tail, palm-branch and rush, in one day. In Matt. 13:25 we have the parable of the tares sown among the wheat. In Luke 22:31 Satan is said to have asked to have Peter that he might sift him as wheat.

d. VEGETABLES.

We shall in the same manner give one reference to each of the vegetables mentioned in the Bible. In 2 Sam. 17:28 it is said that when David was fleeing from Absalom, an Ammonite brought him various kinds of food including beans and lentils and parched pulse. In Isa. 1:8 Jerusalem is compared to a lodge in a garden of cucumbers, as a besieged city. In Num. 11:5 the children of Israel weeping said that they remembered the fish, cucumbers, melons, leeks, onions and garlic of Egypt. In Jonah 4: 6 Jonah was exceeding glad on account of the gourd which the Lord had caused to spring up and furnish a shadow over his head. In Gen. 30:14 Reuben brought mandrakes unto his mother Leah, and these were desired by Rachel.

e. HERBS.

In like manner we shall give herewith one reference to each herb mentioned in Scripture. In Matt. 23:23 Jesus pronounces woe upon the Pharisees for paying tithes of mint and anise and cummin, and having omitted the weightier matters of the Law, judgment, mercy and faith. In Judges 9:14 is the parable of the Bramble. In Isa. 7:24 it is prophesied that Assyria shall become briers and thorns. In Job 31:40 Job protests that if he has not been righteous then may cockle grow up instead of barley. In Num. 11: 7 manna is said to be like coriander seed. In Eccl. 12:5 the time is spoken of when the grasshopper shall be a burden and desire shall fail (desire was a plant eaten as a stimulant to the appetite). In Deut. 29:18 Moses speaks of a root that bears gall and wormwood. In Hos. 10:4 judgment is said to spring up as hemlock in the furrows of the field. In Prov. 15:17 the wiseman says that a dinner of herbs where love is, is better than a stalled ox and hatred therewith. In Ps. 51:7 David pleads with the Lord to purge him with hyssop that he may be clean. In Job 30:4 juniper roots and mallows are mentioned. In

Luke 13:19 the Kingdom of Heaven is likened to a grain
of mustard seed. In Zeph. 2:9 it is prophesied that Moab
and Ammon shall become the breeding place of nettles. In
Luke 11:42 the rue is mentioned as one of the herbs tithed
by the Pharisees. In Matt. 7:16 Jesus says that men do
not gather figs of thistles. In John 19:5 Jesus came forth
wearing a crown of thorns. In Jer. 23:15 it is said concerning the false prophets: "That the Lord will feed them
with wormwood and make them drink water of gall".

f. FLOWERS.

Canaan is a land of flowers even to this day, and yet the
Bible very rarely mentions flowers in general or in particular. The word flower occurs only 34 times in the Bible,
and the blossom only 3 times. Only two flowers are mentioned by name, namely, the lily and the rose. In Matt.
6: 28, in speaking of trusting in God, Christ says: "Consider the lilies of the field, how they grow," etc. In Isa.
35: 1, in speaking of the flourishing of Christ's Kingdom,
the prophet says: "The desert shall rejoice and blossom
as the rose."

g. PERFUMES AND MEDICINES.

Perfumes and medicines are to a large extent made
from vegetable extracts or compounds. Both of these seem
to have been in considerable use among the Hebrews. Perfumes entered into the ritual of the Old Covenant worship,
and incense was burnt every day in the Holy Place. They
were used also as articles of customary adornment and
marks of special honor, as when Mary anointed Christ's
feet (John 12: 3) and head (Matt. 26: 6). In Ezek. 47:12
they were tokens of respect for the living, as when the
wisemen brought Jesus frankincense and myrrh. They
express also affection for the dead, as when the women
brought spices and ointment to the tomb of Jesus.

On page 356 was given a list of the plants mentioned in the Bible as used for perfumes and medicines among the Hebrews. In John 19:39 Nicodemus came to take the body of Jesus away, bringing with him a mixture of myrrh and aloes. In Jer. 8:22 the desperate plight of Jerusalem is set forth in these words: "Is there no balm in Gilead; is there no physician there?" In Ex. 30:23 cinnamon, calamus and cassia are mentioned as the principal spices used together with olive oil for anointing. In the Song of Solomon 12:14 the king compares his lover to a cluster of camphire or of henna flowers. In Jer. 6:20 the Lord protests against the incense from Sheba and the sweet cane from a far country, because the sacrifices of a wicked people were not sweet unto Him. In Matt. 23:23 the Lord rebukes the Pharisees because they tithed cummin, but neglected to do right. In Matt. 2:11 the wisemen gave the child Jesus frankincense and myrrh. In Ex. 30:34 the formula for the Holy perfume to be used in the Tabernacle is given: An equal weight of the four sweet spices frankincense, galbanum, onycha and stacte. In the Song of Solomon 4:14 the king says that the smell of his bride's garments is like the smell of Lebanon...... and like spikenard and saffron, etc. In 2 Chron. 9:1 the Queen of Sheba came to visit Solomon accompanied by a great train of camels that bare spices and gold in abundance and precious stones.

3. ANIMALS.

Palestine combines many very opposite physical features: Mountain and plain, garden and desert, land and sea, hot and cold. This fact accounts for the presence of the great diversity of animals native to the country. The Bible, of course, does not mention all of the beasts and birds, fish and reptiles, that are found in the land. In the list below, for example, are given only 33 of the 80 varieties of quadrupeds and 28 of the 350 kinds of birds now found in Palestine.

a. QUADRUPEDS.

(a) *Domestic Beasts.*

NAMES	TIMES MENTIONED	ILLUSTRATIONS
(1) Ass	136	Matt. 21:7
(2) Camel	59	Gen. 24:19
(3) Cattle (Ox, etc.)	553	Ex. 20:10
(4) Dog	41	Matt. 7:28
(5) Dromedary	4	Esther 8:10
(6) Goat	210	Lev. 9:15
(7) Horse	144	Ps. 147:10
(8) Mule	20	2 Sam. 18:9
(9) Sheep (Ram, Lamb)	497	Matt. 7:15
(10) Swine	20	Matt. 7:6
Total	1684	

(b) *Wild Beasts.*

NAMES	TIMES MENTIONED	ILLUSTRATIONS
(1) Ape	2	1 Kings 10:22
(2) Badger	14	Ex. 25:5
(3) Bat	3	Isa. 2:20
(4) Bear	14	Prov. 17:12
(5) Behemoth	1	Job 40:15
(6) Chamois	1	Deut. 14:5
(7) Coney	4	Lev. 11:5
(8) Elephant (Ebony, Ivory)	14	2 Chron. 9:21
(9) Ferret	1	Lev. 11:30
(10) Fox	9	Matt. 8:20
(11) Hare	2	Deut. 14:7
(12) Hart (Roe, Hind)	38	Ps. 42:1
(13) Leopard	8	Isa. 11:6
(14) Lion	176	Dan. 6:22
(15) Mole	2	Isa. 2:20
(16) Mouse	6	1 Sam. 6:5
(17) Pygarg	1	Deut. 14:5
(18) Unicorn	9	Num. 23:20
(19) Weasel	1	Lev. 11:29
(20) Wild Ass	11	Ps. 104:11
(21) Wild Goat	3	Ps. 104:18
(22) Wolf	12	Matt. 10:16
(23) Beasts	304	Gen. 6:7
Total Quadrupeds	2320	

b. BIRDS.

	NAMES	TIMES MENTIONED	ILLUSTRATIONS
(1)	Bittern	3	Isa. 14:23
(2)	Cormorant	4	Deut. 14:7
(3)	Crane	2	Isa. 38:14
(4)	Cuckoo	2	Lev. 11:16
(5)	Dove (Pigeon)	43	Gen. 8:8
(6)	Eagle (Gier)	34	Isa. 40:41
(7)	Fowl	97	Mark 14:30
(8)	Glede	1	Deut. 14:13
(9)	Hawk	5	Job 39:26
(10)	Heron	2	Lev. 11:19
(11)	Kite	2	Lev. 11:14
(12)	Lapwing	2	Deut. 14:18
(13)	Ospray	2	Deut. 14:12
(14)	Ossifrage	2	Deut. 14:12
(15)	Ostrich	2	Lam. 4:3
(16)	Owl	16	Lev. 11:17
(17)	Partridge	2	1 Sam. 26:20
(18)	Peacock	3	1 Kings 10:22
(19)	Pelican	3	Ps. 102:6
(20)	Quail	4	Ex. 16:13
(21)	Raven	16	Luke 12:24
(22)	Sparrow	6	Matt. 10:29
(23)	Stork	5	Jer. 8:7
(24)	Swallow	4	Ps. 84:3
(25)	Swan	2	Lev. 11:18
(26)	Turtledove	15	Luke 2:24
(27)	Vulture	4	Isa. 34:15
(28)	Birds	51	Gen. 7:14
	Total	334	

c. AQUATIC CREATURES.

	NAMES	TIMES MENTIONED	ILLUSTRATIONS
(1)	Coral	2	Ezek. 27:16
(2)	Fish	60	Gen. 9:2
(3)	Pearl	9	Matt. 13:45
(4)	Whale	4	Matt. 12:40
	Total	75	

d. REPTILES AND AMPHIBIA.

NAMES	TIMES MENTIONED	ILLUSTRATIONS
(1) Adder	5	Prov. 23:32
(2) Asp	5	Isa. 11:8
(3) Chameleon	1	Lev. 11:30
(4) Cockatrice	4	Isa. 14:29
(5) Dragon	33	Isa. 34:13
(6) Frog	14	Ex. 8:6
(7) Leviathan	4	Job 41:1
(8) Lizard	1	Lev. 11:30
(9) Serpent	53	Gen. 3:1
(10) Tortoise	1	Lev. 11:29
(11) Viper	8	Acts 28:3
(12) Creeping Things	28	Gen. 1:26
Total	157	

e. INSECTS AND OTHER SMALL ANIMALS.

	TIMES MENTIONED	ILLUSTRATIONS
(1) Ant	2	Prov. 6:6
(2) Bee	4	Ps. 118:12
(3) Beetle	1	Lev. 11:22
(4) Caterpillar	9	Joel 1:4
(5) Flea	2	1 Sam. 24:14
(6) Fly	2	Eccl. 10:1
(7) Gnat	1	Matt. 23:24
(8) Grasshopper	10	Judg. 6:5
(9) Hornet	3	Ex. 23:28
(10) Horseleach	1	Prov. 30:15
(11) Louse	6	Ex. 8:17
(12) Locust	28	Matt. 3:4
(13) Moth	10	Matt. 6:19
(14) Scorpion	9	Rev. 9:10
(15) Snail	2	Ps. 58:8
(16) Spider	3	Isa. 59:5
(17) Worm (Cankerworm)	25	Ex. 16:20
Total	118	

SUMMARY OF LIST OF ANIMALS.

CLASS	TIMES MENTIONED
a. Quadrupeds	2320
b. Birds	334
c. Aquatic Creatures	75

CLASS	TIMES MENTIONED
d. Reptiles and Amphibia	157
e. Insects and Other Small Animals	118
Total	3004

a. QUADRUPEDS.

The tame animals are mentioned at least 1684 times in the Bible, the wild beasts 626 times, a total of 2310.   Cattle, sheep and goats are mentioned oftenest.   The Hebrews had considerable herds of cattle and sheep, as these were extensively used for food and sacrifices.   At the dedication of the Temple Solomon offered 22,000 oxen and 120,000 sheep (1 Kings 8: 33), and at its cleansing he offered 600 oxen and 3,000 sheep (2 Chron. 29: 33).   The camel and dromedary, the horse, mule and ass, together with the ox, were the beasts of burden.   The dog and swine were both declared unclean and regarded with contempt (Lev. 11:7; 1 Sam. 17:43; Isa. 65:4).   Even in the New Testament the dogs and swine are held in disrepute.   "Beware of dogs, beware of evil workers" (Phil. 3:2).   "The dog is turned to his own vomit" (2 Pet. 2:22).   "Neither cast ye your pearls before swine" (Matt. 7:6).   And the Prodigal Son was sent into the fields to feed swine (Luke 15:15)—the utmost degradation.

Of wild beasts the lion is mentioned oftenest, far outstripping all the rest.   The stories of the personal encounters with the lion by Samson and David and Daniel always interest the young.   The lion was the emblem of the Tribe of Judah.   It typified also ferocity (Ps. 7: 2; 2 Tim. 4:17; 1 Pet. 5: 8).   The hart was reckoned among the clean animals permitted for food.   Its fleetness is spoken of in connection with the Kingdom of Christ: "Then shall the lame man leap as a hart" (Isa. 35:6).   The bear is mentioned in the story of David and of Elisha.   In Daniel's vision it symbolized the Persian Empire.   In Isaiah's proph-

ecy it was made to feed in the same pasture as the cow,
symbolizing the change in the human heart by Christ. The
wolf illustrates cruelty and rapacity. In Isaiah's symbol
of Messianic peace the wolf lives with the lamb (Isa. 11:6;
65:25).

b. BIRDS, FISH, REPTILES AND INSECTS.

Many of the references to the other animals are interesting. The birds are either clean or unclean. All the birds
of prey were unclean. Pigeons and turtle doves were
used for sacrifices and food. The domestic hen and cock
enter into the story of Jesus. The strength and swiftness
of the eagle, his powers of sight and rapacity are often
pictured by the prophets with telling effect. The Bible
divides fish as well as fowl into two kinds. All the fish
without fins or scales were unclean (Lev. 11:9-12). There
was an abundance of fish in the Sea of Galilee, where
Peter and Andrew, James and John were engaged as fish-
ermen before Christ called them to become "fishers of
men." Jonah was swallowed by a great fish, called by
Christ a whale. There have been found about 30 species
of serpents in Palestine. The habits and character of the
serpent is often described in the Bible. Already in the
Garden of Eden he was the most subtile of all the beasts.
In the Wilderness the rebellious pilgrims were bitten by
fiery serpents (Num. 21:6), on account of which Moses
set up a brazen serpent symbolizing the crucified Savior
(John 3:14). In the list of ten plagues upon Pharaoh, frogs
are mentioned as the second plague, lice as the third, flies
as the fourth and the locusts as the eighth. The insects, too,
were used to benefit man—punishing him when disobedient,
providing food for him, or serving as a text for a sermon.
"Go to the ant, thou sluggard". "They compassed me
about like bees". "Lay not up for yourselves treasures
upon earth, where moth and rust doth consume". "And
of which of you that is a father shall his son ask an egg,

will he give him a scorpion?" "Fear not, thou worm Jacob."

4. RACES OF MAN.

Ethnographers divide mankind into several distinct varieties, or races. One of the common classifications is that of Blumenbach, who makes five races:

NAME	NUMBERS	TERRITORY
a. White	725,000,000	W. Asia, Europe, America, etc.
b. Yellow	655,000.000	China, Japan, etc.
c. Black	170,000.000	Africa, Australia, etc.
d. Brown	50,000,000	Java, Sumatra, etc.
e. Red	23,000,000	N. and S. America, etc.
		(Whittaker's "Almanak", 1916).
Total	1,623,000,000	

Their present distribution by continents is as follows:

NAME	NUMBERS	SQUARE MILES
a. Asia	900,000,000	17,000,000
b. Africa	170,000,000	11,500,000
c. Europe	400,000,000	3,750,000
d. N. America	110,000,000	8,000,000
e. S. America	35,000,000	6,800,000
f. Oceanica	8,000,000	3,450,000
g. Polar Regions		5,000,000
Total	1,623,000,000	55,500,000

Their present distribution by descent is approximately as follows (Cf. Gen. 9:27):

NAME	NUMBERS	NATIONS	SQUARE MILES
a. Semitic	80,000,000	1	170,000
b. Japhetic	620,000,000	45	50,037,000
c. Hamitic	923,000,000	6	4,793,000
Total	1,623,000,000	52	55,500,000

It is important to note that race is not identical with people or nation or language. The white race includes many peoples and nations and languages. The Jewish people have now no nation of their own, but are citizens of various countries and speak the languages of these countries as their native tongue. The Canaanites were Hamitics, but spoke a Semitic language; the negroes of the United States are Hamitics, but speak a Japhetic language. The same race, or people even, may speak different languages; and different peoples, or races even, may speak the same language.

It is also important to note that, while man may easily change his language or his nationality, he can hardly remove the traces of his descent or his race. His language is determined by what is spoken in the home and on the street; his nationality is determined by the country he is born in or becomes a citizen of. But descent and race are part of his physiological make-up. A Jew is always a Jew by descent and race. An Englishman is always an Englishman. An Ethiopian can not change his skin. Intermarriage between races does not produce a distinctively new race, for the individuals resulting from such union have a tendency to revert to the racial types of their ancestors on either the paternal or the maternal side. Sometimes, even in the same family it happens that some of the children belong to the father's type, others to the mother's. The racial traits seem to have been fixed for all time already before the beginning of history. Among these traits may be mentioned the color of skin, hair and eyes, shape of skull, jaw, nose, eyes, mouth, lips and teeth. The Jew and the Egyptian of to-day have the same forms, features and other physiological traits as they had 1500 years B. C. This can be proved by an examination of the ancient pictures in stone and coin. The races will always remain distinct. Yet, notwithstanding the differences between the races they are clearly of one blood (Gen. 9; Acts 17:26). They have common wants and weaknesses, hopes and aspirations. They have the Law written in their hearts, and the Gospel is the power unto salvation for all who believe.

The Bible uses about 190 terms to designate what race, people, nation or city a person belonged to. Thus, Egyptian, Hebrew, Samaritan, Moabite, Amorite. All of the languages have been changed. Nearly all of them, including the Hebrew, are dead and spoken no more. All of the nations then in existence have fallen and new ones have risen on their foundations. Some of the peoples have disappeared. But the races and the race traits remain the same. The Semitics are still Semitics, the Hamitics are still Hamitics, and the Japhetics are still Japhetics.

The references to the races of mankind in the Bible are approximately as follows:

RACE	PEOPLES OR TRIBES	TIMES MENTIONED
a. Semitic	46	2328
b. Japhetic	24	122
c. Hamitic	120	1196
Total	190	3646

SUMMARY OF PHYSICAL ANTIQUITIES OF THE BIBLE.

CLASS	TIMES MENTIONED
1. Minerals	2702
2. Plants	1473
3. Animals	3004
4. Races	3646
Total.	10825

What is meant by antiquities? By physical antiquities?

Define natural history. What does Biblical natural history include? How many kingdoms may natural objects be divided into? Illustrate.

Into what classes may objects belonging to the mineral kingdom be divided?

Give a Bible reference in which each of the following mineral substances occurs: Earth, clay, dust, sand, stone, slime, mire, salt, sulphur. How often does each of these words occur in the Bible?

What is meant by metal? Name the metals mentioned in the Bible. Give one Bible reference in which each of the following metals is mentioned: Gold, silver, iron, copper, lead, tin, steel, brass. State how many times each of these metals is mentioned in the Bible.

What is a precious stone? What precious stones are mentioned in the Bible? What precious stones are mentioned in the description of the breastplate? Of the ornaments of the king of Tyre? Of the foundations of the New Jerusalem? Name the symbolic meanings attached to some of the stones.

How many times are mineral substances mentioned in the Bible? Metals? Precious stones?

Into what seven classes may the members of the vegetable kingdom be grouped? Give examples of each of the groups, showing the number of times certain individual species are mentioned in the Bible. Give the total number of references for each group and for the whole vegetable kingdom.

Locate the forests of Palestine. Mention the principal timber trees, and give at least one reference to each in the Bible.

What is said about the orchards of Palestine? Mention the principal fruit trees, and give one reference to each in the Bible.

What was the chief industry of Canaan? Mention some of its grains and grasses, and give a Bible reference to each species.

Mention some of the garden products, and give Bible references.

Mention some of the herbs together with the Bible passages.

What two flowers are mentioned by name in the Bible? Quote a Bible passage for each.

What can you say about the extent to which perfumes were used among the Hebrews? Give illustrations. What plants were used as medicines? Give illustrations.

How can you account for the presence of the great diversity of animals native to Canaan? How many different kinds of animals are mentioned in the Bible?

Name some of the quadrupeds, and tell one Biblical incident connected with each. Likewise mention some of the birds, fish, reptiles and insects, and give appropriate Bible incidents.

Give the common five-fold classification of mankind. Show their present distribution by continents and population. Their present distribution by descent and population. What is the difference between a people and a nation? Show how one people or nation may speak different languages. One's language is determined by what? One's nationality? One's physiological make-up? What are some of the marks of descent to distinguish Semitics, Hamitics, Japhetics?

What does your Bible history say about the physical antiquities? Look up the Bible passages referred to in your lesson, and find additional references to this subject in the Bible. In what ways can the contents of this lesson help you in your Bible study? In your faith and works?

LESSON FORTY-TWO. DOMESTIC ANTIQUITIES.

1. FAMILY RELATIONS.

Human society is divided into various larger and smaller groups, of which the Family is the most important. The Family is the foundation of all other natural associations of mankind. The Family is thus set forth in the Bible, and is in every way protected by the wise Laws of God.

a. MARRIAGE.

God created the human race in two sexes, man and woman. He said that it was not good that man should be alone. Man needed a helpmate. He ordained marriage already in Paradise, and made it a life fellow-ship between the two sexes for the propagation, preservation and spiritual development of the race. The original plan was, that the two should become one flesh (Gen. 2:24; Matt. 19:4; Eph. 5:31). The plan was that a man should have only one wife at a time, and a woman should have only one husband. Having two or more spouses or concubines was not according to God's plan. God forbade the Israelites to intermarry with the heathen Canaanites, lest they seduce the godly to ungodliness and idolatry. He warned Christians, too, to marry within the Church (1 Cor. 7:39; 2 Cor. 6:14). He forbade also marriages between certain near relatives, such as, a man with his mother, sister, etc. (Lev. 18).

The Bible records many variations from the above ideal as to the marriage relationship. Lamech, Jacob, David and Solomon married more than one wife. Solomon had 1000 wives and concubines. Joseph and Moses married outside of the Chosen People. Abraham married his half-sister Sarah. Nevertheless, the Bible is clear as to the ideal marriage and its sacredness as a divine institution for the propagation of the race, the protection of morals, the instruction of the young in the way they should go, and a symbol of the happy union between the Lord and His Church. Even the betrothal was considered sacred, equivalent to marriage.

In the story of Isaac we get a glimpse of how unions were contracted. Abraham sent his trusty servant Eliezer to Haran to find a suitable maiden for Isaac, who was then 40 years of age, and perfectly able to choose for himself. When Eliezer had finally found a maiden suitable for his master's son, he made a contract with her father and brother, whereupon she herself was called in and asked if she would consent to the match (Gen. 24). In Gen. 21:21 the mother of Ishmael took a wife for him out of Egypt. On betrothal, a dowry was paid for the girl (Gen. 24:53), and a present was also given to her. Jacob had to pay for his wives by service rendered. " And Jacob served seven years for Rachel; and they seemed unto him but a few days, for the love he had to her" (Gen. 29:20). His case is no doubt an exception, for the giving of a dowry was not, properly speaking, a price paid for the wife, and the wife was not considered as a slave, but as an equal and a companion, although obedient to her husband as head of the house. "For the husband is the head of the wife, as Christ also is the Head of the Church" (Eph. 5:22; Gen. 3:16). The dowry and present, like the engagement ring of today, were looked upon more in the light of sealing the contract. Parents, too, would bestow presents on their daughters at the time of their engagement (Gen. 29:24,29). The general relations of man and wife are set forth in 1 Cor. 11:3-12; 14:35; Eph. 5:22-33; Col. 3:18-19; 1 Tim. 2:11-15; 1 Pet. 3:1-7.

A special form of marriage was the levirate, from the Latin word levir—brother-in-law. This was the union of a widow who was childless with her brother-in-law. The object of this kind of marriage was to prevent the extinction of the name of any man who was childless and to keep the land within the same family. If a son was born of the levirate marriage he would assume his uncle's name and inherit his estate (Deut. 25:5; Matt. 22:24). A man had the option of refusing to enter such a union. If he did refuse, the widow might expect the next of kin to assume the obligations. In the case of Ruth, Boaz was the second of kin (Ruth 4:7). In the case of the woman in Matt. 22:24-32 seven brothers in turn had had her.

The wedding was a great and joyful event in the Hebrew household. The ceremony was performed before witnesses (Ruth 4:11), although apparently without the presence of a priest. The festival lasted seven days, or even 14 (Judg. 14:12, 17; Tobit 8:20). In Luke 14:17 the guests were first invited and then summoned by special messenger. In Matt. 22:1-10; 25:1-10 the bridal procession is said to have taken place at night. The newly married men were exempt from military duties the first year after their marriage (Deut. 24:5). Such exemption applied also to those who had become engaged (Deut. 20:7). Jesus was present at the marriage in Cana and turned water into wine.

> O happy home, where Thou art loved the dearest,
> Thou loving Friend and Savior of our race,
> And where among the guests there never cometh
> One who can hold such high and honored place.

b. DIVORCE.

God's high moral standard as to marriage was often perverted by plural marriages, adultery and divorce. All three forms of violating the ideal marriage state are displeasing to the Lord.

Adultery was forbidden in the Sixth Commandment (Ex. 20:14; Deut. 5:18; Matt. 5:28). The penalty for adultery was, that both of the guilty parties should be stoned to death (Lev. 20:10; Deut. 22:22-24). All forms of harlotry and prostitution were subject to punishment. The

word adultery is used in Scripture also in a figurative
sense to denote the worship of false gods, the unfaithful-
ness to the Covenant vows (Jer. 3:8-9; Ezek. 23:37-43;
Hosea).

Divorce was permitted in the Mosaic Laws, but not commanded. It is also permitted in the Christian code. Moses
permitted a man to put away his wife if he found "some
unseemly thing in her". Just what is meant by "unseemly
thing" is a matter of dispute. Christ explained this legislation to the Pharisees, saying that Moses had suffered
men to put away their wives on account of their hardness
of heart (Matt. 19:8). Christ held that adultery alone
was an excuse for seeking a divorce (Matt. 19: 9). What
God had joined together, no man should put asunder. In
this country marriage and divorce are considered essentially as affairs under the control of the State, and not the
Church. The State permits a licensed pastor to officiate
at a wedding, but it alone determines the grounds for
divorce. Divorces were a scandal in Israel; every twelfth
home in America is broken up by divorce.

c. CHILDREN.

Children are looked upon in the Bible as a matter of
longing and joy, a heritage and a reward (Gen. 24:60;
30:1; Deut. 28:4; 1 Sam. 1:11; Ps. 113:9; Prov. 17:6;
etc.). Abraham prayed for a son. So did Hannah. Ste-
rility in marriage was deeply lamented as a punishment
from God (1 Sam. 1:6; Luke 1:25; Isa. 47:9; etc.).
Many children was a source of pride (Ps. 127). The Bible contains some very touching scenes portraying par-
ental love, as, for example, Abraham's love for Isaac at
his offering him up (Gen. 22), Jacob's sorrow over Joseph at learning of his supposed death (Gen. 37:35) and David's despairing cries over his lost Absalom (2 Sam. 19:4).

Male children were circumcised on the eighth day and
presented at the sanctuary on the fortieth. First born

males were redeemed. Female children were presented at the sanctuary on the eightieth day. The weaning of the child was celebrated with a feast (Gen. 21:8) or a sacrifice (1 Sam. 1:23-25).

The work of training began in the home. The fear of the Lord was the beginning of wisdom. The Word of God was taught. Reverence for parents was emphasized as a condition of prosperity (Ex. 22:12; Deut. 5:16). Timothy is said by Paul to have known the Holy Scriptures from childhood, having learnt them from his grandmother Lois and his mother Eunice. Other Bible women, too, seem to have had a hand in shaping the destinies of their sons. Among these were the mothers of Moses and Samuel.

The eldest son was entitled to special privileges. After the death of his father, he took his place as the head of the family and the chief heir of the estate. The eldest son might sell his birthright, as in the case of Esau (Gen. 25:33; Heb. 12:17).

d. SERVANTS.

Slavery existed in all of the ancient countries. The servants of antiquity were nearly all slaves, either bought in the markets or captured in war, or children born to slaves already in the house. Joseph was sold as a slave. The Israelites were slaves in Egypt. The Gibeonites became servants to the Israelites. The Mosaic Laws did not seek to abolish slavery, but to soften its severity (Ex. 20:10; Deut. 5:14; 12:18; etc.). Slaves of Hebrew origin might be redeemed at any time by their relatives and might not be sent away empty-handed (Ex. 21:2-11; Deut. 15:12-15). If not redeemed before the Sabbatical year, they were bound to be liberated then. Slaves of foreign origin were freed only when harshly treated or injured by their masters (Ex. 21: 20-27). Although the Mosaic Laws sought to protect the slave, it recognized the great difference between the bond and the free state (Rom. 8: 15;

Gal. 4:1-7). In matters of salvation there is no difference: "There is neither bond nor free......for ye are all one in Christ Jesus" (Gal. 3:28).

At the time of Christ slavery was at its worst in the heathen world. Over one-half of the population was slave. A slave was regarded, not as a person, but as a beast that could talk. He had no legal rights under Rome. He was bought and sold, branded and marked, flogged and crucified, often on the least provocation. Christianity gave liberty to the slave, but not all at once. Christ gave first spiritual freedom, but with that follows civil liberty. He makes free indeed. This is clearly set forth in 1 Cor. 7:21-23 and Philemon.

There were other servants, too, day laborers, who worked for hire, which had to be paid promptly (Deut. 24:14-15; Jas. 5:4). The position of the servant, as well as that of the slave, was much elevated by Christ. In Matt. 20:27 He proclaimed: "And whosoever will be chief among you, let him be your servant." In Matt. 25:21 He said: "Well done, thou good and faithful servant. Thou hast been faithful over a few things; I will make thee ruler over many things. Enter thou into the joy of the Lord".

e. THE FAMILY IN JOY.

The Hebrews had many occasions for social gatherings in addition to the stated services at the sanctuary. There were, for example, the weddings, weanings of children, and funerals, the grain and fruit harvests and sheep shearings, and the ordinary visits of relatives and friends from far and near. The Bible gives us many glimpses of this social life carried on in moderation, as, Jesus at Cana, or in sinful excess, as, Samaria at the time of Amos (Amos 6). The Hebrews were a hospitable people and very demonstrative in their manner of greeting guests (Gen. 18:6; 19:1-10; Matt. 25:35; Rom. 12:13; etc.). The kiss, the embrace, the profound bow to the ground and the

"Peace be with you" were customary forms of greeting (Gen. 29:11-13; 33:4; 1 Sam. 25:6; Mark 5:31; etc.). Goodbyes were said with a bow, a kiss or a benediction (Gen. 32:1; Ruth 1:14; Acts 20:37; etc.).

In addition to social gatherings and banquets the Hebrews amused themselves by various other diversions. Samson put forth a riddle at his wedding feast (Judg. 14:12). Later, the Philistines made "sport" of Samson at their feast to Dagon (Judg. 16:25). Isaiah refers to ball playing (Isa. 22:18); Paul, to the Grecian games (Phil. 3:14; 2 Tim. 2:5), the footrace (1 Cor. 9:24; Heb. 12:1-2) and boxing (1 Cor. 9:26). An instance of a cruel sport in the Old Testament times is the "play" between 12 of the soldiers of Abner and 12 of the soldiers of Joab, in which all were slain by the sword (Cf. bull fights, prize fights, etc., of today). An instance of a very common sport in the Roman times is that of Paul's fighting with beasts in the arena (1 Cor. 15:32). The dance is mentioned 27 times in Scripture, an evidence of its popularity. Miriam danced at the passage of the Red Sea (Ex. 15:20). The Israelites danced around the Golden Calf at Sinai. Jephthah's daughter came out with dances to meet her victorious father (Judg. 11:34). David danced before the Lord when bringing home the Ark (2 Sam. 6:14). The daughter of Herodias danced so well that John the Baptist was beheaded (Matt. 14:6). At the return of the Prodigal Son there was music and dancing (Luke 15:25). It should be noted with respect to the dancing mentioned as pleasing to the Lord, that it was not like modern dances. The dance then was not participated in by the two sexes together, but by men alone or by women alone, an impossibility in our day. Miriam and David danced for the joy they had in the Lord, whereas most people now dance for the joy they seek in the world (Wm. Dallmann's "Dance", C. E. Nordberg's "Modern Amusements"). The most popular form of amusement among the Hebrews was music—both vocal and instrumental—which is mentioned over 650 times in Scripture.

f. THE FAMILY IN SORROW.

Sorrow and joy went hand in hand in the Hebrew as well as in other households. Sickness and suffering, death and burial, are some of the most realistic causes of sorrow. All of these in their deepest source spring from sin and, to a certain extent, are a judgment upon sin. As to sickness, it may be said that in general there was not much sickness among the Hebrews, for their climate and country were healthy, their food was clean and simple, their daily life was well ordered and guarded by sanitary laws and practices. Among the diseases mentioned in the Bible may be noted the following: cancers, consumption, dropsy, epilepsy, fevers, leprosy, lunacy, palsy, piles, etc. In addition to these were physical defects, such as, blindness, deafness, dumbness, lameness, etc. A most singular disease was that of demoniacal possession, very common during the days of our Lord on earth. Jesus spoke on various occasions to the demons, as distinct from the persons possessed by these evil spirits, and received replies. At His command they had to depart from the body of the unfortunates possessed. There are six specific cases in which Jesus cured those possessed by demons. Among his other miracles of healing are given four instances of curing the blind, one of curing the deaf, one of healing a crooked woman, one of dropsy, one of discharges, one of impotency, two of fevers, two of leprosy, two of palsy and one of a withered hand, besides raising three from the dead and healing Malchus' ear.

When sick the Hebrews seem to have had recourse to physicians, as in our own day, although perhaps not to such an extent. The science and art of medicine were as yet in their infancy. In fact, the office of physician was at first not distinct, but a part of the care of the priest or prophet. Back of the priest was the authority of the Lord, "Who healeth all our diseases" (Ps. 103:3). The word medicine is mentioned only 4 times in the Old Testament, and the word physician occurs only 4 times in the Old and 6 times in the New Testament. King Asa, for example, was said to have sought the physicians, and not the Lord (2 Chron. 16:12). The woman with the issue of blood had "suffered many things of many physicians, and had spent all she had", before she had a chance to put her trust in Jesus (Mark 5:24-34). The fame of Jesus went throughout all Palestine and Syria (Matt. 4:24), and "they brought unto Him all sick people that were taken with divers diseases and torments". No wonder He said: "They that are whole have no need of a physician, but they that are sick" (Mark. 2:17). No wonder we sing:

> The Great Physician now is near,
> The sympathizing Jesus.

When death entered the family the corpse was washed and embalmed with spices and perfumes and swathed in linen. So Lazarus was attired when raised to life by Christ's omnipotent voice. So Christ was to be embalmed by Nicodemus and the women. Loud lamentations attended the burial of the dead. There were often paid mourners (Matt. 9:23; Mark 5:38). The burial places were in caves, surrounded by gardens. A funeral feast succeeded the burial (2 Sam. 3:35). The most general token of mourning was a garment of sack cloth, together with rending of the garment and sprinkling ashes on the head.

2. FOOD, CLOTHING AND DWELLINGS.

The Bible is in the first place a book of religion. It shows God's plan of redemption. At the same time it is a history of the Chosen People, and incidentally it tells many facts as to food, clothing and homes of this people.

a. Food.

The articles of food used by men are determined to a

considerable extent by the products of the land and their state of culture. The Hebrews lived in a land flowing with milk and honey, a land of wheat and barley, of vines and fig trees and pomegranates, a land of fish and game. It goes without saying that their food was therefore varied and plentiful, at least as long as the land was favored by the Lord with early and late rains and bountiful increase from the flocks and herds, from the fields and orchards.

Plant foods—grains, fruits and vegetables—constituted the chief articles of diet. Especially was this the case in the Wilderness, for good hygienic reasons. Then the people longed for the fleshpots of Egypt and murmured at the manna. On the whole, the Hebrews lived a simple life, ate simple food, which was simply prepared. The flour from which bread was baked was coarse and made from the whole grain. The baking was thorough. Meat was seldom used for ordinary diet. Fish appears to have been a staple dish at the time of Christ. Only animals which the Law designated as clean—beast, bird or fish— were permitted to be used as food. Animals dying a natural death were prohibited as food. Wine was the chief beverage. Its abuse was clearly recognized and warned against. Drunkenness and gluttony were classified as harmful and sinful. Solomon says: "Be not among winebibbers; among riotous eaters of flesh: for the drunkard and glutton shall come to poverty" (Prov. 23:20-30). Peter spoke also against these excesses (1 Pet. 4:3). So also did Paul (1 Cor. 6:10; etc.) and Christ (Luke 21:34).

The food was placed on tables. In the early times the custom was to sit at the tables (Gen. 27:19). But later, instead of using chairs on which to sit, the Hebrews used special couches on which they reclined at meals. The custom was to lie on the left side, with the head toward the table. This practice was common in the days of Christ and is first mentioned in the book of Amos (6:4). This custom explains many otherwise difficult incidents, such as,

feetwashing during mealtime (Luke 7:36-38; John 13:5).
The custom was to wash and to say grace before meat.

b. CLOTHING.

The dress of the two sexes was almost identical, yet
sufficiently distinct, so that there was a Mosaic Law forbidding men to wear women's clothes, and vice versa (Deut.
22:5).   The dress of males consisted of two main parts—
a tunic, or underdress, extending to the knee, and an upper
dress.   The tunic was made of wool or cotton and worn
on the naked body.   It was fastened round the loins with

No. 103. A Priest and a Levite.

a girdle.   Over the tunic was the upper dress, which was
a square piece of cloth, like a very large shawl or blanket.
It was used by the poor as bed cover (Ex. 22:27).   Trou-

sers and stockings were not used except by the priests.
Sandals served for shoes and a turban for a hat. The
poor had neither head gear nor foot gear. Men of wealth
and rank had finer and costlier garments than the average.

Especially must be mentioned the dress of the high priest.
He had the priest's uniform of four pieces, and outside of

No. 104. A High Priest.

this another special dress, also of four pieces. The priest's
dress was in four colors—white, blue, purple and scarlet,
and consisted of four parts—trousers, coat, girdle and cap.
He was not allowed to wear shoes in the sanctuary. This
indicated that he was on holy ground. The four additional pieces of the high priest's dress were: An upper
robe woven of blue yarn with a lower fringe of pomegran-

ates made of blue, purple and scarlet twined yarn and little gold bells arranged in alternate order; the ephod, or shoulder piece, was made of gold and blue, purple and scarlet twined linen; the breastplate attached to the ephod and containing the 12 precious stones, upon which were engraved the names of the Twelve Tribes, besides the Urim and Thummim, which were possibly two additional stones concealed in the fold of the breastplate; and the head dress, containing a diadem with an inscription upon it, namely, "Holiness to Jehovah" (Ex. 28:1—29: 6).

The dress of the female consisted mainly of two parts— an underdress like that of the men, but as a rule wider, longer, and of finer material, and an upper dress, usually in colors. Women, too, used girdles, sandals, and turbans for hats. The women's dress differed from the men's, then, chiefly in its looseness and material. In the case of the more well-to-do, other distinctions also characterized female dress, namely, the veil and ornaments of gold and silver and other charms, including at times rings, earrings, bracelets, nose jewels, ankle ornaments, etc. (Isa. 8:18-23).

The Hebrews paid particular attention to their body in keeping it clean and healthy. They washed their hands and feet always before eating. They took frequent baths. Cleanliness to them was a symbol of innocence. It was for this reason that Pilate washed his hands when he turned Jesus over to the Jews to be crucified. He meant thereby to say that he was innocent of His blood. The Hebrews bestowed much care on their hair and beard, and their laws forbade any unnatural disfigurement of the body, such as was practised by the heathen nations round about.

c. DWELLINGS.

Most of the types of dwellings known to mankind are mentioned in the Bible. The Horites of Edom lived in caves (Deut. 2:12). Abraham lived in a tent. Jacob made

booths for his cattle, but a house for himself (Gen. 33:17).
The Israelites after the Conquest occupied fixed abodes,
one story houses with walls made of bricks, beams, doors

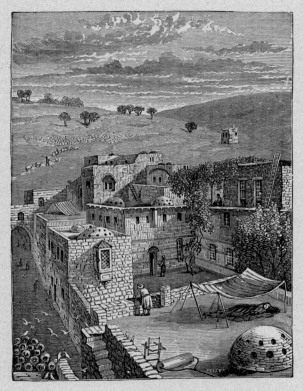

No. 105.   House Tops.

and windows of wood, and flat roofs. The flat roof was
laid with tiles and stone, and the outer edge had a railing
to prevent falling. Only the rich had houses of stone
(1 Kings 7:9; Isa. 9:9) or of marble (1 Chron. 19:2).

The kings had palaces. Solomon's palace was constructed on a grand scale (1 Kings 7:1-12). Among other royal abodes of surpassing magnificence were the palaces of the Persian king at Susa (Esther 1:5-9; 2:3-14; 5:1-2), of Herod (Josephus' "Antiquities", XV-XVI) and of Pilate (Mark. 15:16; John 18: 28, 33). Jesus did not live in any palace. He was born in a manger and buried in a stranger's grave. He once said: "'The foxes have holes, and the birds have nests; but the Son of Man has not where to lay His head" (Matt. 8:20).

The walls were ordinarily whitewashed but not painted. In Haggai's reproof of the people for neglecting to rebuild the Temple he mentions that they lived in cieled houses (Hag. 1:4). The furniture of the average house was of the simplest description. It consisted of a table, stools or chairs, couches and beds, mats, a lamp, water jars, a clay oven and cooking utensils. The poor slept on mattresses or skins. The pillows were made of stuffed goat skin. Chairs were not much in use. Even today the Oriental prefers to sit on the floor with his feet drawn up under him. The lamp was a bowl containing olive oil and a wick (Matt. 25:3-4).

Villages were usually surrounded by hedges for defence, cities by walls (Gen. 4:17; Num. 13:19; Josh. 3:16; etc.). The walls were from 20 to 30 feet thick and 50 feet or more high, with towers for defence. On account of the width of the walls houses were sometimes built on top of them. Rahab lived in such a house (Josh. 2:1-24). Paul escaped by night from Damascus by being let down from a house on the wall (Acts 9:23-25). The walls had gates at regular intervals with strong bars, and, in time of danger, armed guards (2 Sam. 17: 24; 2 Kings 7:10; Neh. 13:19; etc.). The streets were narrow as a rule. Some were wider and used as market places (1 Kings 20:34; Neh. 3:31). The people depended chiefly on wells and cisterns for water. The larger cities had in addition pools and dams, with pipe connections. The pools of Bethesda, Siloam and Gihon were at Jerusalem. In addition to these was the famous dam known as the Pool of Solomon, near Bethlehem, from which an aqueduct supplied Jerusalem and its gardens with water (Eccl. 2:6; Ecclus. 24:30-31).

3. OCCUPATIONS AND CULTURE.

Man is created by God for work. In the sweat of his brow he shall eat his bread. But work is mental as well as physical, hence we group together here the daily occupations and the results of mental application. Work as a necessity became the lot of man through sin, but in itself is a blessing. An idle brain is the Devil's workshop. This can be amply proved also by the history of the Hebrews.

The Bible, on the one hand, ennobles all honest labor. Solomon said: "Seest thou a man diligent in his business? He shall stand before kings" (Prov. 22:29). David was a shepherd, Nehemiah was a butler, Peter was a fisherman, Paul was a tentmaker, Jesus was a carpenter. The Bible, on the other hand, puts its stamp of disapproval on idleness: "Go to the ant, thou sluggard; consider her ways and be wise" (Prov. 6:6). "If any would not work, neither should he eat" (2 Thess. 3:10).

a. OCCUPATIONS.

The patriarchs followed chiefly pastoral pursuits. Abraham was rich in herds and flocks and had at least 318 hired men. In Egypt the Israelites turned to agriculture and the mechanical arts. There are many hundreds of references in the Bible to the occupation of the farmer—the fields, the crops, the sowing and reaping and threshing, the blessings of the Lord through rain and shine and the industry of the farmer. Hunting and fishing also receive due notice. (Gen. 21:20; 1 Sam. 26:20; Hab. 1:15; Luke 5:5; etc.). The chief trades were woodwork, stonework, pottery, metal work. Carpenters, joiners, carvers, basket makers, masons, blacksmiths, goldsmiths, etc., receive frequent mention.

No. 106.　The Fruitful Soil—Num. 13:23　(W. Ebbinghaus).

The architecture of the Tabernacle and the Temples is even to this day in many respects the most wonderful in the world's history.

Palestine was not suited for commerce, except in so far as it lay across the highway of the nations. Palestine lacked harbors, and therefore could not become a maritime nation. It lacked navigable rivers and means of transportation. It was cut up into high mountains and deep valleys, both unfavorable to traffic and trade. Therefore, it never became, except under Solomon, a great commercial nation, although its people, even in Abraham and Jacob, manifested a great capacity for commercial pursuits. Before the monarchy the trade was chiefly local, supplemented by an occasional exchange with a passing caravan. David's conquests greatly increased the wealth of the Hebrews and their opportunities in business. Solomon carried on a vast commerce, by sea as well as by land, through foreign as well as native channels. The division of the Kingdom, of course, put an end to this prestige. After the downfall of Samaria in 722 B. C. and of Jerusalem in 586 B. C. the Hebrews were found dispersed throughout the civilized world. These Jews of the Dispersion were engaged in many occupations, but chiefly those of trade and commerce. This was fortunate in many respects. The Jews were instrumental in making their religion known in all parts of the earth, and they became the nucleus of many of the earlier Christian Congregations.

Besides the shepherds, farmers, artisans and tradesmen enumerated above, a number of the people were also engaged in the professions, such as, lawyers, teachers, doctors, priests, etc.

b. CULTURE.

The Hebrews were in the matter of religion the most cultured and civilized of the ancient nations. In arts and sciences, too, they have made no little contribution to the sum of knowledge.

Moses wrote his Pentateuch at least five centuries before Homer sang his "Iliad". David sang his Psalms to the music of a harp a century or so before the first Greek epic was composed. The books of the Bible, considered as mere literature, have no equal in their class. In music, too, the Hebrews must have been very proficient. Among stringed instruments of music may be noted the harp and psaltery; among wind instruments, the cornet, flute, pipe, sackbut and trumpet; and among instruments that were beaten or shaken to produce sound, the castanet, cymbals, tabret and timbrels. Singing and playing entered into the amusements and religious observances of the Hebrews. Miriam with a choir of women took part in the song of Moses at the Red Sea. The Levites blew in their trumpets. Samuel's schools applied themselves to music as one of the subjects of study (1 Sam. 10:5). David was proficient on the harp and raised song and stringed music to an integral part of the regular worship (1 Chron. 16:4-6; 25:1-31). Each of the three great divisions of the tribe of Levi—the Kohathites, Gershonites and Merarites—was represented. Among the great musicians of David's reign were Heman, Asaph and Ethan, or Jeduthan, one from each of the above divisions. David's chorus had 288 trained singers with 12 leaders. Solomon's chorus had 4000 singers. Solomon had also a court orchestra (1 Kings 10:12).

The artistic skill of the Hebrew is nowhere better displayed than in the workmanship on the Tabernacle and the Temples. The masterworkmen on the Tabernacle were Bezaleel and Aholiab (Ex. 31), and on the Temple of Solomon was Hiram (1 Kings 7:13, 40). Hiram was a Phoenician architect loaned Solomon by King Hiram of Tyre. The plans of the Tabernacle were determined by divine revelation.

The chief science cultivated by the Hebrews was theology. The scribes were the most learned theologians of the Old Covenant. When Jesus began to teach, people marvelled, for He taught them as One having authority, and not as the scribes (Matt. 7:29).

What is the most important unit in human society?

What was God's plan as to marriage? What does the Bible say about bigamy and polygamy? What was the force of the Old Testament betrothals? How were unions contracted in the Old Testament times? What was a Levirate marriage? What was its object? Tell about the Hebrew wedding.

In how many ways was God's standard as to marriage violated? What were the punishments for adultery? What does the Old Testament say about divorce? The New Testament? How are divorces looked upon in our own day?

How did the Hebrews look upon the children? When were children presented before the sanctuary? What instruction did children get at home? In what subjects? What special privileges did the oldest son have? What is meant by birthright? What did Esau sell besides his right to his property inheritance?

Discuss the subject of slavery amongst the Hebrews. Among Christians. What does the Bible teach as to slavery?

Mention some of the social gatherings of the Hebrew family. The hospitality. The forms of greeting and farewell. Discuss their sports in general, the dance in particular. Compare it with the modern dance. What was their most popular amusement?

What sicknesses are mentioned in the Bible? Name a certain peculiar disease common in the days of our Lord on earth. Give instances of Jesus' miracles of healing. What place did the physician have among the Hebrews? Give examples. Describe the Hebrew funeral.

What were the chief articles of diet among the Hebrews? What animals are designated by the Hebrews as unclean? How did they regard drunkenness and gluttony? Tell about the customs of reclining at meals. Of washing before meals and saying grace.

Describe the dress of males. Of females. What was used for head gear and foot gear? Describe the dress of the priest. Of the high priest. To what extent did the Hebrews use jewelry? What attention did they pay to the cleanliness and health of their bodies?

Describe the different types of Hebrew dwellings. Give an illustration from the Bible of each. In what kind of a house was Jesus born? Describe the furnishings of the average house. Find Haggai's reproof in the Bible.

How were the villages protected from their foes? The cities? Describe the Hebrew city wall. A city market place. The city water works.

In what ways is work a blessing? What did Solomon say about a man who is diligent in his business? About a sluggard? Give examples of Biblical characters who were engaged in humble occupations.

What was the chief occupation of the Patriarchs? Of the Chosen People after the Conquest? Mention ten or more occupations that receive frequent mention in the Bible. Why was not Palestine suited for commerce? Under what king did Israel become a great commercial nation? After what event may the Jews be reckoned as a great commercial people? What were the chief professions of the Jews?

In what respect were the Hebrews the most cultured and civilized of ancient nations? Compare the age of the Pentateuch and the Psalms of David with that of Homer's Iliad. What musical instruments are mentioned in the Bible? Name some of the great musicians of David's reign. How many singers in Solomon's chorus? What are the best examples of artistic skill of the Hebrews? What was the chief science of the Hebrews? The chief scientists? Why did people marvel at the teaching of Jesus?

What does your Bible history say about domestic antiquities? Look up the Bible passages referred to in your lesson, and find additional references to this subject in the Bible. In what ways can the contents of this lesson help you in your Bible study? In your faith and works?

LESSON FORTY-THREE. CIVIC ANTIQUITIES.

The Bible teaches that the Home, the Church and the State are divinely instituted—"all the powers that be are ordained of God" (Rom. 13:1). It gives the story of the Chosen People and incidentally refers to the record of the other nations whose course touches that of Israel at one point or another. These nations had many different forms of government; even Israel tried various kinds of civic polity. All of these forms—under patriarchs, judges, kings, emperors, republics—are good and profitable according to Biblical teachings and the experience of the race. All of them fall short of their possibilities for good if God's will is not taken into account.

1. THE CONSTITUTION.

The Constitution of a country is its fundamental, organic law or principles of government, guiding its conduct of affairs. It may be embodied in a written document, as, for example, the "Constitution of the United States"; or, it may be unwritten, implied in the institutions and usages of the country, as, the constitution of England. Some might say that the constitution of the Chosen People was unwritten. We hold rather to the view that it was written and had a three-fold form—moral, ecclesiastical and political, corresponding to the three-fold nature of the Laws and the three-fold character of the Hebrew State and mission. The Hebrew Laws were moral, ecclesiastical and political, and the Hebrew State had a moral, an ecclesiastical and a political mission.

a. THE MORAL LAW.

The Ten Commandments constitute the Moral Law (Ex. 20:1-21; Deut. 5:7-21). They are also known more briefly as the Law, the Decalogue, or the Ten Words (Ex. 34:28). They are really God's Law for all men at all times. They were written in man's heart at creation (Rom. 2:14-15). This Law in the heart we call conscience. When man fell into sin, his understanding became darkened (1 Cor. 2:14), his will became powerless for what is good, and inclined to all that is evil (Rom. 8:7), and the joy and peace of his conscience was disturbed (Gen. 3:8-10). Man in the state of sin gropes about in darkness more or less and can not always distinguish right from wrong. God, therefore, put the Moral Law in writing. This was done through Moses at Mount Sinai, when he was given the Ten Commandments on two tables of stone. These Commandments were confirmed by Christ as valid for all time and binding upon all men (Matt. 5:17-20; 22:37-40). We can not be saved through this Law, for we are not able to keep it perfectly (Rom. 7:18-19; Gal. 3:11). We can be saved only through Christ (Acts 4:12). Nevertheless, the Law is very useful. It convinces us of sin and God's wrath against sin (Rom. 3:20). It alarms us, and drives us to seek Christ (Gal. 3:24). It shows believers the fruits that faith should bear (Ps. 119:105).

The Moral Law may be summarized in the words: "Love to God and love to man" (Deut. 6:1-5; Luke 10:27; Matt. 22:39). It may be divided into two parts or tables: Duties to God and duties to man. The first table according to the Reformed classification has 4 Commandments; according to the Jewish, Catholic and Lutheran it has 3. The second table according to the Reformed has 6 Commandments; according to the Jewish, Catholic and Lutheran it has 7. Each Commandment has a negative side, forbidding something, and a positive side, commanding something.

b. The Ecclesiastical Laws.

The Ecclesiastical Laws are the laws pertaining to the organization and government of the Church. Under the

Old Covenant Church and State were so closely allied that it is not easy to discriminate between the Mosaic code in its ecclesiastical and political aspects. Under the New Covenant very few laws were given, and these again were so general in their nature and so new in practice, that it is difficult at times to state what the New Testament teaches respecting church government.

The Old Covenant Church Laws will be noted more in detail in the lessons on Sacred Persons, Sacred Seasons, Sacred Places, Sacred Sacrifices and Offerings, Other Sacred Obligations and Idolatry. Some of the chief references to them are the following:

(1) Sacred Persons—Lev. 8:1—10: 20; 21:1-24.
    Num. 16:1—18:7.
(2) Sacred Places—Ex. 25:10—30:38; 35:1—40:38.
(3) Sacred Seasons—Ex. 23:10-19; 31:12-18.
    Lev. 16:1-34; 23:1-44; 24:10—25:55.
    Deut. 15:1—16:17.
(4) Sacred Sacrifices and Offerings—Ex. 20:22-26.
    Lev. 1: 6-8; 22:1-33; 26:1—27:34.
    Num. 28:1—29:40.
    Deut. 26:1-19.
(5) Other Sacred Obligations—Ex. 12:48.
    Lev. 12:1—15: 32.
    Num. 19:1-21; 31:14-24.
(6) Idolatry—Ex. 20: 5, 22-23; 32:1—34: 35.
    Deut. 7:1—12:32.

c. THE POLITICAL LAWS.

Jehovah was recognized as the real Ruler of Israel, even as Christ is the Head of the Christian Church. Israel was both a Church and a State. The Christian Church is only a Church, but not a State. The relation between the two has often been misunderstood. The three main types of this relationship are: Church State, in which the Church rules over the State; State Church, in which the State rules over the Church; and Free Church, in which both are free, independent, existing side by side. The State promotes chiefly the temporal welfare of men, protecting the law-abiding and punishing the lawbreakers (Rom. 13:1-7). The Church promotes chiefly the spiritual welfare of men, saving for time and eternity precious souls that were lost.

The main principles of the New Covenant Church Laws are also stated under Sacred Antiquities. As one reads the New Testament he can not help noting the great differences between the Church in the Old and the Church in the New Covenant as to government. The Laws of the Old Testament, for example, are remarkable for their minuteness of detail, while the Laws of the New Testament are very general. There could be only one kind of church polity under the Mosaic regulations, while the number of kinds of church organizations under Christ is well nigh limitless. The priest's dress had to be just so, the Tabernacle must be just so, the Sabbath must be kept just so, the sacrifices must be offered just so, in the Old Covenant Church. All this is different in the New Covenant Church. We are free, indeed, also in this regard. Therefore, the Christian Church down the centuries has developed many kinds of polities, such as, the Papal, the Episcopal, the Presbyterial, the Congregational, etc. In the Papal system the Pope, contrary to Scripture, is the head of the Church on earth. In the Episcopal the Church is governed by a superior body of clergy called bishops. In the Presbyterial the Church is governed by the ministers and presiding elders. In the Congregational each Congregation governs its own affairs. Everyone of these systems has its advantages, and everyone has been subject to abuse. The purpose of the Christian Church is to bring Christ to the masses through the Means of Grace—the Word and the Sacraments. If a system can do that, it is a good one.

The Political Laws of the Hebrews covered questions

of legislation, administration and justice. They will be briefly described under these heads.

2. THE LEGISLATIVE DEPARTMENT.

The so-called higher critics proceed on the theory that legislation as well as all other things has developed from humble beginnings. The Bible states that God gave Moses a complete and perfect set of Laws, so that there was little or no need of legislation afterward. The critics reverse all this. According to them Moses did not get any Laws from God or write any himself. There was no priesthood, no Tabernacle, no Sacred Seasons, no Sacred Sacrifices, in the Wilderness. These things were developed a thousand years later by Ezra, the scribe. We do not believe the higher critics. We believe the plain and direct evidence of the Bible in this matter. The best legislation that the Chosen People ever had was that received through Moses. A thousand years later the scribes commenced, indeed, to make laws, but they were, like all ordinances of men, more or less imperfect. Christ called attention to these defects (Matt. 15:9).

3. THE EXECUTIVE DEPARTMENT.

There was, then, really no lawmaking department in Israel for the reason that the Laws were given them by God. But there was a well-defined law-enforcing, or executive department. Yet, even here, it must be remembered that the Hebrew State was essentially a theocracy—God was the real Ruler. The nominal ruler was only God's representative.

a. THE RULER.

The first government was that of the Family. The father was the apparent ruler, the children were the subjects. The family government is even today the unit and basis of the State and essential to its integrity. The father should, therefore, still perform his duties as a ruler, priest, teacher, of his household, even as God said of Abraham: "I know him, that he will command his children and his household after him, and they shall keep the way of the Lord, to do justice and judgment" (Gen. 18:19).

As the Chosen Family expanded into a people the father of the people became known as the patriarch, and his government is called patriarchal. Naturally he was assisted in the work of governing by appointed assistants. Abraham had an Eliezer as his ambassador, and Moses had 70 elders to represent the Tribes and himself in the transaction of public business (Ex. 3:16; 18:13-22). During the days of the judges the Tribes rarely acted in concert. Judges were raised up by the Lord to meet special demands, such as freeing this Tribe or that from the yoke of some enemy. Meanwhile the office of eldership was kept up and had charge of many civil affairs (Judg. 21:16). The intention was, that God should be considered the Ruler of the Nation. It should be a Theocratic Nation. Moses regarded himself as a servant of the Lord. Joshua held a convocation of the people at which they chose to serve the Lord (Josh. 24). He was to be their Ruler: His Word, their Law. At length, after many ups and downs under the judges, the people demanded a king to rule over them (1 Sam. 8:5). This had been foreseen by Moses, or rather, by the Lord, and He had accordingly prescribed certain laws for the direction of their future kings (Deut. 17:14-20). The truth of the matter was, that the people had really tired of having God for their King, and desired to be like the other nations.

The kings were also intended to be viceroys under Jehovah. This can be seen from the mode in which the king was chosen. The first king—Saul—was chosen from the smallest Tribe, by the Lord's prophet, at the Lord's command and direction. When this king would not obey he was set aside and another king—David—was chosen in the same way. Since David was willing to obey the Lord, and did repent when he went astray, the Kingdom was promised to remain in his family, and from this royal house should come the long-expected Prince of Peace. The king was, furthermore, to be subordinate to the constitution of the land, the Word of God, and to govern in harmony with it (Deut. 17:14-20; 1 Sam. 10:1, 24). He was, of course, given the customary powers of royalty. He made war and peace and had power of life and death, could raise armies and enforce taxation, could erect public buildings and appoint officers, and the like. As an example of the theocratic character of the reigns of David and Solomon we recall that the Lord would not let David build the Temple, but ordered Solomon to do so. Even the plan of the Temple was determined by the Lord.

After the division of the Kingdom the house of David did keep the throne in the Two Tribes. The Ten Tribes seceding elected their own king—Jeroboam. A prophet visited him to tell him that if he would be god-fearing, the Lord would establish him secure on his throne (1 Kings 11:38). As Jeroboam was disobedient, another prophet came to tell him of the sure downfall of his house (1 Kings 14:10). The last prophecy came only too true. The house of Jeroboam fell, and eight other dynasties arose in turn, only to fall on account of their ungodliness. God is King of kings.

After the return from Babylon the Jews were governed by their princes under the direction of the kings of Babylonia, Persia, Greece, Egypt and Syria in turn. The terrible cruelties of King Antiochus caused a revolt under the Maccabees in 166 B. C. For a century the Jews were then independent and governed by their own kings again. In 63 B. C. Rome assumed authority, and the Jews had to submit first to see their own princes degraded and killed, then Herod the Edomite raised to the throne of David, and, finally, Roman governors of the type of Pontius Pilate put in command. Meanwhile the Jews expected the Messiah would come and that He would sit on the throne of David for ever.

They thought that this Messianic Kingdom should be an earthly kingdom, and were disappointed at being told that it was spiritual. Their "Hosannas" speedily changed to "Crucify Him."

b. THE DIVISION OF THE LAND.

The Chosen People were divided into Twelve Tribes, founded by the twelve sons of Jacob. The Tribe of Levi had been set aside to serve in the sanctuary, and the sons of Joseph had been elevated by Jacob to the position of heads of Tribes, hence we have Ephraim and Manasseh instead of Levi and Joseph in the list of the Twelve. These Tribes were subdivided into clans and families. The land of Canaan became their possession and was apportioned to them by lot. Every tribe, every clan and every family received an inheritance for itself and its descendants corresponding to the number of its members. At the time of the distribution of the land not all of Canaan had been taken from the Canaanites. The intention was, that the work of subjugation should go on until not a heathen was left in the land. Not all of the Tribes or parts of Tribes, therefore, came into possession of their allotted territory. The partition of the land is described in Josh. 13:1—21:45.

The land was in the first place the Lord's. The Canaanites who lived there had lost their rights to it by their idolatry. The Israelites were given the land, not by their own cunning or strength, but by the goodness and might of the Lord. They had, furthermore, been given their shares by lot, with the understanding that they could not sell them, but must keep them in the family for an everlasting possession. They should keep them in trust for the Lord, the real Owner. Every seventh year was a Sabbatical Year to remind them of the fact that He gave the increase, and to allow the land that had changed hands on account of debts to revert back to the original family that had it (Lev. 25:1-55; Num. 36:1-13). When daughters inherited land they had to take husbands only of their father's Tribe, so that the land should not be transferred from one Tribe to another (Num. 36). Naboth could not have sold his inheritance to King Ahab even if he had wanted to (1 Kings 21-22). The land was the 'Lord's.

c. INTERNAL AFFAIRS.

The interior affairs of State are many—keeping peace and order, coining money and providing for revenue, establishing roads and encouraging industry and trade, promoting the health, education and opportunities for worship, providing for the poor and administering justice. The Hebrew State sought to take charge of all of these departments of work through local, tribal or national agencies. The father in every family was respected and obeyed. The cities had their watchmen, the kings had their bodyguards. There were representatives from every ten, fifty, hundred and thousand people to look after civic affairs. In the Old Testament money was weighed, in the New it was counted. Under the judges the taxes all went to support the sanctuary. Solomon levied extra heavy taxes to build his palaces and keep up his vast household and idolatry (1 Kings 4). He received also free-will gifts, tributes from subject nations and duties from merchants. Under the Romans the taxes and duties were farmed out to tax collectors called publicans. These men undertook to pay the government a certain amount of money, and in turn they might collect as much as they could get from the people. With some honorable exceptions, as Matthew and Zaccheus, they were extortioners, and hated as a class. It was one of the charges brought against Jesus that He was a Friend of publicans and sinners (Matt. 9:10-13). There is considerable legislation regarding the health of the people. There are laws as to clean and unclean meats, purifications and washings. The scribes and Pharisees added considerably to the Mosaic legislation in this field. In 2 Macc. 7 the story is told of seven brothers who would rather be tor-

tured to death than taste the flesh of swine. In Mark 7:4
Jesus rebukes the Pharisees for their zeal in observing the
commandments of men as to washing, while rejecting the
Commandment of God. Moses commanded parents to instruct the young in the Word of God. This was evidently
neglected at times, for already in Judg. 2:10 we are told
that "there arose another generation that knew not the
Lord". Samuel started a school for the leaders of his
people. David seemed to have acquired a good deal of
knowledge before coming into prominence. The scribes
conducted schools. Nicodemus and Gamaliel were school
masters in the days of Jesus. Jesus Himself went about
teaching for three years. Paul speaks of teachers as one
of the offices and gifts of the Church. The legislation and
practice of the Hebrews is unique amongst the nations of
antiquity for the attempts to help the poor and the oppressed, the orphan and the widow (Deut. 15). Even
kindness to animals is not to be overlooked (Deut. 22:4, 6-7;
1 Cor. 9:9).

d. EXTERNAL AFFAIRS.

Israel, like the Christian Church, was to be in this world
and yet to be not of this world. Israel was to be a Holy
Nation, a Peculiar People, blessed by God and a blessing
unto others. Israel was situated in Canaan along the highway of the nations, consequently it could hardly escape
contact with other nations. At the same time its fastnesses
were on the mountains apart from the highway, consequently it was to a considerable degree secluded and protected. Again, God had commanded Israel to hold aloof
from the heathen nations and at the same time called Israel
to be His servant amongst them. Israel should not hide
its light under a bushel. Jerusalem was a city set on a hill.

International relations express themselves in terms of
treaties and alliances. The Lord was not opposed to such
treaties and alliances in themselves. Abraham and Isaac
concluded treaties with Abimelech of Gerar (Gen. 20:

14; 21:27, 32; 26:28; 31:44). David and Solomon were in alliance with King Hiram of Tyre (2 Sam. 5:11; 1 Kings 5:15). Furthermore, the Mosaic legislation expressly commanded love to the stranger in their midst (Ex. 23:9; Lev. 19:33-34; Deut. 10:18-19), for Israel, too, had been a stranger in Egypt. But the Lord was opposed to certain strangers whose presence in the land would bring Israel into apostasy, and to certain alliances which would result in making Israel a weak vassal of heathen empires. Therefore He commanded that the idolatrous Canaanites should be expelled from Canaan, and therefore He forbade Ahaz and Hezekiah to form alliances with Assyria, Egypt and Babylon (Isa. 7:1—39:8).

International relations express themselves also in the fact that nations are at war or at peace with one another. Israel was not to be a conquering people in a political sense. In a religious sense the duty of the Christian Church to conquer every nation for Christ really already belonged to Israel from the time of Abraham's call. Yet, Israel was at times commanded to wage both offensive and defensive warfare. It had to defend itself against the Amalekites in the Wilderness (Ex. 17:8-13). For this uncalled for and wicked attack the Lord determined to exterminate Amalek (Ex. 17:16; Deut. 25:17). Four hundred years later he ordered Saul to execute this judgment. When Saul disobeyed, the Lord rejected him as king (1 Sam. 14:15). The Amalekites were exterminated as a nation by David (1 Sam. 27:9; 30:17). The Midianites, too, were punished for their offences at Shittim (Num. 25:1; 31:1-54). As to the heathen tribes inhabiting Canaan—the Hittites, Amorites, Canaanites, Perizzites, Hivites and Jebusites— there was only one thing to do, namely, to clear the land of them. They represented heathenism in its most degraded form, and their presence in the land would surely corrupt the faith and morals of Israel. When Israel failed to exterminate them they proved to be an ever present snare and source of corruption (Judges). After the Conquest of Canaan the wars of Israel, even those of David, were of a defensive character.

The original army in the Wilderness consisted of all able-bodied males over 20 years of age (Num. 1:2; 26:2), with the exception of the Levites and the newly engaged or newly married. The soldiers were arranged according to the Tribes and divisions of the Tribes. The whole army was put under a general with subordinate officers. There was no standing army until the time of Saul (1 Sam. 13:2; 24:3), and no paid soldiers before the time of the Maccabees. The booty in people, cattle and goods taken in conquest was variously divided between the sanctuary, the rulers and the fighters.

The weapons of offence were the sword, spear, lance, bow and sling. The weapons of defence were the shield, helmet, coat of mail, brass greaves for the legs and war boots.

A campaign was begun with sacrifices (1 Sam. 7:9). The Ark of the Covenant as a symbol of God's presence accompanied the army in many battles. Priests and Levites always took part, blowing their silver trumpets as signals for the attack (Num. 31: 6; 2 Chron. 13: 12; 1 Macc. 16:8). Spies were used (Josh. 2:1-24; 6:22; Judg. 7:11; etc.). Sometimes the battle was opened with a duel, as when David met Goliath. The battle raged, or the pursuit was continued, until the trumpet gave the signal to halt. When a siege of a walled city was long and protracted the punishment was correspondingly severe. At times captured cities were utterly destroyed (Judg. 9: 45; 1 Kings 14: 26; 1 Macc. 5:51), the males in arms were slain with the sword and the remainder taken as spoil (Deut. 20:10-15). The prisoners were bound together like cattle and held or sold as slaves. War is always cruel. The cruelties in ancient warfare included every kind of torture—eyes gouged out, tongues torn out, skinning alive, etc. War is a terrible thing, and nowhere in the Bible represented as good in itself.

On the contrary, peace is glorified, and the Coming Ruler was to be a Prince of Peace. "He shall judge among many people, and rebuke strong nations afar off; and they shall beat their swords into plowshares, and their spears into pruning hooks; Nation shall not lift sword against Nation, neither shall they learn war any more" (Micah 4:4). With Christ's coming the angels sang: "Peace on earth, good-will to men". Christ gave the rule to love and forgive the enemy (Matt. 5:44). He pronounced also the maxim: "For all they that take to the sword shall perish with the sword" (Matt. 26:52).

4. THE JUDICIAL DEPARTMENT.

The Hebrews have given the world the best laws and the best interpretation of law. It is to be expected that they would have ample provisions for a law-interpreting de-partment in their civic State. This they had. Their laws were based on divine righteousness and God's commands. Their liberty was liberty under law. Their judgments should have been God's judgments, just and righteous al-together. Taking a case to court was therefore regarded as taking it before God (Ex. 18:15; 21:6; 22:8).

a. THE COURTS OF LAW.

In the patriarchal times the judicial power belonged to the patriarchs and judges that God raised up to govern Israel. Moses chose men to assist him as judges over thou-sand, hundreds, fifties and tens (Ex. 18:19-26; Deut. 1:13-18; 16:18). The minor cases were tried by those and the more difficult ones by a higher court, whose seat was at the sanctuary (Deut. 17:8; 19:16-18). In addition to these David appointed 6000 Levites to serve as judges (1 Chron. 23:4). Jehoshaphat created tribunals for every walled city and a supreme court with the high priest as pre-siding head (2 Chron. 19:8). In addition to this he sent the Levites throughout the land to teach the Law of the land to the people (2 Chron. 17:7-9). The lawyers of the New Testament era were teachers of the Law as well as advocates in the courts. The supreme court that tried Christ was known as the Sanhedrin, or the Great Sanhedrin. It originated after the Captivity, and consisted of 70 priests, scribes and lawyers, besides the high priest as president. Jesus was arraigned before this body as a false prophet (John 11:47), Peter, John, Stephen and Paul as false teachers.

b. The Judicial Procedure.

The judges were to judge at all seasons (Ex. 18:22). The place for trial was, in minor affairs, commonly at the city gates (Deut. 21:19; Prov. 22:22; Amos 5:11, 15, etc.), or at the sanctuary. Jesus was tried at the high priest's house, as His case admitted of no delay (Matt. 26:3). The judge was obliged to hear and examine evidence closely and to judge righteously and without respect of persons (Deut. 1:16-17). The declaration of witnesses was valid only if it came from two or more (Deut. 19:15; Matt. 26:60-61). The false witnesses at the trial of Jesus did not agree together (Mark 14:59). In such a case, when a witness testified falsely, the punishment should have fallen on the witness instead of the accused (Deut. 19:18-19). Sometimes the lot was applied to determine guilt (Josh. 7:14; 1 Sam. 14:40). Torture, such as applied to Jesus, was foreign to Jewish Law. After the case was tried the judge pronounced the sentence of guilt or acquittal. Execution was performed before the judge by special officers (2 Sam. 1:15; 1 Kings 2:25-26), or even by the whole city (Num. 15:36; Deut. 22:21). The witnesses were required to begin the work of execution, in case of stoning to cast the first stone (Deut. 13:9; 17:7; John 8:7).

Under Rome the inhabitants of conquered countries were allowed to retain their local courts as well as their religious institutions. All who had obtained Roman citizenship through birth, purchase or reward escaped being condemned and punished without a previous public trial, and escaped also being bound and scourged previous to trial. Paul had occasion to claim these privileges as a Roman citizen (Acts 22:25-29). Such citizens could also appeal to the imperial tribunal. This privilege Paul also exercised (Acts 25:9-12). All cases of a capital nature were to be decided by the Roman court as a last resort. Therefore the Sanhedrin passed Jesus on to Pilate, demanding that a sentence of crucifixion be given. In the execution of Stephen the Jews exceeded their legal authority under Rome.

c. CRIMES AND PUNISHMENTS.

When the law defines a crime it also as a rule provides a punishment. "Life for life, eye for eye, tooth for tooth, hand for hand, foot for foot, burning for burning, stripe for stripe" (Ex. 21:23-25). In the Mosaic Law the principle at the root of the punishment is that of retribution: A life for a life. Evil should be wiped out by punishment. The Old Covenant was one of Law: Do this, and thou shalt live; disobey, and thou shalt die. It was a strict and righteous retribution. The Law knows no mercy or grace, no forgiveness or pardon. Mercy and grace, forgiveness and pardon come with the Gospel, which was proclaimed in the Old as well as in the New Testament. Modern usage in punishing crime does not seek to execute vengeance, but simply to protect society from its repetition and possibly to correct and reform the wrongdoer. In both modern and Hebrew justice the punishment corresponds in some degree to the supposed heinousness of the crime. Both recognize that not every killing of a man is intentional murder. There were, therefore, in Israel six Cities of Refuge to which a manslayer might flee and find shelter.

The chief classes of crime are as follows: Against the

No. 107.   The Stoning of the Blasphemer **(G. Hoet)**.

government, as, treason; against society, as, drunkenness; against a person, as, murder; and against property, as, theft. The following list illustrates the character of the punishments under the Old Covenant.

CLASSES OF CRIMES.

CRIMES AGAINST GOVERNMENT.

CRIME	PUNISHMENT	REFERENCE
(1) Vs. God		
Idolatry . . . . Stoning		Ex. 20:3 Deut. 13:1-11
Blasphemy . . . . Stoning		Lev. 24:10-16
False prophecy . . . . . . Stoning		Deut. 18:20-22
Magic . . . . Stoning		Lev. 20:27
Sabbath breaking . . . . Stoning		Num. 15:32-36
(2) Vs. Parents		
Cursing . . . . Stoning		Deut. 21:18-21
(3) Vs. Magistrates	Discretionary	Ex. 22:28

CRIME AGAINST SOCIETY.

(1) Unchastity . . . . Stoning		Deut. 22:21

CRIME AGAINST PERSONS.

(1) Murder . . . . Death		Ex. 21:14
(2) Homicide . . . . Confinement in City of Refuge		Lev. 24:19-22
(3) Adultery . . . . Death		Lev. 20:10
(4) False Witness . . . . . . Various		Deut. 19:16-21 Deut. 22:13-19

CRIME AGAINST PROPERTY.

(1) Damage . . . . Restitution plus		Ex. 22:4-5 Lev. 24:18
(2) Fraud . . . . Restitution plus		Ex. 22:6-10 Lev. 6:5
(3) Theft . . . . Restitution plus		Ex. 22:1-3 Lev. 6:2-5
(4) Man-stealing . . . . . . Death		Ex. 21:16

What does the Bible teach as to who has instituted the Home? The Church? The State? What different forms of government have been tried by the nations of the world? How many of these tried by the Chosen People? To what extent is each of these forms good? When does each fall short of its possibility for good?

What is meant by the constitution of a country? Did the Chosen People have a written constitution? Explain.

What constituted the Moral Law? Why is this Law serviceable to all men at all times? Where was it first written? When was it first written in words? Describe the giving of the Law on Mt. Sinai. What is the summary of this Law? How may it be divided? Name three of its present uses.

What is meant by Ecclesiastical Laws? Do the Old Testament Ecclesiastical Laws apply to the New Testament Churches? Explain. Illustrate. Under what heads may these laws be noted? Give one important reference to each group of laws.

Who was intended to be the real Ruler of Israel? Who is the real Head of the Christian Church? What was the relationship between the Church and the State among the Chosen People? What main types of relationship between the Church and the State do we find at the present time among the Christians? What is the main purpose of the State? Of the Church? State some of the differences between the Old Covenant laws and the New Covenant laws. What are the three chief departments of political government?

How do the higher critics and the Bible differ as to the origin of Hebrew legislation? What can you say about the perfection of the Political Laws which God gave to Moses? Of the imperfections of the Political Laws which came later from the scribes? Did the Hebrews have a clearly defined Legislature or Congress like ours?

Did the Hebrews have a clearly defined Executive Department of government? Who was the Real Ruler? Who was the nominal ruler? What was the first form of government? Illustrate. Describe the patriarchal form of government. Illustrate. Why did the people demand a king? What position were the kings intended to have under Jehovah? Why was Saul rejected? Why was David accepted? Why was not David allowed to build a temple? Why did the Lord plan the Temple Himself? Show from the record of the Two Tribes that God is King of kings. From the record of the Ten Tribes. What kind of a king did the Jews expect Messiah to be? What do you understand by the Messianic Kingdom?

Why were there Twelve Tribes? Why was not Levi and Joseph known among the Twelve Tribes? How was the land divided among the Twelve Tribes? What right did the Israelites have to the land of Canaan? Why could not Naboth have sold his inheritance to King Ahab?

What are some of the internal affairs of the State? Through what agency did the Hebrew State seek to take charge of its internal affairs? Show that the Hebrews had a representative form of government. How was the money counted? Look in the Appendix for tables of money. Mention some of the Old Testament coins. The New Testament coins. What was the price of Joseph? Of Jesus? How were taxes levied in the Old Testament times? In the New Testament times? Why were publicans hated as a class? Give examples of other legislations, such as, regarding clean and unclean meats, purifications and washings. How did the Hebrews provide for the education of the young? Mention some prominent schools and teachers. In what respect were the legislation and practice of the Hebrews unique amongst the nations of antiquity?

What is meant by calling Israel a peculiar people? Illustrate. Name some of the treaties and alliances concluded by the Hebrews and their neighbors. Why did the Lord command that the Canaanites should be expelled from Canaan? Show that Israel should not be a conquering people in a political sense. Show that it was to be a conquering people in a religious sense. Describe the original army in the Wilderness. The weapons of defence. A typical campaign. Mention some of the defensive wars. Some of the offensive wars of the Chosen People. What does the Bible teach regarding war? Regarding peace? Who is the Prince of Peace?

What people has given the world the best laws? The best interpretation of law? Did the Hebrews have a well defined Judicial Department of Government? Describe the courts of law. What courts tried Christ? Describe the judicial procedure. Describe the procedure at the trials of Jesus. Of Stephen. Of Paul. What was the principle at the root of the punishment under the Old Covenant? What is the principle at the root of punishment under the New Covenant in our own criminal code? Name some of the chief classes and types of crime mentioned in the Bible. Illustrate the character of the punishment for each under the Old Covenant.

What does your Bible history say about civic antiquities? Look up the Bible passages referred to in your lesson, and find additional references to this subject in the Bible. In what ways can the contents of this lesson help you in your Bible study? In your faith and works?

LESSON FORTY-FOUR. SACRED ANTIQUITIES:
I. SACRED PERSONS.

Before the coming of Christ everyone in Israel was in a sense sacred, for He was set apart by covenant and ceremony to belong to God and to live godly. After the coming of Christ everyone who has been baptized into the Christian Church is also in a sense holy, for he, too, has been set apart by Covenant as Christ's own and consecrated to live a holy life. All of God's people might thereby be termed sacred persons. Here we shall notice only those sacred persons who have held sacred offices. The most important offices mentioned in the Bible are those of patriarch, priest, prophet, king, scribe, apostle, deacon, evangelist, teacher and pastor.

1. PATRIARCH.

The patriarchs were the fathers of the early races of mankind, and particularly the fathers of the Jewish race—Abraham, Isaac, Jacob, his twelve sons, Moses, the judges, David. Heb. 7:4 speaks of the patriarch Abraham giving tithes. In Acts 7: 8-9 Stephen calls the sons of Jacob patriarchs, and in Acts 2:29 Peter applies this name to David. The patriarch was not only the head of his family, but of his tribe and race. He was a mediator between God and his people.

In the early ages God had direct dealings with the patriarchs. He promised our first parents salvation in Christ—the seed of woman (Gen. 3:15). He gave Noah the Covenant of the Rainbow that there shall not be another watery flood to destroy the earth (Gen. 9:11-17). It might be added that through the patriarchs—Noah, for example—the Lord taught His will so that the children of men could believe in the coming Messiah and thus escape destruction due to sin.

In the theocratic ages God again made covenants with the patriarchs and placed great responsibilities upon their shoulders. He gave to Abraham what we would call the New Covenant, namely, the Gospel that salvation is by faith in Christ (Gen. 12:3; 17:7; 18:18; 21:12; 22:18; 26:4; Gal. 3:16-18; Heb. 6:13). He renewed this Covenant with Jacob and Moses. Then He gave to Moses also what we know as the Old Covenant, namely, the Law, which promises life to those only who keep it perfectly. This was given in order that the world might be brought to realize its need of the New Covenant. Through Moses He urged the patriarchs in the Wilderness not to forget the things that He had taught them, but to teach it to their sons and sons' sons (Deut. 4:9; 6:6-9; etc.). Through Joshua He repeated the admonition. When the patriarchs forgot to teach their families about Jehovah, they fell into apostasy and bondage under the heathen neighbors. Then God raised up judges to fill the patriarchal office.

The word patriarch is not as a rule applied to the kings or later heads of Israel. Christ, being the second Adam and the Head of the Christian Family, might very appropriately be called our Patriarch. In Isa. 9:6 He is called Everlasting Father, which is the nearest to it.

2. PRIEST.

The word patriarch occurs only 4 times in the Bible; the word priest occurs about 800 times, not including the words for the high priests and assistant priests—the Levites. The fundamental ideas of the priesthood were, that the priest was appointed to represent man before God in sacrifices and prayer (Heb. 5), and also to represent God before man as the mediator of His grace and blessing.

In the early ages the office of priest was not separated from that of patriarch. Noah, for instance, performed the functions of a priest when he built his ark and his altar.

In the patriarchal age Abraham, Isaac and Jacob exer-

cised the same right as Noah. But with the establishment
of the Old Covenant and the Theocratic Nation at Sinai, it
became necessary to make special provision for the priesthood. This was done by separating one tribe for this work
—that of Levi. The office became hereditary, passing from
father to son. The name of Levi is therefore omitted from
the list of the Twelve Tribes. Joseph's name is also
omitted and the names of his two sons, Manasseh and
Ephraim, were substituted for those of Joseph and Levi.
The house of Levi was divided into three general classes—
Levites, priests and high priests. The Levites, divided into
three families, were the assistants of the priests, guarding
the Tabernacle and conveying it from place to place. They
were assigned 35 cities at the Conquest and allowed one
tenth of all the produce and cattle of the country for their
annual support. The priests served immediately at the
altar, keeping up the fires and offering the sacrifices. They
were given 13 cities at the Conquest and one tenth of the
annual income allowed the Levites. The high priest enjoyed peculiar dignities and authority. He alone, for example, could enter the Holy of Holies in the Tabernacle,
and that only once a year.

During the monarchy the priesthood rose to its greatest
heights and sank to its lowest depths. The age began with
confusion as to who should exercise the functions of priest.
Saul attempted to usurp the priest's office (1 Sam. 13:9).
He massacred the priests at Nob (1 Sam. 22:9). But
David and, after him, Solomon, recognized the holy office
of priesthood and sought to elevate it and use it to the
glory of God and the salvation of Israel. David divided
the priests into 24 courses (1 Chron. 24:1-19), each of
which was to serve in rotation one week at a time. He
divided the Levites again into three families as at the time
of Moses, but with subdivisions. These were assigned to
various offices—assistants of the priests, singers and musicians, porters and keepers of the treasury and judges (1

Chron. 23-26). Upon taking a census David found 38,000 Levites over 30 years old, of whom 24,000 served the priests, 4,000 were musicians, 4,000 were porters and 6,000 were judges. Solomon ratified the plans of David. With the division of the Kingdom the Levites as a class fled from the Levitical cities to Jerusalem. The kings of Israel established their own priesthood at the same time as they made calf worship, Baal worship and other heathen beliefs the national religion in place of Jehovah worship. The ideals, work and morals of the priests even in Judah were on a general decline with the fortunes of the rulers. The priests became very corrupt (Isa. 28:7-8; 56:10-12). They were as a class "dumb dogs, who could not bark."

Their position during the centuries that Judah was a vassal state was, on the whole, worthy. They were held in esteem by the Babylonian, Persian, Greek and Egyptian rulers. Ezra 2:36-39 reports that 4,289 priests, besides Levites, returned from Babylonia. In the persons of Jeshua (Joshua) and Ezra they were zealous in rebuilding the Temple, establishing law and order. Ezra completed the Canon of the Old Testament. The Maccabees, a priestly family, threw off the Syrian yoke. Beginning with Simon Maccabaeus the high priestly office was united with that of civil ruler during the Maccabean period. Meanwhile the priests had divided into two sects—the Sadducees, strongly influenced by Greek thought, and the Pharisees, strongly reacting toward the strictest traditions of the Jews. The office of high priest, which was hereditary in the family of Aaron, was captured in every possible way, by hook or crook, and changed hands on the average once in four years.

In the New Testament times the priests appeared as the spiritual leaders of the people and, with few exceptions, the opponents of Jesus. Zacharias, the father of John the Baptist, was a devout priest. But Caiaphas, the high priest, a Sadducee, freethinker and shrewd politician, was the embodiment of hatred against Jesus Christ.

The apostles did not perpetuate the priesthood of the Jews. They recognized that Christ was true Priest after the order of Melchizedek, hence with His coming the priesthood of the Old Testament is abolished. Christ is more sympathetic and perfect than Aaron (Heb. 5: 6-12), with a more solemn and an everlasting consecration and service (Heb. 6:13; 7:28). He is the Mediator of the New Covenant. He has offered His body and blood as a sacrifice for sin once for all (Heb. 9). He ever liveth to make intercession for us (Heb. 7:25). Those who hear His name can therefore go directly to God the Father. They need bring no sacrifice. They may ask whatsoever they will in Jesus' name. They are a royal priesthood (1 Pet. 2:9).

3. PROPHET.

In Hebrew there were three words for prophet: "nabi," "roeh" and "chozeh." The first meant one who had received an announcement from God (hence inspired), or one who had announced what he had heard from God (hence foreteller). The other two meant one who saw (Cf. Engseer). The prophet was one who saw the condition of his times and the future, who was told by God what to say, obeyed God and said it. In addition to this, he often explained what he had said. Hence prophecy means in popular English version, foretelling, forthtelling and interpretation of Scripture.

The prophet, whether speaking or writing, was God's mouthpiece. "For no prophecy ever came by the will of man; but men spake from God, being moved by the Holy Spirit" (2 Pet. 1: 21). Here we are speaking of the true prophets, not the false. God could also speak His will through the unwilling lips of a false prophet. Thus, Balaam thrice blessed Israel, whereas he was hired by Balak to curse, and in his defense he said unto Balak: "Spake I not also to thy messengers that thou sentest unto me, saying, 'If Balak would give me his house full of silver and gold, I can not go beyond the Word of Jehovah, to do either good or bad of mine own mind; what Jehovah speaketh, that will I speak?' " (Num. 24: 13). Balaam's case is, however, exceptional. As a rule the false prophets were messengers of the "Father of Lies," the true prophets were messengers of God, Whose Word is truth.

Prophets are spoken of already by Moses in Deut. 13:1

No. 108. The Prophets (Sargent).
(By permission of Curtis and Cameron).

and 18:20. But there was then as yet no special provision made for the work of the prophets. The people were to be taught by the priesthood mainly through the symbols of the ceremonial law. But during the times of the judges the priesthood degenerated, and the people got little or no instruction in either moral or ceremonial law. The sons of Eli are examples of the corruption of the priesthood, even as Eli is of its weakness. The great reformer, Samuel, judge, priest and prophet in one, set about to get living witnesses for the Lord. He established at Ramah (1 Sam. 19:19-20) what has been called a "school for prophets," what could be called a "theological seminary." Other such schools were later established—one at Bethel, (2 Kings 2:3), one at Jericho (2 Kings 6:1), one at Gilgal (2 Kings 4:38) and elsewhere (2 Kings 6:1). It is particularly in the latter days of the Divided Kingdom (from 800 and down), that prophets are in demand. Corruption was then at its height. Priests and kings were then the most unwilling of God's servants. The prophets, therefore, as divine ambassadors extraordinary, came to teach the will of God without respect of persons, to effect much needed reforms. From the contents of the 17 books usually classified as the prophetical books of the Old Testament we cannot but wonder at the boldness, directness and urgency of their appeal.

The Chosen People was a political Nation as well as a spiritual Kingdom. At first God was their King and ruled through the judges; later, He ruled through their kings, maintaining still that He was their King and they His people, and His Word was the Law. It was the duty of the rulers, priests, Levites and parents to obey His Law and their privilege to teach it. But the duty was often neglected and the privilege scorned. Hence, the people of God forsook their King for the idols of the nations, and the heathen practices in religion and politics became good enough law for them. As the ordinary teachers neglected their duties, God raised up extraordinary teachers, the prophets, who were willing to tell what was what—"Thus saith the Lord."

Theirs had to be a message about sin, because the people disobeyed God, and about punishment for sin, because God is a righteous God. Such messages are hard to hear and harder still to deliver. Jeremiah complained bitterly under his "burden"; Jonah tried to escape from delivering his. No serious spokesman of God delights in

No. 109. The Prophet Amos Preaching (G. Hoet).

denouncing sin and predicting the consequent doom. Neither has God any pleasure in the death of a sinner, but that he repent and live. But, notwithstanding that people hated to be told about their sins, and the prophets would rather not have been given the unpleasant task God saw fit to choose the prophets as his special ambassadors, and they witnessed therefore about sin, sometimes paying for their boldness with their lifeblood.

Theirs was also a message about grace. They were to preach repentance and forgiveness of sins. "Say unto them: 'As I live, saith the Lord God, I have no pleasure in the death of the wicked, but that the wicked turn from his way and live: turn ye, turn ye from your evil ways: for why will ye die, O house of Israel'?" (Ezek. 23:11). These ambassadors are like the ambassadors of Christ in the New Testament, who pray in Christ's stead: "Be ye reconciled to God" (2 Cor. 5:20). The message of grace which they had to offer fill their sad hearts with joy and courage. Like the Apostle Paul they were "sorrowful, yet always rejoicing; poor, yet making many rich; having nothing, yet possessing all things" (2 Cor. 6:10). How delightful it is to learn to know these consecrated men of God, the real statesmen and the teachers of righteousness in the troublous and wicked days of long ago. How real they become to us —Isaiah, Jeremiah, Ezekiel, Daniel and the rest of them, as real as Washington, Lincoln and Wilson. How familiar their times particularly because they are pictured so graphically, their sins being almost the sins of our day, in kind if not always in detail. How important, then, their messages to Church and state, to one and all.

Briefly, their messages as to politics were to recognize God as their God and King, their Defender in war, their Provider in peace, and to make His Word their sole guide. Their supreme statesmanship consisted in just such a message and policy. And as to morals, the message was identical. For the nation's sins the nation was doomed, unless, like Nineveh, it should repent. For the individual's sins the individual was condemned, unless, like David, he should repent. We must never forget that though God is a jealous God, yet He is slow to anger and ready to forgive a contrite sinner. "He is plenteous in mercy unto all them that call upon Him" (Ps. 86:5). This the prophets had in mind. Therefore, in general, it may be said that they preached repentance.

The following themes indicate to some extent the general message of each of the 16 "writing prophets":

The Prophets in Israel.

Jonah: God's Mercy unto Repentant Nineveh.
Amos: The Fall of Israel.
Hosea: The Restoration of an Adulterous Wife (Israel).

A Prophet in Israel and Judah.

Micah: The Trial of God's Chosen.

The Prophets in Judah.

Joel: The Day of the Lord.
Isaiah: Redemption from the World.
Nahum: God's Vengeance upon Wicked Nineveh.
Zephaniah: Sin, the Cause of Judgment.
Habakkuk: Judgment, the Result of Sin.
Jeremiah: The Fall of Jerusalem.
Obadiah: The Fall of Edom and the Restoration of Jerusalem.
Ezekiel: The Fall and Restoration of Jerusalem.
Daniel: God the Ruler of State and Church.
Haggai: The Blessings in Building the House of God.
Zechariah: Judah, Militant and Triumphant.
Malachi: God, Loving, Holy, Righteous.

Of particular interest are the many prophecies about Christ, which are more frequent, full and clear in the prophetical books than in the other portions of the Old Testament. Christ's person, offices, attributes and states are all mentioned. "Each prophet adds a feature, one more, another less clearly: combine the features, and we have the portrait." See the Appendix for a list of prophecies in the Old Testament fulfilled in the New.

4. KINGS.

Kings are mentioned early in Scripture. There were kings a plenty already in the days of Abraham. These had almost absolute authority. They had to be approached with presents, a practice which Jacob observed when he sent his sons to Egypt after corn (Gen. 43:11-26). In like manner the wise men from the East who came to adore Jesus, brought Him presents of gold, frankincense and myrrh (Matt. 2:11). The Israelites, tired of the misrule of Samuel's sons and longing to be like their worldly neighbors, demanded a king (1 Sam. 8:5). He should lead them in war and protect them in peace. God granted their request. Monarchy took the place of theocracy. The story of the Kings of Israel will not be related here. All of them were wicked and misused their office. Even most of the kings of Judah were ungodly, although they were the Lord's anointed and, as such, entitled to reverence, obedience and support. The Lord found in David a king after His own heart and promised to establish his throne for ever (2 Sam. 7:13). This promise was fulfilled in the coming of Jesus, the Son of David, the Messiah, or Anointed. He had been promised to Adam and Abraham as the Seed; to Moses as the Prophet (Deut. 18:15-18) and the Priest; to David as the King (Ps. 132:11; Acts 13:23). During these 4000 years humanity was longing and waiting for His advent. Even the angels waited. And then one night He came.

> Patriarchs and priests aspiring,
> Kings and prophets long desiring,
> Saw not this before they died:
> Lo, the Light to them denied.

According to the promise to Mary, Jesus shall reign for

ever, and of His kingdom there shall be no end (Luke 1:33). He appeared amongst us with power. He spoke as one having authority. At His command the storm ceased and the dead came to life. He was given all power in Heaven and on earth and is with His people always.

5. SCRIBE.

Scribe means writer. During the monarchy the scribe acted as the king's secretary, an office of high rank (2 Sam. 20:25; 2 Kings 12:10). After the Captivity the scribes as a class took the place of the prophets. They were copyists and students of the Law. Ezra is described as a ready scribe (Ezra 7:6). Some of them were priests, and as a class they were closely associated with the priests. Some of them became Pharisees, and as a class they agreed with the Pharisees and took a hostile attitude toward Jesus. Some of them may also have been Sadducees. They became learned in the Scriptures, became teachers and commentators. They began to burden the Scriptures with a mass of explanations, applications and new ordinances that little by little took the place of God's Word. They laid stress on tradition and the letter of the Law, and particularly their own ordinances, which were manifold and worrying. They increased, for example, the number of fasts from one in a year to two in a week, and they discovered 39 different forms of activity which were illegal on the Sabbath. A man might carry a burden of the weight of half a fig on a Sabbath, but if he put it down and lifted it up again it would amount to a whole fig and would be a clear case of Sabbath-breaking. If he were picking up a fruit as the Sabbath overtook him, he would have to drop it then and there (See Edersheim's "Life of Christ," II, 777-787). The scribes made religion a hollow sham. Yet, due to the fact that they had such a reverence for the letter of the Law, we owe them more than we can easily realize, for they were engaged for centuries in copying and guarding the Old Testament text.

6. APOSTLE.

The word apostle means one sent forth, a missionary, an ambassador. One of the first acts of Christ's public ministry was to call disciples, that they might be with Him, and that He might send them forth to preach (Mark 3:13-14). Their training lasted three years as companions

No. 110. Jesus Preaching in Galilee (Hoffman).

of Jesus, the Great Teacher. They were commissioned by Jesus to make disciples of all nations (Matt. 28), and were invested also with power to witness boldly and effectively in His name. On Pentecost Day, ten days after His ascension, the Holy Spirit came upon them, making them altogether different men, clear-eyed, warm-hearted, zealous, brave and faithful to the end. One of the twelve original

disciples—Judas Iscariot—betrayed Jesus. In his place
Matthias was chosen by lot. To these must be added Paul,
the last, but not the least of the apostles. These Thirteen
preached the crucified and risen Christ and planted the
Church in nearly every country of their time. Six of them
wrote 24 (or 23) of the books of the New Testament. The

No. 111. Paul Preaching at Thessalonica (G. Doré).

other 3 (or 4) books were written as follows: Two of the
Gospels by Mark, a disciple of Peter, and Luke, a disciple
of Paul; Acts, by Luke; and Hebrews, either by Paul or
some disciple of his, such as, Apollos, or possibly some co-
worker, such as, Barnabas. The office of apostle ceased
with its first holders.

7. DEACON AND DEACONESS.

Deacon and deaconess are Greek terms for servant.
During the first seven years of the Church the apostles

labored in Jerusalem alone. As the Congregation increased day by day the apostles could not meet all of the demands of their flock. The Grecian Jews complained that their widows were neglected in the daily ministration. It was proposed then that seven men, "full of the Spirit and wisdom, be chosen to assist the apostles, by serving at the tables" (Acts 6) and distributing alms. Seven were thereupon elected and consecrated to this office of "serving". It is supposed that these were the first deacons. It is believed also by some that the early Church soon found it necessary to establish a female as well as a male diaconate. For Paul writes in Rom. 16:1: "I commend unto you Phoebe, our sister, who is a servant of the Church that is at Cenchreae."

8.   EVANGELIST.

This word means Preacher of Good News. It is used three times in the New Testament. Philip, one of the first seven deacons (Acts 6), was later called an evangelist (Acts 21:8). Timothy was bidden by Paul to "do the work of an evangelist" (2 Tim. 4:5). And Paul mentions the evangelist as one of Christ's gifts to the Church (Eph. 4:11). Some hold that this office denoted a field missionary, who went from place to place, preaching Christ and organizing Congregations. Others maintain that the word evangelist, like the words elder, presbyter and bishop, was only another name for pastor. In a special sense the name has been applied to the writers of the Gospels.

9.   TEACHER.

The name teacher occurs many times in Scripture. Jesus was called Didaskalos (Master, Teacher) 51 times. In the early ages parents and patriarchs were commissioned to teach (Deut. 4:9; etc.). In the theocratic ages the work of instruction was also assigned to the priests and Levites (Deut. 24:8; etc.). Down through the centuries judges and kings, prophets and scribes, priests and parents, took upon themselves the responsibilities of teaching. Judge Samuel established regular schools for prophets. During the time of David there were regular schools for singers (1 Chron. 25: 6-8). Moses went to school at the court of Pharaoh; Paul, at the feet of Gamaliel (Acts 22:3). Jesus is the best illustration of the Ideal Teacher, and the hearing of His Word is the one thing needful (Luke 10:42). He gave His disciples the commission to make disciples (learners) of all the nations . . . . teaching them to observe all things whatsoever He had commanded them (Matt. 28:19-20). It seems that the Church very early realized that it had to have teachers, whose whole time should be devoted to instruction. These are mentioned by Paul as one of the gifts of Christ to His Church (1 Cor. 12:28).

10. PASTOR.

The Old Covenant had no pastor. The New Covenant has no priest. The priest was the most conspicuous servant of the Old Testament Church; the pastor is the most conspicuous in the New Testament Church. During the first years of the Christian Church all of the general and local duties fell upon the apostles. They had to organize and govern, to preach and teach, to help the sick and poor. After a few years deacons or elders were chosen to perform some of the more local duties, particularly those of charity. Some years later the duties seem to be still more differentiated. Paul, for instance, in 1 Cor. 12: 28-30, speaks of apostles, prophets, teachers, workers of miracles, gifts of healing, speaking with tongues and interpreting as special gifts or offices. The New Testament is not very clear on the distinction between these offices. Yet it is quite plain that at first the distinctive offices of our present church systems were not marked out, and that they have gradually developed in the course of time. The office of pastor was therefore known by different names expressive of his various duties. His name *pastor* signified that he had to feed his flock with spiritual food (1 Pet. 5: 2; John 21: 15-17). He was known as *bishop* when the work of supervision was had in mind (Acts 20:28; Titus 1:7). He was called an *angel* of the Church, because he was a messenger from God (Rev. 1:20; 2:1). He was called an *ambassador* in Christ's stead, for he was sent to declare the will of God to sinners and to beseech them to be reconciled to God through Christ (2 Cor. 5:20). He was called an *evangelist*, for he was a preacher of the Good News (2 Tim. 4:5). He was called a *minister*, for he served Christ and the Church (1 Cor. 4:1; Eph. 4:12). He was called a *steward* of the mysteries of God, liable to have to give an account of his stewardship (1 Cor. 4:1-2; 1 Pet. 4:10; Luke 12:42). He was called *elder* or *presbyter*, for he should in word and deed be as a father, and an example to the flock (1 Tim. 5:1; Titus 1:5; 1 Pet. 5:1). The word priest is a shortened form of presbyter. It is retained in many Churches (Cf. the Norwegian word prest). But nowhere in the New Testament is the pastor called priest and given the function of sacrificing to God as in the Old Covenant. Christ alone is Priest in the New Covenant.

What is meant by a sacred person? What were the duties of the sacred office of patriarch? Mention some of the patriarchs. What were the chief duties of the sacred office of priest? About how many times is the word mentioned in the Bible? When was the office of priest separated from that of patriarch? How many classes of priests were there in the tribe of Levi? What provision was made for their temporal support? Describe the checkered career of the priesthood, from the time of Moses to the time of Christ. What was the work of the Levites? Of the priests? Of the high priest? What was the attitude of the priests toward Jesus? Why do we not have any priests in the New Covenant? In what sense is every Christian a priest? Show that Christ is our High Priest.

What is meant by prophet? What were the duties of a prophet? What was the difference between writing and speaking prophets? Give a brief history of the prophets of Israel. What was their influence on the politics of the nation? On the religious life of the people? Show that Jesus was a Prophet. Classify the sixteen writing prophets as to country, and state the themes of their books. What was the chief theme of the prophecies of the Old Testament? Mention some of the prophecies concerning Christ's person. His offices. His attributes. His states.

What were the duties of the sacred office of king? Describe briefly the use and abuse of this office by the Hebrew kings. Show that Jesus was a King when on earth. Show that He is a King now.

What is meant by the word scribe? Give a brief history of the scribes. What was their strength and weakness? Their attitude towards Christ? Their contribution to the Church?

What is meant by apostle? What were the duties of the apostles? What did they accomplish? Does the office still exist?

What is meant by deacon and deaconess? When was the office of the diaconate established? What are its duties? Do you have deacons in your Congregation? Deaconesses? If so, what are their duties? If not, who performs these duties?

What is meant by evangelist? Mention some who are called evangelists in the Bible. What were their duties? How is the word now used?

To what office was the duty of teaching assigned at various times in Bible history? Where did Moses go to school? Paul? Who was the Great Teacher? Why?

Give reasons why it is absolutely essential to have religious instruction in the Home, the Church and the State. Give arguments for the different types of religious schools: Sunday schools, parochial schools, confirmation classes, Bible classes, Bible schools, church academies, church colleges, seminaries, etc.

Why did the Old Covenant not have any pastor? Why does the New Covenant not have any priest? Explain. What are the duties of a pastor? What other names is he known by in Scripture?

What does your Catechism say about sacred persons? Your Bible history? Find appropriate hymns in your hymnal bearing on this subject. Look up the Bible passages referred to in your lesson, and find additional references to this subject in the Bible. In what ways can the contents of this lesson help you in your Bible study? In your faith and works?

LESSON FORTY-FIVE. SACRED ANTIQUITIES:
II. SACRED SEASONS.

The sacred times and seasons of the Bible must be divided into two classes—those pertaining to the Old Covenant Jews and those pertaining to the New Covenant Christians. The most familiar sacred season common to both Covenants is the weekly day of rest. Since the period of six days of work with one day of rest conforms to God's method in creation, it has been held that the institution of one day in seven for rest dates back to Creation. The first mention of the week in the Bible is in Gen. 29:27, in connection with Jacob's marriage. The first mention of the Sabbath is in Ex. 16, in connection with the ingathering of manna. Here the Sabbath is mentioned before the giving of the Law on Sinai.

1. JEWISH SACRED SEASONS.

The Jewish sacred seasons may be grouped into seven main classes, as follows:

a. Daily.
b. Seventh Day.
c. Monthly.
d. Seventh Month.
e. Yearly.
f. Seventh Year.
g. Jubilee.

a. DAILY.

Israel celebrated public worship every day. Ex. 29:38-42 gave regulations for burnt offerings on behalf of the Congregation every morning and evening. Ex. 30:7-8 gave rules for the offering of incense daily. This rule was given in the period of the Wandering. In the time of David provision was made for daily song service as well as daily burnt offering (1 Chron. 16). In addition to the daily public worship there was also the daily private worship. The psalmist says: "Evening, and morning, and at noonday, will I complain and moan, and He shall hear my voice" (Ps. 55:17). Daniel prayed on his knees three times a day (Dan. 6:9), on account of which he was thrown into the lions' den. The Pharisees and even the disciples were careful to observe stated periods of private worship every day.

b. SEVENTH DAY.

The Seventh Day, or Sabbath, as already stated, was the keynote of all the sacred seasons, which together form an organic whole. It was based on the sacred number seven, on God's resting on that day, and on the Third Commandment: "Remember the Sabbath to keep it holy. Six days shalt thou labor, and do all thy work, but the Seventh Day is a Sabbath unto Jehovah thy God; in it thou shalt not do any work, thou, nor thy son, nor thy daughter, thy manservant, nor thy maidservant, nor thy cattle, nor thy stranger that is within thy gates" (Ex. 20:8-10). "Verily, ye shall keep My Sabbaths, for it is a sign between Me and you throughout your generations . . . . everyone that profaneth it shall surely be put to death" . . . . (Ex. 31:12-17). The violation of the day was subject to special punishment and God's anger; its observance was followed by God's spiritual and temporal blessings (Isa. 56:2; 58:13; Jer. 17:20-33; etc.). The Israelites, like the heathen round about them and like people of our own day, found it very easy to forget to keep the Sabbath holy. After the Captivity the scribes and Pharisees began to encumber the Third Commandment with their conflicting and annoying ordinances. At the time of Christ this law was a terrible burden. Jesus observed God's Law, but He found occasion time and again to break their rulings. They ruled that one might have feasts on the Sabbath, entertaining friends, but that it was wrong for the disciples to pick grain and eat as they walked through the fields on the Sabbath (Matt. 12). The Pharisees objected to Christ's healing the sick on this day, saying: "There are six days in which men ought to work; in them, therefore, come and be healed, and not on the day of the Sabbath." To this the Lord answered: "Ye hypocrites, doth not each one of you on the Sabbath loose his ox or his ass from the stall, and lead him away to the watering? And ought not this woman (a case before Him), being a daughter of Abraham, whom Satan had bound, lo, these 18 years, to have been loosed from this bond on the day of the Sabbath"? (Luke 13:15-17.) He healed this woman and others on the Sabbath, proclaiming Himself Lord of the Sabbath, explaining that the Sabbath was given for the benefit of man (Mark 2:27; Luke 6:5).

c. MONTHLY.

The first day of every Jewish month was solemnly celebrated. The Jewish month had 29.5 days and began with the new moon, hence the monthly Sabbath was always to be held at every return of the new moon (Num. 28: 11-15). There was the usual daily sacrifice, and in addition two young bullocks, a ram, and seven yearling he lambs as burnt offering with a corresponding meal offering and a goat for sin offering. The worship began with the blowing of trumpets (Num. 10: 10). This feast is frequently mentioned during the period of the kings (1 Chron. 23:31; 2 Chron. 2:4; Neh. 10:33; etc.). It is also mentioned by Paul in Col. 2:16. This day did not in the Old Testament times require rest from all work. In the New Testament times this day was observed as strictly as the Sabbath itself.

d. SEVENTH MONTH.

For the Jewish calendar see the Appendix. The seventh new moon of the year, that is, the first day of the seventh Jewish month, was celebrated as a festival day. It required rest from all work, blowing of trumpets, an assembling of the people and special sacrifices (Lev. 23:23-25; Num. 29:1-6). The day is known in Scripture as the Feast of Trumpets, and in Josephus as the New Year Day of the Jewish secular year. The religious year began with Passover, our Easter week.

e. YEARLY.

In addition to the Feast of Trumpets there were three other great festivals occurring annually, besides a fast day. These were all ordained during the legislation in the Wilderness. To these must be added two festivals ordained by the Jews after the Captivity.

(1) *The Feast of Passover.*—This was an eight-day feast, held in spring, about the time of our Easter. It was really a double festival—the Passover, covering one day, and the Feast of Unleavened Bread, covering seven days. It commemorated the going out from Egypt and was observed with the eating of unleavened bread and a slain lamb or kid (Ex. 12). It derived its name Passover from the passing over, by the angel of death, all those dwellings in Egypt whose doorposts were sprinkled with blood. It was also called the Feast of Unleavened Bread (Lev. 23: 6; Luke 22: 1; Acts 12: 3). On the Passover all males were to appear before Jehovah (Ex. 23: 14-17). If they were prevented from doing so on account of sickness or for other lawful reasons, they might defer their celebration one month. The place of meeting was, at first, the Tabernacle; later, the Temple. The celebration of the Feast is recorded at its foundation, in the wilderness of Sinai, before Jericho on entering Canaan, by Hezekiah, Josiah, the returning exiles, and our Lord and His disciples. The leading feature of the Passover is the slaying of the Paschal lamb. It has a double meaning. It looks back to the freeing from the bondage of Egypt and the angel of death; it looks forward to Jesus, the true Lamb of God, Who frees us from sin, death and the power of the Devil.

Paschal Lamb, by God appointed,
All our sins on Thee were laid;
By almighty love anointed
Thou hast full atonement made.

The morrow after the Passover Day commenced with the bringing of the first of the first fruits of the harvest—a sheaf of barley—to the priest, to be waved by him before the Lord (Ex. 22:29; 23:19; Lev. 23:5-14). This pointed to Christ as the first fruits of God's harvest (1 Cor. 15:23).

(2) *The Feast of Pentecost.*— The Feast of Pentecost was the second great festival of the Jewish church year. It occurred on the Pentecost, or 50th day, after the Passover Sabbath (Lev. 23:15-21). It was called the Feast of Weeks, because it was celebrated seven weeks after the Passover. It was called the Feast of Harvest because it was a festival of thanksgiving for the wheat harvest. It was the Jewish Thanksgiving Day, on which every male had to appear before the Lord, bringing his free will offering of first fruits (Ex. 23:16). Since the giving of the Law on Sinai took place on this day, the older Christian theologians regarded it as the anniversary of that event as well as the harvest feast. The Holy Ghost descended on the waiting disciples on a Pentecost Day, thus making it one of the three great festivals of the Christian Church. The Old Covenant Pentecost had an offering of the first fruits of the wheat harvest in the form of the first two loaves of leavened bread made from the new wheat. This was waved before the Lord by the priest in the same manner as the first sheaves at the Passover (Ex. 34:22; Lev. 23:15-17). These first fruits typified those who were to become the first fruits of the Church at the first Pentecost of the New Covenant.

(3) *The Feast of Tabernacles.*—The third great annual solemnity at which the males had to appear before the Lord was the Feast of Tabernacles. It occurred in the middle of the seventh month (our October) and lasted 8 days. It commemorated God's protecting care during Israel's

40 years in the Wilderness. During the week every male in good health was bound to live in booths made of branches of trees, in remembrance of the life in the Wilderness (Lev. 23: 34-44; Deut. 31: 10-13; Neh. 8: 16; John 7: 2-30). The festival was conducted with singing of hosannas and other signs of rejoicing.

(4) *The Day of Atonement.*—The Day of Atonement was the annual fast day prescribed by Moses. Later, the scribes increased the number of fast days to two a week. It occurred

No. 112.   The Scapegoat (W. H. Hunt).

in the seventh month, five days before the Feast of Tabernacles, and was a day of national humiliation and prayer. It was only on this day that the high priest was permitted to enter the Holy of Holies in the Tabernacle or the Temple. It was on this day that two goats were presented before the Lord, of which one was chosen by lot to become the sacrifice and the other to become the scapegoat and to be sent with the sins of the people into the wilderness. Both goats, the one slain and the one sent away, typify Christ, the Lamb of

God, Who beareth the sins of the world and Who was slain.

(5) *The Feast of Trumpets.*—This festival was described above under Seventh Month.

(6) *The Feast of Purim.*—This was an annual festival instituted, not by divine command, but by the Jews themselves, in commemoration of their deliverance from the intrigues of Haman (Esther 3—9). It is celebrated on the 14th and 15th of the last month of the Jewish church year (our March). All Jews on this day were expected to attend the synagogue services and take part in the reading of the Book of Esther.

(7) *The Feast of Dedication.*—This feast is mentioned in 1 Macc. 4: 52-59 and John 10: 22-23. It was instituted by Judas Maccabaeus to commemorate the purification of the Second Temple, which had been profaned by the Syrian king Antiochus Epiphanes. It commenced on the 25th day of the ninth month (our December) and lasted 8 days.

f. SEVENTH YEAR.

The seventh year was a Sabbatical year. During this year the fields were to lie fallow; there was to be no plowing, or sowing, or reaping, or ingathering. What grew without sowing should not be tended or harvested by the owners, for it was dedicated to charity (Ex. 23:11; Lev. 25:1-7). This year set slaves free, remitted debts, gave property back to heirs (Ex. 21:1-2). At the Feast of Tabernacles falling within this year the Law was to be read at the sanctuary in the presence of all the people (Deut. 31: 10-13). The observance of the Sabbatical year was, as Moses predicted, for centuries disregarded (Lev. 26:34-35; 2 Chron. 36:21). The purpose of the Sabbatical year was to teach trust in the Lord in temporal as well as in spiritual matters.

g. JUBILEE YEAR.

The fiftieth year was called Jubilee (meaning the Ram's Horn), because it was announced by a great blast of rams'

horns on the Day of Atonement. It was a year of grace.
Fields were allowed to rest, servants were released, slaves
were freed, debts were cancelled, property returned to the
original owners. The purpose was, that every Israelite
should come back to the land originally owned by himself
or his fathers. The effect was, that it checked oppression
and poverty, it preserved past memories and love of the
ancestral estates, it filled the land with rejoicing. It foreshadowed the time of grace and refreshing in the Day of
the Lord, when the weary and heavy laden sinner could
come to Jesus and find rest (Isa. 61:1-3; Matt. 11:28-30;
Acts 3:19; Rom. 8:19-24).

It is worth while to consider how much the Jews were
required to give to the Lord. One tribe out of twelve was
set apart exclusively for His service. The first born son
belonged to the Lord, but could be redeemed (Ex. 22:29;
Num. 3:13). Even Jesus was no exception. He had to
be redeemed (Luke 2:23-24).

One twelfth of the people and one tenth of the money
ordinarily should be set aside for the Lord. Abraham
gave tithes (Gen. 14:20). Jacob promised a tenth of his
possessions (Gen. 28:22). Moses commanded that the tenth
of all produce and cattle and flocks should be offered to
God (Lev. 27; Num. 18; Deut. 12). This tithe was to be
the first and best tenth—the first born of the herd and the
flock, the first fruits of the ground and the trees, of corn,
wine, oil, honey, etc. (2 Chron. 31:5; Neh. 10:35-37; Prov.
3:9). The Lord did not want what the people themselves
did not want (Deut. 17:1; Mal. 1:7-8). In addition to the
regular tithe the people had to give a second tithe for
festival purposes and charity (Deut. 12:5-18; 14:22-27;
26:12-13). Under the kings a third tithe was also asked
for the support of the secular government (1 Sam. 8:15-17).
Except when the people fell into open apostasy and neglected the Law, they gave tithes in addition to free-will offerings (Norlie's "United Church Home Missions," 141-200).

One twelfth of the people, one tenth of the money and one seventh of the time of the Jews were to belong to the Lord. This was the general rule. Special regulations called for even greater contributions of men and means and time. The actual time required may be computed as follows:

Let us take a period of 50 years.
The total number of hours is 438,000.
The following hours will be set aside for the Lord:

1 Jubilee year	8,760	hours
7 Sabbatical years	61,320	"
42 other years of yearly festivals	27,056	"
42 other Sabbatical monthly feasts	928	"
2184 other Sabbaths	52,416	"
11970 other days, 3 hours each	35,910	"

Total for worship................186,390
% of total time.................. 42%

2. CHRISTIAN SACRED SEASONS.

The Christian Sacred Seasons of the New Testament times may be grouped into three classes—daily, weekly and yearly.

a. DAILY.

We might expect of the early followers of Christ, filled as they were with love to Him, that they would willingly try to be fully as zealous under the New Covenant as they were required to be under the Old Covenant. Christ had taught daily (Matt. 26:55; Mark 14:49; Luke 19:47; 22:53). The first converts "continued daily with one accord in the Temple, and breaking bread from house to house . . . . praising God" (Acts 2:42-47). The disciples observed the stated hours of prayer (Acts 3: 1). The Congregations tried to observe the admonition of Paul to "let the Word of Christ dwell in them richly in all wisdom; teaching and admonishing one another in psalms and hymns and spiritual songs" (Col. 3:16).   After the preaching service the Agape (Love Feast), or Holy Supper, was celebrated (1 Cor. 11). In other words, the early Christians went to Communion every time they had services, and they had services as a rule every day.

b. WEEKLY.

All of the Jewish festivals were in time discarded by the Christians.   Yet, for some years they observed the Jewish as well as the Christian Sabbath.   The Jews celebrated the seventh day of the week because God had rested from His labors on that day.   The Christians celebrated the first day as Sabbath chiefly because Christ had risen on that day, but also because the work of creation had been begun on that day and the Holy Spirit had descended on a Sunday.   Every Sunday was a weekly Easter Day, a Lord's Day, a day of rejoicing and newness of life.   Paul clearly taught that the requirements of the Law as to the Sabbath were not binding on Christians (Rom. 14:5-6; Col. 2:16-17; see Luther's "Larger Catechism," 3rd Commandment; Sverdrup's "Explanation," 3rd Commandment; A. H. Gjevre's "Sabbaten og søndagen;" K. Grimelund's "Søndagens historie;" F. Mutschmann's "Sabbath or Sunday?"; R. A Torrey's "Ought Christians to Keep the Sabbath?").

c. YEARLY.

The Christian Church has acquired a great number of festival days.   During the Middle Ages, due to the setting aside of days for the saints, the number of festivals increased so rapidly that every day in the year was taken. Hence, a number of such festivals were consolidated and called All Saints' Day, or Hallow E'en.   The Christian church year begins about four weeks before Christmas and is divided into two parts—the Lord's (half) Year and the Church's (half) Year, reproducing the life of Christ and of Christians in the world.   In the first part, the work of the Lord in justification is mainly considered; in the second part, His work in sanctification. There are three great cycles of festivals in the first part—the Father's cycle, beginning with Advent and culminating in Christmas; the Son's cycle, beginning with New Year's and Epiphany and culminating in Easter; and the Holy Spirit's cycle, beginning shortly after Easter and culminating in Pentecost. This part of the year closes with Trinity Sunday. All of these festivals have their origin in the New Testament, yet none of them seem to have been celebrated in the New Testament times. Christmas was not generally celebrated before the fourth century. Pentecost was mentioned as a festival by Irenaeus in the second century. Easter was probably the first of the three to become an outstanding festival. Its keynote was taken from 1 Thess. 4: 13-18 and 1 Cor. 15: 20-58 (A. Neander's "Church History," P. Schaff's "Church History," E. M. Deem's "Holy Days and Holidays," J. C. W. Augusti's "Christian Archaeology").

What is the most familiar sacred season common to both Covenants? Mention the seven main classes of Jewish Sacred Seasons.

Show how the Jews celebrated public worship every day.

Show how the Jews kept the seventh day holy.

Show how the Jews celebrated the first day of every month.

Show how the Jews celebrated the seventh month of each year.

Describe the celebration of the following festivals: The Feast of Passover, the Feast of Pentecost, the Feast of Tabernacles, the Day of Atonement, the Feast of Trumpets, the Feast of Purim, the Feast of Dedication.

Show how the Jews celebrated every seventh year.

Describe the celebration of the Jubilee year.

How many of their people were the Jews required to give to the Lord? Illustrate. How much of their money were the Jews required to set aside for the Lord? Illustrate. How much of their time? Illustrate.

Name the three classes of Christian Sacred Seasons.

Show how the early Christians worshipped the Lord daily. Can this be done now?

Show how the Lord's Day in the course of time superseded the Sabbath.

What are the three great festivals of the Christian Church? What other minor festivals are celebrated by the Church? Why should not Pentecost receive as much notice as Easter? Why should not Easter be as popular a festival as Christmas?

What does your Catechism say about Sacred Seasons? Your Bible history? Find appropriate hymns in your hymnal bearing on this subject. Look up the Bible passages referred to in your lesson, and find additional references to this subject in the Bible. In what ways can the contents of this lesson help you in your Bible study? In your faith and works?

LESSON FORTY-SIX. SACRED ANTIQUITIES:
III. SACRED PLACES.

Five sacred places will be noted—the Altar, Tabernacle, Temple, Synagogue and Church. The first four belonged to the Old Covenant, the last belongs to the New.

1. THE ALTAR.

The word altar has several meanings in Scripture. The first and most common meaning is, that it is a raised structure on which sacrifices are offered or incense burnt to a deity. The word occurs over 400 times in the Old Testament, but only 26 times in the New. The English word altar is from the Latin altus, meaning high, and has reference to the fact that the altar was an elevated or high place employed for offerings. The Hebrew and Greek words most frequently used to denote altar meant slaughter place. We do not know whether the idea of the altar was given by divine revelation or human instinct.

It is not mentioned in connection with the offerings of Cain and Abel (Gen. 4:2-7), although it is believed that they at that early age had built altars on which to place their offerings. It is first mentioned in connection with Noah (Gen. 8:20), when he came out of the Ark. This is the only reference to it in the early ages.

In the theocratic period it is associated with the patriarchs from Abraham to Samuel. Abraham built altars at Shechem (Gen. 12:7), near Bethel (Gen. 13:4), at Mamre (Gen. 13:18) and at Moriah (Gen. 22:9). Jacob built one at Bethel (Gen. 33:20), when departing from Esau, and another when returning (Gen. 35:3-7). Moses built altars at Rephidim (Ex. 17:8-15), at Sinai and elsewhere. Joshua and the judges built altars (Josh. 8:30; 22:10-34; Judg. 6:24-26; etc.). The Lord Himself gave in-

structions that there should be two altars in connection with
the Tabernacle, one in the Outer Court and the other in the
Holy Place. The former was called the Altar of Burnt
Offering; the latter, the Altar of Incense. The Altar of
Burnt Offering was made of acacia wood, 7½ feet square
and 4½ feet high, covered with brass and provided with
rings and staves for carrying. It was placed at the opening
of the Tabernacle to signify that no one could approach

No. 113.   Cain and Abel Sacrificing.

God except through sacrifice. The Altar of Incense was
also made of acacia wood, 1½ feet square and 3 feet
high, overlaid with gold, with two golden rings at each
side. Its position near the veil separating the Holy Place
from the Holy of Holies accounts for its being said to

belong to the Holy of Holies (Heb. 9:3-4). The bloody sacrifices offered on the Brazen Altar were a symbol of Christ's atonement, and the incense offered on the Golden Altar was a symbol of the people's worship (Ex. 30:1-10; Ps. 141:2).

During the monarchy altars were erected not only in the Temple, but also elsewhere. There was to be only one Temple in Israel, but there could be many altars (Ex. 20: 24-36; 25:8). There was to be no association between the altars of Jehovah and the heathen high places (Deut. 16: 21). After the division of the Kingdom, Jeroboam set up special altars at Dan, Bethel and elsewhere, in order to prevent the Ten Tribes from going to Jerusalem to worship. In the famous struggle between Elijah and the priests of Baal on Mount Carmel, Elijah built an altar of 12 stones, symbolizing the Twelve Tribes united in covenant with God (1 Kings 18). Even in Judah and by the kings of Judah themselves heathen altars were set up. Thus Jeremiah complains that in Jerusalem the altars to Baal were as numerous as the streets of the city (Jer. 11:13). Hezekiah, Josiah, Ezra and Nehemiah sought to revive the true Jehovah worship, including the altars.

A second use of the altar was that of a memorial. Laban and Jacob set up such a memorial at Mizpeh (meaning Watch Out), for Laban said: "The Lord watch between thee and me, when we are absent one from another" (Gen. 31:49). Moses wrote all of the Words of the Lord, and built an altar and twelve pillars as a memorial of the Law (Ex. 24:4). Joshua took twelve stones out of the Jordan as Israel was crossing it, and built an altar to commemorate the great event (Josh. 4:5-9). The Two and a Half Tribes built an altar by the Jordan as a memorial of the Conquest (Josh. 22). Joshua built a second memorial altar in witness of the covenant to serve Jehovah (Josh. 24:26).

The chief Old Testament conception of the altar was, as

stated, that it should be a place for sacrificing. There had to be a sacrifice and a priest to perform the ceremony. In the New Testament there is no need of an altar, for there is no priest and no sacrifice, since Christ as our High Priest offered Himself as an atonement once for all. The apostles seem to avoid the use of the terms priest and altar in connection with the New Testament services. Even the Lord's Supper is not called the Sacrament of the Altar in the New Testament. The present usage of calling the Communion Table Altar dates from the first century after Christ. In Heb. 13:10 the word is used symbolically of Christ, Who was offered outside of the gates (on Golgotha). Seven times does the Book of Revelation mention the altar before the throne of God, yet it is not the Brazen Altar of sacrifice that is pictured there, but rather the Golden Altar of Incense, of prayer (Rev. 9:13).

2. THE TABERNACLE.

The Tabernacle was the sanctuary of Israel, the central place of worship for 480 years, that is, from the Exodus to the foundation of the Temple by Solomon. It is rich in symbolical teaching as to how sinful man may approach a righteous and holy God; yet it is but a shadow of the good things to come with Christ (Heb. 10). The pattern for the construction and arrangement and equipment of this house was provided by God Himself (Ex. 25—27; 35—38; 40).

The word tabernacle means tent, dwelling place, meeting place. The Tabernacle was to be God's Tent, His Dwelling Place in Israel, His Meeting Place with His people (Ex. 25:8, 22; 29:42, 45, etc.). The purpose of the Tabernacle was stated by God Himself in such words as these: "Let them make Me a sanctuary that I might dwell among them." "And I will walk among you, and will be your God, and ye shall be My people" (Lev. 26: 9-11). The Tabernacle thus became both a sign and a pledge, a sign that He was their king, and a pledge that He would protect them and permit them to approach Him and receive pardon and fellowship. In accordance with His promise He filled the Tabernacle with His glory by day as well as by night. Thus, He manifested His presence during the wanderings as a pillar of cloud by day and a pillar of fire by night (Ex. 40:34-38).

The Tabernacle proper was surrounded by a Court 150 feet long by 75 feet wide (Ex. 27:9-18). The Court itself was surrounded on its outer edge by sixty pillars 7½ feet

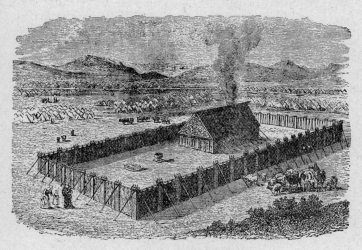

No. 114. The Tabernacle.

high, with curtains hung upon them. The capitals of the pillars of the Court were of silver, and hooks of the same metal held the silver rods on which the side curtains were hung. The Tabernacle was situated at one end of the Court, leaving an open square in front 75 feet by 75 feet. Just within the entrance to the Court stood the Altar of Burnt Offering, and between this altar and the door of the Tabernacle stood the Laver for washings. The people of

Israel were never allowed to enter the Tabernacle itself, as only the priests could do that. The Court, then, was the place where the children of Israel, isolated from all the nations of the earth, assembled to worship God and to present their sacrifices with a view of obtaining from Him forgiveness for their sin. The Altar of Burnt Offering symbolized atonement and consecration. The Laver, at which the priests who had conducted the sacrifices for the people washed their hands and feet before entering the Tabernacle, symbolized regeneration and sanctification. No priest was allowed to enter the Tabernacle or even to approach the Altar to minister who had not first washed his hands and feet at the Laver. The neglect of this duty involved the penalty of death (Ex. 30: 19-21; Tit. 3: 5).

The Tabernacle was a tent divided into two rooms, the Holy Place and the Holy of Holies. The Holy Place was

No. 115.   The Altar of Burnt Offering in the Tabernacle.
(From Bissell's "Sacred Antiquities," by permission).

nearest to the open Court, and the Holy of Holies was at the rear. The dimensions of the Holy Place were 30 by 15 by 15 feet, and of the Holy of Holies 15 feet each way. The frame of the tent consisted of 48 boards of acacia wood, two feet three inches wide and nine inches thick. They were set in sockets of silver and were overlaid with gold. They were held together by five gold-plated bars. The roof consisted of four coverings or curtains, the lowest being

made of fine linen on which were wrought figures of
cherubim or angels, which constituted the ceiling as seen
from the Tabernacle. This ceiling, made up of ten parts,
was in blue, purple and scarlet. The next curtain, spread
over the one just mentioned, was made of goat's hair (Ex.
26:7; 36:7-13). Over this again there was a cover made
of rams' skins dyed red. And, finally, on the top of all
was a covering of badgers' skins to complete the roof of
the tent. The lowest covering symbolized that the priests
who ministered under the figures of the angels were under
the shadow of God's wings, and had the sure protection of
the atoning blood. The three upper coverings, obtained
through the death of animals, also symbolized the atonement. The two rooms of the Tabernacle were separated
by a curtain called the veil. The entrance to the Holy
Place was also covered by a curtain called the outer veil,
which was made of blue, purple and scarlet twined linen
wrought with needlework and hung on five pillars of shittim
wood overlaid with gold.

The Holy Place was the place where the priests as the
consecrated representatives of the people were allowed to
approach God in intercession. The furniture of this room
consisted of the Altar of Incense, a Table of Showbread
and a Golden Candlestick. The Altar of Incense occupied
a middle place near the entrance of the Holy of Holies.
It was made of gold and was used exclusively for burning
on it sweet smelling incense, which symbolized the prayers
of the people rising up to God. The Table for the Showbread was also overlaid with gold. The dishes, bowls,
goblets and cups used for the Showbread and wine of
the Meat and Drink Offerings were all made of pure gold.
Every Sabbath, twelve cakes of Showbread were placed on
this table and not removed until the following Sabbath,
when they were replaced by a fresh supply. This bread
was made of the finest flour and was unleavened. To each
pile, incense was added for a memorial (Lev. 24:5-9).

The twelve cakes symbolized the Twelve Tribes, and the bread itself was a token of sacrifice consecrated to God by the people, and was also a symbol of the spiritual food which Israel was called upon to labor for (John 6:27). When the bread was removed it was given to the priests as food, signifying that they might enjoy the spiritual fruits of His Kingdom. The Candlestick had seven branches supporting seven lamps, which were trimmed every morning and filled with pure olive oil, and lighted every evening

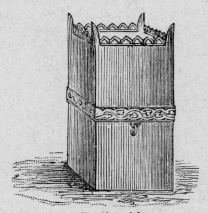

No. 116. The Altar of Incense.

(From Bissell's "Biblical Antiquities", by permission of the American Sunday School Union).

and allowed to burn the whole night (Ex. 27:20; 30:7; Lev. 24:3). The Candlestick was a symbol of the Light of the World, which is Christ (John 8:12), and His disciples (Matt. 5: 14). The Candlestick also pointed to the Seven Churches in Rev. 1-3, representing the Christian Church. Thus the three pieces of furniture in the Holy Place were designed to teach Israel that they should be a people of prayer, of light and of earnest zeal in good works.

Within the Holy of Holies was the Ark, in which were

deposited the two tables of stone on which the Law was written, Aaron's rod and some manna. On top of the Ark stood two cherubim. This Ark was the central object of the Tabernacle. It was a chest made of acacia wood, 3¾ feet long, 2¼ feet wide and 2¼ feet deep. It was overlaid with gold within and without, and was ornamented with a golden border which went around it on all four sides, and was provided with golden rings through which were passed wooden poles covered with gold for the purpose of carrying it. On top of the cover lay a massive gold plate of the same length and width as the Ark itself, on which rested two cherubim with outstretched wings and

No. 117. The Ark.

(From Bissell's "Biblical Antiquities", by permission of the American Sunday School Union).

faces turned toward each other. This Ark containing the Law signified that God entered into a Covenant with Israel, and that this Covenant was based on a righteous Law. The gold plate with the cherubim was called the Mercy Seat, signifying that God is not only a righteous, but also a merciful God. The Holy of Holies was kept dark to show that God dwells in a light unapproachable by man (1 Tim. 6:16). The high priest alone was allowed to enter this room, and that only once a year—on the Day of Atonement—for the purpose of obtaining complete forgiveness of all the sins of his people. He was required to sprinkle the Mercy Seat with the blood of the atoning sacrifice, an act which, together with the whole system of bloody offerings, pointed forward to the sacrifice once made for all by Jesus Christ. The way of the cross is even now the way of approach to the throne of grace.

The New Testament shows that the Tabernacle, in spite of its glories, was but a shadow of the things which were to come with Christ. Christ Himself is the Tabernacle of the New Testament (Cf. John 1:14; 2:19; Col. 1:18-22; Eph. 2:19-22; 1 Tim. 3:15; Heb. 3:6; 1 Pet. 2:5; 2 Cor. 6:16). In the New Covenant we do not then approach the Lord through a Court, a Holy Place and a Holy of Holies, through Burnt Offerings and Mercy Seat, through priests and high priests as mediators, but we go directly to the Throne of Grace in Jesus' name anywhere and at any time we will. This is nowhere more clearly set forth than in the Epistle to the Hebrews, particularly in chapters 4:14—7:28, in which is shown that Christ is a greater priest than the Aaronitic priesthood, and in chapters 8:1—10:18, in which is shown that the Christian Covenant is better than the Jewish (8:1-13), that it has a better sanctuary (9:1-12) and a better sacrifice (9:13—10:18).

The Tabernacle was the sanctuary of Israel for 480 years. It remained in the Wilderness for 38 years. After the Conquest it was at Gilgal for 7 years. It was then set up at Shiloh during the period of the Judges. In the reign of Saul it was located at Nob. In the reign of David it was carried to Gibeon, until David finally erected a new temporary Tabernacle on Mt. Zion. After the building of Solomon's Temple the original Tabernacle was put aside and treasured up in the rooms of the Temple. During the time of the Judges the Ark was sometimes taken out of the Tabernacle to inspire the armies of Israel with its presence. It went in advance of the people of Israel into the Jordan, and was carried for seven days around Jericho before the walls of that city fell. It was captured by the Philistines in the time of Eli, but was soon afterwards sent back into the Hebrew territory (1 Sam. 4-6). It did not find its way back to the Tabernacle for many years. David sought to have it removed, but was at first hindered by the death of Uzzah (2 Sam. 6:1-11). Later David moved it to Jerusalem (2 Sam. 6:12-23), where it was put in the Tabernacle erected for it, and finally placed in the Holy of Holies in Solomon's Temple. It disappeared at the destruction of Jerusalem in 586 B. C.

3. THE TEMPLE.

The Temple (from the Latin templum, meaning a space marked out, a sanctuary) is a house or place dedicated to the worship of some deity. In Jewish history we shall note three temples: the Temple of Solomon, begun in 1012 B. C. and burnt in 586 B. C.; the Temple of Zerubbabel, begun in 436 B. C. and taken down in 19 B. C.; the Temple of Herod, begun in 19 B. C. and destroyed in 70 A. D. In the Christian Church the place of worship is usually not called temple, but merely church. The Temple of Solomon took the place of the Tabernacle and was designed to be the fixed Dwelling Place for the Lord, even as the Tabernacle had been the House of the Lord as long as Israel had moved about from place to place.

a. THE TEMPLE OF SOLOMON.

It was David who first planned to build this Temple (2 Sam. 7:1-16). He reasoned thus: "See now, I dwell in a house of cedar, but the Ark of God dwelleth within curtains." But a message came to David from the Lord through the prophet Nathan, commanding him not to build the Temple, but to leave that work to his successor. The plan of the Temple was divine, following in a general way the pattern and model of the Tabernacle (1 Chron. 28:11-19). David bought a site for the Temple on Mt. Moriah, the same being the threshing floor where he had sacrificed during the great pestilence (1 Chron. 21:25; Josephus' "Antiquities," VII, 13:4). He set about also to collect material for the Temple, such as cedar, gold, silver, copper, iron and precious stones. His son Solomon built the Temple on this site, laying the foundation in the year 1012 B. C. and completing the structure 7½ years later (1 Kings 6:1-38).

The general plan of Solomon's Temple, as stated, was that of the Tabernacle. This consisted of an Outer Court for the people, a Holy Place for the priests, and a Holy of Holies for the Ark. It was on a somewhat larger scale than the Tabernacle, the Holy Place being 60 feet long, 30 feet wide and 45 feet high, and the most Holy Place being a cube of 30 feet. The walls were made of hewn stones. The roof was made of rafters and boards of cedar overlaid with marble. The floors were made of cyprus. The building faced in the same direction as the Tabernacle, namely, the east. The woodwork was covered with carvings representing angels, palms and flowers. These in turn were overlaid with a thin golden plating. In the front of the Temple there was a porch, and in front of the porch on either side was a huge detached pillar of brass. One of these was called Jachin, signifying firmness, and the other was called Boaz, signifying strength. On the top of these pillars were ornaments representing a bunch of lilies (1 Kings 7:15-22; 2 Chron. 4:12). On the sides and at the rear of the Tabernacle were storerooms for holding the furniture and vestments used in the Temple. Between these storerooms and the Temple proper was a narrow court reserved exclusively for the priests. This was called the Inner Court, while the large court outside of the Temple was called the Outer Court (1 Kings 6:36; 2 Chron. 4:9). The furniture of the Temple was exactly the same as in the Tabernacle, with the exception that some of the pieces were larger and more numerous. The Altar of

Burnt Offering had larger dimensions, being 30 feet square and 15 feet high and was approached by three landings. There were 10 Lavers instead of one, besides the Bra-

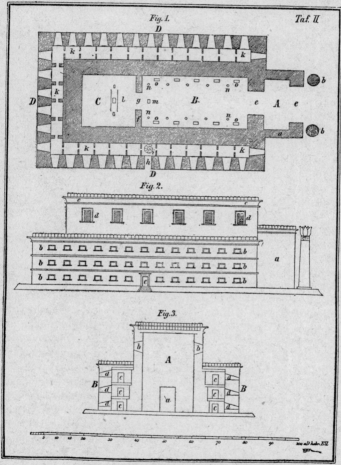

No. 118. The Temple of Solomon (C. F. Keil).

FIGURE 1.

A. Porch.
B. Holy Place
C. Holy of Holies.
D. Store Rooms.
a. Stone walls.
b. Pillars.
c. Open gate.
e. Door to Holy Place.
f. Partition walls.

g. Veil.
h. Side door.
i. Staircase.
k. Side rooms.
l. Ark.
m. Altar of Incense.
n. Ten Golden Candlesticks.
o. Ten Tables for Showbread.

FIGURE 2.

a. Porch.
b. Side rooms, 3 stories high.

c. Side door.
d. Windows.

FIGURE 3.

A. Main building.
B. Store rooms.

a. Entrance.
b. Windows.
c. Side rooms, 3 stories high.
d. Windows.

zen Sea, a huge round water basin, 45 feet in circumference, resting on top of 12 brazen oxen, and containing 15,000 gallons of water. This was the great reservoir for

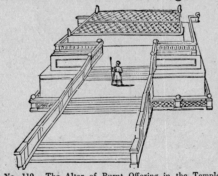

No. 119.   The Altar of Burnt Offering in the Temple.
(From Wm. Smith's "Old Testament History," by permission).

washing before and after sacrificing, from which smaller supplies of water were fetched by the priests according to need. The twelve oxen had reference to the Twelve Tribes of Israel, who as a priestly nation were cleansing them-

selves before the Lord. In the Holy Place there was but
one Altar of Incense as in the Tabernacle, but there were
10 Golden Candlesticks instead of one, five of them on
the right and the other five on the left side (1 Kings 7: 49),
and there were 10 Tables for the Showbread in place of one
(2 Chron. 4:8).

The Temple of Solomon was the sanctuary of the Twelve
Tribes only during his reign. Upon his death the Kingdom was divided, and ten of the tribes under Jeroboam
erected special places of worship at Bethel and Dan,
while only two of the tribes worshipped at Jerusalem.
Under Rehoboam the Temple was plundered of its treasures
by Shishak, king of Egypt (1 Kings 14:26). Soon afterwards Asa, in forming an alliance with Syria, again
stripped the Temple of its gold and silver (1 Kings 15:
18-22). Under most of the succeeding kings of Judah

No. 120. The Brazen Sea.
(From Bissell's "Biblical Antiquities," by permission).

the Temple was allowed to go from bad to worse. Jehoshaphat, however, made some repairs (2 Chron. 20:5). Joash
also tried to repair it (2 Kings 12:5-16). After his death
Jehoash, king of Israel, plundered it (2 Kings 14:14).
Jotham again made some repairs (2 Kings 15:35), but
Ahaz, on the other hand, had the Brazen Altar taken away
and another built after the model of one he had seen in

Damascus and put in its place (2 Kings 16:9-18). Even the pious King Hezekiah was compelled to take the gold from the Temple to pay the tribute imposed by the Assyrian King Sennacherib and to strip the very walls and doors of the Temple of its gold plating (2 Kings 18:14-16). Manasseh built altars for the whole host of heaven in the two courts

No. 121. The Table for Showbread.

of the Temple, and he set the graven image of Astarte in the Temple (2 Kings 21). Josiah exterminated the heathen altars (2 Kings 23), but his own ending was poor. Finally, Nebuchadnezzar came, in 606 B. C., and captured Jerusalem. He came a second time, in 597 B. C., and captured the city again, deporting the treasures of the Temple, including 5,400 gold and silver utensils. He came a third time, in 586, and

set the building on fire.   Thus fell this most glorious and
costly building of antiquity.

b.   The Temple of Zerubbabel.

The Babylonian Captivity may be reckoned from 606
B. C., when the first deportation of the Jews took place, or
from 586 B. C., when the last deportation took place.   The
Captivity lasted 70 years.   The return may be reckoned from
536 B. C., when Cyrus issued an edict that the Jews might return to their native country, or from 516 B. C., when the
Jews who had returned dedicated their new Temple.   The
returning Jews were led by Prince Zerubbabel and the high
priest Joshua. The Temple built after the return has been
called the Temple of Zerubbabel. The people of Samaria re-
quested to be allowed to have a share in the building of the
new Temple, but were flatly refused. Owing to this refusal
they became hostile and opposed the work of building, so that
the work was suspended for about fifteen years. It was again
resumed through the earnest plea of the prophets Haggai and
Zechariah and the consent of the Persian king (Ezra 3—6).
This Temple was larger than the Temple of Solomon,
though much inferior to it in point of splendor (Hag.
2:3; Ezra 3:12).   Particularly should be noted that the
Ark was wanting and that the Holy of Holies remained
empty.   In the Holy Place there was only one Golden
Candlestick and one Table for the Showbread instead of
10 (1 Macc. 1:21; 4:49), and in the Open Court the Altar
of Burnt Offering was not of brass but of stone (1 Macc.
4:45).

In the year 332 Alexander the Great worshipped at this
Temple.   In the year 169 Antiochus Epiphanes plundered
the Temple of its furniture, and in 167 he dedicated it to
Jupiter (1 Macc. 1:57; 2 Macc. 6:2).   In 164 Judas Maccabaeus captured and cleansed the Temple, put new
furniture in it and proclaimed a Feast of Dedication (1
Macc. 4:49-56).   The Roman general Pompey entered the

Holy of Holies in 64 B. C., and the general Crassus plundered the Temple in 54 B. C. In 42 Herod the Great stormed and captured the city and Temple, on which occasion several of the porches were burnt down.

c. THE TEMPLE OF HEROD.

Herod the Great was not a Jew either by nationality or religion, yet he undertook the task of rebuilding the Temple. The purpose of so doing was purely political, as he wished to gain favor with the Jews. Josephus mentions that he employed 1,000 carts, 10,000 skilled workmen and 1,000 priests in preparing metal for the new Temple, and after having made the preparation he tore down the Temple of Zerubbabel and in the year 19 B. C. began the construction of the Temple of Herod. The Temple proper was finished in 18 months, and the courts in 8 years. But the subsidiary buildings were in course of construction for 83 years. This explains John 2: 20, in which the Jews said to Jesus that the Temple had been 46 years in building. This Temple was built on the old site. The Holy of Holies was a cube, each dimension being 30 feet. It was separated from the Holy Place by a veil, which was rent from top to bottom when Jesus died on the cross (Mark 15: 37-38). The Holy Place was 30 feet wide by 60 feet long, containing the Golden Altar at which Zechariah was offering incense when he was promised the birth of John the Baptist. Here also were the Golden Candlestick and the Table for the Showbread. In front of the Holy Place was the porch. It was 120 feet high and covered with golden spikes to keep birds from settling upon it. On the sides of the Temple were chambers for the utensils and the sacrificial articles. In front of the porch was the great Altar of Burnt Offering, which stood in the center of the Court of the Priests. Surrounding the Court of the Priests was the Court of Israel. To the east of the Court of Israel was the Court of Women, also called the Treasury, from the fact that there were treasure chests standing at each of the

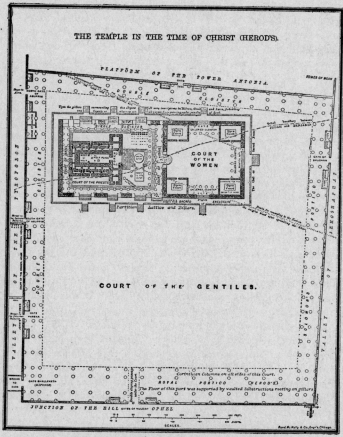

No. 122. The Temple of Herod: Ground Plan.
(From Hurlbut's "Biblical Geography", by permission of
Rand McNally & Co.).

gates on the north, east and south sides (Mark 12:41-42;
John 8:20). This was an open court about 240 feet square,
surrounded by high walls. In each corner of the court was
a room open over head, 60 feet square. The part of the

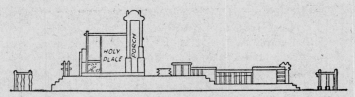

No. 123.   The Temple of Herod: Profile View.
(From Schmauk's "Bible Geography," by permission of the
General Council Publication House).

Temple so far described was called the Sacred Inclosure,
and was intended only for the Jews.   Surrounding the
Sacred Inclosure was the Court of the Gentiles, about 1,000
feet square.   On the east side was a covered porch named after Solomon.   On the south side was another porch named after Herod.   On the west and north sides were walls with double cloisters.   On the north side, next to the wall, was the
fortress of Antonia.   The Court of the Gentiles was entered
on the north by a single gate, on the east by one gate, on
the south by one gate, and on the west by four gates.   On
the floor of this Court was a market for the sale of sacrificial

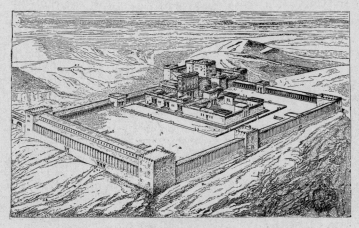

No. 124.   The Temple of Herod: Perspective View (Vogue).

animals, and tables for the money changers, twice broken up by Jesus (John 2:14-16; Matt. 21:12-13).

The Temple of Herod is thus seen to have been built on a much larger scale than the preceding Temples. In another respect, too, it was different from the other temples, namely, that it was built on terraces so that it seemed to be a triple Temple. The first terrace held the Lower Court with its buildings. The second terrace held the Inner Courts of the Women and Men (Israel). The third terrace held the Temple proper. The whole structure was one of the most splendid architectural achievements of the ancient world. It was not in many respects in accordance with the divine model and lacked much of the sacred glory of the Temple of Solomon, especially the Ark. It was destroyed in the year 70 and, in accordance with the prophecy of Jesus, there was not left stone on stone at its fall (F. Josephus' "Antiquities of the Jews," "Wars of the Jews," A. Edersheim's "Temple"). It might be noted that the Jews have not considered Herod's Temple as the third, but as a restoration of the second (Haggai 2:9; Mal. 3:1). Like the Tabernacle, the Temples symbolized the way of salvation and pointed to Christ. They pictured also the splendors of Heaven.

4. THE SYNAGOGUE.

Synagogue means literally a leading together, a meeting place. It was a building in which the Jews assembled for prayer, reading, hearing and expounding the Scriptures. The institution arose during the Babylonian Captivity. The Temple was in ruins, the people were in a strange land and felt the need of a place to worship. The building contained a box for keeping the Sacred Scriptures, a candlestick, a platform with a desk and seat for the reader, seats for the elders and a place hidden by a screen for the women. Each Synagogue had one or more rulers, who appointed the persons to preach (Mark 5:22; Luke 13:14; Acts 13:15), an "angel" who offered up public prayers, a minister, who had charge of the books (Luke 4:20), besides elders (Luke 7:3; Mark 5:22; Acts 13:15).

The services consisted of psalms, prayers, readings of Scripture and addresses. Visitors of renown were often called upon to read and speak. Thus Jesus and Paul were called upon (Luke 4:16-27; Acts 13:15). In Luke 4 we learn that the custom was to stand up while reading and to sit down while preaching.

There were Synagogues in almost every town in which Jews had settled (Acts 6:9). They were found throughout the Roman Empire in the days of Paul. Jerusalem is reported to have had 480 of them just before its fall. They were places of instruction as well as worship. Jesus taught and healed in the Synagogues. Among those he healed were the man with the unclean spirit (Mark 1:23) and the woman sick for 18 years (Luke 13:10-17). Jairus, whose daughter was raised from the dead, was a ruler of a Synagogue (Mark 5:22-38). Crispus, the Corinthian, who accepted Paul's Gospel, was also a ruler (Acts 18:8).

In addition to being a place of worship and instruction, the Synagogue was in certain cases a judicial court. Here trials were held (Luke 12:11); here the punishment of scourging was sometimes inflicted (Matt. 10:17). Here were passed sentences of excommunication, excluding from worship (John 12:42).

The establishment of the Synagogue was also one of the providential means for the spreading of the Gospel. It had made the name of Jehovah known throughout the earth. Its doors were open to the apostles, whose policy it was, when coming to a new town, always to begin preaching the Gospel in the Jewish Synagogue. Thus we find them at work in Damascus, Antioch, Salamis, Iconium, Ephesus, Thessalonica, Athens, Corinth, etc. Besides, the Synagogue furnished to the first Christians many hints as to the organization of the Christian Congregation and its order of worship.

5. THE CHURCH.

The early Christians did not have any special house for worshipping the Lord. The chief reasons for this state of affairs were poverty and persecution. When they were not permitted to use the Synagogues, they met in the homes of the members. When they could not meet there on account of the persecution, they met in some secret place, such as, the cemeteries, caves or catacombs (H. Sienkiewicz's "Quo Vadis"? T. H. Dahl's "Lys fra Katakomberne," Hibsch's "Altchristliche Kirchen"). There was no church building as we know it until after the third century.

In this connection it might be well to remark that these were the times which Jesus referred to when He spoke to the Samaritan woman: "The hour cometh, when neither in this mountain (Gerizim), nor in Jerusalem, shall ye worship the Father, but true worshippers shall worship in spirit and truth" (John 4:21-23).

> Surely in temples made with hands,
> God, the Most High, is not dwelling,
> High above earth His Temple stands,
> All earthly temples excelling;
> Yet He Whom heavens cannot contain
> Chose to abide on earth with men—
> Built in our bodies His Temple.

And yet even in the New Covenant times thus described, it is permissible and profitable to build houses of worship.

> Still we our earthly temples rear,
> That we may herald His praises;
> They are the homes where He draws near
> And little children embraces;
> Beautiful things in them are said,
> God there with us His Covenant made,
> Making us heirs to His Kingdom.

It might also be remarked that the church buildings of the Christians, just as the Tabernacle and Temple of the

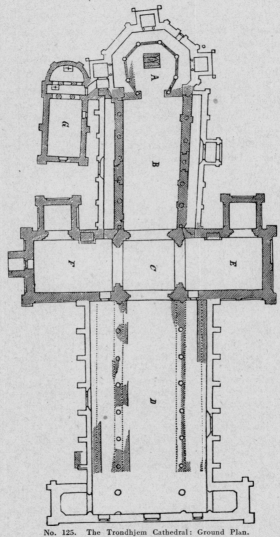

No. 125.   The Trondhjem Cathedral: Ground Plan.

Jews, often have a symbolical message. For example, the steeple points heavenward, holding the cross on high. The ground plan of many of the oldest and finest churches have the design of Jesus on the cross. Thus, Christ's body, the Church, is also represented as in pain because of sin (See the accompanying illustration of the Cathedral at Trondhjem). The furniture inside symbolizes the Means of Grace. There is first the Baptismal Font, at which we were brought to Christ and became members of His Body. There is the Pulpit, from which the Gospel's joyful sound is heard. There is the Altar of the Lord's Supper, at which His disciples may sup (O. Glasoe's "Church Designs," E. Kr. Johnsen's "I Kirken").

> Here stands the Font before our eyes
> Telling how God did receive us:
> Th' Altar recalls Christ's sacrifice
> And what His Table doth give us;
> Here sounds the Word that doth proclaim
> Christ, yesterday, today the same,
> Yea, and for aye our Redeemer.
> (*N. F. S. Grundtvig*).

Mention five sacred places of Scripture. How many of these belong to the Old Covenant? How many to the new?

What are some of the meanings attached to the word Altar? Tell about its use in the early ages. In the theocratic period. During the monarchy. At the present time. Why do we need no Altar under the New Covenant? What was the symbolical meaning of the Old Testament Altar Sacrifices?

What was the Tabernacle? When was it first erected? How long was it maintained? Who gave the pattern for its construction and equipment? What was its purpose? Describe its general plan. Describe the Court with its equipments. The Holy Place. The Holy of Holies and its furniture. Give the symbolical meaning of the Tabernacle service in general and in detail.

What is meant by the word Temple? How many Temples are famous in Jewish history? State when each was built. What was the purpose of the Hebrew Temple? Describe the Temple of Solomon. The Outer Court. The Holy Place. The Holy of Holies.

The Porch. The Pillars. The Storeroom. The Inner Court. The Altar of Burnt Offering. The Brazen Sea. The Altar of Incense. The Golden Candlestick. The Table for the Showbread. Tell briefly the history of the Temple of Solomon.

Describe the Temple of Zerubbabel. The story of its erection. In what did it differ from the Temple of Solomon? Sketch briefly its history from its erection to its remodelling.

Describe the Temple of Herod. The story of its building. Describe the Holy of Holies. The Veil. The Holy Place. The Porch. The Court of the Priest. The Court of Israel. The Court of the Women. What was the Treasury? What was the Sacred Enclosure? What was the Court of the Gentiles? How did this Temple differ from the preceding Temples? What do the Temples symbolize?

What is meant by Synagogue? What is the purpose of the Synagogue? The officers? Describe the services. Give instances of Christ's taking part in synagogue services. How did the Synagogue help to spread the Gospel?

What houses of worship did the early Christians have? What did Jesus say as to the place at which the people should worship Him? Is it right to have church buildings? When were churches first built? Study the diagram of the Cathedral at Trondhjem. What does the ground plan symbolize? What does the furniture of the Christian Church symbolize? What does the spire symbolize? Study the church steeples that you may chance to see, and take note of how many of them hold the cross on high. What is the symbolic message of the cross? What is the message of the other signs on the steeples that you may find? Observe the church buildings in your neighborhood, and note whether the groundplan, steeple, furniture and other parts have any symbolic message or not.

What does your Catechism say about sacred places? Your Bible history? Find appropriate hymns in your hymnal bearing on this subject. Look up Bible passages referred to in your lesson, and find additional references to this subject in the Bible. In what ways do the contents of this lesson help you in your Bible study? In your faith and works?

LESSON FORTY-SEVEN. SACRED ANTIQUITIES: IV. SACRED SACRIFICES AND OFFERINGS.

Sacrifice means literally something made sacred, and offering means something brought or presented, as an act of worship. They are synonymous terms. Here we shall distinguish between them in this way: In the sacrifices the gift is brought to the Altar, while in the offering it is not. Note that the sacrifices are more frequently called offerings. These forms of worship go back to Cain and Abel (Gen. 4). They are ever present down through history, as real to the heathen as to the Jew and the Christian. They might originally have been by divine appointment. At any rate they were commanded in the Old Covenant, and the bitter and bloody death of our Savior was set forth and typified by many sacrifices of many kinds.

1. SACRED SACRIFICES.

We shall call the Sacrifices commanded by God Sacred Sacrifices, for there were also many other sacrifices, of heathen origin, which were not sacred. For example, Jephthah is believed by many commentators to have sacrificed his daughter when he came home victorious (Judg. 11: 34-40). Mesha, king of Moab, sacrificed his eldest son as a burnt offering to Chemosh, when he failed to defeat the allied armies of Judah, Israel and Edom (2 Kings 3:21-27). The Sacred Sacrifices were of seven kinds: Trespass Offerings, Sin Offerings, Burnt Offerings, Peace Offerings, Meat and Drink Offerings, Showbread Offerings and Incense Offerings.

a. THE TRESPASS OFFERING.

The Trespass Offering is described especially in Lev. 5: 14—6: 8; 7: 1-10; 14: 12-19; 19: 20-22; Num. 5: 7-9; Num. 6:12-14; 1 Sam. 6:3-17. This offering was a sacrifice to

get forgiveness for certain special sins by which one had
wronged another, such as by keeping back evidence, violation of trust and swearing falsely. This offering was also
required for acts of ceremonial uncleanliness. The Trespass Offering consisted of a ram without blemish. In addition to bringing this offering the offender had to make
amends for the wrong done, such as, restoring the things
which he had taken violently or by deceit or had found,
and adding one-fifth thereto (Lev. 6:1-7). The priest
would kill the ram near the Altar and place the fat of
the animal upon the Altar of Burnt Offering and sprinkle
the blood about upon the Altar. The skin and the remainder of the animal would belong to the priest who
performed the ceremony.

b. THE SIN OFFERING.

The Sin Offering was very much similar to the Trespass
Offering, and yet distinguished from it. The principal
differences between the two seem to have been: that the Trespass Offering dealt more with special offenses, while the
Sin Offering dealt more with sin in general; that the
Trespass Offering looked more to satisfying the persons
offended, while the Sin Offering looked more to satisfying
the Lord; that the Trespass Offering looked more to the
evil consequences of sin, while the Sin Offering looked
more to the guilt and source of sin. The Sin Offering
symbolized the deep depravity and sinfulness of man and
set forth as its central thought the need of atonement.
The general and special laws relative to Sin Offerings are
found in Lev. 4:1—5:13; 6:24-30; etc. The offering
was made on the part of the individual, the nation and the
high priest at the regular and stated occasion, monthly
and yearly. The animals presented as Sin Offerings differed
according to circumstances. For a private person a female
goat, or kid or lamb was sacrificed. In case of extreme
poverty, two turtle doves or young pigeons might be sub-

stituted for the lamb, or even one-tenth of an ephah of fine white flour might be offered (Lev. 4:24-32; 7:11; Num. 15:24-27). For the Congregation a bullock or a male goat was sacrificed, and in case of the high priest a bullock. In every case the animal was killed, signifying that there is no remission of sins but through the death of the offender and the shedding of blood, and that the wages of sin is death. In case of the Sin Offering by the Congregation or priest, blood was poured before the Altar and sprinkled seven times before the veil, besides being placed on the horns of the Altar. The fat portions were burnt on the Brazen Altar. In the case of Sin Offerings by the Congregation and the priest the remainder of the victim was taken without the camp and there consumed. In the case of a Sin Offering by a private person the remainder of the victim belonged to the priest. Sin Offerings formed a part of every new moon feast and every great yearly feast (Num. 28:15—29:38). This offering was made at the consecration of priests and Levites (Ex. 29: 10-14) and the purification of a leper or a woman after childbirth. On the Day of Atonement two goats were chosen for a Sin Offering for the whole Congregation, and a goat was chosen as a Sin Offering for the high priest. The high priest killed the bullock as an offering for himself, taking of its blood and sprinkling the Mercy Seat (Lev. 16:11-14). Then he took the two goats and presented them before the Lord at the door of the sanctuary. One of the goats he killed, and the other he turned into the Wilderness after having laid his hands upon its head and confessed over him all of the sins of the people. Both of these goats typify the atonement of Jesus Christ, Who was sacrificed as a lamb led to slaughter, and was the Lamb That bore the sins of the world.

c. The Burnt Offering.

The Burnt Offering was also called Whole Burnt Offering, or Perfect Sacrifice, because the victim was wholly burnt up on the Altar. It was not a sacrifice for atonement, but for consecration, signifying that the individual or the Congregation that made the sacrifice completely surrendered unto God. The animals that were sacrificed were a bullock, a lamb or a he goat, all without blemish, or a turtle dove or a pigeon of either sex (Lev. 1:1-17; 6: 9-13). In Rom. 12:1 Paul refers to this type of consecration when he says: "I beseech you therefore, brethren, by the mercy of God, that you present your bodies a living sacrifice, holy, acceptable unto God, which is your reasonable service." The male was chosen as the victim for sacrifice for the reason that he typified greater strength and resistance than the female, and this offering symbolized complete surrender and entire consecration. The sacrifice was made daily, weekly, monthly and yearly, signifying that the people dedicated themselves anew on each of these occasions. The daily offering occurred every morning and evening (Ex. 29:38-42). The fire on the Altar was thus kept continually burning. On the Sabbath the Burnt Offering was twice as large as on the week day (Num. 28:9-10). On the great festivals the offering was still larger, consisting generally of two bullocks, one ram and seven lambs (Num. 28:11—29:39). There were also private Burnt Offerings at the consecration of priests, the purification of women, the removal of leprosy or the performance of a vow. The person who desired to make the Burnt Offering brought the animal to the Altar, laid his hand on its head, thus dedicating it to the slaughter. In the early days he had also to butcher it, but later on this task was performed by the priest or the Levite. The animal was deprived of its skin, which became the property of the attending priest. The blood was sprinkled around the Altar, and the body of the victim was placed on the Altar and entirely consumed by fire. In these sacrifices, as well as in all the others, the priests were assisted by the

Levites, and they eventually slew all the victims and performed all the work (2 Chron. 29:24-34; Ezek. 46:24).
The Burnt Offering was the type of the Perfect Offering
made by Christ, Who on behalf of mankind consecrated
Himself, obeying the will of the Father (Heb. 5:1-7).

d. THE PEACE OFFERING.

Peace Offerings are mentioned eighty-five times in Scripture and are particularly described in Lev. 3:1-17; 7:11-38.
The purpose of this offering was not atonement, but a joyful celebration of peace with God and man. It was really
a thank offering, and was translated thus by Luther. In
this offering only the choicest part of the animal, that is,
the fatty portions, was placed on the Altar and dedicated
to God. To the priests were given those portions which
they during the sacrifice waved back and forth before the
Lord, namely, the breast, shoulder, cheeks, stomach and
right thigh. The remainder of the victim was kept by the
worshipper, who made a sacrificial meal of it for his
friends, including the Levites, strangers, orphans and
widows (Lev. 7:30-32; Deut. 18:3-4). The skin belonged
to the person bringing the sacrifice, and the blood was
sprinkled around the base of the Altar. The animals might
be from the flock or the herd, and of either sex. The
Offerings might be either public or private and might be
brought at any time, although they were prescribed on the
following occasions: At the consecration of priests, the
dedication of the Tabernacle, the purification of a leper
and the expiration of a Nazirite's vow. The word for Peace
Offerings in the original Hebrew is in every case, with the
exception of Amos 5:22, in the plural, denoting the sum
total of the various blessings through which man is at
peace with God and for which he is thankful. The purpose
of the Offering was to establish the Israelite yet more firmly
in fellowship with God. "The whole work of Christ in relation to the believer's peace is here in type. He made

peace (Col. 1:20), proclaimed peace (Eph. 2:17) and is our peace (Eph. 2:14). In Christ, God and the sinner met in peace; God is propitiated, the sinner reconciled—both alike satisfied with what Christ has done. But all this at the cost of blood and fire. The details speak of fellowship. This brings in prominently the thought of fellowship with God through Christ" (Scofield's "Reference Bible," 128).

e. THE MEAL AND DRINK OFFERINGS.

The Trespass, Sin, Burnt and Peace Offerings were animal sacrifices. The Meal Offering was a vegetable sacrifice. It is called Meat Offering in the Authorized Version and Meal Offering in the Revised. The Drink Offering consisted in every instance of wine. The Meal Offering is mentioned 131 times in Scripture and is particularly described in Lev. 2:1-16 and 6:14-23. The Drink Offering is mentioned 59 times, as, for example, in Ex. 29:40; Lev. 23:18 and Num. 15:5. The object of these Offerings was to convey the idea of thanksgiving for blessings received. They were usually associated with Sin Offerings, Burnt Offerings and Peace Offerings, always accompanying and never preceding the animal sacrifice. The Law required a Meal Offering with the daily morning and evening Burnt Offerings, as well as with the special Burnt Offerings on the great festivals of Passover and Pentecost. There was also required a Drink Offering after every morning and evening sacrifice and at the Pentecostal Festival. The Vegetable Offering consisted of grain in the ear or ground into fine flour together with oil, frankincense and salt. The grain should be parched, and the flour might be made into various kinds of cakes without leaven. In the ceremonies of the consecration of the high priest and for the purification of a leper the whole Meal Offering was to be consumed upon the Altar. In every other case the officiating priest was to take only a handful of the flour drenched with oil and seasoned with incense and salt, and burn it upon the Altar for an offering "made by fire of a sweet savor unto the Lord." All of the rest of the offering fell to the priests and was to be eaten by them in the Court (Lev. 6:9). The wine was to be poured out at the foot of the Altar. The bread and wine, which are the principal elements of the Meal and Drink Offerings, are types of human food, and here symbolized the spiritual food which the Chosen People sought to obtain as the fruit of their spiritual labor in the Vineyard of the Lord, following immediately upon the Sin, Burnt and Peace Offerings. They represent also the fruit of sanctification required of those who are members of the Kingdom of God.

f. THE SHOWBREAD OFFERING.

Showbread means literally bread of the presence, from the fact that it was always displayed before the Lord. It consisted of twelve loaves, laid in two piles on top of the golden Table for Showbread. The bread was changed every Sabbath, and the old loaves were eaten by the priests in the Holy Place (Ex. 25:30; Lev. 24:5-9). In the Tabernacle there was only one Table for Showbread, while in Solomon's Temple there were ten (1 Chron. 28:16; 2 Chron. 4:8-19; 13:11). In the later Temples there was only one. In 1 Sam. 21:1-6 Ahimelech the priest supplied David and his followers with this bread, an act which Jesus defended before the Pharisees (Matt. 12:4). The twelve loaves represented the Twelve Tribes. The continual presence signified their constant communion with God and constant support from Him. The Showbread Offering was a thank offering.

g. INCENSE OFFERINGS.

Incense (from the Latin incendere—to burn, to inflame) is the perfume exhaled from spices or gums when burnt in celebrating religious rites. The Altar of Incense was one of the principal pieces of furniture in the Jewish Tabernacle and Temple, occupying a conspicuous place in the

Holy Place, near the veil. On this Altar incense was burnt every day. Once a year the high priest brought incense also within the veil into the Holy of Holies in a censer, enveloping the Mercy Seat in smoke (Lev. 16:12-13). There were two reasons for offering incense—a physical reason and a spiritual. The physical reason was, that the incense purified the atmosphere which was being continually contaminated by the smell of blood from the many slaughtered animals. The spiritual reason was, that it was a type of the intercession of the priests and of the prayers that arose from the worshippers in the Courts outside. The psalmist prayed that his prayers might be set forth before Jehovah as incense. The apostle John saw in a vision an angel burning incense, the smoke ascending with the prayers of the saints (Rev. 8:3-5).

The sacrifices of the Old Covenant have at their foundation the righteousness and holiness, the mercy and love of God. He could not tolerate sin, yet He did not wish the death of any sinner but made provision for his forgiveness, his sanctification and participation in the peace and joy of the saints. All of the sacrifices were shadows, some clearer, others fainter, of the complete sacrifice of Christ (Heb. 9:1-15; 10:1). Since Christ has once for all fulfilled all of the requirements of the Old Covenant Sacrifices, they have all been abolished and we in the New Covenant live, not by sacrifice, but by faith in Christ, "Who gave His life as a ransom for many" (Matt. 20:28), "Who gave Himself a ransom for all" (1 Tim. 2:6).

2. SACRED OFFERINGS.

The Sacred Offerings were such as were not placed on the Altar by the givers. They were of three kinds—free-will, votive and prescribed.

a. THE FREE-WILL OFFERING.

Free-will Offerings were such as one would give to the Lord or His servants of one's own accord, in addition to what was required by law. Thus, on the Feast of Pentecost, or Harvest Feast, Moses required that everyone should come with an offering, but what this offering should be and how large it should be was left to the free will of each individual (Deut. 16:10). The psalmist in Ps. 119:108 sings: "Accept, I beseech Thee, the free-will offerings of my mouth." In Ex. 25:1-9 Moses was commanded to ask of every man a free-will offering for the Tabernacle. The things wanted were gold, silver, brass, precious stones, skins, etc. In 1 Chron. 29:6-8 we read that at David's request the princes and people offered willingly 5,000 talents of gold, 10,000 of silver, 18,000 of brass and 100,000 of iron for the New Temple. "Then the people rejoiced, for they had offered willingly." In Ezra 1:5-6 and 8:24-28 the Jews in Babylonia again brought their silver and gold and brass as a free-will offering for the restoration of the Temple. God has always been a bountiful Giver. The greatest of His Gifts is His Only Begotten Son. "He That spared not His own Son, but delivered Him up for us all, how shall He not also with Him freely give us all things?" (Rom. 8:32). The rule in the New Covenant is this: "Freely ye have received, freely give" (Matt. 10:8). "Let each man do according as he purposed in his heart, not grudgingly, or of necessity, for God loveth a cheerful giver" (2 Cor. 9:7).

b. THE VOTIVE OFFERING.

A Votive Offering is one made according to a promise or vow. The vow sprang from the consciousness of man's dependence upon God and the obligation of thankfulness. Thus Jacob promised God at Bethel that if He would care for him and bring him back home, he would make Bethel a sanctuary and the tenth of his income should belong to the Lord (Gen. 28). Hannah promised the Lord that if He would give her a son, she would give him back to the Lord (1 Sam. 1). One of the vows by which something was set aside for the Lord was called corban, meaning given to God. The Pharisees carried this vow so far as to excuse a man who had said corban from helping his parents in need (Mark 7:11). Christ naturally rebuked such scheming hypocrisy. Vows were in nearly all cases assumed voluntarily, but once made they were regarded as binding, unless sinful (Deut. 23:21-23; Judg. 11; Prov. 20:25). The Lord's promises are all yea and amen in Christ (2 Cor. 1:17).

c. THE PRESCRIBED OFFERING.

The Prescribed Offerings were either first fruits or tithes. Every first fruit—of animals as well as of plants—was to be given to the Lord or His servants (Ex. 22: 29; Num. 18: 12-23; Neh. 10:35-36). In Deut. 18:4 it is stated that the first fruits of corn, wine, oil and sheeps' wool should be given to the Levite. In Deut. 26:1-11 the method of going up to the Temple with the basket of first fruits is described. Very interesting are the words spoken by the giver: "I have brought the first of the fruit of the ground, which Thou, O Jehovah, hast given me." The Jews were not permitted to gather their harvest until they had offered to God the first sheaf, and they were not permitted to make bread for themselves from the new wheat until they had offered the first loaves to the Temple. In 1 Cor. 15:20-23 Christ is called the Firstfruits of them that are asleep, being the first to arise from the dead. The term is also applied to the Jewish Christians and other believers of the early Congregations (Rom. 11:16; 16:5; 1 Cor. 16:15). Besides the first fruits the Jews paid one-tenth of their income to the support of the Levites (Num. 18:21; 2 Chron. 31:5; Mal. 3:8-10; Matt. 23:23). The prescribed first fruits and tithe do not apply to the New Covenant, although there is no reason why people of their own free will might not give at least that much. Jews gladly give their tenth part to the Lord, Mohammedans give 20 per cent to their Allah, and the heathen often give still more to uphold their idolatry. Christians have every reason to give more.   Faith is a hand that receives; love is a hand that gives.   With Paul we should say: "For the love of Christ constraineth us" (2 Cor. 5: 14).

What is meant by sacrifice?   By offering?   Distinguish between these two words.   What is probably the origin of these two acts?

Distinguish between sacred and heathen sacrifices.   Illustrate.

What was the Trespass Sacrifice, or Offering?   State who performed the ceremony.   What was offered in this Sacrifice?   When, where and for what purpose?

Describe the Sin Offering in like manner.   The Burnt Offering. The Peace Offering.   The Metal and Drink Offerings.   The Showbread Offering.   The Incense Offering.

What did the sacrifices of the Old Testament have for their foundation?   What did they typify?

Describe the Free-will Offering.   Give examples of same.

What was the Votive Offering?   Illustrate.

What was the Prescribed Offering?   Give examples of first fruits. Of tithes.   Are there any Prescribed Offerings for Christians?   What was the Old Testament rule for giving?   What is the New Testament rule for giving?

What does your Catechism say about Sacred Sacrifices and Offerings?   Your Bible history?   Find appropriate hymns in your hymnal bearing on this subject.   Look up the Bible passages referred to in your lesson, and find additional references to this subject in the Bible.   In what ways can the contents of this lesson help you in your Bible study?   In your faith and works?

LESSON FORTY-EIGHT. SACRED ANTIQUITIES: V. OTHER SACRED OBLIGATIONS.

In addition to the Sacrifices and Offerings, the Hebrews had several other rites and duties of a sacred character. These were the sacramental rites, purifications and prayers.

1. SACRAMENTAL RITES.

A Sacrament is a holy act instituted by God, in which, by visible means, He bestows and seals His invisible grace. In the New Covenant Protestants recognize two Sacraments —Baptism and the Lord's Supper, while Catholics have five more—confirmation, penance, holy orders, matrimony and extreme unction. In the Old Covenant the Passover corresponds somewhat to the Lord's Supper, and Circumcision of Jews and Baptism of proselytes are antecedents to the Christian Baptism. Circumcision and the Passover prophesied and foreshadowed the Christian Sacraments, but were not such in the proper sense. Circumcision and Baptism are rites of initiation; the Passover and the Lord's Supper are rites of strengthening and communion.

a. Rites of Initiation.

Circumcision was a sacramental rite of initiation. It was a necessary condition of Jewish nationality. After God had made a Covenant with Abraham He commanded that, as a token of this Covenant, every male among them should be circumcized. Boys were therefore circumcized when eight days old (Gen. 17:9-14). The naming of the child accompanied the act (Luke 1:59; 2:21). Slaves and foreigners who wanted to eat of the Passover had to be circumcized (Ex. 12:48). The rite signified approval of God's people, and was a symbol of a pure life and a pure heart (Deut. 10:16; Ezek. 44:7). The reason for beginning the new life on the eighth day lay no doubt in the symbolical meaning of the figures seven and eight. It is worth noting that Easter, with its new life, also began on the eighth day of the Passover Week, and the Pentecost began on the day after the 49th day following the Passover.

In connection with the Hebrew sacrifices the use of water plays an important part. Water was used at the consecration of the priests (Ex. 29:4), at the daily sacrifices and at ceremonial purifications (Num. 19:19-21). It was often spoken of as a symbol of repentance (Isa. 1:16; 4:4; Jer. 4:14; Zech. 13:1). Naaman dipped in the Jordan seven times (2 Kings 5). Israel was said to have been baptized in the cloud and the sea (1 Cor. 10:2). There were at all times strangers who lived in Israel. Many of these accepted the Hebrew faith. In order to enjoy the rights of citizenship and worship they had to subject themselves to the Hebrew laws, including circumcision and ceremonial washings. It seems that these converts from heathenism to Judaism called proselytes (newcomers) were required to be baptized. At any rate, Baptism was not an unknown ceremony when John the Baptist began his ministry. The scribes and Pharisees who came to him expected that the long-looked-for prophet or Messiah would baptize. When John denied that he was the Messiah or the prophet they asked him simply: "Why then baptizest thou?" (John 1:25). On another occasion John said: "I indeed baptize you in water unto repentance, but He That cometh after me........He shall baptize you in the Holy Spirit and in fire" (Matt. 3:11).

The Old Covenant Circumcision and Baptism were symbolical and pointed to the greater fulness of the Christian Baptism. Christian Baptism has supplanted the old rite of Circumcision (Col. 2:11-13). It has been commanded by Christ as the way in which a sinner may be born again and made a partaker of the merits of Christ (Matt. 28:19-20; John 3:5; etc.). Age is never a disqualification for Baptism, although Jesus has commanded that we suffer also little children to come unto Him (J. N. Kildahl's "Infant Baptism", T. S. Kolste's "Daaben og Dens Virkning", O. Lock's "Den Kristelige Daab", A. G. Voigt's "Biblical Dogmatics", etc.).

b. RITES OF COMMUNION.

The partaking of the Passover Feast was the most sacred privilege of the Hebrew, and the partaking of the Lord's Supper is the most sacred privilege of the Christian. But Circumcision preceded the Passover, and Baptism precedes Communion. We must be begotten before we can grow. By Circumcision the Hebrew was received into the Covenant of God; by Baptism the Christian becomes a child of God. By the Passover the Hebrew was preserved in his Covenant; by the Lord's Supper the Christian receives forgiveness of sins, new strength and life. The Passover commemorated the release from the Egyptian bondage. The Angel of Death destroyed the first-born of every house not marked by the blood of the paschal lamb, but passed over every house thus marked (Ex. 12:11-27). The Lord's Supper commemorates our release from the bondage of sin. "Christ our Passover is sacrificed for us" (1 Cor. 5:7). Every Israelite who wanted to escape from Egypt was obliged to sprinkle his doorposts with blood. Every Christian who wants to be free from sin must have a part in Jesus, the Paschal Lamb, Whose body and blood is offered up in the Lord's Supper. The Old Covenant Passover was celebrated only once a year. The New Covenant Lord's Supper may be celebrated often. The first Christians had Communion every time they had divine services. Christ has set no definite time, but that we should go to the Lord's Table often may be seen from these Words of His: "This do, as oft as ye drink it, in remembrance of Me".

2. RELIGIOUS PURIFICATIONS.

The Children of God in the Old Covenant as well as in the

New were to be "an elect race, a royal priesthood, a holy nation, a people of God's own possession" (1 Pet. 2:9). The command to both was: "Be ye holy as I am holy". This principle was enforced upon the Old Testament people by sacrifices and ceremonies and restrictions of many kinds, and is enforced on us by the bitter sufferings and death of Christ for our sins.

The Old Testament Laws were of three kinds—moral, ceremonial and political. All of these deal with purity. The Moral Law forbids every kind of sin—in thought and desire, in word and deed, sins of omission, commission and ignorance, inherited as well as actual sins. The Ceremonial and Political Laws guarded against unclean food, unnatural marriages, lusts, personal disfigurement, injustice, inhumanity, etc., and made provisions for purifications. These rules and regulations were beneficial in a physical way, for they guarded the health and morality of the individual and society, but they were especially intended to convey a spiritual message—concerning the sinfulness of man, the ravages of death and the need of atonement and purification. They all pointed to the need of a Great Physician, a Savior from sin, death and the power of the Devil.

a. PURIFICATION FROM PERSONAL UNCLEANNESS.

The defilement resulting from issues, such as, discharges, menstruation or childbirth, required a Levitical purification in the Old Covenant (Lev. 15). Such uncleanness in a minor degree made it necessary for the unclean person to bathe himself in water and to wash the defiled garments and furniture touched by him. If he should touch anyone before having purified himself, such person touched would also be defiled and be subject to the same process of purification. A woman at childbirth was reckoned unclean for seven days on the occasion of the birth of a boy and fourteen days if a girl was born. In addition to this she had to stay at home a total of 40 days if she had given birth to a boy

and 80 days if it was a girl. And, finally, after this period of cleansing was at an end, she was required to present
a young pigeon or a turtle dove as a Sin Offering and a
lamb as a Burnt Offering, or, if too poor to give a lamb,
then two pigeons or two turtle doves (Lev. 12:2-8).

b. PURIFICATION FROM LEPROSY.

Leprosy is a dreadful skin disease, in Hebrew meaning
scourge, in Greek scabby. It is mentioned 35 times in the
Old Testament and 4 times in the New. Leper is mentioned
19 times in the Old Testament and 9 times in the New. The
symptoms are described in Lev. 13:1-46. The method of
purification and restoration of a healed leper is described
in Lev. 13:47—14:57. Among those who had this disease
were Moses (Ex. 4:6), Miriam (Num. 12:10), Gehazi (2
Kings 5:27), Uzziah (2 Chron. 26:21) and Naaman (2
Kings 5:11-14). Twelve cases of leprosy are mentioned
in the New Testament (Matt. 26:6; Mark 1:40; Luke 5:12;
17:12-19). When a person became a leper he was excluded
from the camp and had to live in the desert apart from
other people. His clothes had to be rent, the hair of his
head had to be uncombed, and upon meeting anyone he
had to cry from a distance: "Unclean!" In the case of
the ten lepers who called upon Jesus to save them, it is
evident that the unfortunates who had thus been excluded
from the society of others naturally sought the company
of those afflicted like themselves. In the case of Simon
the Leper, at whose house Jesus was anointed by Mary,
it is evident that he had been cured of his malady, probably
by Christ. The only instances in which a leper was not
excluded from the camp were those of Moses and Naaman.
In the case of Moses leprosy was only for the moment. In
the case of Naaman, he was a commander in chief of the
Assyrian army and was outside of the regulations of the
Jews (Num. 5:1-4; 12:10-15; 2 Kings 7:3-10; 15:5; 2
Chron. 26:21; Luke 17:12). The story of Naaman coming

to Elisha to be cured and being sent to the Jordan to dip seven times is one of the most dramatic in the Bible history. The story of Gehazi, Elisha's servant who followed after Naaman to take pay for the cure and for this sin was made a leper, is also very significant. The ceremonial prescribed for a purification of a leper is based upon the idea that this disease is a symbol, not only of sin, but especially of death itself. The leper was living dead (Num. 12:12).

The process of purification was as follows: When a person became afflicted or showed symptoms of the disease, but was by the priests pronounced free from it, he was cleansed by washing in water. His affected garments were burnt and the dwellings he had inhabited were torn down and destroyed. He was required to present himself at the entrance of the camp or the gate of the city, and the priests met him and sacrificed two living clean birds, one of which was killed and its blood caught in a vessel with running water. The other bird was dipped into this liquid along with cedar-wood, hyssop and a scarlet thread which bound the wood and the hyssop together. Thereupon the priests sprinkled the leper seven times with the dripping hyssop, pronounced him clean and let the living bird escape into the open field. Finally, the leper washed his clothing and person and shaved off all his hair. At this stage he was allowed to enter the camp, but not to enter his own dwelling for seven days.

The second stage of the ceremony began on the seventh day. First he had to appear at the sanctuary. Again he took a shave and a bath. He brought the appointed sacrifice consisting of a lamb for Sin Offering, another lamb for Trespass Offering and a third lamb for Burnt Offering and, finally, a Meal Offering mingled with oil.

This double ceremony has of course a symbolic meaning. Leprosy, as stated, is a symbol of sin and death. Before the leper could be restored to the camp he had to be reckoned amongst the living. Hence the first part of the ceremony. Before he could be permitted to enter the sanctuary his sins had to be forgiven and he had to be consecrated. This is the second part of the ceremony. David refers to this in Ps. 51:7 when he says: "Purge me with hyssop, and I shall be clean."

c. PURIFICATION FROM DEFILEMENT FROM DEATH.

The Laws of general purification for those defiled by touching the dead are found in Num. 19. The defilement arising from touching the dead of men or animals was regarded as the worst of all, and extending not only to the persons who had touched a corpse or carcass but also to the place where it had lain, the things in the vicinity or the people who came near, and even to everybody and everything they touched. The process of purification in this case was very solemn. The period of purification lasted seven days. A red heifer without blemish and which had never been yoked was taken outside of the camp and slaughtered. The color, age, condition and sex of the animal signified a full, fresh and vigorous life. The priest dipped his finger in the heifer's blood and sprinkled it seven times toward the sanctuary. When this had been done the animal was taken and burnt as a Sin Offering together with some cedar-wood, hyssop and scarlet wool. The ashes of this sacrifice was mixed with running water. Part of the ashes together with water was then used for sprinkling the persons or things defiled by the touch of a dead body. The ashes not used for the occasion might be saved for some other occasion. Thus it will be seen that these ceremonies were very solemn and impressive, and yet they are, as Paul says in Gal. 4:9, "weak and beggarly rudiments". Or, again, as the apostle says in Heb. 8: 5, "a copy and shadow of the heavenly things". "And as the ashes of a heifer sprinkling them that have been defiled, sanctify unto the cleanness of the flesh, how much more shall the blood of Christ, Who through the eternal Spirit offered Himself without blemish unto God, cleanse your conscience from dead works to serve the living God?" (Heb. 9:14).

d. OTHER PURIFICATIONS.

Scripture mentions several other species of impurity which required purification, such as, jealousy and blood guiltiness. All of these had in general the same ceremony for purification. These ceremonies again in every case emphasized the awfulness of sin, the need of atonement and consecration. It is interesting to note that ceremonial cleanness was always associated with cleanliness. Thus the priests and Levites had to wash their hands and feet before entering the sanctuary and after having sacrificed. From the New Testament we learn that the scribes and Pharisees had added largely to the Laws of Moses on this point. Thus, in Mark 7 it is said that they would not eat except they washed their hands diligently, literally up to the elbow, and when they came from the market place they ate not except they bathed themselves. And yet, when one of the Pharisees invited Jesus to eat with him he did not provide Him with water to wash Himself with after the dusty journey. But behold, a woman that was in the city, a sinner, came and began to wet His feet with her tears and wiped them with her hair, and she kissed His feet and anointed them with ointment. The Pharisee was offended at this, but Jesus said unto him: "Thou gavest Me no water for My feet, but she hath wet My feet with her tears and wiped it with her hair. Thou gavest Me no kiss, but she since the time I came in hath not ceased to kiss My feet. My head with oil thou didst not anoint, but she hath anointed My feet with ointment. Wherefore I say unto thee, her sins, which are many, are forgiven."

3. PRAYER.

To pray is to speak with God in our hearts, to mourn our distress before Him, and with earnest longing to seek something of Him. God has commanded His children to pray. He has given many precious promises that He will hear. He has told on what conditions He will hear and in what manner we should pray. In the Bible we have many notable examples of praying men and women and some of the prayers that they offered up. We are told of the answers that came.

a. THE DUTY.

Both the Old and the New Covenant require prayer. Such passages as the following state the position of the Old Covenant: "Seek the Lord while He may be found, call upon Him while He is near" (Isa. 55:6). "So will we render as bullocks the offerings of our lips" (Hos. 14:2). "His House shall be called a House of Prayer for all peoples" (Isa. 56:7). The position of the New Covenant is identical: "Watch and pray" (Matt. 26:41). "Always pray, and never faint" (Luke 18:1). "Pray without ceasing" (1 Thess. 5:17).

b. THE PROMISES.

God has given many promises that He will hear and answer prayer. In Ps. 91:15 He says: "He shall call upon Me, and I will answer him; I will be with him in trouble; I will deliver and honor him". In Isa. 41:17 He says: "When the poor and needy seek water, and there is none, and their tongue faileth for thirst, I the Lord will hear them, I the God of Israel will not forsake them". In Isa. 65:24 He says: "And it shall come to pass, that before they call, I shall answer; and while they are yet speaking, I will hear". In Luke 11:9 He says: "Ask, and it shall be given you; seek, and ye shall find; knock, and it shall be opened unto you". In John 15:7 He says: "If ye abide in Me, and My Words abide in you, ye shall ask what ye will, and it shall be done unto you". In Rom. 8:26 He says: "The Spirit Itself maketh intercession for us."

c. THE CONDITIONS.

The prayer of the Old Covenant people, in order to be acceptable to God, had to be in penitence, humility, child-like confidence, faith, devoutness and sincerity. Thus David speaks: "I said, 'I will confess my transgressions unto the Lord', and Thou forgavest the iniquity of my sins" (Ps. 32:5). And again: "He forgetteth not the cry of the humble" (Ps. 9:12). Also: "I will lift up mine eyes unto the hills, from whence cometh my help" (Ps. 121:1). The Lord said to Solomon: "If My people, which are called by My name, shall humble themselves, and pray, and seek My face, and turn from their wicked ways, then will I hear from Heaven, and will forgive their sin, and will heal their land" (2 Chron. 7:14). The prayer of the New Covenant people has to be of the same general type, and has in addition to be based on the merits of Jesus and His intercession with the Father. Thus we should pray: "Our Father, Who art in Heaven" (Luke 11). Jesus said: "Verily, verily, I say unto you, Whatsoever ye shall ask the Father in My name, He will give it you" (John 16:23). God has not promised to hear the prayers of the ungodly (Deut. 1:45; 2 Sam. 22:42; Isa. 1:15; Micah 3:4). The prayers of His believing children He will answer in His good time (Matt. 7:11; Ex. 33:17).

d. EXAMPLES.

The prayers recorded in the Bible are both public and private. The first indirect reference to prayer is in Gen. 4:26, where it is recorded that a son was born to Seth, and his name was called Enos—"then began men to call upon the name of the Lord". The first recorded prayer is that of Abraham asking for a son (Gen. 15:2). The last recorded prayer is that by the Apostle John in Rev. 22:20, pleading: "Come quickly, Lord Jesus". The examples of prayer in the Bible show a great diversity of objects asked for, of times in which prayer was held, of places, of methods, etc. Solomon prayed for wisdom to govern, for blessing upon his Temple and those who were to worship there. Jesus prayed for blessing upon the food before Him, for the protection and unification of His disciples, for the removal of the bitter cup, if possible, and for the forgiveness of His enemies. Others prayed for a variety of other blessings, temporal as well as spiritual. Prayer was offered up at each public worship (Deut. 26:12-15; Luke 1:10). There were also regular hours set aside for prayer. Daniel observed these (Dan. 6:10). So also did Peter and John (Acts. 3:1) and many more. The hypocrites loved to stand in the Temple or on the streets praying, so that they might be seen of men (Matt. 6:5). The Publican stood afar off, with downcast eyes, smiting his breast and asking God to be merciful to him a sinner (Luke 18:13). Sometimes prayer was offered standing (Mark 11:25), sometimes kneeling (Dan. 6:10) and sometimes with faces to the ground (Neh. 8:6). The Old Covenant people had a fixed form of prayer prescribed to them in connection with the offering of first fruits (Deut. 26:5-15). The disciples of Jesus were taught a fixed form in the well known "Our Father, Who art in Heaven", called also the Lord's Prayer.

As seen from the following table, which is no doubt incomplete, the Bible contains over 2,800 verses referring to prayer in the form of precept, promise or practice. By precept is here meant that prayer is commanded; by promise, that it will be answered; by practice, that somebody was said to pray. Since the Bible has 51,159 verses it will be seen that about one verse out of 19 refers to the subject of prayer. The table does not include benedictions.

PRAYER—TIMES MENTIONED IN THE BIBLE.

SECTION	PLACES	VERSES
Historical	238	488
Didactic	177	1693

Prophetical	159	249
Old Testament	574	2430
Historical	223	280
Didactic	63	67
Prophetical	28	31
New Testament	314	378
Total	888	2808

e. ANSWERS.

All of the greatest characters in the Bible were praying men and women. All of them spoke to God, relying on His promises and expecting to get an answer. All of them found that He was not a man, that He should lie, nor the son of man, that He should repent. They found that He is faithful That promised. They received what they asked for, or something better. They received more than they asked, for God is "able to do exceeding abundantly above all that we ask or think" (Eph. 3:20). To them prayer was power and a recourse never failing. God was "their Refuge and Strength, a very present Help in trouble" (Ps. 46:1). Abraham asked for a son, and—after many years of waiting—a son was born to him. The waiting itself proved good to him and to us, for his faith was tested, he became an example of faith, and they which "be of faith are blessed with the faithful Abraham" (Gal. 3:9). When Israel would not enter the Promised Land the Lord threatened to disinherit them, but Moses interceded, and the Lord heard his plea. Hannah prayed for a son. She got Samuel and five other children. David prayed for forgiveness. His prayer was heard, and he was in addition promised that the Messiah should proceed from his royal house.

Jesus prayed. He prayed much. He needed to pray. He prayed before, during and after the great crises of His life and was heard by the Heavenly Father. In Luke 3:21 He is said to have been praying when He was baptized.

In answer to His prayer, the Heaven was opened and the
Holy Ghost descended and a voice from Heaven came, saying: "Thou art My beloved Son; in Thee I am well
pleased". In Mark 1:35 we find Him departing before
daylight into a solitary place to pray. There was a big
day's work before Him. All men were seeking for Him.
He sought counsel and power from on high and got it. In
Luke 5:16, after a strenuous day of preaching and healing,
He withdrew into the wilderness and prayed. In the next
verse we are told that "the power of the Lord was present
to heal them". In Luke 6:12 He spent the whole night in
prayer. The next day He chose the twelve disciples,
healed and preached. In Mark 8:6 He gave thanks before
meat, and 4000 were fed. In Matt. 14:23, after having
fed the 5000 He went up into the mountain to pass a night
alone with God in prayer. This took place just before the
great break with the Pharisees and the multitude at Capernaum. In Luke 9:28 He spent another night in prayer and
was transfigured. In Luke 10:21, upon the return of the
Seventy, He sent up a prayer of thanksgiving for His disciples. In Luke 11:1-13 His example caused His disciples
to ask Him to teach them how to pray. In John 11:41-43
He thanked the Lord for having heard His prayer, after
which He called Lazarus to life again. In John 12:27-29
His troubled soul pleads: "Father, save Me from this
hour......Glorify Thy name". At once a voice from
Heaven answers: "I have both glorified it, and will glorify
it again". In John 17 He prays to the Father to glorify
Him, to preserve His apostles and all other believers. In
Luke 22:31-32 He tells Peter: "Satan hath desired to have
you, that he may sift you as wheat, but I have prayed for
thee, that thy faith fail not". In Matt. 26:42, while in
such deep agony that His sweat fell as drops of blood, He
prayed: "O My Father, if this may not pass away from
Me, except I drink it, Thy will be done". "And there
appeared an angel unto Him from Heaven, strengthening

Him" (Luke 22:43). In Luke 23:34, while hanging on the cross, He asked His Father to forgive His murderers, for they knew not what they did. In Matt. 27:46 He cried with a loud voice: "My God, My God, why hast Thou forsaken Me?" And a little later (Luke 23:46) He cried again: "Father, into Thy hands I commend My spirit". In all of these examples of prayer from the life of Jesus we note that He was heard and the answer was forthcoming. Jesus is now our High Priest. He sits at the right hand of God and makes intercession for us. "We have an Advocate with the Father, Jesus Christ, the Righteous" (1 John 2:1; Heb. 7:25).

The following list of public and private prayers recorded in the Bible also testify to the fact that God not only promises to hear prayer, but also that all of His promises are yea and amen in Christ.

PUBLIC PRAYERS.

PERSON	REFERENCE	PETITION
(1) Aaron	Num. 6:22-26	The Aaronic blessing of Israel.
(2) Asa	2 Chron. 14:11	Victory over Zerah.
(3) David	1 Chron. 29:10-19	Thanksgiving at close of life.
(4) Elijah	1 Kings 18:36-37	God's attestation of his mission.
(5) Ezra	Ezra 9:5-15	Confession of sin.
(6) Jehoshaphat	2 Chron. 20:6-12	Protection against Moab.
(7) Joshua	Josh. 7:7-9	Confession of Achan's sin.
(8) Joshua, etc.	Neh. 9:5-37	Confession of Judah's sins.
(9) Moses	Num. 10:35-36	Blessing on Israel at the setting forth and stopping of the Ark.
(10) Solomon	1 Kings 8:23-61	Dedication of Temple.
(11) Apostles	Acts 1:24-25	Choosing an apostle.
(12) Bartimeus	Mark 10:47	Sight.
(13) Father of demoniac boy	Matt. 17:15	Help for his son.
(14) Jairus	Matt. 9:18	Help for his dying daughter.
(15) Jesus	Luke 23:34	Forgiveness for His murderers.
(16) Penitent thief	Luke 23:42	To be remembered by Jesus in Paradise.
(17) Paul	Acts 20:36	Farewell intercession at Miletus.
(18) Stephen	Acts 7:59-60	Forgiveness for his murderers.
(19) Ten lepers	Luke 17:13	Cleansing.
(20) The early Church	Acts 4:24-30	Support under persecution.

PRIVATE PRAYERS.

PERSON	REFERENCE	SUBJECT
(1) Abraham . . .	Gen. 15:2	A son.
(2) Daniel	Dan. 9:4-20	Restoration of Jerusalem.
(3) David	Ps. 51	Forgiveness.
(4) Elijah	1 Kings 19:4	Death.
(5) Jacob	Gen. 32:9-12	Deliverance from Esau.
(6) Jeremiah	Jer. 15:15-18	Comfort.
(7) Jonah	Jonah 2:2	Deliverance from the fish.
(8) Moses	Num. 11:11-15	Help in governing Israel.
(9) Nehemiah . . .	Neh. 4:4-5	Protection against Sanballat.
(10) Solomon.	1 Kings 3:5-9	Wisdom to govern Israel.
(11) Anna	Luke 2:37	
(12) Cornelius . . .	Acts 10:2, 30	
(13) Jesus	John 17:1-26	High Priestly Prayer.
(14) Paul and Silas	Acts 16:25	
(15) Peter	Acts 9:40	Restoring Tabitha to life.
(16) Prodigal son . .	Luke 15:18-19	Forgiveness.
(17) Publican . . .	Luke 18:11-13	Mercy.
(18) Samaritan woman	John 4:15	Living Water.
(19) Syro-Phoenician woman . .	Matt. 15:22	Help for her daughter.
(20) The two disciples at Emmaus.	Luke 24:29	Jesus' tarrying.

When in the hour of utmost need,
We know not where to look for aid;
When days and nights of anxious thought
Nor help nor counsel yet have brought:

Then this our comfort is alone,
That we may meet before Thy throne,
And cry, O faithful God, to Thee
For rescue from our misery:

To Thee may raise our hearts and eyes,
Repenting sore with bitter sighs,
And seek Thy pardon for our sin,
And respite from our griefs within.

For Thou hast promised graciously
To hear all those who cry to Thee,
Through Him Whose name alone is great,
Our Savior and our Advocate.
                              (*P. Eber*).

What is a Sacrament in the New Covenant? How many Sacraments were there in the Old Covenant? What are rites of initiation? Of strengthening? What was the rite of initiation in the Old Testament? In the New? What was the rite of strengthening in the Old Testament? In the New? Define Circumcision. What was its purpose? To what extent was water used in connection with Hebrew Sacrifices and other holy rites? Define the Christian Baptism. State its purpose. Who should be baptized?

What was the rite of strengthening and communion in the Old Covenant? In the New? Describe the Passover. The Lord's Supper. State the purpose of each. How often did the first Christians have communion services? Why should Christians often partake of the Lord's Supper?

Why are the Children of God called a holy nation? To what extent do the Old Testament laws deal with purity? What sins does the Moral Law forbid? The Hebrew Ceremonial Law? The Hebrew Political Law? What do these laws show regarding the need of a Savior?

Discuss the question of purification from personal uncleanness. Tell the story of Naaman. Describe the process of purification from leprosy. What was the meaning of the double ceremony? What did David mean by "purge me with hyssop"?

Describe the process of purification for those defiled by touching the dead. What did these ceremonies symbolize? Show that the various kinds of religious purifications emphasize the awfulness of sin and the need of atonement and consecration. What was the attitude of the scribes and Pharisees toward purifications? Of Jesus?

What is meant by prayer? Give examples showing the duty to pray. Of God's promises to answer. Of the conditions for answering. Give examples of Biblical characters that prayed. How many times is prayer mentioned in the Bible? In the Old Testament? In the New? How many verses contain references to prayer? Show that God answers prayer. Illustrate from the Old Testament. From the life of Christ. What is the difference between prayer and intercession? Who is our Advocate?

What does your Catechism say about sacramental rites, religious purification and prayer? Your Bible history? Find appropriate hymns in your hymnal bearing on these subjects. Look up the Bible passages referred to in your lesson, and find additional references to this subject in the Bible. In what ways can the contents of this lesson help you in your Bible study? In your faith and works?

LESSON FORTY-NINE. SACRED ANTIQUITIES:
VI. SACRED NUMBERS.

Letters and numbers are two of the most useful possessions of mankind. By means of a little over two dozen letters of the alphabet man has been able to form millions of different words expressing and recording his thoughts. By means of the ten primary figures he has also been able to make millions of different calculations. He can calculate the distance to the sun about as easily and accurately as to the nearest town. He can determine to a second how long it takes the earth to revolve around the sun. He can determine the law of falling bodies, the proportion of parts in a compound, the shape of the snowflakes, the structure of vegetable and animal life. He can buy and sell, and keep accounts. He can build houses and railroads, drill through mountains and conduct military campaigns. He can in some measure think the thoughts of God the Creator by beholding the orderly work of His hands, Who has created the stars by number, Who has measured the waters in the hollow of His hand and meted out the heavens with a span, Who has weighed the mountains in scales, and the hills in a balance, and Who knows every sparrow that falls to the ground and has numbered every hair on our heads.

Nobody knows when man began to use numbers. The Arabic notation—1, 2, 3, 4, 5, 6, 7, 8, 9, 0—was not in use by any of the ancients. It was introduced into Europe during the Crusades and has been in general use only about 400 years. The cumbersome Roman notation was still in use, and is even now used in numbering chapters and larger divisions in books and volumes of books in sets. The Romans used letters to designate numbers. The Greeks also used letters to represent figures, but did not employ the same letters. The Hebrews, too, gave value to letters as in Latin and Greek. The table below gives a comparison of the four notations mentioned.

NOTATIONS.

ARABIC	LATIN	GREEK	HEBREW
1	I	a	a
2	II	b	b
3	III	g	g
4	IV	d	d
5	V	e (short)	h
6	VI	s	w
7	VII	z	z
8	VIII	e (long)	hh
9	IX	th	t
10	X	i	y
50	L	n	n
100	C	r	q
500	D	ph	qt
1000	M	,a	ä

How much more convenient it is to use the Arabic numerals than the Roman letters can be tried out by writing a few larger numbers. Thus: 948=CMXLVIII. Try also adding a few Roman numbers.

1. THEIR SACRED CHARACTER.

Some commentators dwell a good deal on the sacred character of certain numbers. In the case of the Hebrews, for example, they find especially the numbers 3, 4, 7, 10, 12 and some of their multiples worthy of the title sacred. These numbers are connected with so many sacred events that they have taken on a halo of new meanings not originally connected with them. Thus, the number 3 has been held to represent stability and solidity, because it is used in calculating the three dimensions of a cube. It is held to represent the Deity (E. Kautzsch) and unity (J. Sether), etc. In like manner the other numbers have been given various symbolical meanings. The number 4 has been said to represent the world, the number 7, being 3+4, is said to represent the union of the Triune God with His creatures. It is a peculiarly mystic and sacred number.

The number 10, following the last of the digits, symbolizes completion. The number 12, being 3x4 and the number of the Chosen Tribes, symbolizes holiness (Cf. R. F. Weidner's "Annotations on Revelation").

Some of the multiples of these numbers are also regarded as sacred, as 40, 70, 100.

The number 40 occurs in the Old Testament 122 times; in the New, 21; total, 143. Due to its use in such connections as the following, it has been held that this number signifies a time of trial and temptation before victory.

40 days of rain—at the flood.
40 days of waiting—after the mountain tops appeared.
40 years old—Isaac's age at marriage.
40 years old—Esau's age at marriage.
40 years old—when Moses fled to Midian.
40 years' stay—Moses in Midian.
40 years' wandering—Moses with Israel.
40 days and nights—Moses on Mt. Sinai (twice).
40 times 12—480 years from Exodus to the Temple.
40 years' rest—under Othniel.
40 years' rest—under Deborah and Barak.
40 years' rest—under Gideon.
40 years' servitude—under Philistia.
40 years' rule—of Judge Eli.
40 days—in which Goliath mocked Israel.
40 years' reign—by Saul.
40 years' reign—by David.
40 years' reign—by Solomon.
40 days of grace—until Nineveh's fall.
40 days and nights—Jesus in the Wilderness.

The number 70 occurs 78 times in the Old Testament and 4 in the New, total 82. A partial list is given herewith:
70 elders of Moses.
70 souls with Jacob to Egypt.
70 palm trees at Elim.

70 shekels, weight of silver bowl offered.
70 kings mutilated by Adoni-bezek.
70 sons of Gideon.
70 sons of Ahab.
70 Sabbatical years not kept.
70 years of Babylonian Captivity.
70 years in which Tyre was forgotten.
70 cubits, breadth of Ezekiel's Temple.
70 weeks of Daniel's prophecy.
70 years, a good old age.
70 disciples of Jesus.
70 times 7, the rule for forgiveness.

The following instances illustrate the use of the number 100:

The Court of the Tabernacle (100 cubits long).

The prophets of God protected by Obadiah (100 hid in a cave).

The tribute to Pharaoh-Necho (100 talents of silver).

The treasures of Zerubbabel's Temple (100 talents of silver and 100 of gold).

The Court of Ezekiel's Temple (100 cubits square).

The Parable of the Lost Sheep (1 out of 100).

The Parable of the Unjust Servant (having 100 pence coming).

The Parable of the Sower (some seed bearing 100 fold).

The Parable of the Unjust Steward (100 measures of oil).

The mixture for embalming Jesus (100 weight).

2. EXAMPLES OF THEIR USE.

According to Young's "Analytical Concordance of the Bible" the numbers 1-12 appear in Scripture the following number of times:

Figure	Bible	O. T.	N. T.
1	1245	778	467
2	806	659	147
3	614	512	102
4	285	240	45
5	302	262	40
6	237	215	22
7	544	445	99
8	118	107	11
9	81	66	15
10	256	227	29
11	38	29	9
12	197	122	75
1-12	4723	3662	1061

a. THE FIGURE 1.

Gen. 2:24—"Therefore shall a man leave his father and his mother, and shall cleave unto his wife, and they shall be one flesh."

Deut. 6:4—"Hear, O Israel: The Lord, our God is one Lord" (A. V.).

Josh. 23:14—"Not one thing hath failed of all of the good things which Jehovah your God spake concerning you."

Job 9:3—"If God be pleased to contend with him, he can not answer Him one of a thousand."

Ps. 27:4—"One thing have I asked of Jehovah, that will I seek after: That I may dwell in the House of Jehovah all the days of my life."

Zech. 14:9—"And Jehovah shall be King in all the earth: In that day shall Jehovah be one, and His name one."

Matt. 19:17—"One there is Who is good."

Mark 10:21—"One thing thou lackest."

Luke 10:42—"One thing is needful."

John 9:25—"One thing I know, that, whereas I was blind, now I see."

John 17:22—"And the glory which Thou hast given Me I have given unto them; that they may be one, even as We are one."

1 Cor. 8:4—"Concerning therefore the eating of things sacrificed to idols, we know that no idol is anything in the world, and that there is no god but One."

1 Cor. 10:17—"Seeing that we, who are many, are one bread, one body."

Gal. 3:28—"There can be neither Jew nor Greek, there can be neither bond nor free, there can be no male and female, for ye all are one man in Christ Jesus."

Eph. 4:4-5—"There is one Body and one Spirit, even as also ye were called in one hope of your calling: one Lord, one faith, one Baptism, one God and Father of all, Who is over all, and through all, and in all."

Phil. 3:13—"But one thing I do—I press on toward the goal unto the prize of the high calling of God in Christ Jesus."

1 Tim. 2:5—"For there is one God, one Mediator also between God and men, Himself Man, Christ Jesus."

1 John 5:7—"For there are Three That bear record in Heaven, the Father, the Word and the Holy Ghost, and these Three are One."

b. THE FIGURE 2.

The number two occurs often in Scripture and in many connections. In the beginning God divided time into two parts—day and night. He made two people—Adam and Eve, a man and a woman, each with body and soul, with two hands and two feet, two ears, two eyes, two nostrils, two lungs, etc. He made two Covenants with mankind—the Old and the New, He gave them the Law and the Gospel. There are two parts to the Bible—the Old and New Testaments; there are two Sacraments in the Christian Church—Baptism and Communion. Noah took into the Ark a pair of every unclean animal that could not live in the water. Rebekah had twin sons—Esau and Jacob. Jacob had two wives—Leah and Rachel. Pharaoh had two servants whom he sent to prison—a butler and a baker. Joseph had two sons—Manasseh and Ephraim. Moses received the Law on two tables of stone. The Law may be summarized into two Commandments—love to God and love to man (Luke 10:27). There were two faithful spies—Joshua and Caleb. The Tabernacle and the Temple had two divisions—the Holy Place and the Most Holy. Two goats were taken on the Day of Atonement—the one to be sacrificed and the other to be sent into the desert. Two doves or pigeons might be offered by poor people who could not bring a costlier sacrifice. Two cherubim rested with outstretched wings on the Mercy Seat of the Ark. There were two Kingdoms—Israel and Judah, and the Kingdom of Judah consisted of Two Tribes—Judah and Benjamin. Only two of the Old Testament believers were taken up to Heaven alive—Enoch and Elijah.

Jesus had two natures—human and divine. He was redeemed by His mother Mary by the offering of two pigeons or turtle doves. He sent out His disciples two by two. He fed the multitude with two fishes and some bread. He healed two blind men, told the parable of the Two Sons, stayed with two sisters, Martha and Mary, in Bethany, sent out two disciples to fetch the foal on which He was to ride into Jerusalem, was falsely accused by two witnesses and crucified between two thieves, to the great satisfaction of two rival sects—the Pharisees and the Sadducees. When He arose two angels kept watch at His empty tomb. He walked on the way to Emmaus with two of His disciples. Paul was in a strait betwixt two desires—to depart and be with Christ, and to live and work in the Church (Phil. 1:23).

c. The Figure 3.

Gen. 6:10—"And Noah begot three sons, Shem, Ham and Japheth."

Gen. 18:2—"And he looked, and lo, three men stood over against him" (three angels).

Ex. 2:2—"And when she saw that he was a goodly child, she hid him three months" (Moses).

Ex. 23:14—"Three times shalt thou keep a feast unto me in the year."

Ex. 23:17—"Three times in the year all thy males shall appear before the Lord Jehovah."

Num. 22:28—"And the ass said unto Balaam, 'What have I done unto thee, that thou hast smitten me these three times?'"

Num. 24:10—"And Balak said unto Balaam, 'I called thee to curse mine enemies, and, behold, thou hast altogether blessed them these three times.'"

Josh. 1:11—"For within three days ye are to pass over this Jordan."

Josh. 2:16—"And hide yourselves there three days" (Rahab to the spies).

Judg. 7:20—"And Gideon's three companies blew the trumpets."

Judg. 16:15—"Thou hast mocked me these three times" (Delilah to Samson).

1 Sam. 20:20—"And I will shoot three arrows to the side" (Jonathan to David).

2 Sam. 24:12—"Go and speak unto David, 'Thus saith Jehovah, I offer thee three things'" (seven years of famine, three months of defeat, or three days of pestilence).

1 Kings 17:21—"And Elijah stretched himself upon the child three times."

Esther 4:16—"Fast ye for me, and neither eat nor drink three days."

Job 2:11—"Now when Job's three friends heard of all

of this evil that was come upon him, they came every one from his own place."

Job 42:13—"He had also seven sons and three daughters."

Prov. 30:21—"For three things the earth doth tremble."

Isa. 6:3—"And one (angel) cried to another and said, 'Holy, holy, holy is Jehovah of hosts.'"

Dan. 3:20—"And he commanded . . . to bind Shadrach, Meshach and Abednego, and to cast them into the burning fiery furnace."

Dan. 11:2—"There shall stand up yet three kings in Persia."

Jonah 1:17—"And Jonah was in the belly of the fish three days and three nights."

Matt. 12:40—"So shall the Son of Man be three days and three nights in the heart of the earth."

Matt. 17:4—"If Thou wilt, I will make here three Tabernacles, one for Thee, one for Moses and one for Elijah."

Matt. 26:61—"This Man said, 'I am able to destroy the Temple of God, and to build it in three days.'"

Matt. 28:19—"Baptizing them into the name of the Father and of the Son and of the Holy Spirit."

Luke 2:46—"After three days they found Him in the Temple."

Luke 12:52—"For there shall be from henceforth five in one house divided, three against two, and two against three."

Acts 9:9—"And Saul was three days without sight, and did neither eat nor drink."

Acts 10:16—"And this was done thrice, and straightway the vessel was received up into heaven" (Peter's vision).

1 Cor. 13:13—"But now abideth faith, hope, love, these three; and the greatest of these is love."

Gal. 1:18—"Then after three years I went up to Jerusalem" (Paul in Arabia).

1 John 5:8—"For there are three who bear witness, the Spirit, the water and the blood."

Rev. 16:19—"And the great city (Babylon) was divided into three parts."

Rev. 21:13—"And on the east (of the New Jerusalem) were three gates, and on the north three gates, and on the south three gates, and on the west three gates."

d. The Figure 4.

Mention is sometimes made of the four winds from the four quarters of the heavens (Cf. Jer. 49:36). There were four rivers in Paradise. Four parts of the crops of Goshen should go to Jacob and his sons, the fifth part should fall to Pharaoh. Four plays a prominent part in the construction of the Tabernacle—the altars were square, with four horns and four rings. The veil was hung on four pillars, set in four silver sockets. The decorations of roof and curtains were in four colors—blue, signifying the heavenly origin; purple, signifying the royal glory; crimson, signifying blood and life; white, signifying purity and holiness. It plays also a prominent part in Solomon's Temple, in the Ideal Temple of Ezekiel's vision and in Herod's Temple. In Solomon's Temple, for example, the gates were assigned by lots, four Levites on the north a day, and four on the south. In Ezekiel's Temple there were four tables on each side of the gate, on which to slay the sacrifices, and there were four tables of hewn stone for the Burnt Offering (Ezek. 40:41-42). In Herod's Temple there were four Courts—for the priests, for the men of Israel, for the women of Israel and for the Gentiles, and there were four square rooms, one in each corner of the Women's Court. Jeremiah prophesied four kinds of punishment upon Jerusalem—sword, dogs, fowls, beasts; Ezekiel also prophesied four—sword, famine, beasts, pestilence. Ezekiel had also a vision of four cherubim, every one of which had four faces and four wings (Ezek. 1:5-6). Zechariah had a vision of four horns, signifying the enemies of Judah, and a vision of four smiths, signifying the defeat of these enemies. There are four major prophets in the Old Testament— Isaiah, Jeremiah, Ezekiel and Daniel.

There are four evangelists in the New Testament— Matthew, Mark, Luke and John, and four chief apostles—Peter, James, John and Paul. There are four lists of the disciples, and four accounts of the institution of the Lord's Supper. A man sick of the palsy was carried by four, who let him down through the roof to Jesus. Lazarus had been in the grave four days when Jesus called him to life again. Jesus revealed Himself four times on the first Easter Day. In Peter's vision a great sheet knit at the four corners was let down to the earth, wherein were all manner of four-footed beasts of the earth. In John's vision there were around the throne of God four living beasts, full of eyes before and behind, worshipping God, probably signifying animated nature giving Him glory.

e. THE FIGURE 5.

Gen. 14:8-9—"Four kings against five" (Chedorlaomer etc., vs. Sodom etc.).

Gen. 18:28—"Peradventure there shall lack five of the 50 righteous?" (Abraham praying for Sodom).

Gen. 45:22—"But to Benjamin Joseph gave five changes of raiment."

Ex. 26:3—"Five curtains shall be coupled together one to another; and the other five curtains shall be coupled one to another" (The Tabernacle curtains).

Ex. 26:37—"And thou shalt make for the screen five pillars of acacia, and overlay them with gold; their hooks shall be of gold, and thou shalt cast five sockets of brass for them" (The Tabernacle door).

Lev. 26:8—"And five of you shall chase a hundred" (Israel's prowess, if obedient).

Num. 7:17—"For the sacrifice of Peace Offerings, two

oxen, five rams, five he-goats, five he-lambs a year old."

Josh. 10:17—"And it was told Joshua, saying, 'The five kings are found, hidden in the cave at Makkedah.' "

Josh. 13:3—"The five lords of the Philistines" (Kings of Gaza, Ashdod, Askelon, Gath and Ekron).

2 Sam. 4:4—"He was five years old when the tidings came of Saul and Jonathan out of Jezreel, and his nurse took him up and fled" (Mephibosheth, Jonathan's son).

Ezek. 41:9—"The thickness of the wall, which was for the side chambers, on the outside, was five cubits" (Ezekiel's Temple).

Matt. 14:19—"And He took the five loaves and the two fishes, and looking up to Heaven, He blessed and brake and gave the loaves to the disciples" (Feeding the 5,000).

Matt. 25:2—"And five of them were foolish, and five were wise" (Parable of Ten Virgins).

Matt. 25:15—"And unto one he gave five talents" (Parable of the Talents).

Luke 12:6—"Are not five sparrows sold for two pence? And not one of them is forgotten in the sight of God."

Luke 12:52—"For there shall be from henceforth five in one house divided, three against two, and two against three."

Luke 14:19—"And another said, 'I have bought five yoke of oxen, and I go to prove them; I pray thee, have me excused.' "

Luke 16:28—"For I have five brethren; that he may testify unto them, lest they also come into this place of torment" (The Rich Man's prayer to Lazarus).

John 4:18—"For thou hast had five husbands" (Jesus speaking to the Samaritan woman).

1 Cor. 14:19—"Howbeit, in the Church I had rather speak five words with my understanding, that I might instruct others also, than 10,000 words in a tongue."

f. THE FIGURE 6.

There were six days of creation and of work. Abraham's prayer for Sodom was repeated six times. Jacob worked six years with Laban for cattle. The Golden Candlestick had six branches. The rear of the Holy of Holies was covered by six boards. The posts of Ezekiel's Temple were six feet square. The Sabbath Burnt Offering at this Temple included six lambs without blemish. There were six Cities of Refuge in Israel. The Feast of Unleavened Bread following upon the eating of the Passover lasted six days. Jephthah ruled Israel six years. Boaz gave Ruth six measures of barley. The giant of Gath had six fingers on each hand and six toes on each foot. There were six steps leading to Solomon's throne. The angels in Isaiah's vision had six wings. Jesus called six disciples during the first year of His ministry. There were six waterpots of stone at the wedding in Cana. At the sixth hour Pilate presented Jesus to the multitude, saying, "Behold your King," and they answered, "Crucify Him."

g. The Figure 7.

Gen. 2:2-3—"And on the seventh day God finished His work which He had made; and He rested on the seventh day from all His work which He had made. And God blessed the seventh day and hallowed it."

Gen. 7:2—"Of every clean beast thou shalt take to thee seven and seven, the male and his female."

Gen. 8:4—"And the Ark rested in the seventh month."

Gen. 8:10—"And he stayed yet other seven days and again he sent forth the dove out of the Ark."

Gen. 29:20—"And Jacob served seven years for Rachel; and they seemed unto him but a few days, for the love he had to her."

Gen. 33:3—"And he (Jacob) bowed himself to the ground seven times, until he came near to his brother."

Gen. 41:26—"The seven good kine are seven years; and the seven good ears are seven years."

Lev. 4:17—"And the priest shall dip his finger in the

blood and sprinkle it seven times before Jehovah, before the veil."

Lev. 16:14—"And he shall take of the blood of the bullock, and sprinkle it with his finger upon the Mercy Seat on the east; and before the Mercy Seat shall he sprinkle of the blood with his finger seven times."

Lev. 23:16—"Even unto the morrow after the seventh Sabbath shall ye number 50 days" (Pentecost).

Lev. 23:24—"In the seventh month, in the first day of the month, shall be a solemn rest unto you."

Lev. 25:4—"But in the seventh year shall be a Sabbath of solemn rest for the land, a Sabbath unto Jehovah" (Sabbatic year).

Lev. 25:8—"Thou shalt number seven Sabbaths of years unto thee, seven times seven years" (Jubilee).

Num. 23:1—"And Balaam said unto Balak, 'Build me here seven altars, and prepare me here seven bullocks and seven rams.' "

Deut. 15:9—"The seventh year, the year of release, is at hand."

Deut. 16:13—"Thou shalt keep the Feast of Tabernacles seven days."

Josh. 6:4—"And seven priests shall bear seven trumpets of rams' horns before the Ark; and the seventh day he shall compass the city seven times, and the priests shall blow the trumpets."

Judg. 16:7—"And Samson said unto her, 'If they bind me with seven green withes that were never dried, then shall I become weak, and be as another man.' "

1 Sam. 16:10—"And Jesse made seven of his sons to pass before Samuel."

Job 1:2—"And there was born unto him seven sons and three daughters."

Isa. 30:26—"And the light of the sun shall be sevenfold, as the light of seven days."

Ezek. 39:9—"And they shall make fires of them (weapons) seven years."

Dan. 9:25—"From the going forth of the commandment to restore and to build Jerusalem unto the Anointed One, the Prince, shall be seven weeks, and three score and two weeks."

Zech. 4: 2—"Behold, a Candlestick all of gold, with its bowl upon the top of it, and its seven lamps thereon; there are seven pipes to each of the lamps."

Matt. 12:45—"Then goeth he, and taketh with himself seven other spirits more evil than himself, and they enter in and dwell there."

Matt. 18:22—"I say not unto thee until seven times, but until seventy times seven."

Matt. 22:28—"In the resurrection, therefore, whose wife shall she be of the seven? For they all had her."

Mark 8:6—"And He took the seven loaves, and, having given thanks, He brake, and gave to His disciples to set before them."

Acts 6:3—"Look ye out therefore, brethren, from among you seven men of good report."

Rev. 1:4—"John to the seven Churches which are in Asia."

Rev. 1:20—"The seven stars are the angels of the seven Churches, and the seven Candlesticks are seven Churches."

h. THE FIGURE 8.

There were eight saved by Noah's Ark. Abraham circumcised Isaac on the eighth day. Israel was in bondage to Mesopotamia eight years. Abdon judged Israel eight years. David was the eighth son of Jesse. Jehoram, the son of Jehoshaphat, reigned eight years at Jerusalem. Josiah was eight years old when he began to rule; so also was Jehoiachin. The porch of the gate of Ezekiel's Temple was eight cubits; the ascent to the Court had eight steps; there were eight tables for sacrifices.

Jesus was circumcised when He was eight days old.
Jesus arose on the eighth day of the Passover Week. After
eight days He revealed Himself again to the disciples,
including Thomas, and showed them His pierced hands and
side. Peter healed Aeneas, who had been sick abed of
palsy for eight years. (1 Pet. 3:20.)

i. THE FIGURE 9.

Num. 29:26—"And on the fifth day (of the Feast of
Tabernacles) nine bullocks, two rams," etc. (for a sacrifice).

Josh. 21:13, 16—"And unto the children of Aaron......
nine cities out of those two tribes."

Neh. 11:1—"And the rest of the people also cast lots, to
bring one of ten to dwell in Jerusalem, the holy city, and
nine parts in the other cities."

Matt. 27:46—"And about the ninth hour (12 o'clock)
Jesus cried with a loud voice, saying, "Eli, Eli, lama sa-
bachthani?'—that is, 'My God, My God, why hast Thou
forsaken Me?' "

Luke 17:17—"Were not the ten cleansed? But where
are the nine?"

j. THE FIGURE 10.

There were ten Antediluvian and ten Postdiluvian patriarchs. Abraham prayed God to save Sodom for the sake
of ten righteous that might be found there. Eliezer took
ten camels with him to Haran. He gave Rebekah two golden
bracelets of ten shekels' weight. Jacob accused Laban of
having changed his wages ten times. Joseph was sold by
his ten older brothers. The Israelites crossed the Red Sea
and the Jordan on the tenth of the month. There are ten
Commandments in the Moral Law. The Tabernacle was
built on the principle of 4 and 10 and 3. The boards
were ten cubits long. There were ten pillars in ten sockets.
In the Temple there were ten smaller Lavers and one large
Sea, ten Candlesticks and ten Tables for Showbread. Ten
of the spies encouraged Israel not to enter Canaan. Elon

was judge ten years. Naomi dwelt in Moab ten years. David brought ten loaves of bread to his brothers in the army. The Northern Kingdom consisted of Ten Tribes of Israel. Haman's ten sons were hanged. Daniel was permitted to abstain from meat ten days and gained by it. In matters of wisdom Daniel and his friends were found to be ten times better than all of the king's wise men. The fourth beast of Daniel's vision had ten horns. The Jews gave a tenth of their income to the Levites. The Levites gave one tenth of this tenth to the priests.

In the parable of the Ten Virgins five were wise, five foolish. In the parable of the Talents, one received five talents and gained five, making ten. In the parable of the Lost Penny, the woman had originally ten pieces of silver. In the parable of the Ten Pounds the good and faithful servant who had made ten pounds was placed over ten cities. There were ten lepers cleansed. The Church at Smyrna should have tribulation ten days. The red dragon had seven heads and ten horns. The leopard from the sea had seven heads, ten horns and ten diadems on the horns. In John 15:4-10 the term "Abide in Me" occurs ten times.

k. THE FIGURE 11.

Gen. 37:9—"And Joseph dreamed yet another dream ....and said, 'Behold....the sun and the moon and eleven stars made obeisance to me.' "

Ex. 26:7—"And thou shalt make curtains of goats' hair for a tent over the Tabernacle: eleven curtains shalt thou make them."

Num. 29:20—"And on the third day (of the Feast of Tabernacles) eleven bullocks" (for sacrifice).

2 Kings 23:36—"Jehoiakim....reigned eleven years in Jerusalem."

Ezek. 40:49—"The breadth (of the porch of Ezekiel's Temple) was eleven cubits."

Matt. 28:16—"But the eleven disciples went into Galilee, unto the Mountain where Jesus had appointed them."

Mark. 16:14—"And He was manifested unto the Eleven themselves as they sat at meat."

Luke 24:33—"And they rose up that very hour, and returned to Jerusalem, and found the Eleven gathered together."

Acts 1:26—"And he (Matthias) was numbered with the eleven apostles."

Acts 2:14—"But Peter, standing up with the Eleven, lifted up his voice, saying...."

1. THE FIGURE 12.

Ishmael was promised twelve sons, who should become twelve princes. Jacob's twelve sons became the founders of the Twelve Tribes. At Elim were twelve springs of water to satisfy the thirst of the Twelve Tribes. Moses built an altar under Mount Sinai and twelve pillars, one for each tribe. Joshua took twelve stones from the Jordan and made a memorial altar. The Table for Showbread had twelve loaves, one for each Tribe. The breastplate of the high priest had twelve precious stones, one for each of the Tribes. Twelve spies were sent to inspect Canaan. The land was divided into twelve parts, one for each Tribe. Solomon appointed twelve officers over the Tribes. The Brazen Sea rested on twelve oxen, each one representing a Tribe. There were twelve lions on the steps leading to Solomon's throne. Manasseh became king at twelve years of age. The altar hearth of Ezekiel's Temple was to be twelve cubits square.

Jesus had twelve disciples. He cured the woman who had had an issue of blood for twelve years and had touched the hem of His garment. After feeding the 5,000 with five loaves He took up twelve baskets of fragments. He foretold that the disciples should sit with Him in glory on twelve thrones judging the Twelve Tribes. From each of the Twelve Tribes there were, in John's vision, 12,000 sealed. The woman of Rev. 12: 1 had a crown of twelve stars. The New

Jerusalem had walls resting on twelve foundations, consisting of twelve kinds of precious stones, with twelve gates consisting of twelve pearls, and at the gates twelve angels. The names of the Twelve Tribes were written on the gates, and the names of the twelve apostles were written on the foundations. In the midst of this Paradise was the Tree of Life, bearing twelve manner of fruits, yielding its fruit every month.

———

In what ways are letters and numbers useful to mankind? State some of the wonderful things that can be done by means of the ten primary figures of the Arabic notation. What other means of representing numbers have been used in addition to our Arabic figures? How did the Hebrews represent numbers? The Greeks? The Romans? When was the Arabic notation introduced into Europe? Show that it is more convenient than the Roman.

What numbers are said to have sacred character? What is meant by sacred character of numbers? Illustrate.

How many times is the number 40 used in the Bible? What is the mystic meaning of this number? Give examples of its use. How many times does the number 70 occur in the Bible? Give some examples of its use. Give some instances in which the number 100 occurs.

Study the table showing how many times the numbers 1—12 appear in Scripture.

Give examples from the Old Testament and from the New Testament in which the number 1 occurs. The number 2. The number 3. The number 4. The number 5. The number 6. The number 7. The number 8. The number 9. The number 10. The number 11. The number 12.

What does your Catechism say about sacred numbers? Your Bible history? Find appropriate hymns in your hymnal bearing on this subject. Look up the Bible passages referred to in your lesson, and find additional references to this subject in the Bible. In what ways can the contents of this lesson help you in your Bible study? In your faith and works?

LESSON FIFTY. SACRED ANTIQUITIES:
VII. IDOLATRY AND SECTS.

1. IDOLATRY.

Idolatry is the worship of images representing a divinity. It is, in short, the worship of false gods. Originally man knew the Creator to be the true God. After sin came into the world and man lost the image of God, this knowledge became more and more dimmed. It is therefore recorded that already in the early ages there were two classes of men—sons of God and sons of men. The sons of God learnt about God and walked in His steps; the sons of men did not care about God and filled the earth with corruption. Noah belonged to the first class. His contemporaries drowned in the Flood belonged to the second class.

After the Flood men again forgot the Lord and "glorified Him not as God, neither gave thanks; but became vain in their reasonings, and their senseless heart was darkened" (Rom. 1:21). But they knew in their conscience that there is a God, and they felt in their hearts that He ought to be worshipped. They attempted, therefore, to form an image of Him. As people increased in numbers and spread out over the earth, they separated from one another, and as their original knowledge of God became fainter and fainter, they formed not only one, but many images of Him. These ideas of God were based on their knowledge and views of nature about them and within them. They went on to substitute the things He had created in place of Him. The sun, the moon, the stars, the planets, wind and storm, mountain and vale, the things in nature and the forces thereof, all became gods of one grade or another. These gods fell far short of the glory of the true God, and to a large extent were caricatures of men, emphasizing this or that trait. .As time went on it was found instructive and convenient to make images and idols of these many deities, to have places of worship, forms of service, an appointed priesthood and a regular tax for their maintenance. The worship of images was the commonest form of idolatry in Biblical times. Another form, also quite widespread, was that of magic. Both will be briefly noticed in the following.

a. IMAGES.

NAME	TIMES MENTIONED	ORIGINAL HOME	DATES B. C.	REFERENCES
(1) Teraphim	14	Mesopotamia . .	1739-520	Gen. 31:19
(2) Golden Calf	18	Egypt	1491-722	Ex. 32:1-6
(3) Chemosh	8	Moab	1490-586	1 Kings 11:7
(4) Moloch (Milcom)	14	Ammon	1490-586	2 Kings 23:10
(5) Brazen Serpent	5	Wilderness	1542-722	2 Kings 18:4
(6) Baal Peor (Peor)	10	Moab	1452	Num. 25:3
(7) Chiun	1	Wilderness	1452	Amos 5:26
(8) Remphan	1	Wilderness	1452	Acts 7:43
(9) Baal	68	Canaan	1452-722	Num. 22:41
(10) Ashtoreth (Astarte)	9	Phoenicia	1400-722	2 Kings 23:13
(11) Baal Berith	2	Midian	1200	Judg. 8:33
(12) Dagon	12	Philistia	1100-1055	1 Sam. 5:3
(13) Baal Zebub	3	Ekron	855	2 Kings 1:2
(14) Rimmon	3	Syria	885	2 Kings 5:18
(15) Adrammelech	1	Sepharvaim . . .	722	2 Kings 17:31
(16) Anammelech	1	Sepharvaim . . .	722	2 Kings 17:31
(17) Ashima	1	Hamath	722	2 Kings 17:30
(18) Gad	1	Babylon	722	Isa. 65:11
(19) Meni	1	Babylon	722	Isa. 65:11
(20) Nebo	1	Chaldea	722	Isa. 46:1
(21) Nergal	1	Cuth	722	2 Kings 17:30
(22) Nibhaz	1	Ava	722	2 Kings 17:30
(23) Succoth Benoth	1	Babylon	722	2 Kings 17:30
(24) Tartak	1	Ava	722	2 Kings 17:30
(25) Tammuz	1	Assyria (?) . . .	590	Ezek. 8:14
(26) Jupiter	2	Rome	51 A. D.	Acts 14:12
(27) Mercury	1	Rome	51 A. D.	Acts 14:12
(28) Diana	5	Greece	56 A. D.	Acts 19:24
(29) High Places	101			Lev. 26:30
(30) Idols	59			Lev. 19:4
(31) Images	57			Dan. 3:1
(32) Groves	39			1 Kings 18:19
Total	443			

The worship of images is mentioned in the Bible about 1000 times. In the above list 32 different names are applied to these images. In addition to these is the general name god, which occurs over 500 times.

Image worship flourished in some form amongst the Chosen People or their neighbors from before the call of Abraham to the end of the Apostolic Era. The Chosen People naturally wanted to be like their neighbors. These neighbors, without exception, worshipped false gods. As the Chosen People came in touch with this neighbor or that, they began to delight in the idolatrous practices they saw. In Egypt, for example, they had seen calf worship, therefore they asked Aaron to make a Golden Calf. In Canaan they found Baal worship most popular, therefore they thought that that form of worship was the ideal. King Ahaz formed an alliance with Assyria against Israel and Syria. The king of Assyria captured Damascus, the capital of Syria, and King Ahaz went to Damascus to meet Tiglath-pilezer, the king of Assyria. While at Damascus the king saw the Syrian altar, which he approached and offered upon. He was so captivated by this heathen altar, that when he came home he had the wonderful altar built by Solomon removed and a new one made after the model of the altar at Damascus. This will illustrate how the Israelites came to worship so many different kinds of images. We do not need to wonder at all at this tendency, for it is a part of human nature. If idolatry were the common practice amongst us, we should find also to our sorrow that we would be tempted to fall into this obviously senseless, foolish and ineffective mode of worship. The fashions of dress are not stronger on a person's claim than the fashions of worship. The saying is, that when you are in Rome you should do as the Romans do. There is another saying, that you shall follow the customs or fly the country. This does not in any sense excuse the Chosen People, for they were intended to have the Promised Land all to themselves, and they were taught the true worship of God and were given strength and help in every way to hold fast to it. This does not excuse us either, for we have been taught the essentials of true religion and we should not depart from it (Heb. 10:25).

The first images connected with the Chosen People were the Teraphim. Joshua says that Abraham's father served other gods. Now, Abraham's grandson Jacob, upon fleeing from his brother Esau, went back to the original home in Mesopotamia. There he married his two cousins Leah and Rachel. In Gen. 31 it was recorded that when Jacob departed from Laban together with his family, his wife Rachel had also taken with her secretly her father's gods, known as Teraphim. These were small images in the form of a man, and were household gods for the protection of

No. 126. Moses' Anger at Beholding the Calf Worship—Ex. 32:19.

the family. Laban set out in pursuit of Jacob and overtook him. Then he upbraided him for stealing una-
wares and carrying away his daughters and his gods. With
reference to the gods Jacob, knowing that he was innocent,
answered: "With whomsoever thou findest thy gods, let
him not live". Now, Rachel had taken the images and put
them in the camel's furniture and sat upon them, and Laban
searched all the tent excepting the place where she sat, but
found them not. It is interesting in passing to note that
Jacob's answer to Laban became a doom upon his wife, for
she had the images—and she died shortly after Jacob settled
again in Canaan. These household images seem to have
had a hold upon the Israelites for about fourteen centuries,
for they are mentioned as late as Zech. 10:2.

Another form of idolatrous worship that might be noted
was that of the Golden Calf. From Joshua 24:14 it is
plain that the Israelites worshiped strange gods in Egypt.
This fact is nowhere more clearly set forth than in the action
of the Israelites when Moses was on Mt. Sinai. They had
seen what the Lord could do for them in bringing them
out of Egypt through the Red Sea and through the Wilderness, provided them with food and water, and protected
them from the Egyptians and the Amalekites. They knew
that Moses had gone up on the mountain to meet with the
Lord, and yet they said to Aaron: "Up, make us gods
which shall go before us". They brought their golden
earrings and from these they made a molten calf. The next
day they rose up early and offered Burnt Offerings and
Peace Offerings, after which they sat down to eat and to
drink, and rose up to play. When Moses came down from
the mountain and saw the people dancing, drunken and
naked, around the Golden Calf, he broke in anger the tables
of stone which he had received from the Lord. Then he
took the Golden Calf and ground it into powder and strewed
it upon the water and made the children of Israel drink it.

Thereupon 3000 men were slain and a plague visited the people on account of their sin.

For a long time after that the Israelites refrained from worshiping the idols of Egypt. During the time of Solomon, about 500 years later, Jeroboam, who was the political enemy of the king, escaped to Egypt. When he came back and became the king of the Ten Tribes he introduced the calf worship of Egypt amongst these tribes, making two calves of gold, setting one in Bethel and the other in Dan. The institution of calf worship continued in the Northern Kingdom from its foundation, in 975, until its fall, in 722.

The most popular and evil idolatrous practice recorded in the Bible was Baal worship. Baal was the chief god of the Canaanites and Phoenicians. He was regarded as the male element of the creation, the female counterpart being Ashtoreth, or Astarte. It is quite evident, then, that the worship of Baal and Astarte went hand in hand, and that this worship would make a very strong appeal to the Israelites as well as to the heathen nations round about. Even today the chief elements of this worship are found in the religion of some of the lodges (Mackay's "Encyclopedia of Freemasonry", M. L. Wagner's "Freemasonry"). Altars to Baal were erected on heights or on housetops, hence called in the Bible "high places". The offering consisted of incense, bulls, and even human sacrifices, particularly children. Wild, sensual orgies seem to have been a feature of the worship. A very interesting account of the way the worship was conducted is given in 1 Kings 18 in the story of Elijah and the priests of Baal on Mt. Carmel. At that time Ahab was king of Israel and the Phoenician Princess Jezebel was the queen. The two seem to have been very religious, for it is said in 1 Kings 18:19 that Jezebel fed 850 prophets of Baal and Astarte at her table. By her orders the prophets of Jehovah had been put to death, except a hundred who were hid and fed in a cave by Obadiah, the governor of Ahab's house. The influence of the court did not seem to have corrupted this faithful servant in Israel, and not only Elijah and the other faithful prophets, but also 7000 whose knees had not bowed to Baal (1 Kings 18:3-4; 19:18). The great work of Elijah was to denounce the idolatry of the Israelites and to overthrow the worship of Baal. The 18th chapter of 1 Kings should be read again and again by the Bible student, for it is one of the most romantic and dramatic scenes in the Bible. It has been set to music by Mendelssohn in his celebrated oratorio "Elijah".

Concerning the other idols worshiped, not much will be said here. Dagon was the first god of the Philistines. A rather amusing story is told in the Bible about Dagon. The Philistines captured the Ark of God and brought it into the temple of Dagon and set it up by his side, leaving it there over night. Early in the morning when the people went to their house of worship they found that Dagon was fallen upon his face on the ground before the Ark of the Lord, and that his head and hands were broken off. Furthermore, as long as the Ark remained in the city of Ashdod the people were sick with the plague. They put their heads together, therefore, and consulted with all the lords of the Philistines as to what they should do with the Ark of the Lord. They concluded after due deliberation to remove it from Ashdod to Gath. As soon as the Ark came to this city the inhabitants thereof became afflicted with the plague. They hurriedly sent the Ark on to Ekron, and the Ekronites in panic cried out: "They have brought the Ark to us to slay us and our people". The Philistines then took counsel again as to what to do with the Ark. They concluded not to harden their hearts as Pharaoh had done, but to send the Ark back to Israel as soon as possible. To be sure of their case they made a new cart and placed the Ark on the cart. Then they took two young cows on which had come no yoke, away from their calves and placed them before the cart and sent them away without a driver. It might be supposed that these cows might not know how to pull a cart, for they had not been broken in, and also that they did not want to leave their sucking calves. Still the cows took the straight way up the hills of Judea, turning neither to the right hand nor to the left. The lords of the Philistines followed them into the border of their land. When the cows came into the land of the Israelites they stopped, and the levites took charge of the Ark. Later, when the Philistines had defeated Saul, they took his head and hung it up in the temple of Dagon.

Solomon in his old age took to himself many heathen wives who influenced him to introduce the religions of their various countries. In 1 Kings 11: 5-7 it is told of Solomon that he did evil in the sight of the Lord, for he built high places for Chemosh, the abomination of Moab, and Moloch, the abomination of Ammon, and Ashtoreth, the abomination of the Zidonians, and that his strange wives burnt incense and sacrificed unto these gods. Chemosh of Moab and Moloch of Ammon both required human sacrifices. They were iron furnaces built in the form of a human being with out-stretched arms designed to receive and to store the sacrifices. The worship of these idols was accompanied with a great deal of licentiousness, and was very popular in Israel from the time of Solomon until the downfall of Judah. The good kings of Judah—Jehoshaphat, Hezekiah and Josiah—sought to remove the high places and other traces of this idolatry, but in vain. One of the idols during the reign of Hezekiah was the Brazen Serpent that Moses had made. In 2 Kings 18:4 it is related that Hezekiah removed and destroyed this relic from the days of Moses. (Figure 127). It was not until the Ten Tribes had been taken captive, never to come back, and the Two Tribes had been taken captive and held in bondage for 70 years, that the Chosen People came to their senses and quit worshiping images made with hands. After the return from Babylon,

No. 127. Hezekiah's Removal of the Brazen Serpent from the Temple—2 Kings 18:4.

in 536, you do not find the Jews practising any form of gross idolatry.

In the New Testament times mention is made of one of the idols of the Greeks, and two of the gods of the Romans. When Paul and Barnabas on their first missionary journey came to Lystra in Asia Minor, Paul healed a woman who had been a cripple from birth. When the people saw what Paul had done they cried out: "The gods have come down to us in the likeness of men". They called Barnabas Jupiter, who was the chief Roman god, and Paul Mercurius, because he was the chief speaker. Then a priest of Jupiter who lived in the city brought oxen and garlands to the gates and would have sacrificed to the missionaries. But when the apostles understood this they cried out: "We are men of like passions with you". When they finally had convinced the people that they were indeed men, the people at the suggestion of the Jews stoned Paul, and then dragged him out of the city, supposing he was dead.

On his second missionary journey, when he labored in Ephesus, Paul's preaching occasioned a great riot. There was in the city a man by the name of Demetrius, a silversmith who made silver shrines for the Greek goddess Diana. There were also other craftsmen who made no little money at this profession, but through the preaching of Paul they saw that they would soon have to go out of business if he was permitted to continue. Now, Diana was the goddess of rivers, pools and harbors, besides being invested with many of the attributes of Astarte, and Ephesus was the metropolis of Western Asia, situated at the mouth of the river and on an important harbor. It was a very wicked and licentious city. Conspicuous at the head of the harbor of Ephesus was the great Temple of Diana, whose magnificence was a proverb throughout the civilized world. It is no wonder then that Demetrius was able to appeal to his fellow citizens and to create a riot simply by telling them that their patron goddess was despised, that her magnificence would be destroyed and that their trade would be taken away from them. The result of the uproar was, that Paul had to leave the city and go on to Macedonia.

b. MAGIC.

Image worship is only one form of idolatry. In ancient times and among modern heathen peoples it has assumed some very coarse aspects, including the making of idols of wood, stone and iron. These idols the heathen worship and fear. Their worship as noted above is characterized by unlicensed debauchery, and fear compels them even to offer up their own children as Burnt Offerings. Such idolatry is also accompanied by mystery and superstition. Mystery and superstition are especially present, however, in the other form of idolatry mentioned, namely, that of magic.

The First Commandment of the moral law prohibited the making of any image: "Thou shalt have no other gods before Me". "Thou shalt not make unto thee any graven image or any likeness of anything that is in Heaven above, or that is in the earth beneath; Thou shalt not bow thyself to them, nor serve them, for I the Lord am a jealous God" (Ex. 20:3-5). The Second Commandment prohibited the practice of magic: "Thou shalt not take the name of the Lord thy God in vain: For the Lord will not hold him guiltless that taketh His name in vain". By this is meant, amongst other things, that we should not conjure, or practise magic by His Holy Name. Magic is the wonderful effects produced by mysterious causes. Those who believe in magic are usually superstitious. Superstition (from the Latin words super—above, and stare—to stand) is excessiveness in worship or faith. Excessiveness shows itself especially in fear of the unknown and mysterious and in various practices which arise from such fear and credulity. Cicero defines superstition as a senseless fear of God. He might have added, not only fear of God but also fear of idols, signs, omens, bogies, the dark, ghosts and what not. As the poet Gay says in his "Fables":

> Alas, you know the cause too well;
> The salt is spilt, to me it fell (a token of evil).

Or, as Dryden says in his "Amaryllis": "My right eye itches, some good luck is near". Superstitious people of today are afraid of beginning a journey on Friday, or being one of a company of thirteen. They carry charms and believe in omens; they make journeys to some distant shrine to cure sickness; they have their fortunes told by clairvoyants and burn witches; they would like to see the magician's "Black Book," but they dare not read the Word of God. Superstition must not be confused with faith. Superstition is senseless, faith is sensible. Faith is the substance of things hoped for, the evidence of things not seen. It comes from a Latin word which means to trust. Derivatives of the Latin parent are such words as faithful, fidelity, confide, defy. All men can have faith, but not all men can have saving faith, which is the free gift of the Holy Spirit. Faith is then quite different from superstition. Faith is founded on knowledge and confidence, superstition on ignorance and fear. Superstition led the Israelites to sacrifice their children to Moloch, and the Crusaders to march across Europe to the Holy Land so that by their hardships, or by their view of Jerusalem, or by their possession of a splinter from the Cross, they might obtain merit with God. Faith impelled Abraham at the call of God to go out from his home, not knowing whither he went, and to dwell in tents with Isaac and Jacob, the heirs of the same promise as he had received. Faith impelled also the first Christians to suffer martyrdom for the sake of Christ. Superstition drives the heathen parent to bury children alive if born on an unlucky day. Faith drives the missionary to the heathen land to bear witness of the Truth that shall make free indeed.

O for a faith that will not shrink,
Though pressed by many a foe,
That will not tremble on the brink
Of any earthly woe—
That bears unmoved the world's dread frown,
Nor heeds its scornful smile;
That seas of trouble cannot drown,
Nor Satan's arts beguile.

(W. H. Bathurst).

In the Bible there are at least 16 different synonyms for magician. The list is as follows:

KINDS OF MAGICIANS.

NAME	TIMES MENTIONED	REFERENCES
(1) Astrologer	9	Dan. 1:20
(2) Augurer	1	Deut. 18:10
(3) Chaldeans	9	Dan. 2:2
(4) Charmer	3	Deut. 18:11
(5) Consulter	1	Deut. 18:11
(6) Diviner	13	Jer. 14:14
(7) Enchanter	14	2 Kings 17:17
(8) Familiar spirit	16	1 Sam. 28:7
(9) Magician	15	Gen. 41:8
(10) Mistress of witchcrafts	1	Nah. 3:4
(11) Necromancer	1	Deut. 18:11
(12) Observer of times	5	2 Kings 21:6
(13) Soothsayer	8	Josh. 13:22
(14) Stargazer	1	Isa. 47:13
(15) Witch	9	Ex. 22:18
(16) Wizard	11	Isa. 8:19
Total	117	

There were distinctions between these different types of magicians, yet they are all regarded as a class. They are all branches of the same corrupt tree which is to be hewn down and cast into the fire.

Some of the references to the magical arts are the following: At the court of Pharaoh there was a goodly following of magicians. When Pharaoh had his dreams about the fat and lean cattle and the ears of corn, these magicians were consulted, but there was not one of them that could interpret the dreams for him. Then the chief butler remembered Joseph in the prison, and he was fetched. Pharaoh said to him: "I have heard of thee, that when thou hearest a dream thou canst interpret it". But Joseph answered: "It is not in me. God shall give Pharaoh an answer of peace" (Gen. 41:15-16). When Moses and Aaron came from the Wilderness to demand freedom of Israel they were given power to do miracles before Pharaoh. Aaron's rod, when cast down before the king, became a serpent, and when taken up became a rod again. The magicians of Egypt were commanded to perform the same wonder and did so, but Aaron's rod swallowed up their rods. The Egyptian magicians were permitted to perform only two other wonders similar to those wrought by Moses and Aaron, but no more. At the third plague—that of lice—they had to admit that the finger of God helped Moses (J. H. Ingraham's "Pillar of Fire", G. Norstog's "Moses"). In the same manner the magicians at the court of the Persian king were in no wise able to compete with Daniel, who was found in every matter of wisdom and understanding to be ten times better than all of the magicians and enchanters that were in all his realm (Dan. 1:20).

The best known example in the Bible of apparent witchcraft is no doubt the calling of Samuel to earth again. Saul was in great need. The Philistines were pressing him hard. David had escaped to their side, yet not with the intention of aiding them. Samuel was dead. The Lord did not answer Saul, because he had sinned and had not repented. Saul had in his better days according to God's Law sought to rid his country of magicians. Yet now, when in deepest despair, he said to his servants: "Seek me a woman that hath a familiar spirit, that I may inquire of her". The servants found such a woman in the person of the witch of Endor—and to her Saul went for the help which he might by repenting have had from God. He demanded that she bring up Samuel from the dead. And when Samuel was brought up, she cried with a loud voice, no doubt in astonishment and fear. It was really not the witch that had been able to bring him up from the abode of death, but the Lord. "The more modern orthodox commentators are unanimous in the opinion that the departed prophet did really appear and announce the destruction of Saul, not, however, in consequence of the magical arts of the witch, but through a miracle wrought by the omnipotence of God" (Keil and Delitzsch's "Commentary on the Books of Samuel", 266).

The practice of magic was most severely condemned and punished by the Mosaic Laws. "There shall not be found with thee any one that maketh his son or his daughter to pass through fire, or that useth divination, one that practises augury, or an enchanter, or a sorcerer, or a charmer, or a consulter with the familiar spirit, or a wizard, or a necromancer. For whosoever doeth these things is an abomination unto Jehovah, and because of these abominations Jehovah thy God doth drive them out before thee" (Deut. 18:10-12). In Ex. 22:18 the command is not to suffer a witch to live. In Lev. 20:27 the command is to stone every witch and every wizard.

2. SECTS.

The division of the Church into sects, following this or that leader, or this or that opinion, is of very long standing. The strife and bitterness between the sects, too, are of very ancient date. Some of the most persistently cruel persecutions and the most long drawn out and bloody wars have been fought on account of religious differences, not in accordance with the Word of God, but contrary to its teaching. Such persecutions and wars were plentiful enough already in the Old Testament times.

a. Sects during Old Testament Times.

The sects of the Old Testament times were the Nazirites, Israelites, Samaritans, Pharisees, Sadducees and Essenes.

(1) *The Nazirites.*—The Nazirites bound themselves by a vow to leave their hair uncut, to abstain from wine, and to practice an extraordinary purity of life and devotion. The obligation was for life or for a certain time. They are mentioned only 11 times in the Bible. In Num. 6 the laws relating to the Nazirites are set forth. As to the meaning of the Nazirite vow it might be said that the word Nazir means the separated or consecrated one. The Nazirite separated himself from the rest of mankind in two ways, negatively, by renouncing the world and its pleasures, typified by abstaining from wine, and positively, by letting the hair grow to show that he was set apart for the Lord. If he happened to come into contact with the dead, then he became defiled and had to have his hair shorn. If he again wished to become a Nazirite, he must first have a Sin Offering and a Burnt Offering made, signifying that atonement must be given and his vow must be renewed before he could resume wearing the sign of his consecration, namely, his hair long. When he was to be released from his vow, he had again to bring Sin Offerings and Burnt Offerings in recognition of his sins of ignorance and a desire to live a holy life also as an ordinary member of Zion. Samson was a Nazirite, but in many ways untrue to his holy vows.

(2) *The Israelites.*—The Israelites were the members of the Ten Tribes. Through the political cunning of Jeroboam they were not permitted to go to Jerusalem to worship at the Temple of Solomon. The majority of them worshiped the Golden Calves set up at Bethel and Dan as images of Jehovah. Later, especially under Ahab, they became followers of Baal and Ashtoreth. Naturally, on political, if not for religious grounds, these two neighboring kingdoms carried on for many years bloody warfare. Nevertheless, there

were many in Israel who did not worship the heathen idols set before them by the wicked kings. These continued to worship Jehovah. Elijah was one of these. Micaiah was another. Obadiah and his 100 prophets also belonged to this class. Also the 7000 who had not bent their knees to Baal. These, however, were not in a position to go to Jerusalem to worship at the sanctuary of Jehovah. They can therefore be considered as a sect.

(3) *The Samaritans.*—The Samaritans were the inhabitants of Samaria after the fall of the Ten Tribes. Most of the Ten Tribes were deported into Media and elsewhere, and in their place the Assyrian king planted colonists from the captured provinces of Babylonia, Cutha, Ama, Hamath and Sepharvaim (2 Kings 17:24). These various tribes intermingled, accepted the language and the religion of the Israelites and even wished to take part in the rebuilding of the Temple. As the Jews denied them this privilege, they assumed a hostile attitude toward the Jews. They sought to prevent the Jews from rebuilding the Temple and the city walls. They built their own temple on Mt. Gerizim, which the Jews under John Hyrcanus leveled to the ground. The Samaritans held fast to the Five Books of Moses, making such changes as suited their purposes, and maintained that Gerizim was the proper place for worshiping God. This was one of the points advanced by the Samaritan woman when meeting with Jesus at the well (John 4). They, too, expected the Messiah, not from the tribe of Judah, but from the tribe of Joseph, the father of their race. Samaria lay in Ephraim, and Ephraim was the son of Joseph.

(4) *The Pharisees.*—The Pharisees had taken their rise especially during the Syrian supremacy. Syria was one of the strongest centers of Greek culture. The scribes, following the glorious example of Ezra, had worked hard to preserve the ancient faith of the Jews and to keep their people again from idolatry and deportation. The priests, on the other hand,

seemed to give way to the powerful and fashionable Greek culture. Furthermore, the Syrian king, Antiochus Epiphanes, sought to hasten the utter extinction of the Jewish faith. He stormed Jerusalem and slaughtered about 40,000 of the defenceless population. He entered the Temple, profaning it by offering swine flesh on the Altar of Burnt Offering and throwing filth into the Holy of Holies. Again he came, as a friend, and fell upon the Jews on a Sabbath. He thereupon issued an edict that there should be a uniformity of worship throughout his realm. He forbade Jews to worship according to their faith and commanded that the Greek religion be substituted. The Temple he converted into a temple for Zeus. Its courts were polluted by the phallic revels of the Baal high places and the Ashtoreth groves. Copies of Scripture were burnt and the faithful who resisted were skinned alive and otherwise tortured. Under these painful trials the Maccabees and the Pharisees arose to deliver their country and their faith from extinction. The name Pharisee means to separate. The Pharisees sought to separate themselves from the unholy practices of the Syrian masters and the easy-going worldly ways of the Sadducee party. They laid special stress on the faith of the fathers, on the tradition of the elders and the letter of the Law. In the course of time they had many a conflict in words and in steel with their rivals, the Sadducees, often losing, but usually winning the favor of the people on account of their greater claims to piety. In the course of time, too, their original holy zeal became corrupted, and at the time of Christ they were as a class most detestable hypocrites, fully deserving the seven-fold woe pronounced upon them by Christ Himself (Matt. 23:13-36). Although they looked forward to the coming of a Messiah, they rejected Christ as such, for He did not meet their requirements, and, besides, He was free in condemning their self-righteousness and deep-set unholiness. They joined hearts and hands with their long-time enemies, the Sadducees, to have Him removed. Happy were they when they saw Him crucified. Some of the Pharisees were upright. Among these we recall a Nicodemus and a Joseph of Arimathea, a Gamaliel and a Paul.

(5) *The Sadducees.*—The Sadducees were the religious and political opponents of the Pharisees. The party arose probably about the same time as the Pharisees, during the confusion of the Syrian and Maccabean periods. It is generally believed that the name refers to the high priest Zadok, who officiated in David's reign, and in whose family the high priesthood remained in the Syrian period. The priests, as stated before, were inclined to look upon the introduction of Greek culture and theology with favor. They were therefore the chief occasion for the organizing of the Pharisee party. The two opposing parties were just as active in state as in church affairs, and were just as ready to use the sword as the tongue or the pen. The two sects clashed on many important doctrines. The Pharisees, for example, laid great stress on oral tradition; the Sadducees rejected this. The Pharisees were particular about the letter of the Law; the Sadducees were very liberal, maintaining the right of private judgment. In distinction from the Pharisees, the Sadducees also denied the existence of angels and spirits and the resurrection of the body (Matt. 22:23-33; Acts 23:8). They taught, as Josephus affirms in his "Antiquities of the Jews" (XIII, 5:9), that the events of this world are not at the disposal of the Lord, but are determined by man's own free will, and that God is not concerned in our doing good or refraining from evil. They were thus, in fact, out and out rationalists and free-thinkers. On account of their priestly origin, their up-to-date learning, their liberal views on all questions of doctrine and works, they had a very powerful following, especially amongst the rich and educated. They were able to capture many offices, such as the high priesthood, and to have in their party many educated, rich and otherwise influential men. They united

with the Pharisees in opposing John the Baptist, Christ and the apostles. John the Baptist called them both a generation of vipers (Matt.3:7). Christ refuted their arguments and silenced them with Scripture (Matt. 16). Paul, taking note of the fact that both sects were represented in the Sandhedrin that tried him, cleverly introduced the question of the resurrection of the dead, which brought on a free-for-all fight, from which Paul was rescued by the soldiers (Acts 23:6-10).

(6) *The Essenes.*—The Essenes are not mentioned in the Bible. The Jewish historian Josephus, however, gives considerable information about them. They were ascetics, who betook themselves into the wildernesses and were extremely rigid in selfdenial and devotions. They held property in common. Their food and clothing were very simple. They did not offer sacrifices, on account of which they were excluded from the Temple. They were 4000 in number, all men, and unmarried (Josephus' "Antiquities", XVIII, 1:5). Some have claimed, although without any foundation, that John the Baptist and Jesus belonged to this sect.

b. Sects during New Testament Times.

It was the intention of Christ that His disciples all should be one (John 17:21), "even as Thou, Father, art in Me, and I in Thee, that they also may be one in Us; that the world may believe that Thou hast sent Me". It is, of course, the purpose and work of Satan to try to create divisions among the followers of Christ. These divisions soon became manifest. In the Congregation at Jerusalem some were Jews and others were Grecians. There soon arose a murmuring of the Grecians against the Jews with respect to the care of the poor. This matter was happily settled by the appointment of deacons to look after the poor.

A more serious difficulty then came up, dividing the Christian camp. Both Peter and Paul became convinced that Christianity was intended not only for the Jews, but also for the Gentiles. Even though Peter was an apostle especially to the Jews (Gal. 2:8), he had also done work amongst the Gentiles, including the baptizing of the Roman Cornelius (Acts 10). Paul, on the other hand, was called an apostle to the Gentiles. He came to an agreement with Peter and some of the other apostles as to the reception of the Gentiles into the Church. They were not to be circumcised. They were to be baptized. They were not to be shunned. They were to be accepted on a par with the Jewish Christians. Not all of the Jewish Christians seemed to understand the freedom of the Gospel in this matter. They held that the Gentile had first to become a Jew by circumcision, that the heathen had to become a Christian through the door of Moses. Even Peter at Antioch seemed to hesitate as to what stand to take. Paul on that account withstood him to his face (Gal. 2:11), and a general council was called at Jerusalem, which decided the question in favor of Paul. Nevertheless, there were some, as at Corinth, who seemed to have taken sides with Paul, and others, at the same place, who took sides with Peter. Modern critics maintain that there were two parties, a Pauline and a Petrine, which divided the early Church for centuries. The two leaders do not seem, however, to have disagreed after this matter was settled.

Still the Church was in great danger of being cut up into a large number of sects even during the life of its founders. The day of worshiping idols was about past, but not the day of worshiping ideals and ideas. Christianity was to be preached to every nation, and in a remarkably short time it was diffused by its zealous spokesmen over the whole world. It was an age of thought. The Roman, Greek, Egyptian, Oriental and Jewish religions and philosophies were up for discussion, in addition to the new Christian faith. It was the most natural thing in the world for Christianity to absorb something from the religions that it was displacing. We need not at all wonder at the appearance of sects trying to combine the Christian with one or another religion or teaching. It is true that this tendency did not get full sway during the New Testament times, such as it had during the second and third centuries after Christ and has even in our own day. Yet the New Testament often notices that it is present, and speaks very clearly of the coming heresies, sects and schisms. There were two main groups—Judaizers and Gnostics.

(1) *Judaizers.*—Christianity came into contact with the Jewish religion (Judaism) and resulted in new sects, half Christian and half Jewish. Judaizers is the general name for these heretics. The best example of their dangerous teaching and influence during the New Testament times is found recorded in the Epistle to the Galatians. Paul had organized Congregations in Galatia on his second missionary journey (Acts 16:6). The Gospel was enthusiastically received. Originally, the Galatians had been heathen, then through the Jews they had turned to Judaism, and now through Paul they had become Christians. They were to take one step more. When Paul left the Judaizers came. These accepted Christianity in name, but held that it was necessary to go back to the Jewish Law, including circumcision. As for Paul, they said he had no authority. Paul hastened to stop this falling away by proving that he was an apostle and that they could not be justified if they went back to Moses. Justification is by faith, not by Law.

(2) *Gnostics.*—Christianity came also in contact with the religions and philosophies of the peoples of the Roman Empire. These religions might be called Ethnicism. The attempt to harmonize them and Christianity was called Gnosticism. The adherents of Gnosticism were called Gnostics. The word Gnostic is derived from a Greek word which means good at knowing. The Gnostics claimed to have a deeper wisdom and a truer philosophical interpretation of Christianity. They were divided into smaller sects, such as Simonians,

Ebionites, Cerinthians, Nicolaitanes and many others. The beginnings of Gnosticism are already noted in Acts 8, Colossians, Jude, 2 Peter, 1 John, 2 John and Rev. 2.

The Simonians derive their name from Simon Magus (Acts 8:9), a Samaritan sorcerer and pretender to the Samaritan Messiahship. The Samaritan religion had already from the start a rather strong mixture of heathen elements. Simon introduced considerably more. He was born in Samaria and educated in Egypt. He came back to Samaria, claiming at first to be "some great one", and succeeded in bewitching the people with his sorceries. The preaching of Philip aroused his curiosity, for like all of the Gnostics, he wanted to get something from every religion. He became baptized. Later he witnessed the power with which Peter and John worked. He offered money for the power to give the Holy Ghost to whomsoever he might lay hands upon. As his motive was unholy, he was severely denounced by Peter. Subsequent to this he opposed Peter, claimed for himself that he was the Messiah and the highest God, and for his companion Helena that she was God's partner in creation. He thus sought to unite the main teaching of the Baal and Astarte religions with the Christian teachings concerning the Triune God.

While Paul was a prisoner at Rome he was visited by two Colossians, from whom he learnt that the Congregation at Colosse was threatened by a very grave danger in the form of a new teaching, partly heathen and partly Jewish. The new teachers taught that the merit of Christ was not sufficient to make men holy, therefore they themselves had to do something to attain holiness. They were to observe certain days, deny themselves certain foods, in short, practice self-mortification. Christian freedom was set aside for asceticism. Christ was set aside for angels. Paul wrote to warn the Colossians of the dangers of the speculations and commandments of men and to remind them of the fulness of the grace of God in Christ.

The early Christians were often cruelly persecuted. Persecution was bad, but the danger of heresy was worse. The apostles worked on the Jews and heathen until they secured adherents. The Jewish and heathen teachers started a back fire and sought to win back the Christians or corrupt their faith. False teachers were at work from without and within the Congregations, trying to pursue the same plan as false teachers of all times have pursued—doing away with Christ as the Savior from sin. Among the heretics were a class later known as Ebionites, who taught that Christ was a mere man; the Docetae, who taught that He was only a spirit, and suffered only in appearance; the Cerinthians, who taught that Christ was an emanation from God that descended on the man Jesus, but left Him again only a man before crucifixion. John is said to have written his Gospel partly to refute the Cerinthians. The First Epistle of John is a companion to the Gospel and urges the children of God to shun the lies of the false teachers. The Second Epistle also warns against heresies. The right attitude towards false teachers is to keep away from them and to keep them away. Here we have a glimpse of true pastoral care. In Rev. 2:6 John warns against the deeds of the Nicolaitanes, which he hates. The Nicolaitanes held that Christians could commit the excesses of the heathen (Rev. 2:14-16).

Peter and Jude also warn against the threatening dangers from the sects. In the First Epistle Peter had spoken of the conduct of the Christian pilgrim under trials from without (persecution); in his Second Epistle he speaks of the conduct of the pilgrim under trials from within (heresies). Equally solemn is the warning of Jude.

What is meant by idolatry? What did man originally know about God? How early did there begin to be two classes of men, sons of God and sons of men? Name some persons belonging to the godly class. Name some belonging to the ungodly class. Account for the rise of image worship.

How many times is the worship of images mentioned in the Bible? Study the list of names applied to the images. What induced the Chosen People to worship images? Discuss the worship of the Teraphim. Of the Golden Calf. Of Baal and Astarte. Of Dagon. Of Chemosh and Moloch. Of Jupiter and Mercury. Of Diana. Tell the story of Rachel and her Teraphim. Of the Golden Calf. Of the Brazen Serpent in the Wilderness. Of Elijah and the prophets of Baal on Mt. Carmel. Of the Ark in Ashdod. Of Mesha's sacrificing his eldest son to Moloch. Of Paul and Barnabas at Lystra. Of the riot at Ephesus.

Define magic. What commandment prohibited the making of any image? What commandment prohibited the practice of magic? Define superstition. Give examples of it. Define faith. Give examples of it.

Study the list of names for magician. Give an example of the use of each. Account for the success of the Egyptian magician before Moses. Account for the failure of the Chaldean magician before Daniel. Tell the story of the witch of Endor. What punishments were meted out upon magicians by the Mosaic Law? What is meant by sect? Why is there strife and bitterness between sects? Mention the principal sects during the Old Testament times.

Who were the Nazirites? What was their peculiar teaching and work? Give an example of a Nazirite.

From what date may we look upon the Ten Tribes as a sect? What was the character of their religious worship?

Who were the Samaritans? In what ways did their worship differ from that of the Jews? Give the argument of the Samaritan woman in favor of her sect. What was Jesus' answer?

Give the history of the Pharisees. Why did the Pharisees oppose Jesus? Give the history of the Sadducees. Why did they oppose Jesus? Who were the Essenes?

Was it the intention of Christ that His Church should be divided? What caused the division of the Church in the early times? What different religions and philosophies were up for discussion in those days? What were the two main groups of heresies?

Who were the Judaizers? Give an example of their teaching, and the arguments used by Paul against them.

Who were the Gnostics? Give an example of their teaching, and of the arguments used by Paul against them. Who was Simon Magus? What did he teach?

Why were the early Christians persecuted? Compare the dangers of persecution and of heresy, and the results from these.

What does your Catechism say about idolatry and sects? Your Bible history? Look up the Bible passages referred to in your lesson, and find additional references to this subject in the Bible. In what ways can the contents of this lesson help you in your Bible study? In your faith and works?

PART SIX.

INTERPRETATION OF THE BIBLE.

OUTLINE.

LESSON FIFTY-ONE. MOOD AND MODE IN
BIBLE READING.

It is generally acknowledged that the Bible is the best book and that everyone should own a copy. J. L. Hurlbut relates in his "Story of the Bible" an incident which shows what value great men put on this Book of Books. Some years ago the editor of an English magazine sent a communication to the "100 greatest men in Great Britain," asking them the questions: "If for any reason you were to spend a year absolutely alone, in a prison, for instance, and could select from your library three volumes to be taken with you as companions in your retirement, please inform us what those three books would be". Ninety-eight of the 100 men named the Bible first on the list of the three books to be chosen.

It is to be admitted, however, that the ignorance of the Bible is appalling. We shall give only one illustration, taken from W. F. Craft's "Bible in School Plans of Many Lands": One of the professors of a certain university in the Northwest gave a test to 139 students to determine the extent of their Bible knowledge. The test consisted of 8 questions—by no means hard ones. Twelve (8%) passed with 75%, 90 (about two-thirds) had less than 50%, 10 could not name a single book of the Old Testament. Among those who did name such books, the spelling was brilliantly fantastic. "Duderominy", "Goshua", "Salms" and 'Joob" are examples. Among the Old Testament books a number of the students mentioned "Paul", Timothy", "Babylonians", "Gentiles", "Philistines" and "Xerxes". Others gave as books in the New Testament "Samuel", "Ruth", "Esther", "Simon", "Jacob", "Philipi", "Thomas", "Lazarus", "Ruth", "Samson Agonistes". The question, "Who was the Apostle to the Gentiles?" brought out a variety of answers, including John the Baptist, Methuselah, Judas, Moses, Abraham and Jacob. And the identity of the "Beloved Disciple" was almost as great a mystery. Apollos (Paul's convert and co-worker) was variously explained to be a heathen deity, a mountain, a town, a giant, a judge, a church, a desert and the Promised Land.

Now, it is quite possible to praise the Bible simply because it has become the fashion so to do. It is possible also that some who praise it really know very little about it, even as some who glibly speak of Shakespeare as the greatest poet may never have read a line of his works. It is very unfortunate, to say the least, that there should be such a woeful ignorance of this Book in a Christian land. Everyone ought to have some knowledge of it. Everyone can get such a knowledge. The Book appeals to young and old. Children can learn most of the stories and the way of salvation from their parents long before they are old enough to read. There are no stories more interesting, no teaching more useful. The interest acquired in childhood will be lasting, the benefits derived are for time and eternity.

There are many different ways of reading and studying the Bible. G. C. Morgan, in his book on the "English Bible", says that there are two classes likely to read the Bible—Christian believers and honest inquirers. The believers come to the Bible with a prejudice in its favor, expecting to find therein teachings which will guide in life and service; the inquirers often approach it with a prejudice against it, wanting to find the truth, and yet not prepared to admit anything on mere heresay. These two classes have a different mood of approach and a different mode of study.

1. THE MOOD IN BIBLE READING.

A Bible reader is in a sense a Bible interpreter. He tries to understand what the book says, and possibly he also tries to explain to others what he reads: Now, all of the older Bible interpreters emphasized the proper mood in approaching the Bible.   Luther's rule was: "Oratio, meditatio et tentatio", that is: "Prayer, meditation and

No. 128. Samuel in Prayer.

practice".   The question is asked by U. V. Sverdrup in his "Explanation":   "What must we do to use the Word of God rightly?" And the answer is: "We must first pray to God for the enlightenment of His Spirit (prayer), and then read the Word devoutly (meditation), with an honest purpose to live according to it (practice)". Prayer for enlightenment, reverent meditation and willingness to apply the lesson learnt, constitute the right mood.

a. PRAYER.

One reason for praying for enlightenment is, that we need it. Through sin our understanding is darkened and

No. 129. Peter.

at best we understand only in part. "The natural man receiveth not the things of the Spirit of God; for they are foolishness unto him; neither can he know them, because they are spiritually discerned" (1 Cor. 2: 14). The Bible may be summed up in the one word Jesus. We read it to find Him. But we believe that we can not by our own reason or strength believe in Jesus or come to Him, but it is the work of the Holy Ghost. "No man can say that Jesus is the Lord, but by the Holy Ghost" (1 Cor. 12:3). Another reason for praying for enlightenment is, that the Lord answers our prayers in accordance with our needs and His most gracious promises. "If ye then, being evil, know how to give good gifts unto your children, how much more shall your Heavenly Father give the Holy Spirit to them that ask Him?" (Luke 11:13).

b. REVERENT MEDITATION.

The word reverent is derived from a Latin word which means to fear. It means a profound respect mingled with affection and fear. When one goes to have audience with an earthly king he is apt to show respect and to listen to every syllable. The Bible reader has audience with the King of kings and the Lord of lords and should listen with equal attention, devoutness and respect.

To meditate means to dwell on anything in thought, to muse and to reflect. Meditation is, like mastication, a very necessary step in digestion. It is not how much food we eat but how much we assimilate that counts. We can not assimilate it unless we chew it well. Some years back Charles Fletcher was heralded as a prophet of health because he went around preaching that chewing the food well was the first and chief health law. He had tried out the experiment of chewing his food until he had to swallow it, and had kept up the practice so long that he had regained his health and become remarkably strong, and then he took a notion to preach his secret from the housetops. It is just so in the spiritual world, too. We can not assimilate thoughts very well until we have meditated upon them. It is not how much we read, but how much we assimilate that counts. Paul wrote to the Philippians this golden rule of

No. 130. Luther Meditating on the Bible.

meditation: "Whatsoever things are true, whatsoever things are honorable, whatsoever things are just, whatsoever things are pure, whatsoever things are lovely, whatsoever things are of good report; if there be any virtue, and if there be any praise, *think of these things*" (Phil. 4:8). He himself had tried practicing this rule. Immediately after his conversion, for instance, he went into the desert of Arabia to meditate on the things concerning Christ which he had learnt.

In this connection it is well to remember that "man shall not live by bread alone, but by every Word which proceedeth out of the mouth of God" (Matt. 4: 4). The soul needs spiritual food even as the body needs physical food. The body needs food every day, so also does the soul. It is therefore the proper attitude to take toward the Word of God that it should be read every day. Everyone ought to begin the day with devotion. Everyone ought to take at least one precious verse of the Bible to meditate on during the day. It is a sad commentary on our fear of God and reverence for His Word when we enter a street car day by day and find nearly everyone lost in his newspaper, but scarcely a person reading the Good News in the Bible. A good way is to do as the plowboy: He carried a New Testament on his person. Whenever he saw that his horses were getting tired, he let them rest a minute or two, pulled his Book out and read a Scripture passage, which he meditated on as he was turning the furrows. Such a plowboy is apt to become one of the wisest and happiest of men.

c. WILLINGNESS TO PRACTISE.

The third point under mood was tentatio, which means trial, practice, experience. The reader must be willing to put the Lord to test, to try Him at His Word. The Lord challenges His people squarely to make a test of His truthfulness. In Mal. 3:10 He says: "Bring ye the whole tithe into the storehouse that there may be food in My house, and *prove Me* now herewith, saith Jehovah of hosts, if I will not open you the windows of Heaven, and pour you out a blessing, that there shall not be room enough to receive it". In John 7:17 Jesus says: "If any man *willeth to do His will,* he shall know of the teaching, whether it be of God, or whether I speak from Myself." Bernard of Clairvaux said that he who turns words into deeds rightly reads Scripture. We might add that he who does not turn words into deeds does not rightly read Scripture. The knowledge gained through Bible reading will then be only head-knowledge

No. 131. "At Thy Word"—Luke 5:5.

and theory, good enough in its place. Theory is the guide of practice, but practice is the life of theory. It is dangerous to keep on learning what the Bible teaches and not put it into practice. Such indifference blunts faith and understanding; it often makes the Bible a sealed book and Christian life an impossibility. The teachings that we have tried out we understand doubly well; they fortify us in darkest trial and direst temptation.

Jesus healed on the Sabbath a man that had been blind from birth. The Pharisees found herein a splendid pretext for persecuting Jesus. They examined the healed man whether he had been blind; they examined his parents. They called the man before them a second time to give an explanation of the cure, saying: "Give glory to God; we know that this man (Jesus) is a sinner". He therefore answered: "Whether He is a sinner, I know not; one thing I know, that, whereas I was blind, now I see" (Luke 9:25). This is exactly the way we shall feel when we are beset by the enemies of Christ in this wicked world. We shall often not be able to make any display of great learning as they may do. But if we have tested out some of His precious teachings, we shall be "ready always to give answer to every man that asketh us a reason concerning the hope that is in us, yet with meekness and fear" (1 Pet. 3:15), saying: "This one thing I know, because I have tried it". There are many things in this world which change. Men come and men go like the blossoms of the field and the fashions of dress. There are also things which never change. The multiplication table is always the same. Jesus Christ is the same yesterday and today, yea, and forever (Heb. 13: 8). His Word is the same: "Till heaven and earth pass away, one jot or one tittle shall in no wise pass away from the Law, till all things be accomplished" (Matt. 5:18). The Bible reader should therefore approach the Good Book to find out what it teaches and with an honest purpose to live according to this teaching. In the Arabian Nights' tale of "The Forty Thieves" the robbers came to a mountain, and when they pronounced the magical password "Open Sesame", the mountain opened, admitting them into the robbers' den. Prayer, meditation and practice are the magical passwords which open the door to the Bible treasuries.

2. THE MODE OF BIBLE READING.

A man wants to find out something about our country at

first hand. How shall he proceed? What might he do to get a good, first-hand impression of this great land? Well, he might take a train or an automobile and travel across one state after another from coast to coast. Or, he might in addition to this make a study of the maps of the country and possibly try his hand at surveying and map-making himself. Then, again, he might settle down in some chosen spot and try his hand at farming, for it is clear that the man who has lived on and from the soil for some time has a different, if not also a deeper knowledge of the country than one who has never had this experience. Once more, he might try digging down into the bowels of the earth after water and oil or coal and iron or even more precious metals, such as, silver and gold. This mining experience will add knowledge to his previous store. And, finally— to mention just one more method among many—he might take pictures of places and things of interest.

The Bible, we have said, may be likened to a country. How might one get a good, first-hand impression of this great Land? Well, he might travel to get a general impression of the length and breadth of it, that is, he might read the Book through from cover to cover, and read it again and again. Or, he might in addition to this, study maps and even make maps himself, that is, he might outline the contents of the Bible. Then, again, he might settle down in some fair spot to till the soil, that is, he might take a portion of Holy Writ and analyze it carefully. Once more, he might dig for the hidden treasures, that is, he might search the Scriptures for facts concerning a certain topic, for answers to a definite question. And, finally, he might use his camera to record what is of unusual interest, that is, he might memorize some of the most precious Bible verses. This, then, is the mode of Bible reading we would suggest to the beginner: Get a general impression by reading it through time and again, outline it book by book and as a whole, analyze parts of it, study it topically and memorize choice passages.

a. Just Reading.

Reading the Bible to get a general impression, we shall call simply reading it. It should be read just like a story book, for it contains a story, recording the most thrilling adventures, the most heroic action, the most tender love, the highest ideals, the greatest sacrifices, the most human men and women. It is told in the clearest language and most natural style. And it is a true story, though stranger than fiction. We would never think of reading a novel the way the Bible is read. Nobody opens a novel at random to read a line or two and then close it again, only to repeat the same process at some future reading. This is the commonest mode of reading the Bible, and with many people the only method. It is possible to read the Bible even this way with profit, even though it would be perfectly silly to read a novel in this manner. Yet it is more than passing strange that sensible Christians can not read the Bible as they would read other books through from cover to cover. The whole Bible is not much larger than a Sunday newspaper. It can be read through in about 7 to 14 days, reckoning 10 hours of reading to the day. And yet there are many older people, as well as younger, who have read hundreds and thousands of books through, but they have not yet read the Bible through.

In reading the Bible through to get a general impression the reader should take each book at a time, for each book is a unit, with a special character and message.

If you take Genesis, it is the record of beginnings and involves the rest of the Bible. It covers as many years as all the rest of the Bible. Get an impression of the time covered, of the space given to Abraham and his family, of sin and death, of grace and life. Keep this impression till you get to the Book of Revelation, when sin shall at last be no more and death shall be swallowed up in victory, when those saved by grace shall have life everlasting in a new Paradise.

If you take Job, it is a picture in miniature of human life. Job, at the opening, was in a sense like Adam, a perfect man untried. Then when tried he, too, fell. His three friends sought to comfort him with their worldly wisdom—the consolation that pain is a punishment for sin, while Job stoutly protests his innocence. Then Elihu, the umpire typifying Christ, interposed and set Job aright. After this, God Himself spoke to Job, and Job confessed his vileness in God's sight and repented. This, again, was followed by God's forgiveness and blessing. The whole gives the impression of the testing value of pain.

Or, if you take John's First Epistle, you must regard it as you would a letter that came to you in the mail. You read the letter through from the heading, introduction, down through the message to the complimentary closing and signature. You would not just read a line or two here and there and throw it away without any impression as to whom it was from, when it was written, where, to whom and about what. Now, read John's First Epistle that way. You first note that it is addressed to you, and then that it comes from God. A letter from Home, from the dear Heavenly Father to His child in a strange land. Are letters from home welcome? Do sons and daughters far from home eagerly read such letters? Should we delight in taking up this Epistle and make note of what the good Lord has to say to us through the handwriting of John?

In some such manner as we have indicated with respect to the reading of Genesis, Job and 1 John, should each book in the Bible be read, and the Bible as a whole.

b. OUTLINING.

After having obtained a general impression of the books

of the Bible and of the Bible as a whole, the reader should look at some of the good outlines of the Bible and try his hand at outlining. This means careful meditation, clear thinking. When you are to draw the outline of an object before you, you half close your eyes to see what are the outstanding features. So also in outlining a book. You must reflect on what seem to be the theme and the main divisions. In thinking over the whole Bible story, the theme seems to be Jesus, the main divisions are the Old and the New Covenants. In musing on Genesis the outstanding theme, indicated also in the title, is Beginnings. The divisions answer the question: Beginnings of what? And they are as follows:

Genesis—The Beginnings

(A) Of matter and man. 1: 1—2: 25.
    (I) Of matter (Physical). 1: 1—2: 3.
    (II) Of man (Theocratic). 2: 4-25.
(B) Of sin and grace. 3: 1—6: 12.
    (I) As applied to Adam and Eve. 3: 1-24.
    (II) As applied to Cain and the Cainites. 4: 1-24.
    (III) As applied to Seth and the Sethites. 4: 25—5: 32.
    (IV) As applied to the two lines mingled. 6: 1-12.
(C) Of destruction and deliverance. 6: 13—9: 28.
    (I) Of destruction. 6: 13—7: 24.
    (II) Of deliverance. 8: 1—9: 28.
(D) Of the nations and the Theocratic Nation. 10:1—50:26.
    (I) Of the nations. 10: 1—11: 32.
    (II) Of the Theocratic Nation. 12: 1—50: 26.
        (1) Abraham. 12: 1—25: 10.
        (2) Isaac. 25: 11—27: 4.
        (3) Jacob-Israel. 27: 5—36: 43.
        (4) Jacob's twelve sons. 37: 1—50: 26.

The above divisions can, of course, be subdivided if the

reader wants to make a more detailed outline. It is possible
that the reader will discover, upon reading the book again,
that his first draft of outline is by no means perfect. Subsequent drafts may take on quite a different form from the
first attempts. What has been said of outlining Genesis applies also to any other book.

c. Analyzing.

Analyzing is derived from two Greek words which mean
to loosen up. It is the resolution of an object into its com-
ponent parts, here the examination of the text as to its
meaning in detail. Analysis is a very discriminating and
arduous occupation, but well worth while. The chemist
analyzes the substances of nature and discovers that the
millions of objects can be reduced to less than 100 elements.
He investigates as to what kind of elements enter into each
object and how much of each. Thus, water is made up of
two gases—hydrogen and oxygen, two parts of hydrogen to
one of oxygen. The knowledge obtained through chemical
analysis is put to a thousand uses in every branch of applied
science. In a similar way the Bible reader should examine
the structure of the book before him as a whole and every
smaller division thereof—chapter or poem, paragraph or
stanza, sentence or verse, clause and phrase, word and syllable, and even letter. In many cases the exact meaning
has to be determined by the closest attention to the form of
the letter.

A case in point is the historical controversy between
Arius and Athanasius as to whether Christ was of the same
essence as the Father or of a similar essence or of a different
essence. The Greek word for the same essence was homo-
ousios, that for similar essence was homoi-ousios, and that
for different essence was hetero-ousios. Arius claimed that
Christ was of a different essence from the Father; Athanasius, that He was of the same essence. If Arius were right,
then Christ was only a man; if Athanasius was right, then

He was "Very God of Very God, begotten, not made, being of one substance with the Father" (Nicene Creed, 3). The controversy waged hot and long, dividing Christianity into two bitter camps. A mediating party proposed as a compromise homoi-ousios—similar essence. Everything revolved then around the little letter i. If Athanasius had accepted the compromise, the doctrine concerning Christ would read: Christ is like unto the Father, but really of different nature and inferior dignity. Christ would then, according to this teaching, not be "Very God of Very God." Christianity would then not be a divine institution, and faith in Christ would be worse than vain. This illustrates sufficiently the need of getting at the sense of the words, even the very letters, of Scripture. J. Ruskin puts this same advice this way in his "Sesame": "I tell you earnestly and authoritatively, you must get into the habit of looking intensely at words, and assuring yourself of their meaning, syllable by syllable —nay, letter by letter."

d. Searching.

Another method of reading the Bible is studying it topically, or searching it for information on definite topics. The importance of this method can not be overestimated. Searching implies that you are looking for something in particular and that you go to great pains, if need be, in finding it. Ponce de León crossed the unknown seas and began searching among the swamps of Florida for the fabled Fountain of Youth. Many brave men lost their lives seeking the North Pole before Robert E. Peary reported that he had found it, and many expeditions sought in vain for the South Pole before Roald Amundsen could report that he had at last reached it. What toil and hardships men have endured, what patience and perseverance they have shown who have been really searching for something! And the results of such searching have often surpassed expectations. Columbus re-discovered America and opened the New World.

Luther re-discovered that the just shall live by faith, and started the Reformation and the Modern Age.

In starting out to make a search you must in the first place know what you are going to search for. Luther read the Bible to find out how he could become righteous. In Lesson Forty-Eight is a list of the number of times that prayer is mentioned in the Bible. The one who made the list set out to read the Bible at breakfast devotions with pencil in hand. Whenever he found any passage dealing with the topic of prayer he underscored it. Later, he counted the number of verses and passages he had marked, making the table presented in Lesson Forty-Eight. He was also able to classify these passages in various ways and to get a more thorough and fresh impression of the subject of prayer. After such a first hand study of this topic your reader found new pleasure in reading books on prayer and books of prayer, in attending prayer meetings and in being more faithful in daily devotions, in prayer without ceasing. D. L. Moody tells in his book, "How to Study the Bible," that when he ran through the Scriptures to find out what it had to say about grace, he got so full of grace that he stopped every man and woman he met, and told them how God loved them. He says that if he were going into a court of justice and wanted to carry the jury with him, he would get every witness he could to testify on the one point at stake rather than on everything. In this way he had read the Bible many weeks studying the passages on love, till at least he himself could not help loving people. A Bible reader ought, therefore, also to read topically, to search the Scriptures after something definite, particularly after Jesus, for they testify of Him (John 5:39; Acts 17:11). "Seek, and ye shall find" (Luke 11:9).—After one has marked up a Bible to show what it contains on one or two topics, he should put it aside for reference and start anew, with a new, clean copy. The cost of a new copy is slight; the value of a worked-up copy is to the reader beyond estimation.

e.   Memorizing.

Memorizing is learning by heart. Memory is the tax gatherer of the past, the treasurer of the mind. By means of memory, previous thoughts, impressions and events are retained and recalled. Memory is a source of great power and pleasure unfailing. Want of it is a great misfortune. It is a faculty that can be improved by use even as a prize fighter acquires strength and skill by training. The best time to memorize is in childhood and youth, yet it is never too late to learn. The choice Bible passages found in the Bible histories and catechisms should be learned by heart by the children. We can learn a good deal if we want to. Little and often fills the purse. Many a little makes a mickle. In Norway there was a young girl who wanted to get married to her betrothed. As she was not yet confirmed, her pastor refused to officiate at her marriage. She told him she could not learn Pontoppidan's "Explanation" in ten years. The pastor replied that she would then have to postpone her wedding ten years. But since she wanted to get married and had to be confirmed, she got busy and learned her catechism well. It did not take her ten years, but only eight weeks. Where there is a will, there is a way.

Also other gems from topical and other Bible reading should be memorized. There are many otherwise sensible people who sneer at learning catechisms and Bible verses by heart, although they advocate memorizing the alphabet, the multiplication table, the keys on the piano and typewriter, and a thousand other things. They say: "How much better she sings when she knows the words and the tunes by heart. She seems to sing from the heart and to the heart." We might add that when a song is known by heart it can be used early and late, in the busy hum of work as well as in the assembly of worshipers, that the mind can "think on these things" set forth in the song, be inspired and comforted thereby. This applies especially to Bible verses. Some strive to lay up treasures on earth, which moth and rust doth corrupt and thieves break through and steal. Learning Bible gems by heart is laying up for one's self treasures in Heaven, which neither moth nor rust doth corrupt, and where thieves do not break through nor steal.

Give an instance showing that the Bible is held to be the best book. Give an illustration showing that the ignorance of the Bible is appalling.

What is the difference between mood and mode in Bible reading? What was Luther's rule as to mood? Sverdrup's?

Why is prayer and enlightenment essential to the proper mood in Bible reading? What is meant by reverent meditation? Show that willingness to practise is necessary in order to learn to know the meaning of what one reads.

In what ways may the Bible be likened to a country, and Bible reading to traveling? Discuss the following methods of reading: Just reading, outlining, analyzing, searching, memorizing. Give examples of each method.

What does your Catechism say about mood and mode in Bible reading? Your Bible history? Find appropriate hymns in your hymnal bearing on this subject. Look up the Bible passages referred to in your lesson, and find additional references to this subject in the Bible. In what ways can the contents of this lesson help you in your Bible study? In your faith and works?

LESSON FIFTY-TWO. GENERAL AND SPECIAL PRINCIPLES OF INTERPRETATION.

It can not be denied that there are many things in the Bible which are dark and difficult and seemingly impossible to explain. Peter, for example, admits this in his Second Epistle when, in speaking of Paul, he says that there are some things in his Epistle hard to understand (2 Pet. 3:16). This becomes clear also when we look at the great number of different Denominations in the world, all of which differ from each other on some points of interpretation; also when we read different commentaries on the Bible, all of which presumably try to interpret the Scriptures faithfully and clearly.

It is common to say that there are two great books in which God reveals Himself—the Book of Nature and the Bible. These two books should agree on all the facts they present concerning God, and they differ only in their method of revelation and the extent and clearness of the revelation. Infidels often call attention to the fact that Christians do not agree as to what the Bible teaches. We can also call attention to the fact that scientists do not agree as to what the Book of Nature teaches, not only with respect to God, but also with respect to nature itself. "The age of the earth is variously declared to be ten million years by some, and by others, equally able, it is one thousand million years. The temperature of its interior is stated to be 1,530 degrees by one, and 350,000 degrees by another. Herschel calculated the mountains on the moon to be half a mile high. Ferguson said they were fifteen miles high. The height of the Aurora Borealis is guessed from 2½ to 160 miles, and its nature is still more widely described. The delta at the mouth of the Mississippi was calculated by Lyell to be 100,000 years in forming. General Humphrey of the United States Survey

estimated it at 4,000 years, and M. Beaumont at 1,300 years.
. . . These facts are not cited to discredit science. No
one in his senses would fail to acknowledge our great debt
to the earnest and laborious workers in these varying fields"
(A. Patterson's "Other Side of Evolution," 15). M. Car-
tailhac, the anthropologist, was asked how old he reckoned
a fresco that he had found in a cave. "Between 6,000 and
250,000 years before Christ," he answered (Chr. Bally's
"Le Langage et la Vie," 109). These illustrations suggest
that we ought to approach the conclusion of scientists with
some caution. They show, furthermore, that if scholars of
eminent ability can not agree as to the facts written in the
Book of Nature, it is then no wonder that they do not agree
on every point in the Bible.

In Lesson Eight we learned that the Bible possesses the
property of clearness. It was admitted then, as now, that
there were things in the Bible which were difficult to explain,
and it was maintained then, as we wish to maintain now,
that in all of the things the knowledge of which is necessary
to salvation, the Bible is abundantly clear. What is dark
and difficult in the Bible generally is due to the fact that we
are not well enough acquainted with the original languages
and do not know enough about the geography, chronology,
history and antiquities of the Bible. Again we wish to repeat
that it is not equally clear in all places, to all people and
at all times, even in the things which pertain to salvation.
Yet it is the sentiment of all Protestant theologians, as it is
also the teaching of the Scriptures themselves, that the Bible
is clear and can be understood by the common people, and
should therefore be read and studied by them. The Bible is
indeed a lamp unto our feet and a light unto our path (Ps.
119:105; Prov. 6:23; 2 Pet. 1:19), and is able to make the
man of God perfect and fit for all good work (2 Tim. 3:15-
17). We conclude, then, on this point, that the Scriptures,
being a revelation from God, are clear and intelligible. Now,

if they are intelligible, there must be correct principles of interpretation by which their meaning can be ascertained, even as there must be false principles on which the many false interpretations, debased superstitions, daring heresies and impudent dogmas rest. We shall divide these principles into two classes, general and special.

1. GENERAL PRINCIPLES OF INTERPRETATION.

The Bible, as we have learned in Lesson One, is a work of literature, or rather, a collection of books, a whole library. In general it might be said that it can and should be read exactly the same as any other book and judged on its own merits. The sense, then, would have to be obtained by exactly the same processes as in reading any other book, say, a work on arithmetic, grammar, history, a poem, a novel, etc. What would be some of the general principles to guide one in interpreting any of these books just named? We shall name four principles—finding out the design, scope and class of the book, getting the sense of the author from the text, harmonizing this with the context, and examining the parallel passages.

a. THE DESIGN, SCOPE AND CLASS.

The design of arithmetic is to teach numbers, and its scope is determined by the grade that the book is intended for. The design of grammar is to give a knowledge of the sentence, and its scope likewise is determined by the age and ability of the pupils who are to use it. In like manner every book has a certain design and scope, and it is necessary to discover what the design and scope are in order to interpret them satisfactorily. This is also the case with the Bible. The design of the Bible is to teach the way of salvation, and its scope is to teach this way completely: It is the only book of revelation that we have, and there will be no other such book. It contains all that we ought to know and has given us all that we ever will know on this subject. Some interpreters have approached it as though it were a collection of myths and as though it were not the only source and rule of faith, life and works. These interpreters have been unable to understand and explain the Bible. The first principle for interpreting the Bible, then, is to accept the design and scope; of course this applies also to the reading of any particular book in the Bible. Each book has its own design, scope and form, its own historical setting, its own writer. Who wrote the book, and under what circumstances, and for what purpose, and how much he intended to include— all these things should be determined by the reader, either before he takes up reading any particular book or during the reading of it, usually the latter.

He should also know what class of literature the writing before him belongs to—whether it is prose or poetry, history, law, biography, chronicle, prophecy, epistle, epic, drama, lyric, ode, proverb. It is easier to interpret a book when one knows what class it belongs to. Take, for example, the Hebrew Psalms. In most Bibles they are printed as prose, consequently very few readers think of them as poetry. Hebrew verse is not like English verse. English verse depends on rhythm and uses such devices as letter- and end-rhymes. Hebrew verse depends on thought-rhymes, on symmetry of clauses. "Like the swing of a pendulum to and fro, like the tramp of an army marching in step, the versification of the Bible moves with a rhythm of parallel lines" (R. G. Moulton's "Literary Study of the Bible," 47). The common type of versification in Hebrew poetry is the synonymous couplet, as:

> The heavens declare the glory of God,
> And the firmament showeth His handiwork (Ps. 19:1).

By omitting every other line in such a poem it becomes

quite good prose. Such poetry is often found in the body of the prose sections, as:

> The ox knoweth his owner,
> And the ass his master's crib (Isa. 1:3).

b. THE TEXT.

The second principle of interpretation is, getting the sense of the author from the text. By sense we mean, not how the author's message may be applied, but what the author intended to say.

(1) *Avoiding Applications.*—Each word or passage has one definite sense and only one, but it may have many applications. The reader should distinguish between the sense of a passage and its possible applications. Thus, in Luke 4:16 we read: "As His custom was, He went into the synagogue on the Sabbath day." This sentence states plainly and definitely simply this, that according to custom, Jesus went into the synagogue on the Sabbath day. The sentence as a whole has one definite meaning, and each word in the sentence has one definite meaning, but the whole sentence or any part of it may be variously applied. We may, for example, say that it was a good custom, that it ought to be imitated, and the like. Most preachers spend most of their time making applications rather than explaining the text. Some use the text only as a pretext and say good-bye to it as soon as they have read it; they do not explain it and do not apply it, but preach possibly on some word or topic suggested by the text, and often on topics entirely foreign to it as well as to the Bible itself. The Bible reader should get into the habit of reading the text for each Sunday before going to the Sunday services, and of listening carefully to see whether the text is explained and applied correctly. A pocket Bible and a sermon notebook and a short lead pencil taken along to church, often help to make good Bible students and attentive worshipers in church.

(2) *Avoiding Multiple Meanings.*—The words of Scripture have one definite meaning in each place, and only one. It is true that the language of Scripture is like the language of every day speech, in that it sometimes employs plain words, and at other times figures of speech. In the infancy of races, language is nearly all figure. Our times, too, freely and gladly use figurative language, for it conveys thought often more clearly, forcibly and beautifully than plain speech can. Thus, in Ps. 3:3 David says: "O Lord, Thou art a Shield for me." In this sentence there is not a double sense expressed in the word shield, and that sense is not the literal meaning of the word shield, but the figurative. The Lord is David's protection.

Yet, owing to the circumstance that Scripture employs figurative language as well as plain, many interpreters have tried to discover in every Scripture more than one meaning. Some have insisted that there are mountains of sense in every word of Scripture, that there are in addition to a plain literal sense a great variety of meanings, which they have called by such names as grammatical, moral, mystical, anagogical, allegorical, etc. For example, the numerical letters in the name of Eliezer is 318, which is also the number of Abraham's trained men (Gen. 14:14). "Aha," said the interpreter as the light dawned on him, "now I understand. This means that Abraham's servant Eliezer was as powerful as the other 318 servants together." Again, in the story of Eliezer's seeking Rebekah at the well, it ought to be plain to everybody that this is simply true history. But Origen, a very famous Biblical scholar, is not particularly interested in this history as such, for he is in search of a deeper allegorical meaning in this transaction. "Rebekah," he says, "represents the human soul which Christ wishes to betroth to Himself. While Abraham's servant is the prophetic Word, which unless you first receive, you can not be married to Christ." M. S. Terry relates in his "Biblical Hermeneutics"

(389) that a friend of his thought that it was strange that no mention had been made of the United States in the Bible prophecies. He began to meditate on the subject, and by and by discovered that the United States had not been slighted either in the Old or the New Testament. In the Book of Daniel he held that the United States is the Fifth Kingdom—the stone cut out of the mountain without hands (Dan. 2:34, 44-45). In the Book of Revelations the war in Heaven between Michael and the Dragon, he was sure, must mean our late Civil War (Rev. 12:7-9). J. G. Matteson, in his "Jesu profetier" (321-37), has proved to his own satisfaction that the United States is the "Other Beast" mentioned in Rev. 13:11-18.

The Bible is the Word of God and contains God's Law and Gospel. We expect that words of Law shall not be ambiguous, for then instead of becoming commands they become snares. We expect the Gospel to be not only for the wise and the learned, but also for the simple-minded and babes. The very essence of truth is plainness and clearness. "Thy Word is a lamp unto my feet." Every book of every kind ever written and addressed by one man to his fellow beings can have only one sense, unless it be written in the way of sport or with the intention to deceive.

It is hardly necessary to illustrate further that the theory of double sense in Scripture confuses the Bible reader. This confusion has brought into the Church heresies untold, schisms without number, and many a bitter and bloody battle with the sword. The method of interpretation decides to a large degree the teaching of a Church, the faith and life of the people, and often even the peace of the Church. F. W. Farrar says in his "History of Interpretation" (323) concerning Luther, that he "not only gave the people the open Bible, but taught them and all the world how best it might be interpreted." Luther said concerning the practice of finding a multiple sense in the Bible, that it was from the

Devil. He held that all heresy and errors have originated, not from the simple words of Scripture, but from neglecting the plain literal sense, and trying to discover some mystic and secret meanings. Each passage has one clear, definite and true sense of its own; all other interpretations are doubtful and uncertain opinions.

(3) *Limiting to One Sense.*—Every Scripture word or passage, as stated, has only one definite sense. Where the language is plain there should be no difficult task to determine what this sense is. A word by itself may have many meanings, but only one of these can apply in any particular instance. In the sentence: "In the beginning God created the heaven and the earth," heaven must mean the expanse surrounding the earth where the sun, moon and stars appear. The dictionary gives other definitions, also, as: God's dwelling place; God; any place of supreme happiness; bliss; etc., none of which can very well apply in this sentence. When Ezekiel speaks of stony hearts, the term stony is figurative, but the sense may be regarded as literal. When hardness is ascribed to stone the expression is used literally; when it is ascribed to the heart it is used figuratively. Ezekiel means to state literally that the heart is hard, but he uses figurative language in expressing his thought. In the Old Testament there are many persons and events that foreshadow the coming of greater persons and events in the New. These persons and events in the Old Testament are called types. When they appear in the New Testament they are called anti-types. In Ps. 22, for example, David is the type, and Christ is the anti-type. In the Book of Exodus, the release of Israel from the Egyptian bondage is a type, and its anti-type is the rescue of the Christian from the bondage of sin. This does not mean that Ps. 22 and Exodus convey a double meaning. The language in both places point distinctly to a type. It is the type set forth that prefigures the things to come. A

passage, then, must always have one sense and can have only one, but may have many applications, and may suggest type and anti-type.

(4) *Examining the Etymology of Words.*—By etymology is here meant the original or first meaning of a word. We are assuming that the Bible reader studies his Bible only in translation. Ordinarily, he will have no difficulty in determining what is meant by each word in the text. When he does have trouble it would certainly be to his advantage if he could read and understand the text in the original languages. But this is out of the question in the case of most readers. A distinct help as a substitute for a knowledge of the original text is word-analysis or a study of the etymology of the words with the aid of a larger dictionary. Many words have been so long in use and have become so familiar that their original meanings have worn off or faded away. "Goodbye," for instance, is a contraction of the English sentence, "God be with ye." "Adieu" is from the French "a Dieu"—to God, a prayer at parting. A "forlorn hope" is a mistranslation of the Dutch phrase "verloren hoop"—lost band. "Husband" is from the Scandinavian "husbonde"—master of the house. "Christ" is a Greek word, meaning Anointed. "Messiah" is a Hebrew word, meaning Anointed. Luther discovered that the Greek word for penance was the same as for repentance, a discovery that brought to him a tumultuous joy and an unshakeable conviction that the Bible must be read by theological students in the original text and by the people in the clearest translation possible.

(5) *Finding the True Sense.*—So far the reader has been instructed to look for only one definite, clear, true explanation of any Scripture passage. Said passage may have many uses, many applications, may foreshadow many things to come, but it has only one sense. This sense should be discovered by examining the meaning of the word or words as

intended by the writer, the grammatical construction of the sentence and the historical circumstances which called it forth. When the meaning of the words as then used is not at once apparent, it may usually be ascertained by the help of the context and parallel passages. A careful analysis of the sentence is of inestimable help in arriving at the meaning and force of each part of it. The various circumstances which called forth the writing also shed light on any passage that is dark and difficult.

c. THE CONTEXT.

Context means literally a weaving together, as the web of a garment. Loosely defined, it is that which immediately precedes and follows the given text. More accurately, it is the whole series of statements, arguments and illustrations connected with the text whose meaning is sought. The interpretation of the text must harmonize with the context. It is the business of the reader to be on the lookout so that they do not disagree.

Let us illustrate. We once heard a very brilliant prohibition lecture on Col. 2:21, which reads: "Touch not; taste not; handle not." And yet the interpretation of the text was without any doubt as faulty and false as any interpretation could be. There is probably no poorer prohibition text in the whole Bible than just this one. The meaning of the verse can not be derived from these six words alone, for two good reasons: First, they are only a part of a sentence. The sentence begins with 2:20 and ends with 2:22, and reads as follows: "Wherefore if ye be dead with Christ from the rudiments of the world, why, as though living in the world, are ye subject to ordinances: (Touch not; taste not; handle not; which all are to perish with the using) after the commandments and doctrines of men?" It is clear already from this complete sentence that "Touch not; taste not; handle not," is not given as a prohibition command, but just the opposite: "Touch; taste; handle; for these things are to perish with the using." Second, the context proves decidedly that "Touch not; taste not; handle not," in this verse is not a prohibition law. Paul, then a prisoner in Rome, had learned that a dangerous heresy had like a plague begun to rage in the Church at Colosse. This heresy held forth that men must do something themselves to attain to holiness, for Christ's merit was insufficient. They must observe certain fast days and deny themselves certain foods. They must practise mortifying their flesh. Paul wrote this epistle to the Colossians to show them conclusively that the Church had a sufficiency in Christ. Christ is sufficient as the object of faith and the source of life. The fulness of the Gospel of Christ is contrasted with the emptiness of the world's teachings. In discussing the emptiness of the world's teachings as to asceticism and self-mortification he utters the sentence above quoted, from which this text was taken. He exhorts them to beware of the false teaching of the ascetics and repeats the warning that they be not beguiled by enticing words and a show of wisdom and humility. If said speaker had looked at the context, he would not have chosen this verse as a text for a temperance lecture. He would have selected some other passage in the Bible which would not belie the context, as, for example: "Look not thou upon the wine when it is red. . . . At the last it biteth like a serpent, and stingeth like an adder" (Prov. 23:32). "Wherefore by their fruits ye shall know them" (Matt. 7:20). "It is neither good to eat flesh, nor to drink wine, nor any thing whereby thy brother stumbleth, or is offended, or is made weak" (Rom. 14:21). "Be not deceived . . . . nor thieves, nor covetous, nor drunkards, nor extortioners, shall inherit the Kingdom of God" (1 Cor. 6:10). "All things are lawful unto me, but all things are not expedient; all things are lawful for me, but I will not be brought under the power of any" (1 Cor. 6:12). It will be seen from these illustrative passages that prohibition of liquor, while not commanded by Scripture as a condition for salvation, is highly recommended as expedient. This incident illustrates sufficiently how necessary it is for the reader to harmonize the interpretation of the text and the context. To this we might add that the Revised Version of the Bible groups the verses into paragraphs according to the context, but the Authorized verse division is arbitrary and confusing.

d. PARALLEL PASSAGES.

It happens in many kinds of books, even in text books, that the same subject is taken up more than once. In arithmetic the process of addition comes up again and again; in grammar, the parsing of the parts of speech. In the Bible some events are told more than once and some doctrines or genealogies are repeated. The feeding of the 4,000 is recorded twice—in Matt. 15:32-39 and Mark. 8:1-10. The feeding of the 5,000 is recorded four times—in Matt. 14: 19-21; Mark 6:35-44; Luke 9:10-17; John 6:1-14. Parallel passages are chiefly verbal and real. In verbal parallels the same words occur in similar connections. In real parallels there is a likeness, not in words or sentences, but in subjects or doctrines. Good examples of verbal parallels are 2 Sam. 22 and Ps. 18, which are almost identical throughout. Good examples of real parallels are the Epistles to the Romans and to the Galatians, both devoted to the doctrine of righteousness by faith.

To illustrate how the parallel passages may help determine the sense intended, let us take the word hate in Luke 14:26. In this passage Jesus says: "If any man cometh unto Me, and hateth not his own father, and mother, and wife, and children, and brethren, and sisters, yea, and his own life also, he cannot be My disciple." How shall a Bible reader who is not perfectly at home in his Bible find the parallel passages that bear on the word hate? There are two good ways—by looking up the marginal references and by looking in the Concordance under the word hate.

We turn to our American Revised Bible. It has one marginal reference—Luke 16:13. This is a passage about serving two masters: "For either he will hate the one and love the other, or he will hold to one and despise the other". Two masters so different can not be loved and served at the same time. This thought is set forth by the words hate and despise. We turn to the Oxford edition of the Authorized Version and find one marginal reference—Rom. 9:13. This verse reads: "As it is written, 'Jacob have I loved, but Esau have I hated' ". This passage in turn refers to Mal. 1:2-3 and Matt. 10:37. Mal. 1:2-3 is the Old Testament passage cited in Rom. 9:13. Matt. 10:37 reads: "He that loveth father or mother more than Me is not worthy of Me; and he that loveth son or daughter more than Me is not worthy of Me". No one who loves parents or children more than Christ can be a true disciple. God does not command us to hate our kith and kin, but to love them less. To hate, in the passage means to love less. We examine the Scofield Bible and the Douai Version. The Scofield Bible has two marginal references—Matt. 10: 36; Acts 14:22. The Douai Version has no marginal reference on this point. We examine the Norwegian Versions. They have five references—Luke 14:33; Deut. 13:6-11; 33: 9; Matt. 10:37-38; 19:29. These passages also have further references. By examining these and comparing them we conclude that the word hate means in this connection to love less —but this is the root of hatred. God wills that we shall fear and love and trust in Him above all things (Luke 10: 27).

The second way to find the parallel passages is to use the Concordance. The words hate and hatred are listed 43 times in the Oxford "Helps to the Study of the Bible" and the Oxford "Sunday School Teachers' Bible", 44 times in the

Holman "Pronouncing Bible", 158 times in Cruden's "Concordance" and 210 times in Young's "Concordance". These references include the word "hate" used in the ordinary sense of intense dislike and in the special sense of loving less.

2. SPECIAL PRINCIPLES OF INTERPRETATION.

The general principles of interpretation apply to the Bible as well as to books in general; the special principles to be noted in the following paragraphs apply to the Bible in particular.

a. SELF-INTERPRETATION OF THE SCRIPTURES.

Principle is derived from the Latin principium—beginning. Here it applies to the beginning or fundamental rules of interpretation. The Bible reader should start out with such rules to govern and guide him, first among which should be this one: That the Scriptures must be explained by the Scriptures. The Bible, taken as a whole and allowed to speak for itself, will be its own best interpreter. The New Testament explains the Old better than any commentary; the Old Testament explains the New. The Old Testament is the New Testament veiled; the New Testament is the Old Testament unveiled. That Melchizedek was to be a type of Christ we may see from Ps. 110: 4; Heb. 5: 6, 10; 6: 20—7:1. Matt. 13 explains the Parable of the Sower better than it has ever been explained elsewhere. Men have argued themselves black in the face about the fish which swallowed Jonah. R. G. Moulton settles the whole matter in his "Modern Readers' Bible" by saying that the reference to a great fish does not belong to the Book of Jonah, but is a footnote added by a later editor. Jesus, however, in Matt. 12: 40 says: "For as Jonah was three days and three nights in the belly of the whale; so shall the Son of Man be three days and three nights in the heart of the earth". We shall let the testimony of the Lord of Truth and of the Good Book stand on this and many another question.

b. ANALOGY OF FAITH.

A second special principle in interpreting the Bible is that of the analogy of faith. This means that the Bible, which is the Word of God, must be self-consistent. There is therefore a harmony existing between all parts of Scripture, so that one passage can not clash with or contradict another. There may be seeming discrepancies, especially in minor things, but no real ones, especially in the major doctrines pertaining to salvation. Thus, the Bible everywhere teaches that men are sinners and need a Savior, that God has provided a Savior in His Only Begotten Son, Who suffered and died for our sins, and that salvation is by faith in this Savior, and not by works.

The value of the analogy of faith is negative rather than positive; it tells the interpreter rather what a passage can not mean than what it does mean. In Rom. 3: 24, Gal. 3:11-12, Eph. 2: 8-9 and many other places the Bible teaches that we are justified by faith alone, without the works of the Law. In Jas. 2: 24 it says that by works a man is justified, and not only by faith. This principle tells us that we can not explain Jas. 2: 24 contrary to the rest of the Bible, but it does not tell us how to explain the passage. In order to explain the passage we must discover the historical situation, the scope and design of each book in question. These passages have been harmonized to the satisfaction of Biblical scholars in general. In brief, the difference between Paul and James on the relation of faith and works may be said to be: Paul speaks of faith as something one must have in the first place in order to become saved, while James speaks of the fact that if one has faith it shows itself by works of piety and love; Paul condemns works because he has in mind the works of the Law with reference to legal righteousness, while James praises works because he has in mind the works springing from a believing and pious heart.

c. TRADITION, REASON AND FAITH.

A third special principle in Bible interpretation is, that the reader should believe what the Bible plainly teaches, even if this conflicts with tradition and reason.

Tradition is the oral delivery of information and teaching. It is of value, but it is not always a safe guide. The world had stood about 2500 years before God for the first time commanded anyone to record His Word. But meanwhile he had revealed His will to Adam, Seth, Enoch, Abraham, Isaac, Jacob, Joseph and others. The longevity of mankind in that age made it quite easy to hand down revelations by word of mouth. Adam, for instance, lived 930 years. He lived with his descendants the following number of years:

```
(1) 800 years with Seth.........................................son
(2) 695   "    "   Enos . . ............................grandson
(3) 605   "    "   Cainan . . ......................great-grandson
(4) 535   "    "   Mahalaleel . . ..............great-great-grandson
(5) 470   "    "   Jared . . ..............great-great-great-grandson
(6) 308   "    "   Enoch . . .........great-great-great-great-grandson
(7) 243   "    "   Methuselah  great-great-great-great-great-grandson
(8) 56    "    "   Lamech great-great-great-great-great-great-grandson
```

It would have been a moral impossibility for the Antediluvians not to have known the will of the Lord.

In the history of the Church, tradition has served many a good as well as evil purpose. It has helped to preserve and establish the Canon and the three general creeds of the Church. It was then raised to a par with Scriptures, a fact which in the Middle Ages and since has wrought much confusion. At the time of Christ men set the tradition of the scribes above the Scriptures, for example, in the matter of hallowing the Sabbath, and in the time of the Reformers the Papists set the tradition of the church fathers above the Word of God, for example, in the matter of indulgences and prayers to the saints. Very many traditions are proper and should be taken into account, but none of them ranks with the Word itself in authority.

Reason, too, must be employed in explaining Scripture. It is a precious gift of God, useful to man both in the unrenewed and renewed states. By reason is here meant the capacity of acquiring knowledge and appropriating truths. We can not understand any thing without reason, but we can not understand everything with it. We all see darkly; we all understand only in part. Especially is this true in respect to spiritual things if we have not been enlightened by the Holy Spirit.

Natural human reason is as blind as it is vain with respect to matters of faith (Rom. 1:21; 1 Cor. 3:1; Gal. 4:8; Matt. 11:27; Rom. 8:6; etc.). A man on the train said once to his fellow-passenger: "What's your business?" "I", said the other, "am a preacher". Said the first, who chanced to be a doctor: "I do not believe in the Bible, faith, and the like. I reason, I believe only what I see". "Do you believe that there is such a thing as air?" "Yes". "Can you see it?" "No". "Do you believe that there is a soul?" "Yes", "Have you ever seen one?" "No". To make a long story short, these men argued long and earnestly about the matter, with the result that the doctor had to admit that it was not wise to pin his future entirely to his reason. This applies everywhere, but especially in religion. There are very few things which we can at all understand. The mysteries of vegetation, the workings of the mind, the glory of God and the depth of Christ's suffering we can not fathom with our reason. We are like a child who knows very little and understands less of this world, but it clings in faith for all it is worth to its mother's breast. We are like the sheep, which can not reason why, but they know their master's voice and come at his call. Reason is always a good servant, but a bad master.

Faith opens the Scriptures. The eye of faith pierces the thickest clouds, while reason yet gropes in blackest night. Faith is the substance of things hoped for—the evidence of things unseen. Columbus tried to reason with the great scholars, rulers and merchants of his day about the earth's being round. He was not able to appeal to their reason, and faith in his project they had none. He had faith and a reason for the faith that was in him, therefore he found a path across untried waters. The Gospel was a stumbling block to the Jews and foolishness to the Gentiles of Paul's day, but it was the power of God, the wisdom of God unto anyone, Jew or Gentile, that believed it. We should go to the Bible earnestly seeking to understand the Word, but we should above all accept in faith the plain teachings of the Bible, even when we do not yet understand. It has been said that "human things must be known in order to be believed, but divine things must be believed in order to be known". When Jesus healed the boy with the dumb spirit, He did not say: "If thou canst understand", but: "If thou canst believe. All things are possible to him that believeth". Straightway the father of the boy cried out: "I believe, help Thou mine unbelief" (Mark 9: 23-24). A certain sick man told his pastor he was too weak to pray. "Just hold up your hand", said the pastor, "Jesus will see you and know what it means". The sick man held up his hand. That was faith.

d. TYPES AND SYMBOLS.

A fourth special principle in interpreting the Bible is, that the revelation is not only conveyed by word, but also by the things expressed by the words. These things may be classified into types and symbols. A type is a sign by which one object or event foreshadows a greater to come, as, Abraham's sacrifice of his only begotten son was a type of God's sacrifice of His Only Begotten Son. A symbol is a visible sign of an idea, as, the cross is a sign of salvation. Types have reference to time, symbols have not.

Every *type* is a shadow of something to come, which is called *anti-type*. The types appear in the Old Testament, the anti-types in the New. They may be divided into seven classes, of which some examples are given herewith:

(1) *Typical Persons.*

TYPE	REFERENCE	ANTI-TYPES	REFERENCE
Adam	Gen. 1—3	Christ	Rom. 5:14-21
			1 Cor. 15:45
Enoch	Gen. 4:17	Christ	
Melchizedek	Gen. 14:18	Christ	Heb. 5:6-10;
			7:1-2
Abraham	Gen. 18:3; etc.	Christ	Heb. 7:25; etc.
Abraham	Gen. 15:6	Believers	Rom. 4:10
			Jas. 2:24
Isaac	Gen. 22:7	Christ	Matt. 27:46; etc.
Joseph	Gen. 41—46	Christ	Gospels
Moses	Num. 12:7	Christ	Heb. 3:1-6
Joshua	Num. 14:6	Christ	Heb. 4:8
Samuel	1 Sam.	Christ	Gospels
David	Ezek. 34:23	Christ	John 10:11
Solomon	Ps. 72	Christ	Matt. 22:42
			Heb. 1:5
Elijah	2 Kings 2:11	Christ	1 Cor. 15:52
Elijah	Mal. 4:5	John the Baptist	Matt. 11:14; etc.
Elisha	2 Kings 2—13	Christ	Gospels
Jonah	Jonah 1:17	Christ	Matt. 12:40
Zerubbabel	Zech. 4:4-9	Christ	Hag. 2:23
Israel	Isa 42—44	Christ	Acts 13:34

(2) *Typical Offices.*

TYPE	REFERENCE	ANTI-TYPES	REFERENCE
Priest	Ex. 28	Christ	Rom. 8:34
			Heb. 4:14; 7:27;
			9:12
King	Ps. 2:6	Christ	Luke 1:33
			Heb. 7:2
Prophet	Deut. 18:15	Christ	Luke 24:19

(3) *Typical Seasons.*

TYPE	REFERENCE	ANTI-TYPES	REFERENCE
Sabbath	Gen. 2:2	Everlasting Rest	Heb. 4:4-9
Passover	Ex. 12:3, 11	Easter	1 Cor. 5:7
First Fruits	Lev. 23:15-22	Pentecost	Acts 2
Feast of Tabernacles	Lev. 23:40	Thanksgiving	Zech. 14:16

(4) *Typical Places.*

TYPE	REFERENCE	ANTI-TYPES	REFERENCE
Altars	Gen. 8:20; etc.	Mercy Seat	Heb. 13:10
Tabernacle	Ex. 25–27; etc.	Heaven	Heb. 8:2; 9:2
			Rev. 15:5
Temple	2 Chron. 3—5	Heaven	Rev. 21—22
	Ps. 29:9; etc.		
Cities of Refuge	Num. 35:9-34	Gospel provision for escape	Gospels

(5) *Typical Sacrifices.*

TYPE	REFERENCE	ANTI-TYPES	REFERENCE
Lamb without blemish	Ex. 12:5	Christ	I Pet. 1:19
Lamb for slaughter	Isa. 53:7	Christ	John 1:29
Paschal Lamb	Ex. 12:1-10	Christ	1 Cor. 5:7
Two goats, one for sacrifice, one for Wilderness	Lev. 16:7-10	Christ	Matt. 27:31-33
Incense	Lev. 16:13	Prayers	Rev. 8:3

(6) *Typical Events.*

TYPE	REFERENCE	ANTI-TYPES	REFERENCE
Flood	Gen. 7	End of the world	Matt. 24:37
			2 Pet. 2:5; 3:10
Escape from bondage	Ex. 11—15	Escape from sin	Heb. 2:15; etc.
Passage of the Red Sea	Ex. 14:22	Baptism	1 Cor. 10:2

(6) *Typical Events.*

TYPE	REFERENCE	ANTI-TYPES	REFERENCE
Sojourn in Wilderness	Ex., Num.	The earthly life	1 Cor. 10
Giving of manna	Ex. 16:15	Spiritual food	1 Cor. 10:3
Getting water from the rock	Ex. 17:6	Life from Christ	1 Cor. 10:4
Lifting up of the brazen serpent	Num. 21:9	Crucifixion	John 3:14
Conquest of Canaan	Joshua	Winning of the Kingdom of Heaven	Matt. 11:12
Destruction of Jerusalem	Matt. 24	End of the world	Matt. 24

(7) *Typical Actions (partly typical, partly symbolical).*

Ahijah tears the new garment	1 Kings 11:29-31	Kingdoms divided
Isaiah walks naked 3 years	Isa. 20:2-4	Captivity and shame
Jeremiah soils and hides his girdle by the Euphrates	Jer. 13:1-11	Judah shall be made profitless
Jeremiah puts a yoke on his neck	Jer. 27:1-14	A sign to the nations
Ezekiel eats a book	Ezek. 3:1-3	Conviction of mission
Ezekiel paints a siege of Jerusalem	Ezek. 4:1-3	Siege and exile
Ezekiel prepares unsavory food	Ezek. 4:4-17	Famine and misery
Ezekiel shaves with a sword	Ezek. 5:1-17	Three-fold judgment
Ezekiel eats with trembling	Ezek. 12:3-20	Hasty exile
Hosea marries an adulteress	Hos. 1	Israel's idolatry
Zechariah makes crowns of silver and gold for Joshua	Zech. 6:9-15	Christ's Royal Entry

A type should be taken as such only in so far as the anti-type permits. "David in his royal office is a type of Christ, but not in his sin with Bathsheba; Aaron is a type of Christ in his high-priestly office, but not when he made the golden calf" (G. H. Schodde's "Biblical Hermeneutics," 220).

Types are not very difficult to explain, for the reason that they are nearly all explained in the Scriptures. *Symbols,* however, have occasioned much confusion among

No. 132. The Symbol of the Potter's Vessel (Jer. 18:1—19:15).

interpreters. In a wider sense a symbol is any sign that represents an idea. Every figure, every letter, every word, every picture is a symbol. In a narrower sense a symbol is an emblem suggesting some idea that is not capable of portraiture. The olive is a symbol of peace and the sword is a symbol of war; darkness symbolizes falsehood and ignorance, while light symbolizes the reverse. Among theologians symbol means also creed, but this meaning will not be observed in this book. We shall call attention to some of the different groups of symbols.

In the study of Sacred Places we were often reminded of the fact that the buildings or their furniture symbolized something. The Tabernacle and the Temple were symbols of God's meeting-place with man and His dwelling-place amongst His people. Their whole construction symbolized the approach to God through sacrifice and mediation. The Courts, the Holy Place, the Most Holy, the Altars, the Lavers, the Tables for Showbread, the Candlestick, the Showbread, the Incense, the Ark, the Mercy Seat, the Cherubim, the gold and silver furnishings, the veil, the blood, etc., symbolized some part in God's plan for salvation.

In the prophetic parts of the Bible are quite a number of wonderful signs that have often puzzled the Bible reader. Isaiah mentions several. There was, for example, the sign of the Virgin with Child (Isa. 7), which was fulfilled on Christmas Eve. Jeremiah presents in 1:11-12 a symbol of the Almond Rod, signifying hasty performance, and in 1:12-19 a symbol of a Seething Pot, signifying a deluge of nations over Judah. In Jer. 24 is the symbol of the Two Baskets of Figs, signifying the good and the bad in Judah. Among Ezekiel's symbols may be mentioned the Valley of Dry Bones (Ezek. 37), signifying the resurrection from the dead. Among Daniel's may be mentioned the Great Composite Image (Dan. 2) and the Four Beasts (Dan. 7), both of which depict the succession of world empires. Of the minor prophets Zechariah has the most symbols.

In Zech. 1: 2-17 is the symbol of the Angel's Horsemen, signifying that Judah is watched over. In 1:18-21 the Four Horns and Four Smiths signify that Judah's enemies are defeated. In 4:1-14 the Candlestick Fed by Two Olive Trees signify that Judah is the light bearer of the world, Joshua and Zerubbabel are God's anointed ones, and the oil is the Holy Spirit. In 5: 6-11 the Woman in an Ephah Measure signifies that lawbreakers are sent hence. In 6:1-8 the Four Chariots signify that God's spirits administer righteousness. There are also many symbols in the New Testament.

In addition to the above-mentioned symbols, which are things that can be seen, every observant Bible reader must have wondered at times if there were not also a symbolical meaning attached to certain numbers, colors, names and stones. The whole question is rather vague and possibly of minor value. Lesson Forty-Nine was devoted to Sacred Numbers. The symbolism of colors was mentioned in part in Lesson Forty-Nine, and of stones in Lesson Forty-One. Blue symbolized heavenly origin; purple, royal glory; crimson, blood and life; white, purity and holiness; black, sin and death. There is at least one number that is a perfect riddle and has called forth the most varied answers. This number is 666, "the number of the beast, a man's number" (Rev. 13:18). The usual way of explaining this has been to take some man's name and figure out the numerical value of the letters in that name. If the sum of these letters make up the required number, the interpreter has perhaps said that he has found his man. Among the solutions that have been offered are such names as the following: Lateinos, the Roman Empire, Nero, Trajan, Caligula, Vespasian, the Pope, apostasy, Simon Magus, drunkenness, Antichrist, Paul, the United States and Kaiser Wilhelm. It has also been suggested that this number is not exhausted in one man or power. This illustrates sufficiently that there are some symbols that are really very hard to interpret. It might also be stated as a sort of warning that nearly all interpretations dealing with symbolical numbers are, at best, rather doubtful.

A word might be added about symbolical names. Every name has, or should have, a real meaning apart from the person who bears it. Certain names have in addition to this been assigned to symbolical use. For example, Rev. 17:1-5 speaks of Babylon, the Harlot, and Rev. 21:9-10 speaks of Jerusalem, the Bride. Babylon here stands for the false church and Jerusalem for the true Church.

e. PROPHECIES.

A fifth special principle in Biblical interpretation is the recognition of the presence of prophecy in the Bible. Proph-

No. 133. The Promise of the Messiah (Zech. 9:9).

ecy in this connection means the foreseeing and foretelling of future events. It is a miracle of knowledge beyond the power of any human sagacity. "Holy men of God spake as they were moved by the Holy Ghost" (2 Pet. 1:21). The reader should also recognize the fact that prophecies are not only foretold, but most of them are also fulfilled in the Bible. This fulfillment is the highest evidence that the holy men were inspired and that their words are a revelation from God.

The first prophecy in the Bible refers to the coming of Jesus to crush the serpent's head (Gen. 3:15), and the last is the promise of the Lord Jesus to come quickly (Rev. 22:20). Between these two extremes are many hundred prophecies relating to the world before the Flood, the Hebrews in particular, the neighboring nations, the person and mission of Jesus, the work and lot of His Church, the state of the world after His coming, the end of this world and the state of the world to come. Hundreds of these prophecies are fulfilled, some of them are not, but will be fulfilled in His good time.

A few examples of fulfillment will be noted: Abraham was promised a numerous posterity (Gen. 12:1-3; etc.). He got it (Ex. 1:7-9; etc.). Ishmael should be a wild man (Gen. 16:12). He has maintained that character to this very day (Job 39: 5-8. Arabs). The posterity of Jacob should inherit Canaan (Gen. 13:15). After a long bondage in Egypt the prophecy came true (Joshua). Babylon was made a desolation forever as prophesied by Isaiah (13:4-22). It has been for centuries a mass of ruins. The fall of Jerusalem was foretold, and the return after 70 years in Babylon. These prophecies came true.

Since the great object of all the prophecies is to save mankind, naturally the great subject of prophecy would be Jesus. There are about 175 prophecies about Him in the Old Testament. (See Appendix for list). These prophecies cover such large features of His life as His birth, ministry, passion, resurrection and ascension. They mention many minor details also, such as, the price being paid for Him (Zech. 11:12; Matt. 26:15), this price being given for the potter's field (Zech. 11:13; Matt. 27:7), etc.

There is a world of difference between the Biblical prophecies and the pretended predictions and oracles of heathen priests and soothsayers. The stories of Joseph, Elijah, Jeremiah and Daniel pretty well illustrate the difference. God's prophecies were given without being asked and when not wanted. Ahab did not want to hear Micaiah's prophecies (1 Kings 22). Ahaz did not want to hear Isaiah (Isa. 7). Jerusalem did not want to hear Jeremiah. God's prophets were often hated and hounded. The heathen prophets were men of great influence and might. The greatest difference is, that the prediction of the false prophets did not come to pass, while those of God's prophets were fulfilled or will be accomplished in due season.

Modern critics reject miracles and prophecies as both improbable and impossible. We have before us a sample of their work—the Polychrome Bible, edited by a brilliant set of Bible scholars from different parts of the world. Let us look at the Book of Isaiah, the first of the writing prophets, edited by Prof. T. K. Cheyne of Oxford. This edition is called the Polychrome, meaning many colors, for it is printed in many colors to show the composite structure of the book. The theory of the editor is, that every prophecy was written, not before, but after the event described. Thus, the prophecy about Cyrus (Isa. 44:28) is said to have been written after the Exile by a so-called Second Isaiah, whereas the Bible states that Isaiah wrote it. Isaiah must have spoken the prophecy about 150 years before Cyrus was born. The prophecies on the Fall of Babylon were also pronounced, according to Dr. Cheyne, after the city fell. A prophecy can not possibly be a prophecy if it is to chronicle what has already taken place. If Dr. Cheyne is right, why did not the Lord call it a history instead of a prophecy, and not fool us? If he is right that the prophecies of the Bible were written after the events they pretend to foretell, what shall we say as to the Book of Revelation, which tells about things which are not to happen until the end of time? Or, are they only vain dreams not worth paying attention to? The very definition of prophecy belies these learned editors and commentators. The very appearance of the Polychrome Isaiah is a proof that they are wrong. The book is in many colors, each one pretending to represent the contribution of a certain man. A part of a sentence is in one color, a second part is in another, a third part is in still another color, and so on. The whole thing looks like a crazy quilt, made up of all sorts of odds and ends from far and near. We do not want to read prophecy in this way. We must believe that the Word of God is truth and then try to discover the meaning of the prophecy before us in pretty nearly the same way as we ascertain the meaning of any other passage by discovering the historical position of the prophet, the design and scope of his work, the outline of his book, the analysis of the words and structure of the passage, the study of the context and parallel passages, and reference to the fulfillment of the prophecy. As to the prophecies not yet fulfilled we should not become too positive that we have solved every detail, particularly the year and the day of the fulfillment. Wm. Miller prophesied that April 14, 1844, should be the Day of Judgment (M. Gunther's "Symbolik", 83). J. Steed reckoned that Christ's Advent was due in 1894, M. Baxter, in 1896, and G. Guinness, in 1897. J. B. Dimbleby proved by Scripture and astronomy that Easter, 1898, was the beginning of the Second Advent ("En Ny Tid Er Nær". See also Th. Graebner's "Prophecy and the War"). Jesus said: "But of that day and that hour knoweth no man, no, not the angels of Heaven, but My Father only" (Matt. 24:36-42).

f. ALLEGORIES AND PARABLES.

A sixth principle of special Biblical interpretation is

the recognition of Biblical allegories and parables. In addition to allegories and parables the Bible employs also the riddle and the enigma, the proverb and the fable, as means of conveying thought.

The conspicuous riddle in the Old Testament was Samson's couplet in Judg. 14:14 about honey. It was hard for the Philistines to solve it, but is not hard for the reader. There is no riddle in the New Testament unless it be Rev. 13:18—the number 666. Enigmas are mystic utterances which serve both to conceal and enhance some deep and sacred thought, as, for example: "Except a man be born anew, he can not see the Kingdom of God" (John 3:3). John 4 has several enigmas, as "Living water" (4:10-15), "I have meat to eat" (4:31-34), "fields already white unto harvest" (4:35). The proverbs are a species of Hebrew poetry, expressing briefly and pointedly some practical truth, as: "Physician, heal thyself" (Luke 4: 23). The usual form of the Hebrew proverb is the couplet, in which the second line balances the first in thought, as:

> My son, keep the commandment of thy father,
> And forsake not the law of thy mother (Prov. 6:20).

Proverbs appear in many parts of Scripture, but are mostly confined to the Book of Proverbs. In the Apocrypha the Book of Sirach contains many excellent proverbs. There are only two real fables in the Bible—that of Jotham, in Judg. 9:7-20, and that of Jehoash, in 2 Kings 14:9. In the fable animals are made to speak as human beings, in order to enforce some moral lesson. In Jotham's fable the trees are going to choose a king. They invite the olive, the fig tree and the vine to rule over them, but these all decline. Then they invite the bramble, which accepts and acts the tyrant. The lesson is plain: Israel should not have such a worthless leader as Abimelech.

Another branch of figurative language of Scripture is the allegory, which has been called a continued metaphor.

A metaphor is a figure of speech in which, assuming the likeness between two things, we apply to one of them the term which denotes the other. As, for example, "Ye are the salt of the earth". The allegory is continually using words in a metaphorical sense, and its narrative, however reasonable in itself, is plainly fictitious. Allegory is derived from two Greek words which mean speaking something else, having reference to the fact that it says one thing, but means something else. Thus, in John 15:1-14 Christ says: "I am the True Vine and My Father is the Husbandman. Every branch in Me that beareth not fruit He taketh away," etc. If he had said only, "I am the True Vine", Vine would have been a metaphor, but since He continued speaking figuratively, the discourse became an allegory. Now, when He says that He is the Vine, it is plain that He says it figuratively. And, what the reader can understand with respect to this one word, he can just as easily understand with respect to the whole speech.

The allegories ought not to be very hard to interpret, yet some of those who have tried their hands at interpreting the allegories of Scripture have been guilty of the most extravagant folly. In the investigation of an allegory, the reader must study the meaning of the words in their connection, and the interpretation of the allegory which often subjoins it. The comparison must not be extended to all the circumstances. For example, in the metaphor cited above, "I am the Vine", the comparison between Jesus and the vine does not extend to every detail concerning these two; and in the allegory of which this metaphor is only a part, the comparison must not and can not be extended to all the details. The point in this parable is, that the connection between Christ and Christians should be the same as between a vine and its branches. That is all.

Some interesting examples of parables in the Bible are the following:

Ps. 80:8-15	The Vine from Egypt
Eccl. 12:3-7	Old Age
Song of Solomon 1—8	The Bridegroom and the Bride
Ezek. 13:10-15	The Prophet's Wall
John 10:1-16	The Door of the Sheep Fold
1 Cor. 3:10-15	The Wise Master Builder
1 Cor. 5:6-8	The Leaven
Gal. 4:21-31	The Two Covenants
Eph. 6:11-17	The Christian Armor

The parable bears the same relation to the simile that the allegory bears to the metaphor. The parable is an extented simile. A simile, or comparison, is a figure of speech in which a likeness is pointed out or asserted between things in other respects unlike. A good example of a simile is found in Isa. 55:10-11 and reads as follows: "For as the rain cometh down and the snow from heaven.... so shall My Word be that goeth forth out of My mouth". Similes as well as metaphors are constantly dropping from tongue or pen. The extended similes, that is, parables, are not often met with. The Old Testament has only seven parables, as, for example, the parable of the Ewe Lamb, spoken by Nathan to David (2 Sam. 12:1-4). Jesus is about the only one who has ever successfully made use of this form of speech, and He did not use it continually. He spoke only 40 parables which are recorded in the Gospels, of which 30 are recorded once, 3 recorded twice, and 7 recorded three times. (See Appendix for list). These 40 parables were delivered in groups. There was a series of 8 parables spoken by the seaside in Galilee, during His second year of ministry, after a siege of opposition. Most of the parables were spoken to His disciples during His Perean journeys, and during His last days of public speaking in Jerusalem.

The special reason and purpose for speaking in parables Jesus states in Matt. 13:10-17. The disciples came to Jesus and asked Him why He spoke in parables. He assigned two reasons for this, two objects in view—to reveal and to

conceal the truth. With respect to revealing He said it
was given unto the disciples to know the mysteries of the
Kingdom of Heaven, but it was not given unto the multitude. The word mysteries here means that which we do
not know unless it be revealed, that is, things not necessarily
hard to understand, but whose meaning has not yet been
presented. Jesus says: "Whosoever hath, to Him shall
be given". That is, whosoever understands somewhat shall
be granted to understand more. He who knows arithmetic
can be given algebra; he who knows the abc's can begin
to read. With respect to concealing He said: "Because
seeing they see not, and hearing they hear not, neither do
they understand. For this people's heart is waxed gross,
and their ears are dull of hearing, and their eyes they have
closed; lest at any time they should see with their eyes and
hear with their ears and understand with their heart, and
should be converted". He spoke in parables because so
many were prejudiced against Him and distorted and perverted everything He said when He spoke in plain speech.
Now, the parables which He spoke are remarkable for their
beauty, simplicity, conciseness, and appropriateness to the
time, place and people before whom they were spoken.
Take the parable of the Sower. It was spoken by the seaside in full view of farming scenes. If the listeners did
not at first apprehend the meaning, they might have done
as the disciples did—they came to Jesus and inquired of
Him what this parable might mean. Now the Bible reader
might do likewise. He should by all means study the parable prayerfully and carefully, and meditate upon it late
and early. It will, like a diamond, reveal many new and
precious beauties if seen from the right angle.

g. SCRIPTURE QUOTATIONS IN THE SCRIPTURES.

A seventh principle of special Biblical interpretation
is with reference to the quotations, more or less exact,
made by one Biblical writer from another. These quota-

tions may be divided into four classes: Old Testament quotations from Old Testament sources, New Testament quotations from Old Testament sources, New Testament quotations from New Testament sources, quotations from non-Biblical sources. An example of each of these classes is herewith given in illustration:

(1) 2 Sam. 22—Ps. 18.
(2) Isa. 7:14—Matt. 1: 23.
(3) 2 Pet. 1:12—Jude 1 :5.
(4) The Book of Jasher—Joshua 10:13.

Some readers always have difficulty with the quotations, possibly for the reason that, as they are more or less exact, that is, the quotation is not always identical with the original passage. The most important quotations belong to the 2nd class, the New Testament quotations from the Old Testament. There are 136 direct quotations of this kind, and nearly 500 additional indirect quotations. The direct quotations are of four kinds. Those in which the Greek corresponds exactly with the Hebrew original; those in which the Greek agrees with the Hebrew, excepting in minor details, and not changing the sense at all; those in which the Greek agrees with the Greek translation of the Old Testament called the Septuagint; and those in which the Greek does not agree with the wording of either the Hebrew original or the Septuagint translation. There are 72 passages belonging to the first class, 30 to the second, 17 to the third and 17 to the fourth. It seems then, from this list, that Jesus and His apostles sometimes quoted from the Hebrew original, sometimes from the Greek translation then in use, and sometimes spoke from memory. All of these methods are perfectly legitimate, for the New Testament writers never used the Old Testament contrary to the analogy of faith. If they do not give the exact words of the Old Testament they give the substance and the purpose. In comparison we might say that the quotations in the present book have also been collected from many editions of the Bible. Perhaps most of them have been taken from the Authorized Version of the Bible. A large number of them have been taken from the Revised Version, some have been taken from the Hebrew and Greek originals, and some have been cited from memory, but all of them have been given true to the analogy of faith. Some books, like Bunyan's "Pilgrim's Progress", are quite saturated with Biblical thought and language, even when they do not attempt to quote the Bible at all.

h. APPROPRIATION AND APPLICATION.

Without attempting to exhaust the subject of how to interpret the Bible, we shall mention only one more principle that should be had in mind in reading this book—it is a living Book, whose contents can be appropriated and applied. In power houses one is warned to keep aloof from live wires and dynamos in action. The Word of God can be said to be like the electric currents in that it is powerful, but unlike them in that there is no need of putting up danger signs. On the contrary, there is an urgent standing call to everyone to come near and get into closer touch with the Bible.

In the first place, the Word of God is a Means of Grace. The Means of Grace are the external and visible means by which the Holy Ghost produces in man saving faith accompanied by good works. These Means of Grace are the Word and the Sacraments. The Word, as well as the Sacraments, is endowed with power to produce such supernatural effects as faith, regeneration, renewal of mind and preservation in the faith. The Word of God is always efficacious, but may be frustrated by man's obstinate and continued resistance. Jesus said to Jerusalem: "How often would I have gathered thy children together, even as a hen gathereth her chickens under wings, but ye would not" (Matt. 23: 37; Rom. 10: 21; Acts 7: 51). The Word is always endowed with divine force and accomplishes saving results in every case that it is not resisted, but accepted (Isa. 55:10-11; Rom. 10:17; Jas. 1:18). The power of the Word is grounded in the presence of the Holy Spirit in it.

In the second place, the Word of God is the only source and rule of Christian doctrine. The Bible is "profitable for doctrine, for reproof, for correction and for instruction in righteousness" (2 Tim. 3:16). It does not as such present a system of doctrine, but it contains material from which a doctrinal system can be made. The reason that the Bible does not present a ready-made system at the very outset is, that the Old Testament Church is older than the Old Testament Scriptures, hence the Old Testament Scriptures grew out of the conditions of the Old Testament Church; likewise the New Testament Church is older than the New Testament Scriptures, hence the New Testament Scriptures grew out of the conditions of the New Testament Church. The Lord did not reveal all the truth at once. Even the prophecies are progressive both in their giving and in their fulfilment. Therefore we find the specific doctrines scattered throughout the Bible, some here and some there. Only to a limited extent and only in certain parts can it be said that the Bible attempts to present any doctrinal subject fully and systematically. Examples of these portions are: Leviticus, Deuteronomy, Job, John, Romans, James, Hebrews. The Bible is, like a person, a living organism. You may get a good understanding of the drift of the Bible doctrine without studying its teachings as a system. Yet even as it is profitable to study human anatomy, so also it is of immense value to read the Bible for the sake of its doctrines. Such doctrinal study should be taken from at least two points of view—Biblical Theology and Systematic Theology.

Biblical Theology is a systematic representation of the revealed religion as laid down in the books of the Bible, book by book, or period by period, covering the whole Bible. Thus, what doctrines are taught in Genesis, in Exodus, in Leviticus, and so on?　Or, what is taught about God in the time of Abraham, or of Moses, or of David, and so on? It is a wonderful experience to read the Bible through, outlining and analyzing and marking each book in turn with respect to the teachings it contains.　As one studies in this fashion he will be impressed with the development and expansion of the doctrines and their increasing clearness, especially after the coming of Christ (Weidner's "Biblical Theology of the Old Testament", "Biblical Theology of the New Testament").

Systematic Theology represents the Christian religion as a scientific system.　It finds its material in the Bible and arranges it into an organic whole.　Each Church, each theologian, each reader can make out his own system, although the material in every case should be taken only from the Bible and should in every detail be true to the Bible teaching.　Thus, Luther's "Little Catechism" is a complete system of Bible doctrine, adapted to the wants and capacities of children.　It has five parts—The Law, Faith (the Apostles' Creed), Prayer (the Lord's Prayer), Baptism and Communion (the Lord's Supper).　C. E. Lindberg's "Dogmatik" is also a complete system—for students of theology. It contains seven parts—Theology, Anthropology, Christology, Soteriology, Pneumatology, Ecclesiology and Eschatology.　It is invigorating indeed to read the Bible to get more information on the doctrines held by the Church. Luther was occupied at this when he learnt that the Bible taught differently from the Church on the way of salvation. The Bible will throw light on every Church doctrine, fortify it if it is Biblical, and disprove it if it is merely human. In studying doctrine it is customary to go to the Bible to find out what the Bible teaches, and then use this teaching as proof verses.　Again, some make the mistake of going to the Old Testament only for their teachings. Now, the Old Testament teachings are not always binding on the New Testament Christians, for the New Covenant saves by Grace and not by Law. Therefore many such teachings, while applicable to the Jews of old, have been set aside by later teachings given by the Lord Himself. No teaching ought to be accepted unless it is confirmed by the letter or the spirit of the New Testament. Again, some pluck out passages without any reference to the historical setting or the context. This method is to be avoided, as it leads to no end of misinterpretation and doctrinal controversy. Finally, some spend all of their time on dark passages, entirely disregarding the great, essential teachings concerning which there can be little or no room for controversy. Most of the great controversies in the Church have arisen from the attempts to define what Scripture has left undefined or to answer questions which the Lord has not seen fit to answer.

In the third place, the Word of God is the only source and rule of life and works. It is profitable for "doctrine, for reproof, for correction, for instruction in righteousness, that the man of God may be perfect, thoroughly furnished unto all good works" (2 Tim. 3:16-17). The doctrines give the theory and principles. Theories and principles must be tested out in life. Christ was called the Word. Christians, too, were called Christ's Epistles (2 Cor. 3:3), written not with ink, but with the Spirit of the living God. When we discover the teachings of the Bible, appropriate them and apply them, we become living Bibles writ large. The Bible shows us in its narratives and biographies how to apply the doctrines there given. The personal experiences of Adam, Noah, Abraham, Moses, David, Daniel, Peter, Paul and a host of other Biblical characters, some evil and some good, furnish the reader with ample illustrations of every teaching and ample incentive to put such teaching into practice. Every example of faith and good works, every account of suffering and sacrifice, every triumph of virtue, every defeat of vice, every precept, every promise, every admonition, every warning, every event, may serve in some way to make the Bible reader "perfect, thoroughly furnished unto all good works". In appropriating and applying the Scriptures the reader should always remember that his first duty is to make sure that he has laid hold of the real spirit and meaning of the passage or teaching in question. To build our faith and practice on erroneous interpretations of God's Word may prove fatal. The following incident related by A. Jukes in his "Second Death" illustrates that some interpretations even by good, well-meaning Christian people may be hopelessly wrong, and also that their attitude toward investigating the meaning of perplexing passages may be thoroughly unbiblical. The illustration is this: At a certain Sunday school a class was studying the story of David and Bathsheba. It is related in 2 Sam. 11:2 that David, when walking on the roof of his house, saw Bathsheba. One of the boys said: "But, teacher, how could David walk on the roof of his house?" The teacher happened to be ignorant of the fact that the houses of Israel were built with flat roofs, yet at once checked further inquiry by replying: "Don't grumble at the Bible, boy". Meanwhile the teacher of an adjoining class had overheard the conversation. Leaning over to his fellow teacher he whispered: "The answer to the difficulty is: 'With men it is impossible, but not with God, for with God all things are possible.'" Alas, what an interpretation even in this case. Alas and alas, what dreadful and fatal interpretations are often given of still weightier questions. Therefore the reader should make sure that he has laid hold of the true spirit and the real sense.

In conclusion, we wish to repeat the words with which we began: The Bible is an Open Book. Read it.

To what extent is the Bible dark and difficult? To what extent is it clear? What is meant by the "Book of Nature"? Give examples showing that scholars disagree as to their interpretations of the Bible? Discuss the results of true and false principles of interpretation.

What is meant by general principles of interpretation? Name four general principles. Explain what is meant by the design, scope and class? What is the proper method of studying the text? Explain the principle of avoiding applications. Of avoiding multiple meanings. Of limiting the word to one sense. Of examining the etymology of words. Of finding the true sense. What is meant by context? Show how the text must harmonize with the context. Give an example. What is meant by parallel passages? Give examples of parallel passages. Illustrate how the parallel passages may help to determine the sense intended.

What is meant by special principles of interpretation? Name 8 special principles of interpretation. Define and illustrate each of the following: Self-interpretation of the Scripture, analogy of faith, tradition and reason, types and symbols, prophecies, allegories, parables, riddles, enigmas, proverbs and fables, Scripture quotations in the Scriptures, appropriation and application.

Compare the way the story of Jonah is treated by Moulton and Jesus. Show how the analogy of faith aids in the explanation of Jas. 2:24. Show by the table of Adam's descendants that the Antediluvians must have known the will of the Lord. What are the advantages and disadvantages of tradition? Of reason as applied to Bible reading? What is the value of faith in opening the Scripture? Give examples of types together with antitypes. Distinguish between types and symbols. Give examples of symbols. Discuss the number of the beast. What is the best evidence that the prophecies of the Bible were inspired? Compare these prophecies with human predictions. Give examples of fulfillment. State the object of all the prophecies of the Bible. Why do modern critics reject prophecy, together with miracle, as impossible? What does the Polychrome Bible teach us as to whether the modern critics are right or wrong? Why are allegories so hard to interpret? Give some examples of parables. Show from these the special reason and purpose for speaking in this fashion. In how many ways does the Scripture quote Scripture? Give an example of each. In how many ways is Scripture quoted in this handbook? What is meant by the Word of God as a Means of Grace? The Word of God as the only source and rule of Christian doctrine? What is Biblical theology? Systematic theology? What is meant by the Word of God as the only source and rule of life and works? What should be the first duty of the Bible reader with respect to appropriating and applying Scripture?

What does your Catechism say about the interpretation of the Bible? Your Bible history? Find appropriate hymns in your hymnal bearing on this subject. Look up the Bible passages referred to in your lesson, and find additional references to this subject in the Bible. In what ways can the contents of this lesson help you in your Bible study? In your faith and works?

In what respects is the Bible an Open Book?

APPENDIX.

A. TABLES OF CHRONOLOGY.

NO. OF YEARS	PERIODS	DATES
2083	1. BEFORE THE FOUNDING OF ISRAEL...	4004BC—1921BC
1656	a. *Antediluvian Age*	4004BC—2348BC
427	b. *Postdiluvian Age*	2348 —1921
101	(1) Period of Union.	2348 —2247
326	(2) Period of Dispersion.	2247 —1921
1917	2. DURING THE OLD COVENANT.	1921BC— 4BC
826	a. *Theocracy*	1921 —1095
215	(1) Period of Patriarchs.	1921 —1706
215	(2) Period of Bondage.	1706 —1491
40	(3) Period of Wandering.	1491 —1451
16	(4) Period of Conquest.	1451 —1435
340	(5) Period of Judges.	1435 —1095
509	b. *Monarchy*	1095BC— 586BC
120	(1) Period of Union.	1095 — 975
389	(2) Period of Division.	975 — 586
582	c. *Dependency*	586BC— 4BC
(656)		—(70AD)
70	(1) Period under Babylonia. . . .	586 — 516
186	(2) Period under Persia.	516 — 330
9	(3) Period under Macedonia. . .	330 — 321
123	(4) Period under Egypt. . . . . . :. .	321 — 198
32	(5) Period under Syria.	198 — 166
103	(6) Period under Maccabees. . . .	166 — 63
59	(7) Period under Rome.	63BC— 4BC
		—(70AD)
?	3. DURING THE NEW COVENANT.	4BC— ?AD
104	a. *New Testament Times*.	4BC— 100AD
34	(1) Times of Christ.	4BC— 30AD
70	(2) Times of Apostles.	30AD— 100
?	b. *Dispersion*	70AD— ?

1. BEFORE THE FOUNDING OF ISRAEL.

A. M.	B. C.	a. ANTEDILUVIAN AGE. (1656 YEARS).	Year at birth of son	Rest of life	Total age	AUTHORITY
1	4004					
130	3874	Adam	130	800	930	Gen. 5:3-5
235	3769	Seth	105	807	912	Gen. 5: 6-8
325	3679	Enos	90	815	905	Gen. 5:9-11
395	3609	Cainan	70	840	910	Gen. 5:12-14
460	3544	Mahalaleel	65	830	895	Gen. 5:15-17
622	3382	Jared	162	800	962	Gen. 5:18-20
687	3317	Enoch	65	300	365	Gen. 5:21-24
874	3130	Methuselah	187	782	969	Gen. 5:25-27
1056	2948	Lamech	182	595	777	Gen. 5:28-31
1656	2348	Noah at the Flood	600	350	950	Gen. 7:11; 9:28-29
		b. POSTDILUVIAN AGE (427 YEARS).				
		(1) *Period of Union (101 Years).*				
1658	2346	Shem after the Flood	2	500	502	Gen. 5:32; 11:10-11
1693	2311	Arpachshad	35	403	438	Gen. 11:12-13
1723	2281	Shelah	30	403	433	Gen. 11:14-15
		(2) *Period of Dispersion (326 Years).*				
1757	2247	Eber (Heber)	34	430	464	Gen. 11:16-17
1787	2217	Peleg	30	209	239	Gen. 11:18-19
1819	2185	Reu	32	207	239	Gen. 11:20-21
1849	2155	Serug	30	200	230	Gen. 11:22-23
1878	2126	Nahor	29	119	148	Gen. 11:24-25
2008	1996	Terah at Abraham's birth	130	75	205	Gen. 11:26, 32; 12:4
2083	1921	Abraham at call	75	100	175	Gen. 12:4

2. DURING THE OLD COVENANT (1917 YEARS).
a. THEOCRACY (826 YEARS).
(1) *Period of Patriarchs (215 Years).*

DATE	EVENTS	Age of Abram	Age of Isaac	Age of Jacob	Age of Joseph	AUTHORITY
B. C.						
1921	Call of Abram.........	75	...	...	...	Gen. 12:1-3
1921	His departure to Canaan	75	...	...	...	Gen. 12:4
1920(?)	His removal to Egypt...	76	...	...	...	Gen. 12:10
1919(?)	His return to Canaan...	77	...	...	...	Gen. 13:1-3
1918(?)	Separation from Lot....	78	...	...	...	Gen. 13:10
1918(?)	Abode at Mamre.......	78	...	...	...	Gen. 13:18
1913(?)	Rescue of Lot.........	83	...	...	...	Gen. 14:16
1910	Birth of Ishmael.......	86	...	...	...	Gen. 16:15; 17:25
1897	Change of name from Abram to Abraham....	99	...	...	...	Gen. 17:5
1897	Destruction of Sodom...	99	...	...	...	Gen. 18:20—19:25
1896	Birth of Isaac..........	100	...	...	...	Gen. 21:5
1894(?)	Expulsion of Ishmael...	102	2	...	...	Gen. 21:10-14
1871(?)	Sacrifice of Isaac.......	125	25	...	...	Gen. 22:7
1860	Death of Sarah........	137	37	...	...	Gen. 23:1
1857	Marriage of Isaac......	140	40	...	...	Gen. 25:20
1837	Birth of Esau and Jacob	160	60	...	...	Gen. 25:26
1822	Death of Abraham.....	175	75	15	...	Gen. 25:7
1804(?)	Esau sells his birthright	...	93	33	...	Gen. 25:29
1773	Death of Ishmael.......	...	123	63	...	Gen. 25:17
1760	Jacob steals blessing...	...	137	77	...	Gen. 27:28
1760	Flight of Jacob........	...	137	77	...	Gen. 28:5
1760	Vision at Bethel........	...	137	77	...	Gen. 28:11-15
1753	Marriages of Jacob.....	...	144	84	...	Gen. 29:23-30
1746	Birth of Joseph........	...	151	91	...	Gen. 30:22-24
1739	Return to Canaan......	...	158	98	7	Gen. 31:38-41
1739	Change of name from Jacob to Israel........	...	158	98	7	Gen. 32:28
1739	Reconciliation with Esau	...	158	98	7	Gen. 33:4
1729	Birth of Benjamin......	...	168	108	17	Gen. 35:16
1729	Death of Rachel........	...	163	108	17	Gen. 35:18
1729	Dreams and sale of Joseph	...	168	108	17	Gen. 37:5-28
1716	Death of Isaac.........	...	180	120	29	Gen. 35:29
1716	Exaltation of Joseph....	...	...	121	30	Gen. 41:46
1716	Beginning of 7 years of plenty	...	...	121	30	Gen. 41:26
1709	Beginning of 7 years of famine	...	...	128	37	Gen. 41:27
1706	Departure of Jacob for Egypt	...	...	130	39	Gen. 47:28

(2) *Period of Bondage (215 Years).*

DATE	EVENTS	Age of Jacob	Age of Joseph	Age of Aaron	Age of Moses	AUTHORITY
B. C. 1706	Departure of Jacob for Egypt	130	39	. . .	. . .	Gen. 47:28
1689	Death of Jacob.	147	54	. . .	. . .	Gen. 47:28
1634	Death of Joseph.	. . .	110	. . .	. . .	Gen. 50:26
	Bondage	. . .	. . .	. . .	. . .	Ex. 1:7-22
1574	Birth of Aaron.	. . .	. . .	. . .	. . .	Ex. 7:7
1572 (?)	Order to kill male infants	. . .	. . .	2	. . .	Ex. 1:15
1571	Birth of Moses.	. . .	. . .	3		Ex. 2:2
1531	Exile of Moses.	. . .	. . .	43	40	Ex. 2:15
1492	Return of Moses.	. . .	. . .	82	79	Ex. 7:7
1492	Negotiations with Pharaoh	. . .	. . .	82	79	Ex. 3—11
1492	Ten plagues	. . .	. . .	82	79	Ex. 3—11
1491	Exodus	. . .	. . .	83	80	Ex. 12:40

(3) *Period of Wandering (40 Years).*

DATE	EVENTS	AUTHORITY
B. C.		
1491	Exodus	Ex. 12:40
	1st month: Crossing the Red Sea	Ex. 15
	Marah, Elim	
	2nd month: Wilderness of Sin	Ex. 16:1
	3rd month: Sinai	Ex. 19:1
	40 days on mount	{ Ex. 24:18
		{ Deut. 9:9, 11
	40 days of intercession	Deut. 9:18, 25
	40 days on mount again	{ Ex. 34:28
		{ Deut. 10:10
	Making of Tabernacle, Ark, etc	Ex. 25—39
	Visit of Jethro, organizing, etc	Ex. 18:5-25
1490	1st month: Anointing of tent, etc	{ Ex. 40; Lev. 8:10-12
		{ Num. 7:10, 12, 78
	Celebration of second Passover	Num. 9:1-5
	2nd month: First census	{ Ex. 38:25-28; Num.
		{ 1:1, 3, 18
	Beginning of march to Kadesh	Num. 10:11
	3rd month: Lust for flesh	Num. 11
	Sedition of Aaron and Miriam	Num. 12
	40 days of spying	Num. 13:25
	Beginning of 38 years of wandering	Deut. 2:14
1452	1st month: Death of Miriam at Sin	Num. 20:1
	Moses' offense	Num. 20:10
	5th month: Appointment of Eleazar as high priest	Num. 20:25, 28
	Death of Aaron on Hor, 123 years old	Num. 20:28; 33:38-39
	Serpent of brass	Num. 21:9
	Conquest of Sihon and Og	{ Num. 21:21-35
		{ Deut. 2—3
	Blessing of Balaam	Num. 22-24
	Idolatry at Shittim	Num. 25
	Second census	Num. 26
	Appointment of Joshua as leader	Num. 27:18
	War with Midian	Num. 31
	First assignment of territory	Num. 32:33
	11th month: Moses' addresses	Deut. 1:3
1451	Death of Moses on Nebo; 120 years old . . .	Deut. 31—34
	30 days of mourning	Deut. 34:8

(4) *Period of Conquest (16 Years).*

DATE	EVENTS	AUTHORITY
B.C. 1451	Joshua leader........................	Josh. 1:1-4
	Sending of spies to Jericho............	Josh. 2
	Crossing the Jordan...................	Josh. 3—4
	Celebrating the Passover..............	Josh. 5:10
	Capture of Jericho....................	Josh. 6
	Capture of Ai........................	Josh. 7—8
	Blessing and curse at Shechem........	Josh. 8:30-35
1450	Stratagem of Gibeon..................	Josh. 9
	Conquest of South....................	Josh. 10:28-43
1449	Conquest of North—Jabin, Hazor.......	Josh. 11
1445	Setting up the Tabernacle at Shiloh....	Josh. 18
1452	Division of the land.	
	Reuben	Josh. 13:15-23
	Gad	Josh. 13:24-28
	Half of Manasseh....................	Josh. 13: 29-32
1446	Judah	Josh. 15:1-63
	Ephraim (Joseph)	Josh. 16:1-10
	Half of Manasseh....................	Josh. 17:1-18
1444	Benjamin	Josh. 18:11-28
	Simeon	Josh. 19:1-9
	Zebulon	Josh. 19:10-16
	Issachar	Josh. 19:17-23
	Asher	Josh. 19:24-31
	Naphtali	Josh. 19:32-39
	Dan	Josh. 19:40-48
	6 cities of refuge....................	Josh. 20
	48 cities to Levites...................	Josh. 21
	Return of the 2½ tribes..............	Josh. 22
1437(?)	First convocation at Shechem..........	Josh. 23
1436(?)	Second convocation	Josh. 24
1435(?)	Death of Joshua, 110 years old........	Josh. 24:29
(?)	Supplementary conquests:	
	By Judah and Simeon.................	Judg. 1:1-8
(?)	By Caleb and Othniel.................	Judg. 1:9-20
	By Dan	Judg. 18

(5) *Period of Judges (340 Years).*

DATE	EVENTS	AUTHORITY
B.C. 1435	First apostasy.	
	Servitude 8 years under Mesopotamia...	Judg. 3:8
1427	Rescue by Othniel, with 40 years of peace	Judg. 3:11
1387	Second apostasy.	
	Servitude 18 years under Moab and Philistia............................	Judg. 3:14
1369	Rescue from Moab by Ehud and from Philistia by Shamgar, with 80 years of peace	Judg. 3:30
	Third apostasy.	
1289	Servitude 20 years under Canaanites....	Judg. 4:3
1269	Rescue by Deborah and Barak, with 40 years of rest.........................	Judg. 4:4—5:31
	Fourth apostasy.	
1229	Servitude 7 years under Midian........	Judg. 6:1
1222	Rescue by Gideon, with 40 years of peace	Judg. 8:28
	Fifth apostasy.	
1182	Servitude 3 years under Abimelech, usurper	Judg. 9
1179	Peace under Tola, 23 years...........	Judg. 10:2
1156	Peace under Jair, 22 years............	Judg. 10:3
	Sixth apostasy.	
1138	Servitude 18 years under Ammon, etc...	Judg. 10:8
1132	Rescue by Jephthah, with 6 years of peace	Judg. 12:7
1124	Peace under Ibzan, 7 years............	Judg. 12:9
1117	Peace under Elon, 10 years...........	Judg. 12:11
1107	Peace under Abdon, 8 years...........	Judg. 12:14
	Seventh apostasy.	
1134	Servitude 40 years under Philistia......	Judg. 13:1
1114	Rescue by Samson, with 20 years of peace	Judg. 15:20; 16:31
1154	Rescue by Eli and Samuel, with 40 years of peace.......................	1 Sam. 4:18; 7:2, 15
1095	Beginning of monarchy...............	

b. MONARCHY (509 YEARS).

(1) *Period of Union (120 Years).*

DATE	EVENTS	AUTHORITY
	KING SAUL.	
	First Period.	
B.C. 1095	Saul's visit to Samuel and anointing...	1 Sam. 9:1—10:16
1095	His election by lot, and inauguration....	1 Sam. 10:17-27
1095	His defeat of Ammon and re-inauguration.	1 Sam. 11:1-15
1094	Samuel's retirement at Gilgal..........	
1090(?)	War with Philistines.................	1 Sam. 13:1-7
1090(?)	First case of Saul's disobedience—sacrificing at Gilgal, and first sentence of rejection	1 Sam. 13:8-14
1087(?)	Saul's foolish vow...................	1 Sam. 14:24-31
1087(?)	Jonathan's transgression and rescue....	1 Sam. 14:32-46
	Victories over Moab, Ammon, Edom, etc.	1 Sam. 14:47-48
1085	Birth of David......................	2 Sam. 5:4
	Second Period.	
1079(?)	War against Amalek.................	1 Sam. 15:1-3
1079(?)	Second case of disobedience—sparing king and cattle, and second sentence of rejection	1 Sam. 15:4-35
	Third Period.	
1065(?)	Anointing of David as king...........	1 Sam. 16:1-13
1063(?)	War with Philistines................	1 Sam. 17
1063(?)	David at court and camp.............	{ 1 Sam. 16:18-23; 17:12-31
1063(?)	David's victory over Goliath...........	1 Sam. 17:32-54
1063(?)	Effects of victory: Jonathan's friendship and Saul's hatred....................	1 Sam. 17:55—18:16
1063(?)	Secret persecution of David...........	1 Sam. 18:17-30
1062(?)	David's marriage to Michal...........	1 Sam. 18:27
1062(?)	Open persecution of David............	1 Sam. 19—27
1062(?)	David's first escape and flight to Ramah	1 Sam. 19:1-24
1062(?)	David's second escape and flight to Nob	1 Sam. 20:1—22:23
1062(?)	David's third escape and flight to Keilah	1 Sam. 23:1-13
1061(?)	David's fourth escape and flight to Ziph	1 Sam. 23:14-24

Third Period.

DATE	EVENTS	AUTHORITY
B. C.		
1061(?)	David's fifth escape and flight to Maon	1 Sam. 23:24-28
1061(?)	David's sixth escape and flight to cave at Engedi...........................	1 Sam. 23:29—24:22
1060	David's seventh escape and flight to Paran.............................	1 Sam. 25:1—26:25
1060	Samuel's death....................	1 Sam. 25:1
1059	David's marriage to Abigail and Ahinoam	1 Sam. 25:39-44
1057	David's abode in Ziklag..............	1 Sam. 27:1—28:2
1055	Saul's visit to witch of Endor.........	1 Sam. 28:3-25
1055	David's dismissal from the Philistine army............................	1 Sam. 29:1—30:1
1055	Death of Saul and Jonathan in battle with Philistines..................	{ 1 Sam. 31:1-13 { Acts 13:21
1055	David's lamentation over Saul and Jonathan..........................	2 Sam. 1:1-27

KING DAVID.

First Period: Rise.

1055	King of Judah alone.................	2 Sam. 2:1-4
1055	Message of thanks to Jebusites.......	1 Sam. 2:5-7
1048	Defeat of Abner and Ishbosheth.......	2 Sam. 2:8-31
1048	Break between Abner and Ishbosheth..	2 Sam. 3:6-21
1048	Murder of Abner and Ishbosheth......	2 Sam. 3:22—4:12
1048	King over all Israel.................	2 Sam. 5:1-5
1048(?)	Victories over Jebusites, and establishment of Jerusalem as capital.........	2 Sam. 5:6-16
1047(?)	Victories over Philistines.............	2 Sam. 5:17-25
1042	Transfer of Ark to Mount Zion.......	2 Sam. 6:1-23
1042	David's purpose to build a temple for the Ark...........................	2 Sam. 7:1-29
1038	Extension of the kingdom by conquests of Philistia, Moab, Zobah, Damascus, Hamath, Edom....................	2 Sam. 8:1-14
1038	Organization of the State.............	2 Sam. 8:15-18
	Kindness to Jonathan's son...........	2 Sam. 9:1-13
1036	Victories over Ammonites and allies....	{ 2 Sam. 10:1-19; { 12:26-31

DATE	EVENTS	AUTHORITY
	Second Period: Fall.	
B.C. 1036	David's adultery	2 Sam. 11:1—12:24
1034	Birth of Solomon.	2 Sam. 12:24-25
1027	Amnon's incest	2 Sam. 13:1-22
1023	Absalom's rebellion, David's flight.	2 Sam. 14:25—18:33
	Third Period: Restoration.	
1023	David's victorious return from Gilead. . .	2 Sam. 19:1-40
1023	Suppression of the insurrection of Sheba and Israel	2 Sam. 19:41—20:22
1016(?)	Sinful census and plague.	2 Sam. 24:1-25
1015	Crowning of Solomon.	1 Kings 1:1-53
1015	Death of David, 70 years old.	1 Kings 2:10-11
	KING SOLOMON.	
	First Period: Firmness.	
1015	Execution of Adonijah, Abiathar, Joab, Shimei	1 Kings 2:13-46
1015(?)	First fateful marriage.	1 Kings 3:1
1015(?)	Festival and prayer for wisdom.	1 Kings 3:2-15
1015(?)	First wise judicial decision.	1 Kings 3:16-28
1012	Foundation of the Temple.	1 Kings 6:1
1004	Dedication of the Temple.	{ 1 Kings 5—7 { 2 Chron. 1—8
992	Completion of palace.	1 Kings 9:24
991(?)	Visit of the Queen of Sheba.	1 Kings 10:1-13
	Second Period: Weakness.	
(?)	Three enemies invited by Solomon: polygamy, idolatry, luxury.	1 Kings 11:1-8
(?)	Three enemies stirred up by the Lord: Hadad, Rezon and Jeroboam.	1 Kings 11:14-40
975	Death of Solomon.	1 Kings 11:41-43

(2) Period of Division (389 Years).

TWO TRIBES.

DATE	EVENTS	AUTHORITY
B.C.	*At War with Ten Tribes, Mainly Alone.*	
975	KING REHOBOAM.	
	His foolish reply to people's grievances	1 Kings 12:1-14
	Idolatries and sodomy	1 Kings 14:21-24
	Defeat by Egypt	1 Kings 14:25-28
	Continued war with Ten Tribes	1 Kings 14:29-30
959	Death of Rehoboam, after 17 years of rule	1 Kings 14:31
959	King ABIJAM	1 Kings 15:1-5
	War with Ten Tribes	1 Kings 15:6-7
957	Death of Abijam, after 3 years of rule	1 Kings 15:8
957	King ASA	1 Kings 15:9-11
	Attempt to banish sodomy	1 Kings 15:12-15
	War with Ten Tribes	1 Kings 15:16-17
953	Alliance with Syria	1 Kings 15:18-22

TEN TRIBES.

DATE	EVENTS	AUTHORITY
B.C.	*At War with Two Tribes, Mainly Alone.*	
975	KING JEROBOAM I.	
	Revolt of Ten Tribes	1 Kings 12:1-24
	Institution of calf worship	1 Kings 12:25-33
	Prophecy of man of God vs. this	1 Kings 13:1—14:18
	Ahijah's prophecy vs. house of Jeroboam	1 Kings 14:1-18
954	Death of Jeroboam, after 22 years of rule	1 Kings 14:19-20
954	King NADAB	1 Kings 15:25-26
	War with Two Tribes	1 Kings 15:32
953	Death of Nadab, after 2 years of rule	1 Kings 15:25-31

TWO TRIBES.

DATE	EVENTS	AUTHORITY
917	Death of Asa, after 41 years of rule.............	1 Kings 15:23-24
	In Alliance with Ten Tribes.	
917	King JEHOSHAPHAT. Early reforms.............	1 Kings 22:41-43 2 Chron. 17:6-9

TEN TRIBES.

DATE	EVENTS	AUTHORITY
953	King BAASHA	1 Kings 15:33-34
	Jehu's doom upon his house...	1 Kings 16:1-4
930	Death of Baasha, after 24 years of rule......	1 Kings 16:5-6
930	King ELAH.	
	Jehu's prophecy vs. Elah......	1 Kings 16:7
929	Zimri's conspiracy and murder of Elah, after 2 years of rule..	1 Kings 16:8-10
929	King ZIMRI. Extermination of house of Baasha.............	1 Kings 16:11-14
	Election of Omri by army....	1 Kings 16:15-16
	Cremation of Zimri, after 7 days of rule......	1 Kings 16:17-20
929	King OMRI	1 Kings 16:25-26
	Defeat of Tibni, rival claimant	1 Kings 16:21-22
	Building of Samaria..........	1 Kings 16:23-24
917	Death of Omri, after 12 years of rule......	1 Kings 16:27-28
	In Alliance with Two Tribes.	
917	King AHAB.	1 Kings 16:29-31
	Idolatry..............	1 Kings 16:32-33
	Restoring of Jericho..........	Josh. 6:26

TWO TRIBES.

DATE	EVENTS	AUTHORITY
	First alliance with Ten Tribes	1 Kings 22:44-49 2 Chron. 18:1-34
	Jehu's reproof of alliance with Ahab	2 Chron. 19:1-3
	Later reforms	2 Chron. 19:4-11
	Victory over Moab, Ammon and Syria	2 Chron. 20:1-30
	Second alliance with Ahab, Micaiah's reproof	2 Chron. 20:33-37 1 Kings 22
	Alliance with Ahaziah, Eliezer's reproof	2 Chron. 20:33-37
	Alliance with Ten Tribes	2 Kings 2:4-10

TEN TRIBES.

DATE	EVENTS	AUTHORITY
		1 Kings 16:34
	Elijah's first prophecy—of drought, and flight to Cherith	1 Kings 17:1-24
	Elijah's second prophecy—of rain, and slaughter of priests on Carmel	1 Kings 18:1-46
	Elijah's flight to Paran and Horeb	1 Kings 19:1-18
	Anointing of Elisha	1 Kings 19:19-21
	Ahab's first Syrian campaign	1 Kings 20:1-22
	Ahab's second Syrian campaign	1 Kings 20:26-33
	Elijah's third prophecy—of doom of Ahab and Jezebel	1 Kings 21:1-29
	Ahab's third Syrian campaign	1 Kings 22:1-39
898	Death of Ahab, after 22 years of rule	1 Kings 22:29-40
898	King AHAZIAH	1 Kings 22:51-53
	Moab's secession	2 Kings 1:1
	Elijah's prophecy	2 Kings 1:3-16
896	Death of Ahaziah, after 2 years of rule	2 Kings 1:17-18
396	King JEHORAM	2 Kings 1:17; 3:1-3
	Elijah's departure on chariot of fire	2 Kings 2:1-11
	Elisha, his successor	2 Kings 2:12-13
	Elisha's first appearance as	

TWO TRIBES.

DATE	EVENTS	AUTHORITY
	Elisha's reproof	2 Kings 3:11-15
893	Death of Jehoshaphat, after 25 years of rule	1 Kings 22:42-50
893	KING JEHORAM (Joram)	2 Kings 8:16-19
	Revolt of Edom and Libnah	2 Kings 8:20-23
885	Death of Jehoram, after 8 years of rule	2 Kings 8:17-24
885	King AHAZIAH	2 Kings 8:25-27
	Alliance with Ten Tribes	2 Kings 8:28-29
	Defeat by Jehu	2 Kings 9:14-29
884	Death of Ahaziah, after less than 1 year of rule	2 Kings 9:27-29

TEN TRIBES.

DATE	EVENTS	AUTHORITY
	prophet—healing waters of Jericho, punishing the irreverent children	2 Kings 2:19-25
	Alliance with Two Tribes vs. Moab	2 Kings 3:21-27
	Frequent appearance of Elisha as prophet and helper:	
	Increases a widow's oil	2 Kings 4:1-7
	Restores a boy's life	2 Kings 4:8-37
	Cleanses poisonous pottage	2 Kings 4:38-41
	Feeds 100 men in famine	2 Kings 4:42-44
	Elisha's cure of Naaman, the Syrian	2 Kings 5:1-27
	Gehazi's sin	2 Kings 5:20-27
	Various appearances of Elisha as prophet and helper:	
	Recovers axe	2 Kings 6:1-7
	Blinds the Syrians	2 Kings 6:13-23
	Promises food to the besieged army in Samaria	2 Kings 7:1-20
	Predicts famine	2 Kings 8:1
	Anoints Hazael King of Syria	2 Kings 8:7-15
	War with Syria	2 Kings 8:28-29
884	Death of Jehoram, after 12 years of rule	2 Kings 9:14-26

TWO TRIBES.

DATE	EVENTS	AUTHORITY
884	Queen ATHALIAH.	
	Murder of royal house of David	2 Kings 11:1
	Rescue of Prince Joash.......	2 Kings 11:2-3
	Capture by Jehoiada, the high priest	2 Kings 11:4-21
879	Death of Athaliah, after 6 years of rule	2 Kings 11:20
879	King JOASH	2 Kings 12:1-8; 2 Chro. 24:1-3, 15-21
	Repairing the Temple.......	2 Kings 12:5-16; 2 Chron. 24:4-14
	Despoiling the Temple to pay Syrians	2 Kings 12:17-18; 2 Chron. 24:23-24
840	Death of Joash, after 40 years of rule	2 Kings 12:19-21; 2 Chron. 24:25-27
	At War with Ten Tribes, with Allies.	
B.C. 840	King AMAZIAH	2 Kings 14:1-7; 2 Chron. 25:1-4
	Victory over Edom........	2 Kings 14:5-7

TEN TRIBES.

DATE	EVENTS	AUTHORITY
884	King JEHU	2 Kings 9:1-13; 10:30-31
	Loss of East Canaan to Syria..	2 Kings 10:32-33
856	Death of Jehu, after 28 years of rule	2 Kings 10:34-36
856	King JEHOAHAZ	2 Kings 13:1-7
	Subjection to Syria........	2 Kings 13:3
840	Death of Jehoahaz, after 17 years of rule........	2 Kings 13:8-9
	At War with Two Tribes, with Allies.	
B.C. 840	King JEHOASH (JOASH)	2 Kings 13:10-11

TWO TRIBES.

DATE	EVENTS	AUTHORITY
	War vs. Ten Tribes..........	2 Chron. 25:5-13 2 Kings 14:8-15
811	Death of Amaziah, after 29 years of rule.........	2 Kings 14:17-22 2 Chron. 25:25-28
811	King UZZIAH (AZARIAH)........	2 Kings 15:1-4 2 Chron. 26:1-4
	Victories over Philistines, Arabians, etc............	2 Chron. 26:5-8
	Internal improvements........	2 Chron. 26:9-15
	His leprosy...............	2 Chron. 26:16-21

TEN TRIBES.

DATE	EVENTS	AUTHORITY
	War vs. Two Tribes.........	2 Kings 13:12
	Three victories over Syrians..	2 Kings 13:14-25
825	Death of Jehoash, after 16 years of rule.........	2 Kings 13:13; 14:15-16
825	King JEROBOAM II.............	2 Kings 14:23-24
	Conquests on coast..........	2 Kings 14:25-27

TWO TRIBES.

DATE	EVENTS	AUTHORITY
	Jotham, co-regent	2 Chron. 26:21
	Isaiah's prophecies vs. worldliness	Isa. 1–5
759	Death of Uzziah, after 52 years of rule	2 Kings 15:5-7
759	King JOTHAM	2 Kings 15:32-35
		2 Chron. 27:1-2
	Isaiah's call	Isa. 6
	Defeat of Ammonites	2 Chron. 27:5

TEN TRIBES.

DATE	EVENTS	AUTHORITY
784	Death of Jeroboam, after 41 years of rule	2 Kings 14:28-29
	In Submission to Foreign Nations.	
784	INTERREGNUM.	
762	King ZACHARIAH	2 Kings 15:8-9
762	Destruction of house of Jeroboam II by Shallum; death of Zachariah, after 6 months of rule	2 Kings 15:10-12
762	King SHALLUM	2 Kings 15:13
	Death at hands of Menahem, after 1 month of rule	2 Kings 15:14-15
761	King MENAHEM	2 Kings 15:17-18
	Conquests from Tiphsah to Tirsah	2 Kings 15:16
	Tribute to Assyria	2 Kings 15:19-20
752	Death of Menahem, after 10 years of rule	2 Kings 15:21-22
752	King PEKAHIAH	2 Kings 15:23-24
750	Death of Pekahiah, after 2 years of rule	2 Kings 15:25-26

TWO TRIBES.

DATE	EVENTS	AUTHORITY
	Enmity of Ten Tribes and Syria	2 Kings 15:36-37
742	Death of Jotham, after 16 years of sole rule	2 Kings 15:38 / 2 Chron. 27:8-9
742	King Ahaz	2 Kings 16:1-4 / 2 Chron. 28:1-5
	Enmity of Ten Tribes and Syria	2 Kings 16:5-6 / 2 Chron. 28:6-8
	Isaiah's prophecies vs. alliances	Isa. 7—27
	Vassal of Assyria	2 Kings 16:7-9
	Establishment of Syrian worship in the Temple	2 Kings 16:9-18 / 2 Chron. 28:23-25
	Defeat by Edom and Assyria	2 Chron. 28:16-25
726	Death of Ahaz, after 16 years of rule	2 Kings 16:19-20 / 2 Chron. 28:26-27
726	King Hezekiah	2 Kings 18:1-3 / 2 Chron. 29:1-11
	Cleansing of the Temple	2 Kings 18:4-6 / 2 Chron. 29:12-36
	Celebration of the Passover	2 Chron. 30:1-27
	Other reforms	2 Chron. 31:1-21
	Victory over Philistines	2 Kings 18—8
	Victory over Assyrians	Isa. 36:1-37:38 / 2 Kings 18:9—19:37 / 2 Chron. 32:1-23

TEN TRIBES.

DATE	EVENTS	AUTHORITY
750	King Pekah	2 Kings 15:27-28
	Conquest of Galilee by Assyria	2 Kings 15:29
	First deportation of Israelites	2 Kings 15:29
	Defeat of Two Tribes and release of captives at command of the Prophet Oded	2 Chron. 28:6-15
730	Death of Pekah, after 20 years of rule	2 Kings 15:30-31
730	King Hoshea	2 Kings 17:1-2
	Tribute to Assyria	2 Kings 17:3
	Alliance with Egypt	2 Kings 17:4
722	Last deportation of the Ten Tribes by the Assyrians	2 Kings 17:5-6
	Catalog of sins of Ten Tribes	2 Kings 17:7-23
722	Re-settlement of Samaria	2 Kings 17:24-41

TWO TRIBES.

DATE	EVENTS	AUTHORITY
	Isaiah's prophecies vs. foreign alliances	Isa. 28—39
	Recovery from sickness	2 Kings 20:1-11 / 2 Chron. 32:24-26
	Visit of princes of Babylonia..	2 Kings 20:12-19 / 2 Chron. 32:27-31
697	Death of Hezekiah, after 29 years of rule........	2 Kings 20:20-21 / 2 Chron. 32:32-33
	In Submission to Foreign Nations.	
697	King MANASSEH	2 Kings 21:1, 9, 16 / 2 Chron. 33:1-10
	Prophecy of the fall of Jerusalem	2 Kings 21:10-15 / 2 Chron. 33:11
	His captivity in Babylon......	
	His repentance and restoration.	2 Chron. 33:12-13
	His reforms	2 Chron. 33:14-19
642	Death of Manasseh, after 55 years of rule........	2 Kings 21:17-18 / 2 Chron. 33:20
642	King AMON	2 Kings 21:19-22 / 2 Chron. 33:21-23

TEN TRIBES.

DATE	EVENTS	AUTHORITY
	In captivity.	

TWO TRIBES.

DATE	EVENTS	AUTHORITY
640	Death of Amon, after 2 years of rule	2 Kings 21:23-26
640	King JOSIAH	2 Kings 22:1-2 2 Chron. 34:1-2
632	Seeking the God of David	2 Chron. 34:3
628	Purging Judah	2 Chron. 34:7
622	Repairing the Temple	2 Kings 22:3-7 2 Chron. 34:8-13
	Huldah's prophecy	2 Kings 22:15-20 2 Chron. 34:22-28
	Reading of the Law	2 Kings 23:1-2 2 Chron. 34:14-30
	Renewal of the Covenant	2 Kings 23:3 2 Chron. 34:31-33
622	Keeping the Passover	2 Kings 23:21-23 2 Chron. 35:1-19
	War with Egypt	2 Chron. 35:20-24
609	Death of Josiah, after 31 years of rule	2 Kings 23:28-30
609	Jeremiah's lamentation over him	2 Chron. 35:24-25
609	King JEHOAHAZ (SHALLUM) Vassal of Egypt	2 Kings 23:31-32 2 Kings 23:33 2 Chron. 36:1-4

TEN TRIBES.

DATE	EVENTS	AUTHORITY
	In captivity.	

TWO TRIBES.

DATE	EVENTS	AUTHORITY
609	Removal of Jehoahaz as captive of Egypt, after 3 months of rule..	2 Kings 23:34 / 2 Chron. 36:3
606	King Jehoiakim (Eliakim)..	2 Kings 23:36-37 / 2 Chron. 36:5, 8 / 2 Kings 23:35
	Tribute to Egypt.. Jeremiah's prophecies	Jer. 36
606	Capture of Jerusalem by Nebuchadnezzar and first deportation of Jews .	2 Kings 24:1-5
598	Removal of Johoiakim as captive to Babylon, after 11 years of rule .	2 Chron. 36:6-7
597	King Jehoiachin ..	2 Kings 24:8-9 / 2 Chron. 36:9
597	Capture of Jerusalem by Nebuchadnezzar and second deportation of Jews.. Removal of Jehoiachin as captive to Babylon, after 3 months of rule ..	2 Kings 24:10-16 / 2 Chron. 36:10 / 2 Kings 24:15 / 2 Chron. 36:9-10

TEN TRIBES.

DATE	EVENTS	AUTHORITY
	In captivity.	

TWO TRIBES.

DATE	EVENTS	AUTHORITY
597	King ZEDEKIAH	2 Kings 24:18-19 2 Chron. 36:11-12
	Rebellion vs. Nebuchadnezzar	2 Kings 24:20 2 Chron. 36:13
	Jeremiah's prophecies	Jer. 1-39
586	Capture of Jerusalem and destruction of the Temple by Nebuchadnezzar and third deportation of Jews	2 Kings 25:1-21 2 Chron. 36:17-20
586	Appointment of Gedaliah as governor	2 Kings 25:22-24
586	Removal of Zedekiah as captive to Babylon, after 11 years of rule . . . . Catalog of sins of Two Tribes causing fall	2 Kings 25:7 2 Chron. 36:21
586	Jeremiah's lamentations at fall of Jerusalem	Lam. 1—5

TEN TRIBES.

DATE	EVENTS	AUTHORITY
	In captivity.	

c. PERIOD OF DEPENDENCY (582 YEARS).

DATE	EVENTS	AUTHORITY
	(1) *Under Babylonia (70 Years).*	
B. C. 586	Third deportation by Nebuchadnezzar..	{ 2 Kings 25:1-21 { 2 Chron. 36:17-20
	Murder of Gedaliah and flight of remnant to Egypt.........................	2 Kings 25:22-26
	Abduction of Jeremiah to Egypt........	{ Jer. 40—42 { Jer. 43:1-7
	Prophecies by Jeremiah...............	Jer. 40—52
	Prophecies by Ezekiel................	Ezek. 1—48
	Release of Jehoiachin in Babylon.......	{ 2 Kings 25:27-30 { Jer. 52:31-34
	Prophecies by Daniel.................	Dan. 1—10
	The golden idol and the fiery furnace..	Dan. 3:1-30
	Daniel in the lions' den...............	Dan. 6:1-28
538	Capture of Babylon by Cyrus, the Persian	
	Decree of Cyrus to return and rebuild Jerusalem and the Temple.............	Isa. 44:28—45:1 2 Chron. 36:23; Ezra 1:1-4
536	First return from captivity of 42,360 exiles	Jer. 25:11-12; 29:10 2 Chron. 36:23
	End of first reckoning of 70 years (606-536)	Ezra 1:5—2:70
	Restoration of the Altar worship.......	Ezra 3:1-7
534	First attempt to rebuild the Temple led by Joshua and Zerubbabel.............	Ezra 3:8-13
	Interruption by the Samaritans........	Ezra 4:1-16
	Decree of Artaxerxes to prohibit building	Ezra 4:17-24
520	Second attempt to rebuild the Temple led by Haggai and Zechariah...........	{ Ezra 5:1-2 { Hag.; Zech.
	Threats of Tatnai, the Persian governor	Ezra 5:3-5
	Discovery of the decree of Cyrus.....	Ezra 5:6—6:5
	Decree of Darius to go ahead with the building	Ezra 6:6-12
516	Dedication of Temple................	Ezra 6:13-18
516	Celebration of Passover...............	Ezra 6:19-22
	End of second reckoning of seventy years (586-516).	

DATE	EVENTS	AUTHORITY
B. C.	**(2)** *Under Persia (186 Years).*	
483	Feast of Ahasuerus....................	Esther 1:1-22
479	Elevation of Esther as queen..........	Esther 2:1-23
474	Haman's plot	Esther 3:1—10:3
456	Second return under Ezra............	Ezra 7:1—8:36
	Reforms by Ezra.....................	Ezra 9:1—10:44
444	Nehemiah's commission to restore the walls of Jerusalem...................	Neh. 2:1-10
444	The work of restoration in spite of enemies from without and within.......	Neh. 3:1—6:19
	Reforms by Nehemiah................	Neh. 8:1—12:47
432	Further reforms by Nehemiah........	Neh. 13:1-31
436(?)	Prophecies by Malachi................	Mal. 1—4
400(?)	Completion of Old Testament Canon	
	(3) *Under Macedonia, or Greece (9 Years).*	
330	Conquest of the world by Alexander the Great, bringing the Greek language and culture also to the Jews.	
	(4) *Under Egypt (123 Years).*	
321	Division of Macedonian Empire.......	1 Macc. 1:1-10
320	Capture of Jerusalem by Ptolemy I. Soter, the Egyptian king.	
320	Establishment of Jewish colonies in Alexandria.	
284(?)	Beginning of Septuagint translation of Old Testament.	
246	War with Syria.	
219	Raid of Palestine by Antiochus, of Syria	1 Macc. 1:17-29
217	Recovery of Palestine by Ptolemy IV, of Egypt.	
	Profanation of Temple.	
198	Conquest of Palestine by Syria.	
	(5) *Under Syria (32 Years).*	
198	Conquest of Palestine by Syria.	
170	Tyranny of Antiochus Epiphanes.......	1 Macc. 1:17-67
168	Revolt of Mattathias.................	1 Macc. 2:1-70

(6) *Under Maccabees (103 Years)*.

DATE	EVENTS	AUTHORITY
	First Period: Theocracy.	
B. C. 168	Revolt of the Maccabees..............	1 Macc.; 2 Macc.
166	Judas Maccabaeus, general (1)........	1 Macc. 2:4—9:22
	Capture of Jerusalem; restoration of worship..............................	1 Macc. 4:36-61
	Defeat of Idumea, Ammon, Edom, Philistia.............................	1 Macc. 5:1-68
	Defeat of Syria......................	1 Macc. 7:1-48
	Alliance with Rome	1 Macc. 8:1-32
160	Jonathan, his brother, general (2)......	1 Macc. 9:28-73
	Capture of Joppe, Askalon, etc.........	1 Macc. 10:74-89
	Defeat of Demetrius, the Syrian.......	1 Macc. 11:54-56
	Alliance with Rome and Sparta.......	1 Macc. 12:1-23
143	Simon, his brother, general (3)........	1 Macc. 13:1—16:16
	Alliance with Rome and Sparta........	1 Macc. 14:16-24
	Recognition of Simon as hereditary prince..............................	1 Macc. 14:25-49
	Acknowledgment of Judah's independence	1 Macc. 15:1-24
	Second Period: Monarchy.	
135	His son, John Hyrcanus, his successor. (4).	
125	Annexation of Edom. Rise of opposing sects of the Pharisees and the Sadducees.	
109	Destruction of Samaritan temple on Mt. Gerizim. The supremacy of the Sadducees.	
106	King Aristobulus I. (5). Conquest of Ituraea. Domestic crimes.	
105	King Alexander Janaeus' attack upon Ptolemais, etc. (6). Capture of Gaza, Gilead, Moab. Civil war between the sects. War with Syrians and Arabians.	
78	Queen Alexandra (7). The supremacy of the Pharisees.	

DATE	EVENTS	AUTHORITY
B. C. 69	King Hyrcanus II (8).	
69	King Aristobulus II (9).	
	Victory over Pharisees.	
	Rise of Antipater of Edom, as rival claimant for throne.	
	Refuge in Temple vs. Antipater's army.	
64	Calling in of Roman general Pompey to arbitrate.	
63	Capture of Jerusalem by the Roman general Pompey.	
	(7) *Under Rome, 63 B. C.—4 B. C.* (59 Years).	
63	King Hyrcanus II (restored).	
55	Plunder of Temple by Crassus.	
48	Supremacy of Antipater.	
40	King Antigonus (10).	
	Raid by Parthians.	
37	King Herod the Great (11).	
	Expulsion of Parthians.	
	Capture of Jerusalem by Rome and Herod.	
	Domestic tragedies.	
31	Battle of Actium; defeat of Antony and Cleopatra.	
27	Establishment of Roman Empire.	
19	Building of the Temple.	
4	Alarm at birth of Christ.	
4	Massacre of infants.	
4	Death of Herod.	

3. DURING THE NEW COVENANT.

a. NEW TESTAMENT TIMES (104 YEARS).

(1) TIMES OF CHRIST (34 Years).

NO. EVENTS	PLACE	TIME	MATT.	MARK	LUKE	JOHN
(a) *Thirty Years of Private Life.*						
(aa) INTRODUCTORY.						
1. Luke's Preface					1:1-4	
(bb) ANCESTRY.						
2. Jesus as God's Son..						1:1-18
3. Jesus as David's Abraham's and Adam's son.........			1:1-17		3:23-38	
(cc) ANNUNCIATIONS.						
4. Annunciation to Zacharias	Judea	Sept. B. C. 6			1:5-25	
5. Annunciation to Mary	Nazareth	March B. C. 5			1:26-38	
6. Mary's visit to Elizabeth	Judea	B. C. 5			1:39-56	
7. Annunciation to Joseph	Nazareth	B. C. 5	1:18-25			
(dd) BIRTH OF JOHN THE BAPTIST AND JESUS.						
8. Birth and circumcision of John the Baptist...	Nazareth	June B. C. 5			1:57-80	
9. Birth and circumcision of Jesus	Bethlehem	Dec. B. C. 5			2:1-21	
(ee) INFANCY OF JESUS.						
10. Presentation at the Temple	Jerusalem	Jan. B. C. 4			2:22-38	
11. Visit of wise men...	Bethlehem	Jan. B. C. 4	2:1-12			
12. Flight into Egypt and slaughter of infants..	Egypt Bethlehem	Feb. B. C. 4	2:13-18			
13. Return to Nazareth..	Judea	B. C. 2	2:19-23		2:39-40	
(ff) CHILDHOOD OF JESUS.						
14. Jesus in the Temple	Jerusalem	A. D. 8			2:41-52	

NO.	EVENTS	PLACE	TIME	MATT	MARK.	LUKE	JOHN
(gg)	EIGHTEEN YEARS WITHOUT RECORD, AT NAZARETH.						
(b)	*Preparation for Public Ministry.*						
15	Ministry of John the Baptist	Wilderness of Judea	26	3 :1-12	1 :1-8	3 :1-18	
16	Baptism of Jesus...	Jordan	Jan. 27	3 :13-17	1 :9-11	3 :21-22	1 :31-34
17	Temptation of Jesus	Wilderness of Judea	Feb. 27	4 :1-11	1 :12-13	4 :1-13	
(c)	*First Year of Ministry—Chiefly in Judea.*						
18	First recorded testimony of John concerning Jesus	Bethabara	Feb. 27				1 :19-34
19	First disciples	Bethabara					1 :35-52
20	First miracle—at Cana	Cana	Feb. 27				2 :1-12
21	First cleansing of Temple	Jerusalem	April 11-17, 27				2 :13-25
22	First recorded discourse—with Nicodemus	Jerusalem	April 27				3 :1-21
23	Last recorded witness of John concerning Jesus	Aenon	Fall 27				3 :22-36
24	First convert in Samaria — Samaritan woman	Sychar	Dec. 27				4 :1-42
25	First recorded healing—nobleman's son	Capernaum	Dec. 27				4 :43-54
26	First sign of persecution — imprisonment of John	Macherus	March 28	14 :3-5	6 :17-20	3 :19-20	
27	First conflict with the Pharisees, following the healing at Bethesda	Jerusalem	April 5, 28				5 :1-47
(d)	*His Second Year of Ministry—in Galilee.*						
(aa)	WITH SIX DISCIPLES.						
28	Taking up abode at Capernaum	Capernaum	April 28	4 :12-17	1 :14-15	4 :14-15, 31	
29	Calling four fishermen	Sea of Galilee	April 28	4 :18-22	1 :16-20	5 :1-11	

NO.	EVENTS	PLACE	TIME	MATT.	MARK	LUKE	JOHN
30	Teaching in the synagogue and healing a demoniac	Capernaum	May 28		1 :21-28	4 :31-37	
31	Curing Peter's wife's mother	Capernaum	May 28	8 :14-17	1 :29-34	4 :38-41	
32	Making first preaching circuit of Galilee	Galilee	May 28	4 :23-24	1 :35-39	4 :42-44	
33	Teaching disciples to pray	Desert	May 28			11 :1-13	
34	Teaching concerning the cost of discipleship	Galilee	May 28	8 :18-22		9 :57-62	
35	Stilling the storm . . .	Sea of Galilee	May 28	8 :23-27	4 :35-41	8 :22-25	
36	Restoring the demoniacs	Gergesa	May 28	8 :28-34	5 :1-20	8 :26-39	
37	Healing a paralytic . .	Capernaum	May 28	9 :1-8	2 :1-12	8 :40; 5 :17-26	

(bb) WITH SEVEN DISCIPLES.

NO.	EVENTS	PLACE	TIME	MATT.	MARK	LUKE	JOHN
38	Calling Matthew	Capernaum	June 28	9 :9-13	2 :13-17	5 :27-32	
39	Explaining fasting . . .	Capernaum	June 28	9 :14-17	2 :18-22	5 :33-39	
40	Raising Jairus' daughter to life	Capernaum	June 28	9 :18-26	5 :21-43	8 :41-56	
41	Curing two blind men and one dumb	Capernaum	June 28	9 :27-34			
42	Warning against blasphemy	Capernaum	June 28	12 :22-37	3 :20-30	11 :14-23	
43	Being asked for a sign	Capernaum	June 28	12 :38-45		11 :16, 24-26, 29-32	
44	Defining kinship	Capernaum	June 28	12 :46-50	3 :31-35	11 :27-28; 8 : 19-21	
45	Preaching in parables	Sea of Galilee	June 28	13 :1-52	4 :1-34	8 :4-18	
	The Sower	Sea of Galilee	28	13 :1-23	4 :3-20	8 :4-15	
	The Tares	Sea of Galilee	28	13 :24-30	4 :26-29		
	The Mustard Seed . .	Sea of Galilee	28	13 :31-32	4 :30-32		
	The Leaven	Sea of Galilee	28	13 :33-43			
	The Hidden Treasure	Sea of Galilee	28	13 :44			
	The Pearl of Great Price	Sea of Galilee	28	13 :45-46			

NO.	EVENTS	PLACE	TIME	MATT.	MARK	LUKE	JOHN
	The Drawnet	Sea of Galilee	28	13 :47-52			
	The Candle	Sea of Galilee	28	13 :53-58		8 :16-18	
46	Rejected at Nazareth	Nazareth	June 28		6 :1-6	4 :16-30	
(cc) WITH TWELVE DISCIPLES.			July				
47	Choosing the Twelve	Galilee	28	4 :25; 10 :1-4	3 :7-19	6 :12-19	
48	Preaching on the Mount of Galilee...	Galilee	July 28	5 :1-7, 29		6 :20-49	
49	Healing the leper . .	Galilee	July 28	8 :1-4	1 :40-45	5 :12-16	
50	Healing the centurion's servant.....	Capernaum	28	8 :5-13		7 :1-10	
51	Raising the widow's son to life........	Nain	July 28			7 :11-17	
52	Witnessing concerning John the Baptist	Galilee	Fall 28	11 :2-19		7 :18-35	
53	Anointed by a sinful woman	Galilee	Fall 28			7 :36-50	
54	Making a second preaching circuit of Galilee	Galilee Galilee	Fall 28			8 :1-3	
55	Sending forth the Twelve	Galilee	Winter 28	9 :35-10 : 1; 10 :5- 11 :1	6 :7-13	9 :1-6	
56	Death of John the Baptist	Macherus	March 29	14 :6-12	6 :21-29		
57	Herod's troubled conscience	Macherus	March 29	14 :1-2	6 :14-16	9 :7-9	
58	Feeding 5000.......	Bethsaida	April 29	14 :13-21	6 :30-44	9 :10-17	6 :1-15
59	Walking on the sea	Sea of Galilee	April 29	14 :22-36	6 :45-56		6 :16-21
60	Arguing about the Bread of Life......	Capernaum	April 29				6 :22-71
61	Arguing about the Sabbath	Capernaum	April 29	12 :1-8	2 :23-28	6 :1-5	
62	Healing the man with withered hand on the Sabbath.............	Capernaum	April 29	12 :9-21	3 :1-6	6 :6-11	
63	Laying bare the hypocrisy of the Pharisees	Capernaum	April 29	15 :1-20	7 :1-23		

NO.	EVENTS	PLACE	TIME	MATT.	MARK	LUKE	JOHN
(e) His Third Year of Ministry.							
(aa) To PHOENICIA.							
64	Journeying toward Sidon, healing Syro-Phoenician woman..	Phoenicia	June 29	15:21-28	7:24-30		
(bb) To DECAPOLIS.							
65	Returning through Decapolis, healing deaf mute..........	Decapolis	July 29	15:29	7:31-37		
66	Feeding 4000.......	Decapolis	July 29	15:30-39	8:1-10		
67	Asked again for a sign	Sea of Galilee	July 29	16:1-4	8:11-12		
(cc) To BETHSAIDA.							
68	Taking boat to Galilee	Sea of Galilee	July 29	16:5-12	8:13-21		
69	Healing the blind man near Bethsaida	Bethsaida	July 29		8:22-26		
(dd) To JUDEA.							
70	Celebrating the Feast of Tabernacles	Jerusalem	Oct. 29				7:1--10:21
(ee) To CAESAREA PHILIPPI.							
71	Visiting Martha and Mary	Bethany	Oct. 29			10:38-42	
72	Foretelling His death and resurrection....	Caesarea	Nov. 29	16:13-28	8:27-9:1	9:18-27	
73	Transfigured	Mount	Nov. 29	17:1-13	9:2-13	9:28-36	
74	Curing a demoniac boy		Nov. 29	17:14-21	9:14-29	9:37-43	
(ff) IN GALILEE.							
75	Foretelling again His passion	Galilee	Nov. 29	17:22-23	9:30-32	9:44-45	
76	Paying tribute money	Galilee	Nov. 29	17:24-27			
77	Teaching concerning Christian duties.....	Galilee	Nov. 29	18:1-35	9:33-50	9:46-50; 17:1-4	
(gg) ON FIRST PEREAN JOURNEY.							
78	Rejected by the Samaritans	Samaria	Nov. 29	19:1-2	10:1	9:51-56	

NO.	EVENTS	PLACE	TIME	MATT.	MARK	LUKE	JOHN
79	Healing the 10 lepers	Perea	Nov. 29			17:11-19	
80	Sending forth the Seventy	Perea	Dec. 29	11:20-24		10:1-16	
81	Rejoicing with them on their return	Perea	Dec. 29	11:25-30		10:17-24	
82	Giving parable of the Good Samaritan....	Perea	Dec. 29	*		10:25-37	
83	Answering question concerning divorce..	Perea	Dec. 29	19:3-12	10:2-12		
84	Blessing little children	Perea	Dec. 29	19:13-15	10:13-16	18:15-17	
85	Directing a young ruler to eternal life	Perea	Dec. 29	19:16-26	10:17-27	18:18-27	
86	Giving parable of the Laborers in the Vineyard	Perea	Dec. 29	19:27—20:16	10:28-31	18:28-30	
87	Celebrating the Feast of Dedication.......	Jerusalem	Dec. 20-27, 29				10:22-44
(hh) ON SECOND PEREAN JOURNEY.							
88	Uttering woes against the Pharisees.......	Jerusalem	Jan. 30			11:37-54	
89	Warning against hypocrisy and the unforgivable sin.......	Perea	Jan. 30			12:1-12	
90	Refusing to act as judge	Perea	Jan. 30			12:13-21	
91	Teaching concerning divisions on account of the Gospel.......	Perea	Jan. 30			12:22-59	
92	Commenting on Pilate's slaughter of the Galileans.......	Perea	Jan. 30			13:1-5	
93	Giving the parable of the Fruitless Fig Tree	Perea	Jan. 30			13:6-9	
94	Healing a woman on the Sabbath........	Perea	Jan. 30			13:10-21	
95	Replying to the question whether few are saved	Perea	Jan. 30			13:22-30	

NO.	EVENTS	PLACE	TIME	MATT.	MARK	LUKE	JOHN
96	Replying to the warning against Herod	Perea				13:31-35	
97	Healing the dropsy and discoursing on the Great Supper...	Perea	Jan. 30			14:1-24	
98	Discoursing on counting the cost	Perea	Jan. 30			14:25-35	
99	Giving three parables of Lost Sheep, Lost Penny, Lost Son	Perea	Jan. 30			15:1-32	
100	Giving parable of the Unfaithful Steward.	Perea	Jan. 30			16:1-13	
101	Giving parable of Dives	Perea	Jan. 30			16:14-31	
102	Teaching concerning forgiveness	Perea	Jan. 30			17:1-4	
103	Teaching concerning faith	Perea	Jan. 30			17:5-10	
104	Teaching concerning the nature of His Kingdom	Perea	Jan. 30			17:20-21	
105	Teaching concerning the coming of His Kingdom	Perea	Jan. 30			17:22-37	
106	Giving the parable of the Unrighteous Judge	Perea	Jan. 30			18:1-8	
107	Giving the parable of the Pharisee and the Publican	Perea	Jan. 30			18:9-14	
108	Raising Lazarus to life	Bethany	Feb. 30				11:1-44
109	Withdrawing into Ephraim	Ephraim	March 30				11:45-57
110	Foretelling for the third time His passion	Perea	March 30	20:17-28	10:32-45	18:31-34	
(ii)	ON THIRD PEREAN JOURNEY.						
111	Healing two blind men at Jericho	Jericho	March 30	20:29-34	10:46-52	18:35-43	

NO.	EVENTS	PLACE	TIME	MATT.	MARK	LUKE	JOHN
112	Visiting Zaccheus...	Jericho	March 30			19:1-27	
113	Anointing by Mary..	Bethany	March 30	26:6-13	14:3-9		12:1-11
(f)	*His Last Week.*						
(aa)	SUNDAY—A DAY OF TRIUMPH.						
114	Entering as King...	Jerusalem	April 2, 30	21:1-11	11:1-11	19:29-44	12:12-19
(bb)	MONDAY—A DAY OF AUTHORITY.						
115	Cursing the fig tree	Mt. of Olives	April 3, 30	21:18-19	11:12-14		
116	Second cleansing of the Temple.........	Temple	April 3, 30	21:12-17	11:15-19	19:45-48	
(cc)	TUESDAY—A DAY OF CONFLICT.						
117	Teaching faith from fig tree episode.....	Mt. of Olives	April 4, 30	21:20-22	11:20-26		
118	Questioned as to His authority	Temple	April 4, 30	21:23-27	11:27-33	20:1-8	
119	Giving parable of the Two Sons..........	Temple	April 4, 30	21:28-32			
120	Giving parable of the Wicked Husbandmen		April 4, 30	21:33-46	12:1-12	20:9-19	
121	Giving parable of the Marriage of the King's Son.........	Temple Temple	April 4, 30	22:1-14			
122	Replying to the Herodians' question as to tribute..........	Temple	April 4, 30	22:15-22	12:13-17	20:20-26	
123	Replying to the Sadducees' question as to resurrection......	Temple	April 4, 30	22:23-33	12:18-27	20:27-40	
124	Replying to the Pharisees' question as to the Great Commandment	Temple	April 4, 30	22:34-40	12:28-34		
125	Putting a counter question to the Pharisees	Temple	April 4, 30	22:41-46	12:35-37	20:41-44	
126	Invoking woe upon the hypocritical leaders	Temple	April 4, 30	23:1-39	12:38-40	20:45-47	
127	Praising the widow's two mites	Temple	April 4, 30		12:41-44	21:1-4	

NO.	EVENTS	PLACE	TIME	MATT.	MARK	LUKE	JOHN
128	Sought by Gentiles..	Temple	April 4, 30				12:20-36
129	Rejected by His own	Temple	April 4, 30				12:37-50
130	Prophesying the destruction of Jerusalem and the end of the world..........	Mt. of Olives	April 4, 30	24:1—25:46	13:1-37	21:5-36	
131	Foretelling for the fourth time His passion	Mt. of Olives	April 4, 30	26:1-5	14:1-2	22:1-2	
132	Conspired against by the chief priests and Judas	Jerusalem	April 4, 30	26:14-16	14:10-11	22:3-6	

(dd) WEDNESDAY—A DAY OF RETIREMENT.

(ee) THURSDAY—A DAY OF FAREWELLS.

NO.	EVENTS	PLACE	TIME	MATT.	MARK	LUKE	JOHN
133	Preparing for the Last Supper........	Jerusalem	April 6, 30	26:17-19	14:12-16	22:7-13	
134	Instituting the Lord's Supper......	Jerusalem	April 6, 30	26:20-29	14:17-25	22:14-30	13:1-35
135	Delivering His farewell discourses.....	Jerusalem	April 6, 30				14:1—16:33
136	Offering His intercessory prayer......	Jerusalem	April 6, 30				17:1-26
137	Foretelling Peter's denial	Jerusalem	April 7, 30	26:30-35	14:26-31	22:31-38	13:36-38

(ff) FRIDAY—A DAY OF SUFFERING.

NO.	EVENTS	PLACE	TIME	MATT.	MARK	LUKE	JOHN
138	In agony in Gethsemane	Gethsemane	April 7, 30	26:30, 36-46	14:26, 32-42	22:39-46	18:1-2
139	Betrayed by Judas..	Gethsemane	April 7, 30	26:47-56	14:43-52	22:47-53	18:3-11
140	Tried and condemned by the Jewish authorities..	Jerusalem	April 7, 30	26:57-68	14:53-65	22:54, 63-71	18:12-14, 19-24
141	Denied thrice by Peter	Jerusalem	April 7, 30	26:58, 69-75	14:54, 66-72	22:54-62	18:15-18, 25-27
142	Surrendered to the Roman governor....	Jerusalem	April 7, 30	27:1-2	15:1	23:1	18:28
143	Pronounced innocent by Judas, who in despair kills himself	Jerusalem	April 7, 30	27:3-10			Acts 1:15-20
144	Pronounced innocent by Pilate..........	Jerusalem	April 7, 30	27:11-14	15:2-5	23:2-5	18:29-38

NO.	EVENTS	PLACE	TIME	MATT.	MARK	LUKE	JOHN
145	Questioned and mocked by Herod...	Jerusalem	April 7, 30			23:6-12	
146	Condemned by Pilate	Jerusalem	April 7, 30	27:15-30	15:6-19	23:13-25	18:39-19:16
147	Crucified between two thieves........	Golgotha	April 7, 30	27:31-34	15:20-23 27-28	23:26-33	19:16-18
148	Speaking Seven Words on the cross..	Golgotha	April 7, 30	27:35-50	15:24-37	23:34-46	19:19-30
149	Dead	Golgotha	April 7, 30	27:51-56	15:38-41	23:45-49	19:31-37
150	Buried	Jerusalem	April 7, 30	27:57-66	15:42-47	23:50-56	19:38-42

(gg) SATURDAY—A DAY IN THE TOMB.

(g) *The Forty Days.*

(aa) SUNDAY—THE DAY OF RESURRECTION.

NO.	EVENTS	PLACE	TIME	MATT.	MARK	LUKE	JOHN
151	Appearing, risen, to the women at the tomb	Jerusalem	April 9, 30	28:1-15	16:1-11	24:1-12	20:1-18
152	Appearing to Peter..	Jerusalem	April 9, 30			24:34	1 Cor. 15:5
153	Appearing to two disciples on the way to Emmaus	Emmaus	April 9, 30		16:12-13	24:13-35	
154	Appearing to ten disciples	Jerusalem	April 9, 30		16:14	24:36-43	20:19-23

(bb) LATER APPEARANCES.

NO.	EVENTS	PLACE	TIME	MATT.	MARK	LUKE	JOHN
155	Appearing to eleven disciples		April 16, 30				20:24-29
156	Appearing to seven disciples by the Sea of Galilee..........	Sea of Galilee	30				21:1-23
157	Appearing to over 500	Galilee	May 30	28:16-20	16:15-18		1 Cor. 15:6
158	Appearing to James	Galilee					1 Cor. 15:7

(cc) THE FORTIETH DAY—ASCENSION DAY.

NO.	EVENTS	PLACE	TIME	MATT.	MARK	LUKE	JOHN
159	Ascending to Heaven in presence of the eleven	Bethany	May 18, 30		16:19-20	24:44-53	Acts 1:3-11

(h) *Conclusion.*

NO.	EVENTS	PLACE	TIME	MATT.	MARK	LUKE	JOHN
160	Concerning purpose and omissions.......						20:30-31 21:24-25

(2) Times of the Apostles (70 Years).

THE TWELVE

DATE	EVENTS	AUTHORITY
A.D.	*First Period: In Jerusalem.*	
May	The 120 disciples at prayer awaiting the outpouring of	
30	the Holy Spirit	Acts 1:4-26
	Election of Matthias to succeed Judas Iscariot	Acts 1:26
May	The descent of the Spirit on	
27	Pentecost	Acts 2:1-47
30	Peter's sermon	Acts 3:1-26
30	Hostility of the Jews.	
30	Peter and John in prison	Acts 4:1-22
30	Unity of the Christians	Acts 4:23-37
31	Disciplining of Ananias	Acts 5:1-11
31	Growth of Congregation and	
	persecution	Acts 5:12-42
34	Organization of charity work	Acts 6:1-7
37	Preaching and martyrdom of	
	Stephen	Acts 6:8—7:60
	Second Period: To Judea and Samaria.	
37	Scattering of the Congregation through persecution	Acts 8:1
37	Bringing of Gospel to Judea and Samaria by the dispersed	

PAUL.

DATE	EVENTS	AUTHORITY
37	Paul, a witness of Stephen's death	Acts 7:58

THE TWELVE.

DATE	EVENTS	AUTHORITY
	Christians	Acts 8:1-25
	Third Period: To the Utter-most Parts of the Earth.	
37	Conversion of the Ethiopian eunuch by Philip, the deacon	Acts 8:26-39
	Peter's call to baptize Cornelius and defense of heathen missions	Acts 9:32—11:18
	Spread of the Gospel to Antioch, Cyprus, etc.	
42	The calling of the disciples Christians	Acts 11:26
44	Martyrdom of James, son of Zebedee. Imprisonment of Peter by Agrippa	Acts 12:1-20

PAUL.

DATE	EVENTS	AUTHORITY
37	Conversion of Paul on the way to Damascus	Acts 9:1-31; 22:1-22; 26:12-23
37	Retirement to Arabia	Gal. 1:17-18
41	Introduction to disciples at Jerusalem	Acts 9:27; 22:17-21; Gal. 1:18-19
41	Retirement to Tarsus	Acts 11:25
42	Call to Antioch through Barnabas	Acts 11:19-30
44	Visit to Jerusalem with gifts to the famine sufferers	Acts 11:29-30
45	Paul's first missionary journey, together with Barnabas and Mark	Acts 13—14
	Preaching at Salamis	Acts 13:4-5

THE TWELVE.

DATE	EVENTS	AUTHORITY
50	JAMES ALPHAEUS, at Jerusalem His Epistle. JUDE, in Edessa (?), MATTHEW, in Judea, Persia (?), Libya (?), Ethiopia (?), ANDREW, in Scythia (?), Asia Minor (?), or Greece (?).	

PAUL.

DATE	EVENTS	AUTHORITY
	Rebuking the sorcerer at Paphos	Acts 13:6-13
	Believed by the Gentiles of Antioch in Pisidia	Acts 13:14-52
	Driven out of Iconium by the Jews	Acts 14:1-5
	Stoned at Lystra	Acts 14:6-20
	Teaching in Derbe	Acts 14:20-24
46	Confirming believers on return trip	Acts 14:25-28
	Judaizers in Church at Antioch	Acts 15:1
		Gal. 2:14
51	Council of Jerusalem, determining the question of circumcision	Gal. 2:1
		Acts 15:1-30
51	Paul's second missionary journey, together with Silas, later, Timothy and Luke, but not Barnabas	Acts 15:36-40
	In Asia Minor (Phrygia, Galatia)	Acts 15:36—16:8
52	In Macedonia (Philippi, Thessalonica)	Acts 19:9—17:13
53	In Greece, (Athens, Corinth)	Acts 17:14—18:18
	On return	Acts 18:19-22
53	Epistle to Galatians. First and	

THE TWELVE.

DATE	EVENTS	AUTHORITY
	BARTHOLOMEW, in India (?), Phrygia (?),	
	PETER, in Jerusalem, Palestine, Antioch, Asia Minor, Babylon, Rome.	
	SIMON, in Africa (?), Britain (?).	
	THOMAS, in Persia (?), India (?), Ethiopia (?).	
	PHILIP, in Phrygia (?).	
	MATTHIAS, in Judea (?), Scythia (?).	
62	Matthew's Gospel, in (?) Judea.	
62	Second Peter.	
64	First Peter.	

PAUL.

DATE	EVENTS	AUTHORITY
54	Second Epistles to Thessalonians from Corinth.	
54	Paul's third missionary journey outward, from Antioch to Corinth, with three years at Ephesus.	Acts 19:1—20:1
58	Return, from Corinth to Jerusalem.	Acts 20:2—21:16
57	First Corinthians, from Ephesus.	
57	Second Corinthians, from Macedonia.	
58	Romans, from Corinth.	
58	Arrival in Jerusalem.	Acts 21:17
58	Arrest at the Temple.	Acts 21:27-30
58	Defense at Jerusalem.	Acts 21:31—23:35
60	Defense at Caesarea.	Acts 24:1—26:32
61	Shipwreck of Paul on voyage to Rome.	Acts 27:1—28:10
62	Arrival in chains and preaching while there.	Acts 28:11-31
62	Epistles to Ephesians, Colossians, Philemon and Philippians, from Rome.	
63	Release of Paul.	
64	In Crete and Ephesus.	

THE TWELVE.

DATE	EVENTS	AUTHORITY
65	Martyrdom of James, son of Alphaeus, at Jerusalem.	
67	Mark's Gospel, at Rome.	
67	Martyrdom of Peter.	
70	Siege and destruction of Jerusalem by Titus.	
75	Epistle of Jude, Luke's Gospel and Acts.	
80	Epistle of Hebrews.	
80	John's Gospel, and Epistles,	
90	at Ephesus.	
95	Revelation, at Patmos.	
100	(?) Death of John.	

PAUL.

DATE	EVENTS	AUTHORITY
65	First Epistle to Timothy.	
65	Epistle to Titus.	
	General persecution.	
65	Imprisonment of Paul.	
66	Second Epistle to Timothy.	
67	Martyrdom of Paul.	

B. SOME PROPHECIES CONCERNING CHRIST.

	PROPHECY	FULFILLMENT
I. HIS PERSON.		
1. True God	Ps. 2:7, 12; 45: 6-7, 11; 72:8; 102:24-27; 110:1 Isa. 9:6; 25:9; 40:10 Jer. 23:6 Mic. 5:2 Mal. 3:1	Luke 1:32, 35
2. True Man		
a. Of the seed of the woman....	Gen. 3:15	Gal. 4:4
b. Of the seed of Abraham......	Gen. 12:3; 17:7; 18:18; 22:18; 26:4	Gal. 3:16
c. Of the seed of Isaac.........	Gen. 21:12	Heb. 11:18
d. Of the seed of Jacob........	Gen. 28:14	Luke 3:34
e. Of the seed of Judah........	Gen. 49:10	Luke 3:33
f. Of the seed of David........	2 Sam. 7:12-14 Ps. 89:29, 36; 132:11 Isa. 11:1 Jer. 23:5; 33:15	Acts 13:22
g. Of a virgin..................	Isa. 7:14	Matt. 1:18
II. HIS OFFICES.		
1. Priest.........................	1 Sam. 2:35 Isa. 53:1-12 Ps. 110:4	Heb. 5:5-6 (4:14—10:18)
2. King	Ps. 2:6 Zech. 9:9 Isa. 9:7 Dan. 7:13-14	Matt. 21:1-5
3. Prophet	Deut. 18:15-18	Acts. 3:20-22
III. HIS ATTRIBUTES.		
1. Eternal	Micah 5:2	Col. 1:17
2. Almighty......................	Isa. 9:6	Matt. 28:18
3. All-knowing	Ezek. 11:5	John 2:24 25
4. Holy	1 Sam. 2:2 Isa. 53:9	Luke 1:35 Acts 4:27 1 Pet. 2:22
5. Righteous	Isa. 53:11 Zech. 9:9	John 5:30 Heb. 1:9
6. Faithful	Isa. 11:5	1 Thess. 5:24 1 John 5:20

	PROPHECY	FULFILLMENT
7. Merciful	Isa. 40:11	Luke 19:41 Heb. 2:17
IV. HIS STATES.		
1. OF HUMILIATION.		
a. *Birth in poverty.*		
1. Time	Gen. 49:10	Luke 2:1
2. Place	Micah 5:2	Luke 2:4-6
3. The Wise Men	Ps. 72:10	Matt. 2:1-11
4. The flight into Egypt	Hos. 11:1	Matt. 2:14-15
5. The slaying of the infants	Jer. 31:15	Matt. 2:18
6. Nazarene (Branch)	Isa. 9:1-2; 53:2-4	Matt. 2:23
7. Poverty	Isa. 53:2	Mark 6:3 Luke 9:58
b. *Suffering.*		
1. His forerunner	Isa. 40:3 Mal. 3:1; 4:5	Matt. 3:1-3
2. His anointment	Ps. 45:7	
3. His message	Isa. 11:2-5; 61:1-3	Matt. 3:16 Luke 4:16-21, 43
4. His work in Galilee	Isa. 9:1	Matt. 4:12-16, 23
5. His parables	Ps. 78:2	Matt. 13:34-35
6. His miracles	Isa. 29:18; 32:3- 4; 35:5-6	Matt. 11:4-6
7. His triumphal entry	Ps. 118:26 Zech. 9:9	Matt. 21:1-5
8. His zeal in cleansing the Temple	Ps. 2:7, 12; 69:9 Isa. 59:16-19	John 2:13-17
9. His bearing reproach	Isa. 42:2-3 Ps. 69:9	Matt. 12:19-20 Rom. 15:3
10. His being a stumbling block . .	Isa. 8:14	Rom. 9:32
11. His being hated	Ps. 69:4	Matt. 21:42 John 15:24-25
12. His being rejected by the leaders	Ps. 2:1-3; 118:22	Acts 4:25-26
13. His being rejected by the people	Ps. 69:8	John 1:11
14. His being conspired against . . .	Ps. 2:1-2	Luke 23:12
15. His struggle in Gethsemane . . .	Isa. 63:3	Matt. 26:36-46
16. His being betrayed by a dis- ciple	Ps. 41:9	Matt. 26:49-54 John 13:18, 21
17. His being forsaken by His dis- ciples	Zech. 13:7	Matt. 26:31, 56
18. His being sold for 30 pieces of silver	Zech. 11:12	Matt. 26:15

	PROPHECY	FULFILLMENT
19. His price being given for the potter's field	Zech. 11:13	Matt. 27:7
20. His visage being marred.	Isa. 52:14	Mark 6:1-6
21. His being smitten on the cheek	Micah 5:1	Mark 14:65
22. His being spit on and scourged	Isa. 50:6	Matt. 27:30
		John 19:1
23. His intense sufferings.	Ps. 22:14	Luke 22:44
24. His sufferings being for others	Isa. 53:4-6, 12	Matt. 20:28
25. His patience under sufferings. .	Ps. 22:7-8, 18	Matt. 26:63; 27:
	Isa. 53:7	12-14
		Acts 8:32-35
c. *Crucifixion.*		
1. Nailed to the cross.	Ps. 22:16	John 3:14; 19:18
2. Mocked	Ps. 22:7-8	Matt. 27:39-44
3. Given gall and vinegar.	Ps. 69:21	Matt. 27:34
4. Forsaken by God.	Ps. 22:1	Matt. 27:46
5. Numbered with transgressors. .	Isa. 53:12	Mark. 15:28
6. Intercedes for His murderers. . .	Isa. 53:12	Luke 23:34
7. His garments parted and divided by lot.	Ps. 22:18	Matt. 27:35
d. *Death.*		
1. His spirit yielded up.	Isa. 53:12	Matt. 27:50
2. His side pierced	Zech. 12:10	John 19:34, 37
3. His bones not broken.	Num. 9:12	John 19:33, 36
	Ps. 34:20	
e. *Burial.*		
1. His being buried with the rich	Isa. 53:9	Matt. 27:37-60
2. His flesh not seeing corruption.	Ps. 16:10	Acts 2:31
2. OF EXALTATION.		
a. Descent into hell.	Ps. 16:10	Acts 2:31
		1 Pet. 3:18-19
b. Resurrection	Ps. 16:10; 30:3	Luke 24:34, 46
	Hos. 6:2	John 20:9
		Acts 2:25-33
		1 Cor. 15:4
c. Ascension	Ps. 68:18	Luke 24:51
d. Session at the right hand of the Father	Ps. 110:1	Heb. 1:3
1. As Priest.	Zech. 6:13	Rom. 8:34
		Heb. 10:12; 12:2
2. As King.	Ps. 2;6	Luke 1:33
e. Second coming (Advent).	Ps. 50:3-6	Matt. 24:30
	Dan. 7:13-14	Acts 1:11

C. MIRACLES.

	EVENT	AUTHORITY
	Miracles in Old Testament Times.	
1	Aaron's rod turned into serpent.............	Ex. 7:10-12
2	First plague: Water made blood..........	Ex. 7:20-25
3	Second plague: Frogs....................	Ex. 8:5-14
4	Third plague: Lice......................	Ex. 8:16-18
5	Fourth plague: Flies.....................	Ex. 8:20-24
6	Fifth plague: Murrain...................	Ex. 9:3-6
7	Sixth plague: Boils and blains............	Ex. 9:8-11
8	Seventh plague: Thunder and hail........	Ex. 9:22-26
9	Eighth plague: Locusts..................	Ex.10:12-19
10	Ninth plague: Darkness..................	Ex. 10:21-23
11	Tenth plague: Firstborn slain.............	Ex. 12:29-30
12	Parting of the Red Sea....................	Ex. 14:21-31
13	Curing the waters of Marah...............	Ex. 15:23-25
14	Feeding with manna......................	Ex. 16:14-35
15	Getting water from the rock at Rephidim....	Ex. 17:5-7
16	Death of Nadab and Abihu................	Lev. 10:1-2
17	Burning of the Congregation at Taberah.....	Num. 11:1-3
18	Death of Korah, Dathan, Abiram............	Num. 16:31-35
19	Budding of Aaron's rod, at Kadesh..........	Num. 17:8
20	Getting water from the rock, at Meribah......	Num. 20:7-11
21	The brazen serpent.......................	Num. 21:8-9
22	Parting of the Jordan River...............	Josh. 3:14-17
23	Fall of Jericho...........................	Josh. 6:6-25
24	Staying of sun and moon..................	Josh. 10:12-14
25	Smiting of Philistines, fall of Dagon.........	1 Sam. 5:3-12
26	Death of Uzzah when touching Ark........	2 Sam. 6:7
27	Withering of Jeroboam's hand..............	1 Kings 13:4-6
28	Elijah's staying of the cruse of oil and meal..	1 Kings 17:14-16
29	Elijah's raising the widow's son............	1 Kings 17:17-24
30	Elijah's securing rain at Mt. Carmel........	1 Kings 18:30-38
31	Elijah's burning of the soldiers.............	2 Kings 1:10-12
32	Elijah's parting of the Jordan.............	2 Kings 2:7-8
33	Elisha's parting of the Jordan.............	2 Kings 2:14
34	Elisha's cure of the waters of Jericho.......	2 Kings 2:21-22
35	Elisha's destruction of mocking children....	2 Kings 2:24
36	Elisha's supply of water to armies in Moab..	2 Kings 3:16-20
37	Elisha's increasing widow's oil.............	2 Kings 4:2-7
38	Elisha's raising the Shunammite's son......	2 Kings 4:32-37
39	Elisha's cleansing the deadly pottage.......	2 Kings 4:38-41
40	Elisha's feeding 100 men with 20 loaves......	2 Kings 4:42-44
41	Elisha's cure of Naaman's leprosy..........	2 Kings 5:10-14
42	Elisha's transferring the leprosy to Gehazi...	2 Kings 5:27
43	Elisha's making an axe to swim.............	2 Kings 6:5-7

EVENT	AUTHORITY
44 Elisha's smiting the Syrian army............	2 Kings 6:18-20
45 Resurrection of dead man by touching Elisha's bones	2 Kings 13:21
46 Smiting of Uzziah with leprosy.............	2 Chron. 26:16-21
47 Destruction of Sennacherib's army...........	Isa. 37:36
48 Return of sun by the dial of Ahaz............	Isa. 38:8
49 Deliverance of the three friends from fiery furnace.................................	Dan. 3:19-27
50 Deliverance of Daniel from the lions........	Dan. 6:16-23
51 Deliverance of Jonah from the whale........	Jonah 2:1-10

Miracles of Christ.

EVENT	AUTHORITY
52 Feeding the 5,000.........................	Matt. 14:15-21 Mark 6:35-44 Luke 9:12-17 John 6:5-14
53 Stilling the tempest.......................	Matt. 8:23-27 Mark 4:35-41 Luke 8:22-25
54 The demons in the swine..................	Matt. 8:28-34 Mark 5:1-20 Luke 8:26-39
55 Raising the daughter of Jairus.............	Matt. 9:18-26 Mark 5:22-24, 35-43 Luke 8:41-56
56 Healing the woman with issue of blood.......	Matt. 9:20-22 Mark 5:25-34 Luke 8:43-48
57 Healing the paralytic at Capernaum........	Matt. 9:1-8 Mark 2:1-12 Luke 5:17-26
58 Healing the leper at Gennesaret.............	Matt. 8:1-4 Mark 1:40-45 Luke 5:12-15
59 Healing Peter's mother-in-law..............	Matt. 8:14-17 Mark 1:29-31 Luke 4:38-39
60 Restoring a withered hand..................	Matt. 12:9-13 Mark 3:1-5 Luke 6:6-11

EVENT	AUTHORITY
61 Healing a lunatic child....................	Matt. 17:14-21
	Mark 9:14-29
	Luke 9:37-42
62 Walking on the sea.......................	Matt. 14:22-33
	Mark 6:45-52
	John 6:19-21
63 Healing blind Bartimeus and another near	Matt. 20:29-34
Jericho	Mark 10:46-52
	Luke 18:35-43
64 Healing the Syro-Phoenician damsel........	Matt. 15:21-28
	Mark 7:24-30
65 Feeding the 4,000........................	Matt. 15:32-39
	Mark 8:1-9
66 Withering the fig tree.....................	Matt. 21:17-22
	Mark 11:12-14, 20-24
67 Healing the centurion's servant............	Matt. 8:5-13
	Luke 7:1-10
68 Curing the demoniac in the synagogue.......	Mark 1:23-26
	Luke 4:33-36
69 Healing a blind and dumb demoniac.......	Matt. 12:22
	Luke 11:14
70 Healing two blind men....................	Matt. 9:27-31
71 Healing a dumb demoniac.................	Matt. 9:32-33
72 Finding the stater in the mouth of the fish..	Matt. 17:24-27
73 Healing a deaf mute......................	Mark 7:31-37
74 Healing a blind man at Bethsaida..........	Mark 8:22-26
75 First draught of fishes.....................	Luke 5:1-11
76 Raising the widow's son at Nain............	Luke 7:11-16
77 Healing the woman with an infirmity........	Luke 13:10-17
78 Healing a dropsical man..................	Luke 14:1-6
79 Cleansing of ten lepers...................	Luke 17:11-19
80 Healing the ear of Malchus.................	Luke 22:49-51
81 Turning water into wine...................	John 2:1-11
82 Healing a nobleman's son at Cana..........	John 4:46-54
83 Healing the impotent man at Bethesda......	John 5:1-16
84 Opening the eyes of one born blind........	John 9:1-8
85 Raising of Lazarus.......................	John 11:1-46
86 Second draught of fishes..................	John 21:1-14
87 Noonday darkness on Good Friday..........	Luke 23:44
88 Veil of the Temple rent in twain and earthquake	Matt. 27:51
89 Raising of saints at Jesus' crucifixion........	Matt. 27:52-53

	EVENT	AUTHORITY
90	Demons are subject to the disciples........	Luke 10:17
	Miracles of Apostles.	
91	Place shaken after prayer................	Acts 4:31
92	Peter heals a lame man at the Temple.......	Acts 3:1-10
93	Peter pronounces death upon Ananias and Sapphira	Acts 5:1-11
94	Peter heals Aeneas sick of the palsy........	Acts 9:32-35
95	Peter raises Tabitha-Dorcas from the dead...	Acts 9:36-43
96	Peter liberated from the Jerusalem prison...	Acts 12:7-10
97	Stephen performs signs and wonders.......	Acts 6:8
98	Philip performs signs and wonders.........	Acts 8:6
99	Paul causes Elymas to be blind............	Acts 13:11-12
100	Paul heals a lame man at Lystra............	Acts 14:8-20
101	Paul drives out from a girl a spirit of divination at Philippi...........................	Acts 16:16-18
102	Paul liberated from Philippi prison by angel	Acts 16:25-27
103	Paul heals the sick and demon-possessed at Ephesus	Acts 19:11-12
104	Paul takes no harm from a viper's sting at Malta	Acts 28:1-6

D. PARABLES.

TITLES	AUTHORITY
I. IN THE OLD TESTAMENT.	
1. By Nathan to David.	
(1) The Ewe Lamb...........................	2 Sam. 12:1-4
2. By Widow of Tekoah to David.	
(2) The Two Brethren and the Blood Avengers..	2 Sam. 14:1-11
3. By a Prophet to Ahab.	
(3) The Escaped Captive.....................	1 Kings 20:35-40
4. By Isaiah to Judah.	
(4) The Vineyard and the Grapes...........	Isa. 5:1-7
5. By Ezekiel to Israel.	
(5) The Eagles and the Vine.................	Ezek. 17:3-10
(6) The Lions' Whelps......................	Ezek. 19:2-9
(7) The Boiling Pot..........................	Ezek. 24:3-5
II. IN THE NEW TESTAMENT.	
1. On the Progress of the Kingdom of Christ.	
(1) The Sower	Matt. 13:3-8
	Mark. 4:3-8
	Luke. 8:5-8
(2) The Tares	Matt. 13:24-30
(3) The Mustard Seed......................	Matt. 13:31-32
	Mark 4:30-32
	Luke 13:18-19
(4) The Leaven	Matt. 13:33
	Luke 13:20-21
(5) The Net	Matt. 13:47-48
2. On the Moral Requisites for Entering the Kingdom of Christ.	
(6) The Lost Sheep........................	Matt. 18:12-13
	Luke 15:4-6
(7) The Lost Penny.........................	Luke 15:8-10
(8) The Lost Son...........................	Luke 15:11-32
(9) The Pharisee and the Publican............	Luke 18:9-14
(10) The First Place at Feasts................	Luke 14:7-11
(11) The Two Sons.........................	Matt. 21:28-30
(12) The Hidden Treasure....................	Matt. 13:44
(13) The Pearl	Matt. 13:45-46

TITLES	AUTHORITY
(14) The Tower and the Warring King.........	Luke 14:28-33
(15) The Wedding Garment...................	Matt. 22:11-14
3. *On the Call to Enter the Kingdom of Christ.*	
(16) The Feast	Matt. 22:1-14
	Luke 14:16-24
4. *On the Activity in the Kingdom of Christ.*	
(17) The Vine	John 15:1-8
(18) The Wicked Vine Dressers...............	Matt. 21:33-41
	Mark 12:1-9
	Luke 20:9-18
(19) The Talents	Matt. 25:14-30
	Luke 19:12-27
(20) The Barren Fig Tree....................	Luke 13:6-9
(21) The Laborers	Matt. 20:1-16
5. *On the True Spirit of the Kingdom of Christ.*	
(22) The Good Samaritan....................	Luke 10:30-37
(23) The Unforgiving Servant................	Matt. 18:23-34
	Luke 7:41-42
(24) The Unjust Steward.....................	Luke 16:1-12
(25) The Rich Man and Lazarus...............	Luke 16:19-31
(26) The Ten Virgins........................	Matt. 25:1-13
(27) The Importunate Widow.................	Luke 18:1-8
(28) The Friend on His Journey..............	Luke 11:5-10

E. TABLES OF MEASURES, WEIGHTS, COINS AND TIME.

I. MEASURES.

1. *Long Measure. (Before the Babylonian Captivity).*

HEBREW	METRIC	ENGLISH	REFERENCE
1 span	0.320 meters	12.59 inches	Ex. 28:16
2 spans=1 cubit	0.640 meters	25.19 inches	Gen. 6:15

2. *Long Measure. (After the Babylonian Captivity).*

1 span	0.277 meters	10.92 inches	Ezek. 43:13
2 spans=1 cubit	0.555 meters	21.85 inches	Dan. 3:1
6 cubits=1 reed	3.330 meters	10.92 feet	Ezek. 42:17

3. *Long Measure. (At the Time of Christ).*

ROMAN	METRIC	ENGLISH	REFERENCE
1 cubit	0.444 meters	18 inches	Matt. 6:27
1 furlong	177.4 meters	582½ feet	Luke 24:13
1 mile	1480.0 meters	.919 mile	Matt. 5:41

4. *Surface Measure.*

ROMAN	HEBREW	ENGLISH	REFERENCE
1 furrow	(Larger than	5|16 acre	1 Sam. 14:14
2 furrows=1 acre	Roman)	⅝ acre	Isa. 5:10

5. *Liquid Measure (Earlier).*

HEBREW	METRIC	ENGLISH	REFERENCE
1 log	0.408 liters	0.718 pint	Lev. 14:10
12 logs=1 hin	4.896 liters	1.077 gallons	Ex. 29:40
6 hins=1 bath	29.376 liters	6.465 gallons	1 Kings 7:26
10 baths=1 cor, or homer	293.76 liters	64.65 gallons	Lev. 27:16

6. *Liquid Measure (Later).*

HEBREW	METRIC	ENGLISH	REFERENCE
1 log	0.287 liters	0.523 pints	
12 logs=1 hin	3.570 liters	3.142 quarts	Ezek. 4:11
6 hins=1 bath	21.420 liters	4.714 gallons	Isa. 5:10
10 baths=1 cor, or homer	214.20 liters	47.144 gallons	Ezek. 45:14

7. *Dry Measure (Earlier)*.

HEBREW	METRIC	ENGLISH	REFERENCE
1 cab	1.632 liters	1.436 quarts	2 Kings 6:25
1 omer	2.937 liters	2.586 quarts	Ex. 16:36
10 omers=1 ephah	29.376 liters	3.232 pecks	Lev. 5:11
10 ephahs=1 cor, or homer	293.76 liters	8.081 bushels	Num. 11:32

8. *Dry Measure (Later)*.

HEBREW	METRIC	ENGLISH	REFERENCE
10 omers=1 ephah	21.420 liters	2.357 pecks	Zech. 5:7
10 ephahs=1 cor, or homer	214.20 liters	5.893 bushels	Ezek. 45:13

II. WEIGHTS.

HEBREW	TROY	VALUE IN U. S. MONEY	REFERENCE
1 gerah	11.2 grains	$.032	Ex. 30:13
10 gerahs=1 bekah	112 grains	$.32	Ex. 38:26
20 gerahs=1 shekel	225.5 grains	$.64	Gen. 23:16
50 shekels= 1 maneh, or pound	11,239 grains	$32.00	Neh. 7:71
3000 shekels=1 talent ot silver	674,392 grains	$1,920.00	Ex. 38:27
1 shekel of gold	253 grains	$9.60	1 Chron. 21:25
1 talent of gold	759,000 grains	$28,800.00	Ex. 25:39

GREEK & ROMAN	TROY	VALUE IN U. S. MONEY	REFERENCE
1 libra, or pound	5,050 grains	$14.38	John 12:3
1 mina, or pound	11,239 grains	$32.00	Luke 19:13
1 talent of silver	674,392 grains	$1,920.00	Matt. 25:28

III. COINS.

1. *Old Testament Coins.*

HEBREW	VALUE IN U. S. MONEY	REFERENCE
"A piece of silver"=shekel........	$.64	Gen. 37:28
"A piece of gold"=shekel.........	$9.60	1 Chron. 21:25
1 dram (Persian daric)...........	$5.28	1 Chron. 29:7
First Hebrew coins=shekels.......		1 Macc. 15:6
Egyptian coins in use.............		2 Macc. 4:18

2. *New Testament Coins.*

ROMAN	VALUE IN U. S. MONEY	REFERENCE
"A piece of money"=stater........	$.51	Matt. 17:27
"A piece of silver"=argurion......	$.51	Matt. 26:15
"Tribute money"=didrachmon	$.32	Matt. 17:24
"A piece of silver"=drachme......	$.17	Luke 15:8
"A penny"=denarius	$.17	Matt. 18:28
"A farthing"=assarion	$.01	Matt. 10:29
"A farthing"=kodrantes..........	$.00¼	Matt. 5:26
"A mite"=lepton	$.00⅛	Mark 12:42
Price of Joseph=20 x $.64=$12.80................		Gen. 37:28
Price of Jesus =30 x $.51=$15.30...............		Matt. 26:15
Abraham's price for grave=400 x $.64=$256.00....		Gen. 23:15
Naaman's offering to Elisha=6000 x $9.60=$57,600.00		2 Kings 5:5
The Fellow Servant's 100 pence=$17.00..........		Matt. 18:28
The Debtor's 10,000 talents=$19,200,000.00........		Matt. 18:24

IV. TIME.

1. *The Old Testament Night and Day.*

NAME OF PERIOD	HOURS OF PERIOD	REFERENCE
(1) First watch............	6 P. M.—12:00	Lam. 2:19
(2) Middle watch..........	12:00—3 A. M.	Judg. 7:19
(3) Morning watch........	3 A. M.—6 A. M.	Ex. 14:24
(4) Morning	6 A. M.—10 A. M.	Judg. 16:2
(5) Heat of day............	10 A. M.—2 P. M.	Gen. 18:1
(6) Cool of day............	2 P. M.—6 P. M.	Gen. 3:8

2. *The New Testament Night and Day.*

NAME OF PERIOD	HOURS OF PERIOD	REFERENCE
(1) First watch—evening...	6 P. M.—9 P. M.	Luke 12:38
(2) Second watch—midnight	9 P. M.—12.00	Luke 12:38
(3) Third watch—cock crow	12:00—3 A. M.	Matt. 26:34
(4) Fourth watch—morning.	3 A. M.—6 A. M.	Matt. 14:25
(5) Third hour.............	6 A. M.—9. A. M.	Mark 15:25
(6) Sixth hour.............	9 A. M.—12 Noon	Mark 15:33
(7) Ninth hour.............	12 Noon—3 P. M.	Mark 15:34
(8) Twelfth hour...........	3 P. M.—6 P. M.	

3. *The Old Testament Sacred Year.*

NO. OF MONTH	HEBREW NAME OF MONTH	CORRESPONDING ENGLISH MONTH	FESTIVAL DATES	REFERENCE
1	Abib, or Nisan..	April	1. New Moon 14. Passover (Ex. 12:1-13:10) 16. First Fruits of Barley Harvest (Lev. 23:10-12)	Ex. 12:2
2	Zif, or Iyar.....	May	1. New Moon 14. Second Passover, for those who could not keep the first (Num. 9:10-11)	1 Kings 6:1
3	Sivan	June	1. New Moon 6. Pentecost, or Feast of Weeks, or First Fruits of Wheat Harvest (Lev. 23:17-20)	Esther 8:9
4	Thammuz	July	1. New Moon 17. Fast over Fall of Jerusalem	Ezra 7:9
5	Ab	August	1. New Moon 9. Fast over Destruction of Temple	Ezra 7:9
6	Elul	Sept.	1. New Moon	Neh. 6:15
7	Tisri, or Ethanim	Oct.	1. Feast of Trumpets (Num. 29:1) 10. Day of Atonement (Lev. 16) 15. Feast of Tabernacles (Lev. 23:34) First Fruits of Wine and Oil (Deut. 16:13)	1 Kings 8:2 2 Chron. 5:3

NO. OF MONTH	HEBREW NAME OF MONTH	CORRESPONDING ENGLISH MONTH	FESTIVAL DATES	REFERENCE
8	Bul, or Marche-svan	Nov.	1. New Moon	1 Kings 6:38
9	Chisleu	Dec.	1. New Moon 25. Feast of Dedica-tion (1 Macc. 4:52-59; John 10:22-23)	Neh. 1:1
10	Tebeth	Jan.	1. New Moon	Esther 2:16
11	Shebat	Feb.	1. New Moon	Zech. 1:7
12	Adar	March	1. New Moon 14. Feast of Purim (Esther 9:21-24)	Esther 3:7
13	Veadar	Intercalary	1. New Moon 11. Fast of Esther 14. Feast of Purim	

The Sacred Year is lunar, having 12 x 29.5 + days, or 354 days. It runs behind a little over 11 days a year. In a cycle of 19 years 7 lunar months are introduced to make up for the lost time. These extra months—Veadar—covered the second half of March and the first half of April.

4. *The Old Testament Civil Year.*

NO. OF MONTH	HEBREW NAME OF MONTH	CORRESPONDING ENGLISH MONTH	SEASON AND REFERENCE
1 (7)	Tisri, or Ethanim . .	Oct.	Former, or early rains (Joel 2:23). Plowing and sowing begun.
2 (8)	Bul, or Marchesvan . .	Nov.	Rainy. Wheat and barley sown. Vintage in N. Palestine.
3 (9)	Chisleu . . .	Dec.	Winter begins. Snow on mountains.
4 (10)	Tebeth . . .	Jan.	Coldest month. Hail, snow (Josh. 10:11).
5 (11)	Shebat . . .	Feb.	Weather gets warmer.
6 (12)	Adar	March	Thunder showers. Almond trees blossom.
7 (1)	Abib, or Nisan . . .	April	Latter, or spring rains (Deut. 11:14). Floods (Josh. 3:15). Barley ripe at Jericho.
8 (2)	Zif	May	Wheat getting ripe. Barley Harvest (Ruth 1:2-23).
9 (3)	Sivan	June	Wheat harvest. Dry season begins (1 Sam. 12: 17). Summer begins.
10 (4)	Thammuz .	July	Heat increases.
11 (5)	Ab.	August	Streams dry up. Heat intense. Vintage begins in S. Palestine (Lev. 26:5).
12 (6)	Elul	Sept.	Heat still intense (2 Kings 4: 18-20). Vintage general (Num. 13:23).

F. SOME NAMES AND TITLES OF CHRIST.

NAME	REFERENCE
1. *In the Old Testament.*	
(1) Branch	Zech. 3:8; 6:12
(2) Child (Little Child)...................	Isa. 11:6
(3) Counsellor	Isa. 9:6
(4) David	Jer. 30:9
	Ezek. 34:23; 37:24
	Hos. 3:5
(5) Desire of All Nations.................	Hag. 2:7
(6) Everlasting Father	Isa. 9:6
(7) Fellow (My Fellow)...................	Zech. 13:7
(8) God	Isa. 40:9
(9) Holy (The Most Holy)................	Dan. 9:24
(10) I Am................................	Ex. 3:14
(11) Immanuel	Isa. 7:14
(12) Jehovah	Isa. 26:4
(13) King	Zech. 9:9
(14) Lawgiver	Isa. 33:22
(15) Lord, Our Righteousness..............	Jer. 23:6
(16) Messiah	Dan. 9:25
(17) Mighty God	Isa. 9:6
(18) Mighty One of Jacob.................	Isa. 60:16
(19) Priest	Ps. 110:4
(20) Prince of Peace.....................	Isa. 9:6
(21) Prophet	Deut. 18:15
(22) Redeemer	Job 19:25
	Isa. 59:20
(23) Ruler in Israel.....................	Micah 5:2
(24) Seed of the Woman..................	Gen. 3:15
(25) Servant (My Servant)................	Isa. 52:13
(26) Shepherd in the Land................	Zech. 11:16: 13:7
(27) Shiloh	Gen. 49:10
(28) Star	Num. 24:17
(29) Sun of Righteousness................	Mal. 4:2
(30) Wonderful	Isa. 9:6
2. *In the New Testament.*	
(1) Adam (The Second Adam).............	1 Cor. 15:45-47
(2) Advocate	1 John 2:1
(3) Alpha and Omega.....................	Rev. 1:8; 22:13
(4) Amen	Rev. 3:14
(5) Author and Finisher of Our Faith........	Heb. 12:2
(6) Author of Eternal Salvation............	Heb. 5:9
(7) Beginning of the Creation of God........	Rev. 3:14
(8) Blessed and Only Potentate.............	1 Tim. 6:15
(9) Bread of God.........................	John 6:33

NAME	REFERENCE
(10) Bread of Life............................	John 6:35
(11) Captain of Salvation....................	Heb. 2:10
(12) Child (Holy Child).....................	Acts 4:27
(13) Christ.................................	Matt. 16:16
(14) Corner Stone	Eph. 2:20
	1 Pet. 2:6
(15) David (Son of David)....................	Matt. 9:27; 21:9
(16) Day Spring	Luke 1:78
(17) Day Star	2 Pet. 1:19
(18) Deliverer	Rom. 11:26
(19) Faithful Witness	Rev. 1:5; 3:14
(20) First and Last..........................	Rev. 1:17
(21) First Begotten (First Born)	Heb. 1:6
	Rev. 1:5
(22) First Fruits	1 Cor. 15:23
(23) God	John 20:28
(24) God Blessed for Ever....................	Rom. 9:5
(25) Governor	Matt. 2:6
(26) Head over All Things....................	Eph. 1:22
(27) Heir of All Things......................	Heb. 1:2
(28) High Priest	Heb. 4:14; 5:10
(29) Holy One	Luke 4:34
(30) Horn of Salvation.......................	Luke 1:69
(31) Image of God...........................	2 Cor.4:4
(32) Immanuel	Matt. 1:23
(33) Jesus	Matt. 1:21
(34) Jesus Christ	1 Tim. 1:1
(35) Just One	Acts 3:14; 7:52
(36) King of Israel..........................	John 1:49
(37) King of the Jews........................	Matt. 2:2
(38) King of Kings...........................	1 Tim. 6:15
(39) Lamb of God............................	John 1:29, 36
(40) Life	John 14:6
(41) Light of the World......................	John 8:12; 9:5
(42) Light (True Light)......................	John 1:9; 12:35
(43) Lion of the Tribe of Judah..............	Rev. 5:5
(44) Living Stone	1 Pet. 2:4
(45) Lord	Matt. 3:3
(46) Lord God Almighty......................	Rev. 15:3
(47) Lord God of the Holy Prophets..........	Rev. 22:6
(48) Lord of All.............................	Acts 10:36
(49) Lord of Glory...........................	1 Cor. 2:8
(50) Lord of Lords...........................	1 Tim. 6:15
	Rev. 19:16
(51) Maker and Preserver of All Things.......	John 1:3, 10
	1 Cor. 8:6

NAME	REFERENCE
(52) Man	1 Tim. 2:5
(53) Man (The Second Man)	1 Cor. 15:47
(54) Mediator	1 Tim. 2:5
	Heb. 12:24
(55) Messiah	John 1:41
(56) Morning Star	Rev. 22:16
(57) Nazarene	Matt. 2:23
(58) Passover (Our Passover)	1 Cor. 5:7
(59) Priest for Ever	Heb. 5:6
(60) Prince	Acts 5:31
(61) Prince of Life	Acts 3:15
(62) Prince of the Kings of the Earth	Rev. 1:5
(63) Prophet	Luke. 24:19
(64) Propitiation	Rom. 3:25
	1 John 2:2
(65) Righteous (The Righteous)	1 John 2:1
(66) Rock	1 Cor. 10:4
(67) Root and Offspring of David	Rev. 5:5; 22:16
(68) Same Yesterday, Today and for Ever	Heb. 13:8
(69) Savior	Luke 2:11
	Acts 5:31
(70) Shepherd and Bishop of Souls	1 Pet. 2:25
(71) Shepherd of the Sheep	Heb. 13:20
(72) Shepherd (Chief Shepherd)	1 Pet 5:4
(73) Shepherd (Good Shepherd)	John 10 :11
(74) Shepherd (Great Shepherd)	Heb. 13:20
(75) Son (A Son)	Heb. 3:6
(76) Son (My Beloved Son)	Matt. 3:17
(77) Son (Only Begotten Son)	John 1:14, 18
(78) Son of David	Matt. 9:27; 21:9
(79) Son of God	Matt. 8:29
(80) Son of Man	Matt. 8:20
(81) Son of the Highest	Luke 1:32
(82) Star (The Bright and Morning Star)	Rev. 22:16
(83) Truth	John 14:16
(84) Vine	John 15:1, 5
(85) Way	John 14:6
(86) Witness (The Faithful and True Witness)	Rev. 3:14
(87) Word	John 1:1
(88) Word of God	Rev. 19:13

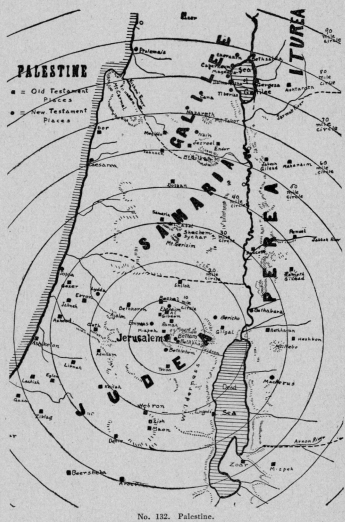

No. 132. Palestine.
(The circles are 10 miles apart).

TEXT INDEX

1 : 9 644
2 : 10 660
2 : 15 582
2 : 17 645
3 : 1–6 581
3 : 6 . . ..454, 661
4 : 4–9 582
4 : 8 581
4 : 14 . . ..581, 660
4 : 14—7 : 28 454
4 : 14—10 : 18 644
5 : 1–7 475
5 : 1–14 416
5 : 5–6 . . ..644, 661
5 : 6–10 581
5 : 6, 10 576
5 : 6–12 419
5 : 9 659
5 : 10 660
6 : 13 . . ..416, 419
6 : 20—7 : 1 576
7 : 1–2 581
7 : 2 581
7 : 4 415
7 : 25 . . ..419, 495, 581
7 : 27 581
7 : 28 . . .. 4.9
8 : 1–13 454
8 : 1—10 : 18 454
8 : 2 582
8 : 5 488
9 : 1–12 454
9 : 1–15 478
9 : 1–28 419
9 : 2 582
9 : 3–4 . . ..446, 447
9 : 4 104
9 : 12 581
9 : 13—10 : 18 454
9 : 14 489
10 : 1 . . ..448, 478
10 : 12 . . ..49, 646
10 : 25 520
11 : 18 644
11 : 9 148
11 : 35–37 225
12 : 1–2 381
12 : 2 . . ..646, 659
12 : 16–17 153
12 : 17 379
12 : 24 661
13 : 8 . . ..553, 661
13 : 10 . . ..448, 582
13 : 20 661

JAMES
1—5 343

1 : 18 597
2 : 24 . . ....577, 581, 601
5 : 4 380
5 : 16 135

1 PETER
1—5 343
1 : 1....264, 265, 268, 326
1 : 10–11 34
1 : 16 485
1 : 19 582
1 : 24–25 70
1 : 25 16
2 : 4 660
2 : 5 454
2 : 6 660
2 : 9 . . ..419, 485
2 : 22 644
2 : 25 661
3 : 1–7 376
3 : 11 . . ..119, 138
3 : 15 553
3 : 18–19 646
3 : 20 513
4 : 3 384
4 : 10 431
5 : 1 431
5 : 2 431
5 : 4 661
5 : 8 369

2 PETER
1 : 1—3 : 18 . . ...343, 539
1 : 12 595
1 : 19......36, 62, 564, 660
1 : 21.. 23, 29, 33, 36, 419, 587
2 : 5 582
2 : 22 369
3 : 10 582
3 : 15–16 60
3 : 16 563

1 JOHN
1—5 . . ....343, 539, 556
2 : 1 . . ..495, 659, 661
2 : 2 661
3 : 10 181
5 : 7 . . ..137, 503
5 : 8 507
5 : 20 644

2 JOHN
1 : 1–13 . . ..343, 539
1 : 7–11 539

3 JOHN
1 : 1–14 343
1 : 13 539

JUDE
1 : 1–25 343
1 : 3–23 539
1 : 5 595

REVELATION
1—3 452
1—22 343
1 : 4 512
1 : 5 . . ..660, 661
1 : 8 659
1 : 9 267
1 : 17 660
1 : 19 23
1 : 20 . . ..431, 512
2 : 1 431
2 : 1–7 266
2 : 1—3 : 13 539
2 : 6 540
2 : 8—3 : 13 266
2 : 12–17 . . ..267, 539
2 : 14–16 540
3 : 14 . . ....659, 660, 661
3 : 14–22 268
4 : 3 354
5 : 5 . . ..660, 661
8 : 3 582
8 : 3–5 478
9 : 10 368
9 : 13 448
9 : 17 354
12 : 1 515
12 : 13 659
13 : 11–18 569
13 : 18 . . ..586, 591
15 : 3 660
15 : 5 582
16 : 19 507
17 : 1–3 587
18 : 12 360
19 : 13 661
19 : 16 660
21 : 9–10 587
21 : 13 507
21 : 19 354
21 : 19–20 . . ..353, 354
21 : 21 351
21 : 22 582
22 : 6 660
22 : 16 661
22 : 18–19 . . ..42, 43
22 : 20 . . ..491, 588

SUBJECT INDEX